A Conflict of Laws Companion

A Conflict of Laws Companion

Essays in Honour of Adrian Briggs

Edited by

ANDREW DICKINSON

MA (Oxon), BCL
Fellow, St Catherine's College and Professor of Law,
University of Oxford

EDWIN PEEL

MA (Oxon), BCL
Fellow, Keble College and Professor of Law, University of Oxford

Assistant Editor
THOMAS PAUSEY
BA (Oxon), BCL

OXFORD
UNIVERSITY PRESS

OXFORD
UNIVERSITY PRESS

Great Clarendon Street, Oxford, OX2 6DP,
United Kingdom

Oxford University Press is a department of the University of Oxford.
It furthers the University's objective of excellence in research, scholarship,
and education by publishing worldwide. Oxford is a registered trade mark of
Oxford University Press in the UK and in certain other countries

© the many contributors 2021

The moral rights of the authors have been asserted

First Edition published in 2021

Impression: 3

All rights reserved. No part of this publication may be reproduced, stored in
a retrieval system, or transmitted, in any form or by any means, without the
prior permission in writing of Oxford University Press, or as expressly permitted
by law, by licence or under terms agreed with the appropriate reprographics
rights organization. Enquiries concerning reproduction outside the scope of the
above should be sent to the Rights Department, Oxford University Press, at the
address above

You must not circulate this work in any other form
and you must impose this same condition on any acquirer

Crown copyright material is reproduced under Class Licence
Number C01P0000148 with the permission of OPSI
and the Queen's Printer for Scotland

Published in the United States of America by Oxford University Press
198 Madison Avenue, New York, NY 10016, United States of America

British Library Cataloguing in Publication Data

Data available

Library of Congress Control Number: 2020951491

ISBN 978-0-19-886895-8

DOI: 10.1093/oso/9780198868958.001.0001

Printed and bound by
CPI Group (UK) Ltd, Croydon, CR0 4YY

Links to third party websites are provided by Oxford in good faith and
for information only. Oxford disclaims any responsibility for the materials
contained in any third party website referenced in this work.

Foreword
Jonathan Mance[1]

The title is a most apposite double-entendre. The book is full of affection for a great companion, whose warmth, care for others, including his students, and sociability shine through the tributes and anecdotes with which it abounds. At the same time, it contains contributions from colleagues worldwide of an excellence that makes it a most worthy tribute to the master of conflicts whom it honours. It is a pleasure both to dip into and to study. There is much to inspire and cite in future academic discussion and in case law.

Under the editorship of Andrew Dickinson and Edwin Peel, the book starts with three vignettes, by Professors Horton Rogers, Derrick Wyatt and Francis Reynolds. The first places Adrian Briggs, briefly, as a lecturer at Leeds University. Another recounts his contribution—'incalculable'—to St Edmund Hall, Oxford; there, he has been for forty years a fellow, as well as becoming the University's Professor of Private International Law and an honorary silk; he has been central to the Hall's life, students, activities and (with his characteristic melding of wit and wisdom) entertainment. The last vignette, in a different dimension, places him as Oxford's third giant in the conflicts field in succession to A V Dicey (to 1922) and J H C Morris (to 1984). On top of all this, and from a London perspective, the writer notes that Adrian Briggs has managed a busy Temple practice (including at the highest levels cases such as *Rubin v Eurofinance*, *The Alexandros T* and *Enka v OOO Chubb*, all discussed in the book) as well as featuring in and contributing valuably to the work of Parliamentary and other committees.

After the vignettes follow thirteen contributions under the heads of jurisdiction, choice of law, recognition and enforcement and, more generally, the role of conflicts principles in the law. The contributors include three members of the highest courts of common law jurisdictions as well as academics worldwide and practitioners. Their distinction is evident. All, without exception, did either the BCL or a DPhil with or under guidance from Adrian Briggs. One reason for this is given by Justice Andrew Bell, President of the Court of Appeal of the Supreme Court of New South Wales, who records that it is 'perhaps not an exaggeration to say that one of the principal reasons why a generation of the brightest law students from around the Commonwealth enrolled year after year to undertake the Bachelor of Civil Law at Oxford was to take his seminars and hear his lectures on Conflicts'.

---

[1] The Rt Hon Lord Mance, former Deputy President of the Supreme Court.

The writer sadly missed that inducement, completing his undergraduate degree before Adrian Briggs arrived at Oxford. The BCL appeared then to consist of an even fuller diet of Roman law than the BA. The writer, who chose to compare legal systems by the more direct method of a *stage* in a Hamburg law firm, also confesses to having been disgracefully late in drawing the distinction, between Adrian Briggs and the now Lord Briggs, that Andrew Bell so carefully makes when discussing *Altimo Holding v Kyrgyz Mobil*. In *Grupo Torras v Al-Sabah* (1994), the writer was, until the then Michael Briggs QC gently corrected him, under the impression that he was receiving particularly authoritative academic submissions on the difficult conflicts points raised by that early case on the Brussels I regime. Both Briggses are now, of course, clearly distinct at the top of their respective pillars.

All thirteen contributions testify to Adrian Briggs' insistence on drilling down into the structure underpinning conflicts of laws, on clarifying the principles supporting its development and showing that it rests on more than mere pragmatism. Thus, they examine, inter alia:

- how far conflicts principles serve private interests of consent and obligation and how far statist interests;
- the proper understanding of comity, which Briggs roots in territoriality;
- the concept of the natural forum, to the development of which the young Briggs contributed so significantly (as recorded by Lord Goff in *The Spiliada* in 1986);
- the extent to which jurisdiction needs to be defined in England or in overseas jurisdictions both by gateways for service out and within these by discretion;
- the scope and operation of the EU rule regarding joinder of co-defendants (Art 8(1) of Brussels 1) in the light of the 'sorry mess' made by the Court of Justice in this area in and after *Owusu v Jackson*;
- the extent to which the anti-suit injunction can really be justified as directed purely *in personam*;
- the extent to which recognition of a foreign decision may, consistently with principles of comity and territoriality, be refused where it was in English eyes clearly obtained in breach of an English choice of jurisdiction clause; and
- as a final example close to Adrian Briggs' heart, the extent to which such a breach may, where necessary as a fall-back, be redressed by the tool of a damages claim, a course recently sanctioned at highest judicial levels in *The Alexandros T*.

It is of particular interest to see the themes of judicial respect for and reluctance to countenance criticism of other jurisdictions now counter-posed so clearly with a discussion of the circumstances in which (in Briggs' words) 'judicial comity should not be allowed to become the enemy of justice'. Already in *The Spiliada* Lord Goff recognised that there would be cases where the interests of justice override the desirability that cases be tried in their natural forum. The 'forum of necessity'

(Briggs' words) has become a feature of English litigation, most recently in *Vedanta Resources PLC v Lungowe* (2019), where the impossibility of funding and finding legal teams for a group claim by impecunious claimants in Zambia justified English, rather than Zambian, proceedings. Cases like *Cherney v Deripaska* and *Altimo Holdings v Kyrgyz* (and *Yukos v Rosneft* and *Belhaj v Straw*) also make clear that, given cogent evidence and the need to do so, English courts will not hold back from identifying a foreign judicial system as corrupt or lacking in independence. Comity or territoriality can be seen to have limits, where fundamental rights are in issue.

A similar realisation has moved the Court of Justice of the European Union from its previous dogma of inviolable and compulsory mutual trust towards the activist stance which it now takes to, in particular, Member State governmental intrusions on the rule of law. It is a pity that this realisation did not dawn before the cases of *Erich Gasser v Misat* and *Turner v Grovit*, where the Court of Justice showed no concern for abuses of the judicial process or for the practical availability of justice in the fora seised by those abusing that process. Maybe Advocate General Léger's nuanced opinion in the former case would today have found a more sympathetic ear. But the Court of Justice rarely reverses course. In a European legal context, that ship has, as Adrian Briggs has said, now sailed.

In future, English conflicts of laws may be less concerned with EU rules and jurisprudence. But, despite all criticisms, the business, financial and legal worlds have become used to and learned to value the Brussels scheme of EU Regulations that prevailed until the end of 2020. The transition period has now ended without any satisfactory resolution of the future arrangements for international civil justice cooperation, though the United Kingdom will have the benefit of three Hague Conventions, including the Choice of Court Convention. The United Kingdom will also continue to seek the consent of the European Union to join the Lugano Convention, that weaker sibling of Brussels I. If it succeeds, the Hague Choice of Court Convention will become largely irrelevant (unless and until it acquires more non-European subscribers). The United Kingdom will voluntarily resubmit itself to the jurisprudence of *Erich Gasser v Misat*, *Turner v Grovit*, *Owusu v Jackson* and *Allianz SpA v West Tankers Inc*—but will, hopefully, also aim towards inciting a re-cast of Lugano. At the same time, under section 6(4) and (5) of the European Union (Withdrawal) Act 2018, both the Supreme Court and the Court of Appeal will be able to depart from that jurisprudence in circumstances where the House of Lords' Practice Statement ([1966] 1 WLR 1234) would justify a departure by the Supreme Court from a prior House of Lords or Supreme Court decision.

There will on any view be plenty of future work for conflicts lawyers. English law and London will remain important for the resolution of international disputes, and, despite Adrian Briggs' formal retirement, we can be sure and be grateful that his insights will continue to enlighten us all. Meanwhile, the present book makes a very good read as well as a very valuable contribution to jurisprudence. Its editors and authors are to be warmly congratulated.

Editors' Preface

Adrian Briggs has been our companion in the Conflict of Laws ever since he first introduced us both to the subject more than a quarter of a century ago. More recently, it has been our great pleasure to share the teaching of the BCL/MJur course in Oxford with him, and we are not sure how we will manage without his knowledge, insight and 'can do' approach. During his tenure, no one wanting to take the course has ever been turned away—if extra resource is needed then Adrian will be the first to volunteer. His inevitable response can be paraphrased as follows: if any student has the settled intention of studying the Conflict of Laws in Oxford, who are we to stand in the way?

This collection was kindled by our admiration and gratitude to Adrian for his boundless wisdom and countless kindnesses. Having gathered a group of authors who shared our view that a collection of essays would serve as a fitting testament to Adrian's many contributions to the subject, as well as his wider contributions to scholarship and legal practice, we provided them with a list of his publications (see the Appendix) and invited them to choose a topic reflecting their own as well as our honorand's interests.

The geographical and intellectual breadth of Adrian's influence is reflected in the range of contributions to this collection. Our authors are domiciled or resident in the legal systems of the United Kingdom (England and Wales), Australia (including New South Wales and Queensland), the United States of America (Louisiana), Canada (Ontario), Japan, Hong Kong, Singapore and the Irish Republic. We have sub-divided their essays, conventionally, under the headings 'Jurisdiction', 'Choice of Law', 'Recognition and Enforcement of Foreign Judgments' and 'Conflict of Laws within the Legal System', although this gives little sense of the variety of their subject matter or the extent to which the individual topics and broad headings that we use are inter-connected.

Adrian Briggs' philosophy of the Conflict of Laws can, perhaps, be summarised as follows: that the subject's function is to provide practical and just solutions to the problems that arise in the relationships between legal systems when adjudicating in cross-border cases; that the legal systems of the common law are well equipped to perform this function but they have no monopoly on elegant solutions and should never be complacent; and that careful study of the solutions adopted in other legal systems and internationally (especially in the institutions of European Union) brings new insights, which can be harnessed by the common law in its quest for just and fair outcomes.

In Part I (Jurisdiction), the collection begins with two essays on the doctrine of *forum non conveniens*. In the first (ch 1), Andrew Bell assesses how the doctrine has fared in its application by the English courts since the seminal decision of the House of Lords in *Spiliada Maritime Corporation v Cansulex*. 'Not as well as might have been hoped' is his assessment, particularly if measured against one of the ambitions set for the doctrine of promoting international judicial comity. He concludes in favour of the more attenuated approach of the High Court of Australia to the question of whether to exercise jurisdiction. In the second (ch 2), Martin Davies expands on a point also made by Andrew Bell, which is the increasing irrelevance, or neutrality, of 'private interest' factors in the application of the doctrine, in light of technological advances that have greatly reduced the significance of the physical location of parties, evidence and witnesses. Notwithstanding the negative comments of Lord Hope in *Lubbe v Cape Plc*, Davies' analysis of the law in England, the United States and Australia leads him to conclude that the future of the doctrine lies in a greater emphasis on the 'public interest' and perhaps, in due course, the need to embrace the exercise of comparative governmental interest.

Janet Walker's essay (ch 3) considers the role of discretion, not in the context of whether to exercise jurisdiction but in determining whether the courts have jurisdiction in the first place. This point is considered principally in the context of 'holiday torts', with a particular emphasis on the travails, of late, of the Canadian courts and the difficulties encountered in abandoning jurisdiction gateways such as 'damage sustained in the forum' and 'necessary or proper party'. This also allows for a comparison with the long running saga of the '*Brownlie* litigation' in the English courts.

In chapter 4, Andrew Dickinson subjects the 'anti-suit injunction' to critical analysis, tracing its history and development to the present where, in his view, the English courts have been guilty of over-reaching themselves. He concludes that this is, in large part, the result of a lack of rigour in identifying the legal bases for the award of an injunction (as embodied in the loose terminology of necessity for the 'ends of justice', or to remedy a party's 'unconscionable conduct'), a failure to appreciate fully the nature and significance of comity and marginalisation of the choice of law issues that often arise.

Andrew Scott's essay (ch 5) is focused specifically on the question of jurisdiction over co-defendants. He compares the evolution, content and application of the rule under the Recast Brussels I Regulation (Art 8(1)) with the jurisdictional gateway under the CPR (Practice Direction 6B, para 3.1(3)), emphasising the uncertainty and deficiencies of the former, described by Adrian Briggs as 'the one part of the Regulation which works badly'.

Koji Takahashi's essay (ch 6) begins Part II on Choice of Law by considering the law applicable to arbitration and jurisdiction agreements and the significance of the principle of 'severability' of such agreements. His argument is that the principle should not be extended to the choice of law analysis. He concludes that the law applicable to the main contract should also regulate any arbitration or jurisdiction agreement contained within it, although he accepts a limited possibility of *dépeçage*. In a postscript, he detects substantial common ground between his approach and that of the Supreme Court in its recent decision in *Enka v Chubb*, which was delivered after the final manuscript of his essay had been submitted.

The essay in chapter 7 is in fact written by one of the minority in the *Enka* case, but Andrew Burrows turns his attention to claims in restitution, principally on the basis of unjust enrichment, but also, more briefly, restitution for 'wrongs'. Although included in Part II on Choice of Law, his essay assesses the principal questions of both jurisdiction and choice of law that have arisen as the conflict of laws has tried to keep pace with developments in the law of restitution. He highlights in particular the tension between a principled approach which recognises the independence of unjust enrichment from other causes of action (especially contract) and pragmatic concerns such as the need to avoid the fragmentation of forum or applicable law.

Maisie Ooi's essay (ch 8) revisits the law applicable to interests in securities, the subject of her doctoral thesis, co-supervised by Adrian. She considers whether conventional approaches to the set of conflict of laws problems in this area are fit for purpose in an era in which technology has created, and will continue to create, a myriad of new forms of securities holding. She rejects the calls of those who advocate bespoke rules for cryptosecurities in favour of solutions based on the *lex creationis*/law of the system that will accommodate both traditional and new forms of holding.

Adam Rushworth also travels back in time to his early encounters with Adrian as a doctoral student in Oxford. His essay (ch 9) examines the evolution of choice of law rules governing private law remedies, seeking enlightenment from case law and commentary on the Rome I and Rome II Regulations over the past decade. He offers some subtle refinements to his supervisor's own suggested ordering of the subject area.

The two essays in Part III of the collection concern the recognition and enforcement of foreign judgments. The topics chosen by Tiong Min Yeo and Máire Ní Shúilleabháin illustrate the diverse range of Adrian's work. In chapter 10, Professor Yeo chooses the topic of the anti-enforcement injunction, a judicial animal less frequently sighted than its close relation, the anti-suit injunction (ch 4, above). He examines recent case law from the courts of England and Singapore, emphasising the need to distinguish between the injunctions restraining the breach of primary obligations not to enforce a foreign judgment and injunctions that serve to reinforce contractual rights not to be sued in the foreign forum in circumstances where an anti-suit injunction has not issued or has been ineffective.

Dr Ní Shúilleabháin's essay (ch 11) builds on Adrian's criticisms of the overseas divorce recognition scheme in Part II of the Family Law Act 1986. Her careful analysis of the case law leads her to condemn the distinctions that the legislative regime seeks to draw between proceedings and non-proceedings divorces and between 'mono-territorial' and transnational divorces.

The collection concludes, in Part IV, with two essays examining, more broadly, the place of the conflict of laws rules within the legal system to which they belong. Adrian Briggs' work on the conflict of law teaches us the importance of contextual analysis: it is not possible to understand or apply rules of jurisdiction or choice of law or recognition and enforcement of foreign judgments without understanding the characteristic features of the legal system of which those rules form part, their particular place within that system and their relationships to other rules. These essays engage with that theme.

Edwin Peel (ch 12) asks the question 'How private is private international law?', focusing on the role of consent and of legal obligation more generally within the field. Adrian's work identifies these private law concepts as underpinning the common law's conception of the conflict of laws, contrasting this with the philosophy underlying the European Union's approach to the subject, in particular within the Brussels-Lugano regime. Although the essay's author sees a strong positive correlation between private law and private international law, he is more hesitant than his colleague in treating choice of law agreements as a source of enforceable legal obligations.

The essay by James Edelman and Madeleine Salinger (ch 13) is inspired by what they describe as the 'ground-breaking series of lectures' delivered by Adrian at the Hague Academy of Private International Law in 2011 on 'The Principle of Comity in Private International Law'. They use the lectures as the foundation for an investigation of the meaning, role and limits of comity, examining its relationship with the forum's fundamental principles of justice, before using the example of privacy to investigate how new fundamental principles of justice might emerge over time to limit the willingness of the courts of one State to respect the legislative and adjudicatory authority of another State.

We have asked our authors to state the law as at 1 January 2021, the first day after the (provisional) entry into force of the new relationship between the United Kingdom and the European Union. It remains, at the time of writing, unclear how this important development will reshape private international law on both sides of the divorce. We can, however, be certain that Adrian's work on private international law in the common law tradition and under EU law will remain an invaluable guide for judges, practitioners, researchers, teachers and students for many years to come.

We would like to thank all of our authors for their enthusiastic support for the project and for reaching the milestones that we have set for them. We are also grateful for the invaluable editorial and other assistance from the team at OUP (in particular Andy Redman, Jordan Burke, Anthuvan Arokia, Fiona Tatham, Penny Dickman and Deborah Shelley), and to Lord Mance for the foreword. We would not have been able to bring the collection together without the excellent work done by our assistant editor, Thomas Pausey, who gave generously of his time and his expertise. While we have shared the editorial duties, an endeavour such as this requires, in some respects at least, a single point of contact and one editor (Edwin Peel) would like to place on record his thanks to the other (Andrew Dickinson) for taking on this role.

This book is dedicated to our colleague, Adrian Briggs.

Andrew Dickinson
Edwin Peel

Oxford
January 2021

Contents

Table of Cases	xix
Table of Legislation and International Conventions	xxxv
Contributors	xliii
Professor Adrian Briggs	xlvii
Biographical note	xlvii
Adrian Briggs and the North of England—A Brief Note	xlvii
Horton Rogers	
Adrian Briggs and the Conflict of Laws in Oxford	xlviii
Francis Reynolds	
Adrian Briggs' Contribution to the Life of St Edmund Hall	liv
Derrick Wyatt	
Recollections	lvii

PART I JURISDICTION

1. The Natural Forum Revisited	3
Andrew Bell	
A. Introduction	3
B. *Spiliada*—a Noble Aim, Rare Praise and a Wide Embrace	5
C. The Natural Forum and 'Unattainable Perfection'—Noble but Naïve?	9
D. The Natural Forum—Australian Iconoclasm	18
E. O Canada, Oh Canada!	21
F. The Natural Forum, Comity and Hard Cases	24
G. The Natural Forum—Final Reflections	30
2. *Forum Non Conveniens*: Now We Are Much More Than Ten	31
Martin Davies	
A. Introduction	31
B. Some Mysteries of Interpretation Found While Digging in the Foundations	33
C. The Convenience of the Parties	38
D. Public Interest Factors	41
E. The Nature of the Decision	47
F. Conclusion	50

3. The Distant Shore: Discretion and the Extent of Judicial
   Jurisdiction ... 53
   Janet Walker
   A. Introduction ... 53
   B. Dipping Our Toes in the Water ... 54
   C. Jurisdiction and Service ... 56
   D. Up to Our Elbows: Eschewing Discretion Has Not Achieved
      Certainty ... 58
   E. In Over Our Heads? Certainty and Denial of Justice ... 60
   F. Feeling the Stones ... 64
   G. Strange New Shores ... 69
   H. Settling In ... 73

4. Taming Anti-suit Injunctions ... 77
   Andrew Dickinson
   A. Introduction ... 77
   B. Terminology ... 79
   C. Legal Basis ... 81
   D. In Search of Principle ... 88
   E. A Way Forward? ... 109

5. Jurisdiction over Co-defendants ... 111
   Andrew Scott
   A. Introduction ... 111
   B. The Domestic Rule ... 112
   C. Art 8(1) of the Recast Brussels I Regulation ... 125

PART II CHOICE OF LAW

6. Putting the Principle of Severability in the Dock: An Analysis in
   the Context of Choice of Law for Arbitration and Jurisdiction
   Agreements ... 139
   Koji Takahashi
   A. Introduction ... 139
   B. Purpose and Structure of This Essay ... 140
   C. Substantive Law Sphere ... 141
   D. Extension to the Sphere of Choice of Law Analysis? ... 143
   E. Possibility of *Dépeçage* ... 153
   F. Preferred Choice of Law Approach ... 156
   G. Illustrations of the Contrasting Approaches ... 156
   H. Analysis of English Cases on Arbitration Agreements ... 162
   I. Compatibility with Existing Instruments ... 165
   J. Concluding Remarks ... 170
   K. Postscript ... 170

7. The Conflict of Laws and Unjust Enrichment 175
   Andrew Burrows
   A. Introduction 175
   B. Jurisdiction 178
   C. Applicable Law 191
   D. Concluding Remarks 198

8. Choice of Law in the Shifting Sands of Securities Trading 199
   Maisie Ooi
   A. Introduction 199
   B. Existing Choice of Law Relating to Securities 200
   C. Appraising the Elephant 203
   D. The Evolution of Securities and Trading Platforms 204
   E. Taxonomy of a DLT System 207
   F. Issues of Entitlement—the Technological Solution 208
   G. Issues of Entitlement—the Conflict of Laws Solution 209
   H. Issues of Title—Canvassed Solutions for Cryptosecurities 211
   I. Conclusion 223

9. Remedies and the Conflict of Laws 225
   Adam Rushworth
   A. Overview 225
   B. What is a '*Remedy*'? 226
   C. Theory 227
   D. Rights Arising by Virtue of Being Involved in Legal Proceedings 230
   E. Inconvenience: The Rule of Exclusion 243
   F. Conclusion 246

PART III RECOGNITION AND ENFORCEMENT OF FOREIGN JUDGMENTS

10. Foreign Judgments and Contracts: The Anti-enforcement Injunction 251
    Tiong Min Yeo
    A. Introduction: From Anti-suit to Anti-enforcement Injunctions 251
    B. The Law on Anti-enforcement Injunctions 253
    C. Interference with Foreign Legal Systems 256
    D. The Importance of Primary Obligations 258
    E. *Ellerman Lines*: Breach of Contract and Fraud 261
    F. Three Modern Cases Involving Breach of Contract 263
    G. Agreements to Discharge Judgment Debts 268
    H. Conclusion 269

11. 'A Peculiarly Pointless Line of Division': Recognition of Proceedings and Non-proceedings Divorces under the Family Law Act 1986 — 273
Máire Ní Shúilleabháin
   A. Introduction — 273
   B. An Historical Exegesis: The Origins of the Distinction between Proceedings and Non-proceedings Divorces — 274
   C. Two Distinct Schemes of Recognition under Section 46(1) and 46(2) of the 1986 Act — 276
   D. Rationality of the Disparate Treatment of Proceedings and Non-proceedings Divorces: A 'Peculiarly Pointless' Line of Division? — 278
   E. Practical Difficulty in Distinguishing Proceedings and Non-proceedings Divorces — 283
   F. Replication in the Civil Partnership Act 2004 — 290
   G. Another Pointless Line of Division? Transnational Divorces — 292
   H. Conclusion — 295

PART IV CONFLICT OF LAWS WITHIN THE LEGAL SYSTEM

12. How Private is English Private International Law? — 299
Edwin Peel
   A. Introduction — 299
   B. Jurisdiction and Jurisdiction Agreements — 301
   C. Choice of Law and Choice of Law Agreements — 319
   D. Brexit — 322
   E. Conclusion — 324

13. Comity in Private International Law and Fundamental Principles of Justice — 325
James Edelman and Madeleine Salinger
   A. Introduction — 325
   B. The Meaning and Role of Comity — 327
   C. Fundamental Principles of Justice as a Limit on Comity — 337
   D. New Fundamental Principles of Justice and the Example of Privacy — 348
   E. Conclusion — 355

Appendix: List of Publications — 357
Index — 363

Table of Cases

UNITED KINGDOM (INCLUDING THE PRIVY COUNCIL)

Abela v Baadarani [2013] UKSC 44; [2013] 1 WLR 2043 ....55, 115
Abidin Daver, The [1984] AC 398. .... 3, 5, 6, 7, 24, 26, 79
Actavis UK Ltd v Eli Lilly & Co [2015] EWCA Civ 555; [2016] 4 All ER 666 ..... 227, 242, 243
Actavis UK Ltd v Eli Lilly & Co [2014] EWHC 1511 (Pat); [2015] Bus LR 154. 236
Adams v Cape Industries plc [1990] 1 Ch 433 (CA). 22, 102, 305, 335
Adhiguna Meranti, The [1988] 1 Lloyd's Rep 384. ....8, 27
AES Ust-Kamenogorsk Hydropower Plant LLP v AES Ust-Kamenogorsk Hydropower
    Plant JSC [2011] EWCA Civ 647; [2011] 1 Lloyd's Rep 233 308
AES Ust-Kamenogorsk Hydropower Plant LLP v Ust-Kamenogorsk Hydropower
    Plant JSC [2013] UKSC 35; [2013] 1 WLR 1889. 252
Agbaje v Agbaje [2010] UKSC 13; [2010] 1 AC 628 335
Aggelki Charis Compania Maritima SA v Pagnan SpA (The Angelic Grace)
    [1995] 1 Lloyd's Rep 87 (CA) 85, 252, 257, 259, 309
Agnew v Lansförsäkringsbolagens AB [2001] 1 AC 223 ....184, 187
Airbus Industrie GIE v Patel [1998] UKHL 12; [1999] 1 AC 119 .... 10, 12, 79, 80,
                                                                     83, 86–7, 93, 102, 252, 255
Air Foyle Ltd v Center Capital Ltd [2003] 2 Lloyd's Rep 753 (QB) 269
AK Investment CJSC v Kyrgyz Mobil Tel Ltd [2011] UKPC 7; [2012] 1 WLR 1804. 46
Aksionairnoye Obschestvo A M Luther v James Sagor & Co [1921] 3 KB 532 ......336, 338
Akai Pty Ltd v People's Insurance Co Ltd [1998] 1 Lloyd's Rep 90 (QB) 85, 256, 257, 258
Al-Bassam v Al-Bassam [2004] EWCA Civ 857 101
Albon v Naza Motor trading Sdn Bhd [2007] EWHC 9 (Ch); [2007] 2 All ER 719 190
Aldington Shipping Ltd v Bradstock Shipping Corp and Marbanaft GmbH
    [1988] 1 Lloyd's Rep 475 8
Alexandros T, The [2013] UKSC 70; [2014] 1 Lloyd's Rep 223 ....312, 313, 316, 323
Alfonso-Brown v Milwood [2006] EWHC 642 (Fam); [2006] 2 FLR 265 ....283, 290
Alfred C Toepfer International GmbH v Molino Boschi Sarl [1996] 1 Lloyd's Rep 510...313
Allen v Flood [1898] AC 1. 346
Alliance Bank JSC v Aquanta Corp [2012] EWCA Civ 1588; [2013] 1 Lloyd's Rep 175 190
Altimo Holdings and Investment Ltd v Kyrgyz Mobil Tel Ltd [2011] UKPC 7;
    [2012] 1 WLR 1804 .... 14, 24, 26, 28, 29, 84, 113, 114, 116, 117, 119, 120, 121, 122
Amin Rasheed Shipping Corporation v Kuwait Insurance Co: The Al Wahab
    [1984] AC 50. ....3, 4, 6, 27, 34, 115
AMT Futures Ltd v Marzillier [2017] UKSC 13; [2018] AC 439. ....108, 127
AmTrust Europe Ltd v Trust Risk Group SpA [2015] EWCA Civ 437;
    [2016] 1 All ER (Comm) 325 49
Andrew Weir Shipping Ltd v Wartsilla UK Ltd [2004] EWHC 1284 (Comm);
    [2004] 2 Lloyd's Rep 377 130
Arab Monetary Fund v Hashim [1996] 1 Lloyd's Rep 589 (CA) 197
Argyll v Argyll [1967] Ch 302. 352
Armstrong v Armstrong [1892] P 98 103
AS Latvijas Krajbanka v Antonov [2016] EWHC 1679 (Comm) 232, 233

TABLE OF CASES

A/S D/S Svendborg v Wansa [1996] 2 Lloyd's Rep 559,
affd [1997] 2 Lloyd's Rep 183 ....101, 102
Aspen Underwriting Ltd v Credit Europe Bank NV [2017] EWHC 1904 (Comm);
[2018] 1 All ER (Comm) 228 185
Aspen Underwriting Ltd v Credit Europe Bank NV [2018] EWCA Civ 2590;
[2019] 1 Lloyd's Rep 221 ....185, 188
Aspen Underwriting Ltd v Credit Europe Bank NV [2020] UKSC 11;
[2020] 2 WLR 919 185
AstraZeneca UK Ltd v Albemarle Int Corp [2010] EWHC 1028 (Comm);
[2010] 2 Lloyd's Rep 61 190
Attorney General v Blake [2001] 1 AC 268 (HL) 260
Attorney General v Guardian Newspapers Ltd (No 2) [1990] 1 AC 109 (HL) 353
Australian Commercial Research and Development Ltd v ANZ McCaughan
Merchant Bank Ltd [1989] 3 All ER 65, affd [1990] 2 WLUK 351 ....100, 105
Avrora Fine Arts Investment Ltd v Christie, Manson & Woods Ltd [2012] EWHC
2198 (Ch); [2012] PNLR 35 322

Babanaft International Co SA v Bassatne [1990] Ch 13.............................104
Baird v Prescott and Co (1890) 6 TLR 231...91
Baku Consolidated Oilfields Ltd, Re [1993] BCC 653 215
Bank of Credit and Commerce International (Overseas) Ltd v Akindele
[2000] EWCA Civ 502; [2001] Ch 347 98
Bank St Petersburg OJSC v Arkhangelsky [2014] EWCA Civ 593;
[2014] 1 WLR 4360 ....263, 264, 265, 268, 269
Bank of Tokyo Ltd v Karoon [1987] AC 45 (CA) 79, 95, 102, 252
Banque Cantonale de Geneve v Polevent Ltd [2015] EWHC 1968 (Comm);
[2016] QB 394...196
Barclays Bank plc v Homan [1992] BCC 757 ....84, 85, 96, 107, 310
Barros Mattos v MacDaniels Ltd [2005] EWHC 1323 (Ch) 195
Bath & North East Somerset DC v Mowlem Plc [2004] EWCA Civ 115; [2004] BLR 153 316
Beauchamp v Huntley (1822) Jac 546; 37 ER 956....................................90, 103
Beckford v Kemble (1822) 1 Sim & St 7; 57 ER 3.....................................90
Beddow v Beddow (1878) 9 ChD 89..81
Belhaj v Straw [2017] UKSC 3, [2017] AC 964 ... 333, 336, 339, 340, 341, 345, 346, 347, 348
Berkovits v Grinberg [1995] Fam 142 (HC) 288, 293, 294
Bernstein v Skyviews & General Ltd [1978] QB 479.................................352
Black Diamond Offshore Ltd v Fomento de Construcciones y Contratas SA
[2016] EWCA Civ 1141; [2017] 1 BCLC 196 321
Booth v Leycester (1837) 1 Keen 579; 48 ER 430 103
Bord Na Mona Horticulture Limited v British Polythene Industries plc
[2012] EWHC 3346 (Comm)..133
Boss Group Ltd v Boss France SA [1997] 1 WLR 351................................185
Bouygues Offshore SA v Caspian Shipping Co (Nos 1, 3, 4 and 5)
[1998] 2 Lloyd's Rep 461 304
Bowling v Cox [1926] AC 751..188
Boys v Chaplin [1971] AC 356 72
Bremer Vulcan Schiffbau und Maschinenfabrik v South India Shipping Corp Ltd
[1981] AC 908..82
British Airways Board v Laker Airways Ltd [1985] AC 58 ....3, 80, 84, 85, 86, 93, 100
British Airways Plc v Spencer [2015] EWHC 2477 (Ch); [2015] Pens LR 519 231
British South Africa Co v Companhia de Moçambique [1893] AC 602 ....103, 331
Brown v Innovatorone plc [2010] EWHC 2281 (Comm); [2001] ILPr 118.............133

TABLE OF CASES xxi

Brownlie v Four Seasons Holdings Incorporated *see* Four Seasons Holdings
  Incorporated v Brownlie
Bunbury v Bunbury (1839) 1 Beav 318; 48 ER 963 .... 91, 106
Bushby v Munday (1821) 5 Madd 297; 56 ER 908 .... 80, 90, 105

C v D [2007] EWCA Civ 1282; [2008] 1 Lloyd's Rep 239 .... 164, 266
Cadre SA v Astra Asigurari SA [2005] EWHC 2626 (Comm); [2006] 1 Lloyd's Rep 560 320
Cammell v Sewell (1860) 5 H & N 728; 157 ER 1371 338
Campbell v MGN Ltd [2004] UKHL 22; [2004] 2 AC 457 353
Carl Zeiss Stiftung v Rayner & Keeler [1967] 1 AC 853 (HL) 269
Carr v Fracis Times & Co [1902] AC 176 336
Carron Iron Co v Maclaren (1855) 5 HLC 416; 10 ER 961 .... 90, 91, 93
Cartier International AG v British Telecommunications plc [2018] UKSC 28;
  [2018] 1 WLR 3259 82
Casio Computer Co Ltd v Sayo (No 3) [2001] EWCA Civ 661; [2001] ILPr 43 183
Castanho v Brown & Root (UK) Ltd [1981] AC 557 (HL); [1980] 1 WLR 833 ... 10, 80, 82, 92, 252
Castrique v Imrie (1870) Law Rep 4 HL 414 331
Catlin Syndicate Ltd v Adams Land & Cattle Co 2065 (Comm); [2006] 2 CLC 425 311
Cavendish Square Holding BV v El Makdessi [2015] UKSC 67; [2016] AC 1172 .... 244, 316
Charrington v Simons & Co [1970] 1 WLR 725 (Ch) 260
Chatelard v Chatelard (CA, 24 October 1988) 16
Chaudhary v Chaudhary [1985] Fam 19 (CA) 275, 280, 284–8
Chung Chi Cheung v The King [1939] AC 160 345
City of Westminster v IC [2008] EWCA Civ 198; [2008] 2 FLR 267 293
Clearlake Shipping Pte Ltd v Xiang Da Marine Pte Ltd [2019] EWHC 1536 (Comm) 93
Clearlake Shipping Pte Ltd v Xiang Da Marine Pte Ltd [2019] EWHC 2284 (Comm) 101, 259
CMA CGM SA v Hyundai Mipo Dockyard Co Ltd [2008] EWHC 2791 (Comm);
  [2009] 1 Lloyd's Rep 213 .... 313, 318
Cohen v Rothfield [1919] 1 KB 410 80
Commerzbank AG v Liquimar Tankers Management Inc [2017] EWHC 161 (Comm);
  [2017] 1 WLR 3497 302
Compagnie d'Armement Maritime SA v Compagnie Tunisienne de Navigation SA
  [1971] AC 572 141
Connelly v RTZ Corporation [1997] UKHL 30; [1998] AC 854 .... 16, 24, 25, 26, 86, 302
Continental Bank NA v Aeakos Compania Naviera SA
  [1994] 1 WLR 588 (CA) 259, 309, 313
Cook v Virgin Media Ltd [2015] EWCA Civ 1287; [2017] 1 All ER 929 33
Corelli v Wall (1906) 22 TLR 532 (Ch) 352
Cox v Ergo Versicherung AG [2014] UKSC 22; [2014] AC 1379 245
Crédit Suisse Fides Trust v Cuoghi [1998] QB 818 327
Curtis v Lockheed [2008] EWHC 260 (Comm); [2008] 1 CLC 219 241

Dallal v Bank Mellat [1986] 1 All ER 239 148
Dalrymple v Dalrymple (1811) 2 Hagg Con 54; 161 ER 665 330
Day v Brownrigg (1878) 10 Ch D 294 354
de Dampierre v de Dampierre [1988] 1 AC 92 .... 9, 27
Dell Emerging Markets (EMEA) Ltd v Systems Equipment Telecommunications
  Services SAL [2020] EWHC 1384 (Comm) 78
Derby & Co Ltd v Larsson [1976] 1 WLR 202 (HL) 203 .... 112, 118, 119
Derby and Derbyshire Angling Association Ltd v British Celanese Ltd [1953] Ch 149 83
Deripaska v Cherney (No 2) [2009] EWCA Civ 849;
  [2010] 2 All ER (Comm) 456 .... 13, 17, 28, 29, 48

xxii TABLE OF CASES

Desert Loan Corp v Hill [1996] 2 All ER 847 317
Deutsche Bank AG v Asia Pacific Broadband Wireless Communications Inc
    [2008] EWCA Civ 1091; [2009] 2 All ER (Comm) 129 140
Deutsche Bank AG v Highland Crusader Offshore Partners LLP
    [2009] EWCA Civ 725; [2010] 1 WLR 1023 .... 82, 84, 85, 99, 252, 310
Dexia Crediop SpA v Comune di Prato [2016] EWHC 2824 (Comm) 195
Doherty v Allman (1878) 3 App Cas 709 (HL) 258, 259, 309
Distiller's Co (Biochemicals) Ltd v Thompson [1971] AC 458 67
Don v Lippmann (1837) 2 Sh & MacL 682 227
Donohue v Armco Inc [2001] UKHL 64; [2002] 1 All ER 749;
    [2002] 1 Lloyd's Rep 25 .... 85, 107, 252, 259, 303, 309, 310, 312
Douglas v Hello! Ltd (No 3) [2007] UKHL 21; [2008] 1 AC 1 353
Dunlop Pneumatic Tyre Co Ltd v New Garage & Motor Co Ltd [1915] AC 79 316
Duval v 11-13 Randolph Crescent Ltd [2020] UKSC 18; [2020] 2 WLR 1167 307

Earl of Feversham v Watson (1678), DEC Yale 97
Earl of Oxford's Case (1615) Rep Ch 1; 21 ER 485 .... 88, 89
Eastern Trader, The [1996] 2 Lloyd's Rep 585 (QB) 253, 257
Ebert v Venvil [2000] Ch 484 95
Eckerle v Wickeder Westfalenstahl GmbH [2013] EWHC 68 (Ch) 203, 206
Ecobank Transnational Inc v Tanoh [2015] EWCA Civ 1309; [2016] 1 WLR 2231 ... 77, 84,
                                               255, 256, 257, 265, 266, 267, 268, 270, 310
ED & F Man (Sugar) Ltd v Haryanto (No 2) [1991] 2 Lloyd's Rep 429 (CA) 104, 253, 256, 262
El Ajou v Dollar Land Holdings plc [1993] 3 All ER 717 195
El Amria, The [1981] 2 Lloyd's Rep 119 .... 5, 304
El Fadl v El Fadl [2000] 1 FLR 175 (HC) 279, 281, 283, 286, 288, 295
Eleftheria, The [1970] P 94 .... 5, 304
Ellerman Lines Ltd v Read [1928] 2 KB 144 .... 101, 261–3, 264, 267, 268, 270, 305, 310, 320
Ellinger v Guinness, Mahon & Co [1939] 4 All ER 16 .... 113, 114, 117, 122
Empresa Exportadora de Azucar v Industria Azucarera Nacional SA
    (The Playa Larga) [1983] 2 Lloyd's Rep 171 338
Enka Insaat ve Sanayi AS v OOO Insurance Company Chubb [2019] EWHC 3568
    (Comm); [2020] 1 Lloyd's Rep 71 .... 86, 108
Enka Insaat ve Sanayi AS v OOO Insurance Company Chubb [2020] EWCA Civ 574;
    [2020] 3 All ER 577 .... 86, 108, 152, 162, 163
Enka Insaat ve Sanayi AS v OOO Insurance Company Chubb [2020] UKSC 38;
    [2020] 1 WLR 4117 .... 86, 108, 152, 162, 165, 170, 171, 172, 258
Erste Group Bank AG v JSC 'VMZ Red October' [2013] EWHC 2926 (Comm);
    [2014] BPIR 81 120
Erste Group Bank AG v JSC 'VMZ Red October' [2015] EWCA Civ 379;
    [2015] 1 CLC 706 (CA) 120, 121, 122
Estate of Fuld, In the, decd (No 3) [1968] P 675 338

Fanti, The [1991] 2 AC 1 312
Fatima, In re [1986] 1 AC 527 (HL) 292, 293, 294
Fearn v Board of Trustees [2020] EWCA Civ 104; [2020] 2 WLR 1081 354
Fibrosa Spolka Akcyjna v Fairbairn Lawson Combe Barbour Ltd [1943] AC 32 347
Finnish Marine Insurance Co Ltd v Protective National Insurance Co
    [1989] 2 Lloyd's Rep 99 188
Fiona Trust & Holding Corporation and others v Privalov and others
    [2007] UKHL 40; [2007] 4 All ER 951 .... 140, 141, 142
Folkes v Generali [2019] EWHC 801 (QB) 237

TABLE OF CASES   xxiii

Forbes v Cochrane (1824) 2 B & C 448; 107 ER 450...........................345, 346
Four Seasons Holdings Incorporated v Brownlie [2017] UKSC 80;
    [2018] 1 WLR 192 ....55, 58, 59, 61, 65, 66, 68, 69, 71, 115
Fourie v Le Roux [2007] UKHL 1; [2007] 1 WLR 320 ....81, 82, 96
FR Lürssen Werft GmbH & Co KG v Halle [2009] EWHC 2607 (Comm);
    [2010] 2 Lloyd's Rep 20 45
FS Cairo (Nile Plaza) LLC v Brownlie [2020] EWCA Civ 996............... 55, 58, 59, 61,
                                                                        65, 66, 68, 69, 71
Fujifilm Kyowa Kirin Biologics Co Ltd v AbbVie Biotechnology Ltd [2016] EWHC
    2204 (Pat); [2017] Bus LR 333, affd [2017] EWCA Civ 1, [2018] Bus LR 228........77

Gard Marine & Energy Ltd v Tunnicliffe [2010] EWCA 1052; [2011] Bus LR 839 (CA) 131
General Star International Indemnity Ltd v Stirling Cooke Brown Reinsurance
    Brokers Ltd [2003] EHWC 3 (Comm); [2003] Lloyd's Rep IR 719 104
Glencore International AG v Exter Shipping Co Ltd [2002] EWCA Civ 528;
    [2002] 2 All ER (Comm) 1 95
Golubovich v Golubovich [2010] EWCA Civ 810; [2011] Fam 88....................104
Gouriet v Union of Post Office Workers [1978] AC 435 102
Governor and Company of the Bank of Ireland v Pexxnet Ltd [2010] EWHC
    1872 (Comm)...195
Grant v Dawkins [1973] 1 WLR 1406..89
Grupo Torras SA v Al-Sabah (No 5) [2001] Lloyd's Rep Bank 36 (CA) 197
Guido van der Garde BV v Force India Formula One Ltd [2010] EWHC 2373 (QB) 315

H v H (The Queen's Proctor Intervening) (Validity of Japanese Divorce)
    [2006] EWHC 2989 (Fam); [2007] 1 FLR 1318 ....283, 286, 288
H v H (Talaq Divorce) [2007] EWHC 2945 (Fam); [2008] 2 FLR 857.........279, 284, 286
H v S (Recognition of Overseas Divorce) [2012] 2 FLR 157 (HC)........... 278, 281, 283,
                                                                        284, 286, 289, 290
Hamed El Chiaty & Co (T/A Travco Nile Cruise Lines) v The Thomas Cook
    Group Ltd [1994] 1 Lloyd's Rep 382...13
Hamilton-Smith v CMS Cameron McKenna LLP [2016] EWHC 1115 (Ch)............259
Hampstead & Suburban Properties Ltd v Diomedous [1969] 1 Ch 248 (Ch D).........258
Harbour Assurance Ltd v Kansa General International Insurance Ltd
    [1993] QB 701 (CA)..142, 147, 149
Harding v Wealands [2006] UKHL 32; [2007] 2 AC 1............................11, 232
Hardinge v Webster (1859) 1 Drew & Sm 101; 62 ER 326 89
Harrison v Gurney (1821) 7 Jac & W 563; 37 ER 743..............................90
Henry v Geoprosco International Ltd [1976] QB 726 (CA) 267
Hewlett Packard Enterprise Company v Manchester Technology Data (Holdings)
    Ltd [2019] EWHC 2089 (Ch) 226
Hill v Hart-Davis (1884) 26 ChD 470..99
Hindocha v Gheewala [2003] UKPC 77 13
Holman v Johnson (1775) 1 Cowp 341; 98 ER 1120................................330
Hyman v Helm (1883) 24 ChD 531 ....91, 92, 99, 100

Ilyssia Cia Naviera SA v Bamaodah (The Elli 2) [1985] 1 Lloyd's Rep 107 (EWCA).......45
Intended Action, Re, Rousou's Trustee v Rousou [1955] 2 All ER 169................188
Iraqi Civilians v Ministry of Defence [2014] EWHC 3686 (QB); [2015] 2 All ER 714....246

Jaggard v Sawyer [1995] 1 WLR 269 (CA)..258
Jervis v Harris [1996] Ch 195 315

xxiv   TABLE OF CASES

Jogia, Re [1988] 1 WLR 484..188, 189, 194
John Russell & Co Ltd v Cayzer, Irvine & Co Ltd [1916] 2 AC 298 (HL)...............114
Johnston v Coventry Churchill [1992] 3 All ER 14...................................72
Jones v Secretary of State for Energy and Climate Change [2012] EWHC
　2936 (QB); [2012] All ER (D) 271 (Oct)...41
JSC BTA Bank v Granton Trade Ltd [2010] EWHC 2577 (Comm)......................15
JSC Commercial Bank Privatbank v Kolomoisky [2019] EWCA Civ 1708;
　[2020] 2 WLR 993...134, 135

Kabab-JI SAL v Kout Food [2020] EWCA Civ 6, [2020] 1 Lloyd's Rep 269.............160
Kennedy v Cassilis (1818) 2 Swans 313; 36 ER 635....................................90
Kitchen v Royal Air Force Association [1958] 1 WLR 563...........................315
Kleinwort Benson Ltd v Glasgow CC [1999] 1 AC 153...................177, 182–8, 193
Kudos Catering (UK) Ltd v Manchester Central Convention Complex Ltd
　[2013] EWCA Civ 38; [2013] 2 Lloyd's Rep 270..................................322
Kuwait Airways Corp v Iraqi Airways Co [2002] UKHL 19; [2002] 2 AC 883.......85, 102,
　　　　　　　　　　　　　　　　　　　　　　　　　　 333, 334, 337, 338, 339, 347, 348
Kuwait Oil Tanker Co v Al Bader [2000] 2 All ER (Comm) 271..................195, 197

Lachaux v Lachaux [2019] EWCA Civ 738; [2019] 4 WLR 86..........................295
Lawrence v Fen Tigers Ltd [2014] UKSC 13; [2014] AC 822......................83, 105
Livingston Properties Equities Inc v JSC MCC Eurochem [2020] UKPC 31..............44
Logan v Bank of Scotland (No 2) [1906] 1 KB 141...................................99
Lorentzen v Lydden & Co [1942] 2 KB 202...337
Love v Baker (1665) 1 Ch Cas 67; 22 ER 698; (1665) Nels 103, 21 ER 801..............90
Lubbe v Cape plc [2000] UKHL 41; [2000] 1 WLR 1545............16, 18, 24–5, 26, 35, 302
Lucasfilm Ltd v Ainsworth [2011] UKSC 39; [2012] 1 AC 208........................103

Macmillan Inc v Bishopsgate Investment Trust (No 3) [1996] 1 WLR 387....200, 201, 222, 223
MacShannon v Rockware Glass Ltd [1978] AC 795; [1977] 1 WLR 376...........3, 18, 79
MAH v ZS [2012] EWHC 3271 (Fam)...281
Mamidoil-Jetoil Greek Petroleum Co SA v Okta Crude Oil Refinery AD
　[2003] 1 Lloyd's Rep 1 (QB)..253
Manifest Shipping Co Ltd v Uni-Polaris Insurance Co Ltd (The Star Sea)
　[2001] UKHL 1; [2003] 1 AC 469...37
Marc Rich & Co AG v Societa Italiana Impianti pA (The Atlantic Emperor) (No 2)
　[1992] 1 Lloyd's Rep 624..318, 319
Mareva Compania Naviera SA v International Bulkcarriers SA [1975] 2 Lloyd's Rep 509.....92
Marks and Spencer plc v BNP Paribas Securities Services Trust Co (Jersey) Ltd
　[2015] UKSC 72; [2015] 3 WLR 1843..160
Masri v Consolidated Contractors International Co SAL [2009] UKHL 43;
　[2010] 1 AC 90..112
Masri v Consolidated Contractors International Co SAL (No 2) [2008] EWCA Civ 303;
　[2009] QB 450..82, 104
Masri v Consolidated Contractors International Co SAL (No 3) [2008] EWCA
　Civ 625; [2009] QB 503................93, 94, 101, 102, 103, 104, 107, 108, 253, 256
Massey & Anor v Heynes & Co and Schenker & Co (1888) 21 QBD 330 (CA)..........116
Mastermelt Ltd v Siegfried Evionnaz SA [2020] EWHC 927 (QB)....................323
McCabe v McCabe [1994] 1 FLR 410 (CA).....................................283, 290
McHenry v Lewis (1882) 22 ChD 397..99
Melvin v Reid (1931) 297 P 91..349
Mercedes Benz AG v Leiduck [1997] AC 284....................................82, 92

MET v HAT [2013] EWHC 4247 (Fam); [2014] 2 FLR 692.....................281, 286
Michael Wilson & Partners v Emmott [2018] EWCA Civ 51, [2018] 1 Lloyd's Rep 299.....82, 96
Midland Bank plc v Laker Airways Ltd [1986] 1 QB 689..........................3, 100
Monson v Tussauds Ltd [1894] 1 QB 671 (CA)....................................352
Morris v Beardmore [1981] AC 446 (HL)..352
Morris-Garner v One Step (Support) Ltd [2018] UKSC 20; [2019] AC 649............315
MRA v NRK [2011] ScotSC CSOH 101..293
Multinational Gas and Petrochemical Co v Multinational Gas and Petrochemical
  Services Ltd [1983] Ch 258 (CA)...................................119, 120, 121, 122

Nabb Brothers Ltd v Lloyds International (Guernsey) Ltd [2005] EWHC 405 (Ch);
  [2005] ILPr 37...190
Navig8 Pte Ltd v Al-Riyadh Co for Vegetable Oil Industry (The Lucky Lady)
  [2013] EWHC 328 (Comm); [2013] 2 Lloyd's Rep 104..........................45, 101
Navitaire Inc v easyJet Airline Co Ltd (No 2) [2005] EWHC 282 (Ch); [2006] RPC 4.....83
Nima Sarl v The Deves Insurance Public Company Ltd [2002] EWCA Civ 1132;
  [2003] 2 Lloyd's Rep 327...17
North London Railway Co v Great Northern Railway Co (1883) 11 QBD 30.........81, 82
Norwich Pharmacal Co v Customs and Excise Commissioners [1974] AC 133..........82
Novus Aviation Ltd v Onur Air Tasimacilik AS [2009] EWCA Civ 122;
  [2009] 1 Lloyd's Rep 576..45, 115
NP v KRP (Recognition of Foreign Divorce) [2013] EWHC 694 (Fam);
  [2014] 2 FLR 1................................. 283, 286, 287, 288, 289, 290
Nursing & Midwifery Council v Harrold [2015] EWHC 2254 (QB)....................95

Ochsenbein v Papelier (1872) LR 8 Ch App 695................................89, 98
OJSC Oil Co Yugraneft v Abramovich [2008] EWHC 2613 (Comm)..............28, 195
OJSC TNK-BP Holding v Beppler & Jacobson Ltd [2012] EWHC 3286 (Ch)......124, 196
OJSC TNK-BP Holding v Lazurenko [2012] EWHC 2781 (Ch).............235, 236, 237
OJSC VTB Bank v Parline Ltd [2013] EWHC 3538 (Comm)....................123, 124
Olib, The [1991] 2 Lloyd's Rep 108...188
Omega Engineering Inc v Omega SA [2010] EWHC 1211 (Ch); [2010] FSR 26........262
Omega Group Holdings v Kozeny [2002] CLC 132................................103
Oppenheimer v Cattermole [1976] AC 249..............................337, 338, 339
OT Africa Line Ltd v Magic Sportswear Corp [2005] EWCA Civ 710;
  [2006] 1 All ER (Comm) 32..85, 259
Overseas Union Insurance v AA Mutual International Insurance
  [1988] 2 Lloyd's Rep 63..147
Owners of the Atlantic Star v Owners of the Bona Spes (The Atlantic Star)
  [1973] 2 QB 364 (CA)...6, 12
Owners of the Atlantic Star v Owners of the Bona Spes (The Atlantic Star and
  The Bona Spes) [1974] AC 436 (HL)..........................3, 6, 29, 31, 79, 100

Pacific International Sports Clubs Ltd v Soccer Marketing International Ltd
  [2009] EWHC 1839 (Ch)...124
Pacific International Sports Clubs Ltd v Surkis [2010] EWCA Civ 753..............28
ParkingEye Ltd v Beavis [2015] UKSC 67; [2016] AC 1172........................187
Peepul Capital Fund II LLC v VSoft Holdings LLC [2019] UKPC 47..................83
Peer International Corporation v Termidor Music Publishers Ltd [2003] EWCA
  Civ 1156; [2004] Ch 212..337
Pell Frischmann Engineering Ltd v Bow Valley Iran Ltd [2009] UKPC 45;
  [2010] BLR 73..315

xxvi TABLE OF CASES

Pena Copper Mines v Rio Tinto Co (1911) 105 LT 846 101
Penn v Lord Baltimore (1750) 1 Ves Sen 444; 27 ER 1132 .... 96, 259, 308
Pennell v Roy (1850) 3 De G, M & G 126; 43 ER 50 91
Peruvian Guano v Bockwoldt (1882) 23 ChD 225 .... 91, 92, 99
Petter v EMC Europe Ltd [2015] EWCA Civ 828, [2015] IRLR 847 102
Phelps v Prothero (1855) 7 De GM & G 722; 44 ER 280 89
Philips Electronique Grand Public SA v BSkyB Ltd [1995] EMLR 472 321
Phillips v Eyre (1870) LR 6 QB 1 11
Phrantzes v Argenti [1960] 2 QB 19 .... 244, 245
Pilcher v Rawlins (1872) LR 7 Ch App 259 96
Pollard v Photographic Co (1888) 40 Ch D 345 352
Polly Peck International Ltd v Nadir (No 3) [1994] 1 BCLC 661 (CA) 189
Portarlington v Soulby (1834) 7 Sim 28; 40 ER 40 90
Prince Albert v Strange (1849) 2 De G & Sm 652; 64 ER 293 352
Princess Paley Olga v Weisz [1929] 1 KB 718 336
Pryce & Son Ltd v Pioneer Press Ltd (1925) 42 TLR 29 352

Quartz Hill Consolidated Gold Mining Co v Eyre (1883) 11 QBD 674 (CA) 311
Quazi v Quazi [1980] AC 744 (HL) 275, 279, 283, 284, 285, 286, 287, 288, 290
Quazi v Quazi [1980] AC 744 (CA) 283, 284
Quazi v Quazi [1980] AC 744 (HC) 290
Qureshi v Qureshi [1972] Fam 173 (HC) 293

R v Hape [2007] SCR 292 333
R v Secretary of State for the Home Dept, ex p Fatima [1985] QB 190 (HC) 275
R (Countryside Alliance) v Attorney-General [2007] UKHL 52; [2008] 1 AC 719 352
R (Unison) v Lord Chancellor [2017] UKSC 51; [2017] 4 All ER 903 .... 78, 80
Raiffeisen Zentralbank Osterreich AG v Five Star Trading LLC [2001] EWCA
    Civ 68; [2001] QB 825 211
Red Sea Insurance v Bouygues SA [1995] 1 AC 190 72
Republic of Angola v Perfectbit Limited [2018] EWHC 965 (Comm) 236, 237
Robinson v Chief Constable of West Yorkshire [2018] UKSC 4; [2018] AC 7 82
Rousou's Trustee v Rousou [1955] 3 All ER 486 .... 188, 194, 195
Royal Bank of Scotland plc v Etridge (No 2) [2001] UKHL 44; [2002] 2 AC 773 101
Royal Bank of Scotland plc v Highland Financial Partners [2013] EWCA Civ 328;
    [2013] 1 CLC 596 83
Rubin v Eurofinance SA [2010] EWCA Civ 895; [2011] Ch 133 335
Rubin v Eurofinance SA [2012] UKSC 467; [2013] 1 AC 236 .... 23, 307, 335

Sabbagh v Khoury [2014] EWHC 3233 (Comm) 133
Sabah Shipyard (Pakistan) Ltd v Islamic Republic of Pakistan [2002] EWCA
    Civ 1643; [2003] 2 Lloyd's Rep 571 311
Sabah Shipyard (Pakistan) Ltd v Pakistan [2002] EWCA Civ 650 93
Sabbagh v Khoury [2017] EWCA Civ 1120 .... 133, 134, 135, 136
Sabbagh v Khoury [2019] EWCA Civ 1219; [2019] 2 Lloyd's Rep 178 93
SAS Institute Inc v World Programming Ltd [2020] EWCA Civ 599 .... 82, 83, 84, 85,
                                86, 87, 101, 103, 104, 254, 255, 256, 263, 265, 266, 267, 310
SAS Institute Inc v World Programming Ltd (No 2) [2019] EWHC 2481 (Comm) 102
Schibsby v Westenholz (1870) LR 6 QB 155 22
Schiffahrtsgesellschaft Detlev von Appen GmbH v Voest Alpine Intertrading
    GmbH (The Jay Bola) [1997] 2 Lloyd's Rep 279 .... 94, 186, 259

TABLE OF CASES　xxvii

Sea Master Shipping Inc v Arab Bank Ltd [2018] EWHC 1902 (Comm);
　[2018] Bus LR 1798 149
Secure Capital SA v Credit Suisse AG [2017] EWCA Civ 1486; [2017] EWCA Civ
　1486 (CA), affirming [2015] EWHC 388 (Comm); [2015] 1 Lloyd's Rep 556. . . . 202, 206,
　　　　　　　　　　　　　　　　　　　　　　　　　　　　209, 211, 219, 222, 223
Seismic Shipping Inc v Total E&P UK plc [2005] EWCA Civ 985;
　[2005] 2 Lloyd's Rep 359 104
Senior Taxi Aereo Executivo Ltda, Synergy Helicopters II LLC v Agusta Westland SpA
　[2020] EWHC 1348 (Comm) 134
Sennar, The (No 2) [1985] 1 WLR 490 .... 304, 306
Settlement Corpn v Hochschild [1966] Ch 10 101
Shierson v Vlieland-Boddy [2005] 1 WLR 3966 12
Sim v Robinow (1892) 19 R 665 (CS) 668 50
Skype Technologies SA v Kasesalu [2009] EWHC 2783 (Ch) 259
SL Claimants v Tesco Plc [2019] EWHC 2858 (Ch) 203
Société Commerciale de Réassurance v Eras International Ltd (formerly Eras (UK))
　(The Eras Eil Actions) [1992] 1 Lloyd's Rep 570 (CA) 13, 123
Société du Gaz de Paris v Société Anonyme de Navigation Les Armateurs Français
　1926 SC 13 (HL) 16, 38, 301
Societe Nationale Industrielle Aerospatiale v Lee Kui Jak [1987] AC 871 .... 10, 79, 80,
　　　　　　　　　　　　　　　　　　　82, 83, 92, 93, 94, 96, 99, 100, 105, 106, 107, 303
Solovyev v Solovyeva [2014] EWFC 1546; [2015] 1 FLR 734 .... 288, 294
South Carolina Insurance Co v Assurantie Maatschappij 'De Zeven Provincien'
　NV [1987] AC 24 .... 82, 92, 93, 94, 96, 103
South West Trains Ltd v Wightman [1997] EWHC 1160 (Ch); [1998] Pens LR 113 262
Southern Foundries (1926) Ltd v Shirlaw [1940] AC 701 307
Southey v Sherwood (1817) 2 Mer 435; 35 ER 1006 352
Spiliada Maritime Corporation v Cansulex Ltd [1987] AC 460 .... 3, 4, 5–9, 10, 11, 12,
　　　　　　　　　　　　　　　　　　　　　　13, 15, 16, 17, 18, 19, 20, 22, 24, 25, 26, 27, 29, 30, 31,
　　　　　　　　　　　　　　　　　　　　　　34, 37, 38, 43, 46, 49, 50, 58, 92, 114, 115, 122
Spire Healthcare Ltd v Royal & Sun Alliance Insurance plc [2018] EWCA
　Civ 317; [2018] 1 CLC 327 321
Sports and General Press Agency Ltd v "Our Dogs" Publishing Co Ltd
　[1917] 2 KB 125 (CA) 353
Stanford International Bank Ltd, Re [2011] Ch 33 12
Star Reefers Pool Inc v JFC Group Co Ltd [2012] EWCA Civ 14;
　[2012] 1 Lloyd's Rep 376 .... 100, 101
Starlight Shipping Co v Allianz Marine & Aviation Versicherungs AG
　[2014] EWCA Civ 1010; [2014] 2 Lloyd's Rep 544 .... 257, 259, 312, 314
Starlight Shipping Co v Allianz Marine & Aviation Versicherungs AG
　[2014] EWHC 3068 (Comm), Piraeus Court of Appeal Nr 89/31.01.2020 257
Stephens v Avery [1988] Ch 449 352
Stichting Shell Pensioenfonds v Krys [2014] UKPC 41; [2015] AC 616 .... 84, 93,
　　　　　　　　　　　　　　　　　　　　　　　　　　　　　　　　95, 96, 103, 104
Stylianou v Toyoshima [2013] EWHC 2188 (QB) 233, 234
Sulaiman v Juffali [2002] 1 FLR 479 293
Sulamérica CIA Nacional De Seguros SA v Enesa Engenharia SA
　[2012] EWCA Civ 638; [2013] 1 WLR 102 .... 163, 164
Sumitomo Heavy Industries Ltd v Oil & Natural Gas Commission
　[1994] 1 Lloyd's Rep 45 165
Sutherland v Her Majesty's Advocate (Scotland) [2020] UKSC 32, [2020] 3 WLR 327 . . . 352

xxviii TABLE OF CASES

Takhar v Gracefield Developments Ltd [2019] UKSC 13; [2020] AC 450 263
Tasarruf Mevduati Sigorta Fonu v Merrill Lynch Bank and Trust Co (Cayman) Ltd
    [2011] UKPC 17; [2012] 1 WLR 1721 82
Texan Management Ltd v Pacific Electric Wire & Cable Co Ltd [2009] UKPC 46 33
Tillman v Egon Zehnder Ltd [2019] UKSC 32; [2020] AC 154 146
Toepfer GmbH v Société Cargill France [1997] 2 Lloyd's Rep 98 313
Tolley v J S Fry & Sons Ltd [1930] 1 KB 467 (CA) 353
Tolley v J S Fry and Sons Ltd [1931] AC 333 (HL) 353
Trendtex Trading Corp v Central Bank of Nigeria [1977] 1 QB 529 345
Trendtex Trading Corp v Credit Suisse [1980] 3 All ER 721 6
Troke v Amgen Seguros Generales Compania de Seguros Y Reaseguros Sau
    [2020] EWHC 2976 (QB), [2020] 4 WLR 159 233
Trustor AB v Smallbone (No 3) [2000] EWCA Civ 150 195
Tufail v Riaz [2013] EWHC 1829 (Fam) 290
Turner v Grovit [2000] QB 345 (CA) 101
Turner v Grovit [2001] UKHL 65; [2002] 1 WLR 107 .... 78, 79, 80, 93, 94, 95, 110, 252
Tyne Improvement Commissioners v Armement Anversois S/A ('The Brabo (No 2))
    [1949] AC 326 (HL) 118, 119

UBS AG New York v Fairfield Sentry Ltd [2019] UKPC 20; [2019] BCC 966 99
Union Discount Co v Zoller [2001] EWCA Civ 1755; [2002] 1 WLR 1517 .... 311, 312
Unwired Planet International Ltd v Huawei Technologies (UK) Co Ltd
    [2020] UKSC 37 .... 15, 17

Vardopulo v Vardopulo (1909) 25 TLR 518 91
Vedanta Resources plc v Lungowe [2019] UKSC 20; [2019] 3 All ER 1013;
    [2019] 2 Lloyd's Rep 399 .... 9, 14, 15, 24, 35, 36, 39, 40, 41, 45, 46, 48, 49, 124, 135
Villiers v Villiers [2020] UKSC 30; [2020] 3 WLR 171 241
Vizcaya Partners Limited v Picard (Gibraltar) [2016] UKPC 5, [2016] 3 All ER 181 23
VTB Capital plc v Nutritek International Corp [2013] UKSC 5; [2013] 2 AC 337 .... 14, 41, 44, 123

Wall v Mutuelle de Poitiers Assurances [2014] EWCA Civ 138;
    [2014] 1 WLR 4263 .... 229, 231, 232, 233, 234
Wallace v Campbell (1840) 4 Y&C Ex 167; 160 ER 964 91
Watson v First Choice Holidays and Flights Ltd [2001] EWCA Civ 972;
    [2001] 2 Lloyd's Rep 339 130
Watson, Laidlaw & Co Ltd v Pott, Cassels & Williamson [1914] SC 18 (HL) 315
Weaver v Clifford (1603) Yel 42, 42; 80 ER 30 88
West Tankers Inc v Ras Riunione Adriatica Di Sicurta SpA [2005] EWHC
    454 (Comm); [2005] 2 All ER (Comm) 240; [2005] 2 Lloyd's 257 .... 84, 149
West Tankers Inc v Ras Riunione Adriatica di Sicurta SpA [2007] UKHL 4;
    [2007] 1 All ER (Comm) 794 .... 77, 85
Wharton v May (1799) 3 Ves Jun 27; 31 ER 454 90
Wicken v Wicken [1999] Fam 224 (HC) 286
Willers v Joyce [2016] UKSC 44; [2018] AC 843 100
Williams v Jones (1845) 13 M & W 628 335
Williams v Settle [1960] 1 WLR 1072 (CA) 352
Witted v Galbraith [1893] 1 QB 431 (CA) 117
WMS Gaming Inc v Benedetti Plus Giocolegale Ltd [2011] EWHC 2620 (Comm) 313
Wood v Capita Insurance Services Ltd [2017] UKSC 24; [2017] AC 1173 321
Wrotham Park Estate Co Ltd v Parkside Homes Ltd [1974] 1 WLR 798 (CA) 260

XX v Whittington Hospital NHS Trust [2020] UKSC 14; [2020] 2 WLR 972...........329

Youell v La Reunion Arienne [2009] EWCA Civ 175; [2009] 2 All ER (Comm) 1071....185
Yukos Capital Sarl v OJSC Rosneft Oil Co (No 2) [2012] EWCA Civ 855;
 [2014] QB 458..29
Yusuf Cepnioglu, The [2016] EWCA Civ 687; [2016] 1 Lloyd's Rep 61 ....93, 94, 107

Z v A (Financial Remedies: Overseas Divorce) [2012] EWHC 467 (Fam);
 [2012] 2 FLR 667 281
Zaal v Zaal [1983] 4 FLR 284 (HC)...275

EUROPEAN COURT OF JUSTICE (IN CHRONOLOGICAL ORDER)

Case 189/87 Kalfelis v Bankhaus Schroeder Munchmeyer Hengst & Co (t/a HEMA
 Beteiligungsgesellschaft mbH) [1988] ECR 5565 ....126, 127, 129, 130, 133, 183, 187
Case 365/88 Kongress Hagen GmbH v Zeehaghe BV [1990] ECR I-1845...............130
Case C-294/92 Webb v Webb [1994] ECR I-1717....................................179
Case C-269/95 Benincasa v Dentalkit Srl Case [1997] ECR I-3767 140
Case C-391/95 Van Uden Maritime BV v Kommanditgesellschaft in Firma Deco
 Line [1998] ECR I-7091 240
Case C-51/97 Réunion Européenne v Spliethoff's Bevrachtingskantoor BV &
 Anor [1998] ECR I-6511...129, 130
Case C-387/98 Coreck Maritime GmbH v Handelsveem BV [2000] ECR I-9337 149
Case C-256/00 Besix SA v Wasserreinigungsbau Alfred Kretzschmar GmbH & Co
 [2003] 1 WLR 1113..184
Case C-116/02 Erich Gasser GmbH v Misat srl [2003] ECR I-14963...............299, 300
Case C-159/02 Turner v Grovit [2004] ECR I-3565 ....5, 79, 251, 252, 299, 303
Case C-281/02 Owusu v Jackson [2005] ECR I-1383;
 [2005] QB 801..5, 9, 123, 299, 301, 314
Case C-103/05 Reisch Montage AG v Kiesel Baumaschinen Handels GmbH
 [2006] ECR I-6827...129, 132, 133, 134
Case C-98/06 Freeport v Arnoldsson [2007] ECR I-8319...........127, 130, 131, 132, 134
Case C-185/07 Allianz SpA (formerly Riunione Adriatica di Sicurta SpA) v
 West Tankers Inc [2009] ECR I-663...................................5, 95, 251, 314
Case C-133/08 Intercontainer Interfrigo v Balkenende Oosthuizen and
 MIC Operations [2009] ECR I-9687..155
Case C-145/10 Painer v Standard Verlags GmbH [2011] ECR I-12533............131, 134
Case C-131/12 Google Spain SL v Agencia Espanola de Proteccion de Datos
 ECLI:EU:C:2014:317...353
Case C-352/13 Cartel Damage Claims (CDC) Hydrogen Peroxide SA v
 Akzo Nobel NV ECLI:EU:C:2015:335; [2015] QB 906.........131, 133, 134, 135, 149
Case C-366/13 Profit Investment Sim SpA v Ossi [2016] 1 WLR 3832 ....180, 181, 185, 187
Case C-536/13 Gazprom OAO, Re [2015] 1 WLR 4937 (ECJ) 251
Case C-102/15 Gazdasági Versenyhivatal v Siemens Aktiengesellschaft Österreich
 [2016] 5 CMLR 14 183
Case C-417/15 Schmidt v Schmidt [2017] ILPr 6..................................180
Case C-149/18 Agostihno da Silva Martins v Dekra Claims Services Portugal SA
 ECLI:EU:C:2019:84..108
Case C-208/18 Petruchová (Jana) v FIBO Group Holdings Limited
 ECLI:EU:C:2019:825..69
Case C-548/18 BGL BNP Paribas SA v TeamBank AG Nürnberg
 ECLI:EU:C:2019:848...217

INTERNATIONAL CASES

Australia

Ace Insurance Ltd v Moose Enterprise Pty Ltd [2009] NSWSC 724 322
Amaca Pty Ltd v Frost (2006) 67 NSWLR 635 11
Ammon v Colonial Leisure Group Pty Ltd [2019] WASCA 158..................... 47, 48
Attorney-General (UK) v Heinemann Publishers Australia Pty Ltd
   (Spycatcher Case) [1988] HCA 25; (1988) 165 CLR 30, ... 46, 336
Australian Broadcasting Corporation v Lenah Game Meats Pty Ltd
   (2001) 208 CLR 199.. 354
Australian Health and Nutrition Association Ltd v Hive Marketing Group
   Pty Ltd (2019) 99 NSWLR 419... 10
Brunoro v Nebelung [2017] ACTCA 26 48
Campbells Cash & Carry Pty Ltd v Fostif Pty Ltd (2006) 229 CLR 386 4
Centrebet Pty Ltd v Baasland [2012] NTSC 100; (2012) 272 FLR 69 38
Church of Scientology v Woodward (1982) 154 CLR 25 354
Colosseum Investment Holdings Pty Ltd v Vanguard Logistics Services Pty Ltd
   [2005] NSWSC 803 49
CSR Ltd v Cigna Insurance Australia Ltd (1997) 189 CLR 345.......... 20, 21, 87, 95, 100
Fleming v Marshall [2011] NSWCA 86; (2011) 279 ALR 737..................... 48, 49
Garsec v His Majesty The Sultan of Brunei (2008) 250 ALR 682; [2008] NSWCA
   211, (2008) 250 ALR 682.. 13, 49
Giller v Procopets (No 2) (2008) 24 VR 1 354
Gomez v Kuhadas (No 2) [2015] FCA 561 269
Habib v Commonwealth (2010) 183 FCR 62................................. 334
Hillam and Barret [2019] FamCA 193..................................... 49
House v R [1936] HCA 40; (1936) 55 CLR 499............................... 47
Jasmin Solar Pty Ltd v Trina Solar Australia Pty Ltd [2015] FCA 1453;
   (2015) 331 ALR 108.. 38
John Pfeiffer Pty Ltd v Rogerson (2000) 203 CLR 503 11
Kuhadas v Gomez [2014] FCCA 1130 269
McGregor v Potts (2005) 68 NSWLR 109 9
McRae v Commonwealth Disposals Commission (1951) 84 CLR 377 322
Minister for Immigration and Border Protection v SZVFW [2018] HCA 30;
   (2018) 264 CLR 541, 357 ALR 408....................................... 47
Murakami v Wiryadi [2010] NSWCA 7; (2010) 268 ALR 377 .... 11, 16, 19, 48, 49
Nationwide News Pty Ltd v Rush [2020] FCFCA 115; (2020) 380 ALR 432 48
Navarro v Jurado [2010] FamCAFC 210; (2010) 44 Fam LR 310 50
Neilson v Overseas Development Corporation (2005) 223 CLR 331................. 11
Oceanic Sun Line Special Shipping Company Inc v Fay (1988) 165 CLR 197...... 5, 8, 18, 19, 64
PCH Offshore Pty Ltd v Dunn (No 2) (2010) 273 ALR 167........................ 19
Pierson and Romilly [2020] FamCAFC 9; (2020) 61 Fam LR 541 49
Potter v Broken Hill Proprietary Co Ltd (1906) 3 CLR 479....................... 331
Puttick v Tenon Ltd [2008] HCA 54; (2008) 238 CLR 265................ 16, 19, 20, 42, 49
Regie Nationale des Usines Renault SA v Zhang [2002] HCA 10;
   (2002) 210 CLR 491.. 11, 19, 36, 49
Reinsurance Australia Corporation v HIH Casualty and General Insurance Ltd (in
   liq) (2004) 254 ALR 29 16
Scarffe v Obannon [2020] FamCA 77 49
Sharif v Sharif (1980) 10 Fam Law 216 (HC)................................. 275
Studorp Ltd v Robinson [2012] NSWCA 382............................ 36, 48, 49
Victoria Park Racing and Recreation Grounds Co Ltd v Taylor (1937) 58 CLR 479 354

Voth v Manildra Flour Mills Pty Ltd [1990] HCA 55; (1990) 171 CLR 538.........5, 8, 13, 18, 19, 20, 21, 25, 26, 30, 32, 35, 36, 38, 46, 49, 50, 51
Warren v Coombes [1979] HCA 9; (1979) 142 CLR 531..............................47
White v Redding [2019] NSWCA 152; (2019) 99 NSWLR 605........................48
Wigmans v AMP Ltd [2019] NSWCA 243; (2019) 373 ALR 323......................48
Yzerman v Schofield [2011] WASC 200..38

Brunei

Syarikat Bumiputra Kimanis v Tan Kok Voon [1988] 3 MLJ 315......................8

Canada

Amchem Products Inc v British Columbia (Workers' Compensation Board)
 [1993] 1 SCR 897..8, 87
Beals v Saldanha [2003] 3 SCR 416..22, 23, 24
Best v Palacios 2016 NBCA 59..65
Brown v Mar Taino SA [2015] NSJ No 516; 2015 NSSC 348..........................66
Club Resorts Ltd v Van Breda (2012) SCC 17....................62, 63, 64, 65, 66, 68, 72
Colavecchia v Berkeley Hotel Ltd [2012] OJ No 3952; 112 OR (3d) 287 (SCJ)............66
Cook v 1293037 Alberta Ltd (cob Traveller's Cloud 9) 2016 ONCA 836.................65
Douez v Facebook Inc (2017) SCC 33...67, 74
Gajraj v DeBernardo (2002) 213 DLR (4th) 651...............................60, 61
Google Inc v Equustek Solutions Inc (2017) SCC 34...............................74
GreCon Dimter Inv v JR Normand Inc [2005] 2 SCR 401 (Québec)..................300
Hunt v T&N plc [1993] 4 SCR 289..60
Kazemi Estate v Islamic Republic of Iran [2014] 3 SCR 176.................340, 345
Laane and Balster v Estonian State Cargo & Passenger SS Line [1949] SCR 530........337
Lapointe Rosenstein Marchand Melançon LLP v Cassels Brock & Blackwell LLP
 [2016] SCJ No 30; [2016] 1 SCR 851...65
Lemmex v Sunflight Holidays Inc (2002) 213 DLR (4th) 627................60, 61, 68
Leufkens v Alba Tours International Inc (2002) 213 DLR (4th) 614..........60, 61, 68
Moran v Pyle National (Canada) Ltd [1975] 1 SCR 393....................66, 67, 70, 72
Morguard Investments Ltd v De Savoye [1990] 3 SCR 1077 (SCC)..........22, 60, 327
Muscutt v Courcelles (2002) 213 DLR (4th) 577.........................56, 60, 61, 62
Nevsun Resources Ltd v Araya 2020 SCC 5.....................................327
Old State Brewing Co v Newlands Service Inc (1998) 155 DLR (4th) 250 (BCCA)......305
Pro Swing Inc v Elta Golf Inc [2006] 2 SCR 612...................................22
Rudder v Microsoft Corp (1999) 40 CPC (4th) 394 (SCJ Ont).........................67
Sinclair v Cracker Barrel Old Country Store, Inc (2002) 213 DLR (4th) 643.........60, 61
Spar Aerospace Ltd v American Mobile Satellite [2002] 4 SCR 205....................331
Teck Cominco Metals Ltd v Lloyd's Underwriters [2009] 1 SCR 321....................74
Wilson v Riu [2012] OJ No 5679, 98 CCLT (3d) 337 (SCJ)...........................66

Cayman Islands

Insurco Int Ltd v Gowan Co [1994–95] CILR 210....................................8
KTH Capital Management Ltd v China One Fin Ltd [2004–05] CILR 213...............8

European Court of Human Rights

Bărbulescu v Romania App no 61496/08 (ECtHR, 5 September 2017).................355
Nunez v Norway (2014) 58 EHRR 17...351
Oliari v Italy (2017) 65 EHRR 26..291

xxxii TABLE OF CASES

P and S v Poland App no 57375/08 (ECtHR, 30 October 2012) 351
Pellegrini v Italy (2001) 35 EHRR 44 295
Ribalda, López v Spain App nos 1874/13 and 8567/13 (ECtHR, 17 October 2019) 355
von Hannover v Germany ECHR 2004-VI 41.....................................355

France

Municipalite de Khoms El Mergeb v Societe Dalico [1994] 1 Rev Arb 116
    (Cour de cassation) 158
SA Banque Worms c/Epx Brachot, Cass civ (1) 19 November 2002, D 2003, 797.........77

Germany

BVerfGE 34, 269 (1973) (Soraya decision) 350
BVerfGE 35, 202 (1973) (Lebach decision) 350, 351

Hong Kong

Bright Shipping Ltd v Changhong Group (HK) Ltd) (The CF Crystal and The Sanchi)
    [2018] HKCFI 2474; [2019] 1 Lloyd's Rep 437, affd [2019] HKCA 246;
    [2019] HKLRD 220; [2020] 2 Lloyd's Rep 1 40
TS Singapore (Owners) v Xin Nan Tai 77 (Owners) [2017] HKCU 1382;
    [2017] 3 HKLRD 387...40

India

Bano v Union of India [2017] INSC 677 290
Interdigital Technology Corp v Xiaomi Corp IA 8772/2020 in CS (Comm)
    295/2020 (Delhi High Court, 9 October 2020) 253
Mayar (HK) Ltd v Owners & Parties, Vessel MV Fortune Express (2006) AIR 1828........8
Modi Entertainment Network v WSG Cricket Pte Ltd (2003) AIR 1177;
    (2003) 1 SCR 480 8

International Arbitration Tribunal

Antoine Fabiani Case (1905) 10 RIAA 83 343
ICC Case No 17176, Final Award [2016] 41 YB Comm Arb 86 256

International Court of Justice

Case Concerning Barcelona Traction, Light and Power Company
    (Belgium v Spain) [1970] ICJ 1...345
Frontier Dispute (Burkina Faso/Republic of Mali) [1986] ICJ Rep 554...............346
North Sea Continental Shelf [1969] ICJ Rep 3 344
Reservations to the Convention on the Prevention and Punishment of the Crime of
    Genocide [1951] ICJ Rep 15..346
Western Sahara [1975] ICJ Rep 12 346

Ireland

Bateman v Willoe (1803) 1 Sch & Lefr 204 89
Bell v O'Reilly (1805) 2 Sch & Lef 430 89
Cooney v Wilson [1913] 2 IR 402 (CA Ireland) 117
Ross v Eason & Son Ltd [1911] 2 IR 459 (CA Ireland)..............................117
Sharples v Eason & Sons [1911] 2 IR 436 (CA Ireland) 117

Japan
Tokyo District Court judgment, 15 February 2016 2016WLJPCA02156001 145

Malaysia
American Express Bank Ltd v Al-Ozeir [1995] 1 CLJ 275. 8

New Zealand
Club Mediterranee NZ v Wendell [1989] 1 NZLR 216. .... 8, 18, 64

Singapore
Ashlock v SetClear Pte Ltd [2012] 2 SLR 625 (CA). 270
BCY v BCZ [2016] SGHC 249. .... 142, 145, 146
Bi Xiaoqing v China Medical Technologies [2019] SGCA 50 92
BNA v BNB [2019] SGCA 84. 157
Dream Star, The [2017] SGHC 220; [2018] 4 SLR 473 40
Goldilocks Investment Co Ltd v Noble Group Ltd [2018] SGHC 108 210
Good Earth Agricultural Co Ltd v Novus International Pte Ltd [2008] 2 SLR 711;
    [2008] SGCA 13 28
Hilton International Manage (Maldives) Pvt Ltd v Sun Travels & Tours Pvt Ltd
    [2018] SGHC 56. 266
Hung Vuong-2, The [2000] 2 SLR (R) 11 30
Koh Kay Yew v Inno Pacific Holdings Ltd [1997] 2 SLR 148 10
Lakshmi v Jhaveri [2019] 2 SLR 372 (CA) 257
Oriental Insurance Co Ltd v Bhavani Stores Pte Ltd [1998] 1 Sing LR 253 8
People's Insurance Co Ltd v Akai Pty Ltd [1998] 1 SLR 206 (HC) 258
Rappo v Accent Delight International Ltd [2017] 2 SLR 265. .... 4, 10, 15, 16, 17
RGA Holdings International Inc v Loh [2017] 2 SLR 997 (CA) 258
Rickshaw Investments Ltd v Nicolai Baron von Uexkull [2007] 1 SLR 377 .... 8, 11
Sembcorp Marine Ltd v PPL Holdings Pte Ltd [2013] 4 SLR 193 (CA) 260
Sun Travels & Tours Pvt Ltd v Hilton International Manage (Maldives) Pvt Ltd
    [2019] 1 SLR 732 (CA). 253, 256, 266, 267, 268
Thahir v Pertamina [1994] 3 SLR 257. 197
Turf Club Emporium Pte Ltd v Yeo Boong Hua [2018] SGCA 44 315
Virsagi Management (S) Pte Ltd v Welltech Construction Pte Ltd [2013] 4 SLR 1097 10

United States
Air Crash Disaster Near New Orleans, Louisiana on July 9, 1982 821 F 2d 1147
    (5th Cir en banc 1987). 43, 46
Air Crash over the Southern Indian Ocean on March 8, 2014, In re 946 F 3d 607
    (DC Cir 2020). 41
Atlantic Marine Construction Co v US District Court for the Western District
    of Texas 571 US 49 (2013) 33, 43
Ayco Farms Inc v Ochoa 862 F 3d 945 (9th Cir 2017) 41
Bachchan v India Abroad Publications Inc 585 NYS 2d 661 (1992). 348
Bangladesh Bank v Rizal Commercial Banking Corp 2020 WL 1322275 (SDNY 2020) 39
Bank of Augusta v Earle 38 (13 Peters) US 519 (1839). 331
Blanchard v Commonwealth Oil Company 294 F 2d 834 (5th Cir 1961) 79
Bodum USA Inc v La Cafetiere Inc 621 F 3d 624 (7th Cir 2010). 42
Carnival Cruise Lines, Incorporated v Eulala Shute 499 US 585 64
Direction der Disconto-Gesellschaft v US Steel Corp 300 F 741 (1925) 332

TABLE OF CASES

Fresh Results LLC v ASF Holland BV 921 F 3d 1043 (11th Cir 2019) 43
Gates Learjet Corp v Jensen 743 F 2d 1325 (9th Cir 1984) 45
Gulf Oil Corp v Gilbert 330 US 501 (1947) 32, 33, 38, 42, 43, 45, 50, 72
Hartford Fire Insurance Co v California 509 US 764 (1993).... 330, 331, 332, 333, 334, 335
Hatch v Baez 7 Hun 596 (1876)... 347
Hilton v Guyot 159 US 113 (1895) 307, 327, 331, 332, 336
Jacobellis v Ohio 378 US 184 (1964).. 46, 51
Johnston v Compagnie Générale Transatlantique 152 NE 121 (NY 1926) 332
Jones v IPX International Equatorial Guinea SA 920 F 3d 1085 (6th Cir 2019) 41
Koster v American Lumbermens Mutual Casualty Co 330 US 518 (1947) 32
Laker Airways v Sabena, Belgian World Airways 731 F 2d 909 (DC Cir 1984)..... 3, 44, 102
Loucks v Standard Oil Co of New York 120 NE 198 (NY 1918) 337
Mannington Mills Inc v Congoleum Corporation 595 F2d 1287 (3rd Cir 1979) 335
Mercier v Sheraton International Inc 935 F 2d 419, 428 (1st Cir 1991) 45
M/S Bremen v Zapata Off- Shore Company 407 US 1 (1972) 305
Nemariam v Federal Democratic Republic of Ethiopia 315 F 3d 390 (DC Cir 2003)...... 43
Nygård v DiPaolo 753 Fed Appx 716 (11th Cir 2018) 45
Oetjen v Central Leather Company 246 US 297 (1917)....................... 336, 347
Pavesich v New England Life Insurance Co 50 SE 68 (Ga 1905)..................... 349
Peck v Jenness (1849) 48 US 612.. 89, 104
Republic of Hungary v Simon 141 S Ct 187 (Mem) (2020) 39
Roberson v Rochester Folding Box Co 64 NE 442 (NY 1902)....................... 349
Shi v New Mighty US Trust 918 F 3d 944 (DC Cir 2019)........................ 39, 40
Sierra Frac Sand LLC v CDE Global Ltd 960 F 3d 200 (5th Cir 2020) 43
Simon v Republic of Hungary 911 F 3d 1172 (DC Cir 2018) 1186 39
Underhill v Hernandez 168 US 250 (1897) 347
US v Various Articles of Merchandise, Seizure No 148 600 F Supp 1383 (ND Ill 1985)....46
Walworth v Harris 129 US 355 (1889) 331
Willendson v Forsoket 29 F Cas 1283 (D Penn 1801) (No 17,682) 1284 31
Wiwa v Royal Dutch Petroleum Co 226 F 3d 88 (2nd Cir 2000)...................... 41

Table of Legislation and International Conventions

STATUTES

Administration of Judgments
  Act 1920 305
Arbitration Act 1996
  s 2(5) 147
  s 7 . . . . 140, 147, 148, 149
  s 89(3) 159
  s 91(1) 159
Bankruptcy Act 1914 189
Civil Jurisdiction and Judgments
  Act 1982
  ss 15A–E 74
  s 16 177
  s 25(2) 240
  s 32 . . . . 85, 251, 304, 308, 309, 310,
                      317, 318, 320, 323
  s 32(1) 304, 308
  s 32(1)(a) 305, 308, 320
  s 32(1)(c) 309
  s 32(3) 304, 305, 306, 317
  s 32(4)(a) 304, 317, 323
  s 33 . . . . 317, 318
  Sch 4 . . . . 177, 182
  Sch 14 305
Civil Partnership Act 2004 . . . . 273, 290, 296
  s 235 291
  s 235(1) 290
  s 235(2) 290, 291, 292
Common Law Procedure
  Act 1852 . . . . 112 177
  ss 18–19 112
Companies Act 2006
  s 145 206
Consumer Rights Act 2015
  s 67 146
Contracts (Applicable Law) Act 1990
  s 2(2) 193
Contracts (Rights of Third Parties)
  Act 1999 209
County Courts Act 1984
  s 69 233
Divorce, Dissolution and Separation
  Act 2020 281

Domicile and Matrimonial
  Proceedings Act 1973 292
European Union (Withdrawal)
  Act 2018 177
European Union (Withdrawal
  Agreement) Act 2020 177
  s 41(4) 178
  Sch 5, para 1 178
Family Law Act 1986 . . . . 281, 285, 288,
                      291, 292, 293, 294, 296
  Pt II 273, 274, 275, 286, 295
  s 44(1) 292, 294
  s 45(1) 276, 292
  s 46 . . . . 276, 279, 280, 283, 291, 292
  s 46(1) 273, 276–8, 279,
                      280, 287, 288, 295
  s 46(1)(a) 276, 288
  s 46(1)(b) 276
  s 46(2) 273, 276–8, 279, 280,
                      289, 290, 291, 296
  s 46(2)(a) 276
  s 46(2)(b) 276
  s 46(2)(c) 276
  s 51 276
  s 51(3)(b)(i) 282, 283
  s 51(3)(b)(ii) 282
  s 51(4) 282
  s 54 . . . . 276, 283
  s 54(1) 273
Fatal Accidents Act 1976
  s 3(3) 245
Foreign Judgments (Reciprocal
  Enforcement) Act 1933
  s 4(3)(b) 305
Human Rights Act 1998
  s 12(3) 235
Law of Property Act 1925
  s 172 189
Law Reform (Married Women and
  Tortfeasors) Act 1935
  s 6 106
Marine Insurance Act 1906
  s 17 37

Matrimonial and Family Proceeding
  Act 1984 283
  Pt III................273, 280, 281, 296
  s 12(1)(a).......................280
Private International Law (Implementation
  of Agreements) Act 2020
  s 1(2) 178
  Sch 3F..........................178
Private International Law (Miscellaneous
  Provisions) Act 1995..........232, 245
Recognition of Divorces and Legal
  Separations Act 1971........275, 276,
                          279, 284, 288, 292
  ss 2–5..........................275
  s 6..........................275, 276
Senior Courts Act 1981 262
  s 19............................81
  s 19(2)(b)......................262
  s 35A 233
  s 37............................245
  s 37(1) 81, 82
  s 37(3) 92
Supreme Court of Judicature
  Act 1873 ....82, 112
  s 16............................81
  s 24(5) 262
  s 25(8) 81
Supreme Court of Judicature Act 1875 .. 112
Supreme Court of Judicature
  (Consolidation) Act 1925
  s 18............................81
  s 41............................262

STATUTORY INSTRUMENTS

Civil Jurisdiction and Judgments
  (Amendment) (EU) Exit
  Regulations (SI 2019/479)
  Pt 2............................177
  Pt 4............................177
  Pt 5............................177
  reg 26...........................74
  reg 82..........................127
  reg 89......................77, 111
Civil Partnership (Jurisdiction and
  Recognition of Judgments)
  Regulations 2005 (SI 2005/3334)...291
Civil Partnership and Marriage (Same Sex
  Couples) (Jurisdiction and Judgments)
  (Amendment etc) (EU Exit)
  Regulations 2019 (SI 2019/495)
  reg 5(6)........................291

Civil Procedure Rules 1998 as amended
  (CPR).........33, 37, 57, 73, 178, 191
  Pt 1............................35
  r 1.1(1) 302
  r 1.1(2)(e) 302
  r 1.2...........................35
  r 1.2(a)........................35
  r 3.11..........................80
  PD 3C...........................80
  Pt 6
  r 6.20..........................114
  r 6.20(3) 114
  r 620(14).......................190
  r 6.20(15) 189, 190
  rr 6.36–6.37 ....54, 73
  r 6.36............114, 123, 188, 189
  r 6.37(3) 34, 37, 122
  PD 6B...........................114
  para 3.1.................54, 178, 188
  para 3.1(3) 114, 120
  para 3.1(3)(a)..........120, 121, 122
  para 3.1(3)(b)..................120
  para 3.1(6) 115, 190
  para 3.1(7) 190
  para 3.1(9) 190
  para 3.1(9)(a)..................58
  para 3.1(11) 190
  para 3.1(15) 189, 190
  para 3.1(16) 189, 190
  para 3.1(16)(a)................190
  Pt 11
  r 11(6)(d) 33
  Pt 35...........................231
Financial Collateral Arrangements (No 2)
  Regulations (SI 2003/3226).......201
Financial Markets and Insolvency
  (Amendment and Transitional
  Provision) (EU Exit) Regulations
  2019 (SI 2019/341)
  paras 4–10......................201
Financial Markets and Insolvency
  (Settlement Finality) Regulations
  (SI 1999/2979) 201
Jurisdiction and Judgments (Family)
  (Amendment etc) (EU Exit)
  Regulations 2019 (SI 2019/519)
  reg 15(7) 288
Law Applicable to Contractual Obligations
  and Non-Contractual Obligations
  (Amendment etc.) (EU Exit)
  Regulations 2019 (SI 2019/834)....108,
                             178, 226, 322

Rules of the Supreme Court (RSC)
Ord XI 112, 114, 128
Ord XI, r 1(g) 112, 117, 120
Ord 11 189
Ord 11, r 1......................34
Ord 11, r 1(1)(c).................113
Ord 11, r 1(1)(j) 118
Ord 11, r 2......................34
Ord 11, r 4(1)(d).................113
Uncertificated Securities Regulations 2001 (SI 2001/3755)
reg 24 211

EUROPEAN UNION
Directives

Directive 91/250/EEC of 14 May 1991 on the legal protection of computer programs [1991] OJ L122/42
Art 5(3) 254
Directive 93/13/EEC of 5 April 1993 on unfair terms in consumer contracts [1993] OJ L95/29
Art 3(1) 159
Annex 1(q) 159
Directive 98/26/EC of the European Parliament and of the Council of 19 May 1998 on settlement finality in payment and securities settlement systems [1998] OJ L166/45, as amended by Directive 2009/44/EC, [2009] OJ L146/37 (Settlement Finality Directive)....224
Art 9............................201
Directive 2001/24/EC of the European Parliament and of the Council of 4 April 2001 on the reorganisation and winding up of credit institutions [2001] OJ L125/5 224
Directive 2002/47/EC of the European Parliament and of the Council of 6 June 2002 on financial collateral arrangements [2002] OJ L168/43, as amended by Directive 2009/44/EC, [2009] OJ L146/ 37 (Financial Collateral Directive) 224
Art 9............................201
Directive (EU) 2015/2302/EU on package travel and linked travel arrangements [2015] OJ L326/1 68
Directive (EU) 2017/828/EU amending Directive 2007/36/EC as regards the encouragement of long-term shareholder engagement [2017] OJ L132/1 (Shareholder Rights Directive II) 206, 209

Regulations

Brussels I Regulation *see* Regulation 44/2001
Brussels I Regulation (recast) *see* Regulation 1215/2012
Brussels II *bis* Regulation *see* Regulation 2201/2003
Maintenance Regulation *see* Regulation 4/2009
Rome I Regulation *see* Regulation 593/2008
Rome II Regulation *see* Regulation 864/2007
Regulation (EC) 44/2001 of 22 December 2000 on jurisdiction and the recognition and enforcement of judgments in civil and commercial matters [2001] OJ 12/1 (Brussels I Regulation).......127, 177, 299, 303
Art 1............................183
Art 5(1) 179, 180, 181
Art 5(3) 179, 181
Art 6(1) 127
Art 23...........................313
Art 24(1) 179
Art 27......................312, 313
Art 54...........................244
Regulation (EC) No 2201/2003 of 27 November 2003 concerning jurisdiction and the recognition and enforcement of judgments in matrimonial matters and the matters of parental responsibility, repealing Regulation (EC) No 1347/2000 [2003] OJ L338/1 (Brussels II *bis* Regulation).............. 288, 291, 296
Regulation (EC) 864/2007 of the European Parliament and of the Council of 11 July 2007 on the law applicable to non-contractual obligations (Rome II) [2007] OJ L199/40 (Rome II Regulation)....... 108, 175, 178, 191, 198, 226, 229, 235, 241, 245, 246
Recital (7) 193, 239
Recital (33) 233, 234, 240
Art 1............................194

Regulation (EC) 864/2007 of the European
  Parliament and of the Council
  of 11 July 2007 on the law applicable
  to non-contractual obligations
  (Rome II) [2007] OJ L199/40
  (Rome II Regulation) (*cont.*)
  Art 1(3) 230, 231, 233, 239, 241, 242
  Art 4. . . . . .72, 196, 197
  Art 4(1) 108
  Art 10. . . . . .192, 193, 195, 196, 197
  Art 10(1) 194, 195, 196
  Art 10(2) 194, 195
  Art 10(3) 194, 195, 196
  Art 10(4) 195, 196
  Art 11. 197
  Art 14. 192
  Art 15. . . . . .231, 235, 243
  Art 15(c)–(d). 108, 230
  Art 15(c) 233, 246
  Art 15(d) . . . 228, 237, 238, 239, 240, 241, 243
  Art 16. 108
  Art 19. 197
Regulation (EC) 593/2008 of the
  European Parliament and of the
  Council of 17 June 2008 on the law
  applicable to contractual obligations
  (Rome I) [2008] OJ L177/6
  (Rome I Regulation) 155, 157,
        165–6, 178, 198, 226, 235,
        241, 246, 268, 321, 322
  Recital (7) 239
  Art 1(2)(c). 228, 230, 232, 238
  Art 1(2)(d). 150, 165
  Art 1(2)(e). 108, 150, 157,
        160, 165, 197, 258
  Art 1(2)(f) 217
  Art 1(2)(h). 151
  Art 1(3) 151, 230, 239
  Art 3. 193
  Art 3(1) 154
  Art 4. 193
  Art 4(1)(a)–(b) .153
  Art 4(2) 153
  Art 6. 166
  Art 6(2) 159, 160, 161, 168
  Art 10.1 235
  Art 12. . . . . .193, 197
  Art 12(1)(c). 178, 191, 193, 197, 243
  Art 12(1)(d). 178
  Art 12(1)(e). 191, 193
  Art 14. . . . . .217, 218

Regulation No 4/2009 [2009] OJ L7/1
  (Maintenance Regulation) 241
Regulation (EU) No 1215/ 2012 on
  jurisdiction and the recognition
  and enforcement of judgments in
  civil and commercial matters
  [2012] OJ L351/1 (Brussels I
  Regulation (recast)). 9, 57, 77, 110,
       111, 115, 149, 177, 305, 317, 323
  Recital (2) 169
  Recital (16) 128
  Art 4. . . . . .135, 186
  Art 4(1) 123, 124, 125
  Art 5(1) 129
  Art 6. 301
  Art 7. .128, 186, 188
  Art 7(1) 179, 180, 185, 186, 187
  Art 7.2 72
  Art 7(2) 130, 186
  Art 7(3) 179
  Art 8(1) 111, 124, 125, 127, 128, 129,
        130, 131, 132, 133, 134, 135, 136
  Art 8(2) 128, 130, 133
  Art 14. . . . . .186, 187, 188
  Art 24. 128
  Art 25. . . . . .128, 313
  Art 25(1) .145, 169
  Art 25(5) 140, 141, 148, 169
  Art 31(2) 300, 313, 323
  Art 45. 305
Regulation (EU) 2015/848 of the
  European Parliament and of the
  Council of 20 May 2015 on
  insolvency proceedings (recast)
  [2015] OJ L141/19 (EU Insolvency
  Regulation). 12

NATIONAL LEGISLATION
Australia
Civil Liability Act 2002 (NSW)
  s 16. 48
Court Procedures Rules 2006 (ACT)
  r 6504(2) 35
  r 6507. 35
Federal Court Rules 2011 (Cth)
  r 10.43 37
Jurisdiction of Courts (Cross-vesting) Act
  1987 (Cth). 11
Rules of the Supreme Court (NT)
  r 7.02 37

Rules of the Supreme Court 1971 (WA)
O 10 r 1(1) 37
O 10 r 1A(2)(a) 37
Supreme Court Civil Rules 2006 (SA)
r 40C(2) 35, 36
r 40F 35
Supreme Court (General Civil Procedure) Rules 2015 (Vic)
r 7.05(2) 35
r 7.07 35
Supreme Court Rules 2000 (Tas)
r 147C(2) 35, 36
r 147F 35
Trans-Tasman Proceedings Act 2010 (Cth)
Pt 3 11
Uniform Civil Procedure Rules 2005 (NSW)
r 11.6(2) 35
r 11.8AA 35

Bangladesh

Muslim Family Laws Ordinance 284, 289

Canada

Charter of Rights and Freedoms
s 7 341
Civil Code of Quebec
Art 3121 158
Court Jurisdiction and Proceedings Transfer Act (CJPTA) 62
s 6 63
Court Jurisdiction and Proceedings Transfer Act, SBC 2003, c 28 (British Columbia) 62
Court Jurisdiction and Proceedings Transfer Act, SNS 2003 (2nd Sess), c 2 (Nova Scotia) 62
Court Jurisdiction and Proceedings Transfer Act SPEI 1997, c 61 (Prince Edward Island) 62
Court Jurisdiction and Proceedings Transfer Act, SS 1997, c C-41.1 (Saskatchewan) 62
Rules of Civil Procedure (Ontario) RRO 1990, Reg 194 (Ontario)
r 17.02(h) 60
r 17.03 63

Germany

Bürgerliches Gesetzbuch (BGB)
s 823 245
s 823(1) 350
s 844 245
Code of Civil Procedure (ZPO)
s 1040 140
Grundgesetz für die Bundesrepublik Deutschland (Basic Law) 1949
Art 1 350
Art 2 350

Greece

Civil Code 312
Criminal Code 312

India

Constitution
Art 14 290

Iraq

Resolution of the Revolutionary Command Council No 369 (RCC 369) 339

Pakistan

Muslim Family Laws Ordinance 279, 284, 285, 286, 287, 289

Singapore

Application of English Law Act (Cap 7A, Rev Ed 1994) 252
Civil Law Act (Cap 43, Rev Ed 1999)
s 3(e) 262
Reciprocal Enforcement of Foreign Judgments Act (Cap 265, Rev Ed 2001) 262, 267
Singapore Convention on Mediation Act 2020, Act No 4 of 2020 270
s 5(2)(a) 271
s 7(3) 271

Switzerland

Federal Act on Private International Law of 18 December 1987
Art 3 63
Art 178.2 158

xl   TABLE OF LEGISLATION AND INTERNATIONAL CONVENTIONS

United States
California Code of Civil Procedure
(Cal Civ Pro)
  § 410.10 . . . . 33, 54
Constitution
  Fifth Amendment. 33
  Fourteenth Amendment 33
Delaware Corporations Law (8 Del C 1953)
  § 224. 221
Federal Rules of Civil Procedure
(Fed R Civ P)
  r 4(d) 33
  r 4(k)(1)(a) 33
  r 30(b)(2). 39
  r 43(a). 39
  r 44.1 42
New York Civil Practice Law and Rules
  § 302. 54
Restatement (Second) on the Conflict
  of Laws (1971) 51
  § 6(b)(2). 43
Rules Enabling Act 1934 (28 USC ss
  2071-2077)
  § 2072 ff 33
Sherman Act 1890
  (15 USC ss 1-7). 20, 332, 333

INTERNATIONAL CONVENTIONS, TREATIES AND AGREEMENTS

American Convention on Human Rights
  (Pact of San José, Costa Rica) (adopted
  22 November 1969, entered into force
  18 July 1978) 1144 UNTS 1979
  Art 11. 352
American Declaration of the Rights
  and Duties of Man 1948 352
Arbitration Rules of the United Nations
  Commission on International
  Trade Law (UNGA Res 31/98 (15
  December 1976) UN Doc A/31/98)
  Art 21(2) 140
Brussels Convention on jurisdiction and
  the enforcement of judgments
  in civil and commercial matters,
  27 September 1968 [1972]
  OJ L299/42 (1968 Brussels
  Convention) 177, 299, 305
  Art 3. 129
  Art 5(1) 182, 183, 184, 185
  Art 5(3) 183, 184
  Art 6(1) 125, 126, 127, 128
  Art 6(2) 126, 127
  Art 22. 126
Charter of Fundamental Rights of
  the European Union
  Art 7. 352
Convention for the Unification of
  Certain Rules for International
  Carriage by Air (Warsaw, 12 October
  1929) (Warsaw Convention) 70
Convention on jurisdiction and the
  enforcement of judgments in civil
  and commercial matters (Lugano,
  16 September 1988 [1988] L319/9
  (Lugano Convention) 125
Convention on jurisdiction and the
  recognition and enforcement of
  judgments in civil and commercial
  matters [2007] (OJ L339/3) (Lugano
  Convention 2007) 9, 127, 177,
          178, 188, 191, 198, 317, 323
  Preamble 179
  Art 2. 179, 182, 184
  Art 5(1) 178, 179, 180, 181, 182, 184
  Art 5(3) 178, 179, 181
  Art 5(6) 179
  Art 5(7) 179
  Art 6(1) 127, 131, 134
  Art 22(1) 179
  Protocol 2, Art 1 323
Convention on the Recognition and
  Enforcement of Foreign Judgments
  in Civil or Commercial Matters
  (2 July 2019) (Hague Judgments
  Convention) 74
Convention on the Rights of the Child
  (adopted 20 November 1989,
  entered into force 2 September
  1990) 1577 UNTS 3
  Art 16. 352
Draft Articles on Responsibility of
  States for Internationally
  Wrongful Acts 2001
  Art 22. 104
  Arts 49-53. 104
European Convention on Human Rights 5
  Art 6. 295
  Art 8. . . . . 291, 295, 351, 352, 355
  Art 8(1) 351
  Art 8(2) 351
  Art 14. 295

Hague Convention on Choice of Court Agreements (2005) (Hague Choice of Court Convention) 149, 169, 178, 188, 191, 317
Art 3(d) 140, 141, 148, 169
Art 5(1) 169
Art 6(a) 169
Art 8(1) 169
Art 9(a) 169
Hague Convention on the Recognition of Divorces and Legal Separations 1970 .... 274, 277
Art 1 274
Art 10 .... 295, 296
Art 17 .... 275, 276, 296
Art 60(c) 296
Hague Convention (IV) respecting the Laws and Customs of War on Land in 1907 344
Hague Principles on Choice of Law in International Commercial Contracts (2015) 157
Art 2(2)(a)–(b) 154
Hague Securities Convention 201, 202, 218, 223
Art 2(3)(c) 206
International Covenant on Civil and Political Rights (adopted 16 December 1966, entered into force 23 March 1976) 999 UNTS 171 (ICCPR)
Art 17 351
Art 49 351
International Convention for the Safety of Life at Sea (SOLAS) (opened for signature 1 November 1974, entered into force 25 May 1980) 1184 UNTS 278 40
International Convention for the Unification of Certain Rules of Law relating to Bills of Lading (Brussels, 25 August 1924) as amended by the protocol done at Brussels on 23 February 1968 (Hague-Visby Rules) 70
Model Law on International Commercial Arbitration of the United Nations Commission on International Trade Law (UNGA Res 40/72 and 61/33 (11 December 1985, as amended 4 December 2006) UN Doc A/40/17, annex I and A/61/17, annex I) (UNCITRAL Model Law) 168
Art 1(2) 166
Art 7, Options I–II 145
Art 16 .... 140, 149
Art 16(1) 141, 143, 148, 167
Art 16(3) 143
Art 34(2)(a)(i) 166
Art 36(1)(a)(i) 166
Rome Convention on the law applicable to contractual obligations (1980) (consolidated version [1998] OJ C27/34) (Rome Convention) 150, 155
Art 4(1) 154, 155
Art 10(1)(e) 193
Statute of the Permanent Court of International Justice
Art 38(1) 344
Art 38(1)(c) 344
UNCITRAL Model Law see Model Law on International Commercial Arbitration
UNCITRAL Model Law on Cross-Border Insolvency 1997 12
UNIDROIT Convention on Substantive Rules for Intermediated Securities 2009 (Geneva Securities Convention) 206
United Nations Convention on the Assignment of Receivables in International Trade 2001 216
United Nations Convention on International Settlement Agreements Resulting from Mediation, GA Res 73/198 (Singapore Convention on Mediation) 270
Art 3(1) 270
United Nations Convention on the Recognition and Enforcement of Foreign Arbitral Awards (New York, 10 June 1958) (New York Convention) 166, 168
Art V(1)(a) 166, 171, 172
Universal Declaration of Human Rights (adopted 10 December 1948) UNGA Res 217 A(III) (UDHR) 351
Art 12 351
Vienna Convention on the Law of Treaties
Art 53 345

Contributors

Professor **Andrew Dickinson**, *Editor*
Andrew Dickinson is a Fellow of St Catherine's College and Professor of Law at the University of Oxford. He is a member of the Mance Committee, which advises the UK Government on private international law issues, and is one of the specialist editors of *Dicey, Morris & Collins: The Conflict of Laws*.

Professor **Edwin Peel**, *Editor*
Edwin Peel is a Fellow of Keble College and Professor of Law at the University of Oxford. He is also a tenant at One Essex Court, Temple.

Thomas Pausey, *Assistant Editor*
Thomas Pausey is a pupil barrister at One Essex Court and a member of Gray's Inn. He studied Law (BA Jurisprudence, BCL) at St Catherine's College, University of Oxford.

The Hon Justice **A S (Andrew) Bell**
Andrew Bell is the President of the Court of Appeal and a Justice of the Supreme Court of New South Wales. He is a co-author of *Nygh's Conflict of Laws in Australia* and an Adjunct Professor at the University of Sydney Law School.

The **Rt Hon Lord Burrows**
Andrew Burrows is a Justice of the UK Supreme Court, a member of the Oxford University Law Faculty and a Quondam Fellow of All Souls College. He was a Law Commissioner for England and Wales (1994–1999) and President of the Society of Legal Scholars (2015–2016).

Professor **Martin Davies**
Martin Davies is Admiralty Law Institute Professor of Maritime Law at Tulane University Law School and Professorial Fellow of Melbourne Law School. He is one of the co-authors of *Nygh's Conflict of Laws in Australia*.

The Hon Justice **James Edelman**
James Edelman is a Justice of the High Court of Australia and Adjunct Professor, Universities of New South Wales, Queensland and Western Australia.

Dr **Máire Ní Shúilleabháin**
Máire Ní Shúilleabháin is an Associate Professor in Law at University College Dublin, specialising in private international law.

Dr **Maisie Ooi**
Maisie Ooi graduated with first class honours in the LLB and BCL and wrote her DPhil under the supervision of Professor Adrian Briggs and Professor Dan Prentice. She practised law for many years and was consultant to the Government of Hong Kong SAR in the

Rewrite of the Companies Ordinance before deciding in a moment of insanity to see if she could teach as well. She currently teaches cross border corporate finance and cross border corporate insolvency at the University of Hong Kong's Faculty of Law.

Professor **Francis Reynolds** DCL, QC (Hon), FBA
Francis Reynolds is Professor of Law Emeritus, University of Oxford and Emeritus Fellow of Worcester College, Oxford.

Professor **W V Horton Rogers**
Horton Rogers was Professor of Law at the University of Leeds from 1977 to 1998 and Senior Fellow at the School of Law, University of Nottingham from 1998 to 2013. He is a member of the European Group on Tort Law. Between 1975 and 2010, he wrote nine editions of *Winfield & Jolowicz on Tort*. From 1998 to 2008 he produced three editions of *Gatley on Libel and Slander* with Patrick Milmo QC.

Dr **Adam Rushworth**
Adam Rushworth is a barrister at One Essex Court, Temple. He was formerly a Lecturer at Lady Margaret Hall and Keble College. His doctorate was concerned with aspects of remedies in private international law.

Madeleine Salinger
Madeleine Salinger is an associate to the Hon Justice Edelman at the High Court of Australia.

Dr **Andrew Scott**
Andrew Scott is a barrister at Blackstone Chambers, London. He was formerly a Fellow of All Souls College, Oxford, where his research focused on various private international law topics, including jurisdiction agreements, upon which he wrote a DPhil supervised by Adrian Briggs.

Professor **Koji Takahashi**
Koji Takahashi is a professor at the Doshisha University Law School in Kyoto, Japan. Prior to taking the appointment in Japan, he was a lecturer at the School of Law of Birmingham University and a Research Fellow at the Institute of Maritime Law of Southampton University.

Professor **Janet Walker**
Janet Walker is a Distinguished Research Professor at Osgoode Hall Law School. She is author of *Canadian Conflict of Laws* and the Conflict of Laws volume of *Halsbury's Laws of Canada*.

Professor **Derrick Wyatt** QC
Derrick Wyatt is an Emeritus Professor of Law at Oxford University, and an Emeritus Fellow of St Edmund Hall. He has published numerous contributions to scholarship in the field of

EU Law, and has appeared before Parliamentary Committees to give evidence on EU Law, and Brexit.

Professor **Tiong Min Yeo**
Tiong Min Yeo is the Yong Pung How Chair Professor of Law at the Singapore Management University, where he was formerly Dean of the School of Law. He has appeared as *amicus curiae* at the request of the Singapore Court of Appeal in complex international commercial cases, and has advised the Singapore Ministry of Law on private international law issues.

Professor Adrian Briggs QC (Hon)

Biographical note

A proud man of Kent, Adrian Briggs was born on 22 September 1956 at Ashford. Having studied at Ashford Grammar School, he came up to Oxford in 1975 to read Jurisprudence at Hertford College. Following success in Finals in 1978, he remained at Hertford to study for the Bachelor of Civil Law, graduating with distinction. It was in that year that he first encountered the Conflict of Laws, the subject area in which he has risen to pre-eminence. In 1979, he briefly took up a post as a lecturer at the University of Leeds before returning the following year to take up a tutorial fellowship at St Edmund Hall (*vice* Robert Venables) and lectureship in Law at the University of Oxford.

Forty years on, Adrian is the Sir Richard Gozney Fellow and Tutor in Law at 'Teddy' Hall and Professor of Private International Law within the University, having been awarded the latter distinction in 2004. In 2016, he was appointed Queen's Counsel (*Honoris Causa*) in recognition of his contributions as an academic, practitioner and expert.

Although Adrian's prodigious record of publication[2] speaks for itself, his major contributions include (presently) six editions of *Civil Jurisdiction and Judgments* (1st edn, 1993), four of his short introduction to the *Conflict of Laws* (1st edn, 2002), a monograph on *Agreements on Jurisdiction and Choice of Law* (2008) and, perhaps most significantly, *Private International Law in English Courts* (2014).

Adrian Briggs and the North of England—A Brief Note

Horton Rogers

It is sobering to realise that it is now more than forty years since I appointed Adrian Briggs to his first academic job. I had only been at Leeds for a year and as I recall both of my professorial colleagues had scarpered overseas, leaving me to manage as best I could. We always seemed to be looking for a lecturer or two. Years later I concluded that if you look at these things in Football League terms our role was

---

[2] See the Appendix to this collection—List of Publications.

that of, say, Leyton Orient to Arsenal: we find a good'un, give the new player a bit of a run in the team and then see him/her be enticed away by a richer club. There was of course one important difference: there was no consolation in the form of a transfer fee. I saw three current members of the Oxford Law Faculty travel this route. Adrian had not been there long when the siren call was heard. We had become fond of him and I think he had become quite fond of us (though his judgements on his colleagues, always discreetly expressed, were remarkably acute for one so young), but I was not in a position to offer any substantial inducement and in any case he would have been mad to stay.

Adrian Briggs and the Conflict of Laws in Oxford

Francis Reynolds

It is common for subjects at universities to be identified with conspicuous figures. This is probably inevitable, given the system of having professors for particular subjects, many of whom are bound to acquire at least a short-term dominance in those subjects.

In Oxford it can be said that the subject Conflict of Laws has, over a period of slightly more than 120 years, been dominated by three teachers, Dicey, Morris and Briggs, though there is at least one more, Cheshire, who achieved great prestige, though not entirely in this field, and certainly other well-known scholars whose contributions, while distinguished, have been less central to the Faculty.

The first of the three was A V Dicey (1835–1922), who is certainly known principally for his work on Constitutional Law, and having invented the term 'Rule of Law'. He was born in 1835, twenty years after the Battle of Waterloo, and became Vinerian Professor and Fellow of All Souls in 1882. His famous constitutional writings (some more controversial than others) can be associated with the publication of *The Law of the Constitution* in 1885.[3] But in addition he produced a major work on private law, *A Digest of the Laws of England with reference to the Conflict of Laws*, which still bears his name, in 1896.[4] He acknowledged the work of Westlake, and the book contained American material added by John Bassett Moore. In 1910 a Lectureship in Private International Law was created for Dicey. He died in 1922, the same year as the third edition was published.[5] So he can be said to have dominated the subject in England for about twenty-five years. He was in fact a somewhat erratic personality who found difficulty in controlling his body movements: an

[3] A V [Albert Venn] Dicey, *Law of the Constitution* (Macmillan & Co 1885). The last edition prepared by Dicey was the 8th (published in 1915). A 9th edition was prepared in 1939 under the editorship of E C S Wade.
[4] Stevens & Sons, 1896.
[5] See n 7.

undergraduate asked about his lectures said that they would be all right if it was not for the state he was always in. Shortly before the First World War he used to travel to All Souls by bus and on one occasion is said to have forgotten where he was and to have given the surprised passengers part of his lecture: his intended audience only got the remainder. Professor Yntema recounted that he had the habit of sitting with a leg on a chair because of gout. On one occasion his housekeeper came in and said 'Mr Dicey, you have got the wrong leg up'.[6]

In the third edition of his book,[7] the last he edited, he cooperated with A Berriedale Keith, described as 'Scottish constitutional lawyer, scholar of Sanskrit and Indologist', though he was also an English barrister and described himself as 'formerly of the Colonial Office'. Keith edited two more editions by himself, but though not incompetent when inspected these do not seem to have improved the reputation of the book.

The next truly dominant figure in the area was in fact Morris, who in 1945, on his return from the Second World War, took on Dicey's book, which was regarded as being in a bad way, and gave it totally new life. However, between Dicey and Morris one must mention the very significant figure of G C Cheshire (1886–1978), the first Oxford law graduate to hold the Vinerian Chair. Cheshire, born in 1886, became a Fellow of Exeter in 1912, and was certainly one of the great Oxford tutors in the first part of the twentieth century. For much of the 1920s he was occupied with explaining in civilised and comprehensible terms the (obviously highly technical) Birkenhead property legislation of 1925 and later, and it is for this that he is probably mainly known. Nonetheless, he succeeded Dicey to the All Souls Lectureship in 1922 and in 1935 published the first edition of his *Private International Law*,[8] in which he displayed the same lucidity of exposition that was beginning to appear in English legal textbooks. He succeeded Holdsworth as Vinerian Professor in 1944 and further deployed his gifts with Fifoot in their book on Contract, which first appeared in 1945,[9] though it would have appeared considerably earlier but for the war. He retired early from the Vinerian chair in 1949, but while handing them over to other editors remained associated with his various books till near his death in a car accident in 1978, when he was 92.

Although Morris much admired him and described him as a 'mentor', and his book on Private International Law is, through several editions, still with us,[10] the sheer breadth of his writings make it more difficult to describe him as dominant in

---

[6] These stories appear in F H [Frederick Henry] Lawson, *The Oxford Law School 1850-1965* (OUP 1968), 70–71.

[7] A V Dicey and Arthur Berriedale Keith, *The Conflict of Laws* (3rd edn, Stevens & Sons 1922).

[8] G C [Geoffrey Chevalier] Cheshire, *Private International Law* (1st edn, Clarendon Press 1935). After writing seven editions, Cheshire was joined for the 8th edition (1970) by Peter North.

[9] G C Cheshire and C H S [Cecil Herbert Stuart] Fifoot, *The Law of Contract* (1st edn, Butterworth & Co 1945).

[10] Now Paul Torremans and others (eds), *Cheshire, North and Fawcett, Private International Law* (15th edn, OUP 2017).

the field of Conflict of Laws. Until the production of *Megarry and Wade* in 1957 he was more clearly authoritative in the field of Real Property, and *Cheshire and Fifoot* was for several years after first publication a leading work in the area of Contract law—though the fact that Fifoot gave (sometimes waspish) lectures on Contract probably made students of the post-war period associate the topic more with him.

J H C (John) Morris (1910–1984)[11] certainly became a dominant scholar in the conflict of laws in England in that post-war period. A very big man physically, he had a surprisingly quiet and cultured voice, though he was willing to direct firm admonitions to students ('Mr X, consider yourself reprimanded') and sometimes others. He was elected a Fellow of Magdalen in 1936, took over the Lectureship in Private International Law in 1939 and became Reader in the Conflict of Laws in 1951. During the 1950s, he was the leader of a very powerful group of three tutors at Magdalen: himself, Rupert Cross and Guenter Treitel, the latter two of whom went on in succession to hold the Vinerian chair (a post which, though he was approached, definitely did not interest Morris himself).

Morris inherited Dicey's book in 1945, a time when law publishers, in this case Stevens & Sons (later merged with Sweet & Maxwell), were setting new standards for their established titles or else letting them go (which certainly happened to some). After preliminary work he told the publishers that the job was too big for one man, and arranged to incorporate a number of other distinguished scholars, including Rupert Cross as well as Zelman Cowen, Otto Kahn-Freund and Kurt Lipstein, with himself as General Editor. His first edition, the 6th, appeared in 1949[12] and was marked by the lucidity and accuracy for which he became famous. He also produced a casebook[13] and later a short textbook[14] within the subject area.

In his teaching of the Conflict of Laws in the 1950s Morris deliberately sought to concentrate on the family law side. This was because in his view the major problem for the subject was that of displaced persons all over Europe and elsewhere. Thus his lectures spent much time on domicile, divorce, nullity, legitimacy, legitimation and adoption. My notes from his lectures at that time had virtually nothing on jurisdiction,[15] little on the enforcement of foreign judgments, and not very much on contract. In respect of the latter one was supposed to accept the notion of the 'proper law of the contract' and then rehearse arguments as to whether this was determined objectively or subjectively (ie by choice of the parties): one was meant to

---

[11] See an extensive memoir by Sir Peter North (1988) LXXIV Proc Br Ac 443.
[12] J H C [John Humphrey Carlile] Morris and others (eds), *Dicey: The Conflict of Laws* (6th edn, Stevens & Sons 1949).
[13] J H C Morris, *Cases on Private International Law* (1st edn, Clarendon Press 1939). The 4th edition was published in 1968. He was joined by Peter North for *Cases and Materials on Private International Law* (Butterworths 1984).
[14] J H C Morris, *The Conflict of Laws* (1st edn, Stevens 1971). Morris wrote three editions of this work before his death. David McClean picked up the baton for the 4th edition (1993).
[15] An American legal writer once commented to me at that time that the most efficient way to explain the jurisdiction of English courts was to establish when they did *not* have jurisdiction.

go over the cases (rejecting with contumely *Vita Food*,[16] where Morris liked to say that all parties involved, including Lord Wright in the Privy Council, were drunk) and come down resoundingly in favour of the objective view, 'to which the arbitration cases are an admitted exception'. The vast increase in international commerce that has occurred since the 1960s soon made this view hardly arguable, as F A Mann made clear in a memorial lecture for Morris,[17] with most of which Morris would have strongly disagreed. My notes on torts were even thinner: about eight lines explaining the rule in *Phillips v Eyre*. *Boys v Chaplin*[18] in 1971 was the first case to set the cat among the pigeons.

Morris throughout conducted a powerful seminar on Conflict of Laws for BCL students: for a considerable period together with P B (Peter) Carter, Fellow of Wadham, another dominating figure while active in this area (Derek Hall, fellow of Exeter, used to describe them as 'the owners of the BCL'). For about ten years subsequently Morris conducted the seminar with P M (now Sir Peter) North, who became a Law Commissioner (being responsible as such for some of the family law legislation in the area) and Vice-Chancellor of the University and took over Cheshire's book for many editions. Carter, who remained throughout active in giving tutorials, in fact returned to the seminar for a period after Morris' retirement.

Morris retired in 1977. His last edition of the book, by then called *Dicey & Morris*, was the tenth, in 1980,[19] though he continued working on supplements till shortly before his death in 1984. Strongly devoted to his College and to the collegiate system, he took some pride in saying that he had never been a professor, and this was true except for a year spent as a visitor at Harvard in 1951–1952 and after his retirement, as Goodhart Professor at Cambridge in 1977–1978.

Morris handed over the work that was at least as much his own as Dicey's to Lawrence Collins, now Lord Collins of Mapesbury, and it is now *Dicey, Morris & Collins*.[20]

Adrian Briggs, who had been an undergraduate at Hertford, returned to Oxford from the University of Leeds in 1980 as a Fellow of St Edmund Hall. My recollection is that he was not absolutely clear when he arrived that he intended to specialise in Conflict of Laws: it was lucky for the Faculty that he resolved any doubts he may have had as he did. He quite soon, in 1983 and 1984, wrote two articles on the topic of *forum non conveniens*,[21] which was at that time becoming a very

---

[16] *Vita Food Products Inc v Unus Shipping Co Ltd* [1939] AC 177.
[17] F A [Frederick Alexander] Mann 'The Proper Law in the Conflict of Laws' (1987) 36 ICLQ 437.
[18] [1971] AC 356.
[19] J H C Morris and others, *Dicey & Morris on the Conflict of Laws* (10th edn, Stevens & Sons 1980).
[20] Lord Collins of Mapesbury and others, *Dicey, Morris & Collins: The Conflict of Laws* (15th edn, Sweet & Maxwell 2012). Lord Collins should certainly be included among those mentioned above as a very distinguished scholar and inheritor of Dicey's work, but the thrust of this essay is towards Oxford teaching, in which Lord Collins was not regularly involved.
[21] Adrian Briggs, 'Forum Non Conveniens—Now We Are Ten?' (1983) 3 Legal Studies 74 and 'The Staying of Actions on the Ground of *Forum Non Conveniens*' [1984] LMCLQ 227.

significant part of the general subject. These were gracefully acknowledged by Lord Goff of Chieveley in the leading case of *Spiliada Maritime v Cansulex* in 1986[22] and in some ways one can say that Adrian's career in the Conflict of Laws took off then.

At that time, less than ten years after British accession to what was then the European Economic Community (EEC), one could see that jurisdiction and judgments were becoming a much more important part of the Conflict of Laws than hitherto. The 1968 Brussels Convention (to be followed by two EU Regulations) came into effect in the United Kingdom in 1987 under the Civil Jurisdiction and Judgments Act of 1982. In 1993 came the first edition of Adrian's book, first named *Norton Rose on Civil Jurisdiction and Judgments* and initially co-authored with Peter Rees, a partner in that firm.[23]

When the operation of the *forum non conveniens* doctrine within the Brussels Convention regime (preserved by the Court of Appeal in *Re Harrods (Buenos Aires)*[24]) became untenable by reason of the European Court of Justice's decision in *Owusu v Jackson*[25] in 2005, it became clear how much of the English conflict of laws was being dismantled by the activities in the field of the EEC, a change of which *Erich Gasser*[26] and *Turner v Grovit*[27] had already given clear indications. The Rome Convention of 1980 on the law applicable to contractual obligations[28] came into effect by virtue of the Contracts (Applicable Law) Act 1990, also to be superseded later by an EU Regulation. Until case law began to develop in the 1990s, it remained possible to expound the choice of law part of the subject (which had completely dominated in Morris' day) on the basis that the English methodology of the conflict of laws was still valid subject to various changes, welcome or unwelcome, made by accession to the EEC's instruments. The contract case law certainly did not and does not have the same dramatic differences from the existing English law as were to be found in the area of jurisdiction and judgments. But there were some: and of course the Rome II Regulation[29] subsequently produced what were in effect new rules for tort and other non-contractual private law. Beyond this, there were plenty of indications that the EU had further ambitions to harmonise private international law and even substantive private law.

---

[22] *Spiliada Maritime Corp v Cansulex Ltd* [1987] AC 460, 488. Lord Goff also refers approvingly to an article by Rhona Schuz ('Controlling Forum-Shopping: The Impact of *MacShannon v Rockware Glass Ltd*' (1986) 35 ICLQ 374).

[23] Adrian Briggs and Peter Rees, *Norton Rose on Civil Jurisdiction and Judgments* (1st edn, LLP Professional 1993). From the 5th edition (2009) the work, which he had always led, was published under Professor Briggs' name alone. It is now in its 6th edition (2015) with the 7th forthcoming.

[24] [1992] Ch 72.

[25] (C-281/02) [2005] ECR I-1383.

[26] *Erich Gasser GmbH v MISAT SRL* (C-116/02) [2005] ECR I-1383.

[27] (C-159/02) [2005] ECR I-3565.

[28] [1980] OJ L266/1.

[29] Regulation (EC) No 864/2007 on the law applicable to non-contractual obligations (Rome II) ([2007] OJ L199/40).

Some of Adrian's reactions to this in the early 2000s were articulately hostile, and expressed in his highly recognisable uncompromising style[30] (though he also has a much more favourable one available[31]). In 2003 he wrote that 'the common law conflict of laws is being overtaken by legislative events over which we now find we have little or no control'.[32] More emphatically in 2005 he began a paper presented to the Swiss Jurists Association: 'Let me introduce this paper by observing that, as seen from London, the European Court has just completed fifteen months of infamy.'[33] And ranging on to the Draft Common Frame of Reference he wrote in 2009 that 'the idea that there will never be a properly functioning single market until a single and comprehensive civil code is imposed across 27 states whose approaches to private law and its adjudication are (to put it neutrally) far more divergent than anyone else dare admit, is something which would recommend itself only to the deranged'.[34] Further ambitions had already been warned against in a reference to a proposed Rome IV to regulate the law of succession: 'evidently the internal market cannot be complete without the free movement of the dead.'[35]

But although his views in the early part of this century were clear from these and similar firm comments Adrian, seemingly, had a change of heart about this sometime around 2010, and in 2014 published a pioneering work, *Private International Law in English Courts*, which set out a fresh approach to the subject.[36] Abandoning, or at least archiving, some (although not all) of his previous disapproval of EU law in the area, he set out to explain what he called 'his own perspective on the subject', how the now established EU approach required most of previous English ideas on the Conflict of Laws to be shelved and replaced by a careful study of EU Regulations and other legislative instruments as well as the jurisprudence of the European Court. Not only is the explanation of what may be called the new position remarkable (a point not always recognised when the book came out, and which in present circumstances may remain partly unrecognised), the explanation in chapter 3 of the common law methodology that is being superseded is full of insight and perception for common lawyers as to what they had been doing, which would remain relevant even if the whole EU structure were abandoned. Of course the withdrawal

---

[30] There are some good examples in book reviews. For example: 'One grows wearily, and warily, accustomed to the techniques of comparative law and those who profess it: to make assertions about law and lawyers which are simplistic and sloppy and to pass this off as some form of legal science': book review [2005] LMCLQ 119, 121.
[31] 'This is a marvellous book ... There is no need to read any more of this review: just buy it': [2015] LMCLQ 597, 597 (of Michael McParland, *The Rome I Regulation* (OUP 2015)).
[32] 'The Real Scope of European Rules for Choice of Law' (2003) 119 LQR 352, 357.
[33] "The Impact of Recent Judgments of the European Court on English Procedural Law and Practice" (2005) 124 *Zeitschrift fur Schweizerisches Recht* 231, 232.
[34] Book review [2009] LMCLQ 157, 158–159.
[35] Ibid 158.
[36] Adrian Briggs, *Private International Law in English Courts* (OUP 2014). This was foreshadowed in the 3rd edition of his short book *The Conflict of Laws* (3rd edn, OUP 2013). The 1st edition was published in 2002, and the 4th and most recent in 2019.

of the United Kingdom from the EU puts all this in a state of flux, and we shall have to wait and see what happens. His own words give the best indication of the present position as he sees it: 'When the dust settles, and it is possible to see the outlines of private international law after secession from the European Union, it will be time to return to the task of writing monographs on the subject.'[37] We may be sure that whatever Adrian writes will be, as ever, original and perceptive.

Adrian Briggs is undoubtedly a worthy successor to John Morris, himself a successor to Dicey. John Morris' Readership was allocated elsewhere on his retirement, but more recently Adrian became Professor of Private International Law in 2004 and was appointed QC (*honoris causa*) in 2016. A review of one of Adrian's books rightly referred to 'the typically engaging, effective, critical and authoritative manner of the writing'.[38] Through his writings, and presiding over the BCL Conflict of Laws seminar over a period approaching forty years, and also by his teaching and former pupils in Oxford, Australasia and Singapore, he has maintained a personal ascendancy over instruction in the subject in Oxford which matches that of his illustrious predecessors. We wait with admiration to see what comes next.

Adrian Briggs' Contribution to the Life of St Edmund Hall

Derrick Wyatt

Fate was kind to St Edmund Hall when Adrian, a law lecturer at the University of Leeds, applied for a university post at Oxford combined with a Fellowship at St Edmund Hall. The College Magazine announced at the time that he was an Oxford man, who had read law with great distinction at Hertford College. It might have added that he was a man of Kent, who had also found Yorkshire to his taste, having enjoyed his time at Leeds, before coming to the Hall. He took up his Fellowship in 1980 (transformed into the Sir Richard Gozney Fellowship in Law in 2012), and so began forty years of energetic and exemplary service to the College. I was a grateful beneficiary of all this, as the Law Tutor already in post when Adrian arrived, and I could not have wished for more in the way of support and friendship than that he gave me over the years we served together. Adrian's impressive stint has made him the longest serving of all the Law Fellows at the Hall to date. From the College's point of view, his contribution has been simply incalculable, and no account of his career can do it full justice.

---

[37] Biography, Oxford Law Faculty website (<https://www.law.ox.ac.uk/people/adrian-briggs-qc-hon> (accessed 9 September 2020)).

[38] Barry Rodger [2003] LMCLQ 544, reviewing the 3rd edition of *Civil Jurisdiction and Judgments* (n 23).

Shortly after his arrival, Adrian and I presided over the inauguration of the Portia Society, or rather the rebranding of the existing law students' annual dinner into an organisation dedicated to the year-round socialising of the Hall lawyers. It was on such occasions that Adrian's pupils encountered the witty and companionable human being who shared a body with the sharp and forthright scholar who ambushed them in tutorials on a weekly basis. The annals of the Portia Society contain regular references to 'entertaining' speeches from Mr Briggs at the annual dinner. 'Entertaining' is actually quite an understatement. Adrian's speeches were the highlights of Portia dinners. He somehow managed to acquire an encyclopaedic knowledge of the extramural activities of our students, and he would pepper his speeches with revelations of their dalliances, escapades and mishaps, amid gales of laughter from all present. After dinner we would retire to Adrian's room in front quad for fruit and chocs, banter, and perhaps a sing-along or two. In latter years the dinner and its jolly aftermath became staging posts to late night clubbing sessions for our students. To this day I can only wonder at their staying power, and at that of Adrian, who would at the end of the evening cycle cheerfully off home while I sleepily negotiated the High to catch a bus back to Abingdon.

Adrian made a distinctive contribution to the ethos of undergraduate law teaching at the Hall. He taught our undergraduates Criminal Law, Roman Law, Contract Law and Land Law. Taking into account revision classes for finalists, he taught the Hall lawyers in all three of the years they spent with us. He expected students to read cases thoroughly, but did not expect them to be content with parroting the analysis of the judges. Rather, he pressed them to advance some analysis of their own. This can be quite a big ask for undergraduates. Former students recall the intellectual rigour of his tutorials, with an ever-present undertone of hazard for the unwary. Adrian certainly lacked patience with those who turned up unprepared or late for tutorials, or wanted to change tutorial times in order to participate in sporting activities (the word 'sport' was always something of a red rag to a bull where Adrian was concerned). But he showed great kindness in his dealings with pupils he felt needed a helping hand, whether academically or otherwise. One overseas Hall lawyer was taken seriously ill and required major surgery in Oxford. Adrian visited him frequently in hospital, and gave daily support to his mother, who spoke no English, when she arrived in Oxford to be with her son. I vividly remember a rather wonderful dinner in Oxford at which mum entertained a much-recovered son, along with his law tutors. Adrian and the (then) young man are still in touch.

For a good number of years, we incorporated a mooting competition for second years into the tutorial timetable. Adrian did the lion's share of judging, which I suppose means I did less than I should, but he made a splendid job of it. He unfailingly got the best out of our student advocates, who took the exercise very seriously and often surprised us with the efforts they made preparing and presenting their arguments. Adrian interrogated them fairly robustly, as would be expected, but with such an air of cerebral affability, that he encouraged and brought them on rather than intimidated them. In another life, it is my strong conviction Adrian would have made an outstanding judge. The Commercial Court would probably have been to his taste, at least before the inevitable elevation. He would have been quick, funny and good at *ex tempore* judgments, just as he was in our moots.

Adrian was always lead tutor for the BCL at the Hall, and was assiduous in encouraging our own best-qualified undergraduates to stay on for it, as well as in spotting the most promising applicants from outside Oxford. BCL students who took tutorials in the Conflict of Laws with Adrian probably appreciated him most of all as an academic and as a teacher. But he took all the BCL students at the Hall under his wing, whether he taught them or not, and they all benefited from his readiness to find time for them and make sure that the system worked for them. I remember one outstanding BCL student attending an early lecture in one of his chosen subjects, only to find it far from what he had expected and hoped for. He visited Adrian in a state of anxiety, fearing he had made an irreversible mistake. Adrian quickly reassured him that the situation could be remedied, and within a few hours had ensured not only the student's transfer to a different subject, but also a meeting with the course convener in that subject to receive and discuss the relevant reading materials. Being under Adrian's wing meant more than receiving academic support. One graduate student who was admitted to hospital in some haste was the grateful recipient of one of Adrian's generously tailored night-shirts, delivered personally by Adrian, just in time for lights out.

It is not surprising that so many of Adrian's undergraduate and graduate students appreciated so much the contribution he made to their time at Oxford. After he took Honorary Silk in 2016, a dinner was arranged for him by former students, which Adrian described as 'utterly joyful'.

Adrian's elevation to Queen's Counsel, *Honoris Causa*, was also proudly celebrated by his College, in a packed Senior Common Room, after dinner, as is the custom. Adrian's Honorary Silk was awarded for his major contribution to the law of England and Wales outside practice in the courts. Adrian's closer colleagues at the Hall were aware that his contribution to the law of England and Wales was not confined to that made by his outstanding legal writing, but also comprised practice as a barrister from a prestigious set of chambers in the Temple and expert witness evidence in foreign jurisdictions. All this wealth of experience enriched his teaching at undergraduate and graduate level, as many of his students are aware.

Adrian's contribution to the life of St Edmund Hall far surpassed teaching, admissions, marking collections and judging moots. He invariably talked calming good sense in the College's Governing Body, and for his pains was appointed repeatedly to college office, serving for many years in the roles of Tutor for Admissions, Senior Tutor and Tutor for Undergraduates. He served briefly as Dean of Chapel, and he involved himself in the selection of the College Chaplain. He contributed to Professor Lucy Newlyn's 'Chatter of Choughs, A St Edmund Hall

Anthology', and it was probably this literary venture which emboldened him to rewrite the College Statutes and By-Laws, and make them (almost) a pleasure to read. Despite being at best lukewarm in his enthusiasm for formal occasions, he attended numerous Old Members' dinners, reflecting his conviction that at least one of the Law Fellows should be present at such events, and his own liking for keeping in touch with former students. He took special pleasure in this, and shared their sense of achievement as they passed the milestones that were of significance in their various careers.

I had reason to be grateful to Adrian on more occasions than I could ever begin to count. When the least sought responsibility that ever falls to a Vice-Principal, that of organising a Principalian election, fell to me, one major consolation was that I knew I could count on Adrian's advice and support in the weary months that would follow. I took full advantage of both before the final vote was counted, and metaphorical white smoke emerged from the metaphorical Sistine Chapel chimney in the Senior Common Room.

Floreat Aula—may the Hall flourish—is the salute offered by members and fellows of the Hall on those occasions when glasses are raised to toast the College. After his many years of distinguished service, Adrian has earned many times over the right to a similar salute from Teddy Hall, and I have no hesitation whatsoever in assuming full authority to provide it—*Floreas* Adrian Briggs, and may any retirement you allow yourself be long, and utterly joyful.

Recollections

Andrew Bell

The endlessly fascinating world of what Dicey described as 'the Conflict of Laws' and Cheshire characterised as 'Private International Law' has perhaps never had as clear an expositor, or as creative a thinker, as the great Briggs. The one time wunderkind and occasional *enfant terrible* of private international law—with his ability to bring fresh insight and challenge orthodoxy often matched by an arresting or provocative title to a case note or article or quirky turn of phrase—leaves, on his retirement, an enormous legacy: not only a body of work upon which practitioners, scholars and students draw daily, but a legion of students from around the common law world, many of whom are now judges and senior practitioners, who have benefited directly from his guidance. Indeed, it is perhaps not an exaggeration to say that one of the principal reasons why a generation of the brightest law students from around the Commonwealth enrolled year after year to undertake the Bachelor of Civil Law at Oxford was to take his seminars and hear his lectures on Conflicts.

I had the great good fortune to be Adrian's first doctoral student as long ago as 1992. Our interactions were lively, robust, challenging and stimulating. Famously, they also involved the consumption of much baklava, purchased from 'Parmenters' on the High Street, almost equidistant between my lodgings at Magdalen and his turret at Teddy Hall.

Our mutual interest in the Conflict of Laws, particularly on the jurisdictional side, has continued to this day. For many years we spoke fortnightly, at length and from different sides of the globe about cases in which we were engaged (occasionally together), or in respect of recent decisions or enduring conundrums. Former students of his sit on the Supreme Courts of nearly every Australian State as well as on the Federal Court of Australia. His Australian students hold him in the highest regard and affection and the Oxford Law Faculty is fortunate indeed to have had, for so many years, such a scholar of the highest skill and the utmost dedication to his vocation.

Andrew Burrows

I have known Adrian for over forty years. We were exact contemporaries at Oxford, he at Hertford and I at Brasenose. Both of us stayed on to do the one-year BCL (1979–1980) where together we studied Conflicts and Restitution each for the first time. It may be apparent from our subsequent academic careers which subject each of us preferred! While Adrian then started his long attachment to St Edmund Hall, as Fellow and Law Tutor, I departed Oxford first for Harvard and then, for five years, to be a lecturer at Manchester University. But our paths merged again, and we became colleagues, when I returned to Oxford as Law Fellow at Lady Margaret Hall. Adrian's observations on all goings-on in the Faculty have provided me with many happy hours of entertainment over the years. We have also often discussed legal points, whether in person or over the phone, and I have invariably found his views helpful, whether I agreed with him or not. Throughout he has been a stalwart of his college and faculty and, above all, has selflessly devoted himself to his students to whom he has rightly become something of a legend. It was a particular pleasure a few years ago to join with him on the Faculty of Law's project to help revive legal education in Myanmar and it was a special delight to be his co-author for a book on the Law of Contract in Myanmar. He may have found my own pedantry on grammar and punctuation somewhat tedious, but he bore it all with the sort of amused bemusement that he had previously reserved for my obsession with the law of unjust enrichment (or as he might prefer to say, to wind me up, the law of quasi-contract).

Martin Davies

Adrian Briggs and I were exact contemporaries at Oxford, studying for both the BA and the BCL at the same time in the same college (Hertford). I spent a lot of time with Adrian as we learned the law together, and the resulting mutual familiarity has given me the great advantage (not shared by all, as I have seen over the years) of not being intimidated by his great intellect and sometimes-sharp tongue. We stood together on the threshold of Peter Carter's rooms at Wadham for our first tutorial on Conflict of Laws and were told, sternly, to wipe our feet before we entered. That put us both in our place, which was, of course, the point. (Adrian always removes his shoes before entering his own house. Can these facts possibly be related?) We have stayed in touch, usually distantly, often intermittently, ever since, for what is now an exceedingly long time. Adrian has been one of the few constants in my life as an academic. For that, I am both grateful, and very fortunate.

Andrew Dickinson

One's path in life is not always carefully chosen. As a sixth former, my school—irrationally predisposed to the other place—told me that they did not advise an application to Oxford, but added that if I insisted (I did) I should mark my card with St Edmund Hall, where one of my predecessors, a Metallurgist, had ventured with some success. It was for this reason that, little more than seventeen years of age, I first stepped into Adrian's room in the front quad in December 1988. He gave me a small slip of paper, no more than 1cm tall, containing the text of what I later came to recognise as section 1(1) of the Theft Act 1968. There followed a tale about a borrowed season ticket, and some searching questions. Almost two years later, having passed muster, I arrived at Teddy Hall where I spent four happy years (BA and BCL) under the tutelage of Adrian and his colleague, Derrick Wyatt. As well as instructing me in Criminal Law, Contract and Land Law, Adrian trained me to think ('Really?'), to enquire ('So?') and to write ('Ugh!').

But for Adrian, I would not have considered applying for the BCL, studying the Conflict of Laws or writing my first casenote. Nor, in 2013, would I have applied for tutorial fellowships in Oxford. Close family members apart, he has had a bigger influence on my life than any individual. He has guided me as a tutor, colleague and friend. Like many others, I was fortunate to cross the threshold.

James Edelman

Twenty years ago, whilst I was a graduate student, Adrian gave me a job as a lecturer at St Edmund Hall to teach his undergraduate students during his sabbatical. He has been a close friend and colleague for more than two decades since, but teaching for him that year, together with later teaching alongside him and even writing with him, brought into sharp focus the qualities that make him such an extraordinary academic: his strict discipline, but with a heart of compassion; his great depth of learning, but with the humility and agility to adapt and develop his thinking; his diligence and attention to detail, but without punctiliousness. Perhaps his most endearing quality is his generosity in giving of his time, at any time, to assist those in need, especially colleagues, students and former students. He has brought provisions and comfort to a student in hospital after a bicycle accident; spoken at all hours of the day and night to students having pre-exam crises; travelled afar to comfort a former student in hard times whom others had forsaken and, so far as I have ever seen, never declined any request for assistance. With decades of energetic devotion to the law and all of those around him it is hard to imagine him tiring, still less retiring.

Máire Ní Shúilleabháin

I arrived in Oxford as a BCL student in 1998, having never previously studied private international law, and intent on a career in legal practice. I joined the Conflict of Laws class, taught by Adrian Briggs, in that first term, and discovered an academic law subject which intrigued me in a way that no other law subject ever had. In those early lectures, and later on in the seminars of the second term, Adrian Briggs imparted his immense enthusiasm for this branch of law, navigating its twists and turns and conceptual complexities, with characteristic style and clarity. I recall, in particular, a seminar in the second term on divorce recognition under the Family Law Act 1986 (the subject of my contribution to this book). BCL students could choose to focus on property or family aspects of private international law, and only two students (including myself) chose the latter. Nonetheless, Briggs gave the seminar his complete attention, working through a series of carefully crafted problem questions which exposed the deficiencies in the scheme of the Act. I left Oxford determined to try to carve out an academic career in private international law, a plan which happily came to fruition, and to this day I use the same kind of mini problems to help my students gain a grasp of the subject. I feel privileged to have enjoyed such wonderful teaching in my BCL days and to have discovered an academic discipline which is so endlessly stimulating.

Maisie Ooi

Adrian Briggs introduced me to the world of Conflict of Laws, and to an entirely different way of looking at securities and finance, my then areas of practice. Adrian was my lecturer and tutor for the Conflict of Laws when I read for the BCL, and later co-supervisor with Professor Dan Prentice of my unscheduled DPhil when I took up Sir Roy Goode's challenge to find a viable solution for intermediated securities in the alternative to that in the then proposed Hague Convention on the law applicable to certain rights in respect of securities held with an intermediary, which he was advancing.

Thanks to Adrian I have spent much of the last two decades since Oxford obsessing about the choice of law for securities, finance and insolvency (which I both practise and teach) and developing my various theses on the multifaceted issues that arise from securities trading and changes to securities. The essay which considers the challenges that cryptosecurities bring to the conflict of laws is my way of thanking Adrian for the guidance that continued beyond Oxford, and for the unstinting generosity, good humour and wisdom that he brought to it.

Edwin Peel

Although the early years of Adrian Briggs' fellowship at Oxford overlapped with my three years as an undergraduate (1983–1986), our paths did not cross until the summer of 1992 in the first of several unsuccessful interviews for a fellowship of my own. On that occasion, I was grilled principally by Adrian, acting on behalf of the Faculty rather than the college. I was set the then customary task of treating him as if he was a second year undergraduate and asked to explain the law on the effect of mistaken identity on the formation of a contract. I have no idea how it was received (other than not well enough to be appointed), but I can say that he is, to this day, the cleverest 'second year' I have encountered. Later that year, I returned to Oxford (after a period of time in practice and teaching at Leeds University) to read for the BCL, Adrian having made it clear over the post-interview dinner that this was probably necessary if I was to be appointed, and I became the student to him as tutor in the Conflict of Laws. The first two tutorials were memorable. In the first, I was described as resembling a provincial solicitor on the partners' golf day (I was dressed for an MCR dinner). I later discovered that a firm I had worked for had booked Adrian for a lecture on the day the partners were all playing golf. I took the riposte with the good humour with which it, and others, were always intended. In the second, my penchant for closing my eyes to concentrate on a point led to the room falling silent and my finding that Adrian was staring at me intently. I denied what I assume was the impression I had created of dropping off, but was cut off with the observation: 'and how do you explain the dribble running down your chin'.

None of this put me off my pursuit of a fellowship, which was encouraged by Adrian, nor my interest in the Conflict of Laws. In 1994 I was finally successful and was very grateful to be invited by Adrian and Francis Reynolds to teach on the Conflicts course. Thereafter, if space would allow, there are countless episodes of support, advice and encouragement one could recount, not all confined to the development of my academic career, and many of them imbued with the same good humour already referred to (such as the hand drawn and coloured 'Italian torpedo' produced from the stage while speaking with Adrian to an audience of practitioners, as an antidote to my use of the not yet ubiquitous power-point presentation). My academic career has been one of the utmost good fortune, but I can safely say that my greatest stroke of luck was to fall under the guidance of Adrian Briggs.

Adam Rushworth

I first met Adrian Briggs as my personal tutor on the BCL, during which he also taught me the Conflict of Laws. Memory may be playing tricks but, as I recall, when I first met Adrian he used to offer coffee freshly brewed from '$7/$8 mix', which he obtained on his visits to the Far East. Inflation appears to have had its effect and, a decade and a half later, he recently offered me some '$10/$11 mix'. It is difficult to overestimate the support I received over that decade and a half. Adrian was responsible for my first academic job (as a college lecturer replacing his teaching whilst he was on sabbatical), he examined my doctorate and he subsequently encouraged me in my wish to pursue a career at the Bar.

One memory remains particularly vivid and which illustrates both his sense of humour and kindness. He was acting as my MPhil internal examiner. There had been an error at the printers and three or four pages were garbled in the submitted version. I apologised profusely and offered immediately to re-submit a corrected version. He accepted the offer and explained that it was not the first time it had happened but, on the previous occasion, the accidentally enclosed love letters had been more interesting. I left his room thinking catastrophe had been averted and also feeling immensely sorry for my predecessor. Characteristic of all conversations with Adrian, I felt much better after it.

Andrew Scott

Although difficult to capture in a few lines, I owe my academic career (such as it was) to Adrian and likewise my practice now. Of all the many excellent lawyers and teachers I had the fortune of encountering at Oxford, he stands out: a true common lawyer in the best of its traditions, discerning from the detail of the case law (of which he was a master) principles by which to explain, justify or criticise the law. It was the highlight of my education at Oxford to listen to Adrian and read his work, and to watch him make sense of the EU jurisdictional regime as articulated in cases like *Owusu*, *Turner* and *West Tankers*; and where sense could not be made of it, to say so clearly and compellingly.

Having finished the BCL, I thought it would be a good idea to write a thesis on the law of unjust enrichment. Adrian cured me of that misapprehension and was kind enough to agree to supervise me. He was the perfect supervisor: unfailingly generous with his time and constructive with his criticism. And although he was always many steps ahead of me as we each tried to make sense of the law on jurisdiction agreements from different perspectives, he was kind enough never to say.

When it came time to leave Oxford for the Bar, I joined Adrian's Chambers. As I began practising in the Commercial Court and the Chancery Division, it was striking how frequently its judges would ask 'what does Briggs say?' when a difficult private international law issue arose. On a few occasions, I have had the pleasure of working with or against Adrian on these issues on appeals to the Supreme Court. On every occasion, his contribution was characterised by creativity and clarity of thought in deriving answers from the case law that others could not see.

Koji Takahashi

In the opening part of my essay, I have described my first encounter with Adrian, which took place while I was doing my PhD research. After I obtained a PhD, it was Adrian and Trevor Hartley who patiently supported me through an arduous process of finding my first full-time academic job in the UK. Each time my application ended in failure, I was consoled by Adrian's words, 'It is their loss'.

Years later, I had an opportunity to invite Adrian to give seminars at my university in Kyoto, Japan. I have touched on the academic aspect of this story in the introduction to my essay. Here is the personal aspect of it. Adrian's rating in the opinion of the clerical staff of my university mounted as he showed great responsiveness in his dealing with them. In the presence of my secretary, he told me, 'Making your secretary's life easy is the quickest way to make your own easy', an advice I have since tried to abide by. Kyoto is a historic city full of touristic attractions and it was Adrian's first visit there. Yet, he spent most of the day doing what he would be doing at home—reading English cases. Maybe that was what made him a great scholar, I gathered. It is, however, not that Adrian lacked interest in culture. On a frosty winter morning, I took him out on a hike to a famous temple. To avoid the crowd, I scheduled it very early and in fact too early as it proved—when we reached the temple, it was closed and there were still hours before its opening. Thoroughly unfazed, Adrian behaved generously despite that we had to come back empty-handed. A few days later, I redeemed myself by taking him to another temple, one famous for its garden. Adrian apparently had done some homework reading about moss in the temples of Kyoto. Strolling in the garden, he said that he came to appreciate it while he had been wondering what the fuss was about it. During his short stay,

Adrian also exhibited his daring character by venturing to North Korea to watch a football match. The hermit country, despite its geographical proximity to Japan, is so much shrouded in mystery that its law is a favourite example when we discuss the classic conflicts topic of failure to prove foreign law in Japan. Accounting for his motivation to make the trip, Adrian said 'It was an opportunity not to miss', having come a long way to the Far East.

Contributing an essay to this collection has allowed me to refresh my memory of the time spent with Adrian. No one questions his great scholarship. My recollection of him illustrates that he also has an endearing personality.

Janet Walker

As with some of the other contributors to this volume, my personal reflection of Adrian is as a doctoral student who benefitted enormously from his urbane and thoughtful supervision, not to mention his pastoral care as the following vignette reveals. In one early term of my residence, I had my 9-year-old daughter staying with me from Canada, and it happened that I was scheduled to meet with Adrian to discuss my progress at a time when she was not at the local school. Through the pigeon post came his response that it would be possible for me to bring her along to the meeting.

It was a bright and chilly day. We climbed the narrow circular staircase leading to his room in Teddy Hall's front quad. Anxious not to be late, we had arrived a few minutes early and we listened in case there was another meeting in progress. Hearing nothing, I tapped gently on the door and waited. No response. We looked at one another wondering whether he might be elsewhere or, perhaps, might not have heard. I knocked a little more firmly. The command to 'Enter!' made us jump. (These were meetings that I approached with some trepidation.)

As we peeked around the door, Adrian's face went from frustration to delight. Bidding us to sit, he turned back to the desk and tapped out the last few words of what was undoubtedly a brilliant article. Then turning to us, he decried the impertinence of undergraduates, making me feel quite relieved not to have been one of them. Having explained his impatience, he gave us such a welcome that my daughter curled up in the comfy chair in the warmth of his rooms and was soon asleep, while we enjoyed a stimulating discussion on judicial jurisdiction.

As unfailingly 'cruel but fair' as was Adrian in his appraisal of legal analysis, he could not have been kinder or more generous to me during my time in Oxford.

Tiong Min Yeo

It is perhaps not uncommon for doctoral candidates to defy their supervisors, but I was at the receiving end of a demonstration of Adrian's omnipresence and omniscience. I had completed my residence requirement at Oxford University and had returned to my home country to complete the writing of my thesis. Some days after I had a draft manuscript couriered to Teddy Hall (he did not accept electronic transmissions at least in those days), I was relaxing at home on a weekend when suddenly the doorbell to my apartment buzzed. My jaw nearly dropped to the floor when Adrian's voice boomed over the intercom demanding that I open the door to receive the reviewed manuscript. I stood in a daze as I struggled to comprehend the situation. Why was my supervisor who was supposed to be half the world away at my door, and how did he even know my home address? It turned out that he was spending a few days in Singapore on his way to Australia, and a mutual friend had driven him to my apartment. No doubt he was having some fun at my expense, but how many doctoral students can boast of this level of dedication and service from their supervisors?

PART I
JURISDICTION

1
The Natural Forum Revisited

Andrew Bell

A. Introduction

Thirty-five years was once considered half a lifetime. By that metric, *Spiliada Maritime Corporation v Cansulex Ltd*[1]—synonymous with the concept of the natural forum and the ultimate reception of the doctrine of *forum non conveniens* into English law—was decided half a lifetime ago. How the world has changed in that period: in so many ways, more interconnected; in so many ways, less internationalist.

In 1986, the year *Spiliada* was decided, Mikhail Gorbachev articulated the twin policies of *glasnost* and *perestroika* and the Berlin Wall was soon to fall; the European Economic Community (as it then was) was expanding with the admission that year of Spain and Portugal; Deng Xiaoping was in his prime as paramount leader of China, opening up the economy of that sleeping giant; Sir Freddie Laker had opened up cheap and mass international air travel, challenging entrenched national carriers, many of which were to disappear in the decades that followed;[2] and, most significantly, advances in technology were about to facilitate the launch of the world wide web, email on a commercial scale and the rise of electronic funds transfer. These quotidian features of life in 2021 were largely inchoate in 1986—the founder of Facebook, for example, was only two years old in the year Lord Goff delivered his famous speech in *Spiliada*.

And yet, as I write this essay, some thirty-five years after *Spiliada* was decided, the internationalist spirit which animated that decision and its immediate progenitors,[3] and which was relevantly embodied in the concept of international judicial comity,[4] may be seen to be on the wane: Britain has left the European Union; the

---

[1] [1987] AC 460 (hereafter *Spiliada*).
[2] *British Airways Board v Laker Airways Ltd* [1985] AC 58; *Laker Airways v Sabena, Belgian World Airways* 731 F 2d 909 (DC Cir 1984); *Midland Bank plc v Laker Airways Ltd* [1986] 1 QB 689.
[3] *Owners of the Atlantic Star v Owners of the Bona Spes* [1974] AC 436 (hereafter *The Atlantic Star*); *MacShannon v Rockware Glass Ltd* [1978] AC 795 (hereafter *MacShannon*); *Amin Rasheed Shipping Corporation v Kuwait Insurance Co* [1984] AC 50 (hereafter *Amin Rasheed*); *The Abidin Daver* [1984] AC 398 (hereafter *The Abidin Daver*).
[4] In *The Abidin Daver* (n 3) 411, Lord Diplock famously observed that:

> [T]he essential change in the attitude of the English courts to pending or prospective litigation in foreign jurisdictions that has been achieved step-by-step during the last 10 years as a result of the successive decisions of this House ... is that judicial chauvinism has been replaced by judicial comity...'

United States of America has withdrawn from the World Health Organization; nationalism is on the rise accompanied by its first cousin, economic protectionism; the West's embrace of China is very much in retreat; and the COVID-19 pandemic has crippled the international aviation industry and left few, if any, countries socially and economically untraumatised.

There have also been very significant changes in the world of dispute resolution, including international and transnational dispute resolution, in the decades since *Spiliada* was decided. Many of these changes have been the direct by-product of technological advances: documents can be imaged and interrogated by powerful search engines; witnesses can be interviewed using audio-visual technology whose quality has improved exponentially; hearings may be conducted remotely with participants in different venues; legal research is greatly enabled by online resources which include what were once described as 'unreported decisions'[5] and judgments from many jurisdictions are available instantaneously on the click of a mouse within seconds of their being pronounced in a courtroom anywhere in the world.

Institutionally, many common law jurisdictions have adopted far more active judicial case management than was historically the case; class actions have been introduced in some jurisdictions accompanied by the rise of litigation funding;[6] and much transnational commercial dispute resolution has effectively been privatised through the imperial march of arbitration, a march which may well have been hastened by the adoption of the natural forum doctrine in *Spiliada*, as explained more fully below in Section C.

So-called 'international commercial courts' nowadays compete with domestic courts and the arbitral institutions for 'business',[7] and the very status of such courts as 'international commercial courts' has been held in Singapore (which has one) to be relevant to their suitability to determine particular disputes for which there may be competing, available forums.[8] And, doctrinally, English law has been overlaid

---

[5] A term which has lost all meaning. As Professor Briggs observed in his preface to Adrian Briggs, *Private International Law in English Courts* (OUP 2014) (hereafter Briggs, *Private International Law in English Courts*), this phenomenon is not wholly desirable:

> The fact that practically every judgment, regardless of provenance, utility, or quality control now makes it into the public domain shows the ubiquity of the Law of Unintended Consequences. The law is drowning itself at the same time as overwhelming the professional judgment of those who dare not risk the accusation of having overlooked something.

[6] *Campbells Cash & Carry Pty Ltd v Fostif Pty Ltd* (2006) 229 CLR 386.
[7] The Hon Justice Andrew Bell, 'An Australian International Commercial Court—Not a Bad Idea or What a Bad Idea?' (2020) 94 ALJ 24; Man Yip, 'The Singapore International Commercial Court: The Future of Litigation?' [2019] Erasmus L Rev 81.
[8] *Rappo v Accent Delight International Ltd* [2017] 2 SLR 265 [122] (hereafter *Rappo*). Also, TM Yeo, 'Staying Relevant: Exercise of Jurisdiction in the Age of the SICC', Yong Pung How Professorship of Law Lecture (Singapore, 13 May 2015). Interestingly, in *Amin Rasheed* (n 3) 67, Lord Diplock rejected the view expressed by Lord Donaldson MR in the Court of Appeal that the London Commercial Court should be regarded as an 'international commercial court' and that any consideration of comity should keep this matter in mind.

both by the European Convention on Human Rights[9] as well as innumerable European directives, all overseen by an apex court (pre-Brexit) of a very different character to either the House of Lords or, since 2009, the Supreme Court.[10] It was that apex court which, in *Turner v Grovit*,[11] *Owusu v Jackson*[12] and *Allianz SpA v West Tankers Inc*,[13] effected 'a bit of a battering' of '[s]ome cherished aspects of English civil procedure'.[14]

It is against the backdrop of these broad geopolitical, technological and institutional observations that this essay considers and revisits the 'natural forum'. It is a topic and a concept with which Professor Adrian Briggs has frequently grappled throughout his distinguished career. It is, as an Australian conflicts lawyer might quip, a 'not clearly inappropriate'[15] topic with which to commence this most well-deserved collection of essays celebrating the career and contribution of the most prolific, dynamic and provocative private international law scholar of his generation.

B. *Spiliada*—a Noble Aim, Rare Praise and a Wide Embrace

The background to the decision in *Spiliada* has been traced elsewhere[16] and is likely to be well known to readers of this book. It stands as a classic example of how the common law develops and evolves incrementally through a series of decisions, and how that development can be driven by strong judicial personalities[17] or affected by the identity of the judges who sat on particular cases.[18] In this context,

---

[9] JJ Fawcett, 'The Impact of Article 6(1) of the ECHR on Private International Law' (2007) 56 ICLQ 1.
[10] The impact of that influence on private international law in England was charted (and chartered) by Professor Briggs in Briggs, *Private International Law in English Courts* (n 5).
[11] Case C-159/02 [2004] ECR I-3565.
[12] Case C-281/02 [2005] ECR I-1383 (hereafter *Owusu*).
[13] Case C-185/07 [2009] ECR I-663.
[14] Edwin Peel, '*Forum Non Conveniens* and European ideals' [2005] LMCLQ 363, 377 (hereafter Peel, 'European Ideals').
[15] *Voth v Manildra Flour Mills Pty Ltd* (1990) 171 CLR 538 (hereafter *Voth*).
[16] See Adrian Briggs, '*Forum Non Conveniens*—Now We Are Ten?' (1983) 3 Leg S 74 (hereafter Briggs, '*Forum Non Conveniens*') and 'The Staying of Actions on the Ground of *Forum Non Conveniens* in England Today' [1984] LMCLQ 227 (hereafter Briggs, 'The Staying of Actions') and Andrew Bell, *Forum Shopping and Venue in Transnational Litigation* (OUP 2003) [3.71]–[3.174] (hereafter Bell, *Forum Shopping*). This book was based on the first doctoral thesis, written some ten years earlier, which Professor Briggs supervised. See also Ardavan Arzandeh, *Forum (Non) Conveniens in England: Past, Present and Future* (Hart Publishing 2018) ch 3.
[17] An example in a related field is supplied by the trilogy of decisions by Brandon J, Brandon LJ and Lord Brandon in *The Eleftheria* [1970] P 94; *The El Amria* [1981] 2 Lloyd's Rep 119; and *The Abidin Daver* (n 3).
[18] Had Sir Anthony Mason, for example, sat instead of Brennan J in *Oceanic Sun Line Special Shipping Company Inc v Fay* (1988) 165 CLR 197 (hereafter *Oceanic Sun*), the distinctive line of jurisprudence in this area that developed in Australia and which is discussed later in this essay may have been rather different. The subsequent decision in *Voth* (n 15) in which Mason CJ presided was explicitly stated to be something of a compromise decision with the likely differences in outcome between the application of the *Voth* approach and the *Spiliada* natural forum doctrine predicted to be 'rare'.

it is perhaps no coincidence to note that the successful counsel in *The Atlantic Star*[19] was Robert Goff QC who, as Goff J in *Trendtex Trading Corporation v Credit Suisse*,[20] outlined in strikingly similar language the test that was given authoritative status in *Spiliada*.

Spiliada yielded a test—the more appropriate or natural forum test—that, from 'an abstract (and international) standpoint', had 'much to be said' for it.[21] *Spiliada's* prequels had exposed major philosophical differences between some large figures in the English judiciary of the second half of the 20th century. In one corner of the ring lined up Lords Denning,[22] Simon[23] and Donaldson[24] but they were trumped by Lords Reid,[25] Diplock[26] and Brandon[27] with the latter group's commitment to a form of judicial diplomacy and délicatesse, namely 'international judicial comity', besting the former group's unalloyed pride and confidence in the centrality of London and the English legal profession in the commercial, shipping and insurance worlds.[28]

This dialectic was perhaps best captured in Lord Brandon's response to the observations of Sir John Donaldson (as he then was) about the merits and experience of the Turkish judiciary in *The Abidin Daver*:[29]

> I hope that I shall not be thought discourteous to Sir John Donaldson MR if I say that, while paying lip service to the avoidance of any comparisons of that kind, his

---

[19] *The Atlantic Star* (n 3).
[20] [1980] 3 All ER 721, 734.
[21] *Voth* (n 15) 557. It is important to bear in mind that the short-hand description—'the more appropriate or natural forum test'—must be understood as involving the second leg requirement that proceedings will not be stayed in favour of that forum in circumstances where justice requires that a stay should nevertheless not be granted: *Spiliada* (n 1) 478.
[22] Who famously said in the Court of Appeal in *The Atlantic Star* [1973] 2 QB 364, 382 (hereafter *The Atlantic Star* (CA)) that 'if the forum is England, it is a good place to shop, both for the quality of the goods and the speed of service …'.
[23] *The Atlantic Star* (n 3) 471: '"Forum-shopping" is a dirty word; but it is only a pejorative way of saying that, if you offer a plaintiff a choice of jurisdictions, he will naturally choose the one in which he thinks his case can be most favourably presented: this should be a matter neither for surprise nor for indignation.'
[24] *The Abidin Daver* [1983] 1 WLR 884, 889; *Amin Rasheed Shipping Corporation v Kuwait Insurance Co* [1983] 1 WLR 228, 240.
[25] *The Atlantic Star* (n 3) 453.
[26] *The Abidin Daver* (n 3) 411–12.
[27] Ibid 424–5.
[28] Most interestingly, in his Hague lectures (Adrian Briggs, 'The Principle of Comity in Private International Law' (2012) 354 *Recueil des Cours* 65, ch 3), Professor Briggs does not equate the natural forum doctrine with an embrace of comity but quite the opposite: the effect of the doctrine was that 'the English court can be said to be insisting that the foreign court do the work, take on the task of adjudication, and so forth, and that this passive transfer of cases to a foreign court's list is not at all consistent with comity, but is instead a form of dumping, possibly of toxic waste'. Of course, much depends upon one's definition of comity: Professor Briggs sees it not in terms of deference but rather as a 'logical and legal deduction from the principle of territorial sovereignty'. See also Thomas Schultz and Jason Mitchenson, 'Rediscovering the Principle of Comity in English Private International Law' (2018) 26 Eur Rev Priv L 311 and the essay by James Edelman and Madeleine Salinger in this collection (ch 13).
[29] *The Abidin Daver* (n 3) 424–5.

heart was not really in what he felt obliged to concede. Thus on p 889 of his judgment he said this:

> 'I share entirely the reluctance of Sheen and Brandon JJ. to express any view as to the relative merits of particular courts. That must be a matter of subjective judgment which I, as a judge of an English court, and an ex Admiralty judge, do not feel that I should make. What I think can be said—and I doubt whether it would be controverted by anybody—is that the English Admiralty Court has a vast amount of international maritime experience in this field going back over the centuries. While I do not doubt for one moment that the Turkish courts have long maritime experience, I doubt very much whether it is as international or extensive. This is not a criticism, and should not be taken as a criticism, of the Turkish courts; it is an accident of geography. The English courts are situated on an island off Europe. That has led, as a matter of history, to their being involved in far more maritime disputes than Turkey or any country similarly situated.'

The Master of the Rolls will, I trust, forgive me if I say that, having paid lip service to the need to avoid comparison between English and foreign courts, he then proceeded to make just such a comparison.

As will be observed later in this essay, there has been something of a retreat from the commitment to international judicial comity writ large in this memorable appellate 'put down' complete with its twice emphasised reference to 'lip service', although that retreat may represent less of a return to parochialism and more of a concern with the individual justice of particular cases in a very different world.

But to return to 1986 and *Spiliada*. Adrian Briggs was a young, possibly (*sed quaere*) idealistic scholar when he penned two articles[30] which attracted high judicial praise by Lord Goff (as Goff QC had become) in *Spiliada*. In a postscript to his leading judgment, Lord Goff generously observed that he could not:

> ... conclude without paying tribute to the writings of Jurists which have assisted me in the preparation of this opinion. Although it may be invidious to do so, I wish to single out for special mention articles by Mr. Adrian Briggs in (1983) 3 Legal Studies 74 and in [1984] LMCLQ 227, and the article by Miss Rhona Schuz in (1986) 35 ICLQ 374. They will observe that I have not agreed with them on all points; but even when I have disagreed with them, I have found their work to be of assistance. For jurists are pilgrims with us on the endless road to unattainable perfection; and we have it on the excellent authority of Geoffrey Chaucer that conversations among pilgrims can be most rewarding.

---

[30] Briggs, '*Forum Non Conveniens*' (n 16) and Briggs, 'The Staying of Actions' (n 16).

The noble aspiration towards 'unattainable perfection' to which Lord Goff referred was one that was evidently shared by, or at least inspired courts in, the vast majority of common law jurisdictions, and the doctrine of the natural forum associated with *Spiliada* was rapidly and widely adopted throughout most of the Commonwealth including in Canada,[31] New Zealand,[32] Hong Kong,[33] Singapore,[34] Malaysia,[35] Brunei,[36] Gibraltar,[37] the Cayman Islands[38] and India.[39]

Of the common law jurisdictions to embrace *Spiliada*, Canada was perhaps the most explicit in expressing the reasons for so doing at the level of policy. Thus, in *Amchem*, Sopinka J observed:[40]

> [T]he business of litigation, like commerce itself, has become increasingly international. With the increase of free trade and the rapid growth of multi-national corporations it has become more difficult to identify one clearly appropriate forum for this type of litigation. The defendant may not be identified with only one jurisdiction. Moreover, there are frequently multiple defendants carrying on business in a number of jurisdictions and distributing their products or services world wide. As well, the plaintiffs may be a large class residing in different jurisdictions. It is often difficult to pinpoint the place where the transaction giving rise to the action took place. Frequently, there is no single forum that is clearly the most convenient or appropriate for the trial of the action but rather several which are equally suitable alternatives. In some jurisdictions, novel principles requiring joinder of all who have participated in a field of commercial activity have been developed for determining how liability should be apportioned among defendants. *In this climate, courts have had to become more tolerant of the systems of other countries.*

Australia was a conspicuous exception to the otherwise Commonwealth-wide embrace of *Spiliada*.[41] As Sir Anthony Mason subsequently reflected, '*Voth* and its Australian line of authority was to stand in lonely isolation'.[42] This was notwithstanding the (perhaps) diplomatic attempt in *Voth* to predict that:

---

[31] *Amchem Products Inc v British Columbia (Workers' Compensation Board)* [1993] 1 SCR 897 (hereafter *Amchem*).
[32] *Club Mediterranee NZ v Wendell* [1989] 1 NZLR 216 (hereafter *Club Mediterranee*).
[33] *The Adhiguna Meranti* [1988] 1 Lloyd's Rep 384.
[34] *Oriental Insurance Co Ltd v Bhavani Stores Pte Ltd* [1998] 1 Sing LR 253; *Rickshaw Investments Ltd v Nicolai Baron von Uexkull* [2007] 1 SLR 377.
[35] *American Express Bank Ltd v Al-Ozeir* [1995] 1 CLJ 275.
[36] *Syarikat Bumiputra Kimanis v Tan Kok Voon* [1988] 3 MLJ 315.
[37] *Aldington Shipping Ltd v Bradstock Shipping Corp and Marbanaft GmbH* [1988] 1 Lloyd's Rep 475.
[38] *Insurco Int Ltd v Gowan Co* [1994–95] CILR 210; *KTH Capital Management Ltd v China One Fin Ltd* [2004–05] CILR 213.
[39] *Modi Entertainment Network v WSG Cricket Pte Ltd* (2003) AIR 1177; (2003) 1 SCR 480; *Mayar (HK) Ltd v Owners & Parties, Vessel MV Fortune Express* (2006) AIR 1828.
[40] *Amchem* (n 31) 911–12 (emphasis added).
[41] *Oceanic Sun* (n 18); *Voth* (n 15).
[42] Bell, *Forum Shopping* (n 16) foreword.

The 'clearly inappropriate forum' test is similar and, for that reason, is likely to yield the same result as the 'more appropriate forum' test in the majority of cases. The difference between the two tests will be of critical significance only in those cases—probably rare—in which it is held that an available foreign tribunal is the natural or more appropriate forum but in which it cannot be said that the local tribunal is a clearly inappropriate one.

That prediction has not always been borne out, particularly, as shall be seen, where the moving party in Australia was a badly injured individual.[43]

Of course, within the model adopted in the European instruments, the Brussels I Regulation and the 2007 Lugano Convention, the allocation of jurisdiction and the problems presented by concurrent proceedings are dealt with far more mechanistically than in common law jurisdictions (or 'arbitrarily', as Lord Goff bluntly described it in *de Dampierre v de Dampierre*).[44] There was 'no room at the inn' for the doctrine of *forum non conveniens* within the black letter rules of the European scheme as the Court of Justice's much lamented[45] decision in *Owusu*[46] made apparent. The paralysing effect of that decision on English *forum conveniens* jurisprudence and the scope it lends for forum manipulation through so-called 'anchor' defendants continues to be a running sore.[47]

C. The Natural Forum and 'Unattainable Perfection'—Noble but Naïve?

Just what or how abstract the 'unattainable perfection' was to which Lord Goff alluded in his paean to academic pilgrims in the *Spiliada* postscript is unknown. Given his Lordship's strong commitment to and interest in comparative legal scholarship,[48] however, he may well have been familiar with Rabel's observation that 'since Savigny it has been customary to regard the attainment of uniform solutions as the chief purpose of private international law'.[49] As I have previously observed,

---

[43] The decision of Brereton J in *McGregor v Potts* (2005) 68 NSWLR 109 stands as an exception to this trend.
[44] [1988] 1 AC 92, 107 (hereafter *de Dampierre*).
[45] See eg Peel, 'European Ideals' (n 14) 372: 'For the most part, the impact of the ruling in *Owusu* on the practice of the English courts is self-evident; a valuable tool against the worst excesses of forum shopping is no longer available.'
[46] *Owusu* (n 12).
[47] *Vedanta Resources plc v Lungowe* [2019] UKSC 20, [2019] 3 All ER 1013 [15]–[16]; [2019] 2 Lloyd's Rep 399 (hereafter *Vedanta*).
[48] Jack Beatson, 'Robert Goff', *Biographical Memoirs of Fellows of the British Academy* (British Academy 2019) vol XVIII, 241–73; see also Lord Goff, 'Judge, Jurist and Legislature" (1987) 2 Denning 79; Lord Rodger, 'Judges and Academics in the United Kingdom' (2010) 29 UQLJ 29, 30.
[49] Ernst Rabel, *The Conflict of Laws: A Comparative Study* (2nd ed, University of Michigan Press 1958) vol 1, 94.

the intuitively attractive corollary of this succinct statement of the guiding aspiration of the modern conflict of laws is that the venue in which a piece of litigation is tried should not affect the outcome or result of that litigation.[50]

The doctrine of the natural forum in many respects was and is a mechanism designed to minimise the scope for forum-dependent outcomes. It was not adopted for the purposes of 'mere practical convenience' to parties[51] but out of greater tolerance and respect for other countries' legal systems and their claims (articulated or not) to be able to provide parties with substantial justice in their courts in matters with which they had the closest and most real connection.

The spectre of a multiplicity of proceedings about or relating to the same underlying dispute and the possibility of inconsistent results is unseemly and unsatisfactory because, if the same legal question is answered differently according to the venue or forum in which it is asked, fundamental respect for the rule of law may be undermined as the outcome of a dispute may be manipulated by jockeying over jurisdiction, and forum shopping is encouraged. Driving litigation to the 'natural forum' by staying proceedings or refusing to assert and exercise jurisdiction in a forum that does not merit this moniker reduces the risk of parallel proceedings or concurrent litigation and the possibility of inconsistent decisions.

Returning to the common law's technique for minimising the scope for litigation in more than one forum, the growth of anti-suit injunctions can to some extent be explained by that goal.[52] Whilst Lord Goff made clear in *Societe Nationale Industrielle Aerospatiale v Lee Kui Jak*[53] that the adoption of the 'natural forum' as the criterion for the grant of an anti-suit injunction—a step which Lord Scarman in *Castanho v Brown & Root (UK) Ltd*[54] may have been thought to have endorsed—was a step too far,[55] the natural forum was still adopted by the House of Lords in *Airbus Industrie GIE v Patel*[56] as a jurisdictional prerequisite to the grant of this powerful and, in the view of some,[57] controversial remedy. So too, what the Singapore Court of Appeal has described as 'forum election' is directed to the same end of minimising the scope for inconsistent results.[58]

Other common law techniques have developed and been deployed in the years since *Spiliada* directed to a similar end, namely to minimise the possibility of inconsistent results depending on choice of venue. It is perhaps unsurprising that

---

[50] Bell, *Forum Shopping* (n 16) [2.01].
[51] *Spiliada* (n 1).
[52] See *Australian Health and Nutrition Association Ltd v Hive Marketing Group Pty Ltd* (2019) 99 NSWLR 419 [87].
[53] [1987] AC 871.
[54] [1981] AC 557.
[55] A view that Briggs had expressed with characteristic force: Adrian Briggs, 'No Interference with Foreign Courts?' (1982) 31 ICLQ 189.
[56] [1998] UKHL 12, [1999] 1 AC 119 (hereafter *Airbus*); also *Koh Kay Yew v Inno Pacific Holdings Ltd* [1997] 2 SLR 148 [18]–[19].
[57] See eg the essay by Andrew Dickinson in this collection (ch 4).
[58] *Virsagi Management (S) Pte Ltd v Welltech Construction Pte Ltd* [2013] 4 SLR 1097; *Rappo* (n 8).

many of these techniques have been embraced in Australia which, as already noted and as is developed more fully below in Section D, adopted something of an iconoclastic attitude to *Spiliada* (although at a statutory level, both between its constituent states[59] and in relation to New Zealand,[60] the natural or clearly more appropriate forum rubric has been adopted).

These other common law techniques include the refinement of the substance/procedure dichotomy which is directed to minimising the prospect of differential results depending upon the choice of forum[61] and the development or recognition of choice of law rules that reduce the scope for application of the law of the forum. This is seen most notably in the statutory rejection (in England) of the double actionability rule in *Phillips v Eyre*[62] and the repudiation of the same rule at common law by the High Court of Australia in *John Pfeiffer Pty Ltd v Rogerson*[63] and *Regie Nationale des Usines Renault SA v Zhang*,[64] coupled with the embrace in Australia of the doctrine of *renvoi* in *Neilson v Overseas Development Corporation*.[65] Professor Briggs identified the functional similarity between the embrace of the natural forum and *renvoi* in his brilliant short article 'In Praise and Defence of Renvoi'.[66]

Also significant in this respect has been the recognition of the role of choice of law in equity, most powerfully seen in the decision of the Singapore Court of Appeal in *Rickshaw Investments Ltd v Nicolai Baron von Uexkull*,[67] drawing heavily upon the scholarship of Professor Tiong Min Yeo in *Choice of Law for Equitable Doctrines*,[68] and the rejection of the notion that the application of equitable doctrines and remedies is a matter for the law of the forum.[69]

---

[59] Jurisdiction of Courts (Cross-vesting) Act 1987 (Cth) and state analogues. The statutory scheme is discussed in Martin Davies, Andew Bell, Paul Le Gay Brereton and Michael Douglas, *Nygh's Conflict of Laws in Australia* (10th ed, LexisNexis Butterworths 2019) ch 6 (hereafter Davies et al, *Conflict of Laws in Australia*).
[60] Trans-Tasman Proceedings Act 2010 (Cth) pt 3.
[61] Richard Garnett, *Substance and Procedure in Private International Law* (OUP 2012). cf *Harding v Wealands* [2006] UKHL 32, [2007] 2 AC 1.
[62] (1870) LR 6 QB 1.
[63] (2000) 203 CLR 503.
[64] (2002) 210 CLR 491 (hereafter *Renault*).
[65] (2005) 223 CLR 331 (hereafter *Neilson*). This important but complex decision is noted by Andrew Dickinson in 'Renvoi: The Comeback Kid?' (2006) 122 LQR 183. See also David Hughes, 'The Insolubility of Renvoi and its Consequences' (2010) 6 Journal of Private International Law 195. In two subsequent decisions of the New South Wales Court of Appeal, Spigelman CJ described *Neilson* as establishing the 'no advantage principle', that is to say, it operated to preclude a plaintiff from bringing an action in tort in Australia that would not have been available had it been brought in the place where the tort had occurred and whose law governed the question of tortious liability: see *Amaca Pty Ltd v Frost* (2006) 67 NSWLR 635 [93]–[100]; *Murakami v Wiryadi* (2010) 268 ALR 377 [94], [119] (hereafter *Murakami*).
[66] (1998) 47 ICLQ 877. Professor Briggs revisited this theme in a case note on *Neilson* (n 65), Briggs, 'The Meaning and Proof of Foreign Law' [2006] LMCLQ 1, 3, describing the approach of the majority as 'a brilliant illumination of renvoi as a vital element in the overall search for the most appropriate outcome'.
[67] [2007] 1 SLR 377.
[68] (OUP 2004). See also *Murakami* (n 65) [128]–[149].
[69] Davies et al, *Conflict of Laws in Australia* (n 59) ch 21.

As a sidenote, the use of the notion of a (or the) natural forum as a technique for securing or striving for at least a measure of uniformity of outcome may be seen to have its statutory equivalent in the form of a 'foreign main proceeding', being an insolvency proceeding taking place in the state where the debtor has its 'centre of main interest'. These concepts lie at the core of the UNCITRAL Model Law on Cross-Border Insolvency which was issued on 30 May 1997 and has been widely adopted.[70] It is perhaps not a stretch to describe the 'centre of main interest' as the 'natural forum' for the winding up of a company or group of companies with transnational spheres of operation and for the administration of their insolvency. As with the 'natural forum', however, there will sometimes be scope for controversy as to the identification of the 'centre of main interest' and the criteria for its identification.[71]

There is no doubt that the desire that litigation should occur in its natural forum has a superficial attraction and certain nobility from an abstract and internationalist perspective—after all, what could be a superior forum in which to litigate than the *natural* forum? Underpinning that concept are, as have been seen, considerations of international judicial comity and recognition and respect for other legal systems. Reduction in the scope for forum shopping and the potential for conflicting or inconsistent results and the insidious damage that may be done to respect for the rule of law thereby also underscore the value of driving litigation to the natural forum.

The leveraging of substantive, procedural, institutional or cultural differences or any combination thereof between potentially available forums is what feeds and drives forum shopping,[72] and although Lord Denning famously celebrated the practice[73] and there is a case to be made for its revival,[74] 'forum shopping' is a term that generally carries pejorative connotations and certainly did at the time *Spiliada* was decided. It is a practice that is all but inevitable, however, given the 'jungle'[75] of separate, broadly based jurisdictions all over the world.[76]

In this context, it was perhaps somewhat naïve to hope or believe, as Lord Templeman certainly did in *Spiliada*, that parties with significant commercial interests at stake would be content merely to furnish a list of connecting factors to a judge to consider 'in the quiet of his [or her] room without expense to the parties', without reference 'to other decisions on other facts' and with submissions

---

[70] *Shierson v Vlieland-Boddy* [2005] 1 WLR 3966 [55]. Within Europe, see EU Insolvency Regulation (Regulation (EU) 2015/848 of the European Parliament and of the Council of 20 May 2015 on insolvency proceedings (recast) [2015] OJ L141/19).
[71] *Re Stanford International Bank Ltd* [2011] Ch 33.
[72] Andrew S Bell, 'The Why and Wherefore of Transnational Forum Shopping' (1995) 69 ALJ 124; Bell, *Forum Shopping* (n 16) ch 2.
[73] *The Atlantic Star* (CA) (n 22) 382.
[74] Sir Peter Gross, 'A Good Forum to Shop In: London and English Law Post-Brexit' [2018] LMCLQ 222 (hereafter Gross, 'A Good Forum to Shop In').
[75] *Airbus* (n 56) 132.
[76] Bell, *Forum Shopping* (n 16) ch 1.

being measured 'in hours and not days'[77] (or even minutes not hours)[78] with appeals to be 'rare' and appellate intervention reluctant. That has simply not been the experience of the courts in England and the myriad other countries around the Commonwealth which embraced *Spiliada* so enthusiastically. Indeed, the time, cost and degree of engagement of the courts in jurisdictional disputes has over many years been the subject of repeated comment and complaint by senior judges.[79]

Thus, in 1992, the Court of Appeal comprising Mustill, Nourse and Nicholls LJJ saw irony in the fact that they were making reference to Lord Templeman's remarks about the need for summary disposition of *forum non conveniens* applications 'on the 39th page of a judgment, resulting from argument which spread over all or some part of 14 days', wryly observing that 'it seems that something must have gone wrong' and commenting that 'the parties have allowed the zeal with which they have explored all the labyrinthine features of the merits to obscure the fact that the applications and the appeal are concerned with questions which lie within a short compass'.[80] In the following year in another case, Neill LJ expressed his concern that the hearing (albeit on some issues in addition to *forum non conveniens*) before the primary judge took eight days and before the Court of Appeal over three days.[81]

A decade later, Lord Walker, delivering the advice of the Privy Council on an appeal from Jersey, described the litigation before the Board as 'regrettably far from Lord Templeman's ideal', noting that more than six years had elapsed fighting the issue as to whether or not the dispute should be heard in Jersey or Kenya.[82] In 2009, in *Deripaska v Cherney (No 2)*,[83] Waller LJ said that 'disputes as to forum should not become state trials' and that:

> ... here we are with an appeal to this court with a mountain of material; an appellant's skeleton argument of 69 pages; respondent's skeleton of 53 pages; a reply skeleton from the appellant of 39 pages. It surely would have been better for both parties and better use of court time if they had expended their money and their energy on fighting the merits of the claim.

---

[77] *Spiliada* (n 1) 460, 465.
[78] *Voth* (n 15) 565; cf for the failure to achieve this aspiration in Australia, *Garsec v His Majesty The Sultan of Brunei* (2008) 250 ALR 682; [2008] NSWCA 211 at [93]–[94].
[79] It would be interesting to conduct a detailed quantitative study as to the number of applications for stays of proceedings and service *ex juris* in England on *Spiliada* grounds to ascertain the number of applications which have succeeded and the number of appeals that have been allowed from such decisions. This would serve to update the survey undertaken by David Robertson, '*Forum Non Conveniens* in America and England: A Rather Fantastic Fiction' (1987) 103 LQR 398.
[80] *Societe Commerciale de Reassurance v Eras International Ltd (formerly Eras (UK))* [1992] 1 Lloyd's Rep 570, 614.
[81] *Hamed El Chiaty & Co (T/A Travco Nile Cruise Lines) v The Thomas Cook Group Ltd* [1994] 1 Lloyd's Rep 382.
[82] *Hindocha v Gheewala* [2003] UKPC 77.
[83] [2009] EWCA Civ 849, [2010] 2 All ER (Comm) 456 [6]–[7] (hereafter *Cherney*).

Four years later, Lord Neuberger vented his frustration in *In VTB Capital plc v Nutritek International Corp*,[84] stating that:

> [H]earings concerning the issue of appropriate forum should not involve masses of documents, long witness statements, detailed analysis of the issues, and long argument. It is self-defeating if, in order to determine whether an action should proceed to trial in this jurisdiction, the parties prepare for and conduct a hearing which approaches the putative trial itself, in terms of effort, time and cost. There is also a real danger that, if the hearing is an expensive and time-consuming exercise, it will be used by a richer party to wear down a poorer party, or by a party with a weak case to prevent, or at least to discourage, a party with a strong case from enforcing its rights.
>
> Quite apart from this, it is simply disproportionate for parties to incur costs, often running to hundreds of thousands of pounds each, and to spend many days in court, on such a hearing. The essentially relevant factors should, in the main at any rate, be capable of being identified relatively simply and, in many respects, uncontroversially. There is little point in going into much detail: when determining such applications, the court can only form preliminary views on most of the relevant legal issues and cannot be anything like certain about which issues and what evidence will eventuate if the matter proceeds to trial.

In 2019, Lord Briggs (no relation to Adrian Briggs), echoing Lord Collins in *Altimo Holdings and Investment Ltd v Kyrgyz Mobil Tel Ltd*,[85] expressed his concern at the length, cost and complexity of stay applications in terms of the 'requirement for proportionality, and for respect to be given to first instance decisions on jurisdiction', observing that 'unless condign costs consequences are made to fall upon litigants, and even their professional advisors, who ignore these requirements, this court will find itself in the unenviable position of beating its head against a brick wall.'[86]

To put the matter bluntly, for thirty-five years and notwithstanding enhanced powers of case management, judges at the highest levels have remonstrated that fights over jurisdiction on natural forum grounds should be brief and disposed of in virtually a summary fashion and, for the same amount of time, experienced counsel and solicitors representing sophisticated commercial clients have consistently honoured Lord Templeman's injunction in *Spiliada* more in the breach than the observance. It is necessary to grapple frankly with the reasons for this, reasons which, with respect, may not always have been fully comprehended in judicial complaints about the time and expense involved in jurisdictional disputes

---

[84] [2013] UKSC 5, [2013] 2 AC 337 [82]–[83].
[85] [2011] UKPC 7, [2012] 1 WLR 1804 [7] (hereafter *Altimo*).
[86] *Vedanta* (n 47) [9], [14].

and concomitant exhortations to 'get to the merits'. At least seven such reasons can be identified.

First, notwithstanding some doctrinal developments in some jurisdictions that have reduced the scope for the leveraging of strategic advantages as between forums as discussed above, venue still matters and sophisticated commercial parties assess it to be worth fighting about, and fighting hard. Rationality dictates that, even where 'substantial justice' may be available in two or more forums, parties often perceive that the difference in potential outcome as between jurisdictions, whether measured in terms of money or risk or both, is still worth fighting over. And substantial justice may not in truth be available in an alternative posited forum but it may be very difficult to establish this so that the outcome of the forum dispute will often be more significant than may appear to be the case.

Second, the identification of the natural forum in any given case may be far from obvious, and that will especially be so where the dispute involves more than two parties and arises from events over a long period of time involving multiple transactions. Moreover, the full canvass of facts and points of contention will not necessarily have emerged or fully emerged at the early stage of proceedings at which a stay must be applied for. This presents a problem, particularly but not exclusively in cases of service out of the jurisdiction.

In this context, the *Spiliada* test requires a nuanced assessment to be made not only as to connecting factors but of their relative significance. This demands a proper understanding of the case and the ambit of the dispute. In complex commercial cases, this cannot always be done simply, quickly or cheaply and, as the Supreme Court has recently recognised, too hasty a characterisation 'runs the risk' in complex litigation 'that the court will by choosing a particular definition prejudge the outcome of the *forum conveniens* analysis'.[87] Further, as the Singapore Court of Appeal has correctly pointed out, a court asked to stay proceedings is not engaged simply in a mechanistic or quantitative exercise of 'counting up' connecting factors: rather the court should always be astute to determine the particular incidences of the case that are likely to be material to the fair determination of the dispute, and to ascribe greater weight to those over others.[88] In a similar vein, in *JSC BTA Bank v Granton Trade Ltd*,[89] Christopher Clarke J, conscious no doubt of the attempt to anchor jurisdiction with particular defendants, expressed the view that 'a decision as to the appropriate forum must necessarily take account of the relative importance within a case of different defendants and particularly those against whom proceedings in England are practically bound to continue'.

---

[87] *Unwired Planet International Ltd v Huawei Technologies (UK) Co Ltd* [2020] UKSC 37 [94] (hereafter *Unwired Planet*).
[88] *Rappo* (n 8) [71]. *Vedanta* (n 47) provides a good example of this.
[89] [2010] EWHC 2577 (Comm) [28].

Third, expressed in the rather open-ended terms of the identification of the 'forum which is more suitable for the ends of justice',[90] the natural or more appropriate forum may be apt to be manipulated by the proffering of undertakings,[91] shrewd pleading involving selective choice of defendants or causes of action (especially statutory)[92] or the making of claims of varying degrees of contestability as to the suitability of the proffered foreign forum or, to use Lord Goff's language in *Spiliada*, its '*availability*'. The open-textured nature of this concept, left undefined in *Spiliada*, has opened up the scope for much interlocutory debate.[93] Arguments in respect of a foreign court's 'availability' cannot take place in an evidentiary vacuum. The twin decisions of the House of Lords in *Connelly v RTZ Corporation*[94] and *Lubbe*,[95] for example, were both decisions in which the arguments were heard in the House of Lords over three and four days respectively, and the decision to refuse a stay of proceedings was ultimately made over four years after the commencement of proceedings. Four years is a very long period to determine a question of venue, especially in a case where claims of injured persons are at stake.

Fourth, the open-ended nature of the *Spiliada* test lends itself to assessments which are not necessarily discretionary in nature,[96] thereby opening up and increasing the possibility of appellate interference. And successful appeals beget further appeals. An early application of *Spiliada* in England saw the Court of Appeal reverse a decision to stay English proceedings in favour of France in a case involving a matrimonial dispute notwithstanding Lord Templeman's observation in *Spiliada* the previous year that appeals should be rare.[97]

Fifth, in some cases, the identification of the governing law may be far from straightforward[98] and indeed sometimes incapable of clean or definitive assessment short of a final hearing when all of the facts have come out.[99] Moreover, an inquiry as to what law would be applied in the alternative forum, if the proceedings were stayed or service out refused, and whether or not the application of this law would deliver 'substantial justice', will require evidence of the alternative forum's choice of law rules and an understanding as to how they apply. In some cases, those rules will, depending on the alternative posited forum, be non-existent or in an inchoate stage of development. In others, differences asserted to exist in the

---

[90] *Société du Gaz de Paris v Société Anonyme de Navigation 'Les Armateurs Francais'* (1926) Sess Cas (HL) 13, 22 per Lord Sumner, quoted by Lord Goff in *Spiliada* (n 1) 474–5.
[91] As occurred in *Lubbe v Cape plc* [2000] UKHL 41, [2000] 1 WLR 1545 (hereafter *Lubbe*).
[92] See eg *Reinsurance Australia Corporation v HIH Casualty and General Insurance Ltd (in liq)* (2004) 254 ALR 29.
[93] This point is well made in Louise Merrett, 'Uncertainties in the First Limb of the *Spiliada* Test' (2005) 54 ICLQ 211.
[94] [1997] UKHL 30, [1998] AC 854 (hereafter *Connelly*).
[95] *Lubbe* (n 91).
[96] This question is discussed by Martin Davies in his essay in this collection (ch 2).
[97] *Chatelard v Chatelard* (CA, 24 October 1988).
[98] See eg *Rappo* (n 8); *Murakami* (n 65) [150].
[99] See eg *Puttick v Tenon Ltd* (2008) 238 CLR 265 (hereafter *Puttick*).

potentially applicable foreign law will need to be determined, and questions of the jurisdiction of the foreign forum may also arise and need to be determined.[100] This last point is illustrated by the Supreme Court decision in *Unwired Planet*.[101]

Sixth, the quality of justice available in the foreign forum *is* made relevant on the *Spiliada* test, albeit that that test calls for deference to differences in procedures of foreign courts. But frequently, a court asked to stay proceedings or authorise service out of the jurisdiction, in order to ascertain both the availability and appropriateness of the proffered foreign forum, will need to make at least some form of assessment of how proceedings in that forum may proceed, not only procedurally but also, as indicated above, in terms of what law the foreign court would apply.[102] It is neither unknown nor uncommon for there to be detailed foreign law (including foreign choice of law) issues to be debated, including by reference to expert evidence, within such an application.

Seventh, as shall be seen below in Section F, an increasing willingness on the part of English courts to engage with the suitability or availability of what is contended to be the natural forum, and the proper insistence on the need for cogent evidence in this regard, only encourages 'litigation about where to litigate' on an elevated scale because the consequences of losing such an argument are not unlike the consequences (real or imagined) of making an unsuccessful application to a judge to disqualify him or herself for bias. Life may be more than a little uncomfortable for a party who has made such an application and failed. Related to this, the relatively rapid emergence of new economies, the maturity and sophistication of whose legal (and political) systems is not always commensurate with their economic growth, may be apt to generate forensic anxiety in corporate plaintiffs for whom the prospect of litigating in such a forum may be far from attractive, especially when there have been dealings with assets which the foreign government may be looking to renationalise.[103]

It is interesting to ponder in this regard the extent to which the adoption of the natural forum doctrine and the jurisdictional litigation which it has nurtured has contributed to the growth of international commercial arbitration in the last three decades. By committing to arbitration, parties that may, pre-*Spiliada*, have been content to litigate in the Commercial Court in London are not exposed to the risk of having their proceedings stayed in favour of a different forum with less or no expertise or experience in commercial dispute resolution. Agreement to arbitrate also largely immunises commercial parties from preliminary disputes about forum which, as experience has taught and contrary to Lord Templeman's aspiration in

---

[100] *Rappo* (n 8) [92]–[96].
[101] *Unwired Planet* (n 87) [97].
[102] eg *Nima Sarl v The Deves Insurance Public Company Ltd* [2002] EWCA Civ 1132, [2003] 2 Lloyd's Rep 327.
[103] *Cherney* (n 83) [66].

Spiliada, can frequently delay resolution of the ultimate dispute quite significantly, with concomitant increases in costs.

Whether or not the natural forum test as enunciated in *Spiliada* would promote extensive and expensive adjectival litigation of this nature was one of the reasons why the High Court of Australia did not fully embrace the natural forum doctrine and only adopted an attenuated version of it in *Voth*. For reasons that are, it is hoped, rather more than parochial, it is worth revisiting that decision in the context of a retrospective consideration of the natural forum doctrine.

D. The Natural Forum—Australian Iconoclasm

I have often pondered (as has Professor Briggs[104]) whether or not the failure to adopt *Spiliada* and embrace the concept of the natural forum in Australia had something to do with the fact that the first opportunity for the High Court of Australia to consider *Spiliada* arose in a personal injury case—*Oceanic Sun*—in which an injured individual was pitted against a substantial (and no doubt well-insured) Greek shipping company.[105] By way of contrast, with the exception of *MacShannon*, all of the cases in the House of Lords leading up to and including *Spiliada* were commercial or collision cases. *Lubbe*,[106] in which a stay was not granted and the justice exception engaged, involved personal injury claims on a mass scale.

As a sidenote, as with *Oceanic Sun*, the first New Zealand case to apply *Spiliada* also involved a personal injury claim but, although the plaintiff's injury occurred at a resort in Noumea where the plaintiff was treated by a doctor, the New Zealand Court of Appeal held in that case that it had not been shown that the case had a greater connection with New Caledonia (which on the face of matters, might have been thought to be the natural forum) than New Zealand.[107]

Returning to the position in Australia, although *Spiliada* had been warmly embraced by Wilson and Toohey JJ in *Oceanic Sun*, their Honours formed the minority in a five judge bench. Given that Greece was fairly obviously the natural forum in a case arising from an injury sustained on board a passenger liner whilst cruising the Greek Islands, a stay of proceedings would have consigned a badly injured plaintiff to litigate in an unfamiliar forum halfway around the world. That

---

[104] Adrian Briggs, 'The Death of *Harrods: Forum Non Conveniens* and the European Court' (2005) 121 LQR 535, 536: 'The doctrine of *forum non conveniens* causes the most palpable sense of unease where a corporate defendant raises it against an individual claimant who has sustained personal injury, and most of all if the claimant is a local. All doctrinal analysis aside, this may be the real explanation for its repudiation by the High Court of Australia …'.

[105] *Oceanic Sun* (n 18). On this perspective, see further the essay of Janet Walker in this collection (ch 3).

[106] *Lubbe* (n 91).

[107] *Club Mediterranee* (n 32).

this outcome did not recommend itself to the members of the majority was, perhaps, hardly surprising (although it was not welcomed in academic circles).[108]

The majority in *Oceanic Sun* analysed the matter rather differently as between themselves with Brennan J taking the most conservative line, namely that a court invested with jurisdiction should exercise it unless the invocation of that jurisdiction was vexatious or oppressive. The other members of the majority, Deane and Gaudron JJ, whilst not embracing *Spiliada*, laid the groundwork for the clearly inappropriate forum test which was adopted a few years later by four members of the Court in *Voth*.[109] Although that was a professional negligence case, the die had in many respects been cast and the members of the plurality 'put aside individual differences of emphasis in order to participate in this majority judgment'.[110]

A later personal injuries case which, in its use of the language of vexation, oppression and abuse of process, arguably took the High Court closer to the approach favoured by Brennan J in *Oceanic Sun* was the decision in *Renault*.[111] There, a post-graduate Chinese student, studying in Australia and rendered quadriplegic in a motor vehicle accident in New Caledonia, was pitted against the might of the French industrial behemoth, Renault. In refusing to grant a stay in a case which was really concerned with the adequacy of the design and manufacture of the motor vehicle in which Mr Zhang was driving (which took place in France), the High Court made the point that the fact that a matter may be governed by foreign law will not alone make a forum inappropriate. There was a need to establish that the proof and application of foreign law would be a positive source of prejudice.[112]

Also significant is the fact that it was in yet another personal injuries case, *Puttick*,[113] involving a claim by a New Zealand widow of a man who died of mesothelioma in New Zealand, that the High Court of Australia declined to revisit its rejection of *Spiliada* in favour of the 'clearly inappropriate forum' test.[114] Had the litigation, which had been commenced in Victoria, been stayed on the basis that New Zealand was the natural forum, Mrs Puttick would have been consigned to compensation assessed under the New Zealand accidents compensation regime which was perceived to be far less generous than an award of common law damages by an Australian court.

It was pointed out by French CJ, Gummow, Hayne and Kiefel JJ in *Puttick* that:[115]

---

[108] See eg Michael Pryles, 'Judicial Darkness on the Oceanic Sun' (1988) 62 ALJ 774.
[109] *Voth* (n 15). By the time *Voth* was decided, Wilson J had left the Court but Toohey J expressed himself as remaining 'impenitent' in adhering to his previous support for *Spiliada*: 590.
[110] Ibid 552. See also *Puttick* (n 99).
[111] *Renault* (n 64).
[112] Ibid 510–1 [78]–[82]. *PCH Offshore Pty Ltd v Dunn (No 2)* (2010) 273 ALR 167 is an illustration of a case where this was clearly established. For a perhaps more nuanced view to the effect that the very need to prove foreign law is a source of prejudice, adding complexity, expense and uncertainty and the risk of error in application (the 'lost in translation' risk), see *Murakami* (n 65) at [150].
[113] *Puttick* (n 99).
[114] Ibid 277 [29]–[30], 280 [38]–[41].
[115] Ibid 277 [29] (emphasis added, footnotes omitted).

It may readily be accepted that ... the power to stay proceedings, regularly commenced, on inappropriate forum grounds, is exercised 'in accordance with the general principle empowering a court to dismiss or stay proceedings which are oppressive, vexatious or an abuse of process' and that 'the rationale for the exercise of the power to stay is the avoidance of injustice between parties *in the particular case*'.

The only decisions of the High Court of Australia that have resulted in a stay of proceedings on 'clearly inappropriate forum grounds' have been *Voth* itself which, as noted above, was a professional negligence case, and *CSR Ltd v Cigna Insurance Australia Ltd*,[116] a significant commercial case in relation to insurance coverage.

It is not without irony that the two leading protagonists in *CSR* both had their head offices in Sydney, less than a kilometre from the Supreme Court of New South Wales, and the principal dispute related to a contract negotiated in Sydney, circumstances which suggested, as emphasised by Brennan CJ in his powerful dissent, that New South Wales was not only *not* a clearly inappropriate forum but indeed was overwhelmingly the natural forum, and yet the proceedings were held to have been brought in a 'clearly inappropriate forum' and stayed.

This decision was heavily influenced by the fact that there were overlapping albeit not completely parallel proceedings that had been commenced in New Jersey where a claim had been brought under the Sherman Act and a concession had been made in the NSW proceedings, by reference to the then Australian choice of law rule for tort, that that claim could not be heard in New South Wales. As I have explained elsewhere:[117]

> [T]he availability of a remedy in a foreign jurisdiction not available in the local forum will largely be a function of the local forum's choice of law rules and how internationalist the local forum is in its approaches to characterisation of foreign causes of action. Thus, there is no reason in principle why a foreign statutory claim may not be entertained in Australia. In this context, the only reason why the critical concession in relation to the inability to litigate the Sherman Act claim in Australia was made in *CSR v Cigna* was because the then Australian choice of law rule for tort required double actionability and, in particular, required that the 'foreign ' cause of action be actionable in Australia. It was not until *Renault v Zhang* was decided, some five years after *CSR v Cigna*, that the choice of law rule in tort was altered to provide for application of the law in the place of the wrong.

---

[116] (1997) 189 CLR 345 (hereafter *CSR*).
[117] Andrew Bell, 'Transnational Commercial Litigation and the Current State of Australian Law' in KE Lindgren (ed), *International Commercial Litigation and Dispute Resolution* (Sydney University Press & Ross Parsons Centre of Commercial, Corporate and Taxation Law 2010) 61.

In light of this development, the concession made in *CSR v Cigna* would not need to have been made.

The *CSR* litigation, as with some of the English cases referred to above in Section C, entailed a two week mini-trial at first instance on the question of stay and anti-suit injunction. It highlighted that, even under the *Voth* test, the resolution of jurisdictional disputes may be far more complex than the simple exercise contemplated by Lord Templeman's observation in *Spiliada* as to how such applications should be dealt with. *CSR* illustrates the potential significance of foreign law in a stay application, the complexity introduced by the existence of statutory causes of action not necessarily available in the alternative forum and the complications arising from overlapping but not absolutely concurrent proceedings in the determination of stay applications.

Thirty years on from *Voth*, some of the reasons identified by the plurality for not embracing the natural forum and following *Spiliada* resonate with the reasons why it has been suggested that Lord Templeman's hope in *Spiliada* as to how stay applications would be dealt with have not been realised. Thus, their Honours emphasised that:[118]

- in some cases, the question 'what is the natural and appropriate forum' will be 'by no means easy to answer, particularly at an interlocutory stage of proceedings';
- 'the complexity of modern transnational transactions and relationships between parties is such as to indicate that in a significant number of cases there is more than one forum with an arguable claim to be the natural forum';
- it is desirable to discourage the litigation of such a potentially difficult question; and that
- 'there are powerful policy considerations which militate against Australian courts sitting in judgment upon the ability or willingness of the courts of another country to accord justice to the plaintiff in the particular case.'

E. O Canada, Oh Canada!

Australian scepticism directed towards *Spiliada* and the natural forum was in one sense counterbalanced by Canadian enthusiasm for the doctrine. Indeed, in Canada, the natural forum has, in effect and radically, been elevated into something of an organising principle in the context of the recognition and enforcement of foreign judgments. Thus, a foreign judgment will be enforced in Canada which

---

[118] *Voth* (n 15) 558–9.

has been given by a court of a jurisdiction which has a 'real and substantial connection' with the dispute, irrespective of whether or not the defendant/judgment debtor has been served with process in that jurisdiction or otherwise submitted to it, whether contractually or by entering an appearance and participating in the proceedings that led to the judgment: see *Beals v Saldanha*.[119]

Beals constituted a radical extension of the conventional understanding of 'jurisdiction in the international sense'. It, in some ways, represented a modern resurrection of the use, long repudiated elsewhere, of comity as a basis for the recognition and enforcement of foreign judgments.[120] The radicalism of the decision is illustrated by the observation that rules 'based on territoriality, sovereignty, independence and attornment' were 'outmoded'.[121] These concepts might fairly be said to be foundational to received conflicts of law doctrine elsewhere in (and throughout) the common law world.

Of most significance for present purposes was the plurality's justification in *Beals* for what it candidly recognised was a change in the law. This was sourced in the Court's perception of the nature and needs of the contemporary global economy, the self-same justification that almost certainly underpinned but which was not explicitly stated in *Spiliada*. Thus in *Beals* it was said that, '[i]nternational comity and the prevalence of international cross-border transactions and movement call for a modernisation of private international law'[122] and the earlier observations of La Forest J in *Morguard* were elevated and adopted in the transnational context:[123]

> The business community operates in a world economy and we correctly speak of a world community even in the face of decentralized political and legal power. *Accommodating the flow of wealth, skills and people across state lines has now become imperative.*

There is room for a separate essay as to the propriety of an appellate court, even an ultimate appellate court, so explicitly seeking to change and modify the law. For more conservative jurisdictions, the *Beals* approach was and remains a step too far and the banner of 'comity' cannot conceal naked and radical law making.

The radical development of the common law in Canada[124] represented by *Beals* has not been taken up elsewhere in the common law world. Indeed, it would be

---

[119] [2003] 3 SCR 416 (hereafter *Beals*). The real and substantial connection test had been 'road-tested' as it were federally in a series of decisions originating with *Morguard Investments Ltd v De Savoye* [1990] 3 SCR 1077 (hereafter *Morguard*).
[120] *Schibsby v Westenholz* (1870) LR 6 QB 155, 159; *Adams v Cape Industries plc* [1990] 1 Ch 433, 513.
[121] *Beals* (n 119) 434 [20].
[122] Ibid 437 [28].
[123] Ibid 436 [26] (emphasis added), quoting *Morguard* (n 119) 1098.
[124] Not the only recent challenge to orthodoxy in the field of recognition and enforcement of foreign judgments by the Supreme Court of Canada: *Pro Swing Inc v Elta Golf Inc* [2006] 2 SCR 612.

fair to say that it has been politely but firmly rejected, both by the United Kingdom Supreme Court[125] and by the Privy Council.[126]

Professor Briggs' response to *Beals*, having at its fulcrum the 'real and substantial connection' test, was always going to be interesting. One finds it set out in the Singapore Year Book of International Law of 2004. In an article entitled 'Crossing the River by Feeling the Stones: Rethinking the Law on Foreign Judgments', his 'submission' was that 'cautious and incremental development of the law on foreign judgments, especially by reference to broad and general principles of the common law, has much to recommend it'.[127] This was not, however, his conclusion about what the Supreme Court of Canada had done in *Beals*.

By the end of a familiarly provocative article, Professor Briggs concludes with the characteristic robustness for which he is well known, stating that those who 'proclaim that foreign courts and foreign judgments are to be treated as the equivalent of local ones, and that a foreign judgment should be regarded as having the same conclusiveness, the same likelihood of being correct, and the same immunity from challenge as a local judgment does', as the Supreme Court had in *Beals*, betray a:[128]

> ... *bien-pensant* cast of mind [is] based more on sentiment and optimism than on reason and analysis. The price which is paid for giving spurious equality of treatment to local and foreign judgments is paid by those individuals who seek relief from a local court in its adjudicating and receiving functions.... Though there may be no bright line which marks the transition from comity to political correctness, some cases plainly cross it. In the present submission, *Beals v Saldanha* lies far to the wrong side of it, and how it got there teaches a lesson which needs to be learned.

Rather curiously, however, Professor Briggs' criticism of the decision was far from absolute. On the one hand, whilst he opined that 'the Supreme Court of Canada was right to do as it did in widening the grounds of acceptable international jurisdictional competence', his thesis was that the Court should have developed the defences available at common law to the recognition and enforcement of foreign judgments to accommodate what was, on the facts in *Beals* and, to borrow Professor Briggs' language, an outcome that 'beggar[ed] belief'.[129]

---

[125] *Rubin v Eurofinance SA* [2012] UKSC 46, [2013] 1 AC 236 [109]–[110].
[126] *Vizcaya Partners Limited v Picard (Gibraltar)* [2016] UKPC 5, [2016] 3 All ER 181 [54] fn 1.
[127] (2004) 8 Singapore Yearbook of International Law 1, 1 (hereafter Briggs, 'Crossing the River').
[128] Ibid 21.
[129] Ibid 13. Writing ten years later, Professor Briggs was less balanced in his assessment, describing the Supreme Court's decision in *Beals* as taking 'Canadian common law off on a frolic of its own': Adrian Briggs, 'Recognition of Foreign Judgments: a matter of obligation' (2013) 129 LQR 87, 94.

F. The Natural Forum, Comity and Hard Cases

Professor Briggs concluded his discussion of *Beals* with the statement that 'judicial comity should not be allowed to become the enemy of justice'.[130] The reality is that the 'natural forum', as a jurisdictional *grundnorm*, is often incapable of accommodating hard or sympathetic cases. Lord Goff can be seen to have recognised as much in *Spiliada* by carving out a caveat where the ends of justice required the denial of a stay of proceedings notwithstanding the existence of the natural forum elsewhere or the authorisation of service even though England did not merit that description. Leading early examples of this 'carve out' being availed of are the two decisions of the House of Lords in *Connelly* and *Lubbe*. *Altimo* and *Vedanta* are more recent examples.

In both *Connelly* and *Lubbe*, Namibia and South Africa were overwhelmingly the natural forum. Exceptional circumstances in both cases were invoked to justify the refusal to stay proceedings that had been commenced in England. In the former case, Lord Goff said, '[t]here is every reason to believe that this case calls for highly professional representation, by both lawyers and scientific experts, for the achievement of substantial justice, and that such representation cannot be achieved in Namibia.'[131] The factual accuracy of these observations at the time they were made may be accepted but one cannot help but observe how remote they seem to be from the polite concerns with international judicial comity that animated Lord Brandon's attack on Sir John Donaldson in *The Abidin Daver*, for example, as noted earlier in Section B. Indeed, it may be thought that a conclusion expressed in terms that 'substantial justice' may not be available in the foreign but, *ex hypothesi*, natural forum may only be to elevate the affront to comity.

In *Lubbe,* Lord Bingham cloaked his observations about the South African judicial system by considering whether or not certain features may operate as a disincentive to a third party funder to finance the proceedings. He put the matter this way:[132]

> I do, however, think that the absence, as yet, of developed procedures for handling group actions in South Africa reinforces the submissions made by the plaintiffs on the funding issue. It is one thing to embark on and fund a heavy group action where the procedures governing the conduct of the proceedings are known to and understood by experienced judges and practitioners. It may be quite another where the exercise is novel and untried. There must then be an increased likelihood of interlocutory decisions which are contentious, with the likelihood of appeals and delay. It cannot be assumed that all judges will respond to this new

---

[130] Briggs, 'Crossing the River' (n 127) 22.
[131] *Connelly* (n 94) 854, 874.
[132] *Lubbe* (n 91) 1560.

procedural challenge in the same innovative spirit. The exercise of jurisdiction by the South African High Court through separate territorial divisions, while not a potent obstacle in itself, could contribute to delay, uncertainty and cost. The procedural novelty of these proceedings, if pursued in South Africa, must in my view act as a further disincentive to any person or body considering whether or not to finance the proceedings.

The success of his Lordship's deft attempt not to reflect adversely on another legal system may be open to question. Restraint in the criticism of other legal systems is no doubt simpler out of court than in a judgment of the court. Thus liberated from the constraints of the immediate facts of a hard case, Lord Bingham observed that: '[t]here are countries in the world where all judicial decisions find favour with the powers that be, but they are probably not places where any of us would wish to live.'[133]

The High Court of Australia, in its rather different way, perhaps recognised the reality of the need to retain and exercise jurisdiction in 'hard cases' by adopting the more attenuated clearly inappropriate forum test in *Voth*. A refusal to grant a stay of proceedings because the local forum is not clearly inappropriate does not require the same focus to be fixed on the procedures and experience of foreign courts, still less the more problematic charge that the courts of particular countries are creatures of government or beset with endemic corruption or administered with gross incompetence. As the plurality said in *Voth*,[134] in a passage that is worth recalling in the context of the decisions in *Connelly* and *Lubbe*:

> [A] conclusion that some suggested foreign tribunal is, in the judgment of the local court, the appropriate or more appropriate forum necessarily involves assumptions or findings about the comparative claims of the competing foreign tribunal, including the standards and impartiality of its members. Thus, Lord Goff recognised in Spiliada (at p 478) that one factor to be considered in determining whether a stay should be granted under the Spiliada test 'can be the fact, if established objectively by cogent evidence, that the plaintiff will not obtain justice in the foreign jurisdiction'. In a context where the relevant test will fall to be applied in accordance with the individual perception of a primary judge, the courts of this country are better adapted to apply a test which focuses upon the inappropriateness of the local court of which the local judge will have both knowledge and experience than to a test which focuses upon the appropriateness or comparative appropriateness of a particular foreign tribunal of which he or she is likely to have little knowledge and no experience.

---

[133] Tom Bingham, *The Rule of Law* (Penguin Books 2010) 65, cited in Gross, 'A Good Forum to Shop In' (n 74) 226.
[134] *Voth* (n 15) 559.

As noted above in Section D, the plurality in *Voth* also said that 'there are powerful policy considerations which militate against Australian courts sitting in judgment upon the ability or willingness of the courts of another country to accord justice to the plaintiff in the particular case'.[135] In his Hague Lectures, Briggs draws attention to these passages from *Voth* as being more attuned to comity, perhaps reflecting an evolving respect for the High Court of Australia's refusal fully to embrace *Spiliada*.[136]

This leads to a consideration of a series of decisions in recent years in which English courts, applying *Spiliada*, have been asked to do just what the High Court of Australia was anxious to avoid, with the consequence that, in the application of a doctrine designed to *promote* comity, precisely the opposite may be seen to have resulted. These cases, together with *Connelly* and *Lubbe*, reveal that the practical operation of *Spiliada* is not as straightforward or as faithful to the policy goals which so explicitly underwrote its development as had been hoped by those responsible for the promotion of the natural forum doctrine.

In *Spiliada* it will be recalled that Lord Goff said:[137]

> If however the court concludes ... that there is some other available forum which prima facie is clearly more appropriate for the trial of the action, it will ordinarily grant a stay unless there are circumstances by reason of which *justice requires* that a stay should nevertheless not be granted. In this inquiry, the court will consider all the circumstances of the case, including circumstances which go beyond those taken into account when considering connecting factors with other jurisdictions. One such factor can be the fact, if established objectively by cogent evidence, that the plaintiff will not obtain justice in the foreign jurisdiction; see the *The Abidin Daver* [1984] A.C. 398, 411, per Lord Diplock, a passage which now makes plain that, on this inquiry, the burden of proof shifts to the plaintiff.

The requirement for 'cogent' evidence was pointed. The requirement, moreover, was that there be cogent evidence that the plaintiff *will not* obtain justice in the foreign jurisdiction as opposed to cogent evidence of a *real risk* that substantial justice will not be able to be obtained.[138] In *The Abidin Daver*, Lord Brandon had made it plain that an affidavit filed in opposition to the grant of a stay of proceedings by a solicitor from 'the distinguished firm of solicitors acting for the Cuban owners' was inappropriate: it 'cast aspersions on the capacity of the Turkish court to try the Turkish action properly, and on the independence from the executive of any Turkish lawyer acting for the owners of a foreign ship against the owners of a

---

[135] Ibid 559; cf Lord Collins in *Altimo* (n 85).
[136] Adrian Briggs, '*Forum Non Conveniens* in Australia' (1989) 105 LQR 200 and Adrian Briggs, 'Wider Still and Wider: The Bounds of Australian Exorbitant Jurisdiction' [1989] LMCLQ 216.
[137] *Spiliada* (n 1), 478 (emphasis added).
[138] *Altimo* (n 85).

Turkish ship' As no sufficient grounds were supplied to found these aspersions, Lord Brandon made it clear that they 'should never have been made'.[139]

Earlier, in *Amin Rasheed*, in the context of a contention that the ability of a Kuwaiti court to decide matters of disputed fact was markedly inferior to that of the Commercial Court in England, Lord Diplock had warned of the invidious nature of the 'task of making a comparison of the relative efficiency of the civil law and common law procedures for the determination of disputed facts'.[140] His Lordship expressed the opinion that:[141]

> ... it would have been wholly wrong for an English court, with quite inadequate experience of how it works in practice in a particular country, to condemn as inferior to that of our own country a system of procedure for the trial of issues of fact that has long been adopted by a large number of both developed and developing countries in the modern world. So a natural prejudice in favour of a procedure with which English lawyers are familiar is not a consideration to which any weight ought to be given in determining whether a Kuwaiti court or the Commercial Court in England is the forum conveniens for the present litigation.

It was no surprise, therefore, that in *de Dampierre v de Dampierre*,[142] Lord Goff did not permit the residual 'ends of justice' discretion to be used to undermine the high principle immanent in the very idea of directing litigation to the natural forum, and as a backward route to the parochialism that had marked the traditional English approach to the assertion and retention of jurisdiction in cases with a transnational element. This was even though the availability of financial provision to the wife in France depended upon her establishing an absence of fault, a circumstance that Lord Goff described as 'no longer acceptable in this country' where maintenance was available irrespective of fault. The absence of this remedy in France was not such as to stand in the way of a stay of the English proceedings the wife had commenced. No judgment was cast on the merits of the French insistence on the establishment of an absence of exclusive fault.

But the 'justice exception' to the natural forum doctrine was invoked early by the Hong Kong Court of Appeal in the very decision in which *Spiliada* was adopted by that Court. In *The Adhiguna Meranti*,[143] the Court of Appeal refused to grant a stay of proceedings notwithstanding what it considered to be 'the comparatively tenuous connection' between Hong Kong and the shipping casualty in circumstances where it considered that it would be unjust to the plaintiffs to deprive them

---

[139] *The Abidin Daver* (n 3) 425.
[140] *Amin Rasheed* (n 3) 67.
[141] Ibid.
[142] *de Dampierre* (n 44) 110.
[143] [1988] 1 Lloyd's Rep 384.

of the Hong Kong limitation on liability which was said to reflect international public policy.

Writing in 2009 after his retirement as Chief Justice of Australia, Murray Gleeson referred to the textbook observation by the Singapore Court of Appeal in *Good Earth Agricultural Co Ltd v Novus International Pte Ltd*[144] that the Singapore courts have 'nothing but unreserved respect for the Hong Kong legal system' and then wryly observed that this sentiment was 'not surprising, but one can imagine some rather more challenging possibilities'.[145] The challenge was about to present itself to the English courts in a way which Professor Briggs has characterised as revealing cracks in the edifice and 'the breaking of the dam'.[146]

In *Cherney*,[147] the English Court of Appeal granted leave to serve out of the jurisdiction in a case where England was palpably not the natural forum in the sense of having the closest and most real connection with the dispute but Russia was. Notwithstanding this uncontroversial fact, the Court of Appeal affirmed a decision that England was the appropriate forum to hear a dispute between two Russian businessmen. Litigation in the natural forum, it was held, would have exposed Mr Cherney to increased risks of assassination, prosecution on trumped-up charges and state interference in the judicial process. For a court to make such findings in an interlocutory hearing is remarkable but it is not to say that such findings were not justified or not open. They were made by reference not only to evidence particular to Mr Cherney but by more generalised evidence about the Russian legal system, unrelated interference by the Russian government with the judicial process and the use by the Russian government of trumped-up criminal charges. Moreover, the decision involved a degree of speculation as to the extent to which the Russian government may take an interest in the significant commercial subject matter of the dispute, concerning control of a 13 per cent stake in what Moore-Bick LJ described as 'an industrial giant of national importance in Russia'.[148]

In *Altimo*,[149] Lord Collins made the following points. First, that where a party asserts that justice will not be done in the natural or more appropriate forum, it is sufficient that that party simply show that there is a real *risk* that it will not be done whether 'by reason of incompetence or lack of independence or corruption'.[150] Second, that, 'comity requires that the court be extremely cautious before deciding that there is a risk that justice will not be done in the foreign country by the foreign

---

[144] [2008] 2 SLR 711; [2008] SGCA 13 [27].
[145] Anthony Murray Gleeson, 'Transnational Litigation—Forensic Pathologies' in Hugh Dillon (ed), *Advocacy and Judging: Selected Papers of Murray Gleeson* (Federation Press 2017) 323.
[146] Adrian Briggs, 'Forum Non Satis: *Spiliada* and an Inconvenient Truth' [2011] LMCLQ 330.
[147] *Cherney* (n 83).
[148] Ibid [65].
[149] *Altimo* (n 85).
[150] Ibid [95], referring to *Cherney* (n 83) [28]–[29]; *Pacific International Sports Clubs Ltd v Surkis* [2010] EWCA Civ 753 [34]–[35]; *OJSC Oil Co Yugraneft v Abramovich* [2008] EWHC 2613 (Comm) [496].

court, and that is why cogent evidence is required'.[151] Third, his Lordship cited United States authority for the proposition that '[e]vidence of corruption in the foreign court system is admissible ... but it must go beyond generalised, anecdotal material'.[152] Fourth, the act of state doctrine did not preclude an English court from being able to find that justice will not, or may not, be done in a posited alternative forum because of endemic corruption in the foreign system.[153]

On the facts of *Altimo*, Lord Collins held that 'there was substantial evidence of specific irregularities, breach of principles of natural justice, and irrational conclusions, sufficient to justify a conclusion that there was considerably more than a risk of injustice'.[154] Although that was not the precise basis upon which the appeal was dismissed, the fundamental point being that 'if there is no trial in the Isle of Man, there will be no trial anywhere',[155] this decision, in conjunction with *Cherney v Deripaska (No 2)*, opened up the prospect in a very real way of English courts being dragged, under the guise of stay or service out applications, into invidious inquiries as to the quality and integrity of foreign legal systems. Large questions are left unanswered. How great does the risk need to be? Moore-Bick LJ's observation in *Cherney* that '[i]n most ordinary cases a person cannot reasonably be expected to accept more than a slight degree of increase in the risk of assassination, but a greater degree of risk of government interference in the judicial process might be thought acceptable'[156] highlights the utterly invidious nature of the exercise on any number of levels.

These decisions, coupled with the deterioration of confidence in the integrity of the judicial systems of many states around the world—the same loss of confidence that has fuelled the growth of international commercial arbitration—may have signalled the return of forum shopping or at least acted as a very significant fillip to that practice. As Professor Briggs memorably put it, commenting on *Cherney*, '[t]he whoops of delight at the Commercial Bar must be audible in caviar canneries the length and breadth of Russia'.[157] The 'forum of necessity'[158] is far removed both from the natural forum championed in *The Atlantic Star* and *Spiliada* and the centrality of the concept of comity in those decisions. The approach disclosed in a number of English decisions in the last decade is also in stark tension with

---

[151] *Altimo* (n 85) [97].
[152] Ibid [102].
[153] Ibid [101]. In *Yukos Capital Sarl v OJSC Rosneft Oil Co (No 2)* [2012] EWCA Civ 855, [2014] QB 458 [87], the Court of Appeal held that the act of state doctrine 'has never referred to judicial acts of state', meaning that 'the judicial acts of a foreign state are judged by judicial standards, including international standards regarding jurisdiction, in accordance with doctrines separate from the act of state doctrine, even if the dictates of comity still have an important role to play'.
[154] *Altimo* (n 85) [142].
[155] Ibid [151].
[156] *Cherney* (n 83) [59].
[157] Adrian Briggs, 'Decisions of British Courts 2009' (2010) 80 BYIL 575, 577.
[158] Ibid 578.

observations made by the Singapore Court of Appeal in *The Hung Vuong-2*[159] with which, one suspects, Lord Goff would fully have concurred:

> We must point out at once that it is not for this court or any court in Singapore to pass judgment on the competence or independence of the judiciary of another country, all the more so of a friendly country. Comity between nations would be gravely undermined if such a wholly invidious pursuit is embarked upon.

G. The Natural Forum—Final Reflections

This essay began with a reflection on the changed nature of the world at the beginning of the third decade of the 21st century as compared to the world as it stood when *Spiliada* was decided. The doctrine of the natural forum, originally so widely and warmly embraced, has not fared particularly well as times have changed. It was and is a doctrine whose success, to a large extent, depends upon mutuality of adoption, and it works best as between jurisdictions which share a common legal tradition. It is a self-denying ordinance but works less effectively if other jurisdictions do not subscribe to its underlying architecture and conceptual footings, or are at different stages of institutional development and repute. It was strangled for twenty years by European hostility and, beyond Europe, has not lived up to the expectations of those who thought that its application would be short, simple and straightforward. Far from advancing comity, ironically it has contributed to its infraction and exposed the judiciary to the most invidious of tasks, all the while representing a massive 'own goal' as far as the English legal profession is concerned. Hard cases, the best test for any principle of law, have rather shown it up and the clearly articulated reservations of the High Court of Australia in *Voth* have largely been vindicated. That is, at least, my assessment, some thirty-five years on.

---

[159] [2000] 2 SLR (R) 11 [27].

2
Forum Non Conveniens: Now We Are Much More Than Ten

Martin Davies

A. Introduction

One of Adrian Briggs's first published works was entitled '*Forum non conveniens—now we are ten?*'.[1] The article was written in 1983, ten years after the decision of the House of Lords in *The Atlantic Star*,[2] which, to use Professor Briggs's words, 'touched off the process of reconsideration' of the proposition, which had hitherto been 'clear beyond argument', that 'English law denied the idea that an action brought in English courts could be stayed on the ground that a foreign court was more suitable for the case to be adjudicated in'.[3] With memorable grace, Lord Goff acknowledged his debt to 'Now we are ten?' and another article by Professor Briggs[4] in his seminal speech in *Spiliada Maritime Corp v Cansulex Ltd*,[5] which remains the starting point for a consideration of the doctrine of *forum non conveniens* in the United Kingdom.

Application of the doctrine had a rather earlier start in the United States, where federal admiralty courts had been exercising a discretion to decline jurisdiction in cases involving foreigners since the early nineteenth century.[6] The doctrine was popularized by a New York attorney named Paxton Blair, in a 1929 article[7] that is

---

[1] Adrian Briggs, '*Forum non conveniens—now we are ten?*' [1983] Legal Studies 74 (hereafter Briggs, 'Now we are ten?').

[2] *Owners of the Atlantic Star v Owners of the Bona Spes (The Atlantic Star and The Bona Spes)* [1974] AC 436 (HL).

[3] Briggs, 'Now we are ten?' (n 1) 74.

[4] Adrian Briggs, 'The staying of actions on the ground of '*forum non conveniens*' in England today' [1984] LMCLQ 227. Lord Goff also included Rona Schuz in his thanks, for her article 'Controlling forum-shopping: The impact of *MacShannon v Rockware Glass Ltd*' (1986) 35 ICLQ 374. Professor Schuz, fellow pilgrim with Adrian Briggs and Lord Goff, is now Professor of Law and Co-Director of the Center for the Rights of the Child and the Family at Sha'arei Mishpat Law School in Hod Ha Sharon, Israel.

[5] [1987] AC 460 (HL) 488 (hereafter *Spiliada*).

[6] See, eg, *Willendson v Forsoket* 29 F Cas 1283 (D Penn 1801) (No 17,682) 1284, which begins with the splendidly no-nonsense statement: 'It has been my general rule not to take cognizance of disputes between the masters and crews of foreign ships. I have commonly referred them to their own courts'. The history of the American admiralty doctrine is traced by Alexander Bickel, 'The doctrine of *forum non conveniens* as applied in federal courts in matters of admiralty' (1949) 35 Cornell L Rev 12.

[7] Paxton Blair, 'The doctrine of *forum non conveniens* in Anglo-American law' (1929) 29 Colum L Rev 1. Blair has been described as having 'an imperious writing style and brilliant timing' (a phrase that

generally credited with influencing and shaping the adoption of the doctrine by the US Supreme Court.[8] The American doctrine was crystallized[9] in the form that it has to this day by a pair of cases decided by the Supreme Court on the same day in 1947.[10]

The Australian version of the *forum non conveniens* doctrine took the form that it has today in 1990, when the High Court of Australia decided, in *Voth v Manildra Flour Mills Ltd*,[11] to part ways with *Spiliada* by adopting a version of the test that asks whether the plaintiff's[12] chosen forum is 'clearly inappropriate'.

So, in the three countries that will be considered in this essay, the *forum non conveniens* test has remained almost completely unchanged since 1947 (in the United States), 1986 (in the UK), and 1990 (in Australia). A great deal has changed since then, whichever 'then' one looks at.[13] Now, we are much more than ten, to borrow a turn of phrase. The manner in which litigation is conducted has changed enormously, as has the ease of transmission of information around the world. One might have expected such fundamental changes to have changed the *forum non conveniens* tests, but that has not happened in any of the three countries. What has happened, not surprisingly, is a change in the way that they are applied, which is the subject of this essay.

In *Gulf Oil Co v Gilbert*,[14] the US Supreme Court distinguished between private interest factors, which are concerned with the convenience of the parties in conducting the litigation, and public interest factors, which are concerned with the administration of justice in the plaintiff's chosen forum. My main contention in this essay is that modern methods of presenting evidence and argument in court have so reduced the significance of the private interest factors that it is the public interest factors that now carry most of the weight, in all three of the countries

---

seems apt in a volume in honour of Adrian Briggs): see Gary Born and Peter Rutledge, *International Civil Litigation in United States Courts* (6th edn, Wolters Kluwer 2018) 352. Born in New Orleans, Blair spent his entire legal career in New York, becoming both a state Supreme Court justice and, later, state Solicitor-General.

[8] Blair's influence on the Supreme Court's adoption of the doctrine is described by Allan Stein, '*Forum non conveniens* and the redundancy of court-access doctrine' (1985) 133 U Pa L Rev 781, 811–12.
[9] This was the word used by the Supreme Court itself in *Piper Aircraft Co v Reyno* 454 US 235 (1981) 248 (hereafter *Piper*).
[10] *Gulf Oil Corp v Gilbert* 330 US 501 (1947) (hereafter *Gilbert*); *Koster v American Lumbermens Mutual Casualty Co* 330 US 518 (1947). Both decisions were handed down on 10 March 1947.
[11] [1990] HCA 55, (1990) 171 CLR 538 (hereafter *Voth*).
[12] At the risk of causing confusion, I will use the word 'plaintiff' generically throughout this essay, because that is the word still used in the United States and Australia, and 'claimant' only when writing specifically about the UK.
[13] When *Gilbert* (n 10) was decided, Jackie Robinson, the first African-American to play baseball in the major leagues, was soon to make his debut for the Brooklyn Dodgers, and the Nuremberg Trials were still in progress: see Martin Davies, 'Time to change the federal *forum non conveniens* analysis' (2002) 77 Tulane L Rev 309, 311.
[14] *Gilbert* (n 10) 508–9.

under consideration. Increased focus on the public interest factors requires a court to make comparisons between national interests that are difficult to explain rationally. However, before considering how courts now use the various factors in making *forum non conveniens* decisions, it is worth reflecting on the source of their power to make those decisions in the first place, which is the focus of the next section.

B. Some Mysteries of Interpretation Found While Digging in the Foundations

The source of the court's power to make *forum non conveniens* dispositions varies among jurisdictions. In the United States, *forum non conveniens* has no statutory or constitutional basis, but is based on nothing but the inherent discretionary power of the court to administer proceedings before it.[15] That is because the jurisdiction of American courts is not founded on service of process, but on the scope of the relevant 'long arm' statute[16] and constitutional notions of due process.[17] Service of process merely serves the due process function of giving the defendant notice of the proceedings.[18] Because the invocation of the court's jurisdiction does not depend on valid service of process, *forum non conveniens* dismissal[19] of pending proceedings is, thus, the doctrine in perhaps its purest form, an entirely judge-made exercise of discretionary power that derives simply from the fact of being a judge.[20]

---

[15] *Gilbert* (n 10) 504.

[16] When the subject-matter jurisdiction of federal courts is based on diversity of citizenship (properly called 'alienage' in cases involving foreigners), personal jurisdiction is based on the 'long arm' statute of the state in which the federal district court sits: see Fed R Civ P 4(k)(1)(A). In many states, the 'long arm statute' is not a statute at all, but a judge-made rule of procedure: see Zachary Clopton, 'Long arm "statutes"' (2020) 23 Green Bag 2d 89 (hereafter Clopton, 'Long arm'). When the plaintiff invokes a cause of action based on federal law, the court's personal jurisdiction is based on the federal 'long arm' statute, which is also not a statute but rules made by the Supreme Court under the Rules Enabling Act (28 USC § 2072ff): see Clopton, 'Long arm', ibid; Benjamin Spencer, 'The territorial reach of federal courts' (2019) 71 Fla L Rev 979.

[17] In combination, the Fifth and Fourteenth Amendments to the US Constitution limit the personal jurisdiction of state and federal courts by reference to the constitutional guarantee of due process. In many states, the 'long arm statute' simply extends personal jurisdiction as far as the US Constitution permits. See, eg, Cal Civ Pro Code § 410.10: 'A court of this state [California] may exercise jurisdiction on any basis not inconsistent with the Constitution of this state or of the United States.'

[18] In domestic cases in federal court, actual service of process is the exception, rather than the rule, because the rules provide that the defendant has 'a duty to avoid unnecessary expenses of serving the summons' and must pay the expenses of service if it refuses to waive service when requested to do so: Fed R Civ P 4(d). Service is still necessary in international cases, because foreign defendants cannot be required to waive service in the same way, and without service, the due process element of adequate notice would not be satisfied.

[19] Dismissal of the proceedings, not a permanent stay, is the appropriate order in the United States if the court concludes that it is *forum non conveniens*: see *Gilbert* (n 10); *Atlantic Marine Construction Co v US District Court for the Western District of Texas* 571 US 49 (2013) (hereafter *Atlantic Marine*).

[20] Before the Civil Procedure Rules 1998 (CPR), the power of courts in England and Wales to stay proceedings on *forum non conveniens* grounds was similarly inherent, but it is now understood to derive from CPR r 11(6)(d): see *Texan Management Ltd v Pacific Electric Wire & Cable Co Ltd* [2009] UKPC 46 [58]-[66] (hereafter *Texan Management*); *Cook v Virgin Media Ltd* [2015] EWCA Civ 1287; [2017] 1 All ER 929 [38]-[40].

Where the court's jurisdiction is founded upon effective service of originating process, and where leave of the court is required before process can be served in another country, *forum non conveniens* decisions are usually 'frontloaded' into a decision at a preliminary stage about whether leave should be given or, if given *ex parte*, should be set aside as improperly given. In 'frontloaded' decisions of that kind, the power to make *forum non conveniens* dispositions arises, at least in theory, from the words of the relevant rules of court governing the service of process, rather than solely from the residual power of the court to administer proceedings.

The words of the relevant UK rules were changed in 1998, without any discernible change in the courts' approach to *forum non conveniens* cases. *Spiliada* itself involved an application to set aside leave that had been given under what was then Ord 11, r 1 of the Rules of Supreme Court (RSC). The Court's power to set aside the grant of leave derived from RSC Ord 11, r 4(2), which provided: 'No such grant of leave shall be granted unless it shall be made sufficiently to appear to the Court that the case is a proper one for service out of the jurisdiction under this Order.' The *Spiliada* factors were, thus, an elaboration of whether and how a court should decide that the case before it was 'a proper one for service out of the jurisdiction'.

The relevant phrase in the UK rules was changed in 1998 in a way that would have seemed, at least on its face, to be quite significant. The 'frontloading' of the *forum non conveniens* inquiry now arises because of CPR r 6.37(3), which provides: 'The court will not give permission unless satisfied that England and Wales is the proper place in which to bring the claim.' So, until 1998, it was necessary to show that the *case* was a proper one for service; now it is necessary to show that the court is the proper *place* for the claim to be brought. Factors such as those listed by Lord Wilberforce in *Amin Rasheed*[21] and quoted by Lord Goff in *Spiliada*[22]— the nature of the dispute, the legal and practical issues involved, such questions as local knowledge, availability of witnesses and their evidence and expense— are concerned with the nature of the *case*. They are what US courts call 'private interest factors', which are principally concerned with the dispute itself and how the claimed right to recovery must be established by the plaintiff and countered by the defendant. It would seem that the question of whether the court is the proper *place* in which to bring the claim should turn more on what American courts call 'public interest factors', which are concerned with the administration of justice in, and by, the court chosen by the plaintiff, rather than with the manner in which the parties themselves must present their arguments. Inconvenience to either of the parties surely does not make the *place* an improper one to hear the case, or at least not in the same way that it used to indicate that the *case* was not a proper one to be heard by the forum court. Consideration of public interest factors in this context

---

[21] *Amin Rasheed Shipping Corp v Kuwait Insurance Co: The Al Wahab* [1984] AC 50, 72 (HL) (Lord Wilberforce).
[22] *Spiliada* (n 5) 479 (Lord Goff).

would seem to be consistent with the mandate in CPR Part 1 for courts to consider overriding objectives that include keeping the expense incurred proportionate to the complexity of the issues and the amount involved, and also the need for the case to be disposed of expeditiously and fairly.[23] Curiously, courts seldom seem inclined to consider those objectives in this context, presumably because they pay more attention to the objections to the use of public interest factors stated by the House of Lords in *Lubbe v Cape plc*[24] than to the clear mandate set out in the CPR.[25] If that is right, it is just one of many examples in this essay of courts paying more attention to precedent than to the statutory language that confers the relevant power on them.

Purely as a textual matter, the phrase '*the* proper place' also suggests a hurdle rather higher than is actually found in the English cases. *A* proper place is one in which it is appropriate to proceed. *The* proper place is surely the *only* one in which it is appropriate to proceed. Nevertheless, the UK Supreme Court recently reassured us that use of the phrase 'the proper place for the claim' did not reflect an intention to change the underlying meaning of the *forum non conveniens* concept 'in any way', and that the question is still to be answered by applying the *Spiliada* test.[26]

A similar textual curiosity is to be found in Australia, which is like the UK and unlike the United States in the fact that the jurisdiction of courts is founded upon effective service of process. In five Australian jurisdictions, originating process can be served outside Australia without the permission of the court, but leave to proceed must be obtained if the defendant fails to appear.[27] Before or after leave to proceed has been granted, the defendant may apply to set aside service of the originating process or to stay the proceedings on grounds that include that the forum selected by the plaintiff was 'an inappropriate forum'.[28] On the face of it, this statutory choice of words is significant in light of the fact that the High Court of Australia famously (or infamously, depending on one's point of view) adopted a '*clearly* inappropriate forum' test in *Voth*,[29] preferring it to the *Spiliada* 'clearly or distinctly

---

[23] See Andrew Dickinson, 'Faulty Powers: One-star service in the English courts' [2018] LMCLQ 190, 192–3 (hereafter Dickinson, 'Faulty Powers').

[24] [2000] 1 WLR 1545 (HL(E)) (hereafter *Lubbe*). See, eg, Lord Hope (at 1566): 'In my opinion, the principles on which the doctrine of *forum non conveniens* rest leave no room for considerations of public interest or public policy which cannot be related to the private interests of any of the parties or the ends of justice in the case which is before the court.'

[25] CPR r 1.2(a) requires the court to give effect to the overriding objectives listed in CPR r 1.1(2) whenever it 'exercises any power given to it by the Rules'—as it does when it considers whether to give leave to serve a claim form outside the jurisdiction. On the inconsistency between *Lubbe* (n 24) and the CPR mandate, see Edwin Peel, '*Forum non conveniens* revisited' (2001) 117 LQR 187, 191.

[26] *Vedanta Resources plc v Lungowe* [2019] UKSC 20, [2019] 3 All ER 1013 [66] (Lord Briggs) (Lady Hale P, Lords Wilson and Hodge and Lady Black agreeing) (hereafter *Vedanta*).

[27] Court Procedures Rules 2006 (ACT) r 6507 (hereafter CPR (ACT)); Uniform Civil Procedure Rules 2005 (NSW) r 11.8AA (hereafter UCPR (NSW)); Supreme Court Civil Rules 2006 (SA) r 40F (hereafter SCCR (SA)); Supreme Court Rules 2000 (Tas) r 147F (hereafter SCR (Tas)); Supreme Court (General Civil Procedure) Rules 2015 (Vic) r 7.07 (hereafter SC(GCP)R (Vic)).

[28] CPR (ACT) r 6504(2); UCPR (NSW) r 11.6(2); SCCR (SA) r 40C(2); SCR (Tas) r 147C(2); SC(GCP)R (Vic) r 7.05(2).

[29] *Voth* (n 11) 559–60 (Mason CJ, Deane, Dawson, Gaudron JJ).

more appropriate forum' test. Isn't a *clearly* inappropriate forum somehow *more* inappropriate than a plain old inappropriate forum?[30] Nevertheless, a majority of the High Court in *Regie National des Usines Renault SA v Zhang*[31] held that the phrase 'inappropriate forum' in the New South Wales court rules about service outside the jurisdiction should be informed by 'the same concepts and considerations ... in the same way' as the *Voth* 'clearly inappropriate forum' test.

Kirby J protested in vain in *Zhang*, saying that the phrase 'inappropriate forum' should be interpreted to mean just that, because:[32]

> I dissent from the notion that judges are authorised to adhere to their 'doctrine' where a superior law making power, whether in the form of the Constitution or legislation or rules validly made under legislation, has entered the field. In such cases, 'judge-made doctrine' yields. It then becomes impermissible for judges to adhere to their doctrine if the written law is in any way different. Their duty is to obey the written law.

In the light of these comments, what is one to make of the fact that South Australia and Tasmania only added the phrase 'an inappropriate forum' to their rules in 2016 and 2017, respectively?[33] When the 'superior law making powers' in those states enacted a rule saying that a court can set aside service of process if it thinks itself to be 'an inappropriate forum', were they saying, 'Of course, we know that "an inappropriate forum" really means "a *clearly* inappropriate forum" because the judges have told us so', or were they saying, 'We know that judges have previously used a clearly inappropriate forum test, but we really do want the test to be just "an inappropriate forum"'? Similarly, what are we to make of the UK Supreme Court's breezy assertion in *Vedanta* that the form of words now used in the CPR is merely the latest in a series of different ways of saying the same thing?[34] To echo Kirby J's complaint: ought there not be at least *some* serious focus on the exact form of words chosen by the 'superior law making power'?[35]

In a recent book chapter, Adrian Briggs reflected on the extent to which it is permissible or appropriate for judges to go beyond the conditions set out in what he called 'not unless' legislative rules.[36] He argued that it would be better for judges

---

[30] In *Studorp Ltd v Robinson* [2012] NSWCA 382 [5] (hereafter *Studorp*), Allsop P observed that the use of the adverb 'clearly' in the *Voth* test evinced a 'difference in quality and emphasis' from the statutory test.

[31] *Regie National des Usines Renault SA v Zhang* [2002] HCA 10, (2002) 210 CLR 491 [25] (Gleeson CJ, Gaudron, McHugh, Gummow and Hayne JJ) (hereafter *Zhang*).

[32] Ibid [144] (Kirby J).

[33] SCCR (SA) r 40C(2) (n 28) came into force on 1 September 2016; SCR (Tas) r 147C(2) (n 28) came into force on 11 January 2017.

[34] *Vedanta* (n 26) [66], [73]–[74] (Lord Briggs).

[35] See also Dickinson, 'Faulty Powers' (n 23) 195.

[36] Adrian Briggs, 'Private international law and the Privy Council' in Charles Mitchell and Stephen Watterson (eds), *The World of Maritime and Commercial Law: Essays in Honour of Francis Rose* (Hart 2020) (hereafter *The World of Maritime and Commercial Law*).

in small jurisdictions such as Bermuda or the Bahamas to be allowed to decide for themselves whether their legislatures had intended to proscribe judges' ability to go beyond a statutory form of words by crafting analogous extensions, rather than for the Privy Council to interpret a 'not unless' statute as meaning just that, 'applying ... a rule of statutory construction which [makes] sense in England'.[37] Briggs said that the effect of statutes should be different in small jurisdictions like Bermuda or the Bahamas than in England (or, one might add, South Australia and Tasmania), where the legislature has greater 'resources to think through and make ... statutory changes' and the 'duty of keeping the law in good working order' may not fall solely on local judges.[38] The Woolf Report certainly thought through at length the changes that led to the Civil Procedure Rules, and its authors had twenty-two years' worth of experience of the *Spiliada* test when they chose the form of words in CPR r 6.37(3). Is it really for a court, even the Supreme Court, to say that the words chosen in 'rules validly made under legislation' in 1998 really mean much the same thing as the House of Lords said in 1987?

Of course, these are idle reflections, as the possibility of a change in the judicial interpretation of the statutory rules in the UK and Australia is 'past praying for', to quote from Lord Clyde's speech in *The Star Sea*,[39] reflecting on another context in which a statute seemed clearly to say one thing but had long been interpreted to say another.[40] Nevertheless, it should still be said that the form of words used in the rules creates a legitimate expectation that those rules about the scope of the court's jurisdiction will be applied as written. That legitimate expectation is thwarted if the court applies not the words of the rules but a judicial doctrine derived from previous cases, some of which predate the creation of the rules. In three Australian jurisdictions, leave is still required to serve originating process outside Australia, but (unlike the UK's CPR) the rules in those three jurisdictions make no mention of setting aside service because of the appropriateness or otherwise of the invocation of that court's jurisdiction.[41] Although the drafting of the relevant rules gives the impression that leave *must* be given if the applicant satisfies the stated preconditions, which say nothing that would 'frontload' a *forum non conveniens* inquiry, there are many authorities that either say or assume that the court has a residual discretion to refuse leave if the proceeding is liable to be stayed on *forum non*

---

[37] Ibid 124–5.
[38] Ibid 128.
[39] *Manifest Shipping Co Ltd v Uni-Polaris Insurance Co Ltd (The Star Sea)* [2001] UKHL 1; [2003] 1 AC 469 [6] (Lord Clyde) (hereafter *The Star Sea*).
[40] The headings and the context of the Marine Insurance Act 1906 (UK) s 17 suggested that its effect should be confined to pre-contractual relations, but the House of Lords in *The Star Sea* (n 39) held that that was no longer possible, given the many years' worth of decisions interpreting the section otherwise.
[41] Federal Court Rules 2011 (Cth) r 10.43 (hereafter FCR); Rules of the Supreme Court (NT) r 7.02 (hereafter RSC (NT)); Rules of the Supreme Court 1971 (WA) O 10 rr 1A(2)(a), 1(1) (hereafter RSC (WA)).

conveniens grounds.[42] Indeed, that is what *Voth* itself held.[43] In the three jurisdictions where leave is still required, the rules say one thing and judge-made practice says another.

Whatever the source of the court's power to make *forum non conveniens* dispositions, there is considerable agreement among the three countries under consideration about the factors to be considered. Although it has long been noted that the Latin word *conveniens* is better translated as 'appropriate' than 'convenient',[44] convenience to the litigants unquestionably plays a part in the court's consideration. How much of a part is the focus of the next section.

C. The Convenience of the Parties

The convenience of the parties is much less significant in the *forum non conveniens* inquiry than it used to be, given the impact of modern technology on methods of case presentation. Two of the items listed among the 'private interest' factors by the *Gilbert* Court were 'the relative ease of access to sources of proof' and 'the cost of obtaining attendance of willing witnesses'.[45] Similarly, Lord Goff in *Spiliada* referred generically to 'factors affecting convenience or expense (such as availability of witnesses)'.[46]

In commercial matters, at least, most proof is documentary and most documents are electronic, as readily available in one country as another, and easily transferable from one country to another at virtually no expense. In 1986, Lord Goff in *Spiliada* conjured up an image of blizzards of paper when he observed that each of the fifteen counsel involved in the 'Cambridgeshire' trial was equipped with seventy-five files of documents;[47] in contrast, in 2020, the Courts and Tribunals Judiciary issued general guidance on how to present 'bundles' of documents in electronic form, stipulating, among other things, that PDF documents must be the subject of optical character recognition (OCR) so that they are readily word-searchable, and giving details of how 'e-bundles' should be delivered by e-mail.[48] In 1947, when the US Supreme Court listed 'ease of access to sources of proof' as a relevant factor in the *forum non conveniens* analysis,[49] American courts still applied the 'best

---

[42] For an example from each of the three jurisdictions, see: *Jasmin Solar Pty Ltd v Trina Solar Australia Pty Ltd* [2015] FCA 1453, (2015) 331 ALR 108 [66]–[67] (Edelman J); *Yzerman v Schofield* [2011] WASC 200; *Centrebet Pty Ltd v Baasland* [2012] NTSC 100; (2012) 272 FLR 69.

[43] *Voth* (n 11) 561–4 (Mason CJ, Deane, Dawson, Gaudron JJ).

[44] *Société du Gaz de Paris v SA de Navigation Les Armateurs Français* 1926 SC (HL) 13, 18 (Lord Dunedin), quoted in *Spiliada* (n 5) 474 (Lord Goff).

[45] *Gilbert* (n 10) 508.

[46] *Spiliada* (n 5) 478.

[47] Ibid 467.

[48] Courts and Tribunals Judiciary, 'General Guidance on PDF bundles' <https://www.judiciary.uk/wp-content/uploads/2020/05/GENERAL-GUIDANCE-ON-PDF-BUNDLES-f1-1.pdf> accessed 4 August 2020.

[49] *Gilbert* (n 10) 508.

evidence' rule, which generally required production of the original documents, rather than copies;[50] in 2020, the very notion of an 'original' document makes little sense. These days, most documents and photographic images have no single location: all readers have surely been nagged by someone at some time to back up all of their computer files in several different locations. Businesses that use 'cloud' storage of documents and images probably do not even know in which country the 'server farm' on which they are stored is located and do not greatly care, provided that the computer files are secure and accessible where and when needed—which is anywhere in the world with an internet connection.

Predictably, and appropriately, it is now fairly routine for courts to note that 'Digitization ... has eased the burden of transcontinental document production and has increasingly become the norm in global litigation',[51] so that the location of documents is 'not a powerful factor'[52] in the *forum non conveniens* analysis because 'Much of the relevant evidence is in electronic form accessible from either forum'.[53] The need for translation of some documents will always be undeniably inconvenient for the parties, but it is worth noting that its effect may be largely neutral if a comparison is to be made between party convenience in the forum court and an alternative foreign court, because it may be necessary to translate some documents whichever forum hears the case.[54]

So far as the evidence of witnesses is concerned, the exigencies of the coronavirus lockdowns in 2020 and 2021 have taught us all quite how much can be achieved by remote connection, including the provision of evidence, if necessary. In England and Wales, emergency provision was made for as much use of video or audio hearings as possible during the coronavirus pandemic,[55] but even before the pandemic lockdowns, the use of such technology was increasingly common. Federal courts in the United States have long been permitted to take witness testimony by live video-conferencing link,[56] and depositions are routinely conducted remotely and video-recorded.[57] Similarly, all Australian jurisdictions have made provision for

---

[50] Edward Cleary and John Strong, 'The best evidence rule: an evaluation in context' (1966) 51 Iowa L Rev 825.

[51] *Simon v Republic of Hungary* 911 F 3d 1172 (DC Cir 2018) 1186 (hereafter *Simon*). The US Supreme Court granted *certiorari* (special leave to appeal) in this case—see *Republic of Hungary v Simon* 141 S Ct 187 (Mem) (2020). Oral argument was heard on 7 December 2020, but as of 1 January 2021, the Court had not given judgment.

[52] *Vedanta* (n 26) [85](viii) (Lord Briggs).

[53] *Bangladesh Bank v Rizal Commercial Banking Corp* 2020 WL 1322275 (SDNY 2020).

[54] *Simon* (n 51) 1186; *Shi v New Mighty US Trust* 918 F 3d 944 (DC Cir 2019) 951 (hereafter *Shi*).

[55] 51Y PD, 'Video or Audio Hearings during Coronavirus Pandemic' <https://www.judiciary.uk/wp-content/uploads/2020/03/CPR-116th-PD-Update-video-or-audio-hearings-for-coronavirus-period.pdf> accessed 4 August 2020. See also Judiciary of England and Wales, 'Civil Justice in England and Wales: Protocol Regarding Remote Hearings' (26 March 2020) <https://www.judiciary.uk/wp-content/uploads/2020/03/Remote-hearings.Protocol.Civil_.GenerallyApplicableVersion.f-amend-26_03_20-1-1.pdf> accessed 4 August 2020.

[56] Fed R Civ P 43(a) (permitting evidence to be given 'in open court by contemporaneous transmission from a different location').

[57] Fed R Civ P 30(b)(2) (depositions 'may be recorded by sound, sound-and-visual, or stenographic means'), 43(a).

the taking of evidence from witnesses outside Australia directly by audio or video link.[58] Taking evidence remotely from witnesses in other countries may raise concerns about the requirement (in the United States, a constitutional requirement) that court proceedings be public,[59] and there are technical issues about the administration of the oath, privileges and immunities, and how to punish perjury or contempt by the distant witness,[60] but the recent ubiquity of Zoom, GoToMeeting, and similar platforms during the pandemic lockdowns has shown beyond doubt that there may now be little or no expense and inconvenience involved in taking evidence remotely from people in other countries. In *Vedanta*, Lord Briggs referred to an English court's ability to take evidence from witnesses in Zambia by video conference and the ability of the Zambian public to follow proceedings in England as being relevant to the court's *forum non conveniens* inquiry in that case.[61] Simply put, logistical hurdles to obtaining voluntary testimony from witnesses present much less of a problem than they used to.[62]

In any event, electronic evidence in documentary form is very often to be preferred to the evidence of human witnesses, which can be notoriously unreliable.[63] For example, in two recent ship collision cases in Singapore and Hong Kong, both courts preferred computer evidence from shore-based vessel traffic systems and the voyage data recorders (VDRs) and electronic chart displays (ECDIS)[64] on the ships involved to the eyewitness testimony of the various officers and crew.[65] In such cases, the location of crew witnesses is regarded as relatively unimportant in a court's *forum non conveniens* analysis, given the availability of the ship's electronic documentary records, which can be produced in any forum.[66] Human testimony is

---

[58] Martin Davies, Andrew Bell, Paul Brereton and Michael Douglas, *Nygh's Conflict of Laws in Australia* (10th edn, LexisNexis Butterworths 2020) [11.24] (hereafter *Nygh*).

[59] Stephen Smith, 'The right to a public trial in the time of COVID-19' (2020) 77 Washington & Lee L Rev Online 1, 13–4.

[60] *Nygh* (n 58) [11.28]–[11.34].

[61] *Vedanta* (n 26) [86] (Lord Briggs).

[62] *Shi* (n 54) 951.

[63] For a comprehensive addition to an already extensive literature, see Barbara Spellman and Charles Weaver, 'Memory in the law' in Michael Kahana and Anthony Wagner (eds), *Handbook of Human Memory, Volume 2: Applications* (OUP forthcoming).

[64] Mandatory carriage of ECDIS (Electronic Chart Display and Information System) on all ocean-going ships was phased in from 1 July 2012 to 1 July 2018; it is required by the International Convention for the Safety of Life at Sea (SOLAS) (opened for signature 1 November 1974, entered into force 25 May 1980) 1184 UNTS 278. See International Maritime Organization, 'Electronic Nautical Charts (ENC) and Electronic Chart Display and Information Systems (ECDIS) <https://www.imo.org/en/OurWork/Safety/Pages/ElectronicCharts.aspx>accessed 6 January 2021.

[65] *The Dream Star* [2017] SGHC 220, [2018] 4 SLR 473 [45] (Ang J) ('The bridge team's reconstruction of events does not square with the electronic data recorded on board the vessels'); *TS Singapore (Owners) v Xin Nan Tai 77 (Owners)* [2017] HKCU 1382, [2017] 3 HKLRD 387 [64] (Ng J) (rejecting master's testimony).

[66] *Bright Shipping Ltd v Changhong Group (HK) Ltd (The CF Crystal and The Sanchi)* [2018] HKCFI 2474, [2019] 1 Lloyd's Rep 437 [30]–[31] (Chan J), *affd* [2019] HKCA 246, [2019] HKLRD 220, [2020] 2 Lloyd's Rep 1.

usually preferable only when credibility is of central importance, such as in family law cases, which generally raise rather different considerations.[67]

American courts give more deference to the choice of an American forum by an American resident plaintiff than a foreign one,[68] a preference not given—or not given quite so explicitly—by their British and Australian counterparts. That preference stems not (or not solely) from chauvinism or bias in favour of American residents but from an assumption that the greater the plaintiff's ties to the chosen forum, the more likely it is that he or she would be inconvenienced by a requirement to bring the claim in a foreign jurisdiction.[69] Thus, the extra deference is not shown to American citizens who have made their home abroad,[70] or to Americans resident in states other than that of the chosen forum.[71] Like any other assumption, it can be outweighed by contradictory evidence, particularly of a greater public interest in having the case heard in the alternative foreign forum. For example, litigation arising out of the still-unexplained disappearance of Malaysian Airlines flight MH370 was recently dismissed on *forum non conveniens* grounds, even for the families of American-resident passengers against an American defendant (Boeing), because 'Malaysia's public interest in hearing claims arising out of Flight MH370's disappearance far outweighs that of the United States, even as to the tort claims asserted against US-based manufacturer Boeing'.[72] It is to the role of public interest factors that we now turn.

D. Public Interest Factors

When it comes to the mechanics of presenting the case, either the claim or the defence, there is not much difference between a polluting copper mine in Zambia[73] and a polluting coal mine in South Wales,[74] whether the case is heard in London or New York or Melbourne. However near or far away the mine is, the relevant evidence must still be brought within the confines of the courthouse, either in the form of documents, images or the testimony of witnesses. Similarly, most commercial

---

[67] See also, eg, *VTB Capital plc v Nutritek International Corp* [2013] UKSC 5, [2013] 2 AC 337 [62] (Lord Mance) (hereafter *VTB*), noting the 'core' significance of the evidence of witnesses in that case, a relatively unusual circumstance in a commercial dispute.
[68] *Piper* (n 9) 255–6.
[69] *Wiwa v Royal Dutch Petroleum Co* 226 F 3d 88 (2nd Cir 2000) 102.
[70] *Jones v IPX International Equatorial Guinea SA* 920 F 3d 1085 (6th Cir 2019) (no extra deference given to choice of American forum by American citizen living in Equatorial Guinea).
[71] *Ayco Farms Inc v Ochoa* 862 F 3d 945 (9th Cir 2017) (no extra deference given to choice of California forum by Florida-based corporate plaintiff).
[72] *In re Air Crash over the Southern Indian Ocean on March 8, 2014* 946 F 3d 607 (DC Cir 2020) 613 (hereafter *Air Crash*).
[73] *Vedanta* (n 26).
[74] See, eg, *Jones v Secretary of State for Energy and Climate Change* [2012] EWHC 2936 (QB), [2012] All ER (D) 271 (Oct), a case about a South Wales coal mine but not about *forum non conveniens*.

cases turn on documentary evidence about contracts and business communications, which is usually now presented to the court in an electronic form. As we have seen, evidence of this kind is just as easily sent from the other side of the world as from around the corner—as easily from Zambia as from South Wales. If the place of the occurrence of an alleged tort or the context of contested business dealings still has much significance in an increasingly connected world, it is because of their possible impact on the national law that should govern the dispute.

The very existence of choice-of-law rules is enough in itself to show that the identification of a foreign *lex causae* is not necessarily fatal to the exercise of jurisdiction by the forum court.[75] So what is it about the need to apply foreign law that suggests that the case has not been properly (or appropriately) brought in the forum court? If foreign law must be proved as fact, it can be as easily proved as any other fact that depends largely on documentary evidence. If foreign law can be established as law, as is the case in the United States,[76] it can be briefed and argued to the court without the need to rely on the evidence of expert witnesses.[77] The main concern about hearing cases governed by foreign law is no longer principally one of *establishing* the relevant law, but one of *understanding* it. It is not the convenience of the parties that is important (if it ever was), but a concern that the judge will get the right answer. As Judge Diane Wood of the US Court of Appeals for the Seventh Circuit has put it:

> Exercises in comparative law are notoriously difficult, because the US reader is likely to miss nuances in the foreign law, to fail to appreciate the way in which one branch of the other country's law interacts with another, or to assume erroneously that the foreign law mirrors US law when it does not.[78]

There is a *public* interest in having courts apply their own country's law and, conversely, in having a country's law applied by its own courts.

As noted above, the *Gilbert* Court listed 'public interest factors' about the administration of justice separately from convenience factors relevant to 'the private interest of the litigant'.[79] Tellingly, the possible relevance of a foreign *lex causae* is listed among the public interest factors, the concern being not with the convenience of the litigants, but with the task facing the court, which might have to 'untangle problems in the conflict of laws, and in law foreign to itself'.[80] Similarly, in

---

[75] *Puttick v Tenon Ltd* [2008] HCA 54, (2008) 238 CLR 265 [31] (French CJ, Gummow, Hayne, Kiefel JJ) (hereafter *Puttick*).

[76] Fed R Civ P 44.1 provides that in determining foreign law, 'the court may consider any relevant material or source, including testimony, whether or not submitted by a party'.

[77] For an interesting debate between judges about the extent to which it is even desirable to consider the evidence of expert witnesses about foreign law, see *Bodum USA Inc v La Cafetiere Inc* 621 F 3d 624 (7th Cir 2010) (hereafter *Bodum*).

[78] Ibid 638–9.

[79] *Gilbert* (n 10) 508–9.

[80] Ibid 509.

Spiliada, Lord Goff wrote that the law governing the transaction might *also* be a relevant factor, in addition to those affecting convenience or expense.[81]

Although it listed the public and private interest factors separately in *Gilbert*, the US Supreme Court gave no indication about the relative weight or importance of the two categories. It has since been established that the public interest factors should still be considered even if most or all of the private, convenience-related, factors point towards dismissal.[82] That highlights the significance of the *lex causae* as a public interest factor in the court's inquiry, at least in the United States. It also foreshadows what a future *forum non conveniens* analysis might look like in all common law countries, as factors of private convenience to the parties decline in importance. The public interest in applying the proper law in the proper way remains a significant factor, perhaps the predominant one.

The relevance to the *forum non conveniens* inquiry of the law governing the dispute transcends technical concerns about whether and how the court will apply foreign law. There is a larger sense of *rightness* in 'having localized controversies decided at home', as the *Gilbert* Court put it.[83] That is not just because the parties and the judge are more comfortable applying their own law to 'localized disputes', it is also because the country itself has an interest in having its law applied properly to the cases that it governs. Although no judge outside the United States would probably feel comfortable admitting it, the court's consideration of governing law as part of the *forum non conveniens* inquiry implicitly involves a kind of comparative interest analysis that is very similar to one of the most controversial aspects of the 'choice of law revolution' in the United States.[84]

Choice of law based on comparative interest analysis requires the court to answer the almost impossibly difficult question of which jurisdiction has a greater interest in having its law applied to the dispute.[85] That approach has been roundly

---

[81] *Spiliada* (n 5) 478.
[82] *Nemariam v Federal Democratic Republic of Ethiopia* 315 F 3d 390, 393 (DC Cir 2003); *Fresh Results LLC v ASF Holland BV* 921 F 3d 1043 (11th Cir 2019). The Fifth Circuit previously took the position that there was no need to consider the public interest factors if the private ones favoured dismissal (see *In re Air Crash Disaster Near New Orleans, Louisiana on July 9, 1982* 821 F 2d 1147, 1165 (5th Cir *en banc* 1987)) but that position must now be regarded as incorrect after *Atlantic Marine* (n 19), where the US Supreme Court held that the presence of an enforceable foreign forum selection clause 'changed the dynamic' in relation to the private interest factors, making them all point toward dismissal, but nevertheless remanded the case to the district court below for consideration of the public interest factors. The Fifth Circuit's decision in *Sierra Frac Sand LLC v CDE Global Ltd* 960 F 3d 200 (5th Cir 2020) is consistent with *Atlantic Marine* in considering public interest factors notwithstanding the presence of an enforceable forum selection clause.
[83] *Gilbert* (n 10) 509.
[84] See generally Symeon Symeonides, *The American Choice of Law Revolution: Past, Present and Future* (Martinus Nijhoff Publishers 2006).
[85] Although 'interest analysis' in choice of law is often associated with the writings of Currie, he actually refused to countenance any balancing of competing national interests, writing that if more than one country had an interest in having its law applied, the forum court should simply apply its own law: see Brainerd Currie, 'Notes on methods and objectives in the conflict of laws' [1959] Duke LJ 171 (hereafter Currie, 'Notes'). The *balancing* of governmental interests is part of the choice of law test recommended in the *Restatement (Second) on the Conflict of Laws* (1971), particularly § 6(b)(2), which

criticized for asking the court to compare the incommensurable,[86] and because countries do not obviously have 'a deep-seated concern in the implementation of their legal rules',[87] but the fact remains that legislatures and courts do regard it as important to have their substantive law applied in at least some defined category of cases having international contacts.[88] If governing law is relevant at all in the context of a *forum non conveniens* inquiry, it is relevant because of the proposition that foreign law should, where possible, be decided by the relevant foreign court, not just because that court would be better at it than the plaintiff's chosen forum would be, but because it would be *proper* for it to do so—not just proper in the sense of being right or fitting, but proper in the older sense of *belonging*.[89] As Lord Mance SCJ observed in *VTB Capital plc v Nutritek International Corp*,[90] it is generally preferable, other things being equal, that a case should be tried in the country whose law applies, particularly if issues of law are likely to be important. In *Vedanta*, the obvious desirability of having Zambian law apply to pollution allegedly occurring in Zambia was outweighed principally by the *public* interest factor of the need to provide access to justice—conditional fee arrangements and lawyers experienced in complex litigation—for indigent Zambian plaintiffs.[91]

The now old-fashioned phrase 'the proper law of a contract' used 'proper' in both senses—proper because it was the law belonging to the contract, but proper also because it was the right or fitting law to govern the parties' rights. If the parties themselves have chosen the law belonging to their contract, that is the right law to apply to it (in the absence of some overriding mandatory law pronounced by a legislature), although one might sometimes question whether acceptance of 'boilerplate' choice of law clauses constitutes genuine agreement, even among commercial parties.[92] Although 'particular caution' may be required when requiring a foreign defendant to litigate in England and Wales where the only basis is that

---

calls for consideration of 'the relevant policies of other interested states and the relative interests of those states in the determination of the particular issue'.

[86] See, eg, *Laker Airways Ltd v Sabena* 731 F 2d 909 (DC Cir 1984) 949 ('We are in no position to adjudicate the relative importance of antitrust regulation or nonregulation to the United States and the United Kingdom').

[87] Friedrich Juenger, *Choice of Law and Multistate Justice* (Martinus Nijhoff Publishers 1993) 135.

[88] Symeon Symeonides, 'The choice-of-law revolution fifty years after Currie: An end and a beginning' [2015] U Ill L Rev 1847, 1853–60.

[89] The *Oxford English Dictionary* tells us that the etymology of 'proper' is the Latin *proprius* and the old French *propre*, which both meant 'one's own, special, peculiar': Oxford University Press, 'proper, adj., n., and adv.' (*OED Online*, June 2020) <https://www.oed.com/view/Entry/152660?rskey=NBpmhz&result=1&isAdvanced=false> accessed 4 September 2020.

[90] *VTB* (n 67) [46] (Lord Mance SCJ), cited in *Livingston Properties Equities Inc v JSC MCC Eurochem* [2020] UKPC 31 [12].

[91] *Vedanta* (n 26) [89]–[90] (Lord Briggs).

[92] Sir David Foxton, 'The boilerplate and the bespoke: Should differences in the quality of consent influence the construction and application of commercial contracts?' in *The World of Maritime and Commercial Law* (n 36) 266–71.

English law is the governing law of the contract,[93] it has been held that much less caution is called for when the parties have chosen English law to be the governing law, expressly or impliedly, particularly when the case is likely to turn on questions of law, rather than fact.[94] Although other countries' courts might legitimately apply English law if that has been chosen by the parties, it surely cannot be said to be *improper* for an English court to apply its own law when the parties have chosen that law to govern their contract.

The other public interest factors listed in *Gilbert* are less familiar to non-American eyes: the administrative burden on congested courts, and the burden on local juries considering foreign cases.[95] The burden on local juries is simply no longer significant in transnational cases in the United States, because only a tiny percentage of diversity cases in federal court end up being tried to a jury.[96] The administrative burden for a busy court having to hear non-local disputes is a public interest factor *par excellence*, concerned quite explicitly with the convenience of the court, rather than that of the parties. Some, but not all, American courts undertake a comparative analysis of docket congestion when considering this factor, anxious not to worsen the plaintiff's position by sending it to an even slower or more congested foreign forum.[97]

The possibility of a court considering whether it is busier than a court in the Philippines, Turkey or the Bahamas may make some non-American readers feel uneasy.[98] Nevertheless, something very like this lies at the heart of the threshold *forum non conveniens* inquiry into whether the alternative forum is an adequate one, which is also ultimately concerned with public factors, rather than with private convenience. The *Vedanta* Court declared that the question of the adequacy of the alternative forum required 'anxious scrutiny', because it involves consideration

---

[93] *Novus Aviation Ltd v Onur Air Tasimacilik AS* [2009] EWCA Civ 122, [2009] 1 Lloyd's Rep 576 [32] (Lawrence Collins LJ); *FR Lürssen Werft GmbH & Co KG v Halle* [2009] EWHC 2607 (Comm), [2010] 2 Lloyd's Rep 20 [49](2) (Simon J).

[94] *Ilyssia Cia Naviera SA v Bamaodah (The Elli 2)* [1985] 1 Lloyd's Rep 107 (EWCA) 113 (Ackner LJ); *Navig8 Pte Ltd v Al-Riyadh Co for Vegetable Oil Industry (The Lucky Lady)* [2013] EWHC 328 (Comm), [2013] 2 Lloyd's Rep 104 [28] (Andrew Smith J).

[95] *Gilbert* (n 10) 509.

[96] The federal courts' annual report *Judical Business 2019* shows that 114,799 cases based on diversity of citizenship were commenced in 2019; only 523 of them (0.17 per cent) culminated in a jury trial: see Table C-4 at <https://www.uscourts.gov/sites/default/files/data_tables/jb_c4_0930.2019.pdf> accessed 4 August 2020. Diversity cases include cases based on citizenship of different US states, as well as cases (properly called 'alienage') based on the involvement of foreigners, so the percentage is likely to be smaller still in cases with an international element. Cases commenced in state courts, where jury trials are more common, can be removed to federal court if there is diversity of citizenship: see 28 USC § 1444.

[97] See, eg, *Gates Learjet Corp v Jensen* 743 F 2d 1325, 1337 (9th Cir 1984) (hereafter *Gates Learjet*) ('The real issue is not whether a dismissal will reduce a court's congestion but whether a trial may be speedier in another court because of its less crowded docket'); *Mercier v Sheraton International Inc* 935 F 2d 419, 428 (1st Cir 1991) (hereafter *Mercier*); *Nygård v DiPaolo* 753 Fed Appx 716, 728 (11th Cir 2018) (hereafter *Nygard*).

[98] In *Gates Learjet* (n 97), the alternative foreign forum was in the Philippines; in *Mercier* (n 97), it was in Turkey; in *Nygård* (n 97), it was in the Bahamas.

of 'whether substantial justice is obtainable in one of the competing jurisdictions'.[99] Even considering the adequacy of the law or administration of justice in another country is a task so fraught with political value judgements that it sits oddly with the proper role of a court,[100] as the *Voth* majority pointed out, likening a consideration of the comparative appropriateness of a foreign court to the principle of judicial abstention that precludes the courts of one country from 'passing upon the provisions for the public order' of another.[101] That is one of the main reasons why the *Voth* majority preferred a test that asks a court to make a decision about its own appropriateness, rather than the *Spiliada* test, which would require it to consider the comparative appropriateness of other possible fora in other countries.[102]

An explicitly comparative analysis of public interest—'Malaysia's public interest in hearing claims arising out of Flight MH370's disappearance far outweighs that of the United States', for example[103]—may seem or feel intuitively sound, but it is almost impossible to explain or justify in rational terms. Such a decision brings to mind an apt, if somewhat over-used, analogy. In *Jacobellis v Ohio*,[104] a majority of the US Supreme Court struggled to explain how to decide whether a motion picture fell on one side or the other of the 'dim and uncertain line that often separates obscenity from constitutionally protected expression'.[105] In his concurring opinion, Potter Stewart J was rather more succinct:[106]

> I shall not today attempt further to define the kinds of material I understand to be embraced within that shorthand description [hard-core pornography]; and perhaps I could never succeed in intelligibly doing so. But I know it when I see it, and the motion picture involved in this case is not that.

Like many a test formulated in the highest of appeal courts, Stewart J's approach might work tolerably well at the highest level, but it may be rather more troublesome for a judge at first instance, for reasons explained in a later case also concerned with seizure of material alleged to be pornographic:[107]

---

[99] *Vedanta* (n 26) [11] (Lord Briggs).

[100] Currie's version of interest analysis (Currie, 'Notes' (n 85)) refused to countenance the balancing of competing national interests on the ground that it involved a 'political function of a very high order [which] is a function that should not be committed to courts in a democracy': see Brainerd Currie, *Selected Essays on the Conflict of Laws* (Duke University Press 1963) 182.

[101] *Voth* (n 11) 559 (Mason CJ, Deane, Dawson, Gaudron JJ), citing *Attorney-General (UK) v Heinemann Publishers Australia Pty Ltd (Spycatcher Case)* [1988] HCA 25, (1988) 165 CLR 30, 40–4.

[102] cf *AK Investment CJSC v Kyrgyz Mobil Tel Ltd* [2011] UKPC 7, [2012] 1 WLR 1804 [97]-[102], where Lord Collins expressed reservations about the High Court's analogy to the act of state doctrine.

[103] *Air Crash* (n 72).

[104] 378 US 184 (1964) (hereafter *Jacobellis*)

[105] Ibid 187.

[106] Ibid 197.

[107] *US v Various Articles of Merchandise, Seizure No 148* 600 F Supp 1383 (ND Ill 1985) 1384.

Whenever a case is an obvious 'I know it when I see it' candidate, with the seized material compelling an equally obvious affirmative conclusion as to obscenity, it is extraordinarily difficult if not impossible to articulate any meaningful findings of fact of a kind that would ease the task of appellate review.

The related questions of the nature of the court's decision about *forum non conveniens* and standards for appellate review are considered in the next section.

E. The Nature of the Decision

When there is no statutory basis for a *forum non conveniens* disposition, a primary judge's order is a 'pure' exercise of discretion, and so is entitled to an appropriate degree of deference on appeal (if there is one). That is the position in the United States, for example, where all decisions about *forum non conveniens* are 'committed to the sound discretion of the trial court', rather than being based on any statutory or constitutional formula, and so the primary judge's decision 'may be reversed [on appeal] only when there has been a clear abuse of discretion'.[108] When the primary judge's decision is based, at least in theory, on whether the facts conform to a statutory form of words, it is not so obvious that such broad appellate deference is appropriate.

There has recently been a resurgence of interest about standards of appellate review in Australian courts, thanks largely to a judgment of Gageler J, which distinguished between what he called the 'correctness standard' and the 'deferential standard'.[109] Under the deferential standard, an appeal court should not change a primary judge's discretionary decision simply because it would have decided the case differently, but can only do so if it thinks that the primary judge's decision shows that the discretion was not properly exercised.[110] The deferential standard recognizes that there are some value judgements about which there is room for reasonable differences of opinion, no particular opinion being 'right'. In contrast, the correctness standard allows an appeal court to substitute its opinion for that of the primary judge if it would have decided the case differently. According to the correctness standard, there can be only one uniquely correct outcome to the application of a legal standard.[111]

Importantly for present purposes, the deferential standard does not apply to every question that may be characterized as evaluative.[112] Not every decision that

---

[108] *Piper* (n 9) 257.
[109] *Minister for Immigration and Border Protection v SZVFW* [2018] HCA 30, (2018) 264 CLR 541, 357 ALR 408 [35]–[50] (Gageler J).
[110] *House v R* [1936] HCA 40, (1936) 55 CLR 499, 504–5.
[111] *Warren v Coombes* [1979] HCA 9, (1979) 142 CLR 531.
[112] *Ammon v Colonial Leisure Group Pty Ltd* [2019] WASCA 158, 55 WAR 366 [128]–[129] (Murphy, Mitchell, Beech JJA) (hereafter *Ammon*).

requires a process of balancing of conflicting considerations is properly described as 'discretionary' in the strictly accurate sense; the word 'discretion' is often used where the word 'judgement' would be more appropriate.[113] For example, the correctness standard has recently been applied to the question whether an interference with use and enjoyment of property constituted a private nuisance,[114] but the deferential standard to the question whether damages for non-economic loss caused by defamation were manifestly excessive.[115] The New South Wales Court of Appeal split, two to one, over which standard to apply to an appeal from a trial judge's assessment of damages for non-pecuniary loss in a personal injury case, which is not 'at large' in the judge's discretion but depends upon an evaluative consideration of statutory formulae.[116] The majority preferred the deferential standard because of the evaluative nature of the primary judge's decision, despite the fact that it did not, strictly speaking, depend upon the exercise of discretion.[117] In dissent, Macfarlan JA said that although the primary judge's application of the statutory formula in such cases 'will involve the exercise of a value judgment', it is a question to which there can be only one correct answer.[118]

Even before Gageler J's reanimation of interest in standards of appellate review, doubt had been expressed in Australian courts about whether a primary judge's *forum non conveniens* decision should be subject to what has now been dubbed the correctness standard, rather than the deferential standard. The New South Wales Court of Appeal has considered that question no less than four times, without yet finding the need to make a final choice,[119] most recently asking (rhetorically) whether the right answer might not properly lie somewhere between the two alternatives.[120]

Whenever a primary judge's decision requires an evaluative assessment of several disparate factors, it is natural to resort to metaphors of 'weighing' and 'balancing' when describing the deliberative process. 'Balancing of the connecting factors ... lies at the heart of the issue as to proper place' in England and Wales,[121]

---

[113] *Murakami v Wiryadi* [2010] NSWCA 7, (2010) 268 ALR 377 [33]–[34] (Spigelman CJ) (hereafter *Murakami*).

[114] *Ammon* (n 112).

[115] *Nationwide News Pty Ltd v Rush* [2020] FCFCA 115, (2020) 380 ALR 432 [472] (White, Gleeson and Wheelahan JJ).

[116] *White v Redding* [2019] NSWCA 152, (2019) 99 NSWLR 605 (hereafter *White*). The statutory formulae for the assessment of damages for non-pecuniary losses are set out in the Civil Liability Act 2002 (NSW) s 16.

[117] *White* (n 116) [61] (Gleeson JA), [96] (White JA). See also *Brunoro v Nebelung* [2017] ACTCA 26 [15]–[16], where the Australian Capital Territory Court of Appeal unanimously adopted the deferential standard in relation to the same question.

[118] *White* (n 116) [21] (Macfarlan JA).

[119] *Murakami* (n 113) [32]–[34] (Spigelman CJ); *Fleming v Marshall* [2011] NSWCA 86, (2011) 279 ALR 737 [58]–[59] (Macfarlan JA) (hereafter *Fleming*); *Studorp* (n 30); *Wigmans v AMP Ltd* [2019] NSWCA 243, (2019) 373 ALR 323 (hereafter *Wigmans*).

[120] *Wigmans* (n 119) [34] (Bell P).

[121] *Vedanta* (n 26) [88] (Lord Briggs). See also *Cherney v Deripaska* [2009] EWCA Civ 849, [2010] 2 All ER (Comm) 456.

with the consequence that the exercise carried out by the judge is an evaluative one, sometimes with a predictive element, with more than one possible right answer.[122] In contrast, a majority of the High Court of Australia has stated emphatically that the correct approach '[is] not a question of striking a balance between competing considerations' and that the primary judge in that case had erred by stating that his conclusion had been arrived at 'after weighing all the factors'.[123] The difference of approach lies in the (rather notorious) difference between the *Spiliada* 'clearly and distinctly more appropriate forum' test and the *Voth* 'clearly inappropriate forum' test. Under the *Voth* test, the primary judge's focus should be 'upon the inappropriateness of the local court and not the appropriateness or comparative appropriateness of the suggested foreign forum'.[124] Although it is difficult even for Australian judges to avoid using metaphors of balancing and weighing,[125] the evaluative process under *Voth* should simply be one of assessing whether enough of the relevant factors indicate that the forum is clearly an inappropriate one.[126] A decision of that kind does not look like an exercise of discretion in the strict sense,[127] but rather an evaluative decision that an appellate court is just as well placed to make as a trial judge is.[128] Even under the 'more appropriate forum' test in England and Wales, which more obviously calls for a balancing of factors, the 'frontloading' of the question into one about the grant of leave to serve outside the jurisdiction seems also to call for an evaluative judgement about whether the facts as found by the primary judge satisfy a statutory description.

In Australia and in England and Wales, judges at the highest level have expressed the hope that *forum non conveniens* submissions should be brief and cogent, with the decisions of primary judges reached quietly and speedily in chambers, and seldom appealed.[129] However realistic these calls for proportionality in argument and length of reasons,[130] they would lead if successful to the rather ironic result that the more fully the primary judge explains her or his decision, the more

---

[122] *AmTrust Europe Ltd v Trust Risk Group SpA* [2015] EWCA Civ 437, [2016] 1 All ER (Comm) 325 [33] (Beatson LJ).
[123] *Zhang* (n 31) [78]–[79] (Gleeson CJ, Gaudron, McHugh, Gummow and Hayne JJ).
[124] *Voth* (n 11) 565 (Mason CJ, Deane, Dawson, Gaudron JJ); *Puttick* (n 75) [27] (French CJ, Gummow, Hayne, Kiefel JJ).
[125] For example, *Garsec Pty Ltd v His Majesty the Sultan of Brunei* [2008] NSWCA 211, (2008) 250 ALR 682 [6] (Spigelman CJ), describing the process as 'weighing of disparate and incommensurable factors for purposes of formulating an overall judgment'.
[126] *Colosseum Investment Holdings Pty Ltd v Vanguard Logistics Services Pty Ltd* [2005] NSWSC 803 [77]–[78] (Palmer J) (hereafter *Colosseum*); *Hillam and Barret* [2019] FamCA 193 [50] (Wilson J); *Scarffe v Obannon* [2020] FamCA 77 [62] (Wilson J); *Pierson and Romilly* [2020] FamCAFC 9, (2020) 61 Fam LR 541 [14] (Strickland, Kent, Watts JJ).
[127] *Fleming* (n 119) [59] (Macfarlan JA); *Studorp* (n 30) [7] (Allsop P).
[128] *Murukami* (n 113) [33] (Spigelman CJ).
[129] *Voth* (n 11) 565, 571 (Mason CJ, Deane, Dawson, Gaudron JJ); *Spiliada* (n 5) 465 (Lord Templeman); *VTB* (n 67) [82]–[83] (Lord Neuberger); *Vedanta* (n 26) [6]–[7] (Lord Briggs).
[130] In *Colosseum* (n 126) [72], Palmer J said that a first instance judge should be permitted a wry smile because 'in the present judicial climate, a judgment following that advice would receive a frosty welcome in the Court of Appeal'.

likely there are to be grounds for appeal.[131] The fact that doubt remains, at least in Australia, about the very nature of a first instance court's *forum non conveniens* disposition speaks volumes about the extent to which the doctrine has been adequately theorized.

F. Conclusion

Unlike the child in the poem that gave Adrian Briggs the title for 'Now we are ten?', it is impossible not to be changed by the times.[132] Some people try, of course. We all know people (usually older people) who refuse to use email or the latest developments on the internet, or who remain stuck in their ways in other respects, listening to the music that they listened to when young, waiting for new novels from the same old favourite authors, disapproving vaguely of any new development as not quite as good as things used to be. Conversely, it is rather pitiful to see older people who attempt to keep up with every passing fashion or fad. (Anyone who has been a parent of a teenager can tell you that you will always be behind the times—*always*.) It is part of growing old to find one's place along this spectrum. It is not only acceptable, but fitting, to live in the world of the present but as what we are, shaped by our experience of the past.

Gilbert, *Spiliada* and *Voth* are aging but they have served their respective countries well enough, and there is no obvious need for them to be remade completely, even though they would probably look very different if they were created for the first time now. Fittingly, they are the same as they always were but they no longer act in the way that they once did. Like some people of similar vintage, they have learned to make much better use of computers and the internet, which have substantially changed the relative importance of the private interest factors of convenience to the parties.

A frank acceptance of the decline in significance of the private interest factors would focus more attention on the public interest factors. The goal of *forum non conveniens* analysis has always been to find the place 'in which the case may be tried more suitably for the interests of all the parties and for the ends of justice'.[133] An increased focus on 'the ends of justice' leads to the realization that there has never really been much of an underlying explanatory theory about what kind of justice is being sought. Distributive justice? Corrective justice? Something else? Mere expediency? Even 'I know it when I see it' changes with the eye of beholder

---

[131] *Navarro v Jurado* [2010] FamCAFC 210, (2010) 44 Fam LR 310 [13] (Thackray J).
[132] The last poem in AA Milne's *Now We Are Six* (First published Methuen 1927; Methuen Children's Books 1989) is aptly called 'The End' (at 102), which ends with the couplet:
> But now I am six, I'm as clever as clever.
> So I think I'll be six now for ever and ever.

[133] *Sim v Robinow* (1892) 19 R 665 (CS) 668 (Lord Kinnear).

and over time. (Much of what now streams daily on Netflix might have seemed like pornography to some, but perhaps not all, of Potter Stewart J's colleagues on the Supreme Court bench in 1964.)[134]

In another context in which it is notoriously difficult to provide rational explanations for decisions that feel intuitively right, Jane Stapleton has reminded us that it has traditionally been unacceptable merely to assert a conclusion on the basis of intuition or common sense.[135] A thorough rationalization of the role of 'the ends of justice' in *forum non conveniens* may (and probably should) end up leading to an intellectual grapple with comparative governmental interest analysis. Perhaps that way madness lies.[136] Perhaps it may lead instead to the kind of abstention recommended by the High Court in *Voth*.[137] Either way, it is time to recognize that things are not as they used to be, and to engage with the task that lies ahead. After all, now we are much more than ten.

---

[134] *Jacobellis* (n 104).
[135] Jane Stapleton, 'Choosing what we mean by "causation" in the law' (2008) MLR 433, 446.
[136] In relation to the comparative interest analysis approach to choice of law (n 85), it has been said that '[I]t hardly comes as news that the *Second Restatement* is flawed. But one needs to read a lot of opinions in a single sitting fully to appreciate just how badly the *Second Restatement* works in practice ... ': see Larry Kramer, 'Choice of law in the American courts in 1990: trends and developments' (1991) 39 Am J Comp L 465, 486–7.
[137] Text to nn 100–101.

3
The Distant Shore: Discretion and the Extent of Judicial Jurisdiction

Janet Walker

A. Introduction

One of the finest analyses of Canadian conflict of laws questions is Professor Adrian Briggs' article 'Crossing the River by Feeling the Stones: Rethinking the Law on Foreign Judgments'.[1] It is remarkable for there to be such a depth of appreciation for the subtleties of the law in Canada in an article written by an English conflicts scholar, particularly when, in spite of a shared common law foundation, the rules of jurisdiction in England and Canada have evolved so differently. The question considered in this essay, like that considered in Professor Briggs' 'Crossing the River', is one that has caused conflicts scholars to pause and re-think some of the underlying approaches to established doctrines. Like fording a river, it calls for different techniques and resources from those that enable common lawyers to continue along the road in the ordinary course. As with a number of Professor Briggs' writings, this essay hopes to draw on comparisons between recent developments in two legal systems, in this case England and Canada, to shed light on challenges that they both face.

The question considered in this essay is 'What role is played by discretion in determining the extent of judicial jurisdiction?' This is different from the question of the role played by discretion in determining on a case-by-case basis which cases of those that are within the courts' jurisdiction they will decline to decide.[2] The inherent authority of common law courts to control their own process in particular cases to prevent abuse by exercising discretion to decline jurisdiction is well accepted. But that is a discretion to *decline* jurisdiction, and it is a discretion to be exercised, in *exceptional cases*. Is there also a role for discretion to play in determining the *extent* of jurisdiction as well, either in particular cases, or in particular classes of cases—or is the extent of jurisdiction a matter for legislators? This is a river that the common law in Canada and in England and Wales has

---

[1] Adrian Briggs, 'Crossing the River by Feeling the Stones: Rethinking the Law on Foreign Judgments' (2004) 8 Singapore Yearbook of International Law 1.
[2] Which is discussed in Andrew Bell's essay in this collection (ch 1).

been crossing in recent years. This essay hopes to mark some of the stones that might help to feel the way.

Section B documents the tendency of common law courts to insist that the extent of their jurisdiction is defined by the law and that their discretion is limited to determining which of the cases that are within their jurisdiction they will decide and which they will not decide. This tendency is surprising in light of the traditional common law approach to determining jurisdiction based on service and the court's assessment of whether it is a proper forum. Section C observes that in some situations, the certainty sought to be achieved by this seemingly errant approach may nonetheless be elusive or achieved only at the expense of access to justice. Section D describes the unfortunate consequences of the Canadian courts' attempts to grapple with this. Section E remarks on the extraordinary coincidence that this fundamental issue arises peculiarly from holiday torts, and suggests opportunities that this might provide for identifying new ways forward. Section F asks whether some of the bases of jurisdiction, or gateways, by their nature, are exceptional and, therefore, should be treated as discretionary. Section G suggests some of the implications for larger questions of comity of adopting an approach in which some gateways are treated as inherently a matter of discretion.

B. Dipping Our Toes in the Water

1. Jurisdiction and proper forum

In the English courts, the plaintiff requires leave to serve a defendant abroad with the notice of proceeding. This is different from some other common law jurisdictions, including in Canada, in which the rules of procedure identify a number of situations in which the suitability of service outside the forum is presumed.[3] The *ex parte* application in the English court practice requires the plaintiff to show that the claim falls within one of the 'gateways' listed in Practice Direction 6B, para 3.1 and, then: that England is the proper place in which to bring the claim; that it would not be unjust to require the defendant to defend in England; and that there is a serious issue to be tried on the merits.[4] This suggests that discretion is exercised in each case of service outside the forum to determine whether the court has jurisdiction. As Professor Briggs has observed, if reliance on the heads (or 'gateways')

---

[3] In the United States, where jurisdiction is subject to the due process standard of the Constitution, some of the State rules of procedure provide generally for service out, such as §410.10 of the California Code of Civil Procedure, which provides: 'A court of this state may exercise jurisdiction on any basis not inconsistent with the Constitution of this state or of the United States'; while other State rules of procedure provide lists of grounds on which service out is permitted, such as §302 of the New York Civil Practice Law and Rules: 'Personal jurisdiction by acts of non-domiciliaries'.

[4] Civil Procedure Rules (hereafter CPR), rr 6.36–6.37.

of jurisdiction is always subject to a determination that the English courts are the proper forum, what purpose is served by the heads? Isn't the extent of jurisdiction, as a question ultimately of *forum conveniens,* a matter of discretion?[5]

Despite his observation in *Abela v Baadarani*,[6] that jurisdiction established by service out was exorbitant, Lord Sumption disagreed strenuously in his judgment in *Four Seasons Holdings Incorporated v Brownlie* with the suggestion that the extent of jurisdiction was to be guided primarily by discretion:[7]

> The gateways identify relevant connections with England, which define the maximum extent of the jurisdiction which the English court is permitted to exercise. Their ambit is a question of law. The discretion as to *forum conveniens* authorises the court to decline a jurisdiction which it possesses as a matter of law, because the dispute, although sufficiently connected with England to permit the exercise of jurisdiction, could be more appropriately resolved elsewhere. The main determining factor in the exercise of the discretion on *forum conveniens* grounds is not the relationship between the cause of action and England but the practicalities of litigation. The purpose of the discretion is to limit the exercise of the court's jurisdiction, not to enlarge it and certainly not to displace the criteria in the gateways.

Despite the fact that the gateways are found, not in legislation or even in the CPR, but in Practice Direction, 6B, para 3.1,[8] and despite the fact that they have evolved over time,[9] the English courts, as illustrated in Lord Sumption's opinion above, regard them as setting the legal parameters for jurisdiction. It is only within those externally defined parameters that the courts may, in matters brought against defendants served abroad, exercise discretion to hear cases or not to hear them. The courts prefer to understand the gateways as fixed by a legislative or regulatory body, and to limit their task to interpreting the gateways and reserving the use of discretion for logistical considerations affecting the litigation of the instant case. In other words, the courts use their discretion to determine which of the cases that

---

[5] Adrian Briggs, 'Service Out in a Shrinking World' [2013] LMCLQ 415.
[6] *Abela v Baadarani* [2013] UKSC 44, [2013] 1 WLR 2043.
[7] *Four Seasons Holdings Incorporated v Brownlie* [2017] UKSC 80, [2018] 1 WLR 192 [31] (Lord Sumption SCJ) (hereafter *Brownlie I*).
[8] A point observed by Arnold LJ in *FS Cairo (Nile Plaza) LLC v Brownlie* [2020] EWCA Civ 996 [71] (hereafter *Brownlie II*): 'The gateways represent the considered judgment of the Civil Procedure Rules Committee as to the classes of case in which it may (but not necessarily will) be appropriate to bring a foreign defendant before the courts of England and Wales. (Although the gateways are contained in a Practice Direction rather than in a rule of the Civil Procedure Rules, which may be thought somewhat questionable from a constitutional perspective, they nevertheless need, and receive, the approval of the Committee.)' See *Brownlie II* [161] (Underhill LJ); also Andrew Dickinson, 'Faulty Powers—One Star Service in the English Courts' [2018] LMCLQ 189, 191–2 (hereafter Dickinson, 'Faulty Powers').
[9] As reviewed by McCombe LJ in *Brownlie II* (n 8) [24]–[26].

fall within their jurisdiction they will decide, and not which cases fall within their jurisdiction.[10]

The latter formulation, in which the courts determine the maximum extent of their jurisdiction across the range of cases on a case-by-case basis, seems to present an unwelcome indeterminacy. Concern about this indeterminacy has been evident in the decisions of Canadian judges as well. Even in developing elaborate and fluid tests for exercising jurisdiction over foreign defendants, Canadian courts have emphasized that these tests for jurisdiction in cases of service outside the forum[11] represent *legal* standards and are to be distinguished from the exercise of discretion in determining jurisdiction on grounds of *forum non conveniens,* which is limited to *declining* to exercise jurisdiction: [12]

> While the real and substantial connection test is a legal rule, the *forum non conveniens* test is discretionary. The real and substantial connection test involves a fact-specific inquiry, but the test ultimately rests upon legal principles of general application. The question is whether the forum can assume jurisdiction over the claims of plaintiffs in general against defendants in general given the sort of relationship between the case, the parties and the forum. By contrast, the *forum non conveniens* test is a discretionary test that focuses upon the particular facts of the parties and the case. The question is whether the forum should assert jurisdiction at the suit of this particular plaintiff against this particular defendant.

As discussed further below, the jurisdictional test enunciated in the case from which the passage above is excerpted provided for such an extensive exercise of discretion that it had to be revised. Nevertheless, the court emphasized that this test, as a test of jurisdiction *simpliciter*, was intended to be a legal test and to be distinguished from the test for *forum non conveniens* which was intended to be discretionary.

C. Jurisdiction and Service

This apparent inconsistency between what the courts seem to be doing and what they say they are doing bears a surprising relationship to another of Professor

---

[10] This point is emphasized in Dickinson, 'Faulty Powers' (n 8) 195 ('It is vital to isolate the factual basis for asserting adjudicatory jurisdiction from the factors affecting its exercise. Questions of the former kind should not be determined, or influenced, by such matters as access to documents or witnesses, the court's familiarity with the law to be applied, the court's expertise, the efficiency of the justice system (or the inefficiency of an alternative legal system), the availability of legal representation or the ease of enforcement of an eventual judgment.' (citations omitted).

[11] The 'real and substantial connection test' is the Canadian equivalent of the gateways.

[12] *Muscutt v Courcelles* (2002) 213 DLR (4th) 577 [43] (hereafter *Muscutt*); in the various jurisdictions in Canada, service out of the jurisdiction does not require leave and hence, an *ex parte* determination of *forum conveniens*, but leaves the question of proper forum to be raised on an *inter partes* basis by the defendant.

Briggs' astute observations on the recent confusion in the English jurisprudence between the approaches to jurisdiction in the common law and the civil law. He described one of the distinctions that has been confused as follows: [13]

> Common law: If service is made, there is jurisdiction—Regulation: If there is jurisdiction, service may be made.

This description of the operation of the 'common law'[14] clearly reflects the underlying logic of the Civil Procedure Rules. Why then would the English courts proclaim this approach while adopting the Regulation model? Why is the 'authority piling up' in which they do so, and will there come a day when it 'is going to have to be shovelled up and taken away'?[15] Why are the courts in England and, as will be seen, in Canada motivated to insist, regardless of the traditional method of ascertaining their jurisdiction as a function of service, that the outer contours of jurisdiction are defined by the law and not through the courts' own assessment of whether they are the proper forum?

The confusion of these approaches is all the more puzzling, as has been noted by Professor Briggs, because the common law and the Brussels I Regulation systems of jurisdiction are designed to serve different purposes. The systems are different from one another not merely because the majority of the member state courts for which the Brussels system was designed are civil law courts. The systems are different also because the Brussels system is designed to *allocate* jurisdiction among member state courts in a way that supports a regime that includes a fixed obligation of recognition and enforcement of the resulting judgments; whereas the common law system is designed to be guided, at best, by a much more vague and diffuse principle concerning the appropriate exercise of jurisdiction, one that has been described in Canada as 'comity'.[16] The question arises as to why common lawyers (at least in England and Canada) operating on the high seas of international litigation (ie, beyond the scope of a regional regime for jurisdiction and judgments) are inclined to confine every discretionary determination of their own jurisdiction within clearly defined limits that are prescribed by law.

If this tendency to drift from the traditional common law approach towards an approach more closely resembling the Brussels system—one in which jurisdiction is a fixed legal standard—is not a mere misstep or mistake, then surely it hints at a more profound issue of judicial jurisdiction. The emphasis on the certainty that

---

[13] Adrian Briggs, 'The Hidden Depths of the Law of Jurisdiction' [2016] LMCLQ 236, 237 (hereafter Briggs, 'Hidden Depths').

[14] ie under the CPR as opposed to the (formerly applicable) recast Brussels I Regulation (Regulation (EU) No 1215/2012 on jurisdiction and the recognition and enforcement of judgments ([2012] OJ L351/1) (hereafter Brussels I Regulation), rather than the statutory grounds of assumed jurisdiction as opposed to the traditional *common law* grounds: Andrew Dickinson, 'Keeping up Appearances: The Development of Adjudicatory Jurisdiction in the English Courts' (2016) 86 BYBIL 6.

[15] Briggs, 'Hidden Depths' (n 13) 243.

[16] Adrian Briggs, 'The Principle of Comity in Private International Law' (2012) 354 *Recueil des Cours* 65.

might be gained through the acceptance of an externally defined scope of jurisdiction as occurs through a legal standard is perplexing when it fails to yield the desired result, and especially so when it threatens, as it has done in Canada, to prevent courts from exercising jurisdiction in particular situations where they are inclined to do so for the interests of justice. This is where the riverbed starts to drop away.

D. Up to Our Elbows: Eschewing Discretion Has Not Achieved Certainty

The failure of the application of a legal standard for jurisdiction to yield the desired result of greater certainty became evident in the English law of jurisdiction when, some ten years after the death of Sir Ian Brownlie in a road accident during an excursion in a chauffeur driven car provided by his hotel in Egypt, jurisdiction over the action brought by his widow in the English courts against the hotel has still to be determined.[17] From a distance, one might imagine that a straightforward and seemingly commonplace question such as this would have a clear and easily ascertained answer, but it does not.

The question of whether the facts of the case fit into the relevant gateway has been contested all the way to the Supreme Court,[18] and following a determination on other grounds that required an amendment to the claim, it has risen again to the level of the Court of Appeal with no clear resolution yet in sight. To underscore the point, the differences of opinion in the judgments do not relate to whether England is 'the proper forum' within the formulation of the Practice Direction, as a matter of the practical logistics of the litigation. The persistent differences of opinion relate to whether the facts of the case fall within the gateway described in Practice Direction 6B, para 3.1(9)(a) for 'a claim in tort where—(a) damage was sustained ... within the jurisdiction'.

On the one hand, some of the judges in the various courts have supported an expansive interpretation of 'damage sustained in the jurisdiction' because the common law has the 'valuable safety valve' of discretion. They say that this is a discretion that need not be limited to the *Spiliada* principles, but can concentrate on the real question of which is 'the proper place for the resolution of the dispute ... [and while] the claimant should not be in the position of choosing where to bring the claim ... the discretion should be robust enough to prevent that'.[19]

On the other hand, some of the judges have supported a narrower interpretation—one that was limited to 'direct'[20] damage because:[21]

---

[17] *Brownlie II* (n 8); Dickinson, 'Faulty Powers' (n 8) 196.
[18] *Brownlie I* (n 7).
[19] *Brownlie I* (n 7) [51], [54] (Lady Hale SCJ).
[20] cf *Brownlie II* (n 8) [53] (McCombe LJ).
[21] *Brownlie I* (n 7) [28] (Lord Sumption SCJ).

[A] principle which located damage in the place where the pecuniary consequences of the accident were felt or where any continuing pain, suffering or loss of amenity were experienced would in the great majority of cases confer jurisdiction on the country of the claimant's residence. It would confer on the English courts what amounts to a universal jurisdiction to entertain claims by English residents for the more serious personal injuries suffered anywhere in the world.

In testing the practical implications of the second of these two approaches in the instant case, one judge remarked:[22]

[T]here is certainly nothing remarkable in the Egyptian arm of the multinational organisation to which this defendant belongs, and which looks for customers from all over the world, being the potential subject of litigation in a country other than that of its incorporation.

However, a devil's advocate might counter this by saying that it could indeed seem remarkable, if this were a small Cairo hotel, with lodgings patronized almost exclusively by local persons, for it to find itself defending proceedings in London at the suit of a traveller simply because the traveller happened to be English. Are we to distinguish between foreign providers of goods and services on the basis of the size of the enterprise or the size of its web presence? Are hospitality venues meant to adjust their tariffs to accommodate the varying expense posed by the risk of having to defend or to compensate patrons based on their places of origin?

Accordingly, despite the apparent anomaly noted by Professor Briggs, after many years of litigation at all levels of the English courts in the *Brownlie* case, there seems to be a trend towards the view that jurisdiction is a fixed legal standard marking the scope of jurisdiction—one that is merely caveated by judicial discretion concerning the practicalities of litigation in the forum in particular cases. However, there is no clear answer, not even a prevailing view on whether one can sue in England for a tort that has occurred[23] abroad. Perhaps the best that can be said on this question is 'sometimes' or 'it depends'—but 'when' and 'on what basis' have yet to be articulated in any compelling way. Nevertheless, as demonstrated by the *Brownlie* litigation, the decision to treat jurisdiction as a legal standard and not a discretionary determination of proper forum has not produced the certainty desired; nor has it secured results that inspire confidence that they will be widely accepted.

Ironically, there may be some light to be shed on this issue by considering the plight of the plaintiffs in Canadian courts who seem to have found themselves in over their heads.

---

[22] *Brownlie II* (n 8) [51] (McCombe LJ).
[23] This term is not parsed here as it is in Adrian Briggs, 'Holiday Torts and Damage within the Jurisdiction' [2018] LMCLQ 196.

E. In Over Our Heads? Certainty and Denial of Justice

It became clear that the common law courts in Canada had been pushed into the water on the questions raised by the gateway 'damage sustained in the forum' when, in 2002, the Court of Appeal for Ontario issued a compendium of five related appeals on this gateway in one series of decisions. As the Court explained at the beginning of the lead decision in *Muscutt v Courcelles*,[24] '[t]his appeal, argued together with four other appeals, involves the important issue whether the Ontario courts should assume jurisdiction over out-of-province defendants in claims for damage sustained in Ontario as a result of a tort committed elsewhere'.[25]

At the time, the state of the law in Canada provided the courts with little choice but to confront the issue. About a decade earlier, the Supreme Court had held that the standards for direct and indirect jurisdiction[26] should be correlatives;[27] and that, in cases involving service outside the forum of defendants who had not consented to the court's jurisdiction, this, in effect, required courts to exercise jurisdiction only where there was a 'real and substantial connection' between the matter and the forum.[28] Although not argued in constitutional terms, the Court later confirmed that the 'principles of order and fairness' that dictated this result were constitutional principles.[29] Unfortunately, 'constitutional' was not generally taken to mean 'structural' or 'fundamental' but, rather, 'absolute' or 'overriding'. This suggested that a court accepting jurisdiction over a matter in a case of service out where the defendant had not consented and where there was no 'real and substantial connection' between the matter and the forum would be acting *ultra vires*. The further complicating factor was that in Ontario's equivalent to the gateways, the gateway for 'damage sustained in the forum' was a standalone gateway, distinct from the gateway for torts.

As a result, the jurisdictional objection to the gateway for 'damage sustained in the forum' was not directed at cases such as the negligent manufacture abroad of consumer products acquired and used in the forum. Those cases would be admitted through the tort gateway. Rather, the objection was directed specifically at

---

[24] *Muscutt* (n 12); *Leufkens v Alba Tours International Inc* (2002) 213 DLR (4th) 614 (hereafter *Leufkens*); *Lemmex v Sunflight Holidays Inc* (2002) 213 DLR (4th) 627 (hereafter *Lemmex*); *Sinclair v Cracker Barrel Old Country Store, Inc* (2002) 213 DLR (4th) 643 (hereafter *Sinclair*); *Gajraj v DeBernardo* (2002) 213 DLR (4th) 651 (hereafter *Gajraj*).

[25] *Muscutt* (n 12) [1]; Rules of Civil Procedure (Ontario) RRO 1990, Reg 194 (hereafter Ontario Rules), Rule 17.02(h).

[26] *Direct* jurisdiction refers to the jurisdictional standards of a court in deciding a case; *indirect* jurisdiction refers to the jurisdictional standards for courts that have issued judgments that the court is asked to recognize and enforce.

[27] *Morguard Investments Ltd v De Savoye* [1990] 3 SCR 1077 (SCC) (hereafter *Morguard*).

[28] The decision in *Morguard* (n 27), in fact, addressed the obligation to recognize and enforce judgments, but it was generally accepted to have implications for the standards for direct jurisdiction as well: Vaughan Black, 'The Other Side of *Morguard*: New Limits on Judicial Jurisdiction' (1993) Canadian Business LJ 4.

[29] *Hunt v T&N plc* [1993] 4 SCR 289.

claims like that brought in *Brownlie*, by the relatives of a person fatally injured while outside the forum or by persons injured abroad who had returned to the forum. The argument ran as follows: the Supreme Court of Canada had held that the exercise of jurisdiction must conform to the constitutional principles of order and fairness[30] and, beyond the traditional bases of jurisdiction over local defendants and those who submit, the requirements for service out are met only where there is a real and substantial connection between the matter and the forum; 'damage sustained in the forum' does not constitute a real and substantial connection and, accordingly, a Canadian court is constitutionally incapable of exercising jurisdiction in cases in which service is based on this ground.

The logic of this argument was difficult to gainsay. It placed the courts in a quandary. If they accepted it, they were bound to regard themselves as incapable of exercising jurisdiction in a case such as the *Brownlie* case even if they regarded it as just to do so. The challenge was to articulate a coherent legal standard that would distinguish the cases that fell within this gateway over which they would have jurisdiction from those over which they would not. Without this, in some cases, the constitutional principles of order (the certainty of the legal standards of jurisdiction) and fairness (the desire to exercise jurisdiction as the proper forum) arguably could be at odds with one another.

As mentioned, the Court of Appeal combined the jurisdictional challenge in the *Muscutt* appeal with four other appeals to undertake a broad-based review of the use of the 'damage sustained in' ground. Of the five cases, two dealt with excursion torts. In *Leufkens v Alba Tours International Inc*,[31] a man was badly injured while rappelling from a platform while on an excursion purchased during a package holiday in Costa Rica. In *Lemmex v Sunflight Holidays Inc*,[32] a man suffered carbon monoxide poisoning in a taxicab on a shore excursion on the Island of Grenada while on a Caribbean cruise. In both cases, the package tour operators from whom the plaintiffs had purchased the basic holiday had accepted jurisdiction, but the local tour operators in Costa Rica and Guyana from whom the plaintiffs had purchased the excursion during the holiday did not.[33] This focused the analysis of the 'damage sustained in' ground of jurisdiction on cases in which the injury had occurred in the provision of a service arranged while the plaintiff was away from the forum on vacation.

---

[30] *Morguard* (n 27).
[31] *Leufkens* (n 24).
[32] *Lemmex* (n 24).
[33] The other three cases did not deal with holiday excursion torts: *Muscutt* (n 12) involved a motor vehicle accident in another province (but the auto insurance arrangements in Canada provide for access to the courts of the place where the insured is located); *Sinclair* (n 24) involved a slip and fall in an American chain restaurant a short distance from the US–Canada border; and *Gajraj* (n 24) involved a car accident in the United States in which the Canadian insurer accepted jurisdiction, but the individual American drivers did not. Of the five cases, *Muscutt* was the only case in which jurisdiction was upheld in relation to the defendant challenging it, and arguably this was because the defendant in the case, an insurer, was bound to defend in the plaintiff's residence in any event.

The Court held that rules for service out of the province, such as 'damage sustained in the forum' were only a rough guide to the kinds of cases in which persons outside Ontario will be regarded as subject to the jurisdiction of the Ontario courts and that the decision about whether a court had jurisdiction, which was described as a question of law, not discretion, was, nonetheless, a question, that should be decided on the basis of a flexible, non-hierarchical examination of eight factors.[34]

This was an unfortunate result. This ostensibly legal test—the flexible, non-hierarchical examination of eight factors—produced considerable uncertainty. Although it was adopted throughout the common law provinces in jurisdictional determinations across the range of cases,[35] it soon became clear that such a multifactorial case-specific analysis would not produce certainty. The factors of 'unfairness to the defendant in accepting jurisdiction' and 'fairness to the plaintiff in denying jurisdiction' required an exercise of discretion as extensive as that involved in determining convenient forum.[36] Academics complained,[37] the courts struggled on and, in time, some provinces gave up and adopted a statute on jurisdiction to clarify the law.[38]

Under that statute—the Court Jurisdiction and Proceedings Transfer Act—the courts exercise jurisdiction where 'there is a real and substantial connection between [the enacting province] and the facts on which the proceeding against that

---

[34] The eight factors were: (1) the connection between the forum and the plaintiff's claim; (2) the connection between the forum and the defendant; (3) unfairness to the defendant in assuming jurisdiction; (4) unfairness to the plaintiff in not assuming jurisdiction; (5) the involvement of other parties to the suit; (6) the court's willingness to recognize and enforce an extra-provincial judgment rendered on the same jurisdictional basis; (7) whether the case is interprovincial or international in nature; and (8) comity and the standards of jurisdiction, recognition and enforcement prevailing elsewhere.

[35] *Muscutt* (n 12) was cited (directly and indirectly) in more than 400 decisions across Canada in the years before the Supreme Court of Canada rendered its decision in *Club Resorts Ltd v Van Breda* (2012) SCC 17 (hereafter *Club Resorts*).

[36] Janet Walker, 'Beyond Real and Substantial Connection: The *Muscutt* Quintet' (2002) Annual Review of Civil Litigation 61 (hereafter Walker, 'Beyond').

[37] The Court of Appeal cited in its subsequent review of the law: Vaughan Black and Mat Brechtel, '*Muscutt v Courcelles* Revisited: The Court of Appeal for Ontario Takes Another Look' (2009) 36 The Advocates' Quarterly 35; Vaughan Black and Stephen GA Pitel, 'Reform of Ontario's Law on Jurisdiction' (2009) 47 Canadian Business LJ 469; Janet Walker, '*Muscutt* Misplaced: The Future of Forum of Necessity Jurisdiction in Canada' (2009) 48 Canadian Business LJ 135; Jean-Gabriel Castel, 'The Uncertainty Factor in Canadian Private International Law' (2007) 52 McGill LJ 555; Tanya J Monestier, 'A "Real and Substantial" Mess: The Law of Jurisdiction in Canada' (2007) 33 Queen's LJ 179; Stephen GA Pitel and Cheryl D Dusten, 'Lost in Transition: Answering the Questions Raised by the Supreme Court of Canada's New Approach to Jurisdiction' (2006) 85 Can Bar Rev 61; Joost Blom QC and Elizabeth Edinger, 'The Chimera of the Real and Substantial Connection Test' (2005) 38 UBC L Rev 373; Cheryl D Dusten and Stephen GA Pitel, 'The Right Answers to Ontario's Jurisdictional Questions: Dismiss, Stay or Set Service Aside' (2005) 30 The Advocates' Quarterly 297; Elizabeth Edinger, '*Spar Aerospace*: A Reconciliation of *Morguard* with the Traditional Framework for Determining Jurisdiction' (2003) 61 The Advocate 511; Walker, 'Beyond' (n 36).

[38] Uniform Law Commission of Canada *Court Jurisdiction and Proceedings Transfer Act, Proceedings of the 1994 Annual Meeting* at 48 (hereafter *CJPTA*); Saskatchewan: *Court Jurisdiction and Proceedings Transfer Act*, SS 1997, c C-41.1 (in force 2004); British Columbia: *Court Jurisdiction and Proceedings Transfer Act*, SBC 2003, c 28; Nova Scotia: *Court Jurisdiction and Proceedings Transfer Act*, SNS 2003 (2nd Sess), c 2; Prince Edward Island: *Court Jurisdiction and Proceedings Transfer Act* SPEI 1997, c 61.

person is based'. What constitutes a 'real and substantial connection' is elaborated in the statute through a list of bases that is similar to the gateways. Notably absent, though, are 'damage sustained in the province' and 'necessary and proper party'.

Eventually, following a discussion paper prepared in association with the Law Commission of Ontario on these issues,[39] the Court of Appeal resumed its efforts to clarify the law. This time, it combined two appeals that it had on reserve, and asked counsel to make submissions on the framework of the law.[40] The result of this combined appeal was reviewed by the Supreme Court of Canada, and the 2012 decision in *Club Resorts*[41] continues today as the leading decision on judicial jurisdiction in Canada.

Before considering that result and the way in which it might assist the analysis in this essay, it is helpful to provide a brief note on the follow-on developments in the common law provinces, as exemplified by Ontario. In 2014, the Ontario Rules Committee, whose amendments are promulgated without any formal notice and comment or regulatory impact statement, decided that it should tidy up the bases on which service out are permitted (ie the gateways) to reflect these jurisprudential developments. There had been widespread complaint that the term 'real and substantial connection' provided no clear indication of its application: What counts as a *real* connection? What makes that connection *substantial*? Drawing on some academic commentary suggesting that most of the gateways, such as 'tort occurring in the jurisdiction' and 'contract breached in the jurisdiction' referred roughly to events that occurred in the forum and that this was to be contrasted with 'damage sustained in the province' and 'necessary and proper party',[42] the Rules Committee simply omitted these gateways.

Comfort might have been taken in the jurisdictional savings provision found in another rule of procedure that permitted plaintiffs to seek leave where none of the named gateways applied.[43] Indeed, the statute that had been adopted by some of the provinces also included a provision similar in function to this.[44] It was inspired by a provision in the Swiss Private International Law Act[45] for the courts to have 'residual jurisdiction' to serve as a forum of necessity in order to prevent a denial of justice.

The unfortunate result in Ontario was that the Rules Committee eliminated the gateways for cases involving 'damage sustained in the province' and 'necessary and proper party', without indicating that jurisdiction on these grounds might still

---

[39] Janet Walker, 'Reforming the Law of Crossborder Litigation: Judicial Jurisdiction' (Consultation Paper, Law Commission of Ontario 2009) prepared in consultation with a number of leading scholars in the field, some of whom are participants in this symposium.
[40] Letter from the Court of Appeal for Ontario to Counsel in C49188—*Van Breda v Village Resorts Limited* and C49632—*Charron v Bel Air Travel Group Ltd* (6 June 2009).
[41] *Club Resorts* (n 35).
[42] Walker, 'Beyond' (n 36).
[43] Ontario Rules (n 25) rule 17.03.
[44] *CJPTA* (n 38) s 6.
[45] Federal Act on Private International Law of 18 December 1987 (Switzerland), Art 3.

be exercised on the residual discretionary basis with leave pursuant to the other rule. Since then, without legislative encouragement to do so, the courts have not reinvigorated this previously little used residual provision for granting leave. Certainty had been achieved, but at the demonstrable expense of fairness. The various occasions, rare though they may be, in which plaintiffs once would have relied on 'damage sustained in the forum' to enable them to gain access to the local courts, or 'necessary and proper party'[46] to enable them to avoid a multiplicity of actions, no longer had a gateway permitting suit in Ontario. The elimination of these bases might seem to have enabled the courts to keep their heads above water, but it has not brought the other shore any nearer.

F. Feeling the Stones

1. Holiday torts: A coincidence?

How can any of this help in giving guidance on the role of discretion in determining the extent of jurisdiction? One surprising feature of this debate might provide a clue. The jurisdictional challenges in England and Canada that have proved so difficult to resolve, and that have provoked a fundamental and protracted review of the approach to jurisdictional analysis have both arisen from the same narrow set of circumstances—those of holiday torts. In fact, like the cross-border car accidents that once dominated conflict of laws jurisprudence, it seems that holiday torts have been the subject of considerable interest in many common law systems,[47] without much attention being paid to the potential significance of the specificity of the pattern of events that they entail.

One possible conclusion that might be drawn from this recognition is that the jurisdictional issues that arise from holiday torts are in a category of their own—a mere anomaly that has beguiled the courts. If that were so, we might reassure ourselves that all is otherwise well in the law of jurisdiction, and it is not necessary or helpful to develop a solution to this challenge that seeks to have wider relevance. A rather different observation might be that, in the process of working out why this particular fact scenario has proved so difficult for common lawyers, we might be able to identify some subtle but significant refinements to our approach to jurisdiction that could assist more generally.

It is worth having a closer look at the two appeals that were decided by the Supreme Court of Canada. These appeals involved the same defendant, Club Resorts. In *Van Breda*, a woman was playing on the beach with her fiancé at a resort

---

[46] In 'Jurisdiction Over Defences and Connected Claims' [2006] LMCLQ 447, Adrian Briggs bemoans a similar development in the European jurisprudence on the related articles in the Brussels I Regulation.
[47] *Carnival Cruise Lines, Incorporated v Eulala Shute* 499 US 585; *Oceanic Sun Line Special Shipping Company Inc v Fay* (1988) 165 CLR 197; *Club Mediterranee NZ v Wendell* [1989] 1 NZLR 216.

in Cuba when she did a chin-up on a metal structure that collapsed rendering her a paraplegic,[48] and in *Charron*, a man at a Cuban resort drowned while scuba diving.[49] Perhaps guided by its desire to accept jurisdiction in these cases and to design a simpler and more coherent jurisdictional test, the Supreme Court reduced the eight-factor test of the Court of Appeal for Ontario to four 'presumptive connecting factors'. These factors were: the defendant is domiciled or resident in the province; the defendant carries on business in the province; the tort was committed in the province; and a contract connected with the dispute was made in the province.

It is possible to see how these factors happened to exist in the instant cases. However, they bear little resemblance to any established doctrine relating to situations in which an injured plaintiff now in the jurisdiction seeks to sue a foreign plaintiff in connection with a harmful event that occurred in the foreign jurisdiction. The first two presumptive connecting factors[50]—that the defendant is based in the forum or operates in the forum—are not specific to holiday torts. They are factors that exist in most cases involving local service. The third factor—committing a tort in the forum—would not apply to torts that have occurred abroad, such as is the case with 'holiday torts'. The fourth factor—a contract connected with the dispute was made in the forum—is difficult to understand.[51] Conflicts scholars will know that the place where a contract is made was once presumed to indicate the proper law of the contract where none had been selected by the parties, but that presumption has long been abandoned as meaningless in a world where contracts are routinely concluded in counterpart via the internet, and that presumption had related to applicable law and not to jurisdiction. What relevance could there be for this fourth factor?

This is the point at which all else has failed, when we may need to think laterally about the problem. As common lawyers, one useful starting point may be to consider sample scenarios of holiday torts and to note the instinctive reaction that might be given to them. One scenario is suggested by the *Brownlie* case: persons who have arranged from their place of residence with a multinational hospitality provider for transportation and accommodations in another country and are injured in the course of their stay in that country. A second scenario is slightly different: persons spending extended periods of time travelling the world and

---

[48] *Club Resorts* (n 35) [4].
[49] Ibid [7].
[50] Although the Supreme Court of Canada acknowledged the possibility of recognizing other presumptive connecting factors and it provided a test for doing so: ibid [91], Canadian courts have been unwilling to do so: see *Cook v 1293037 Alberta Ltd (cob Traveller's Cloud 9)* 2016 ONCA 836; *Best v Palacios* 2016 NBCA 59. Although the Court specified that these factors were relevant only for claims in tort, they have been cited across the range of cases involving defendants served abroad: *Club Resorts* (n 35) [90].
[51] This factor has since been described in a Supreme Court of Canada judgment as: 'unprecedented': *Lapointe Rosenstein Marchand Melançon LLP v Cassels Brock & Blackwell LLP* [2016] SCJ No 30, [2016] 1 SCR 851 [88] (Côté J, dissenting); and by at least one commentator as 'odd': Vaughan Black, 'Simplifying Court Jurisdiction in Canada' (2012) 8 J Priv Int L 411, 425, 426.

enjoying an authentic cultural experience by using the local transportation and accommodations that they find in the countries that they visit. A third scenario is different again: non-residents suffering loss or injury and then moving to the forum, settling in the forum and wishing to sue in the courts of the forum. Each scenario involves residents of the forum suing in the forum for injuries suffered abroad, but in each case the foreseeability for the defendant of the need to be accountable to the plaintiff in this forum is different. The *Club Resorts* and *Brownlie* cases suggest a strong inclination on the part of the courts to exercise jurisdiction in the first scenario, but there might be less confidence in doing so in the second scenario,[52] and there seems to be little if any justification for doing so in the third scenario.

If there is a meaningful distinction to be made between these scenarios, it has little to do with where the harm was suffered. The fact that the victims all suffered their injuries while away from the forum is a constant factor. Rather, the difference between the scenarios seems to relate to the dealings between the parties when they reached agreement on the services to be provided. It may also be helpful to consider the way in which our understanding of that relationship has changed in recent years. Clearly, tourism has increased rapidly (at least until the pandemic restricted it), but what else has changed? And how have these changes affected our approach to judicial jurisdiction? It could help to consider other situations in which changes in the world around us have prompted changes in our approach to jurisdiction to see if that provides any guidance.

2. Developments in other areas of consumer law

Half a century ago, there was a significant increase in international trade in consumer products, and with it issues of jurisdiction arose in respect of product liability arising from products that caused harm in the forum but had been manufactured abroad. In Canada, the leading case was an interprovincial case and it involved a spent lightbulb. When a widow in Saskatchewan, whose husband had been electrocuted removing a spent lightbulb, wanted to sue the Ontario manufacturer, the manufacturer challenged the jurisdiction of the Saskatchewan courts on the basis that the requirement for the gateway was not met because the tort was *committed* in Ontario.[53] The Supreme Court of Canada did not agree, instead adopting the view that a tort could be regarded 'as having occurred in any country

---

[52] In particular, the use of an online booking facility from the forum has been held not to constitute a contract made in the forum for this purpose because this would condone universal jurisdiction by virtue of online booking websites: *Colavecchia v Berkeley Hotel Ltd* [2012] OJ No 3952, 112 OR (3d) 287 (SCJ); *Brown v Mar Taino SA* [2015] NSJ No 516, 2015 NSSC 348; and the purchase at a concierge desk of an excursion in a hotel booked from the forum has also been held not to be a contract connected with the forum: *Wilson v Riu* [2012] OJ No 5679, 98 CCLT (3d) 337 (SCJ).

[53] *Moran v Pyle National (Canada) Ltd* [1975] 1 SCR 393 (hereafter *Moran*).

substantially affected by the defendant's activities or its consequences and the law of which is likely to have been in the reasonable contemplation of the parties'.[54]

Applying that principle to product liability, the Supreme Court held that a court has jurisdiction:[55]

> where a foreign defendant carelessly manufactures a product in a foreign jurisdiction which ... he knows or ought to know both that as a result of his carelessness a consumer may well be injured and it is reasonably foreseeable that the product would be used or consumed where the plaintiff used or consumed it. This rule recognizes the important interest a state has in injuries suffered by persons within its territory.

Local recourse in cases of products negligently manufactured abroad seems obvious today and yet, at the time, it was not obvious that consumers should be permitted to sue foreign manufacturers of products in the courts where they had acquired and used the products. A similar threshold in jurisdictional approach was crossed in the Privy Council jurisprudence with *Distiller's Co (Biochemicals) Ltd v Thompson* concerning liability for harm to those in New South Wales prescribed a drug manufactured in the United Kingdom containing thalidomide.[56]

A comparable evolution of thought concerning consumer services occurred more recently in respect of the rights of consumers using social media. Two decades ago, the Ontario courts showed little sympathy for a group of consumers who paid to subscribe to a social media service called 'MSN Messenger' and who wished to challenge the enforceability of a jurisdiction agreement that prevented them from seeking recovery in the local courts for frequent outages and other deficiencies in the service provided.[57] The internet was in its infancy and the claimants were regarded as adventurous early adopters exploring a novel service. The forum selection clause in their click-wrap agreement that required them to sue in a foreign forum was accepted as valid and binding on them, and the court did not exercise jurisdiction. While there continue to be jurisdictional battles over local court access for consumers of internet services, such claimants are now widely regarded as consumers deserving of the protections afforded to them under the laws of their place of residence.[58]

The fundamental changes in the world that brought about the expectations that consumers should be able to rely upon the standards in their residence for products and services acquired and consumed there seems also to be at play in the jurisdictional issues posed by holiday torts. We are far less certain today than we might

---

[54] Ibid 409.
[55] Ibid.
[56] *Distiller's Co (Biochemicals) Ltd v Thompson* [1971] AC 458.
[57] *Rudder v Microsoft Corp* (1999) 40 CPC (4th) 394 (SCJ Ont).
[58] *Douez v Facebook Inc* (2017) SCC 33.

once have been that the courts should not grant access to plaintiffs in situations like that described in *Brownlie*. What has changed?

A clue to this might be found in the otherwise mysterious fourth presumptive connecting factor articulated by the Supreme Court of Canada in *Club Resorts*— that of 'a contract connected with the dispute was made in the forum'. Of course, as mentioned, it is far from obvious what kind of contract and what kind of connection is involved in this factor, and equally unclear what suffices to demonstrate the 'making of the contract *in* the forum', but the notion of contracting in the forum for a service that is ultimately provided during the holiday seems to resonate with the treatment of these cases as local consumer claims that are entitled to be heard by the courts of the consumers' residence.

In today's (pre-pandemic) world of package holidays and five-star resorts, many of the tourists are far more like travel *consumers* than they are seasoned adventurers. They thumb through glossy magazines at the travel agents' shop or click through online advertisements, and they imagine themselves whisked away to exotic destinations to enjoy exciting adventures and then transported home again magically without the need to assume any greater responsibility for the logistics or the safety of their travel than they would when boarding a ride at the local amusement park. The jurisdictional confusion arises not from the amenability of the package tour provider or cruise operator who has sold the package tour or vacation stay to the tourist before the holiday begins. They are likely to be subject to the jurisdiction of the courts of the tourist's residence.[59] Rather, the jurisdictional confusion concerns the ability to bring within the jurisdiction of the plaintiff's home forum the service providers at the holiday destination to whom the traveller has been referred while at that location.[60] Those defendants may regard themselves as providing a service to a person in that locale and not in the tourist's residence. However, it is also understandable how the tourist could be lulled into the false sense of security that these 'add-on' tours and excursions are being provided on the same basis as the main tour, particularly when the tourists have been directed to the excursions by the main tour provider.

In short, critical to the growth of the travel industry has been the transformation of international travel into a consumer product. Ordinary people now go regularly to places that they have scarcely heard of and do things that they would never otherwise do. It does not occur to them that, in the event of an accident on an excursion during their trip, they might need to seek recourse in the local courts there. Once home, apart from having visited the country in question, they would no more imagine having to rely on the courts in that distant place than they would

---

[59] Directive (EU) 2015/2302/EU on package travel and linked travel arrangements ([2015] OJ L326/1).
[60] See discussion of *Lemmex* and *Leufkens* at text to nn 31–32 above.

have to rely on the courts in the country of a foreign manufacturer for an injury suffered upon the breakdown of a household appliance in their residence.

G. Strange New Shores

1. The place of the tort or the relationship between the parties?

Where does this leave us? Some travellers, particularly those who are engaged in adventures of the more 'off road' variety, might be regarded as having the capacity to assess and voluntarily accept the responsibility of managing the risk of injury, whether through insurance, self-insurance or reliance on the local authorities in the place where they are injured.[61] Other travellers, whether it is because they have purchased an all-inclusive holiday marketed to them in the place of their residence, or have made the arrangements with a major hotel chain from their place of residence, may be less likely to be regarded as having accepted this responsibility. Some cases, like that of Lady Brownlie, may involve a more complex combination of events—a call from home in one's place of residence to the concierge of the hotel at the holiday destination based on a leaflet obtained in a previous visit. Similarly, some accommodations may be multinational enterprises that have structured their operations to cater to the needs of a particular kind of traveller in a particular country who is within their target market. This appears to have been the general tenor of the argument made in the *Brownlie* litigation about Fairmont Hotels and five-star travellers from Britain such as the Brownlies. Others, like the example considered by the Court of Appeal for Ontario, the local wilderness canoe rental operator,[62] are obviously incapable of assuming a similar level of responsibility to respond to claims brought by customers who have arrived from distant countries around the world.

Somewhere along this spectrum is a dividing line that indicates when it might be reasonable for a court to accept jurisdiction in the place of the plaintiff's residence and when it might be regarded as reasonable to decline jurisdiction. Furthermore, even if this premise is accepted in principle, the courts of one forum might be inclined to favour the interests of holiday makers in a given scenario where the courts of another forum are more inclined to favour the interests of hospitality providers.

---

[61] Although the European Union does not distinguish between sophisticated and non-sophisticated consumers. See, eg, Case C-208/18 *Jana Petruchová v FIBO Group Holdings Limited* ECLI:EU:C:2019:825.

[62] *Leufkens* (n 24) [33].

It might be argued that the logical consequence of assigning the risk to hospitality providers would be the need to price services according to the relative cost of defending in the various home jurisdictions of their patrons. This would militate in favour of assigning the risk to tourists and encouraging them to purchase insurance, as was the generally the arrangement that was adopted in respect of carriage of goods by sea[63] and air.[64] But even if this particular issue could be resolved through travel insurance, it stands as yet another instance when the courts have confronted questions of the extent of their own jurisdiction that required an exercise of judgement, one that they would not necessarily expect to accord with the judgement that might be exercised by a court in another forum. Would this be understood as a question of law, or of discretion and, if discretion, would that discretion be exercised on a category-by-category, or case-by-case basis?

It is worth returning to the passing observation of the Supreme Court of Canada some fifty years ago, as the Court broadened jurisdiction in product liability. The Court said that, for jurisdictional purposes, a tort could properly be regarded 'as having occurred in any country substantially affected by the defendant's activities or its consequences *and the law of which is likely to have been in the reasonable contemplation of the parties*'.[65] This observation highlights the nature of the relationship between the parties and the law that might reasonably have been in their contemplation when they entered into the agreement for the product or service. Without presuming to decide the question in any particular case,[66] one can imagine why, for example, Lady Brownlie, speaking on the telephone with a major hotel, might think that it was understood that she was arranging for services intended to have safety standards consistent with those she enjoyed in the United Kingdom, even if the hotel understood the situation differently. In contrast, it might be imagined that had she wandered down the street from the hotel in Cairo to hail a local cab, her understanding might have been otherwise. Of course, what happened in her case, as with what happens in many cases, might be more nuanced and must be considered on its own particular facts.

If, indeed, we are finally approaching the far shore, what a strange vista it presents. For this last observation relates not so much to the exercise of jurisdiction, but to applicable legal standards that the parties might have in mind. These are usually considered to be very different issues. Have we lost sight of

---

[63] International Convention for the Unification of Certain Rules of Law relating to Bills of Lading (Brussels, 25 August 1924) as amended by the protocol done at Brussels on 23 February 1968 (hereafter Hague-Visby Rules).
[64] Convention for the Unification of Certain Rules for International Carriage by Air (Warsaw, 12 October 1929) (hereafter Warsaw Convention).
[65] *Moran* (n 53) 409 (emphasis added).
[66] And acknowledging that 'the reasonable contemplation of the parties' may, in circular fashion, be driven by the law as it comes to be known.

the relevance of discretion in determining appropriate forum—or has it just become a question of a court exercising judgement in respect of particular facts?

To be clear, this is a different exercise of judgement from the role of discretion in determining *forum conveniens* in the English civil practice, which is usually concerned with the parties' logistical capacities to commence or defend the action in the forum of the opposing party. There is no doubt that once upon a time, logistical challenges were an important consideration. However, today, with the steady increase in the cost of litigation before the English and Canadian courts, and the transformative impact of modern communications, the difference in suing at home or abroad is likely to be relevant in far fewer cases. For example, in *Brownlie,* it is difficult to imagine how, if Lady Brownlie had accepted that she had to sue in Cairo, this would have resulted in litigation that was more expensive or more protracted than it proved to be by seeking to sue in London. This is not to suggest that someone in Lady Brownlie's position should be required to sue in Cairo. Rather it is to say, as has been said in other essays in this collection,[67] that logistical considerations are likely to be significant to questions of the proper forum only in exceptional cases; and it goes without saying, that where logistical considerations are relevant, they should inform the court's discretion to exercise or to decline jurisdiction, whether on a leave application or a stay application.

However, if the reason why Lady Brownlie and plaintiffs like her should be entitled to assert that the English courts are the proper forum is not logistical, does that mean that it is because she is entitled to the application of English law? Perhaps not, but even if Egyptian law governs, and the English courts are capable of applying it, and even if the quality of justice in the Egyptian courts is not to be impugned, there may still be a benefit sought by suing in London.

2. The comforts of (suing at) home

For those preparing and presenting cross-border claims there are myriad benefits, quite apart from the application of forum law to various aspects of the case, that make it attractive to sue at home. It is easy to see why a plaintiff such as Lady Brownlie might wish the triers of fact and law to be those who might more readily appreciate her situation and her perspective on the issues. Plaintiffs in that position naturally want to be seen as 'travel consumers' entitled to assurances of safety similar to consumers of products acquired in their country of residence. It is easy to see why they might be anxious about having the matter determined in a forum in which they might be seen as wealthy foreigners indulging in extravagant pastimes and expecting inappropriately high and reliable levels of service. Could courts that

---

[67] See Martin Davies' essay in this collection (ch 2), 38 ('The convenience of the parties is much less significant in the *forum non conveniens* inquiry than it used to be...'); and Andrew Bell's essay (ch 1).

sympathize with these concerns and consequently support the choice of forum of someone like Lady Brownlie, be said to be 'recogniz[ing] the important interest a state has in injuries suffered by persons within its territory',[68] albeit having suffered the injury while away on vacation? Could this be an expression of the 'public interest factors'[69] that Martin Davies, in his essay, says now carry most of the weight in the analysis of appropriate forum?[70]

Perhaps so. Although these situations may be distinguished as torts in which the harm has been *suffered*, but which did not *occur* in the forum,[71] the gateway for cases involving damage sustained in the forum following injury that has occurred abroad will need to be exercised with caution. It differs from most of the other gateways, which may be more easily fitted into a notional allocation of cases to fora based on the geographically located occurrence of a particular event. In this way, this particular gateway will necessarily entail exercising a jurisdiction that overlaps with that of the place in which the harmful event occurred. For this reason, it is possible that, unlike the other gateways, this gateway ought to be understood as inherently discretionary (or more accurately, 'exceptional', and warranting a careful exercise of judgement)—not merely as also subject to the usual determination of proper forum as a question of the balance of logistical convenience between the parties.

Strangely, this approach would echo the approach taken in choice of law in tort. In choice of law in tort in many places in the common law, and under the Rome II Regulation,[72] the courts generally apply the law of the place where the tort occurs unless the parties' relationship (either through a common habitual residence or a pre-existing legal relationship) suggests otherwise.[73] Under the approach to jurisdiction considered here for holiday torts, the court would ordinarily regard the place where the tort occurred as the proper forum unless the parties' relationship suggested otherwise. Could this have been the impetus for the Supreme Court of Canada to include the strange factor of 'a contract connected with the dispute having been made in the forum'?[74]

The resemblance between this formulation of the jurisdictional analysis and that of the traditional doctrine of the flexible exception in tort,[75] echoes the

---

[68] *Moran* (n 53) 409.
[69] *Gulf Oil v Gilbert* 330 US 501 (1947).
[70] Ch 2.
[71] To adopt the formulation used in interpreting Art 7.2 of the recast Brussels I Regulation (n 14).
[72] Regulation (EC) 864/2007 of 11 July 2007 on the law applicable to non-contractual obligations (Rome II) [2007] OJ L199/40, Art 4 (hereafter Rome II Regulation).
[73] *Club Resorts* (n 36) [90].
[74] Or the thinking in *Boys v Chaplin* [1971] AC 356, as explained by the Privy Council in *Red Sea Insurance v Bouygues* SA [1995] 1 AC 190, or even *Johnston v Coventry Churchill* [1992] 3 All ER 14?
[75] And the further exceptions to the *lex loci damni* in the Rome II Regulation (n 72) found in Art 4.2, 4.3 for common habitual residence and pre-existing relationship between the parties, advocated for in Janet Walker, 'Are We There Yet: Towards a New Rule for Choice of Law in Tort' (2000) 38 Osgoode Hall LJ 331.

tendency of judges to combine (or confuse) analysis based on choice of law in tort with jurisdiction in cases of holiday torts. Perhaps it is time to consider the possibility that the traditional territorial structure of our field, one in which so much of the analysis of the physical location of relevant events and persons at particular moments, is giving way to a structure that is more conceptual. In a post-territorial world, in private law matters, parties may be less often understood as reasonably expecting questions of law and forum to be determined in accordance with the geographical location of physical events as much as they might reasonably expect those questions to be determined in accordance with the legal system with which their relationship is most closely connected. In the situation of a holiday tort, this might result in some cases being analysed as the provision of holiday services in the place of the tourist's residence notwithstanding that the services are performed—and the injuries suffered—at the travel destination.

This would not affect the confident exercise of jurisdiction permitted by gateways relating to torts where the harmful event has occurred in the forum, subject of course to the moderating influences of *forum conveniens* and *forum non conveniens* found in the determination of proper forum.[76] However, it would entail the recognition that jurisdiction founded on gateways involving events that occur abroad and persons based abroad, such as that arising from 'damage sustained in the forum' and 'necessary and proper party', are inherently exceptional. Where the majority of the gateways would be based on a legal presumption of jurisdiction that was subject to the court's discretion to decline where another forum was better placed logistically to hear the instant case, these exceptional gateways would not be presumed but would be available to be exercised only on a discretionary basis where the interests of justice so dictated. It does not fit neatly with the current analytic structure of the CPR to treat certain gateways differently from the others, but as an alternative to eliminating them, as has been done in Canada, or consigning cases involving them to decades of litigation over the question of jurisdiction, as has occurred with Lady Brownlie's case, it could provide a habitable resting place for this journey.

H. Settling In

To acknowledge that some jurisdictional bases, though exceptional, are defensible even if the presumption is against them is to accept that the extent of the court's jurisdiction must necessarily be fashioned in a way that does not match perfectly the contours of the jurisdiction of other courts. There will necessarily be areas of overlap with the potential for differences of view. These differences might result in

---

[76] Pursuant to leave sought under CPR rr 6.36–6.37.

parallel litigation; they might result in refusal on occasion to recognize a judgment. This is not an exercise in allocating jurisdiction—it is part of a maturing understanding of the scope of judicial jurisdiction in a more interconnected world.

These are the complexities of international jurisdiction that Canadian courts and court regulators are only now exploring.[77] It has taken some time for them to question the concern that fuelled the desire to eliminate gateways such as 'damage sustained in the forum' and 'necessary and proper party', which denied access to the courts in situations where it had traditionally been afforded and continued to be afforded in many other legal systems. Canadian courts have never operated within a system, like the European Union, in which jurisdiction is allocated among member state courts even if Canadian courts seemed driven to shape their jurisdiction as if it was part of some notional international double convention. The reciprocal benefits that might warrant restricting jurisdiction based upon exceptional gateways such as these do not exist internationally, absent a treaty. Where matters of pressing local importance for consumers, workers or other protected classes of persons are at stake, exercising jurisdiction may be necessary to ensure that local mandatory laws are not subordinated to the different interests of another forum. Such concerns appear to have prompted the inclusion of specific provisions in the Regulations adapting the law on jurisdiction in the United Kingdom following Brexit for consumer and employee protection, corresponding closely to those in the Brussels I regime.[78]

Accepting that the alignment between direct and indirect jurisdiction on the international plane is imperfect is part of a maturing understanding of international jurisdiction. Some gateways are 'entirely unobjectionable', and others might be described as 'exorbitant', as has been observed by Lord Collins.[79] The idea that not all gateways should be treated equally is reflected in the revised approach to the Hague Judgments Convention[80] in which the initial aim to develop a double convention[81] was amended to make possible a multilateral system for the recognition and enforcement of judgments.

One might wonder whether the requirement of a positive showing of proper forum in a leave application might be unnecessary for gateways that are entirely unobjectionable, with objections to the exercise of jurisdiction that relate to the convenience of the forum to be left to motions to stay on grounds of *forum non conveniens*. This could result in retaining a requirement of leave only

---

[77] *Teck Cominco Metals Ltd v Lloyd's Underwriters* [2009] 1 SCR 321; *Douez v Facebook Inc* (2017) SCC 33; *Google Inc v Equustek Solutions Inc* (2017) SCC 34.
[78] See SI 2019/479, reg 26 inserting new ss 15A–E in the Civil Jurisdiction and Judgments Act 1982.
[79] Lord Collins of Mapesbury, 'Sovereignty and Exorbitant Jurisdiction' (2014) 130 LQR 555.
[80] Convention on the Recognition and Enforcement of Foreign Judgments in Civil or Commercial Matters (2 July 2019).
[81] Peter Nygh and Fausto Pocar, *Report on the Preliminary Draft Convention on Jurisdiction and Foreign Judgments in Civil and Commercial Matters* (Hague Conference on Private International Law, Preliminary Document, No 11 of August 2000).

for gateways that have the potential to be regarded as exorbitant. The 'discretionary' feature of granting leave in respect of these gateways would not address only the balance of convenience between the parties to the instant case, but could include the larger questions that are captured by the concept of 'public interest factors' that have been part of the United States' jurisprudence on *forum conveniens*. Whether this analysis is described as exercising discretion, or exercising judgement, cases such as the holiday tort cases considered here highlight the critical importance, as the world changes around us, of the role of the courts. That role goes well beyond interpreting and applying the existing rules of jurisdiction to shaping jurisdiction to meet the needs of this changing world.

4
Taming Anti-suit Injunctions

Andrew Dickinson

A. Introduction

Courts everywhere are in the business of doing justice. While competing with one another and with international arbitral bodies for a share of the lucrative global litigation market, they engage in a common venture with the object of the fair and just resolution of disputes.[1] Indeed, without collaboration between legal systems, litigation would likely prove fruitless in many cases. In recognising each other's judgments, granting protective measures in support of each other's proceedings and managing proceedings so as to reduce the risk of conflicting decisions, legal systems contribute—by individual contributions or through reciprocal arrangements[2]—to this common enterprise.

At the same time, many legal systems, including but not limited to[3] those of a common law tradition, continue to assert the power to grant what is now conventionally albeit rather unsatisfactorily termed an 'anti-suit injunction', that is to say an order restraining a person over whom the court asserts judicial authority from commencing or continuing legal proceedings or from taking a particular step in a legal proceeding before another court or tribunal. Far removed from its original role within the English legal system, the modern anti-suit injunction targets proceedings in other legal systems.[4]

---

[1] *Ecobank Transnational Inc v Tanoh* [2015] EWCA Civ 1309, [2016] 1 WLR 2231 [132] (Christopher Clarke LJ) (hereafter *Ecobank*).

[2] Notably, Regulation (EU) 1215/2012 of 12 December 2012 on jurisdiction and the recognition and enforcement of judgments in civil and commercial matters (recast) [2012] OJ L351/1 (hereafter the Recast Brussels I Regulation), which no longer applies in the UK after 1 January 2021 (Civil Jurisdiction and Judgments (Amendment) (EU) Exit Regulations (SI 2019/479), reg 89).

[3] eg *West Tankers Inc v Ras Riunione Adriatica di Sicurta SpA* [2007] UKHL 4, [2007] 1 All ER (Comm) 794 [18] (Lord Hoffmann) (hereafter *West Tankers*), referring to *SA Banque Worms c/Epx Brachot*, Cass civ (1) 19 November 2002, D 2003, 797 (the latter case noted by H Muir-Watt (2003) 62 CLJ 573); also Adrian Briggs, 'Anti-suit injunctions and Utopian ideals' (2004) 120 LQR 529, 530–1; Louis Perreau-Saussine, '*Forum conveniens* and anti-suit injunction before French courts: recent developments' (2010) 59 ICLQ 519, 523–5.

[4] For an account of the rules and practice of the English courts in granting injunctions restraining proceedings before domestic courts, see Thomas Raphael, *The Anti-Suit Injunction* (2nd edn, OUP 2019) ch 6 (hereafter Raphael, *The Anti-Suit Injunction*); *Fujifilm Kyowa Kirin Biologics Co Ltd v AbbVie Biotechnology Ltd* [2016] EWHC 2204 (Pat), [2017] Bus LR 333 [45]–[62], affd [2017] EWCA Civ 1, [2018] Bus LR 228 [107]–[108].

Andrew Dickinson, *Taming Anti-suit Injunctions* In: *A Conflict of Laws Companion*. Edited by: Andrew Dickinson and Edwin Peel, Oxford University Press. © Andrew Dickinson 2021.
DOI: 10.1093/oso/9780198868958.003.0004

In contrast with his enthusiastic advocacy of the principle of *forum conveniens*,[5] Adrian Briggs' writing on the subject of the anti-suit injunction takes a more cautious approach, acknowledging its ominous[6] presence within the judicial arsenal[7] while seeking to rationalise the procedures and conditions for its use.

Even to a seasoned observer of the conflict of laws, the anti-suit injunction is—as Professor Briggs puts it—'a remarkable thing'.[8] Its innocuous title belies its character as a heavy fetter on the exercise of constitutional rights of access to the courts so prized and jealously defended by English judges within their own realm.[9] In granting an anti-suit injunction, an English court imposes a duty upon the restrained party that prohibits it[10] from seeking judicial protection to which it claims to be entitled within a constitutional order of which the enjoining court forms no part. That duty is accompanied by the threat that, if the restrained party does not comply, it or its officers will be imprisoned or fined or its corporate assets sequestered as punishment for its contempt.[11]

In many cases, the ostensible reasons for granting an injunction suggest that the restrained party has behaved in a legally and morally reprehensible manner in seeking to bring forward a matter for determination by a foreign court: that it has done so 'unconscionably', or 'vexatiously' or 'oppressively', and that its wrongdoing must be restrained.[12]

In view of its character, one would expect the legal basis of the power to grant an anti-suit injunction, and its boundaries, to be clearly defined and controlled. Regrettably, courts in England and elsewhere in the common law world have not sought refuge in legal certainty, preferring to keep the anti-suit injunction to hand as a tool available 'when the ends of justice require it'[13] and to avoid even working definitions of the vituperative adverbs used to castigate the restrained party's conduct.[14] This attitude, scented with the 'innate

---

[5] See the essays by Andrew Bell (ch 1) and Martin Davies (ch 2) in this collection.

[6] 'It looks very much like an act of interference with proceedings before [the] foreign court, and the appearance does not mislead' (Adrian Briggs, *Private International Law in English Courts* (OUP 2014) [5.89] (hereafter Briggs, *Private International Law in English Courts*)).

[7] In addition to the work collected in the List of Publications (see Appendix) under the heading 'Anti-Suit Injunctions', see also Adrian Briggs, *Civil Jurisdiction and Judgments* (6th edn, Informa Law 2015) [5.32]ff (hereafter Briggs, *Civil Jurisdiction and Judgments*); Briggs, *Private International Law in English Courts* (n 6) [5.89]ff; Adrian Briggs, *The Conflict of Laws* (4th edn, OUP 2019) 119–23 (hereafter Briggs, *The Conflict of Laws*); Adrian Briggs, *Agreements on Jurisdiction and Choice of Law* (OUP 2008) ch 6; *The Principle of Comity in Private International Law* (2011) 354 Recueil des Cours 77, 125–32.

[8] Briggs, *Private International Law in English Courts* (n 6) [5.89].

[9] *R (Unison) v Lord Chancellor* [2017] UKSC 51, [2017] 4 All ER 903 [66]–[83] (Lord Reed) (hereafter UNISON).

[10] The singular, neutral pronoun is used here for convenience as most (but by no means all) anti-suit injunctions are targeted at corporate bodies.

[11] *Dell Emerging Markets (EMEA) Ltd v Systems Equipment Telecommunications Services SAL* [2020] EWHC 1384 (Comm) [16] (Henshaw J).

[12] *Turner v Grovit* [2001] UKHL 65, [2002] 1 WLR 107 [24] (Lord Hobhouse) (hereafter *Turner v Grovit*).

[13] Section D.3(a).

[14] Section D.3(c).

superiority'[15] professed by English courts in the 19th century,[16] presents a second challenge to the rule of law, by undermining the principle that the law must be accessible, intelligible, clear and predictable.[17]

The existence of the anti-suit injunction, and much of the current judicial practice, sit uneasily with assurances that we live in an era in which judicial comity has replaced judicial chauvinism.[18] This contribution critically assesses the current state of English law, drawing on experience elsewhere in the common law world. It considers how the law relating to anti-suit injunctions might be recast to support, rather than undermine, the rule of law within the global legal order.

B. Terminology

The term 'anti-suit injunction' is a relatively modern one, understood to have originated in the United States[19] and to have been imported, reluctantly, by Robert Goff LJ (as he then was) in *Bank of Tokyo Ltd v Karoon*.[20] Since then its use has become widespread among judges and commentators.[21]

In *Turner v Grovit*, Lord Hobhouse objected that 'the terminology is misleading since it fosters the impression that the order is addressed to and intended to bind another court'.[22] He continued:[23]

> It suggests that the jurisdiction of the foreign court is in question and that the injunction is an order that the foreign court desist from exercising the jurisdiction given to it by its own domestic law. None of this is correct.

---

[15] cf *Owners of the Atlantic Star v Owners of the Bona Spes (The Atlantic Star and The Bona Spes)* [1974] AC 436, 453 (Lord Reid) (hereafter *The Atlantic Star*); *Macshannon v Rockware Glass Ltd* [1977] 1 WLR 376, 380 (Lord Denning MR).
[16] Text to nn 114–23
[17] Lord Bingham, *The Rule of Law* (Allen Lane 2010) ch 3.
[18] *The Abidin Daver* [1984] AC 398, 411 (Lord Diplock).
[19] References to an 'antisuit injunction' can be found in the judgment of Circuit Judge Rives in *Blanchard v Commonwealth Oil Company* 294 F 2d 834 (5th Cir 1961) 839; also Charles H Helein, 'Foreign Recognition of Foreign Antisuit Injunctions' (1960) St Louis ULJ 552.
[20] [1987] AC 45, 58–59 (hereafter *Bank of Tokyo*). The term does not appear in his Lordship's influential opinion in *Société Nationale Industrielle Aerospatiale v Jak* [1987] AC 871 (hereafter *SNI Aerospatiale*), where he referred (at 892) to 'injunctions restraining a party from commencing or pursuing legal proceedings in a foreign jurisdiction'.
The editors of the best known English work on the conflict of laws did not use the term until relatively recently and then only with quotation marks accompanied by the comment that 'the terminology may not be altogether accurate or elegant' (Lawrence Collins and others (eds), *Dicey & Morris: The Conflict of Laws* (13th edn, Sweet & Maxwell 1999) [12-057]; currently Lord Collins of Mapesbury and others (eds), *Dicey, Morris & Collins: The Conflict of Laws* (15th edn Sweet & Maxwell 2012) [12-078] (hereafter Dicey, Morris & Collins)).
[21] *Airbus Industrie GIE v Patel* [1999] 1 AC 119, 127 (Lord Goff) (hereafter *Airbus Industrie*); also Case C-159/02 *Turner v Grovit* [2004] ECR I-3565, Opinion of AG Colomer, para 1 (hereafter *Turner*).
[22] *Turner v Grovit* (n 12) [23].
[23] Ibid.

This provided his Lordship with an opportunity to advance the well-worn claim that an injunction of this kind 'is not directed against the foreign court'.[24]

This criticism is unconvincing.[25] Although the word 'suit' can refer to the passive object of judicial control, it more naturally refers to the claimant's action in pursuing a judicial remedy.[26] Moreover, insofar as the label can also be understood in the sense that Lord Hobhouse postulated, it serves as a valuable reminder that orders of this kind do interfere with the functioning of foreign legal systems, in the same way that the term 'freezing injunction' reminds one of the impact of that form of relief on the assets subject to the order.

A more fundamental objection to the current terminology is its benign, euphemistic tone. In cases of the kind here under consideration, the anti-suit injunction is a drastic remedy. It prohibits the restrained party from exercising rights of the most fundamental kind within the constitutional order of a legal system that is entirely independent of the English legal system. Its intended effect, backed by penal sanctions, is that the foreign court will be deprived of the opportunity to exercise its constitutional function of conferring legal protection. Although English courts have long acknowledged that orders of this kind produce an 'indirect' interference with foreign judicial proceedings, leading to ostensible judicial restraint in granting them,[27] they have been unwilling to recognise the extraordinary character of the direct interference with rights that within their own legal order are considered to be 'inherent in the rule of law',[28] operating in the public interest and not only in the interests of the parties before the court.[29]

A small first step in the renovation process would be to replace 'anti-suit' with a label that more openly acknowledges the invasive character of the remedy. Lord Hobhouse's preference for 'restraining order'[30] seems, if anything, less expressive, offering only a synonym for 'injunction'. The term 'overseas civil restraint order (or injunction)' more aptly captures the nature of the injunction.[31] Without prejudice

---

[24] Ibid, referring to *SNI Aerospatiale* (n 20) 892 (Lord Goff). Lord Goff in turn drew support from the words of Sir John Leach VC in *Bushby v Munday* (1821) 5 Madd 297, 307; 56 ER 908, 918 (hereafter *Bushby*), while pointing out that '[t]here are, of course, many other statements in the cases to the same effect'.

[25] Dicey, Morris & Collins (n 20) [12-078] fn 360.

[26] Bryan A Garner and others (eds), *Black's Law Dictionary* (11th edn, Thomson Reuters 2019) ('Suit stresses the sense of campaign—originally a lover's persistent efforts to win love as a suitor but now a complainant's attempt to redress a wrong, enforce a right, or compel application of a rule.').

[27] *Cohen v Rothfield* [1919] 1 KB 410, 413 (Scrutton LJ); *Castanho v Brown and Root (UK) Ltd* [1980] 1 WLR 833, 869 (Brandon LJ) (hereafter *Castanho*); *British Airways Board v Laker Airways Ltd* [1985] AC 58, 95 (Lord Scarman) (hereafter *British Airways*); *SNI Aerospatiale* (n 20) 892 (Lord Goff); *Airbus Industrie* (n 21) 138, 141 (Lord Goff).

As Professor Briggs notes, however, '[t]his note to self is far from effective ... [The cases] can leave the impression that little more than lip-service was paid to such concerns' (Briggs, *Private International Law in English Courts* (n 6) [5.95]).

[28] *UNISON* (n 9) [66] (Lord Reed).

[29] Ibid [70]–[73].

[30] *Turner v Grovit* (n 12) [16].

[31] The term 'civil restraint order' is used in Civil Procedure Rules 1998 (CPR) r 3.11 and CPR PD 3C for orders operating domestically to restrain vexatious proceedings.

to that observation, this essay will use the label 'anti-suit injunction' to describe orders restraining a party from commencing or continuing proceedings before a foreign court.

C. Legal Basis

1. Introduction

Although section 37(1) of the Senior Courts Act 1981 sets out the bare bones of the court's general power to grant an injunction (including an anti-suit injunction), it is a mere conduit.[32] Understanding its effect requires a closer examination of the meaning of the statutory conditions: that it be both 'just' and 'convenient' to grant the injunction.

2. 'Just'

Section 37(1) traces its ancestry to section 25(8) of the Supreme Court of Judicature Act 1873, the terms of which referred only to interlocutory orders. In *Beddow v Beddow*, Jessel MR suggested that section 25(8), in combination with the transfer to the High Court of the powers formerly exercised by the courts of common law and of equity,[33] gave the newly established court 'unlimited power to grant an injunction in any case where it would be right or just to do so'.[34] Importantly, however, he immediately qualified that statement with the following words:[35]

> [W]hat is right or just must be decided, not by the caprice of the Judge, but according to sufficient legal reasons or on settled legal principles.

This important proposition was emphasised by the members of the Court of Appeal in *North London Railway Co v Great Northern Railway Co*.[36] The Court rejected the contention that section 25(8) had given the High Court a general power to grant injunctions, unfettered by precedent. The section removed procedural constraints, but did not authorise the granting of an injunction without a sufficiently identified basis in law.[37]

---

[32] *Fourie v Le Roux* [2007] UKHL 1, [2007] 1 WLR 320 [25] (Lord Scott) (hereafter *Fourie*).
[33] Supreme Court of Judicature Act 1873, s 16; Supreme Court of Judicature (Consolidation) Act 1925, s 18; Senior Courts Act 1981, s 19.
[34] (1878) 9 ChD 89, 93.
[35] Ibid.
[36] (1883) 11 QBD 30.
[37] Ibid 36–7 (Brett LJ), 39–40 (Cotton LJ).

Although the *North London Railway* case has never been overruled, it has proved controversial.[38] It does not, despite occasional submissions to the contrary, support the proposition that the 1873 Act ossified the law on injunctions, rendering it incapable of incremental development in the same way as any unwritten rule of English law (whether originating in the practice of the courts of common law or equity).[39] The rise of the freezing injunction[40] and the growth of injunctive relief against those innocently mixed up in wrongdoing[41] are testament to that. The decision, however, retains its significance in emphasising that the court's power to grant an injunction is not unfettered, and does not depend on a judge's own free-flowing ideas as to what justice requires, but is founded on legal principle, established by precedent.[42]

Accordingly, the temptation[43] to assert that the court's jurisdiction[44] to grant an injunction is limited only by its ability to compel the defendant to appear before it and by judicial 'practice' capable of being moulded 'in the interests of justice' must be resisted. The judicial power embodied in section 37(1) is not 'unfettered by statute', as Lord Goff once infelicitously suggested.[45] To adapt the words of Sir George Jessel, justice demands that the court identify a sufficient legal reason for the injunction, according with settled legal principles. A judge cannot sidestep principle and precedent by the incantation that an anti-suit injunction may be granted whenever necessary (or appropriate) 'to avoid injustice' or 'in the interests of justice',[46] any more than one can invoke 'justice' alone to justify imposing a duty of care in negligence.[47] Equally, statements that the categories of situation in which an anti-suit injunction may be granted are not 'confined'[48] should be understood as

---

[38] In *Bremer Vulcan Schiffbau und Maschinenfabrik v South India Shipping Corp Ltd* [1981] AC 908, Donaldson J (at 924) described it as a 'troublesome case'; also ibid 959 (Roskill LJ), 961 (Cumming Bruce LJ), 979–80 (Lord Diplock).

[39] *Masri v Consolidated Contractors International (UK) Co SAL (No 2)* [2008] EWCA Civ 303, [2009] QB 450 [143]–[148], [162], [174]–[184] (Lawrence Collins LJ) (hereafter *Masri (No 2)*); *Tasarruf Mevduati Sigorta Fonu v Merrill Lynch Bank and Trust Co (Cayman) Ltd* [2011] UKPC 17, [2012] 1 WLR 1721 [55]–[58] (Lord Collins) (hereafter *Tasarruf Mevduati*).

[40] *Fourie* (n 32) [30] (Lord Scott).

[41] *Norwich Pharmacal Co v Customs and Excise Commissioners* [1974] AC 133; *Cartier International AG v British Telecommunications plc* [2018] UKSC 28, [2018] 1 WLR 3259.

[42] *Tasarruf Mevduati* (n 39) [56]–[58] (Lord Collins, with whom Lords Hope, Mance, Clarke and Reed joined). cf *Michael Wilson & Partners v Emmott* [2018] EWCA Civ 51, [2018] 1 Lloyd's Rep 299 [36] (Sir Terence Etherton MR) (hereafter *Michael Wilson*).

[43] *Mercedes Benz AG v Leiduck* [1997] AC 284, 307–8 (Lord Nicholls, in a dissenting opinion) (hereafter *Mercedes Benz v Leiduck*); *Fourie* (n 32) [30] (Lord Scott).

[44] In the strict sense described by Lord Scott in *Fourie* (n 32) [25].

[45] *South Carolina Insurance Co v Assurantie Maatschappij 'De Zeven Provincien' NV* [1987] AC 24, 44–5 (hereafter *South Carolina*). cf ibid 40 (Lord Brandon, with whom Lords Brightman and Bridge agreed).

[46] *Castanho* (n 27) 573; *South Carolina* (n 45) 44–5 (Lord Goff); *SNI Aerospatiale* (n 20) 892 (Lord Goff); *Deutsche Bank AG v Highland Crusader Offshore Partners LLP* [2009] EWCA Civ 725, [2010] 1 WLR 1023 [50] (Toulson LJ) (hereafter *Deutsche Bank v Highland*); *SAS Institute Inc v World Programming Ltd* [2020] EWCA Civ 599 [90] (Males LJ) (hereafter *SAS Institute*).

[47] *Robinson v Chief Constable of West Yorkshire* [2018] UKSC 4, [2018] AC 736 [26]–[29] (Lord Reed).

[48] *SNI Aerospatiale* (n 20) 892, 896 (Lord Goff).

referring to the capacity of unwritten rules of law to evolve over time, subject to the limits imposed by the doctrine of precedent.

3. 'Convenient'

The second statutory condition for granting an injunction must not be overlooked—it must be 'convenient' as well as 'just' to grant an injunction.

If it is 'just' to grant an injunction (ie there exists a sufficient legal reason for the court to restrain a party[49]), the point of departure is that the court should act upon that reason and make the order.[50] The burden then lies on the defendant to identify one or more countervailing 'special circumstances'[51] justifying the refusal of the injunction, reserving the court's power to award damages *in lieu*.[52] Although the granting or refusal of a final injunction is not merely a question of the balance of convenience,[53] the court may consider other circumstances which reinforce the case for granting an injunction. In this evaluation, it is relevant to consider not only the conduct[54] and interests of the parties, and in particular the impact on them of granting or refusing the injunction (although mere hardship to the defendant will not of itself constitute a sufficient countervailing reason), but also the interests of third parties[55] and the public interest.[56]

For anti-suit injunctions, the public interest in the due administration of justice is obviously a significant factor to be taken into account, but (importantly) this is not solely a concern with the due administration of justice in England. Additionally, the acknowledged impact of the injunction on the foreign legal system, and in particular on the foreign court's ability to perform its constitutional role, make it a highly significant 'third party'.

It is at this stage of the enquiry that considerations of 'comity' exert a strong countervailing force against the granting of an injunction.[57] Comity is not a matter

---

[49] Section C.2.
[50] *Lawrence v Fen Tigers Ltd* [2014] UKSC 13, [2014] AC 822 [101], [121] (Lord Neuberger) (hereafter *Lawrence*).
[51] *Derby and Derbyshire Angling Association Ltd v British Celanese Ltd* [1953] Ch 149, 181 (Evershed MR).
[52] *Lawrence* (n 50) [121], [124].
[53] *Navitaire Inc v easyJet Airline Co Ltd (No 2)* [2005] EWHC 282 (Ch), [2006] RPC 4 [104] (Pumfrey J).
[54] The 'clean hands' maxim applies to anti-suit injunctions (*Royal Bank of Scotland plc v Highland Financial Partners* [2013] EWCA Civ 328, [2013] 1 CLC 596; *Peepul Capital Fund II LLC v VSoft Holdings LLC* [2019] UKPC 47 [52]).
[55] *SAS Institute* (n 46) [82].
[56] *Lawrence* (n 50) [124]–[126].
[57] *SNI Aerospatiale* (n 20) 892 (Lord Goff); *Airbus Industrie* (n 21) 133 (Lord Goff). On comity more generally, see the essay by James Edelman and Madeleine Salinger in this collection (ch 13).

of judicial collegiality or *'amour propre'*.[58] Instead, it mandates respect for the adjudicatory authority of the foreign court that is both equal in status as a matter of public international law[59] and ostensibly serving the same public interest in the due administration of justice as the English court.[60]

Comity demands that:[61]

> [T]he normal assumption is that an English court has no superiority over a foreign court in deciding what justice between the parties requires...

That assumption will be falsified, and the force of 'comity' as a factor in the evaluation of convenience, will be diminished if there is cogent evidence that the foreign court itself has acted or is likely to act[62] in excess of its jurisdiction under international law,[63] in violation of the requirements of natural justice,[64] or otherwise in a manner manifestly incompatible with the forum's fundamental policies,[65] or that its proceedings are likely significantly and irreversibly to interfere with the administration of justice in England.[66] By contrast, comity's countervailing force will be strengthened if the applicant has encouraged or allowed the foreign proceedings to progress significantly before seeking an injunction.[67] In that case, the likelihood that the resources that the defendant and the foreign judicial system have invested in the proceedings will be wasted if the injunction is granted weighs against the grant of an injunction.[68]

Whenever the injunction is founded on violation of a contractual right (such as an exclusive choice of court or arbitration agreement), the English courts require

---

[58] *Ecobank* (n 1) [132] (Christopher Clarke LJ); *SAS Institute* (n 46), [105] (Males LJ). cf *British Airways* (n 27) 185–6 (Lord Donaldson MR); *West Tankers Inc v Ras Riunione Adriatica Di Sicurta SpA* [2005] EWHC 454 (Comm), [2005] 2 Lloyd's 257 [51] (Colman J); *SAS Institute* (n 46) [101], [125].

[59] Robert Jennings and Arthur Watts (eds), *Oppenheim's International Law* (9th edn, Longman 1996), §107; also Joseph Story, *Commentaries on Equity Jurisprudence* (6th edn, Little & Brown 1853) vol II, 238 (hereafter Story, *Commentaries*).

[60] *Ecobank* (n 1) [132]; Timothy Endicott, 'Comity among Authorities' (2015) 68 Current Legal Problems 1.

[61] *Barclays Bank plc v Homan* [1992] BCC 757, 762 (Hoffmann J) (hereafter *Barclays Bank v Homan*); *Deutsche Bank v Highland* (n 46) [56] (Toulson LJ).

[62] This mirrors the approach to the *forum conveniens* enquiry when the claimant asserts that the interests of justice will not be served in the *prima facie* natural forum. In such cases, the claimant must advance cogent evidence of a real risk that justice will not be done in that forum (*Altimo Holdings and Investment Ltd v Kyrgyz Mobil Tel Ltd* [2011] UKPC 7, [2012] 1 WLR 1804 [89]–[97] (Lord Collins)). The more invasive character of an anti-suit injunction, as contrasted with refusal of a stay, supports the stricter test of likelihood proposed here.

[63] *Barclays Bank v Homan* (n 61) 762; *Deutsche Bank v Highland* (n 46) [56]; *SAS Institute* (n 46) [104], [111]–[112], [125].

[64] Elaborated, most clearly, in the recognition and enforcement of foreign judgments at common law (Dicey, Morris & Collins (n 20) [14R-162]).

[65] *Barclays Bank v Homan* (n 61) 762; *Deutsche Bank v Highland* (n 46) [56]; *Stichting Shell Pensioenfonds v Krys* [2014] UKPC 41, [2015] AC 616 [42] (Lord Sumption) (hereafter *Stichting Shell*).

[66] Section D.3(e).

[67] *Ecobank* (n 1) [132]–[137].

[68] Ibid; also *SAS Institute* (n 46) [104]–[106], [113]–[117].

'strong reasons' for the refusal of an anti-suit injunction.[69] In such cases, the case for an injunction is reinforced by the public interest in encouraging parties to make and respect such agreements to promote the efficient conduct of litigation (and in maintaining England's place as a leading centre for dispute resolution).[70] Moreover, in assessing the injunction's impact upon the injunction defendant, little weight will be given to circumstances foreseeable at the time of the agreement.[71] In recent years, however, English judges have taken to asserting that the 'true role' of comity in these cases is to ensure that the parties' agreement is respected.[72] Statements of this kind mischaracterise comity. They fail to give sufficient weight to the fact that the adjudicatory authority asserted by the foreign court does not depend on the parties' agreement and will, one may assume, withstand a challenge based upon that agreement. Just as the English common law does not treat a foreign choice of court agreement as ousting the jurisdiction of its courts, or as requiring the English courts to decline jurisdiction,[73] and as Parliament has imposed further restrictions on the effectiveness of such clauses,[74] other legal systems may also legitimately seek to control their use, and mere differences in approach between two legal systems should not bring their legislative or adjudicative authority into question.[75] Here, as elsewhere, comity requires the English court to accept that 'different judges operating under different legal systems with different legal policies may legitimately arrive at different answers, without occasioning a breach of customary international law or manifest injustice'.[76] Although the defendant's agreement to litigate or arbitrate in England diminishes the force of any argument it may make of prejudice to its own financial or other interests arising from an injunction,[77] that is distinct from the argument based on comity which pertains to the legitimate interests of the foreign court in administering justice within its own constitutional order. The

---

[69] *Donohue v Armco Inc* [2001] UKHL 64, [2002] 1 All ER 749 [24] (Lord Bingham), [53] (Lord Scott) (hereafter *Donohue*).

[70] *West Tankers* (n 3) [17]–[23] (Lord Hoffmann), [29]–[30] (Lord Mance); also *Grace Ocean Private Ltd v MV 'Bulk' Poland* [2020] EWHC 3343 (Comm) [45] (Bryan J), describing the parties' freedom of contract as 'a system-transcendant value'.

[71] *Deutsche Bank v Highland* (n 46) [102] (Toulson LJ).

[72] *Aggelki Charis Compania Maritima SA v Pagnan SpA (The Angelic Grace)* [1995] 1 Lloyd's Rep 87, 95–6 (Millett LJ); *OT Africa Line Ltd v Magic Sportswear Corp* [2005] EWCA Civ 710, [2006] 1 All ER (Comm) 32 [32] (Longmore LJ); *Deutsche Bank v Highland* (n 46) [50(5)] (Toulson LJ). cf *Ecobank* (n 1) [98]–[100], [131] (Christopher Clarke LJ), rejecting the submission that comity has 'no place other than to give effect to the rights of the parties to have the dispute determined by arbitration'.

[73] Briggs, *Civil Jurisdiction and Judgments* (n 7) [4.41].

[74] Ibid [4.49].

[75] *Barclays Bank v Homan* (n 61) 765–6; also *Kuwait Airways Corp v Iraqi Airways Co* [2002] UKHL 19, [2002] 2 AC 883 [15]–[17] (Lord Nicholls) (hereafter *Kuwait Airways*). cf *Akai Pty Ltd v People's Insurance Co Ltd* [1998] 1 Lloyd's Rep 90.
The existence of s 32 of the Civil Jurisdiction and Judgments Act 1982 does not call this proposition into question, for its effects are limited to the reception of the judgment in England.

[76] *Deutsche Bank v Highland* (n 46), [50(5)] (Toulson LJ); *SAS Institute* (n 46) [103] (Males LJ); also Thomas Raphael, 'Do as you would be done by? System-transcendent justification and anti-suit injunctions' [2016] LMCLQ 256, 260–4; Raphael, *The Anti-Suit Injunction* (n 4) [1.55]–[1.59].

[77] Text to n 71.

view that 'comity ... has little if any role to play where anti-suit injunctive relief is sought on the grounds of breach of contract'[78] rests upon the twin misconceptions that comity concerns itself with the risk of causing offence to the foreign court and that it aligns with the parties' agreement.

Comity acknowledges and embraces differences between legal systems in the pursuit of their common purpose of administering justice, and such differences do not in any way diminish its force.[79] Absent cogent evidence that the foreign proceedings imperil the due administration of justice in some fundamental respect,[80] the foreign court's legitimate claim to exercise its adjudicatory authority is a factor which should in all cases weigh heavily against the granting of an anti-suit injunction.

4. *Airbus*—'sufficient interest'

In *Airbus Industrie v Patel*, Lord Goff concluded that 'comity requires that the English forum should have a sufficient interest in, or connection with, the matter in question to justify the indirect interference with the foreign court which an anti-suit injunction entails'.[81] He distinguished 'alternative forum' cases from 'single forum' cases. In the former category, Lord Goff laid down the general rule[82] that England must be the natural forum for the resolution of the dispute, a test that he thought unsuitable for the latter category.[83]

The single/alternative forum distinction, originating in the speech of Lord Diplock in *British Airways v Laker Airways*,[84] has justifiably been criticised by Professor Briggs and others[85] for its apparent focus on the availability of a cause of action in the foreign forum rather than the 'availability' of that forum in the technical sense of being competent to determine the matters in issue between the parties.[86]

---

[78] In *Enka Insaat ve Sanayi AS v OOO Insurance Company Chubb* ([2020] UKSC 38, [2020] 1 WLR 4117 [180], [184] (Lords Hamblen and Leggatt, with whom Lord Kerr agreed; also [293] (Lord Sales) (hereafter *Enka*)).
At first instance ([2019] EWHC 3568 (Comm), [2020] 1 Lloyd's Rep 71, Andrew Baker J had suggested ([7]-[10], [81]-[82]) that the doctrine of *forum conveniens* (Section C.4) could play a decisive mediating role in such cases, but this approach was flatly rejected by the Court of Appeal ([2020] EWCA Civ 574, [2020] 3 All ER 577 [42]-[66]), with whose reasoning the Supreme Court agreed (*Enka*, above, [179], [184], [293]).

[79] *Connelly v RTZ Corporation plc* [1998] AC 854, 872-3 (Lord Goff) (*forum conveniens*).

[80] Text to n 63-6.

[81] *Airbus Industrie* (n 21) 138.

[82] *SAS Institute* (n 46) [108]-[110] (Males LJ).

[83] *Airbus Industrie* (n 21) 137-40. His Lordship put to one side (at 138) cases involving a contractual choice of forum (text to nn 69-78).

[84] *British Airways* (n 27) 80.

[85] Adrian Briggs, 'Anti-suit Injunctions in a Complex World' in Francis Rose (ed), *Lex Mercatoria: Essays in International Commercial Law in Honour of Francis Reynolds* (LLP 2000) 240-2 (hereafter Briggs, 'Anti-suit Injunctions in a Complex World'); Dicey, Morris & Collins (n 20) [12-089].

[86] Dicey, Morris & Collins (n 20) [12-032].

Although Lord Goff correctly emphasised the restraining effect of comity,[87] the focus in his 'general rule' on the suitability of the English forum for the trial of the injunction defendant's substantive claims seems misplaced—the court's focus at this juncture should instead be on the matters relied on to support and oppose the injunction.[88] Indeed, one questions whether there is any value in borrowing the concept of the 'natural forum' or the principle of *forum conveniens* more generally[89] from the set of rules governing questions of personal jurisdiction in order to answer a question concerning the legitimacy of judicial interference with the affairs of a foreign sovereign State.[90] Comity requires that the administration of justice in a foreign legal system should ordinarily be left to the courts of that system. If, however, the conditions for granting an injunction are met,[91] an English court may still conclude that it would not be an appropriate exercise of the judicial function to make the order, potentially affecting relations between the UK and a foreign State, if the forum's interests are not sufficiently engaged.[92] If, as in *Airbus*, the interests of a third legal system are also engaged in the matter, that is a factor to be taken into account in reaching that decision, but it is not of itself a reason for the exercise of restraint. So viewed, the question of 'sufficient interest' is merely one facet of the requirement that it be 'convenient' to grant the injunction.

5. Combining the conditions

The two conditions, justice and convenience, are cumulative. Accordingly, even if there are compelling reasons why the court considers that the public interest would be served by the granting of an anti-suit injunction, it cannot rest its decision on those considerations alone, but must identify a sufficient legal basis for the injunction.[93]

---

[87] Section C.3.
[88] *CSR Ltd v Cigna Insurance Australia Ltd* (1997) 189 CLR 345, 397 (hereafter *CSR*).
[89] cf *Amchem Products Inc v British Columbia (Workers' Compensation Board)* [1993] 1 SCR 897 (Sopinka J), piling complexity on complexity.
[90] Of course, the court may act only if it has personal jurisdiction over the defendant, and the principle of *forum conveniens* will often be relevant to that question.
[91] Sections C.2 and C.3.
[92] eg *SAS Institute* (n 46) [129].
[93] See Section D.3(e), considering whether an injunction may be granted in aid of the forum's public policy.

D. In Search of Principle

1. Emergence of the anti-suit injunction

At the turn of the 19th century, the jurisdiction of courts of equity to grant injunctions restraining proceedings before the common law courts and inferior local courts was well-established, and its contours well-defined.[94] That, of course, had not always been the case, the power secured only by the intervention of the King some two hundred years earlier, after a long and heated debate.[95]

In that debate, the arguments of Chancery lawyers in favour of the 'common injunction' were essentially threefold: first, that the injunction was directed to the person, or more accurately the conscience,[96] of the defendant rather than to the court in which the defendant was proceeding—it was not a writ of prohibition and acknowledged rather than denied the jurisdiction of the courts of common law;[97] secondly, that the courts of common law had long tolerated more direct interferences with their exercise of jurisdiction by the Chancery;[98] and, thirdly, that only the courts of equity were in a position to do complete justice in the case by reason of their extensive, and exclusive, jurisdiction to investigate certain matters (those of conscience) and their more extensive powers to discover the true circumstances of the case by eliciting evidence known only to the defendant.[99]

The first argument was wafer-thin from the outset. Lord Ellesmere's resort to the second line of defence betrays his lack of conviction in the 'no interference' rhetoric. Although Ellesmere did not rely on the second argument in the *Earl of Oxford*'s case, he did boast that 'the Precedents of [Chancery] shall close up the Mouths of the Judges of the Common Law', answering the (over-confident) claim to the contrary by Sir Christopher Yelverton, a justice of the Court of King's Bench.[100] Moreover, by the early 19th century, the Court of Chancery had begun to assert exclusive jurisdiction over the entire subject matter of the suit before it.[101] Indeed, the prosecution of proceedings at law during the pendency of the

---

[94] Section D.3(b).
[95] *The Earl of Oxford's Case* (1615) Rep Ch 1; 21 ER 485 (hereafter *Earl of Oxford's Case*), reproduced with notes in W J Whittaker and others, *A Selection of Leading Cases in Equity* (8th edn, Sweet & Maxwell 1910) vol I, 773ff; L A Knapfla, *Law and Politics in Jacobean England* (CUP 1977) ch VI-VII (hereafter Knapfla, *Law and Politics*).
[96] See n 179.
[97] *Earl of Oxford's Case* (n 95), 5-11, 486-7; Robert Henley Eden, *A Treatise on the Law of Injunctions* (W Gould & Co 1821) 4 (hereafter Eden, *Injunctions*).
[98] 'A Breviate of Direccion for the Kinges Learned Councell Collected by the Lord Chancellor Ellesmere' (September 1615) (hereafter Ellesmere, 'A Breviate'), reproduced in Knapfla, *Law and Politics* (n 95) ch XVI (esp 321-2).
[99] *Earl of Oxford's Case* (n 95), 5-7, 486; Ellesmere, 'A Breviate' (n 98) 321; Eden, *Injunctions* (n 97) 3-4.
[100] *Weaver v Clifford* (1603) Yel 42, 42; 80 ER 30, 30-1; Knapfla, *Law and Politics* (n 95) 163-4.
[101] William W Kerr, *A Treatise on the Law and Practice of Injunctions in Equity* (Blackstone 1867) 103-4 (hereafter Kerr, *Injunctions*).

Chancery proceedings was treated as a contempt of that court even if no injunction had yet been issued.[102] Chancery considered itself to be 'the Superior Court'.[103]

Neither of the first two arguments offers a persuasive justification for granting an injunction to restrain proceedings in a legal system that is independent of the legal system granting the injunction, as the United States' Supreme Court forcefully observed in *Peck v Jenness*:[104]

> [W]here the jurisdiction of a court, and the right of a plaintiff to prosecute his suit in it, have once attached that right cannot be arrested or taken away by proceedings in another court. These rules have their foundation, not merely in comity, but on necessity.[105] ... The fact ... that an injunction issues only to the parties before the court, and not to the court, is no evasion of the difficulties that are the necessary result of an attempt to exercise that power over a party who is a litigant in another and independent forum.

The third argument, which represented the most persuasive explanation for the common injunction within the English legal system, must also be adapted when applied to a foreign legal system. In domestic cases, equity fixed on a deficiency in the competence of the common law courts to adjudicate upon a particular subject matter, or in their mechanisms for delivering justice.[106] If the matters raised in Chancery could effectively be considered by the court seised, or another court with the power to review its decision, there was no equitable jurisdiction to intervene: the injunction defendant did not act unconscionably by pursuing his remedy at law.[107]

By contrast, unless the matter is one with respect to which the English court claims exclusive jurisdiction,[108] the English courts must act on the assumption that the courts of the foreign legal system are omnicompetent to determine the matters in dispute and will act justly, absent cogent evidence to the contrary.[109] The relationships between the English legal system and foreign legal systems were (and

---

[102] *Phelps v Prothero* (1855) 7 De GM & G 722, 734; 44 ER 280, 285 (Turner LJ), referring to the judgment of Lord Redesdale in the Irish case of *Bell v O'Reilly* (1805) 2 Sch & Lef 430; also Story, *Commentaries* (n 59) vol II, 226–7; *Grant v Dawkins* [1973] 1 WLR 1406, 1409 (Goff J).

[103] Anon, 'A Vindication of the Judgment Given by King James in the Case of the Jurisdiction of the Court of Chancery', reproduced in F Hargrave, *Collectanea Juridica* (London 1791) 23ff, 32; 1 Ch Rep (App) 576ff, 579.

[104] *Peck v Jenness* (1849) 48 US 612, 625 (Grier J) (hereafter *Peck*).

[105] The court pointed, in particular, to the possibility of each court granting an injunction, resulting in a denial of justice to both parties.

[106] Section D.3(b).

[107] *Hardinge v Webster* (1859) 1 Drew & Sm 101, 62 ER 326; *Ochsenbein v Papelier* (1872) LR 8 Ch App 695 (hereafter *Ochsenbein*); *Bateman v Willoe* (1803) 1 Sch & Lefr 204; Kerr, *Injunctions* (n 101), 14–15; Story, *Commentaries* (n 59) vol II, 231–4.

[108] Text to nn 237–9.

[109] Text to nn 61–6.

are) fundamentally different from those between the Court of Chancery and other courts within the English legal system prior to the Judicature Acts.

From the 17th century onwards, litigants nonetheless sought to extend the equitable jurisdiction to proceedings brought in legal systems outside England. In an early case, the Earl of Clarendon LC expressed the view that this would set a 'dangerous' precedent, but his opinion did not command universal support[110] and merely postponed equity's advance. Subsequently, in 1799, Lord Loughborough LC granted an injunction restraining proceedings before the Court of Session pending the taking of an account in English proceedings, although the question of jurisdiction was not argued.[111] Some twenty years later, in *Kennedy v Cassilis*, Lord Eldon did not doubt that he had the power to make such an order, but was not willing to restrain 'another Court of competent jurisdiction',[112] influenced by a finding that the Scots action was *bona fide* and the fact that the case was one in which co-operation between the two systems was needed to do justice.[113]

A very different attitude prevailed in *Bushby v Munday*.[114] In that case, Sir John Leach asserted that he had 'full authority to act upon [the defendants] personally with respect to the subject of the suit, as the ends of justice require; and with that view, to order them to take, or to omit to take, any steps and proceedings in any other Court of Justice, whether in this country, or in a foreign country',[115] there being, he thought, no pretence of interference with the foreign court.[116] Having considered the powers of the Scots court to gather evidence, he granted the injunction on the basis that the 'substantial ends of justice' required that the Chancery Court 'should pursue its own better means of determining both the law and the fact of the case'.[117]

Although *Bushby* was later described as going to the 'very verge of the law',[118] it opened the gates.[119] In *Portarlington v Soulby*, involving Irish proceedings, Lord Brougham LC declined to follow the Earl of Clarendon's earlier opinion.[120] In his view, the matter was no different in principle from any case involving an injunction to do, or refrain from doing, an act abroad.[121] It was, he thought, no answer to argue that an injunction could equally have been sought from the Courts of Equity

---

[110] *Love v Baker* (1665) 1 Ch Cas 67, 22 ER 698 ('all the Bar was of another opinion'); (1665) Nels 103, 21 ER 801 ('all the Barons were of another Opinion').
[111] *Wharton v May* (1799) 3 Ves Jun 27, 31 ER 454; also Raphael, *The Anti-Suit Injunction* (n 4) [2.05].
[112] (1818) 2 Swans 313, 318; 36 ER 635, 637.
[113] Ibid 322–3; 638.
[114] *Bushby* (n 24).
[115] Ibid 307; 913.
[116] Ibid; also 309; 914.
[117] Ibid 308; 913.
[118] *Carron Iron Co v Maclaren* (1855) 5 HLC 416, 446; 10 ER 961, 973 (Lord Brougham) (hereafter *Carron Iron*).
[119] eg *Harrison v Gurney* (1821) 7 Jac & W 563, 37 ER 743; *Beauchamp v Huntley* (1822) Jac 546, 37 ER 956 (hereafter *Beauchamp v Huntley*); *Beckford v Kemble* (1822) 1 Sim & St 7, 57 ER 3.
[120] (1834) 7 Sim 28, 107; 40 ER 40, 41.
[121] Ibid 108; 42.

in Ireland.[122] In *Bunbury v Bunbury*, Lord Langdale MR took the extraordinary step of making an order restraining proceedings in Demerara on terms which enabled him to manage the proceedings for the English court's benefit.[123] In the same period, however, there were also notable examples of judicial restraint, founded upon a declared willingness to assume that justice could and would be done in the foreign forum.[124]

In *Carron Iron Co v Maclaren*,[125] the jurisdictional question was debated before the House of Lords, which affirmed the power to grant an injunction restraining foreign proceedings, but discharged the injunction made in that case. Having reviewed the authorities, Lord Cranworth LC concluded that:[126]

> [I]f the circumstances are such as would make it the duty of the Court to restrain a party from instituting proceedings in this country, they will also warrant it in restraining proceedings in a foreign court. But though they will justify such a course, yet they will not ... make it the duty of the Court so to act, if from any cause it appears likely to be more conducive to substantial justice that the foreign proceedings should be left to take their course.

This passage must be approached with care. In suggesting an alignment of the grounds for granting injunctions to restrain local and foreign proceedings, it overlooks the point that the two situations differ greatly.[127] By demanding positive proof that the foreign proceedings advance the interests of justice, it undermines comity.[128]

Greater heed was paid to these considerations in two important decisions of the Court of Appeal shortly after the Judicature Acts. In *Peruvian Guano v Bockwoldt*,[129] the Court of Appeal acknowledged that different considerations applied to domestic and foreign cases. Jessel MR warned of the danger of depriving foreign claimants of the opportunity to assert their rights *bona fide*.[130] Lindley MR noted that the English court is not and cannot be alive to all the advantages a person may expect to derive from suing abroad.[131] Bowen LJ emphasised the need

---

[122] Ibid 109; 42.
[123] (1839) 1 Beav 318, 335–6; 48 ER 963, 969.
[124] *Wallace v Campbell* (1840) 4 Y&C Ex 167, 168; 160 ER 964, 964 (Lord Abinger CB: 'I must take for granted that the Court in Madeira will do justice as well as the Court here'); *Pennell v Roy* (1850) 3 De G, M & G 126, 140; 43 ER 50, 56 (Turner LJ: 'the duty of this Court to give credit to foreign Courts for doing justice in their own jurisdiction'); *Hyman v Helm* (1883) 24 ChD 531, 539 (Brett MR) (hereafter *Hyman*); *Baird v Prescott and Co* (1890) 6 TLR 231, 233 (Lord Esher MR); *Vardopulo v Vardopulo* (1909) 25 TLR 518 (Cozens-Hardy MR).
[125] *Carron Iron* (n 118).
[126] Ibid 439; 971.
[127] Text to nn 106–9.
[128] Text to nn 61–6.
[129] (1882) 23 ChD 225 (hereafter *Peruvian Guano*).
[130] Ibid 232.
[131] Ibid 232.

for care in exercising 'this sort of dictatorial power of interfering with actions'.[132] In *Hyman v Helm*, the Court of Appeal emphasised that the burden lay on the injunction claimant to justify the intervention. As Bowen LJ put it, 'it lies on the person who wishes to stop a foreign litigation to make out a clear case'.[133]

Although the jurisdiction of the English High Court to grant an injunction to restrain foreign proceedings was recognised by the end of the 19th century, one searches in vain for guiding principles. It was, with respect to Lord Goff, unsatisfactory to conclude that these cases establish a 'fundamental principle' that 'the jurisdiction is to be exercised when the "ends of justice" require it'.[134] The search turns to the more recent past.

2. Framework uncertainty

In *South Carolina Insurance Co v Assurantie Maatschappij de Zeven Provincien NV*, Lord Brandon asserted that:[135]

> [T]he power of the High Court to grant injunctions is, subject to two exceptions ... limited to two situations. Situation (1) is when one party to an action can show that the other party has either invaded, or threatens to invade a legal or equitable right of the former for the enforcement of which the latter is amenable to the jurisdiction of the court. Situation (2) is where one party to an action has behaved, or threatens to behave, in a manner which is unconscionable.

Several points follow from this formulation.

First, the 'two exceptions' to which Lord Brandon referred were (i) the freezing (*Mareva*) injunction,[136] and (ii) the view expressed by the House of Lords in *Castanho v Brown & Root*[137] that proceedings could be restrained if brought in an inappropriate forum, mirroring the courts' evolving power to stay proceedings on *forum conveniens* grounds.[138] *Castanho* proved to be a wrong-turning, corrected

---

[132] Ibid 234.
[133] *Hyman* (n 124) 544.
[134] *SNI Aerospatiale* (n 20) 892.
[135] *South Carolina* (n 45) 40.
[136] *Mareva Compania Naviera SA v International Bulkcarriers SA* [1975] 2 Lloyd's Rep 509; Senior Courts Act 1981, s 37(3).

The latter provision, affirming the High Court's power to grant an injunction restraining dealings with locally situate assets, had the (unhappy) effect of stymying debate as to the juridical nature and basis of the freezing injunction (cf *Mercedes Benz v Leiduck* (n 43) 299–301 (Lord Mustill), 306–12 (Lord Nicholls); also *Bi Xiaoqing v China Medical Technologies* [2019] SGCA 50).

[137] *Castanho* (n 27) 575 (Lord Scarman, with whom Lords Wilberforce, Diplock, Keith and Bridge agreed).

[138] *South Carolina* (n 45) 40. The development of the *forum conveniens* doctrine was completed in *Spiliada Maritime Corp v Cansulex Ltd* [1987] AC 460.

by the Privy Council (led by Lord Goff[139]) in *Société Nationale Industrielle Aerospatiale Appellants v Lee Kui Jak*.[140] These cases now fall under Lord Brandon's 'situation (2)' (unconscionability).[141]

Secondly, in *SNI Aerospatiale*, the Board accepted the proposition that (absent violation of a legal or equitable right—situation (1)) the court will generally grant an injunction only if the pursuit of litigation abroad is 'vexatious or oppressive'.[142] In *South Carolina*, Lord Brandon had treated 'conduct which is oppressive or vexatious or which interferes with the due process of the court' as the paradigm examples of 'unconscionable conduct'.[143] Thirty years on, the role that vexatious or oppressive conduct plays in this framework remains uncertain. It has been treated variously as a synonym for unconscionable conduct[144] and as an alternative to it.[145] It has also occasionally been suggested that the concepts of vexation and oppression underpin both of Lord Brandon's 'situations'.[146] In *Turner v Grovit*, Lord Hobhouse treated 'vexatious' and 'oppressive' as merely colourful labels for individual cases of 'unconscionable' (in the sense of equitably wrongful) conduct.[147] By contrast, the Privy Council in *Stichting Shell Pensioenfonds v Krys* suggested a separation between 'vexatious harassing of the opposing party', proceedings that are 'vexatious in a larger sense' and 'cases which do not turn on the vexatious character of the foreign litigant's conduct ... in which foreign proceedings are restrained because they are "contrary to equity and good conscience"'.[148]

Thirdly, the relationship between equitable right and unconscionable conduct remains equally uncertain. In *British Airways v Laker Airways*, Lord Diplock appeared to treat the two as indistinguishable.[149] By contrast, in *Masri v Consolidated Contractors (No 3)*, Lawrence Collins LJ (as was) sought to distinguish 'a cause of action based on a legal or equitable right not to be sued' from 'an equitable remedy to protect the plaintiff against the consequences of unconscionable conduct'.[150]

---

[139] Alongside Lords Keith, Griffiths and Mackay and Sir John Megaw.
[140] *SNI Aerospatiale* (n 20) 894–7. See Section D.2(f) below.
[141] *Masri v Consolidated Contractors International Co SAL (No 3)* [2008] EWCA Civ 625, [2009] QB 503 [41], [48] (Lawrence Collins LJ) (hereafter *Masri (No 3)*).
[142] *SNI Aerospatiale* (n 20) 896.
[143] *South Carolina* (n 45) 41; also *CSR* (n 88) 393–4.
[144] eg *Sabah Shipyard (Pakistan) Ltd v Pakistan* [2002] EWCA Civ 650 [29] (Clarke LJ); *Sabbagh v Khoury* [2019] EWCA Civ 1219, [2019] 2 Lloyd's Rep 178 [105] (David Richards LJ).
[145] eg *Masri (No 3)* (n 141) [19], [39], [48] (Lawrence Collins LJ); *The Yusuf Cepnioglu* [2016] EWCA Civ 687, [2016] 1 Lloyd's Rep 61 [55] (Moore Bick LJ) (hereafter *The Yusuf Cepnioglu*); also *Airbus Industrie* (n 21) 134 (Lord Goff), contrasting 'single forum' and 'alternative forum' cases (see text to nn 84–6).
[146] eg *Clearlake Shipping Pte Ltd v Xiang Da Marine Pte Ltd* [2019] EWHC 1536 (Comm) [32] (Bryan J), but compare the reasoning of Andrew Burrows QC (now Lord Burrows) in a later decision in the same case, [2019] EWHC 2284 (Comm) [18].
[147] *Turner v Grovit* (n 12) [24].
[148] *Stichting Shell* (n 65) [18], referring to the judgment of Lord Cranworth in *Carron Iron* (n 118) 437–9; 971.
[149] *British Airways* (n 27) 81.
[150] *Masri (No 3)* (n 141) [46]–[59].

To illustrate a case in which there was an equitable remedy but no equitable right (cause of action), his Lordship cited *The Jay Bola*[151] in which an insurer subrogated to the insured sub-charterer's rights under a charterparty was restrained from suing the charterer otherwise than in accordance with the charterparty's arbitration clause. The reasoning in that case does not, however, support the distinction suggested in *Masri (No 3)*: Hobhouse LJ considered the insurer's disregard of the charterer's 'equitable right' to insist upon arbitration to be 'unconscionable conduct' justifying the equitable remedy of an injunction.[152] He sought to distinguish this equitable remedy for 'failing to recognise the equitable rights of the ... charterers' from a claim that the insurer had breached the charterparty giving a right to sue for damages: the claim for an injunction was not a cause of action 'of the same character' as a damages claim, but it was a cause of action founded on an equitable right of the claimant not to be sued by the defendant otherwise than in accordance with the terms of the charterparty.[153]

Fourthly, the High Court of Australia has distinguished cases involving the exercise of 'equitable jurisdiction' from those in which anti-suit injunctions are granted in the exercise of the court's inherent power to protect the integrity of its proceedings.[154] In *South Carolina*, Lord Goff suggested that the general purpose of anti-suit injunctions was to protect the court's jurisdiction,[155] but he was unable to persuade either the majority of his colleagues in that case or his Privy Council colleagues in *Aerospatiale* of the correctness of that view.[156] In *South Carolina*, Lord Brandon referred to conduct 'which interferes with the due process of the court' as an example of unconscionable conduct.[157] In *Masri (No 3)*, Lawrence Collins LJ seized on this and other *dicta*[158] to support the proposition that:[159]

> As a matter of English law, once the court has jurisdiction over the substance of the case, it has jurisdiction to make ancillary orders, including anti-suit injunctions to protect the integrity of its process.

Even so, the precise legal basis, and limits, of this asserted power to protect the court's adjudicatory jurisdiction[160] remain unclear. From time to time, English

---

[151] Ibid [46].
[152] *Schiffahrtsgesellschaft Detlev von Appen GmbH v Voest Alpine Intertrading GmbH (The Jay Bola)* [1997] 2 Lloyd's Rep 279, 286 (Hobhouse LJ).
[153] Ibid; also *The Yusuf Cepnioglu* (n 145) [33] (Longmore LJ), [55] (Moore Bick LJ).
[154] CSR (n 88) 391–2.
[155] *South Carolina* (n 45) 45.
[156] *SNI Aerospatiale* (n 20) 892–3; also *Bank of Tokyo* (n 20) 60, describing the protection of the court's jurisdiction as 'the golden thread running through the rare cases where an injunction has been granted'.
[157] *South Carolina* (n 45) 41.
[158] *Masri (No 3)* (n 141) [83]–[88].
[159] Ibid [59].
[160] Section D.3(e).

judges have suggested that the court has an inherent jurisdiction to grant anti-suit injunctions to aid its own process.[161] In *Stichting Shell*, however, the Privy Council identified protection of the jurisdiction as a basis for granting an anti-suit injunction, distinct from cases of vexatious or oppressive conduct, but equally rooted in the equitable jurisdiction founded in 'good conscience'.[162] It is unclear, therefore, whether and, if so, how injunctions issued to protect the court's own jurisdiction fall within Lord Brandon's attempted categorisation.

Fifthly, in *Bank of Tokyo v Karoon*, Robert Goff LJ (as he then was) also suggested that anti-suit injunctions could be granted 'to protect the litigant's evasion of the important public polices of the forum'.[163] If that suggestion, which has attracted occasional judicial support, is correct, it represents another 'exceptional' category.[164]

Taking these points into account, the defects in Lord Brandon's framework are such that it seems desirable to set it aside in the search for principle. That was, in effect, what Lord Hobhouse sought to do in *Turner v Grovit*. He explained the power to grant an anti-suit injunction as resting upon 'wrongful conduct of the party to be restrained of which the applicant is entitled to complain and has a legitimate interest in seeking to prevent',[165] separating cases of contractual and non-contractual wrongdoing, and classifying 'unconscionable conduct' as an equitable species of non-contractual wrongdoing.[166] The High Court of Australia's analysis of its equitable jurisdiction in *CSR v Cigna* supports a similar distinction between injunctions in the aid of legal rights and injunctions restraining unconscionable conduct.[167] Although the High Court also asserted the Australian courts' distinct (inherent) power to regulate their own proceedings,[168] Lord Hobhouse relegated protection of the jurisdiction to a factor of secondary importance in his own framework.[169] That subordination is, perhaps, explained by their Lordships' wish in *Turner* to persuade the European Court of Justice that the anti-suit injunction was a straightforward private law remedy rather than an act of judicial pre-emption.[170]

In his own writing, Professor Briggs has suggested a tripartite scheme. His first two categories, breach of contract and vexatious or oppressive behaviour, are classed under 'private law wrongdoing'; the third (protection of the court's jurisdiction) under 'public law wrongdoing'.[171] This is an appealing starting point for

---

[161] eg *Glencore International AG v Exter Shipping Co Ltd* [2002] EWCA Civ 528, [2002] 2 All ER (Comm) 1 [23] (Moore Bick J), [60] (Rix LJ); also *Ebert v Venvil* [2000] Ch 484, 496–7 (Lord Woolf MR). cf *Nursing & Midwifery Council v Harrold* [2015] EWHC 2254 (QB) [27] (Hamblen LJ).
[162] *Stichting Shell* (n 65) [18]–[24].
[163] *Bank of Tokyo* (n 20) 60.
[164] Section D.3(e).
[165] *Turner v Grovit* (n 12) [24].
[166] Ibid [24]–[25].
[167] *CSR* (n 88) 392–3.
[168] Section D.3(e).
[169] *Turner v Grovit* (n 12) [26]–[29], [34].
[170] The Court of Justice saw through the attempted disguise: *Turner* (n 21) [27]–[29]. See also Case C-185/07 *Allianz SpA v West Tankers Inc* [2009] ECR I-663.
[171] Briggs, *Private International Law in English Courts* (n 6) [5.114]–[5.120].

further analysis, but (as Professor Briggs is quick to recognise[172]) is neither complete nor free from difficulty.

3. Rule uncertainty

Analysis of the law concerning anti-suit injunctions requires one to strip away the layers of the judicially created onion. At each stage, one encounters a fear of definition and an aversion to fleshing out the detail of the law.

(a) The 'ends of justice'

Although the 'ends of justice' may be 'a deliberately imprecise expression', as Lord Sumption has suggested,[173] it does not (and should not) follow that the underlying rules are themselves imprecise.[174] The need for legal certainty is particularly important given that the effect of the order is to prevent a party from exercising rights of access to a court under threat of penal sanctions.

The influential decision of the Privy Council in *SNI Aerospatiale*[175] is a case in point. For as much as the opinion given by Lord Goff contains an erudite summary of several aspects of the law on anti-suit injunctions, it is difficult to extract a single reason or set of reasons to explain why the widow and personal representatives of Mr Yoon were prevented from pursuing their claims in Texas. Before returning to this point, let us consider possible reasons, and the uncertainties surrounding them.

(b) 'Unconscionable conduct'

That category of 'unconscionable conduct' could never be captured by a single definition,[176] as the word 'unconscionable' does no more than signify the presence of circumstances warranting the exercise of equitable jurisdiction.[177] That jurisdiction (inherited from the former courts of equity[178]) depends upon the court having sufficient reason to act upon the defendant's conscience,[179] and that is a matter not of individual moral judgement but of applying rules and principles developed

---

[172] Ibid [5.104] ('even the degree of organization proposed here may be unhelpful').
[173] *Stichting Shell* (n 65) [18].
[174] Section C.1. cf *Michael Wilson* (n 42) [36].
[175] Section D.3(f).
[176] *South Carolina* (n 45) 41.
[177] *Barclays Bank v Homan* (n 61) 762 (Hoffmann J).
[178] Section C.2.
[179] *Penn v Lord Baltimore* (1750) 1 Ves Sen 444, 447; 27 ER 1132, 1134–5 (Lord Hardwicke LC); *Pilcher v Rawlins* (1872) LR 7 Ch App 259, 266 (Lord Hatherley LC).
A judicial tendency to assume that the equitable jurisdiction to grant an injunction rests only on the court's ability to exercise power over the defendant's person (eg *Fourie* (n 32) [30]) misses this point: it is the defendant's 'soul' not his body with which equity is concerned.

by the courts over centuries and covering a wide range of subject matter.[180] The following statement, written in the middle of the 19th century, remains valuable today:[181]

> In determining whether the remedy given by the Courts of ordinary jurisdiction comes up to the requisitions of complete justice, a Court of equity does not exercise a mere arbitrary discretion. Complete justice, as understood by a Court of equity, though originally founded on the principles of natural justice and reason, has by authority, decision and statute long grown into a system, and assumed a technical consistency and shape, and must be contradistinguished from all considerations of discretion, fairness, and equal justice in the popular sense of the word. The principles of equity are as fixed and certain as the principles upon which the Courts of common law proceed.

The modern judicial reluctance to unpack 'unconscionability' may be contrasted with the detailed treatment in 19th-century legal texts of the equitable jurisdiction to grant injunctions to restrain proceedings at common law. The account in Robert Eden's valuable 1821 treatise begins with the following general statement:[182]

> It frequently happens that a person, in consequence of some circumstance of which judicial notice can only be taken in a court of equity, has an advantage in proceeding in a court of ordinary jurisdiction, which must make that court an instrument of injustice. There are so many cases in which the legal defence to a claim set up at law rests either exclusively, or in a great degree, within the knowledge of the party advancing the claim, by which means, that defence can only be obtained through the assistance of a court of equity. As it is against conscience therefore that the party should in the one case, make any use of the advantage of which he is thus inequitably possessed, or that he should in the other proceed in the assertion of his claim, without communicating the information, it has become one of the most ordinary modes of equitable interposition to afford relief by Injunctions to stay proceedings at law ... An Injunction ... is granted on the sole ground that from certain equitable circumstances, of which the court that issues it has cognizance, it is against conscience for the party to proceed in the cause.

---

[180] DR Klinck, 'Lord Nottingham and the Conscience of Equity' (2006) 67 Journal of the History of Ideas 123, 124, describing Lord Nottingham as 'the father of *systemic* equity' and noting his objection to 'the kind of conscience that amounted only "to the pleasure of a Court which took upon itself to be purely arbitrary"' (see *Earl of Feversham v Watson* (1678), DEC Yale (ed), *Lord Nottingham's Chancery Cases* (London 1961) vol 2, 639).
[181] Kerr, *Injunctions* (n 101) 3–4.
[182] Eden, *Injunctions* (n 97) 3–4; also Story, *Commentaries* (n 59) vol II, 216–8.

The remainder of Eden's chapter, running to over forty pages, describes the cases in which the court will (or will not) assume to act upon the defendant's conscience in restraining common law actions. This account is sub-divided into cases of accident, mistake, fraud (including duress, undue influence and improper conduct by fiduciaries), 'underhand agreements' (including transactions contrary to statutes), discovery, relief against forfeiture and penalties, injunctions in the nature of specific performance, account, the administration of assets, election between remedies in equity and at common law, relief after a decree in equity, marshalling of securities, protection of sureties and criminal cases.[183] The topic of 'injunctions to restrain vexatious litigation' is covered separately in a later chapter.[184]

Although anti-suit injunctions stand apart from common injunctions in terms of the detail,[185] the point worth emphasising here is that there was no reticence, of judges or legal commentators, in the 19th century to specify the grounds upon which common injunctions would issue. They were not content to rest with an ill-defined category of 'unconscionable conduct', but sought to identify particular circumstances in which the common law court was ill-equipped, in terms of the substantive legal rules being applied or the court's procedural powers, to deliver justice in the parties' dispute.[186] Far from being a guiding principle, use of the language of 'conscience' served in 19th-century accounts either to acknowledge the Court of Chancery's origins or as a label to signal the presence of a sufficient (and identified) ground for equitable intervention.

Today, a century and a half after the Judicature Acts, it is time to discard the language of unconscionability here and elsewhere in the (wider) common law. A vestige of an earlier monotheistic society, it no longer performs any useful role and obscures the real reasons for granting injunctions. The contention that 'unconscionability' offers an 'essentially objective' standard 'reflecting a societal norm for acceptable and unacceptable conduct'[187] overlooks modern pluralistic usage of conscience to describe inner, personal reflection on what is right and wrong,[188] and underplays the significance of defendant's subjective knowledge in defining the limits of equitable jurisdiction.[189]

---

[183] Eden, *Injunctions* ch II; also chs IV–VIII.
[184] Ibid ch XVI.
[185] Text to nn 106–9.
[186] *Ochsenbein* (n 107) 697 (Lord Selbourne LC).
[187] Sir Terence Etherton MR, 'Equity and Conscience' (Eldon Professor's Lecture, Northumbria University, 25 October 2017), <https://www.judiciary.uk/wp-content/uploads/2017/10/sir-terence-etherton-mr-eldon-lecture-20171030.pdf> accessed 1 October 2020 [44], [50], [57]; also S Agnew, 'The Meaning and Significance of Conscience in Private Law' (2018) 77 CLJ 479.
[188] Alberto Guibilinim 'Conscience' (Stanford Encyclopaedia of Philosophy, 14 March 2016), <https://plato.stanford.edu/entries/conscience/> accessed 1 October 2020.
[189] eg *Bank of Credit and Commerce International (Overseas) Ltd v Akindele* [2000] EWCA Civ 502, [2001] Ch 347, 455 (Nourse LJ).

(c) 'Vexatious' and 'oppressive' conduct

At the next layer, the obfuscation extends to the category of vexatious or oppressive conduct. In the late 19th century, Bowen LJ suggested that it was 'unwise' to lay down a definition, or 'draw a circle' around the court's powers to intervene 'to prevent the administration of justice being perverted for an unjust end'.[190] In *SNI Aerospatiale*, Lord Goff took this as a mandate to exemplify, treating the terms 'vexatious' and 'oppressive' as labels for conduct warranting the English court's intervention.[191] In *UBS AG New York v Fairfield Sentry Ltd*, the Privy Council asserted that the 'general nature' of 'vexatious and oppressive litigation' was 'clear', but again offered only examples rather than a definition.[192] Although others (including Professor Briggs) have endorsed this approach,[193] it takes reticence too far. An understandable wish not to tie the hands of judges in future cases has translated to a refusal to capture even the essence of the reason for intervention.

The modern approach also overlooks the significance of Bowen LJ's characterisation of the power to intervene to prevent 'vexation or oppression' by reference to the improper purpose of the proceedings in question.[194] That is a critical feature in the earlier case law. In the same case, Jessel MR (with the concurrence of Cotton and Bowen LJJ) declined to characterise concurrent litigation in England and the United States as 'vexatious' as there existed a 'very strong ground for saying that the actions are not only brought *bona fide*, but with a decided intention to enforce the remedy to which the Plaintiff believes himself entitled'.[195] Subsequently, in *Peruvian Guano Co v Bockwoldt*, the Master of the Rolls referred to an action 'so utterly absurd that the Judge sees it cannot possibly succeed, and that it is brought only for annoyance'[196] while asserting that 'it is not vexatious to bring an action in each country where there are substantial reasons of benefit to the plaintiff'.[197] Bowen LJ, while acknowledging that the courts would interfere 'to prevent a plaintiff under colour of asking for justice from harassing others', asserted that the court had 'no sort of right, moral or legal, to take away from a plaintiff any real chance he may have of an advantage'.[198] A century later, the High Court of Australia cited *McHenry* and *Peruvian Guano*, among other cases, to support the

---

[190] *McHenry v Lewis* (1882) 22 ChD 397, 407–8 (hereafter *McHenry*); also *Hill v Hart-Davis* (1884) 26 ChD 470, 473 ('It is better to determine in each case whether the circumstances are such as to come within a perfectly intelligible expression').

[191] *SNI Aerospatiale* (n 20) 893–4 (Lord Goff).

[192] [2019] UKPC 20, [2019] BCC 966 [20].

[193] *Deutsche Bank v Highland* (n 46) [50(3)] (Toulson LJ); Briggs, *Private International Law in English Courts* (n 6) [5.12].

[194] 'perverted for an unjust end' (text to n 190).

[195] *McHenry* (n 190) 403.

Note, however, that the defendant's *bona fide* belief in its rights does not necessarily excuse: *Logan v Bank of Scotland* (No 2) [1906] 1 KB 141, 151 (Gorell Barnes P, referring to 'a mind which held a distorted view of the matter such as no reasonable person ought to entertain').

[196] *Peruvian Guano* (n 129) 230.

[197] Ibid 225; also *Hyman* (n 124).

[198] *Peruvian Guano* (n 129) 233–4 (Bowen LJ); 232–3 (Lindley LJ).

proposition that 'foreign proceedings are to be viewed as vexatious or oppressive only if there is nothing to be gained by them over and above what may be gained in local proceedings'.[199]

In *The Atlantic Star*, Lord Kilbrandon (presciently) thought the terms 'vexatious' and 'oppressive' to be inappropriate in defining the limits of the court's power to grant a stay.[200] He offered, however, the following working definitions of the two concepts, describing them as 'grave allegations':[201]

> 'Oppressive' is an adjective which ought to be, and today normally is, confined to deliberate acts of moral, though not necessarily legal, delinquency, such as an unfair abuse of power by the stronger party in order that a weaker party may be put in difficulties in obtaining his just rights. 'Vexatious' today has overtones of irresponsible pursuit of litigation by someone who either knows he has no proper cause of action, or is mentally incapable of forming a rational opinion on that topic.

These working definitions accord with the earlier case law, and offer valuable insights. The essence of 'vexation' is the use of judicial process in the absence of a genuine purpose of securing a just determination of one's legal entitlement[202] whereas 'oppression' involves acts of interference to impede another in securing such a determination. In each case, the foreign proceedings are being used as an instrument of injustice.

If the injunction claimant demonstrates to the court's satisfaction that there is no advantage, pursued for good reason,[203] in the foreign proceedings, the English court (having considered all relevant circumstances) may justifiably infer that the foreign claimant has an ulterior, improper purpose in pursuing the claim. The English court may also reach that conclusion if, for example, the foreign proceedings are manifestly without merit[204] or substantially duplicate the subject matter of proceedings already pending elsewhere.[205] The injunction defendant's conduct may also be characterised as vexatious if it sues in a forum lacking any significant connection with the parties or the subject matter of the claim.[206] Otherwise—unless

---

[199] *CSR* (n 88) 393.
[200] *The Atlantic Star* (n 15) 477.
[201] Ibid.
[202] So defined, it is an equitable counterpart to the common law tort of malicious prosecution (*Willers v Joyce* [2016] UKSC 44, [2018] AC 843).
[203] *Hyman* (n 124) 538 (Brett MR), 543–4 (Bowen LJ).
[204] eg *British Airways* (n 27) 86–7 (Lord Diplock); *SNI Aerospatiale* (n 20) 893 (Lord Goff); *Star Reefers Pool Inc v JFC Group Co Ltd* [2012] EWCA Civ 14, [2012] 1 Lloyd's Rep 376 [31], [36] (Rix LJ) (hereafter *Star Reefers*).
[205] eg *Hyman* (n 124) 538 (Brett MR), 539–40 (Cotton LJ); *SNI Aerospatiale* (n 20) 893–4; *Australian Commercial Research and Development Ltd v ANZ McCaughan Merchant Bank Ltd* [1989] 3 All ER 65, affd [1990] 2 WLUK 351 (hereafter *Australian Commercial Research*).
[206] eg *Midland Bank plc v Laker Airways Ltd* [1986] QB 689 (CA).

the available evidence establishes that the injunction defendant has an ulterior purpose,[207] has interfered with the due administration of justice or is likely to do so[208]—a foreign claimant does not act vexatiously or oppressively if it pursues its interest in securing an advantageous determination, using whatever advantages, procedural or substantive, the foreign legal system may confer on it.[209] The court should not 'search for darker motives'.[210]

(d) Anti-suit injunctions as a remedy for wrongdoing

There is no need for the courts to strain these bases for equitable intervention when others are more appropriate. A party who brings proceedings abroad in breach of a contractual promise to do so acts wrongfully[211] irrespective of its purpose in bringing those proceedings, and there is no need for its conduct to be characterised as 'vexatious' or 'oppressive'.[212] So too if a party commits perjury to secure a favourable foreign judgment: common law or equitable doctrines of fraud offer a more than adequate basis for the injunction.[213] In these cases, as well as in cases of vexation and oppression, the injunction defendant's commission of a legal or equitable wrong against the injunction claimant makes the granting of the anti-suit injunction just, as a private law remedy.

If that proposition is accepted, two questions remain. First, a logically prior choice of law question, as to whether English law or a foreign law should be applied to the claim of wrongdoing. Secondly, whether the injunction is the appropriate remedy. The first question will be considered below.[214] The second takes us back to the section 37(1) conditions. The injunction defendant's wrongdoing towards the injunction claimant makes it 'just' to issue an injunction, but it must also be 'convenient' to do so.[215]

This essay contends that the English court must account for the substantial impacts that the injunction will have on the foreign court's relationships with the litigating parties and its ability to carry out its constitutional functions, and

---

[207] eg *Turner v Grovit* [2000] QB 345 (CA), although the injunction granted in that case was held contrary to EU law (see n 170 above).
The technique proposed here, combining direct proof of wrongdoing with a willingness to draw inferences from the evidence in particular circumstances, has also found favour in the equitable doctrine of undue influence (*Royal Bank of Scotland plc v Etridge* (No 2) [2001] UKHL 44, [2002] 2 AC 773).
[208] cf *A/S D/S Svendborg v Wansa* [1996] 2 Lloyd's Rep 559, affd [1997] 2 Lloyd's Rep 183 (hereafter *Svendborg v Wansa*) with *Al-Bassam v Al-Bassam* [2004] EWCA Civ 857.
[209] *Star Reefers Pool* (n 204) [32]–[39], a rare beacon of lucidity in the modern English case law; also *Navig8 Pte Ltd v Al-Riyadh Co for Vegetable Industry* [2013] 2 Lloyd's Rep 104 [22] (Andrew Smith J). cf *Cood v Cood* (1863) 33 Beav 314, 55 ER 388.
[210] *SAS Institute* (n 46) [44] (Males LJ).
[211] *Pena Copper Mines v Rio Tinto Co* (1911) 105 LT 846 is an early example.
[212] *Clearlake Shipping Pte Ltd v Xiang Da Marine Pte Ltd* [2019] EWHC 2284 (Comm) [18] (Andrew Burrows QC). cf *Settlement Corpn v Hochschild* [1966] Ch 10; *Masri (No 3)* (n 141) [39].
[213] *Ellerman Lines Ltd v Read* [1928] 2 KB 144.
[214] Section D.4.
[215] Section C.5.

that an English court should refrain from issuing an anti-suit injunction unless there is cogent evidence that the foreign proceedings seriously undermine the due administration of justice, or are likely to do so.[216] In addressing the question of 'convenience' in cases of allegedly wrongful conduct on the part of the injunction defendant, the English court must also consider, in particular, whether the foreign forum provides the injunction claimant with an adequate remedy for the conduct complained of, for example, by staying or striking out proceedings, the exclusion of evidence, the setting aside of a judgment obtained by fraud or an order for costs. In that enquiry, the court 'must have regard to fundamental principles of justice and not to the letter of the rules which, either in our system, or in the relevant foreign system, are designed to give effect to those principles'.[217]

If the foreign court does offer an adequate remedy, which it would be reasonable for the injunction claimant to pursue, the English court should leave it to do so, and refuse the injunction.[218] This accords with the line taken by the courts of equity, in their relationship with the common law courts, in the 19th century.[219]

(e) Beyond private law

The aforementioned cases do not exhaust the well of precedent, for the English courts have asserted the power to grant anti-suit injunctions in two categories of case independently of any private law wrongdoing: (i) to protect the English courts' own jurisdiction (the integrity of English court proceedings),[220] and (ii) more controversially, to protect the forum's important public policies.[221]

Notwithstanding supportive *dicta*,[222] it is doubtful whether violation of English public policy[223] constitutes an independent reason for granting an anti-suit injunction. Injunctions cannot be granted in ordinary civil proceedings on the ground that they would serve the public interest.[224] The incompatibility of a foreign system's laws with fundamental principles of English public policy may be significant in overcoming 'comity' concerns or in characterising the foreign proceedings as 'vexatious' or 'oppressive',[225] but it is not of itself a sufficient reason to intervene.

---

[216] Section C.3.
[217] *Adams v Cape Industries* [1990] Ch 433, 459 (CA).
[218] Ibid 568–70; *Svendborg v Wansa* (n 208) 189 (Staughton LJ), with respect to the allegation of fraud.
[219] Text to n 107.
[220] Text to nn 154–62.
[221] Text to nn 163–4. Note that these represent the two cases specifically referred to by Judge Wilkey in his influential judgment in *Laker Airways Ltd v Sabena* 731 F 2d 909 (DC Cir 1984); also *Bank of Tokyo* (n 20) 58; *Airbus Industrie* (n 21) 136–7.
[222] *Masri (No 3)* (n 141) [86] (Lawrence Collins LJ); *Petter v EMC Europe Ltd* [2015] EWCA Civ 828, [2015] IRLR 847 [51]–[61] (Sales J); *SAS Institute Inc v World Programming Ltd (No 2)* [2019] EWHC 2481 (Comm) [76]–[78], [107]–[117] (Cockerill J), revd [2020] EWCA Civ 599) without considering this point.
[223] Understood here in its international sense, as a reference to 'the fundamental values of English Law' (Briggs, *The Conflict of Laws* (n 7) 192; *Kuwait Airways* (n 75) [16] (Lord Nicholls); Dicey, Morris & Collins (n 20) [5-003]).
[224] *Gouriet v Union of Post Office Workers* [1978] AC 435.
[225] Sections C.3 and D.3(c).

There is, however, no reason to doubt that anti-suit injunctions may be granted to protect the integrity of proceedings before the English courts.[226] Indeed, it would be surprising if the English courts were defenceless in the face of external interference with the due execution of their own constitutional mandate. The power to restrain such interference is inherent in the judicial role, and there is no need to rest it upon ideas of 'unconscionability'.[227]

Caution is nonetheless required on three fronts.

First, the English courts have tended to take a broad view of 'interference' as extending to foreign proceedings that (a) seek to re-litigate subject matter already determined by the English court in proceedings between the parties,[228] or (b) have as their object the recovery by a creditor of individual assets falling within the body of assets under administration by the English court.[229] Such claims require close scrutiny. It may be that there is evidence upon which the court can conclude that the foreign proceedings will likely have a significant practical impact upon the English court's ability to administer justice *in England*. That would be the case, for example, if the foreign court sought to prevent a successful claimant from enforcing its judgment against English assets.[230] In such cases, the English court reacts to preserve its autonomy.

In other cases, the 'interference' complained of is of a more abstract character: that the foreign court's adjudication with respect to a particular subject matter jeopardises the effectiveness or integrity of the judgments and orders of the English court or obtrudes upon the English court's exercise of its own adjudicatory jurisdiction. However, a claim of the latter kind is sustainable only if the English court can justifiably assert that its own jurisdiction is exclusive in an international sense. It may be doubted whether any claim of this kind may legitimately be advanced except in relation to locally situate immovable property[231] and, possibly, the validity of registered intellectual property rights[232] and measures of enforcement against locally situated assets.[233] A claimant who seeks to re-litigate before a foreign court a claim determined by the English court, or a creditor who seeks to recover for its own benefit assets located outside England, does not interfere with the adjudicatory jurisdiction of the English court, but instead seeks to take

---

[226] eg *Armstrong v Armstrong* [1892] P 98 and *Omega Group Holdings v Kozeny* [2002] CLC 132, but cf *South Carolina* (n 45).

[227] cf text to n 162.

[228] *Masri (No 3)* (n 141) [85], [95] (Lawrence Collins LJ). *Booth v Leycester* (1837) 1 Keen 579, 48 ER 430 is an early example.

[229] *Stichting Shell* (n 65), [23]–[25] (Lord Sumption). *Beauchamp v Huntley* (n 119) is an early example.

[230] That was not the case in *Masri (No 3)* (n 141).

[231] cf *British South Africa Co v Companhia de Moçambique* [1893] AC 602.

[232] cf *Lucasfilm Ltd v Ainsworth* [2011] UKSC 39, [2012] 1 AC 208, [101] (Lord Walker and Lord Collins).

[233] *SAS Institute* (n 46). For a more detailed discussion of anti-enforcement injunctions, see Tiong Min Yeo's essay (ch 10) in this collection.

advantage of limitations upon that jurisdiction. A more satisfactory basis for the grant of an injunction in such cases would be to treat it—analogously to a post-judgment freezing injunction or receivership order[234]—as ancillary to the court's prior judgment or decree, in order to maintain its effectiveness as between the parties.[235] Whichever view is taken, the injunction should not extend to the determination by a foreign court of a matter outside the adjudicatory jurisdiction of the English court, such as whether the conditions for recognition or enforcement of an English judgment in a foreign legal system have been met.[236]

Secondly, the anti-suit injunction should be a measure of last resort. Other options, including communication with the foreign court with a view to co-ordinating the proceedings,[237] case management to minimise the interference or seeking appropriate undertakings from the parties[238] should first be exhausted.

Thirdly, the English courts must face up to the paradox created by their assertion of the power to grant anti-suit injunctions to defend the English legal system from outside interference.[239] In such cases, the anti-suit injunction is, potentially, a justifiable countermeasure[240] responding to interference arising from the operations of a foreign State's judicial system.[241] It is, however, difficult to imagine a greater practical interference with the administration of justice than external measures of compulsion applied to prevent a party from bringing or pursuing proceedings in the courts of that system. If a foreign legal system were to grant an injunction restraining proceedings before the English courts, the English courts may legitimately respond by issuing an 'anti-anti-suit injunction'.[242] By the same force of reasoning, however, an English court should treat foreign legal systems as equal partners in a global system of justice, and should not subject those legal systems to interferences to which the English legal system would forcefully object,[243] or provoke them to adopt countermeasures of their own (with the prospect that no legal system will be able to administer justice).[244]

---

[234] *Babanaft International Co SA v Bassatne* [1990] Ch 13; *Masri (No 2)* (n 39).
[235] *Masri (No 3)* (n 141) [26], [60]–[62], [99] (Lawrence Collins LJ).
[236] *ED & F Man (Sugar) Ltd v Haryanto (No 2)* [1991] 1 Lloyd's Rep 429, 440 (Mann LJ); *Seismic Shipping Inc v Total E&P UK plc* [2005] EWCA Civ 985, [2005] 2 Lloyd's Rep 359 [51] (Clarke LJ), [66] (Rix LJ); *Masri* (No 3) (n 141) [93] (Lawrence Collins LJ); *SAS Institute* (n 46) [120], [129] (Males LJ); Raphael, *The Anti-Suit Injunction* (n 4) [4.69].
[237] *Golubovich v Golubovich* [2010] EWCA Civ 810, [2011] Fam 88 [96] (Thorpe LJ).
[238] *Stichting Shell* (n 65) [40].
[239] Andrew Dickinson, 'The Interference Paradox' (2020) 136 LQR 569, commenting on the decision of the Court of Appeal in *SAS Institute* (n 46).
[240] See, however, Arts 22 and 49–53 of International Law Commission, *Draft Articles on Responsibility of States for Internationally Wrongful Acts* (2001) YbILC vol 2(1), 14–18; vol 2(2), 128–39.
[241] *SAS Institute* (n 46) [111]–[112] ('comity is a two way street').
[242] Ibid [133]–[136]; also Raphael, *The Anti-Suit Injunction* (n 4), [5.57]–[5.64].
[243] eg *General Star International Indemnity Ltd v Stirling Cooke Brown Reinsurance Brokers Ltd* [2003] EHWC 3 (Comm), [2003] Lloyd's Rep IR 719, noted by Adrian Briggs (2003) 74 BYIL 532–5.
[244] *Peck* (n 104) 625.

(f) SNI Aerospatiale: a troubling case?

In *SNI Aerospatiale*,[245] Mr Yong, an international businessman resident in Brunei, was killed in a helicopter crash in Brunei in 1980. Later that year, his widow and personal representatives started proceedings in three countries: in Brunei, against SNI (the French helicopter manufacturer) and Bristow (its Malaysian operator and servicer); in France, against SNI; and in Texas, against SNI and two of its United States associate companies, Bristow and two of its US associates, and others. The French proceedings were soon discontinued. In 1983, the claims against all defendants other than the SNI parties were settled. Subsequently, the SNI parties unsuccessfully challenged the jurisdiction of the Texas court, exhausting all avenues of appeal by the end of 1986. Depositions were taken to gather evidence, and a trial date fixed for June 1987. At this point, six years into the litigation, SNI decided to seek an anti-suit injunction in Brunei. It failed in its application before the High Court and Court of Appeal. During the hearing before the Court of Appeal, SNI served a contribution notice on Bristow, which indicated a willingness to submit to the jurisdiction of the Brunei court while objecting to the jurisdiction of the Texas court. On the same day, SNI accepted service of Brunei proceedings issued by the helicopter's owner and hull insurer.

One might have thought that SNI's considerable delay in seeking an injunction would have been fatal to its application,[246] but the injunction defendants' counsel does not appear to have pressed this point before the Privy Council. Instead, they argued that the superior means of gathering evidence in Texas,[247] the expertise of local counsel there, the contingency fee system and the prospect of an earlier trial date were 'distinct practical advantages'[248] which explained their wish to proceed to trial in Texas. That argument was a powerful one: the courts in both Brunei and Texas were both available fora with respect to claims arising from Mr Yong's death. Although it would have been vexatious for his widow and representatives to refuse (if pressed) to elect in which forum they wished to proceed to trial,[249] the injunction was not pursued on that basis. Why then were the injunction defendants not at liberty to seek justice in Texas? SNI might well have argued that the limited connection that the subject matter had to Texas rendered the claimants' manifest advantages illegitimate, justifying the conclusion that the proceedings were vexatious,[250] but it did not do so. In concluding that Brunei, not Texas, was the natural forum for the trial of the action, Lord Goff observed that 'there was nothing to

---

[245] (n 20) 883–7. See Adrian Briggs, 'Restraint of Foreign Proceedings' [1987] LMCLQ 391.
[246] Text to nn 67–8.
[247] Similar evidential advantages in the English court had been relied on to support the injunction in *Bushby* (n 24); see text to n 117.
[248] *SNI Aerospatiale* (n 20) 880–1. It was conceded that no substantive advantage would be secured, as Brunei law would be applied in Texas to questions of liability and quantum (ibid 888).
[249] *Australian Commercial Research* (n 205).
[250] Text to n 206.

connect the action with Texas at all',[251] but this point assumed no overt significance in his reasoning.

Instead, the injunction claimants were allowed, several years after being sued in Texas, to erect their own scaffold. By giving undertakings to the Brunei court,[252] they 'neutralised'[253] the advantages on which the injunction defendants relied to explain their choice to proceed in Texas. By actively pursuing the contribution claim against Bristow, they laid the foundation for the Privy Council's conclusion that the injunction defendants' 'conduct in continuing with their proceedings in Texas ... should properly be described as oppressive' insofar as it would potentially lead to a multiplicity of proceedings and the risk of irreconcilable judgments.[254]

This conclusion is troubling on several counts. First, the Board appears to have leant in SNI's favour on evidential matters. For example, it assumed that an early trial of all claims in Brunei was possible,[255] overturned the Court of Appeal's finding that SNI's pursuit of the contribution claim was designed to buttress its case for an injunction[256] and inferred that Bristow's objection to the jurisdiction of the Texas court was well founded.[257] Secondly, its conclusion that the continuation of proceedings in Texas 'could indeed lead to serious injustice'[258] was founded principally[259] on a defect not in the laws of Texas but in the laws of Brunei, insofar as its contribution legislation (modelled on earlier English legislation[260]) arguably[261] failed to recognise liability established by the judgment of a competent foreign court.[262] Thirdly, by giving significant weight to the undertakings, it allowed SNI to generate the circumstances supporting the conclusion that the injunction defendants were acting 'oppressively'.[263] Moreover, in an echo of *Bunbury v Bunbury*,[264] the Board made the Texas court the involuntary servant of the Brunei court, by taking advantage of the evidence gathered under Texas law for trial in Texas and, indeed, encouraging pre-trial discovery in Texas to continue.[265] Finally, having refused to define the concept of 'oppression',[266] the Board did not even attempt to explain why the 'serious injustice' to SNI that it considered might result from the

---

[251] *SNI Aerospatiale* (n 20) 897; also ibid 895, criticising legal systems exercising an exceptionally broad jurisdiction' offering 'great inducements' to litigants to pursue claims there.
[252] Ibid 888, 903–4.
[253] Ibid 899, 902.
[254] Ibid 899–903.
[255] Ibid 899, 903 (cf the contrary submission by the injunction defendants' counsel, at 879).
[256] Ibid 900.
[257] Ibid 900.
[258] Ibid 902.
[259] Ibid 901 ('even greater importance').
[260] Law Reform (Married Women and Tortfeasors) Act 1935, s 6.
[261] The Board declined to decide the point (*SNI Aerospatiale* (n 20) 902).
[262] Ibid 901–2. It appears that, following rejection of its jurisdiction challenge, SNI had submitted to the jurisdiction of the Texas court.
[263] cf *Lawrence* (n 50) [53]–[58] (private nuisance).
[264] Text to n 123.
[265] *SNI Aerospatiale* (n 20) 888 (undertakings 5 and 7).
[266] Ibid 893.

continuation of the Texas proceedings constituted wrongdoing on the injunction defendants' part. Could they, to use Lord Kilbrandon's formulation,[267] be said to have engaged in unfair abuse of power 'in order that [SNI] may be put in difficulties in obtaining [its] just rights'? As a matter of English law, (a) if SNI and Bristow were both liable for Mr Yong's death, they were liable as several tortfeasors, albeit for the same damage, and (b) in such a case, a claimant may choose whom to sue leaving the defendant to pursue a claim for contribution against others liable for the same damage. The 'injustice' in *SNI Aerospatiale* arose not in the assertion by the injunction defendants of their rights against SNI, but in the relationship between SNI and Bristow that was *res inter alios acta* so far as the injunction defendants were concerned. There was nothing whatsoever to suggest that they had sought to put SNI in difficulty as a means of applying pressure in settlement negotiations. The Board's reasoning nonetheless labelled them as wrongdoers and compelled them to withdraw their action in Texas, but not before taking advantage of the mechanisms available there to gather evidence.

4. Choice of court and choice of law

A theme in Professor Briggs' writing on anti-suit injunctions has the insistence that they operate within the broader framework of the conflict of laws, requiring careful attention to questions of jurisdiction and choice of law.[268] Although the English courts have acknowledged the need to establish adjudicatory jurisdiction with respect to the injunction defendant,[269] the choice of law toolbox has been little used.[270] English courts, with the acquiescence of the parties and their legal advisers, default to English law to determine the injunction claimant's entitlement to relief.[271]

That approach is perfectly understandable if the injunction protects the integrity of proceedings before the English court.[272] The injunction, granted in the exercise of the court's inherent jurisdiction, protects the court's procedural autonomy and is

---

[267] Text to n 201.
[268] Briggs, 'Anti-suit Injunctions in a Complex World' (n 85) 243; Briggs, *Private International Law in the English Courts* (n 6) [5.101]–[5.103], [5.107], [5.113]; also Andrew Dickinson, *The Rome II Regulation* (OUP 2008) [4.107]–[4.111]; Raphael, *The Anti-Suit Injunction* (n 4) [4.08]–[4.18]; Cameron Sim, 'Choice of Law and Anti-Suit Injunctions: Relocating Comity' (2013) 62 ICLQ 703. cf Jonathan Harris, 'Anti-Suit Injunctions: A Home Comfort?' [1997] LMCLQ 413.
[269] *Donohue* (n 69) [21] (Lord Bingham); *Masri (No 3)* (n 141) [27]–[31], [55]–[59] (Lawrence Collins LJ).
[270] eg *The Yusuf Cepnioglu* (n 145), noted Adrian Briggs [2016] LMCLQ 327 and Andrew Dickinson (2016) 132 LQR 541.
[271] eg *Barclays Bank v Homan* (n 61) 687–8 (Hoffmann J); Raphael, *The Anti-Suit Injunction* (n 4) [4.08]–[4.09].
[272] Section D.3(e).

addressed to an injunction defendant who is already a party.[273] English law applies as the law of the forum.

A more complex picture emerges when the injunction responds to private law wrongdoing, including (to use the examples given above[274]) breach of a dispute resolution provision, vexatious or oppressive conduct or fraud. In such cases, a procedural characterisation, supporting application of the *lex fori*, is no longer appropriate. As choice of court and arbitration agreements fall outside the Rome I Regulation, matters of remedy will be governed principally by the law of the forum[275] if a breach is established under the agreement's governing law.[276] Non-contractual obligations, by contrast, have since 2009 been subject to the Rome II Regulation,[277] which points in a different direction.[278] Not only are remedies subject principally to the law applicable to a tort/delict,[279] but the general rule favours application of the law of the country in which damage directly occurred.[280] When proceedings are wrongfully brought in a foreign court, damage occurs in that place.[281]

Even so, English law can still be applied to a claim for an anti-suit injunction founded on non-contractual wrongdoing if the rules of English law supporting the grant of an injunction constitute overriding mandatory provisions.[282] That provision, however, sets a high bar, requiring that the rule be shown to be one considered essential for safeguarding the public interests of the State concerned.[283] An English court might conclude that the threshold had been met if the requirement of 'convenience' were to be interpreted, as this essay suggests, as demanding cogent evidence that the foreign proceedings imperil the due administration of justice in some fundamental respect, so undermining the rule of law.[284] If, however, the threshold is set at a lower level, the case for applying English law becomes much weaker.

---

[273] *Masri (No 3)* (n 141) [59], [99].

[274] Section D.3(c)–(d).

[275] Dicey, Morris & Collins (n 20) [7-011]–[7-012]). See Regulation (EC) 593/2008 on the law applicable to contractual obligations (Rome I) [2008] OJ L177/6, Art 1(2)(e).

[276] This will usually, although not always, be English law (ibid [32-021], a topic considered in great detail by the Supreme Court in *Enka* (n 78)).

[277] Regulation (EC) 864/2007 (11 July 2007) on the law applicable to non-contractual obligations (Rome II) [2007] OJ L199/40 (hereafter Rome II Regulation).

The Rome II Regulation continues to apply, alongside the Rome I Regulation, following the UK's departure from the European Union: see Law Applicable to Contractual Obligations and Non-Contractual Obligations (Amendment etc.) (EU Exit) Regulations (SI 2019/834).

[278] The neglect of choice of law analysis in earlier cases may be explained by the (then) predominant view that equitable claims were governed exclusively by the forum's own principles of equity (Dicey, Morris & Collins (n 20) [34-083]–[34-086]).

[279] Rome II Regulation (n 277) Art 15(c)–(d). See the essay by Adam Rushworth (ch 9) in this collection.

[280] Rome II Regulation (n 277) Art 4(1).

[281] *AMT Futures Ltd v Marzillier* [2017] UKSC 13, [2018] AC 439.

[282] Rome II (n 277) Art 16.

[283] *Agostihno da Silva Martins v Dekra Claims Services Portugal SA* [2019] ECLI:EU:C:2019:84.

[284] Section C.3.

E. A Way Forward?

Unless and until the English courts address the uncertainty surrounding the legal basis for granting anti-suit injunctions,[285] and address the 'interference paradox',[286] this area of the English conflict of laws will remain in a most unsatisfactory state. In recent decades, the highest English courts have mostly failed to engage with these issues and have lost sight of the extraordinary character of the remedy. This essay suggests a possible way forward, representing a modern interpretation of longstanding equitable principles, as follows:

1. An anti-suit injunction (or, more appropriately, 'overseas civil restraint order'[287]) should issue only (a) if there is a sufficient legal reason making it 'just' to grant the order, and (b) it is a 'convenient' remedy.[288]
2. Statements that injunctions of this kind are permissible whenever the ends of justice require are question begging, and should be avoided.[289]
3. The language of 'unconscionability' also serves no valuable purpose and should be abandoned here.[290]
4. The set of sufficient legal reasons for issuing injunctions to restrain overseas proceedings can be sub-divided into cases of (a) private law wrongdoing, and (b) protection of, or support for, the administration of justice in England.[291]
5. The English courts must work harder to define the contours and limits of private law wrongdoing as a foundation for injunctions of this kind, in particular as regards 'vexatious' or 'oppressive' conduct.[292]
6. Closer attention should be paid to the choice of law issues that arise.[293]
7. The interests of the foreign legal system in administering justice within its own territory (aptly captured by the term 'comity') should ordinarily weigh heavily against the issue of an injunction to restrain overseas proceedings, absent cogent evidence of a likelihood that justice cannot or will not be done in the foreign forum or that the administration of justice in England is imperilled.[294]
8. The court should, in any event, not issue an injunction if its own legal system does not have a sufficient interest in the matter.[295]

---

[285] Sections C.1–5, D.2.
[286] Text to n 239–44.
[287] Section B.
[288] Sections C.1–5.
[289] Sections D.1 and D.3(a).
[290] Section D.3(b).
[291] Sections D.2 and D.3(d)–(e).
[292] Section D.3(c).
[293] Section D.4.
[294] Section C.3.
[295] Section C.4.

The conflict of laws in England might well have been in a more satisfactory state today if the courts had heeded the advice of Earl of Clarendon and declined to set a 'dangerous precedent'. For better or worse, however, the anti-suit injunction is here to stay.[296] Happily, Professor Briggs' work in the field will remain to guide us through these hazardous waters.

---

[296] Its prominence will likely increase following the UK's departure from the European Union, as the Recast Brussels I Regulation (n 2) which underpinned the European Court's decision in *Turner* (n 21) no longer applies.

5
Jurisdiction over Co-defendants

Andrew Scott

A. Introduction

For more than 130 years, English courts have been empowered to permit service outside the jurisdiction on necessary or proper parties to the proceedings. As Professor Briggs explains, the power:[1]

> ... depends for its successful operation on a number of textual requirements, and on a flexible judicial discretion which is capable of responding to all manner of issues and sub-issues which need to be considered before a proposed co-defendant is subject to a jurisdiction from which he is otherwise safe.

Insofar as EU law has a functional equivalent, it is Art 8(1) of the Recast Brussels I Regulation.[2] It provides for special jurisdiction over EU-domiciled co-defendants, but only where one of the defendants is sued in its domicile; and subject to the proviso that 'the claims are so closely connected that it is expedient to hear and determine them together to avoid the risk of irreconcilable judgments resulting from separate proceedings'.

This essay considers the two regimes. Section B traces some of the key developments of the domestic law power and the principles governing its exercise. Section C does likewise in respect of the EU law rule, identifying some of the principal limitations and difficulties that arise in relation to it, and the extent to which these have been addressed in the case law. While progress has been made in this regard, particularly in the English Courts, much force remains in Professor Briggs' assessment that 'Article 8(1) is the one part of the Regulation which works badly'.[3] A principal deficiency is that Art 8(1) is confined to cases in which the 'anchor' defendant is sued in its domicile with the result that it is too narrow fully to achieve

---

[1] Adrian Briggs, *Civil Jurisdiction and Judgments* (6th edn, Informa 2015) [2.226] (hereafter Briggs, *Civil Jurisdiction and Judgme*nts).
[2] Regulation (EU) No 1215/2012 of the European Parliament and of the Council of 12 December 2012 on jurisdiction and the recognition and enforcement of judgments in civil and commercial matters ([2012] OJ L351/1) (hereafter Recast Brussels I Regulation), which no longer applies in the UK after 1 January 2021 (Civil Jurisdiction and Judgments (Amendment) (EU) Exit Regulations (SI 2019/479), reg 89).
[3] Briggs, *Civil Jurisdiction and Judgments* (n 1) [2.226].

the purpose of the provision in terms of facilitating the sound administration of justice. It is difficult to see how that can be remedied without legislative reform that the EU legislator has so far declined to make. A further deficiency is the lack of clarity in the European Court's case law as to whether it is relevant to enquire into the merits of the claimant's claim against the 'anchor' defendant and his motives in bringing it; and if so, how this is to be done.

B. The Domestic Rule

1. Origins and development

The domestic rule (the Rule) has its origins in the great legislative reforms of English civil procedure that occurred in the nineteenth century. The detail does not matter for present purposes and is set out elsewhere.[4] The development may be broadly summarised as follows.

At common law, English Courts recognise no power to permit service of originating process outside the jurisdiction, regarding the matter as one for Parliament.[5] In the course of the nineteenth century, Parliament conferred on the English Courts the power they had declined to recognise at common law. Following on from initial reforms under the Common Law Procedure Act 1852,[6] the Judicature Acts 1873 and 1875 introduced a scheme whereby English Courts were empowered to permit service of a writ outside the jurisdiction in certain cases. The cases were initially those set out in rules scheduled to the 1875 Act, as RSC Order XI. As enacted, they were confined to cases where the subject matter of the action was connected to England and made no distinct provision for co-defendants. The position changed in 1883 with the introduction of RSC Order XI, r 1(g). This provided that the court could permit service out where: 'Any person out of the jurisdiction is a necessary or proper party to an action properly brought against some other person duly served within the jurisdiction'.

The Rule represented a concern to balance potentially conflicting considerations: the international law principle that Courts generally do not exercise extra-territorial jurisdiction; and the desirability of having before the court all persons required for justice to be done.[7] The concern results from the anomalous nature

---

[4] Andrew Dickinson, 'Keeping Up Appearances: the Development of Adjudicatory Jurisdiction in the English Courts' (2016) 86 BYIL 6.
[5] In *Masri v Consolidated Contractors International Company SAL* [2009] UKHL 43, [2010] 1 AC 90, the House of Lords rejected the idea of an inherent power to permit service on a non-party. Lord Mance (with whose speech each other member of the Appellate Committee agreed) observed (at [32]) that 'It has long been established that service out of the jurisdiction requires express authorisation either by statute or in the Rules'.
[6] Which empowered the English Court to permit service of a notice of writ on British or foreign subjects outside the jurisdiction (see ss 18 and 19).
[7] *Derby & Co Ltd v Larsson* [1976] 1 WLR 202 (HL) 203 (Lord Simon).

of the necessary and proper party head of jurisdiction, which is not founded upon any territorial connection to the claim, or the subject matter of the action; but instead on considerations of sound administration of justice. The balance is achieved by a combination of: (i) the Rule's requirements, which identify the cases in which the court may permit service out under this head; (ii) the further requirement that England be the proper forum for the case; and (iii) a residual judicial discretion to determine whether it is appropriate to permit service out in all the circumstances.

So far as concerns its requirements, the Rule remained in much the same form until 1987, when it was amended in several important respects. The changes were summarised by the Privy Council in *Altimo Holdings and Investment Ltd v Kyrgyz Mobile Tel Ltd*.[8] The case concerned the Manx version of the Rule, which was in the form originally enacted in England. Giving the Board's advice, Lord Collins said this:[9]

> [The Manx Rule] corresponds to the former RSC Order 11, r 1(1)(c) in England. There were three changes to that rule in England which came into effect in 1987, which were not made in the Isle of Man. First, Ord 11, r 1(1)(c) was extended so that it applied where the original claim was brought against a person 'duly served within or out of the jurisdiction' and not only as regards a person 'duly served within the jurisdiction' as the Manx rules continue to provide. Second, the word 'properly' in the phrase 'properly brought' against that person was omitted. This made no substantive difference, particularly in the light of the third change, which was that a new RSC Ord 11, r 4(1)(d) provided that where an application was made under RSC Ord 11, r 1(1)(c), the applicant for leave had to show grounds for belief that there was between the plaintiff and the person on whom a writ had been served 'a real issue which the plaintiff may reasonably ask the court to try'. No such change was made in the Isle of Man, but it was declaratory of the principle established in *Ellinger v Guinness, Mahon & Co* [1939] 4 All ER 16, 22, where Morton J said:
>
>> 'I do not think it is part of the function of the court, in considering whether an action is "properly brought" against a party within the jurisdiction, to arrive at a conclusion as to whether the plaintiff will or will not succeed against that party. It is enough if the court is satisfied that there is a real issue between the plaintiff and that party which the plaintiff may reasonably ask the court to try.'

It will be necessary to consider in further detail below the role that the phrase 'properly brought' has played in the development of the law in managing assessment of the merits of the claims brought and the claimant's motives in bringing

---

[8] [2011] UKPC 7, [2012] 1 WLR 1804 (hereafter *Altimo*).
[9] Ibid [65].

them; and in that connection, the further guidance that *Altimo* provides on this issue.

In 2000, RSC Order XI was replaced by r 6.20 of the Civil Procedure Rules (as amended), with the necessary or proper party head of jurisdiction appearing, in revised form, as CPR r 6.20(3). The revisions had two main effects. First, CPR r 6.20(3)(a) expressly incorporated the principle established in *Ellinger*, which had been formerly reflected in RSC Order 11, r 4(1)(d) rather than in the head of jurisdiction itself. Second, the head was further broadened: it was no longer necessary for service on the 'anchor' defendant to have been effected by the time permission to serve out was sought, it sufficing that the claim form 'will be served' on that defendant. In 2004, the Rule was further amended to clarify that the 'anchor' defendant had to be served 'otherwise than in reliance on this paragraph'. It was in this form that the Rule stood in 2008 when, along with the other heads of jurisdiction, it was relegated to Practice Direction 6B (PD 6B). The necessary or proper party head now appears as para 3.1(3) of that Practice Direction, as follows:

The claimant may serve a claim form out of the jurisdiction with the permission of the court under rule 6.36 where— ... (3) a claim is made against a person ('the defendant') on whom the claim form has been or will be served (otherwise than in reliance on this paragraph) and—(a) there is between the claimant and the defendant a real issue which it is reasonable for the court to try; and (b) the claimant wishes to serve the claim form on another person who is a necessary or proper party to that claim.

The thrust of these developments was thus to broaden the court's power to permit service outside the jurisdiction in the case of necessary or proper parties. However, that was subject always to the protection for foreign defendants that arose from the requirement that the action against the 'anchor' defendant had to be properly brought;[10] that is to say, raise real issues which it was reasonable for the court to try.

Alongside these developments in the Rule's requirements, the court developed principles governing the exercise of the power to permit service out. Chief among these was that service out would not be permitted unless the claimant satisfied the court that England was the proper forum. The (now) classic statement of that principle is Lord Goff's speech in *Spiliada Maritime Corpn v Cansulex Ltd*,[11] which paid just tribute to Professor Briggs' contribution to this branch of the law.[12] Among the many insights contained in this speech is the recognition that the word

---

[10] It has been long-established that this requirement enures to the protection of the foreign defendant: see eg *John Russell & Co Ltd v Cayzer, Irvine & Co Ltd* [1916] 2 AC 298 (HL) 304 (Lord Sumner).
[11] [1987] AC 460 (HL) 475–484.
[12] Ibid 488.

'exorbitant' does little useful work in the context of the law on service out of the jurisdiction.[13] Lord Goff described it as an 'old-fashioned word which perhaps carries unfortunate overtones' confining it to the sense described by Lord Diplock in *Amin Rasheed Shipping Corpn v Kuwait Insurance Co*,[14] that is, a jurisdiction 'which, under general English conflict rules, an English court would not recognise as possessed by any foreign court in the absence of some treaty providing for such recognition'. Lord Diplock made those observations in the context of a head of jurisdiction (now found in para 3.1(6) of Practice Direction 6B) that permits service out where English law is the applicable law of a contract. While that head of jurisdiction might fairly be characterised as having the potential for exorbitance in the sense described by Lord Diplock,[15] the same is not necessarily true of other heads of jurisdiction. Moreover, the English Court will only permit service out where it is the proper forum. Lord Goff's insight was taken further by the Supreme Court in *Abela v Baadarani*, Lord Sumption JSC (with whose judgment each of the other justices agreed) stating that, 'It should no longer be necessary to resort to the kind of muscular presumptions against service out which are implicit in adjectives like "exorbitant". The decision is generally a pragmatic one in the interests of the efficient conduct of the litigation in an appropriate forum.'[16] The insight is important in the context of the necessary or proper party head of jurisdiction, where the requirements of that head, the requirement that England be the proper forum, and judicial discretion, all serve to ensure that the jurisdiction is kept within proper bounds. It will be necessary to consider below the impact that EU law has had in this context by depriving the English Court of the power they would otherwise have to decline jurisdiction over claims against English-domiciled 'anchor' defendants on *forum non conveniens* grounds.

---

[13] Ibid 481–482.

[14] [1984] AC 50, 65.

[15] For example, there is no equivalent in the Recast Brussels I Regulation or the instruments that precede it; and English courts have recognised that the weight to be attached to English governing law in identifying the proper forum very much depends on the circumstances: see eg *Novus Aviation Ltd v Onur Air Tasimacilik AS* [2009] EWCA Civ 122, [2009] 1 Lloyd's Rep 576 [77]–[79] (Lawrence Collins LJ).

[16] [2013] UKSC 44, [2013] 1 WLR 2043 [53]. For a critical view of Lord Sumption's observations regarding exorbitance, and a defence of them, see, respectively: A Dickinson, 'Service abroad—an inconvenient obstacle?' (2014) 130 LQR 197 and L Collins 'Sovereignty and exorbitant jurisdiction' (2014) 130 LQR 555. Professor Briggs' assessment in Briggs, *Civil Jurisdiction and Judgments* (n 1) was characteristically pragmatic: 'It is sufficient to say that the court will not grant permission to serve out unless England is the proper place to bring the claim—notice, the proper place—and if it is, arguing about use of the 'e' word is an odd thing to be doing when there is work to be done' (at [4.57]). Writing elsewhere, Professor Briggs reflected on whether Lord Sumption's observations in *Abela* might suggest that *forum conveniens* could become the sole criteria for service out: A Briggs 'Service out in a shrinking world' [2013] LMCLQ 415. Lord Sumption dismissed that suggestion in *Brownlie v Four Seasons Holdings Inc* [2017] UKSC 80, [2018] 1 WLR 192 [31]. Not everyone will find Lord Sumption's observations in *Brownlie* easy to reconcile with what he had said in *Abela*.

2. The scope of the domestic rule

Consistently with its purpose in terms of facilitating the administration of justice, the domestic rule is broad in scope. Two aspects are notable. They stand in sharp contrast to the EU law rule.

First, as described above, whereas the domestic rule was initially confined to cases in which the 'anchor' defendant was served within the jurisdiction, that restriction was removed in 1987. That is not to say that the basis for jurisdiction over that defendant is irrelevant. Rather, it is a factor that goes to the court's discretion to permit service out. As will be seen below in Section C, the EU law rule is fundamentally different: it is a necessary condition for relying on that rule that proceedings have been brought where one of the defendants is domiciled.

Second, the domestic rule permits service outside the jurisdiction not just on 'necessary' parties but also on 'proper' parties. The concept of a 'proper' party is an inherently broad and malleable one. From the outset, English Courts have rejected attempts to restrict it. In an important early case, *Massey v Heynes*,[17] decided in 1888, the Court of Appeal rejected the submission that a foreign defendant could not be a proper party where relief against it was sought in the alternative to relief against the local defendant. Lord Esher MR explained that the application of the Rule could not turn on the outcome of the case at trial and laid down a broad test as follows: 'supposing both parties had been within the jurisdiction would they both have been proper parties to the action?'[18] Lindley and Lopes LJJ concurred, the former observing that 'when the liability of several persons depends upon one investigation ... they are all 'proper parties' to the same action'.[19] It is this same broad test that still applies in the modern law.[20] The breadth of the test is beneficial in the context of a rule concerned with facilitating the sound administration of justice. As further described below in Section C, the EU law rule is again narrower, its scope being defined by a proviso that is concerned solely with protecting against the risk of irreconcilable judgments resulting from separate proceedings.

3. Merits and motives

Though broad in scope, the Rule was premised from the outset, and for almost a century, on there being an 'action properly brought' in the English Court. This served as an important tool in the development of the necessary or proper party head of jurisdiction and as a counterbalance against its breadth. In particular, and

---

[17] *Massey & Anor v Heynes & Co and Schenker & Co* (1888) 21 QBD 330 (CA).
[18] Ibid 338.
[19] Ibid 338–339.
[20] *Altimo* (n 8) [65] (Lord Collins).

in a precursor to debates that arose later in the context of the EU law rule, the requirement that the action be 'properly brought' provided the occasion to consider the relevance of the merits of the claim against the local defendant, the claimant's motive in suing that defendant, and the interrelationship between these considerations. The courts have not spoken with one voice on this topic.

For example, in *Witted v Galbraith*,[21] decided in 1893, service was set aside where there was no 'apparent cause of action' against the 'anchor' defendant. The Court of Appeal inferred from its lack of merit that the claim against that defendant was brought for the sole purpose of joining the foreign defendant; and on that basis held that the case fell outside RSC, Order XI, r 1(g). This appeared to treat the claimant's motive for suing the 'anchor' defendant as a relevant criterion in determining whether the action was 'properly brought', with the merits of the claim being a factor that shone a light on that motive.[22] By contrast, other courts have treated the merits of the claim as the relevant criterion. For example, in *Cooney v Wilson*, the claim against the local defendant was a viable one, but he was a 'no mark for damages or costs'.[23] The Irish Court of Appeal held that the action was nonetheless 'properly brought' against him, Eason O'Brien LC (with whom the other members of the Court concurred) said that:[24]

> If there is a real substantial cause of action against both defendants, it would be most dangerous to hold that the mere fact the one within the jurisdiction is a pauper can make any difference.

A similar approach is apparent from *Ellinger v Guinness, Mahon & Co*, decided in 1939, in which Morton J stated the principle quoted in the passage from *Altimo* set out above in Section B.1. It is that statement of principle which underlies the modern formulation of the necessary or proper party head of jurisdiction, insofar as it asks whether there is as between the claimant and the 'anchor' defendant a 'real issue which it is reasonable for the court to try'. As *Cooney* illustrates, the fact that the 'anchor' defendant has no assets does not of itself make it otherwise than reasonable for a claimant to seek judgment against him on such 'real issues' as arise.

---

[21] [1893] 1 QB 431 (CA).
[22] For further examples, see *Ross v Eason & Son Ltd* [1911] 2 IR 459 (CA Ireland) and *Sharples v Eason & Son* [1911] 2 IR 436 (CA Ireland) in which plaintiffs asserted weak or unviable claims against local newsagents in an attempt to establish jurisdiction over foreign publishers of alleged defamatory material. The abuse was particularly plain in the latter case, in which notice of discontinuance was served on the local defendant the same day as proceedings were served on the foreign defendant, Holmes LJ observing (at 449) that: 'The only inference I can draw is that the plaintiff had never any cause of action against [the local defendant], and only sued them for a collateral object, namely, so as to get the order to serve this [foreign defendant]'.
[23] [1913] 2 IR 402 (CA Ireland).
[24] Ibid 407.

118 JURISDICTION OVER CO-DEFENDANTS

The interrelationship between motive and merit was considered in *The Brabo (No 2)*, decided in 1939.[25] The House of Lords held by a majority that since the action against the 'anchor' defendant was bound to fail, it was not 'properly brought', rejecting the submission that it was sufficient for the claimant to show that it had brought that action in good faith.[26] Lord Porter clearly expressed the view that the plaintiff's motive was not the true criterion: what mattered was whether the action raised issues to be tried.[27] The other members of the majority gave speeches that were more or less consistent with this.[28] Dissenting, Lord MacDermott emphasised the claimant's good faith in bringing the action and held that consideration of the merits of the claim was a matter going to the exercise of discretion to permit service out rather than whether the action was 'properly brought'.[29]

The House of Lords returned to the issue in *Derby & Co v Larsson*, decided in 1976.[30] It held that a counterclaim brought in accordance with the prevailing procedural rules was 'properly brought' for the purposes of the Rule. At first sight, that might be thought to suggest a limited role for the 'properly brought' requirement. However, there was no suggestion of lack of merit or improper motive in that case and so consideration of such issues did not directly arise. Lord Russell (with whose speech each other member of the Appellate Committee agreed) said that whether the requirement was concerned with the claimant's motives or compliance with the rules, it was satisfied.[31] Nonetheless, in *obiter dicta*, Viscount Dilhorne recorded his doubts about enquiry into a claimant's motives, stating as follows:[32]

> I doubt very much whether the court has to consider whether or not the claim or counterclaim is made *bona fide* or for some improper purposes. For a court to do that appears to be likely to involve something of the nature of a trial before the trial of action. I am inclined to think that 'properly brought' in Ord. 11. r 1(1)(j) means no more than brought in accordance with the rules of court. But it is not necessary to decide as to that in this appeal for there is no question as to the genuineness of the appellants' counterclaim.

This illustrates the familiar concern of the appellate courts that questions of jurisdiction should be dealt with in a proportionate way. Bearing the context in mind, it is often difficult for the Court accurately to assess a claimant's motivations at

---

[25] *Tyne Improvement Commissioners v Armement Anversois S/A (The Brabo (No 2)* [1949] AC 326 (HL).
[26] Ibid 330, the report recording the claimant's submission as follows: '... in law the chances of success or failure [as against the 'anchor' defendants] are irrelevant, provided the claim was brought bona fide and the parties within the jurisdiction are proper bona fide parties to the action'.
[27] Ibid 338–339.
[28] Ibid 347–348 (Lord Simonds), 353–356 (Lord Du Parcq), 357 (Lord Normand).
[29] Ibid 359–360.
[30] [1976] 1 WLR 202 (HL).
[31] Ibid 205.
[32] Ibid 203.

the jurisdictional stage; and difficult for a claimant fully to describe them without risking a waiver of legal professional privilege.

The issue of motive was further discussed by the Court of Appeal in *Multinational Gas and Petrochemical Co v Multinational Gas and Petrochemical Services Ltd*,[33] decided in 1983. There, the 'anchor' defendant was in liquidation, there was no prospect of recovery against it, and the judge had concluded that the predominant reason for suing it was to establish jurisdiction over the foreign defendants; and on that ground, he set aside the order permitting service on those defendants under (among others) the necessary or proper party head. The judge's decision was upheld by a majority of the Court of Appeal (Lawton and Dillon LJJ), the *ratio* of their decision being that the claim against the foreign defendants was not viable, the other member of the Court (May LJ) having dissented on that issue. On the question whether the action was 'properly brought' against the local defendant, different views were expressed. Lawton LJ held that the judge was entitled to take account of the plaintiff's motive in the exercise of his discretion whether to permit service and that was sufficient to dismiss the appeal.[34] Dillon LJ said it was 'well established that an action is not properly brought against a defendant within the jurisdiction if that defendant has been made a party to the action solely in order to found an application under [the necessary or proper party head]', but concluded that that was not the plaintiff's sole motivation in that case.[35] May LJ concluded that in circumstances where there was a viable case against the local defendant, and no suggestion of *mala fides*, the action against it was 'properly brought' notwithstanding that the main or predominant purpose of suing it was to establish jurisdiction over the foreign defendants, observing that the plaintiff's motive was 'much more relevant' to the question of discretion.[36]

With the authorities in this somewhat unsatisfactory state, the Privy Council considered the issue in *Altimo*, decided in 2012. Giving the advice of the Board, Lord Collins said that 'the mere fact that D1 is sued only for the purpose of bringing in D2 is not fatal to the application for permission to serve D2 out of the jurisdiction' relying on Lord Porter's observations in *The Brabo (No 2)* and Viscount Dilhorne's observations in *Derby*, considering that these were not adequately taken into account in *Multinational Gas*. Having analysed that latter decision, Lord Collins concluded as follows:[37]

> The better view, therefore, is that the fact that D1 is sued only for the purpose of bringing in the foreign defendants is a factor in the exercise of the discretion and

---

[33] [1983] Ch 258 (CA).
[34] Ibid 268.
[35] Ibid 287.
[36] Ibid 273–279.
[37] *Altimo* (n 8) [79].

not an element in the question whether the action is 'properly brought' against D1, provided that there is a viable claim against D1.

It is to be noted that, although Lord Collins reached this conclusion in the context of the Manx rule described above in Section B.1, he detected no material difference between its formulation (which reflected RSC Order XI, r 1(g) and its successors) and the reformulation of the necessary or proper party head contained in para 3.1(3) of Practice Direction 6B, observing that 'none of these changes affects the questions of law which arise on this appeal, each of which applies equally to the amended RSC and to the current CPR'.[38]

The question of motive again arose for consideration in *Erste Group Bank AG v JSC 'VMZ Red October'*, decided in 2015.[39] Simplified somewhat, the facts were as follows. The claimant was an Austrian bank and an unpaid creditor under instruments governed by English law and subject to the English Court's jurisdiction. The defendants were Russian debtors under those instruments and associated Russian entities. In the English Court, the claimant brought: (i) contractual claims against the debtors to recover the sums due under those instruments; and (ii) tortious claims against all the defendants, based on an alleged conspiracy among them to prevent the debtors paying those debts. The claimant served the debtors in the jurisdiction, relying on service provisions in the relevant instruments. The debtors did not engage with the proceedings and were liable to judgment in default by the time the claimant sought permission to serve the other defendants outside the jurisdiction. Summary judgment was later obtained on the contractual claims. In addition, the claimant had proved for the relevant debts in a Russian insolvency process. Despite the claimant's various efforts, no recoveries had been made against the debtors. In the circumstances, it appeared that they had been sued in England for the sole purpose of bringing in the other defendants. Flaux J nonetheless granted permission to serve those defendants outside the jurisdiction, concluding (among other things) that the requirements under para 3.1(3) of Practice Direction 6B were met where all the claims were viable on the merits.[40] The Court of Appeal overturned the decision, including on the basis that Flaux J had erred in principle in his approach to para 3.1(3).

So far as concerns the claimant's motive, the Court followed *Altimo*, holding that the fact the claimant's only reason for suing the 'anchor' defendants was to establish jurisdiction over the foreign defendants was a discretionary consideration and 'not an element in deciding the question whether the gateway requirements of paragraph 3.1(3)(a) or (b) [of Practice Direction 6B] have been satisfied'.[41] The Court

---

[38] *Altimo* (n 8) [67].
[39] [2015] EWCA Civ 379, [2015] 1 CLC 706 (CA) (hereafter *Erste*).
[40] [2013] EWHC 2926 (Comm), [2014] BPIR 81.
[41] *Erste* (n 39) [43].

did so despite its 'reservations on this point' noting that to revisit the issue would require reconsideration of *Multinational Gas*, which was thought to be a matter for the Supreme Court.[42] The Court did not elaborate on these 'reservations' and it is not obvious why it would be preferable to treat a claimant's motive as a jurisdictional requirement rather than a discretionary consideration. That is particularly so bearing in mind that: (i) the Rule does not in terms lay down such a requirement; (ii) given the rationale for the rule in terms of facilitating administration of justice, such a requirement seems unduly restrictive, as the rationale may be engaged irrespective of the claimant's particular motivation in suing a particular defendant; (iii) practical difficulty would arise if the Court were required accurately to ascertain a claimant's motivation in the interlocutory context; (iv) motivations for suing come in various shades of nuance, particularly in complex commercial litigation, and it is difficult to capture these in a jurisdictional requirement; and (v) whereas the difficulties and nuances that arise as regards a claimant's motives can be managed with flexibility in the context of a judicial discretion, that is not so in the context of a jurisdictional requirement—at least, not unless the requirement is formulated in terms akin to a discretion.

Despite following *Altimo* as regards the approach to motive, the Court of Appeal in *Erste* alighted on the requirement under para 3.1(3)(a) of Practice Direction 6B that the claim against the 'anchor' defendant raise a 'real issue which it is reasonable for the court to try'. It treated this as entailing distinct requirements such that it was not sufficient that (as Flaux J had found, and as the defendants accepted on appeal) the claims were viable, in the sense that they raised issues that could not be disposed of without a trial. Rather, a claimant had to go further and show that it was 'reasonable' for the Court to conduct that trial. The Court of Appeal rejected the submission that *Altimo* precluded consideration of such 'wider issues of reasonableness' under para 3.1(3)(a). Flaux J having failed to consider them in that context, the Court approached the matter afresh and concluded that the requirements of the paragraph were not satisfied.

It is impossible within the confines of this essay fully to summarise the Court's detailed reasoning on that issue. In essence, the Court concluded as it did because: (i) disagreeing with Flaux J, it found that by the time the claimant sought permission to serve out, it had submitted to the jurisdiction of the Russian Courts in the context of the insolvency processes there; and (ii) in any case, the Court held that there were no 'real issues' that it was 'reasonable' for the English Court to try as against the debtors. In that latter respect, the Court focused on the fact that the claimant's contractual claims against the debtors were undisputed, the tortious claims duplicated them in quantum terms such that they afforded no greater prospect of recovery, and even if the claimant wished to pursue these claims in

---

[42] Ibid.

England, it was not 'reasonable' for the claimant to do so, including having regard to the overriding objective, and the Court's concern to avoid wasteful litigation.

Standing back from the detail of the Court's reasoning in *Erste*, it appears that the sorts of consideration that would have been relevant to an assessment of the claimant's motives were taken into account as part of the enquiry into 'wider issues of reasonableness' that para 3.1(3)(a) was construed to require. It is debatable how far that approach is consistent with *Altimo*, *Multinational Gas*, or Morton J's statement of principle in *Ellinger*.[43] It is also debatable whether it is a positive development in the law. The practical consequence is to elevate matters that would otherwise be discretionary considerations to matters relevant to the question of law as to whether the Court has the power to permit service out at all; and thereby to increase the prospect of such matters being further debated on appeal, with attendant additional cost and delay for litigants, not to mention impact on the Court's resources. Furthermore, the Court of Appeal's approach has these consequences without the benefit of increasing certainty in the law: as the Court conceded, and its analysis reveals, its construction of para 3.1(3)(a) results in incorporating as jurisdictional issues questions that are 'finely nuanced' and 'soft-edged'. It might be thought that such matters are better dealt with as discretionary considerations, alongside the claimant's motives and other such nuanced issues.

4. The proper forum

The final topic addressed in this section is the requirement that England be shown to be the proper forum before service out is permitted. This is now contained in CPR r 6.37(3), which imports, by the requirement that England be the 'proper place in which to bring the claim' the principles authoritatively stated in *Spliada*. As Lord Collins explained in *Altimo*, the 'task of the court is to identify the forum in which the case can be suitably tried for the interests of all the parties and for the ends of justice'.[44]

In the context of the necessary or proper party head of jurisdiction, the application of this requirement is often relatively straightforward. That is because the prospect of a multiplicity of proceedings is ordinarily inimical to the interests of the parties and the ends of justice, not least owing to the risk of irreconcilable judgments. Thus, the fact that the English Court is capable of determining the claim as against all proper parties is typically a weighty consideration in favour of its being

---

[43] The Court contrasted the language of CPR PD 6B para 3.1(3)(a) ('a real issue which it is reasonable for the court to try') with what was thought to be 'the more subjective formulation' of Morton J in Ellinger (ie 'a real issue ... which the plaintiff may reasonably ask the court to try'): *Erste* (n 39) [48]. Some may think that a distinction without a difference; and it is notable that the supposed difference was not detected in *Altimo* (n 8) [65]–[66].

[44] *Altimo* (n 8) [88].

the proper forum: 'in practice the factors which make the party served a necessary or proper party ... will also weigh heavily in favour of granting leave to make the foreigner a party, although they will not be conclusive'.[45] Where the claimant may proceed in England against the 'anchor' defendant in any event, that is often a decisive factor in favour of England as the proper forum for claims against other proper parties, even if the case otherwise exhibits connecting factors elsewhere, at least where the decision is between determination of the dispute against all proper parties in England and a multiplicity of proceedings in England and elsewhere.[46] By contrast, where it is possible for the dispute against all proper parties to be resolved in England or in a foreign forum,[47] identification of the proper forum ordinarily depends on considering the connecting factors to the competing jurisdictions and the relative convenience of dispute resolution there. In the end, however, the question of 'proper place' is an evaluative one,[48] and the Court retains a residual discretion under CPR r 6.36. The scheme is a flexible one enabling the Court to exercise its powers to permit service out, or stay its proceedings, in a manner that is sensitive to all the circumstances.

The flexibility in this scheme was called into question in cases where jurisdiction over English-domiciled 'anchor' defendants was established under Art 4(1) of the Recast Brussels I Regulation. The Court of Justice of the EU (CJEU) having held in *Owusu v Jackson*[49] that the English Court has no power to decline such jurisdiction on *forum non conveniens* grounds, it followed that a claimant would be entitled to proceed against such a defendant irrespective of whether England was the proper forum. Professor Briggs observed that this was liable to produce 'remarkable' and 'startling' consequences for foreign defendants joined as necessary or proper parties: a claimant could rely on his entitlement under Art 4(1), coupled with the English Court's traditional concern to avoid a multiplicity of proceedings, to argue that England was the proper forum.[50]

English Courts approached the argument with varying degrees of enthusiasm. Some Courts were unwilling to treat *Owusu* as a 'trump card' as against foreign defendants, drawing attention to the fact that insofar as a risk of a multiplicity of proceedings arose, that was a result of the claimant's choice to proceed against the 'anchor' defendant in England notwithstanding that there was an available

---

[45] *Société Commerciale de Réassurance v Eras International Ltd (formerly Eras (UK)) (The Eras Eil Actions)* [1992] 1 Lloyd's Rep 570 (CA) 591 (Mustill LJ).
[46] eg *OJSC VTB Bank v Parline Limited* [2013] EWHC 3538 (Comm) [16] (Leggatt J) (hereafter *Parline*).
[47] eg because the evidence showed that all the defendants could be sued in that foreign forum, or they would undertake to submit to its jurisdiction.
[48] *VTB Capital plc v Nutritek International Corp* [2013] UKSC 5, [2013] AC 337 [97].
[49] Case C-281/02 [2005] ECR I-1383, [2005] QB 801.
[50] Briggs, *Civil Jurisdiction and Judgments* (n 1) [4.65].

and more appropriate forum for the dispute elsewhere.[51] Other Courts took the view that this gave insufficient weight to the fact that the claimant was entitled as a matter of EU law to sue the 'anchor' defendant in England. For example, in *OJSC VTB Bank v Parline*, Leggatt J (as he then was) said that:[52]

> [I]t is a matter of entitlement on the claimant's part to sue the ['anchor' defendants] in England. There is no reason why the claimant should be expected or required to relinquish that right in order to avoid duplication of proceedings. Rather, it seems to me that the existence of that right and the fact that it is being exercised is the starting point and the background against which I ought to consider the question of whether England is also the appropriate forum for the claim against the [foreign defendant].

In *Vedanta Resources plc v Lungowe*,[53] the Supreme Court was required to choose between these approaches. The claimants were Zambian citizens, resident in Zambia. They brought claims in tort against an English company and its Zambian subsidiary in respect of alleged negligence causing damage in Zambia. The defendants challenged jurisdiction. One of the issues that arose was whether England was the proper forum for the claim so as to justify service out on the Zambian subsidiary as a proper party to the proceedings. The issue arose in circumstances where jurisdiction had been asserted over the English company pursuant to Art 4(1) of the Recast Brussels I Regulation, but it had undertaken to submit to the Zambian Court's jurisdiction to enable the case to be resolved there against both defendants. In a judgment with which the other Justices agreed, Lord Briggs JSC concluded 'after anxious consideration'[54] that Leggatt J's approach in *Parline* (which had been followed by the lower courts in *Vedanta*) was wrong in principle.

Lord Briggs held that Art 4(1) could not be interpreted 'to confer upon claimants a right to bring proceedings against an EU domiciliary in the member state of its domicile in such a way that avoids incurring the risk of irreconcilable judgments'. In support of that, his Lordship reasoned that in the intra-EU context, a claimant with claims against co-defendants domiciled in different Member States had the choice whether to sue them in separate proceedings, in each of their domiciles, with the attendant risk of irreconcilable judgments, or to rely on Art 8(1) to bring a single proceeding and thereby mitigate that risk. He considered that the claimants were faced with a similar choice in *Vedanta*. Lord Briggs said that his approach did not reintroduce *forum conveniens* considerations in the context of Art 4(1). Rather,

---

[51] eg *Pacific International Sports Clubs Ltd v Soccer Marketing International Ltd* [2009] EWHC 1839 (Ch) [111]–[112] (Blackburne J); *OJSC TNK-BP Holding v Beppler & Jacobson Ltd* [2012] EWHC 3286 (Ch) [313] (Andrew Sutcliffe QC).
[52] *Parline* (n 46) [10].
[53] [2019] UKSC 20, [2010] 2 WLR 1051 (SC) (hereafter *Vedanta*).
[54] Ibid [79].

it recognised that the claimants had a choice whether or not to avoid the risk of irreconcilable judgments by suing the English company in England (as was their right under Art 4(1)) or in Zambia (as was their right in the light of the defendants' agreement to that forum). He accordingly considered the question of proper forum afresh, treating the risk of irreconcilable judgments as a relevant factor but not a 'trump card'. Bearing in mind the overwhelming connections to Zambia, and the fact that any risk of irreconcilable judgments would be the result of the claimants' choice to sue the defendants separately, he would have concluded that the claimants had failed to establish that England was the proper forum, had he not gone on to find that substantial justice was unavailable to the claimants in Zambia.

C. Art 8(1) of the Recast Brussels I Regulation

1. Origins and development

Art 8(1) of the Recast Brussels I Regulation has its origins in the 1968 Brussels Convention.[55] Art 6(1) of that Convention provided for special jurisdiction over co-defendants as follows: 'a person domiciled in a Contracting State may also be sued: 1. where he is one of a number of defendants, in the courts for the place where any one of them is domiciled.' The provision remained in this form in subsequent versions of the Brussels Convention and in the initial version of the Lugano Convention adopted in 1988.[56]

According to the Jenard Report, Art 6(1) of the Brussels Convention reflected the internal law of the original Contracting States, other than Germany.[57] Mr Jenard explained that it was adopted by the Contracting States to address the risk of irreconcilable judgments resulting from separate proceedings, and said this regarding its application:[58]

> In order for this rule to be applicable there must be a connection between the claims made against each of the defendants, as for example in the case of joint debtors. It follows that action cannot be brought solely with the object of ousting the jurisdiction of the courts in which the defendant is domiciled.

---

[55] Convention on jurisdiction and the enforcement of judgments in civil and commercial matters (Brussels, 27 September 1968) ([1972] OJ L299/42) (hereafter 1968 Brussels Convention).
[56] Convention on jurisdiction and the enforcement of judgments in civil and commercial matters (Lugano, 16 September 1988 ([1988] L319/9).
[57] Report on the Convention on jurisdiction and the enforcement of judgments in civil and commercial matters ([1979] OJ C 59/1) 26.
[58] Ibid 26–27.

126   JURISDICTION OVER CO-DEFENDANTS

Art 6(1) did not in terms require such a connection, however; and Mr Jenard did not precisely define the connection envisaged. Nor did he further elaborate on its interrelationship with the concern to prevent ouster of the jurisdiction of a defendant's domicile; and in particular, whether this latter concern amounted to a separate requirement in the context of Art 6(1), or merely the rationale for the connection envisaged. In that regard, it is notable that whereas Art 6(2) of the Convention[59] was expressly subject to such a requirement, Art 6(1) was not so subject. It fell to the courts to resolve these ambiguities.

The matter was addressed in *Kalfelis v Bankhaus Schroeder Munchmeyer Hengst & Co (t/a HEMA Beteiligungsgesellschaft mbH)*.[60] The European Court imposed a connection requirement on Art 6(1), holding as follows:

> For Article 6(1) of the Convention to apply there must exist between the various actions brought by the same plaintiff against different defendants a connection of such a kind that it is expedient to determine the actions together in order to avoid the risk of irreconcilable judgments resulting from separate proceedings.

The Court reasoned that:[61] (i) as a head of special jurisdiction, Art 6(1) was an exception to the general principle under the Convention that a defendant shall be sued in his domicile; (ii) it was accordingly necessary to construe Art 6(1) so as not to call the very existence of that principle into question; (iii) that possibility could arise if an action could be brought under Art 6(1) with the sole object of ousting the jurisdiction of the defendant's domicile; (iv) the Jenard Report made clear the Contracting States' concern to protect against this by requiring a connection between the claims made against each of the defendants in order to invoke Art 6(1); (v) to ensure the uniformity of the Convention, it was necessary to define this connection independently of national law; and (vi) in circumstances where the purpose of Art 6(1) (as appeared from the Jenard Report) and the Convention more generally (as appeared from Art 22, on related actions) was to address the risk of irreconcilable judgments resulting from separate proceedings, the connection set out in the passage quoted above was appropriate.

While the Court relied in *Kalfelis* on the concern to protect against a claimant whose sole object or motive in invoking the co-defendant rule was to oust the jurisdiction of a defendant's domicile, it did so as part of the rationale for the connection requirement that it imposed; it did not suggest that Art 6(1) was itself subject

---

[59] Which provides for special jurisdiction as against a 'third party in an action on a warranty or guarantee or in any other third party proceedings, in the court seised of the original proceedings, unless these were instituted solely with the object of removing him from the jurisdiction of the court which would be competent in his case'.
[60] Case 189/87 [1988] ECR 5565.
[61] Ibid [7]–[12].

to an anti-ouster requirement such as appears in Art 6(2) of the Convention.[62] The same approach was adopted by the EU legislator when it adopted the Brussels I Regulation in 2001.[63] Codifying the connection requirement laid down in *Kalfelis*, Art 6(1) of the Regulation provided that:

> A person domiciled in a Member State may also be sued: 1. where he is one of a number of defendants, in the courts where any one of them is domiciled, provided that the claims are so closely connected that it is expedient to hear and determine them together to avoid the risk of irreconcilable judgments resulting from separate proceedings.

Art 6(1) did not, however, adopt the anti-ouster requirement that continued to appear in Art 6(2) of the Regulation. The EU legislator regarded the connection requirement as preferable in this context, because it was thought to be more objective than the anti-ouster requirement the European Commission had proposed.[64] The same approach was adopted when the EU entered into the revised Lugano Convention in 2007,[65] Art 6(1) of which is in terms materially identical to Art 6(1) of the Brussels I Regulation, adopting the connection requirement laid down in *Kalfelis*, but without any anti-ouster requirement such as appears in Art 6(2). As appears from the Pocar Report on the 2007 Lugano Convention, this was again a conscious decision, taken against the advice of the Commission, on the express basis that the connection requirement was thought 'sufficient to avoid misuse of the rule'.[66] The EU legislator followed the same approach when it adopted the Recast Brussels I Regulation in 2012. Art 8(1) of that Regulation is in terms materially identical to those of Art 6(1) of its predecessor, and of the 2007 Lugano Convention. Like its predecessors, the text imposes two requirements. First, that one of the defendants be sued in his domicile. Second, that the connection requirement derived from *Kalfelis* be satisfied. There are no further textual requirements.

---

[62] The importance of distinguishing between the terms of a derogation such as the co-defendant rule and its rationale is perhaps self-evident bearing in mind the importance that the EU regime attaches to legal certainty. If authority were needed, see eg *AMTF Futures v Marzillier, Dr Meier & Dr Guntner Rechtsanwaltsgesellschaft mbH* [2017] UKSC 13, [2018] AC 439 [14] and [29] (Lord Hodge JSC, with whose judgment the other justices agreed).
[63] Council Regulation (EC) No 44/2001 of 22 December 2000 on jurisdiction and the recognition and enforcement of judgments in civil and commercial matters ([2001] OJ 12/1) (hereafter Brussels I Regulation).
[64] *Freeport v Arnoldsson* (C-98/06) [2007] ECR I-8319 [51] (hereafter *Freeport*) (recording the Commission's observation to that effect).
[65] Convention on jurisdiction and the recognition and enforcement of judgments in civil and commercial matters [2007] (OJ L339/3), which no longer applies in the UK after 1 January 2021 (Civil Jurisdiction and Judgments (Amendment) (EU) Exit Regulations (SI 2019/479), reg 82. The UK's application to rejoin the Convention is pending.
[66] Explanatory Report on the 2007 Lugano Convention by Professor Fausto Pocar ([2009] OJ C 319/1) [70].

It will be necessary to consider below some of the case law on the claimant's motive in invoking what is now Art 8(1) and the difficulties that have arisen in reconciling the CJEU's observations on this issue. But it bears emphasis at the outset that at no stage in the genesis of Art 8(1) has enquiry into these matters been required by the express terms of the legislation. It is difficult to regard that as an oversight or an irrelevance in circumstances where what is now Art 8(2) and its predecessors have always expressly required that enquiry.

2. The Scope of Art 8(1)

As with the domestic rule, the purpose of Art 8(1) is to facilitate the sound administration of justice.[67] However, the provision is subject to two restrictions that undermine its ability to achieve this purpose.

First, as noted above in Section C.1, like its predecessors, Art 8(1) is confined to cases where the 'anchor' defendant is sued in his domicile. Insofar as that reflected the position in the internal law of most of the original Contracting States to the Brussels Convention, it did not reflect the internal laws of at least some of the states that subsequently acceded;[68] and nor did it reflect English domestic law following the changes to RSC, Order XI that were made in 1987. Moreover, the restriction is difficult to justify bearing in mind the purpose of the provision. It has the effect that even though jurisdiction over the 'anchor' defendant may be established on the basis of a provision of the Regulation that takes precedence over the general domicile rule, a co-defendant cannot be joined under Art 8(1). For example, a Member State may have jurisdiction by agreement under Art 25 of the Regulation, or exclusive jurisdiction pursuant to Art 24; but in neither case does Art 8(1) apply. Nor does the provision apply where special jurisdiction arises under Art 7, notwithstanding that such jurisdiction is necessarily premised on there being a close connection with the dispute.[69]

As Professor Briggs has observed regarding the narrow scope of Art 8(1), 'One has to wonder why this should be'.[70] It cannot be justified on the ground that considerations of the sound administration of justice *only* arise in cases in which a defendant is sued in his domicile. Nor can it be justified on the ground that it is *only* in such cases that jurisdiction is proper, given that the Regulation itself recognises various exceptions to the general principle of jurisdiction by domicile. It

---

[67] Recast Brussels I Regulation (n 2) Recital (16).
[68] eg it did not reflect Greek law: see the Report on the accession of the Hellenic Republic [1986] OJ C298/1 [56](a), explaining with reference to Art 6(1) of the 1968 Brussels Convention (n 55) that 'Greek law goes further and permits the institution of joint proceedings before the court which is vested with either general or some special form of jurisdiction in respect of any one of the defendants'.
[69] Recast Brussels I Regulation (n 2) Recital (16).
[70] Briggs, *Civil Jurisdiction and Judgments* (n 1) [2.227].

is also difficult to see how a concern for the foreign defendant might justify the restriction. True enough, the European Court has said that heads of special jurisdiction (Art 8(1) included) must be interpreted such that a defendant can reasonably foresee before which Member State court he may be sued.[71] But that concern cannot sensibly be regarded as satisfied *only* where proceedings are brought in another defendant's domicile.

Given the clear terms of the legislation which it has to interpret, it is difficult to see what the European Court could do to remedy this particular deficiency; and it has declined the invitation to do so. In *Réunion Européenne v Spliethoff's Bevrachtingskantoor BV & Anor*,[72] the French Cour de Cassation asked whether what is now Art 8(1) could be interpreted to apply in proceedings brought otherwise than in a defendant's domicile, on the ground that the claims against the various defendants were not merely connected, but were 'indivisible'. The European Court held that it could not be so interpreted. The Court gave various reasons for this conclusion, certain of which have been the subject of some controversy[73] and clarification in its subsequent case law.[74] But the principal, sufficient, and incontrovertible reason for the Court's decision in *Réunion* was the terms of the Article itself, coupled with the fact that one of the fundamental protections under the Brussels regime is that persons domiciled in a Member State may only be sued elsewhere pursuant to the common jurisdictional rules that the regime lays down.[75] The problem is that what is now Art 8(1) has always been cast in terms too narrow fully to ensure the sound administration of justice in the case of co-defendants. That is a matter for the EU legislator, which has regrettably been unwilling to extend the rule beyond cases in which at least one of the defendants is sued in his domicile.[76]

The second feature of Art 8(1) that undermines its ability to facilitate the sound administration of justice is the connection requirement derived from *Kalfelis*. As set out above in Section C.1, the requirement is concerned with and confined to

---

[71] *Reisch Montage AG v Kiesel Baumaschinen Handels GmbH* Case C-103/05 [2006] ECR I-6827 [25].
[72] Case C-51/97 [1998] ECR I-6511 (hereafter *Réunion Européenne*).
[73] Andrew Scott, '*Réunion* revised?' (2008) LMCLQ 113 (hereafter Scott, '*Réunion* revised?').
[74] See further text to nn 80–86.
[75] Recast Brussels I Regulation (n 2) Art. 5(1); 1968 Brussels Convention (n 55) Art. 3.
[76] That is so despite the fact that the so-called 'Heidelberg Report' procured by the European Commission for the purpose of considering reforms to the Brussels I Regulation recognised the deficiencies in Art 6(1) as it stood and recommended that further consideration be given to expanding its scope beyond cases in which a defendant is sued in its domicile: Hess, Schlosser and Pfeiffer, 'The General Report of the Study on the Application of Regulation Brussels I in the (former) 25 Member States' (Study JLS/C4/2005/03) [226]–[227]. However, no proposals in this regard were made in the European Commission's report on the Brussels I Regulation adopted on 21 April 2009: European Commission, 'Report from the Commission to the European Parliament, the Council and the European Economic and Social Committee on the application of Council Regulation (EC) No 44/2001 on jurisdiction and the recognition and enforcement of judgments in civil and commercial matters' COM (2009) 174 final; and when the Recast Brussels I Regulation was adopted, Art 8(1) retained the same scope as its predecessor.

protecting against the risk of irreconcilable judgments. That is an important consideration in the context of a rule providing jurisdiction over co-defendants, as the English Court's practice in relation to the domestic rule well-illustrates. But it is not the only consideration that informs the question whether the sound administration of justice requires multiple claims to be determined together. For example, considerations of cost, convenience, and conserving judicial resources also play a role. Whereas the domestic rule is sufficiently broad to accommodate these considerations, the equivalent rule under EU law is not. It might be said that to take account of such broader considerations would be inimical to the Regulation's purpose in terms of achieving legal certainty. But that would be difficult to sustain where it is also a purpose of the Regulation—and a specific purpose of Art 8(1)—to facilitate the sound administration of justice. Furthermore, it is notable that Art 8(2) is not confined to cases in which there is a risk of irreconcilable judgments resulting from separate proceedings, and the European Court has held a Member State court seised under that provision may apply its own procedural law to determine whether or not to allow the third-party proceeding to be brought.[77] If such flexibility can be tolerated in that context, why would it be intolerable in the context of Art 8(1)?

Again, the European Court is constrained by the text it has to interpret, which codifies the connection requirement that was laid down in *Kalfelis* with reference to the risk of irreconcilable judgments and goes no further. The Court accordingly has limited room for manoeuvre, confined to providing further guidance on what that requirement entails. That said, and as Professor Briggs has observed 'the approach of the European Court to this issue has not been easy to follow'.[78] Particularly challenging were observations in *Réunion*, which appeared to suggest that the claims must share the same legal basis in order to exhibit the requisite connection.[79] Few found that suggestion persuasive,[80] and the Court was asked to provide clarification.[81] It did so in *Freeport*.[82] It explained that the observations in *Réunion* were not directed at what is now Art 8(1), which, as noted above, was straightforwardly not engaged in that case; rather, they were directed at what is now Art 7(2), under which the referring court was seised in *Réunion*, the Court's point being that that provision applied to claims in tort and did not extend to claims in contract[83]—and

---

[77] *Kongress Hagen GmbH v Zeehaghe BV* Case C-365/88 [1990] ECR I-1845; Briggs, *Civil Jurisdiction and Judgments* (n 1) [2.238].
[78] Briggs, *Civil Jurisdiction and Judgments* (n 1) [2.229].
[79] *Réunion Européenne* (n 72) [50].
[80] *Andrew Weir Shipping Ltd v Wartsilla UK Ltd* [2004] EWHC 1284 (Comm), [2004] 2 Lloyd's Rep 377, in which Cooke J stated (at [69]) that 'if the [Court's] intention was to lay down a general principle applicable to art. 6.1, it is simply wrong' and endorsed Professor Briggs' observations to that effect in Adrian Briggs and Peter Rees, *Civil Jurisdiction and Judgments* (4th edn, Informa 2004) [2.175].
[81] eg *Watson v First Choice Holidays and Flights Ltd* [2001] EWCA Civ 972, [2001] 2 Lloyd's Rep 339 [28]-[40] (in which the case settled before the questions referred were answered).
[82] *Freeport* (n 64).
[83] As the European Court had specifically held in *Kalfelis* (n 60) Operative Part, [2](a), Judgment, [19]-[20].

it was in that context that such claims could not be regarded as connected.[84] It is debatable how persuasive the explanation was;[85] but nothing of any practical significance turns on that. What matters is that *Freeport* makes clear that there is no requirement under Art 8(1) that the claims have the same legal basis: the question is whether there is a risk of 'divergence in the outcome of the dispute ... [arising] in the context of the same situation of law and fact', it being for a national court to determine whether there is the requisite connection between the claims taking account of 'all the necessary factors in the case file', which may, or may not, include the legal bases for the claims.[86] The Court has subsequently followed this formulation, identifying further potentially relevant considerations, and emphasising that, in order for the requisite connection to be established, it must be foreseeable by the co-defendants that they may be sued in the Member State where at least one of them is domiciled.[87] Depending on the context, the Court has been more or less prescriptive in the guidance that it has given in that regard.[88]

Guided by this case law, English courts have generally approached the connection requirement under what is now Art 8(1) in a common sense and pragmatic way. The approach is well-illustrated by the Court of Appeal's decision in *Gard Marine & Energy Ltd v Lloyd Tunnicliffe*.[89] The case concerned reinsurance governed by English law, under which the claimant brought claims against various participants for sums said to be due, later adding claims against the brokers that placed the reinsurance. One of the defendant participants, a Swiss-domiciled entity, challenged jurisdiction, maintaining (among other things) that there was no sufficient connection between the claims for the purposes of Art 6(1) of the Lugano Convention. It relied in this regard on the particular terms of its participation and the circumstances in which it had been induced to participate, which were said to give rise to distinct defences. Thomas LJ (with whose judgment Richards and Ward LJJ agreed) took the law as set out in *Freeport* and concluded that the requisite connection was made out; in essence, because: (i) the principal issue against all participants turned on the proper construction of the reinsurance; (ii) the secondary issues arose in the same factual context as one another, as they concerned

---

[84] *Freeport* (n 64) [42]–[45].
[85] Professor Briggs described it as 'reverse ferret': Briggs, *Civil Jurisdiction and Judgments* (n 1) [2.229] fn 1358. cf Scott, '*Réunion* revised?' (n 73).
[86] *Freeport* (n 64) [39]–[41].
[87] eg *Painer v Standard Verlags GmbH* Case C-145/10 [2011] ECR I-12533 [81] (hereafter *Painer*); *Cartel Damage Claims (CDC) Hydrogen Peroxide SA v Akzo Nobel NV* Case C-352/13 [2015] ECLI:EU:C:2015:335, [2015] QB 906, [20]–[25] (hereafter *Cartel Damage Claims*).
[88] For example, in *Cartel Damage Claims* (n 87), which concerned claims arising out of a European Commission decision on competition law infringement, the Court held that the requisite connection was made out bearing in mind that the Commission had found a single and continuous infringement of EU law ([24]–[25]). For discussion of the Court's case law in the intellectual property context, see Briggs, *Civil Jurisdiction and Judgments* (n 1) [2.230] 285–286, in which Professor Briggs notes that a more prescriptive approach would appear to apply in the context of patents than other intellectual property rights.
[89] [2010] EWCA 1052, [2011] Bus LR 839 (CA).

the circumstances in which the placement occurred and alleged misrepresentations made in that regard; (iii) the brokers had been sued in England; (iv) it made obvious sense for all these interconnected issues to be tried together; and (v) the English Court was the proper forum to conduct that trial. One might add that it would have been readily foreseeable to a participant in a reinsurance governed by English law, placed on the London market, and involving London-based participants, that it might be sued alongside them in England.

3. Merits and motives

Until recently, it was difficult to state with confidence how Art 8(1) dealt with the merits of a claim against the 'anchor' defendant, the claimant's motive for suing him, or the interrelationship between these considerations. That was so for two main reasons.

First, Art 8(1) does not expressly incorporate a requirement that the claim against the 'anchor' defendant has merit; and it is difficult to discern from the European Court's case law a clear answer to the question whether the merits are relevant (at all) when applying the provision. Particularly challenging was the Court's decision in *Reisch Montage*, in which it held that what is now Art 8(1) could be relied on notwithstanding that the claim against the 'anchor' defendant was inadmissible under the law of the Member State court seised with the proceedings. In *Freeport*, the referring court asked whether it was relevant for the purpose of the connection requirement to enquire into the likelihood of success against the 'anchor' defendant; but the European Court declined to answer the question.[90] It was thus unclear whether the Court agreed with its Advocate General that enquiry into such matters was relevant to the extent of ascertaining whether the claim was 'manifestly inadmissible or unfounded in all respects'.[91]

Secondly, Art 8(1) does not expressly incorporate a requirement that directs attention to the claimant's motive in suing the 'anchor' defendant; and the European Court's case law gives guidance on this issue that is difficult to reconcile. In *Reisch Montage*, the Court appeared to suggest that motive was a relevant enquiry, observing that whereas the provision could not be interpreted to permit a claimant to rely on it for the sole purpose of ousting the jurisdiction of the foreign defendant's domicile, that did not appear to be the claimant's purpose in that case.[92] By contrast, in *Freeport*, the Court held that it is sufficient that the connection requirement is satisfied and there is no need to establish separately that the claim against the 'anchor' defendant was brought otherwise than with the sole object of ousting

---

[90] *Freeport* (n 64) [55]–[58].
[91] *Freeport* (n 64) Opinion of AG Mengozzi [70].
[92] *Reisch Montage* (n 71) [32].

the jurisdiction of the foreign defendant's domicile. In this regard, the Court drew attention to the legislative development of what is now Art 8(1) and the fact that a conscious decision was taken by the EU legislator not to subject the provision to an anti-ouster requirement such as appears in what is now Art 8(2), the legislator preferring to adopt the connection requirement that derives from *Kalfelis* as the means of protecting the domicile principle in the context of Art 8(1).[93] However, in the Court's subsequent decision in *Cartel Damage Claims*, it held that a Member State court nonetheless could conclude that Art 8(1) is inapplicable provided that there is 'firm evidence to support the conclusion that the applicant artificially fulfilled, or prolonged the fulfilment, of that provision's applicability'.[94]

It has fallen to national courts to attempt to reconcile this guidance. In the English context, some clarity has been provided by two recent decisions of the Court of Appeal; though in each case, the Court did not speak with one voice and there are tensions between the two decisions.

In *Sabbagh v Khoury*,[95] one of the issues was whether what is now Art 8(1) can be relied on where the claim against the 'anchor' defendant is hopeless. At first instance, it was conceded that it could not be relied on in such a case, given the well-established practice of the English Court in requiring the claim to raise serious issues to be tried.[96] On appeal, the claimant contended that that practice had no proper foundation in EU law. The issue did not ultimately arise for decision because (disagreeing with the lower court) the Court of Appeal unanimously concluded that the claim raised serious issues to be tried. However, full argument was heard on the issue, and reasoned conclusions were given regarding it. Beatson and Patten LJJ concluded that a hopeless claim against the 'anchor' defendant cannot engage Art 8(1), in summary reasoning that: (i) there is no material risk of irreconcilable judgments resulting from separate proceedings;[97] and (ii) it is properly to be inferred that the claimant's sole object is to oust the jurisdiction of the foreign defendant's domicile, such that it would be an abuse of the provision to allow the claimant to invoke it.[98] Bearing in mind the status of the provision as a derogation, the terms in which the European Court had expressed itself in *Reisch Montage* and *Cartel Damage Claims*, the majority rejected the submission that to establish abuse it was necessary to show fraud or bad faith.[99] Gloster LJ gave a powerful dissenting judgment on the issue. It is impossible here fully to summarise her

---

[93] *Freeport* (n 64) [51]–[53].
[94] *Cartel Damage Claims* (n 87) [28].
[95] [2017] EWCA Civ 1120 (hereafter *Sabbagh*).
[96] [2014] EWHC 3233 (Comm) [97]–[98] (Carr J).
[97] *Sabbagh* (n 95) [43], [44], [66], where the Court endorsed reasoning to that effect in first instance decisions (see *Brown v Innovatorone plc* [2010] EWHC 2281 (Comm), [2001] ILPr 118, [25] (Hamblen J); and *Bord Na Mona Horticulture Limited v British Polythene Industries plc* [2012] EWHC 3346 (Comm) [83] (Flaux J)) and, following those decisions, distinguished *Reisch Montage* (n 71) as a case concerned with a procedural bar.
[98] *Sabbagh* (n 95) [67]–[69].
[99] Ibid [47], [57], [67]-[69].

reasoning. Among other things, she reasoned that: (i) the European Court's case law as a whole supported the proposition that Art 8(1) could be invoked even if the claim against the 'anchor' defendant will not proceed, subject only to questions of fraudulent abuse;[100] (ii) it was impermissible to introduce a merits test as part of the connection requirement under Art 8(1), which was concerned with the connection between the claims as brought, not as to what would become of them as the case progressed;[101] and (iii) lack of merit was insufficient to establish abuse, which depended on showing fraud or bad faith.[102] The *obiter* observations in *Sabbagh* were recently considered in *Senior Taxi Aereo Executivo Ltda, Synergy Helicopters II LLC v Agusta Westland SpA*,[103] in which Waksman J endorsed and followed the majority view. For now, at least, it seems that that merits test is here to stay in the context of Art 8(1).

Motive again arose for consideration in *JSC Commercial Bank Privatbank v Kolomoisky*.[104] One of the issues for the Court of Appeal was whether a claimant could rely on Art 6(1) of the Lugano Convention in circumstances where it had a viable claim against the 'anchor' defendant, which it intended to pursue to judgment, but the claim had been brought with the sole object of suing the foreign defendants. The issue did not ultimately require determination, because the Court unanimously concluded that the lower court was wrong to conclude that that was the claimant's object. However, full argument was heard on the issue, and reasoned conclusions were given regarding it. David Richards and Flaux LJJ concluded that a claimant could rely on Art 6(1) in such circumstances. Their essential reasoning was that: (i) the terms of Art 6(1) and its legislative history did not support the imposition of a 'sole object' test; (ii) the concern about ouster was instead addressed in the context of Art 6(1) by the connection requirement derived from *Kalfelis*; (iii) to impose an additional requirement based on the claimant's intention would introduce unwelcome uncertainty; and (iv) such requirement was unsupported by European Court authority, *Freeport* being treated as authority for the proposition that there was no 'sole object' test and *Cartel Damages Claims* and *Reisch Montage* being treated as concerned with the narrower notion of abuse of law.[105] Newey LJ dissented, in essence because he disagreed with the majority's analysis of the European Court's decisions: in short, he treated *Reisch Montage* and *Cartel Damages Claims* as establishing a 'sole object' test rather than a narrower notion of abuse of law; and treated *Freeport* as (in essence) a decision that satisfaction of the

---

[100] Ibid [172]–[200].
[101] Ibid [201]–[209]. Gloster LJ's reasoning in this regard echoes the observation of Adv Gen Trstenjak in *Painer* (n 87) Opinion of AG Trstenjak [101]: 'Article 6(1) of the [Brussels I] regulation proceeds for the assumption of the abstract risk that the transfer of two judgments to two courts may result in inconsistencies between these judgments'.
[102] *Sabbagh* (n 95) [210]–[212].
[103] [2020] EWHC 1348 (Comm).
[104] [2019] EWCA Civ 1708, [2020] 2 WLR 993.
[105] Ibid [104]–[111].

connection requirement presumptively establishes that the claimant does not have the sole object of ousting the jurisdiction of the foreign defendant's domicile, but subject to proof to the contrary.

Taken together, the approaches adopted by the majorities in *Sabbagh* and *Privatbank* yield a scheme whereby it is necessary and sufficient for the claimant to show that the claim against the 'anchor' defendant is viable; provided that it is, sufficiently connected claims against foreign defendants may be brought under what is now Art 8(1). That is a workable scheme which goes some way to align the EU law rule with the domestic rule. In that sense, the Court of Appeal's judgments are to be welcomed.

Nonetheless, it is difficult to reconcile the reasoning adopted in the majority judgments in *Sabbagh* and *Privatbank*. In *Sabbagh*, the claimant conceded that there is a 'sole object' test in the context of Art 8(1)[106] and that was an important part of the majority's justification for the merits test they endorsed. But if there is no 'sole object' test, as the majority held in *Privatbank*, then it is more difficult to justify the merits test endorsed in *Sabbagh*. Two potential justifications can be identified. Neither is without difficulty.

First, the merits test might be justified based on the connection requirement under Art 8(1). The argument would be that where the English Court considers the claim against the 'anchor' defendant to be a hopeless one, it can safely be assumed that other Member State courts will view it the same way, such that there is no material risk of irreconcilable judgments.[107] However, some may think that a questionable assumption: as *Sabbagh* well-illustrates, judges often reach different views as to whether a claim is not a hopeless one. That is among the reasons that underlie the powerful argument, set out in Gloster LJ's dissenting judgment in *Sabbagh* and supported by Professor Briggs,[108] that enquiry into the merits is no part of the enquiry which the connection requirement entails.

Secondly, it might be said that the general principle against abuse of EU law justifies the merits test.[109] As articulated in *Cartel Damages Claim*, the principle applies in the context of Art 8(1) where a claimant has 'artificially fulfilled, or prolonged the fulfilment, of that provision's applicability'. In a case where a claim is brought against an 'anchor' defendant without any intention to pursue it to judgment, one can see how that principle is engaged: Art 8(1) expressly requires there to be a 'claim' and the bringing of proceedings against the 'anchor' defendant without intending to pursue them is fairly characterised as an artifice, particularly when the purpose of the provision is borne in mind. But if the claimant intends to pursue the 'claim' and the connection requirement is made out, it is difficult to see how its lack

---

[106] *Sabbagh* (n 95) [169(i)].
[107] This is the reasoning in the first instance authorities referred to at n 97 above.
[108] Briggs, *Civil Jurisdiction and Judgments* (n 1) [2.228].
[109] The principle was analysed, in the context of Art 4 of the Recast Brussels I Regulation, in *Vedanta* (n 53), Lord Briggs referring (among other things) to the case law on Art 8(1): [27]–[41].

of merit could of itself yield the conclusion that the requirements for Art 8(1) have been 'artificially fulfilled'. Lack of merit might be a factor from which the Court might in an appropriate case infer that there was no genuine intention to pursue the 'claim'. But that is not the same thing as the merits test that the English Court applies. For example, in *Sabbagh*, the lower court had rejected the suggestion that the claimant was acting in bad faith in bringing the claim and had found that its lack of merit was due to evidence that subsequently emerged. These were among the reasons why Gloster LJ considered that the abuse principle was not engaged.[110]

It remains to be seen what the European Court's position on these issues will be; as well as the final resting place of a claimant's motives within the scheme under Art 8(1). Whatever the European Court's answer, it is to be hoped that it is clearly expressed. A further, striking, feature of the judgments in *Sabbagh* and *Privatbank* is the extent to which the Court's decisions in this context are capable of being interpreted in very different ways. There is much force in Professor Briggs' observation that the Court's case law in this area has become a 'sorry mess'.[111] It will remain so until the Court clearly and precisely says what role (if any) a claimant's motives and the merits of its claim has in this context.

---

[110] *Sabbagh* (n 95) [211]).
[111] Briggs, *Civil Jurisdiction and Judgments* (n 1) [2.232].

PART II
CHOICE OF LAW

6
Putting the Principle of Severability in the Dock: An Analysis in the Context of Choice of Law for Arbitration and Jurisdiction Agreements

Koji Takahashi

A. Introduction

My first encounter with Professor Briggs was through his book, *Civil Jurisdiction and Judgments* (1993),[1] the first of many in his name. I was at that time writing a PhD thesis in London and the book was among the very few materials shedding useful light on the niche area of my research. Much excited, I approached him with a list of queries. The generosity and hospitality with which he received my visit in Oxford are still vivid in my memory.

Years later, after I had returned to my home country, Japan, I invited Professor Briggs to give seminars at my university. Writing in an article subsequently published from my university's law journal, he explained the ambitious goal of his trip as follows:[2]

> It is sometimes said of the common law conflict of laws that it lacks a fundamental theory, or that it develops pragmatically rather than in developing in accordance with a grand scheme. It did not generate jurists of the stature of Savigny; it did not produce treatises of abstract theory. The purpose of my coming to Japan is to explain how wrong and misconceived this criticism is. My intention is to lay before you an account of certain aspects of the English conflict of laws, and to seek to show you the really profound theory which explains it all.

---

[1] Adrian Briggs and Peter Rees, *Norton Rose on Civil Jurisdiction and Judgments* (1st edn, Lloyd's of London Press 1993).

[2] Adrian Briggs, 'Distinctive Aspects of the Conflict of Laws in Common Law System: Autonomy and Agreement in the Conflict of Laws' (2005) 57–3 同志社法学 [Doshisha Law Review] 21 [3].

Anyone curious to find out how Professor Briggs successfully accomplished this task should consult the article. He recalled the experience as a 'challenge for all concerned' in the preface of his book, *Agreements on Jurisdiction and Choice of Law*.[3] One of the distinguishing features of the book is its thorough discussion of damages for breach of jurisdiction agreements. It is in fact a topic I specifically requested him to address in his seminars in Japan as the granting of that remedy was to my mind characteristic of the common law approach. Inspired by his analysis, I myself managed to write a set of articles on the same topic.[4] In theoretical terms, the remedy of damages brings to light the substantive character of jurisdiction agreements of which attention is usually centred on the procedural character.[5] The appreciation of the substantive character of such dispute resolution agreements further stimulated me to write an article, 'Autonomy of Arbitration Agreements and Choice-of-Court Agreements: Re-evaluation in Choice-of-Law Context'.[6] It was written in Japanese, using primarily Japanese materials and caused some heated debate in Japan. This essay will examine the same topic, using materials drawn primarily from the common law and European law.

B. Purpose and Structure of This Essay

The principle of severability (or separability) is a principle widely accepted in the legislation and case law on arbitration agreements and jurisdiction agreements (hereafter 'arbitration and jurisdiction agreements' for short).[7] It signifies that these agreements should be treated as being severable from the contract in which they are contained (hereinafter 'matrix contract').

---

[3] Adrian Briggs, *Agreements on Jurisdiction and Choice of Law* (OUP 2008) (hereafter Briggs, *Agreements*).

[4] Koji Takahashi, 'Damages for Breach of a Choice-of-Court Agreement' (2008) 10 Yearbook of Private International Law 57; and Koji Takahashi, 'Damages for Breach of a Choice-of-Court Agreement: Remaining Issues' (2009) 11 Yearbook of Private International Law 73.

[5] See further Edwin Peel's essay in this collection (ch 12).

[6] 「仲裁合意・管轄合意の独立性原則―準拠法決定プロセスにおける再検討」(2012) 147-3 民商法雑誌 255.

[7] With respect to arbitration agreements, see eg Art 21(2) of the Arbitration Rules of the United Nations Commission on International Trade Law (UNGA Res 31/98 (15 December 1976) UN Doc A/31/98), Art 16 of the Model Law on International Commercial Arbitration of the United Nations Commission on International Trade Law (UNGA Res 40/72 and 61/33 (11 December 1985, as amended 4 December 2006) UN Doc A/40/17, annex I and A/61/17, annex I) (hereafter UNCITRAL Model Law), s 1040 of the German Code of Civil Procedure (ZPO) and s 7 of the English Arbitration Act 1996; also *Fiona Trust & Holding Corporation v Privalov* [2007] UKHL 40, [2007] 4 All ER 951 [17], [18] (hereafter *Fiona Trust*). With respect to jurisdiction agreements, see eg Art 3(d) of the Hague Convention on Choice of Court Agreements (2005) (hereafter Hague Choice of Court Convention) and Art 25(5) of the Regulation (EU) No 1215/2012 of the European Parliament and of the Council of 12 December 2012 on jurisdiction and the recognition and enforcement of judgments in civil and commercial matters [2012] OJ L351/1 (hereafter Recast Brussels I Regulation); also *Benincasa v Dentalkit Srl* Case C-269/95 [1997] ECR I-3767 and *Deutsche Bank AG v Asia Pacific Broadband Wireless Communications Inc* [2008] EWCA Civ 1091, [2009] 2 All ER (Comm) 129 [24].

The principle of severability also has the potential of influencing the choice of law analysis for determining the law applicable to arbitration and jurisdiction agreements. While this essay will accept that this principle is useful and defensible in the sphere of substantive law (Section C), it will challenge the assumption, often formed on the basis of this principle, that arbitration and jurisdiction agreements should be treated as a distinct contract severed from the matrix contract for the sake of determining their governing law[8] (Section D). This essay will, however, accept that arbitration and jurisdiction agreements are, like any other terms in the same matrix contract, subject to the choice of law technique known as *dépeçage* (splitting), though it will be suggested that the possibility of involuntary *dépeçage* should be circumscribed (Section E). After the summing up of the preferred choice of law approach based on the preceding analysis (Section F), an illustration will be given to show how it will operate in different scenarios in comparison with a rival approach (Section G). After giving an analysis to English cases on arbitration agreements (Section H), the essay will conclude by examining the compatibility of the preferred approach with existing instruments (Section I).

C. Substantive Law Sphere

In this section, we will observe how the principle of severability operates in the sphere of substantive law before proceeding to the next section where we will consider whether this principle should be extended to the sphere of choice of law analysis.

The principle of severability, that arbitration and jurisdiction agreements should be treated as being severable from the matrix contract, means in the sphere of substantive law that these agreements can only be found invalid on grounds which relate directly to them and not merely as a consequence of the invalidity of the matrix contract. This proposition is accepted in many jurisdictions[9] and adopted by various instruments. The UNCITRAL Model Law, for example, provides, 'A decision by the arbitral tribunal that the contract is null and void shall not entail *ipso jure* the invalidity of the arbitration clause' (Art 16(1)). The Hague Choice of Court Convention also provides, 'The validity of the exclusive choice of court agreement cannot be contested solely on the ground that the contract is not valid' (Art 3(d)). The Recast Brussels I Regulation contains essentially the same provision (Art 25(5)).

---

[8] This essay will not address the relevance of an arbitration or jurisdiction agreement to the determination of the law applicable to the matrix contract. For this question, see eg *Compagnie d'Armement Maritime SA v Compagnie Tunisienne de Navigation SA* [1971] AC 572.

[9] In England, see eg *Fiona Trust* (n 7).

The principle of severability is useful since a challenge to the jurisdiction of an arbitral tribunal or, as the case may be, the court chosen by a jurisdiction agreement often takes the form of an allegation that the matrix contract is invalid for fraud, mistake, misrepresentation, duress, or the like.[10] In the event that the tribunal or, as the case may be, the chosen court comes to accept that the matrix contract is indeed invalid, it would lose its competence if the validity of the arbitration agreement or, as the case may be, jurisdiction agreement (hereafter 'arbitration (or jurisdiction) agreement') automatically followed that of the matrix contract. However, by virtue of the principle of severability, it is open for the tribunal (or the chosen court) to form the view that the arbitration (or jurisdiction) agreement is validly concluded and proceed on that basis to hear the disputes consequent upon the finding of invalidity of the matrix contract. In many instances, the parties to an arbitration (or jurisdiction) agreement intend to have such issues resolved in their chosen forum. They may make it plain by stating along the lines that 'any disputes arising in connection with this contract, including any issues consequent upon the finding of invalidity of this contract, shall be referred to arbitration'. Such an agreement can be given effect thanks to the principle of severability.

The principle of severability is defensible as it leaves open for the tribunal (or the chosen court) to come to the conclusion that the given arbitration (or jurisdiction) agreement is invalid on the same ground that renders the matrix contract invalid. In *Fiona Trust*, a leading case which confirmed the severability of arbitration agreements in English law, Lord Hoffmann acknowledged[11] that an arbitration agreement might be hit by the same ground of invalidity as the matrix contract where, for example, a forged signature was used or the agent who concluded the contract lacked any authority to contract on the principal's behalf. This is unsurprising since an arbitration agreement is usually negotiated at the same time as other terms in the same contract and included in the same signed document. In *Harbour Assurance Ltd v Kansa General International Insurance Ltd*,[12] a case predating *Fiona Trust* in which the principle of severability was established for the first time in English law, Hoffmann LJ acknowledged[13] that the cases of *non est factum* and mistake as to the identity of the other contracting party were examples of cases in which a claim that no matrix contract came into existence would necessarily entail a denial that there was any agreement to arbitrate. It follows that in terms of outcomes, arbitration and jurisdiction agreements are not always 'severed' from the matrix contract but are only 'severable'.[14] While the word 'autonomy' is sometimes used to denote

---

[10] *BCY v BCZ* [2016] SGHC 249 [61] (Steven Chong J) (hereafter *BCY*).
[11] *Fiona Trust* (n 7) [17]. Lord Hope made the same point at [34] and [35].
[12] [1993] QB 701 (CA) (hereafter *Harbour Assurance*).
[13] Ibid 723.
[14] Adrian Briggs, *Private International Law in English Courts* (OUP 2014) [14.37] (hereafter Briggs, *Private International Law in English Courts*).

the same principle,[15] the expression 'severability' better captures this nuance.[16] It should, however, be noted that in terms of analytical methodology, these agreements are treated as being severed from the matrix contract since only the grounds for invalidity which relate directly to them may be taken into account.

The principle of severability should not be confused with its twin principle, Kompetenz-Kompetenz, which allows an arbitral tribunal to rule on its own competence. It is a principle just as widely accepted. The UNCITRAL Model Law, for example, provides that '[t]he arbitral tribunal may rule on its own jurisdiction, including any objections with respect to the existence or validity of the arbitration agreement' (Art 16(1)). In contrast to the principle of severability which operates in the sphere of substantive law, the principle of Kompetenz-Kompetenz operates in the sphere of procedural law.[17] Since a tribunal derives its competence solely from an arbitration agreement,[18] it ought in theory to have no power to rule on the validity of the agreement. The Kompetenz-Kompetenz principle is a convenient fiction since an arbitral process could otherwise be sabotaged too easily by a spurious claim that the arbitration agreement is invalid. The fiction is defensible as the arbitral tribunal's ruling on its own competence is only provisional: while the tribunal has the initial competence to rule on its own competence, the final determination is reserved with a State court. The UNCITRAL Model Law, for example, provides that if a tribunal rules that it has jurisdiction, any party may request the local court to decide the matter (Art 16(3)).

D. Extension to the Sphere of Choice of Law Analysis?

Let us now come to the core question of this essay. If, as observed in Section C, the principle of severability is useful and defensible in the sphere of substantive law, should it also guide the choice of law analysis? To borrow a line from one author,[19] should we assume that 'there are two separate contracts ... for which an applicable law must be selected, ie, the arbitration agreement and the substantive or main contract'?

---

[15] Emmanuel Gaillard and John Savage (eds), *Fouchard Gaillard Goldman on International Commercial Arbitration* (Kluwer Law International 1999) [389] (hereafter *Fouchard Gaillard Goldman*) notes that it is the accepted terminology in continental Europe.
[16] Pierre Mayer, 'The Limits of Severability of the Arbitration Clause' (1999) 9 ICCA Congress Series 261 (hereafter Mayer, 'The Limits of Severability').
[17] Jan Paulsson, *The Idea of Arbitration* (OUP 2013) [3.1(c)]. For a further comparison between these two principles, see *Fouchard Gaillard Goldman* (n 15) [416].
[18] A State court, by contrast, does not need the principle of Kompetenz-Kompetenz to rule on its competence since a jurisdiction agreement is not the only source of its competence. That a court is competent to examine its bases of jurisdiction including an agreement on its jurisdiction is, therefore, beyond question.
[19] Julian David Mathew Lew, 'The Law Applicable to the Form and Substance of the Arbitration Clause' (1999) 9 ICCA Congress Series 114, 136.

It is suggested that for the purpose of choice of law analysis, arbitration and jurisdiction agreements should not be treated as a distinct contract severed from the matrix contract save in exceptional cases where the given arbitration (or jurisdiction) agreement is concluded as a free-standing agreement. This suggestion rests on the following grounds.

First, since these agreements are usually negotiated and accepted as a vital part of the matrix contract, the parties would expect them to be treated in the same way as the other terms of the same contract.

Secondly, these agreements are not the only terms in a contract which are severable from the rest of the contract. Substantive terms may also survive the finding of invalidity of other terms of the same matrix contract. Yet, no suggestion is made that such terms should be treated as a distinct contract severed from the matrix contract for the purpose of choice of law analysis.

Thirdly, it is a matter for the governing law of an arbitration (or jurisdiction) agreement to determine, in the course of evaluating its validity, whether the principle of severability is accepted in the sphere of substantive law. It would accordingly be wrong to start from the assumption that arbitration and jurisdiction agreements are a priori severed from the matrix contract when embarking on the choice of law analysis.

Fourthly, whether the principle of severability should be a guiding principle depends on the purpose for which it is invoked. It is not anomalous to reject it in the context of choice of law analysis and then apply the governing law which, in the sphere of substantive law, endorses it.

Fifthly, the procedural character of arbitration and jurisdiction agreements does not warrant referring their validity to a law different from that which governs the matrix contract.

Finally, the proposition that arbitration and jurisdiction agreements should be treated as a distinct contract could not be ultimately sustained unless we could satisfactorily answer the difficult question of what generally constitutes a single contract for choice of law purposes. This question does not confront us if we argue for the opposite proposition supported by this essay since it should be sufficient to show that there are no good reasons to sever arbitration and jurisdiction agreements from the matrix contract.

These grounds will be elaborated in turn in the remainder of this section. Parenthetically, it should be noted that the mere mentioning of 'the law governing an arbitration (or jurisdiction) agreement' does not imply an admission that such an agreement should be treated as a distinct contract since that expression leaves open the question of how that law should be determined.

1. Expectation of the parties

Sometimes called 'midnight clauses',[20] arbitration and jurisdiction agreements are often negotiated as a vital part of the matrix contract and accepted without additional formality. The method of dispute resolution is an important element of the rights and obligations negotiated in a contract. Severability would be far from the minds of the ordinary parties engaged in negotiation. They would expect these agreements to be treated in the same way as the other terms in the same contract.[21]

Could the same be said if the given arbitration (or jurisdiction) agreement is concluded at a time or place different from the contract it relates to? A *compromis*, a post-dispute arbitration agreement, is a typical example of such an agreement. But a *clause compromissoire*, a pre-dispute arbitration agreement, could also be concluded at a time or place different from the contract it relates to. The temporal or spatial difference does not, however, detract from the fact that the arbitration (or jurisdiction) agreement is related to the specific contract in respect of which it is concluded.[22] It is, therefore, possible to view it as forming part of that contract. It is no different from the situation where substantive terms are separately negotiated. Take, for example, a term on the place of delivery of goods concluded after the contract of sale to which it relates. That term will no doubt be treated as forming part of the sale contract for the purpose of choice of law analysis.

It is a different story if the given arbitration (or jurisdiction) agreement is concluded as a free-standing agreement. Consider a jurisdiction agreement which reads, 'Should any dispute arise between the parties, irrespective of whether it arises in connection with this contract, each party may submit it to the courts of State X'. Such an agreement does not specify the disputes which it purports to cover. While it is rare to encounter a free-standing arbitration (or jurisdiction) agreement like this, it is not unknown.[23] Since there is no specific contract with which it is associated, a free-standing arbitration (or jurisdiction) agreement can only be treated as a distinct contract for the purpose of choice of law analysis. At the end of the day, however, such agreements may not be given effect. The UNCITRAL Model Law, for example, only gives effect to an agreement to arbitrate disputes arising 'in respect of a defined legal relationship' (Options I and II of Art 7). The Recast Brussels I Regulation likewise only gives effect to a jurisdiction agreement for disputes arising in connection with 'a particular legal relationship' (Art 25(1)).

---

[20] See *BCY* (n 10) [61] (per Steven Chong J).
[21] Edwin Peel, 'The Proper Law of an Arbitration Agreement' (2020) 136 LQR 534, 539.
[22] Arbitration and jurisdiction agreements concluded solely for non-contractual disputes are outside the purview of this essay since they do not raise the question whether they should be treated as being severed from the matrix contract.
[23] eg a jurisdiction agreement featured in the case of the Tokyo District Court's judgment on 15 February 2016 (available on Westlaw Japan at 2016WLJPCA02156001).

The expression 'free-standing arbitration (or jurisdiction) agreement' is often used in a broader sense. In a Singapore case, *BCY v BCZ*,[24] Chong J noted that there were two types of free-standing arbitration agreements: the first type was an arbitration agreement related to several contracts constituting a highly complex transaction and the second type was a post-dispute arbitration agreement.[25] The judge considered that an arbitration agreement of either type was free-standing because it was 'not intended to be a term of any other contract'. On that basis, the judge concluded that there was 'no question of any express choice of governing law of a main contract to govern the arbitration agreement'. As discussed, however, an arbitration agreement of the second type does relate to a specific contract, albeit on an *ex post facto* basis. An agreement of the first type, too, is associated with a specific contract, namely each of the constituent contracts. It is, therefore, suggested that an agreement of these types should also be treated as forming part of the contracts to which it relates for the purpose of choice of law analysis.[26]

2. Severability of substantive terms

Though the principle of severability has particular significance for arbitration and jurisdiction agreements, severability is not unique to them. A contract may contain a clause known as a 'severability clause' which reads something like 'If any term of this contract is found to be invalid or unenforceable, the remaining terms shall remain valid and enforceable, unless the invalid or unenforceable term is essential to either party'. Even without such a clause, some terms in a contract may remain valid and enforceable even if other terms in the same contract are found to be invalid or unenforceable. Thus, under the Consumer Rights Act 2015, where an unfair term of a consumer contract is not binding on the consumer, the contract continues, so far as practicable, to have effect in every other respect (s 67). More generally, in the English case law, where illegality renders part of a contract unenforceable, the remainder of the contract may be enforceable.[27] In *Tillman v Egon Zehnder Ltd*, a leading case concerning restraint of trade, the Supreme Court observed that '[w]here part of a contract is unenforceable, the enforceability of the remainder represents an issue which arises far more widely than in contracts of employment'.[28]

---

[24] *BCY* (n 10) [66].
[25] An agreement of the second type is also considered to be free-standing in Briggs, *Private International Law in English Courts* (n 14) [14.42].
[26] If it is feared that this might create complexity, the parties to a complex transaction should be vigilant to avoid the fragmentation of the governing law of the constituent contracts or care to make, by means of voluntary *dépeçage*, a specific choice of law for the arbitration agreement. As regards voluntary *dépeçage*, see discussions below at Section E.
[27] Jack Beatson, Andrew Burrows, and John Cartwright, *Anson's Law of Contract* (OUP 2020) 423.
[28] [2019] UKSC 32, [2020] AC 154 [54] (Lord Wilson).

Despite the severability of substantive terms, no suggestion is made that such terms should be treated as a distinct contract severed from the matrix contract for the purpose of choice of law analysis. It is true that these terms may, by virtue of *dépeçage*, be referred to a law different from that governs the matrix contract. However, as will be explored in the following Section E, splitting up terms within a contract by means of *dépeçage* is not the same, in terms of a choice of law methodology, as treating a term as a distinct contract severed from the matrix contract.

3. Dependence on the applicable law

While the principle of severability has come to be accepted widely, it does not necessarily mean that every legal system has embraced it. English law, for instance, had long been reluctant to do so[29] until the Court of Appeal accepted it in 1993 in *Harbour Assurance*.[30] Whether the principle of severability is accepted depends, therefore, on its governing law.[31]

What, then, is the governing law of the principle of severability? As we have seen in the preceding Section C, this principle concerns the question whether the validity of an arbitration (or jurisdiction) agreement could only be challenged on the grounds which directly relate to that agreement and not merely on the ground that the matrix contract is invalid. This question arises in the course of addressing whether the given arbitration (or jurisdiction) agreement is validly concluded, a question which is answered by the law applicable to the agreement in question. It follows that the governing law of the principle of severability is the law applicable to the arbitration (or jurisdiction) agreement in question. This suggestion is consistent with the English Arbitration Act 1996: its provision on severability (s 7) applies where English law is applicable to the arbitration agreement even if the seat of the arbitration is outside England (s 2(5)).

One author argues that both the severability principle and the Kompetenz-Kompetenz principle should be subject to the law of the country of the arbitral seat, reasoning that both principles address the kind of allocation-of-authority questions and pertain directly to the arbitral process.[32] It does make sense that the Kompetenz-Kompetenz principle, being a principle of procedural law, should

---

[29] See eg *Overseas Union Insurance v AA Mutual International Insurance* [1988] 2 Lloyd's Rep 63, 66, in which Evans J cited an earlier case as establishing the rule that 'arbitrators can never have jurisdiction to decide whether there was or was not a valid contract under which, if it exists, that jurisdiction arises' and commented that 'This rule owes as much to logic as it does to authority'. The quoted rule appears to reject both the principle of Kompetenz-Kompetenz and the principle of severability.
[30] *Harbour Assurance* (n 12).
[31] Briggs, *Agreements* (n 3) [3.10]; Trevor Hartley and Masato Dogauchi, 'Explanatory Report on the 2005 Hague Convention on Choice of Court Agreements' (2007) [115] (hereafter Hartley and Dogauchi, 'Explanatory Report').
[32] George Bermann, *International Arbitration and Private International Law* (The Hague Academy of International Law 2017) [135] and [137] (hereafter Bermann, *International Arbitration*).

be subject to the curial law of arbitration, which is normally the law of the seat.[33] A distinction should, however, be made with the principle of severability which, as noted in the preceding Section C, operates in the sphere of substantive law.

Another author argues that in order to decide whether an arbitration agreement is severed from the matrix contract in a given case, a preferable course is to ascertain the parties' intent rather than conducting an analysis through the prism of the governing law.[34] There is a lot of sense in this argument as many legal systems will in any event look to the parties' intent. If, however, there is no common intent between the parties, a solution could only be found in the applicable law. Where, for example, the matrix contract is procured by bribe and found to be invalid for illegality, it will not always be possible to ascertain the parties' common intent as to whether an arbitration (or jurisdiction) agreement contained in that contract should also be rendered invalid for the same reason.

4. Purpose specificity

Whether the principle of severability should be a guiding principle depends on the purpose for which it is invoked. This proposition seems widely accepted by various instruments and in the case law.

Some instruments which enshrine the principle of severability use words like 'independent' and 'distinct' to describe the relationships between an arbitration (or jurisdiction) agreement and the matrix contract. The UNCITRAL Model Law, for example, provides that 'an arbitration clause which forms part of a contract shall be treated as an agreement *independent* of the other terms of the contract' (Art 16(1) (emphasis added)). The English Arbitration Act 1996 provides that 'an arbitration agreement which forms or was intended to form part of another agreement ... shall ... be treated as a *distinct* agreement' (s 7 (emphasis added)). And the Hague Choice of Court Convention provides that 'an exclusive choice of court agreement that forms part of a contract shall be treated as an agreement *independent* of the other terms of the contract' (Art 3(d) (emphasis added)). The Recast Brussels I Regulation contains a similar provision (Art 25(5)). These words may strengthen the impression that an arbitration (or jurisdiction) agreement is severed from the matrix contract.

A closer reading, however, reveals the drafters' intention to qualify the operation of the principle of severability. In the UNCITRAL Model Law, Art 16(1) begins with an endorsement of the principle of Kompetenz-Kompetenz by providing that

---

[33] *Dallal v Bank Mellat* [1986] 1 All ER 239, 252 ('The curial law is normally, but not necessarily, the law of the place where the arbitration proceedings are held').

[34] Mayer, 'The Limits of Severability' (n 16) 267. The author accepts that in theory, there is a merit in identifying the governing law.

an arbitral tribunal may rule on its own jurisdiction even where the existence or validity of the arbitration agreement is called into question. It then continues that 'For that purpose', the arbitration agreement must be treated as independent. The same words 'for that purpose' appear in s 7 of the English Arbitration Act 1996. It is no coincidence. The Departmental Advisory Committee which prepared the draft stated in its report:[35]

> [W]e have redrafted [what is now s 7] in order to follow the relevant part of Art 16 of the UNCITRAL Model Law more closely, and to make clear that the doctrine of separability is confined to the effect of invalidity etc of the main contract on the arbitration agreement, rather than being, as it was in the July 1995 draft, a free-standing principle.

It is, accordingly, possible to say that these instruments do not purport to extend the principle of severability to the sphere of choice of law analysis. The intention of the drafters of the Hague Choice of Court Convention is less clear. But the provision quoted above is immediately followed by the sentence which reads, 'The validity of the exclusive choice of court agreement cannot be contested solely on the ground that the contract is not valid'. And it would be possible to interpret this sentence as qualifying the context in which to treat a jurisdiction agreement as independent. The same may be said of the Recast Brussels I Regulation.

The proposition that the principle of severability is not an all-purpose principle is also accepted in the case law. In *Harbour Assurance*, Hoffmann LJ acknowledged that an arbitration agreement might form part of the matrix contract for some purposes and might constitute a separate agreement for other purposes.[36] For instance, where an assignment is made under a contract, Colman J held in *West Tankers Inc v RAS Riunione Adriatica di Sicurta SpA*[37] that the duty to submit to arbitration is an 'inseparable' component of the subject matter assigned. Similarly, the Court of Justice of the European Union held in *Cartel Damage Claims (CDC) Hydrogen Peroxide v Evonik Degussa*[38] that where a party not privy to the original contract had succeeded to an original contracting party's rights and obligations, that third party could nevertheless be bound by a jurisdiction clause to which it had not agreed.

Since the principle of severability is purpose-specific, it is not anomalous to reject it in the context of choice of law analysis and then apply the governing law

---

[35] The Departmental Advisory Committee on Arbitration, 'Report on the Arbitration Bill' (1996) [44].
[36] *Harbour Assurance* (n 12) 722.
[37] [2005] EWHC 454, [2005] 2 All ER (Comm) 240 [33]. Also *Sea Master Shipping Inc v Arab Bank Ltd* [2018] EWHC 1902 (Comm), [2018] Bus LR 1798 [28].
[38] Case C-352/13 [2015] ECLI:EU:C:2015:335 [65], citing its own judgment in *Coreck Maritime GmbH v Handelsveem BV* Case C-387/98 [2000] ECR I-9337.

which, in the sphere of substantive law, endorses it. Thus, even if an arbitration (or jurisdiction) agreement is considered to be subject to the same law that governs the matrix contract, that law may see the validity of the agreement unaffected by the factor invalidating the matrix contract.

Many authors accept that the principle of severability should not be extended to the sphere of choice of law analysis.[39] One author[40] agrees that this principle is purpose-specific but draws a distinction within the sphere of choice of law analysis depending on the way the jurisdiction of an arbitral tribunal is challenged. In cases where the respondent contends that the dispute falls outside the scope of the arbitration agreement, he considers that the principle of severability is inapplicable, with the result that an express choice of law for the matrix contract constitutes a choice of law for the arbitration agreement. Where, on the other hand, the respondent contends that there is no valid, existent, or effective arbitration agreement, he considers that the principle of severability is applicable, resulting in the opposite outcome. As the author himself admits, these are absurd results since the respondent would be able to influence how the governing law of an arbitration agreement is determined by the vagaries of jurisdictional challenges. A better approach would be to reject the extension of the principle of severability to the sphere of choice of law analysis altogether, irrespective of the way in which jurisdiction is challenged.

5. The dual character of arbitration and jurisdiction agreements

The procedural character of arbitration and jurisdiction agreements is sometimes cited as a ground for giving them a special treatment in the choice of law analysis. For example, the Rome I Regulation[41] excludes these agreements from its scope of application (Art 1(2)(e)). It inherited this position from its predecessor, the Rome Convention,[42] which similarly excluded these agreements from its scope (Art 1(2)(d)). According to the Report of Professors Giuliano and Lagarde on the Convention,[43] the exclusion was based in part on the view that the matter

---

[39] See eg Ian Glick and Niranjan Venkatesan, 'Choosing the Law Governing the Arbitration Agreement' in Neil Kaplan and Michael Moser (eds), *Jurisdiction, Admissibility and Choice of Law in International Arbitration* (Kluwer Law International 2018) 131 [9.02] (hereafter Glick and Venkatesan, 'Choosing the Law') and Briggs, *Private International Law in English Courts* (n 14) [14.37].

[40] Blake Primrose, 'Separability and stage one of the *Sulamerica* inquiry' (2017) 33 Arbitration International 139.

[41] Regulation (EC) No 593/2008 of the European Parliament and of the Council of 17 June 2008 on the law applicable to contractual obligations (Rome I) [2008] OJ L177/6 (hereafter Rome I Regulation).

[42] Rome Convention on the law applicable to contractual obligations (1980) (consolidated version [1998] OJ C27/34) (hereafter Rome Convention).

[43] Mario Giuliano and Paul Lagarde, 'Report on the Convention on the law applicable to contractual obligations' [1980] OJ C282/11 (hereafter Giuliano and Lagarde Report).

lay within the sphere of procedure. Procedure was excluded from the scope of the Convention (Art 1(2)(h)) and is likewise under the Regulation (Art 1(3)).[44] As will be discussed later in this essay (Section I), the exclusion of arbitration and jurisdiction agreements from the scope of these instruments does not preclude the possibility for the courts of Member States to treat these agreements as forming part of the matrix contract for the purpose of choice of law analysis.

There is no doubt that arbitration and jurisdiction agreements have procedural character since they concern the method of dispute resolution and hence possess procedural dimensions. The fact that an agreement has a procedural character, however, does not warrant the assumption that each and every issue pertaining to it is a procedural issue since the agreement also has substantive dimensions. As put by one author:[45]

> [A] choice-of-court agreement has a hybrid nature. On the one hand, it is a private-law contract: to this extent it falls under the law of contract; on the other hand, it has procedural (jurisdictional) consequences: to this extent, it falls under the law of procedure. In order to be valid, it must comply with the normal requirements for a private-law contract. If it is not valid as a contract, it can have no jurisdictional effects. However, once it is decided that it is valid, we then move from the law of contract to that of procedure to determine what its effects are ...

It is, therefore, unhelpful to pin a procedural label on arbitration and jurisdiction agreements. For the purpose of determining applicable laws, a better approach would be to consider which issues are procedural and which are substantive. Only the issues which directly implicate the resources of the forum State in the administration of justice should be characterised as procedural and be submitted to the *lex fori* (the law of the forum) in accordance with the maxim '*forum regit processum*' (the law of the forum governs procedure). Other issues should be characterised as substantive and be submitted to the *lex causae* (the governing law of the agreement) as ascertained by the normal choice of law analysis.

In fact, arbitration and jurisdiction agreements are not the only agreements possessing both procedural and substantive characters. Other agreements, such as an anti-suit agreement (ie an agreement not to sue), an agreement to discontinue an action, an agreement to desist from executing a judgment, an agreement to abstain from disputing particular facts, and an agreement to refrain from adducing

---

[44] When consulted on a draft text of the Regulation, the European Economic and Social Committee also observed that the exclusion of arbitration and jurisdiction agreements was based on the same reasoning as the exclusion of procedure: Opinion of the European Economic and Social Committee on the Proposal for a Regulation on the law applicable to contractual obligations (Rome I) [2006] OJ C318/58 [3.1.4].

[45] Trevor Hartley, *Choice-of-court Agreements under the European and International Instruments* (OUP 2013) [7.01].

particular evidence, possess the dual characters. It may, therefore, be said generally that with respect to any agreement, the appropriate question to ask is which, if any, are procedural issues and which are substantive issues.[46]

Among the issues pertaining to arbitration and jurisdiction agreements, their effects of conferring or depriving jurisdiction are obviously procedural issues and should accordingly be subject to the *lex fori* (the law of the forum where a suit is brought pursuant to or, as the case may be, regardless of an arbitration (or jurisdiction) agreement). The formation, validity, and interpretation of these agreements, on the other hand, have less direct implications for the resource of the forum State and should, therefore, be regarded as substantive issues, in view also of the fact that they do not pertain uniquely to arbitration and jurisdiction agreements but can be relevant to any contract. These issues should accordingly be submitted to the *lex causae*.

As a side note, a distinction should also be made between the curial law of arbitration and the law applicable to arbitration agreements.[47] The curial law of arbitration means the law applicable to arbitral proceedings, which may hardly be described as an aspect of arbitration agreements. It governs both the tribunal's conduct of arbitral proceedings and the national court's supervision, support, and control of arbitral proceedings.[48] There is a broad consensus that the curial law is normally the law of the country where the arbitration is seated.[49]

While reference to the *lex fori* or the law of the seat would automatically sever arbitration and jurisdiction agreements from the matrix contract, reference to the *lex causae* would not. It may, therefore, be concluded that the procedural character of these agreements is not a sufficient reason for treating them as a distinct contract severed from the matrix contract for the purpose of choice of law analysis.

6. Question of what generally constitutes a single contract for the choice of law purposes

If we were to argue for the proposition that arbitration and jurisdiction agreements should be treated as a distinct contract, we would be confronted with

---

[46] For further analysis, see Koji Takahashi, 'Law Applicable to Choice-of-Court Agreements' (2015) 58 Japanese Yearbook of International Law 384, 391–4.

[47] cf *Enka Insaat Ve Sanayi AS v OOO Insurance Company Chubb* [2020] EWCA Civ 574, [2020] 3 All ER 577 (hereafter *Enka* (CA)). The Court of Appeal's decision and reasoning in this case will be discussed in Section H below. Work on this essay was completed before the UK Supreme Court delivered its own ruling in the case ([2020] UKSC 38) in October 2020. That ruling is addressed separately in Section K (Postscript) below.

[48] Gary Born, *International Commercial Arbitration* (2nd edn, Kluwer Law International 2014) 1531 (hereafter Born, *International Commercial Arbitration*).

[49] Ibid 1604.

the question of what generally constitutes a single contract for choice of law purposes. That proposition could not be ultimately sustained unless we could satisfactorily answer this question, which is theoretically difficult. Where, for example, an agreement for the sale of goods and an agreement for the provision of services are concluded in the course of the same transaction and their terms are set out in the same document, do they constitute a single contract or two distinct contracts? The Rome I Regulation sets forth a rule for determining the governing law of a contract containing multiple elements such as those of sale of goods and the provision of services (Art 4(2)). The Regulation would not, however, exclude the treatment of those elements as two distinct contracts especially if in the circumstances one may be performed independently of the other. This is apparent from the listing of these two categories of contracts in sub-paras (a) and (b) of Art 4(1).

If one argues, as this essay does, for the opposite proposition, namely that arbitration and jurisdiction agreements should be treated as forming part of the matrix contract, it is unnecessary to answer the question what generally constitutes a single contract for the choice of law purpose. Since arbitration and jurisdiction agreements are, save those concluded as a free-standing agreement, related to a specific contract, it suffices to show that there is no good reason to treat them as a distinct contract. This much has been attempted throughout this section.

E. Possibility of *Dépeçage*

In the last section (Section D), it has been suggested that arbitration and jurisdiction agreements should be treated, for the purpose of choice of law analysis, as forming part of the matrix contract. This means submitting these terms to the choice of law analysis in the same way as other terms of the same matrix contract. It follows that to the extent the applicable choice of law rules employ the technique of *dépeçage*, it is possible for an arbitration (or jurisdiction) agreement to be referred to a law different from that which governs the matrix contract.[50] But splitting up terms within a contract by means of *dépeçage* is not the same as treating a term as a distinct contract in terms of choice of law methodology. In this section, we will first explain the difference and then consider to what extent *dépeçage* should be embraced in principle.

---

[50] See also Glick and Venkatesan, 'Choosing the Law' (n 39) [9.02].

1. *Dépeçage* distinguished from treating a term as a distinct contract

The word 'severability' is sometimes used to indicate that parts of a contract are severable for the sake of *dépeçage*. The Rome Convention, for example, provided that 'a severable part of the contract which has a closer connection with another country may by way of exception be governed by the law of that other country' (Art 4(1)).[51] It should be noted, however, that splitting up terms within a contract by means of *dépeçage* is not the same as treating a term of a contract as a distinct contract severed from the matrix contract. The question of what constitutes a contract logically precedes the question of whether the splitting up of terms within a contract for choice of law purposes is permissible.

For an illustration of the point, consider a typical scenario where the parties make no specific choice of law for an arbitration (or jurisdiction) agreement. If the agreement is treated as a distinct contract severed from the matrix contract, its governing law would have to be ascertained independently of the matrix contract and the possibility of *dépeçage* would not arise for consideration. If, on the other hand, the agreement is treated as forming part of the matrix contract, it would be governed by the same law as the latter, subject to the possibility of involuntary *dépeçage* with all its limitations as suggested below.

2. Voluntary and involuntary *dépeçage*

There are two types of *dépeçage*: voluntary and involuntary. Voluntary *dépeçage* allows the parties to a contract to choose the law applicable to a part or parts only of the contract. It is in the form of either a partial choice of law or multiple choices of law.[52] Involuntary *dépeçage* (or objective *dépeçage*) allows the court to apply different laws to different parts of a contract.

Voluntary *dépeçage* is widely accepted. The Rome I Regulation, for example, provides that '[b]y their choice the parties can select the law applicable to the whole or to part only of the contract' (Art 3(1)). Involuntary *dépeçage* is less widely accepted. The possibility existed under the Rome Convention, which contained a provision permitting involuntary *dépeçage* (Art 4(1), quoted above in Section E.1). But the Giuliano and Lagarde Report on the Convention states that 'the court must have recourse to severance as seldom as possible'.[53] Citing this Report, the European Court of Justice took a strict stance to involuntary

---

[51] Giuliano and Lagarde Report (n 43) 17 also makes mention of 'the question whether severability (*dépeçage*) was to be allowed'.
[52] See Art 2(2)(a) and (b) of the Hague Principles on Choice of Law in International Commercial Contracts (2015) (hereafter Hague Choice of Law Principles).
[53] Giuliano and Lagarde Report (n 43) 23.

dépeçage, holding in one case[54] that 'the possibility of separating a contract into a number of parts in order to make it subject to a number of laws runs counter to the objectives of the Convention', by which the Court meant raising the level of legal certainty. The Rome I Regulation did not inherit from the Rome Convention the provision permitting involuntary *dépeçage*.

Voluntary *dépeçage* makes sense as a logical extension of the party autonomy, a principle which enjoys near-universal acceptance in the field of contract law. It should, therefore, be possible, by means of voluntary *dépeçage*, to refer an arbitration (or jurisdiction) agreement to a law different from that which governs the matrix contract.

Then, what about involuntary *dépeçage*? Should it be accepted at all and in what circumstances? The main objection to involuntary *dépeçage* is its unpredictability. It is all very well to say that a severable part of a contract *may* be referred to a law different from that which governs the contract. But it is not clear when it *should* or *must* be so referred. The test under the Rome Convention of 'a severable part of the contract' having 'a closer connection with another country' (Art 4(1)) was too general and too vague. It is suggested in principle that the court should only be allowed to resort to involuntary *dépeçage* if the applicable choice of law rules provide in clear language what specific terms are referred, separately from the remainder of the matrix contract, to what laws. Thus, the applicable choice of law rules may provide that an arbitration agreement should be subject to the law of the country of the arbitral seat or that a jurisdiction agreement should be subject to the law of the country of the chosen court. Only if there is such a clear and specific provision in the applicable choice of law rules, should the court be allowed to resort to involuntary *dépeçage* to refer an arbitration (or jurisdiction) agreement to a law different from that which governs the matrix contract.

It is suggested that there should be a further limitation to the operation of involuntary *dépeçage*: the court should only be allowed to resort to it where the parties have made no choice of law for the matrix contract. Where the parties have chosen a law to govern the matrix contract, it appears hardly defensible to refer a part of it to a different law by means of involuntary *dépeçage*. The Rome Convention, too, only permitted involuntary *dépeçage* where the parties made no choice of law for the matrix contract

---

[54] *Intercontainer Interfrigo v Balkenende Oosthuizen and MIC Operations* Case C-133/08 [2009] ECR I-9687 [43]–[47].

F. Preferred Choice of Law Approach

From the foregoing analysis, it is suggested that the following choice of law approach should be adopted to ascertain the governing law of arbitration and jurisdiction agreements.

Arbitration and jurisdiction agreements should not be treated as a distinct contract severed from the matrix contract. The principle of severability, which is useful and defensible in the sphere of substantive law, should not be extended to the sphere of choice of law analysis. These agreements should be treated as forming part of the matrix contract.

It should, however, be accepted that arbitration and jurisdiction agreements may, by virtue of *dépeçage*, be referred to a law different from that which governs the matrix contract. Accordingly, the parties should be allowed to make a specific choice of law for such agreements by means of voluntary *dépeçage*. The court, on the other hand, should be allowed to resort to involuntary *dépeçage* only where the parties have not made a choice of law for the matrix contract and only if the applicable choice of law rules contain a clear and specific provision for such agreements.

G. Illustrations of the Contrasting Approaches

This section will illustrate how the preferred approach, summarised in the last section (Section F), will operate in different scenarios. In the course of analysis, comparison will be made with the rival approach, that is, the approach of treating arbitration and jurisdiction agreements as a distinct contract severed from the matrix contract.

At its most basic level, the difference between the contrasting approaches lies in whether the governing law of the matrix contract, in and of itself, constitutes the governing law of the arbitration (or jurisdiction) agreement contained therein. The question is answered affirmatively if we follow the preferred approach of treating arbitration and jurisdiction agreements as forming part of the matrix contract, whereas it is answered negatively if we follow the rival approach.

The following analysis will illustrate these contrasting approaches more fully with the implications of *dépeçage*. It will examine (1) the cases where the parties have made, expressly or impliedly, a choice of law for the matrix contract, and (2) the cases where the parties have made no choice of law for the matrix contract. But before embarking on the analysis, it is necessary to set out the analytical premise regarding the applicable choice of law rules.

1. Analytical premise

The analysis in this section will illustrate the operation of the contrasting approaches based on a certain premise with respect to the applicable choice of law rules. Rather than proceeding on the basis of any concrete example of choice of law rules, this section will, with a view to retaining a wider relevance, base its analysis on hypothetical choice of law rules sharing the following traits with the conventional and mainstream choice of law rules.

First, it is presupposed that the applicable choice of law rules for contracts in general consist of (i) a rule giving effect to the parties' express choice of law, if any; (ii) in the absence of any express choice, a rule giving effect to the parties' implied choice of law, if any; and (iii) in the absence of any choice, a rule specifying the governing law by objective connecting factors. This set of rules reflects the near-universal acceptance of party autonomy as the primary choice of law principle for contracts. It is also consistent with the common law choice of law rules for contracts[55] and the Rome I Regulation.

Secondly, it is presupposed that the rule giving effect to the parties' implied choice of law (rule (ii) above) may only be triggered if the choice is actually made at the time the parties concluded the contract. It does not give effect to a fictional choice, namely a choice which the parties did not actually make but would have made if they had addressed their minds to the choice of law issue at the time of the conclusion of the contract. This presupposition should be supported since confounding an implied choice with a fictional choice would make rule (ii) an objective rule in all but name, leading to the confusion of rules (ii) and (iii). Properly confined to an actual choice, rule (ii) would only be different from rule (i) on the point of whether the choice is expressed or tacit. It would be safe to say that this presupposition is widely supported and consistent with the common law[56] and the Rome I Regulation[57] as well as the Hague Choice of Law Principles.[58]

Thirdly, it is presupposed that the applicable choice of law rules for contracts also guide the determination of the law applicable to arbitration and jurisdiction agreements. Comparatively, this is the mainstream methodology,[59] though there are, on

---

[55] Lord Collins of Mapesbury and others (eds), *Dicey, Morris & Collins: The Conflict of Laws* (15th edn, Sweet & Maxwell 2012) [32-006].

[56] Ibid [32-007], though it is also observed that 'before the objective close connection test became fully established, the test of inferred intention was in truth an objective test designed not to elicit actual intention but to impute an intention which had not been formed'.

[57] Giuliano and Lagarde Report (n 43) 17 stated that the courts were not permitted 'to infer a choice of law that the parties might have made where they had no clear intention of making a choice'.

[58] Hague Choice of Law Principles (n 52). Its official commentary states at [4.6] that 'the choice must be a real one although not expressly stated in the contract.... A presumed intention imputed to the parties does not suffice'.

[59] As is the case in England and Singapore, as observed in *BNA v BNB* [2019] SGCA 84 [45] (Steven Chong JA). The English case law applies the common law choice of law rules, rather than the rules of the Rome I Regulation (See Art 1(2)(e)).

the other hand, States adopting special rules for such agreements. Switzerland, for example, has special choice of law rules for arbitration agreements, with its Federal Act on Private International Law setting forth alternative connecting factors (Art 178.2).[60] The Civil Code of Quebec does likewise (Art 3121).[61] The French courts, for their part, apply a substantive rule of international arbitration ('règle matérielle du droit international de l'arbitrage'), instead of engaging in the normal choice of law analysis, to assess the validity of arbitration agreements.[62] The evaluation of such approaches is beyond the scope and purpose of this essay.

2. Where there is a choice of law for the matrix contract

(a) Preferred approach

Where the parties have made, expressly or impliedly, a choice of law for the matrix contract, if we follow the preferred approach of treating an arbitration (or jurisdiction) agreement as forming part of the matrix contract, the choice of law for the matrix contract, in and of itself, constitutes the choice of law for the arbitration (or jurisdiction) agreement. This conclusion is subject to the possibility of voluntary *dépeçage*: the parties may choose a separate law for the arbitration (or jurisdiction) agreement.

An express choice of a separate law is, however, hardly ever made in practice.[63] This is because the parties do not usually address their minds to the law applicable to arbitration and jurisdiction agreements when they conclude the matrix contract.[64] It is, therefore, unlikely for the parties to resort to voluntary *dépeçage* by means of an express choice.

What is commonly done in an arbitration agreement is to specify the seat of arbitration.[65] The seat is sometimes specified in a country other than the country whose law is chosen as the governing law of the matrix contract. Since voluntary *dépeçage* may be implemented by way of an implied choice, this begs the question whether it is possible to elicit an intention to choose the law of the seat as the governing law of the arbitration agreement. The choice of an arbitral seat is generally made to anchor the arbitration in a trusted jurisdiction supportive of arbitration.

---

[60] It reads, 'Die Schiedsvereinbarung ist im Übrigen gültig, wenn sie dem von den Parteien gewählten, dem auf die Streitsache, insbesondere dem auf den Hauptvertrag anwendbaren oder dem schweizerischen Recht entspricht'.

[61] It reads, 'En l'absence de désignation par les parties, la convention d'arbitrage est régie par la loi applicable au contrat principal ou, si cette loi a pour effet d'invalider la convention, par la loi de l'État où l'arbitrage se déroule'.

[62] Judgment of the French Cour de cassation in *Municipalite de Khoms El Mergeb v Societe Dalico* [1994] 1 Rev Arb 116.

[63] Born, *International Commercial Arbitration* (n 48) 580.

[64] Bermann, *International Arbitration* (n 32) [164].

[65] Born, *International Commercial Arbitration* (n 48) 497.

It is, therefore, a reliable indicator of the parties' intention to choose the curial law of arbitration. But it is not a good indicator of their intention to choose the law governing the validity of their agreement to arbitrate.[66] Similarly, sometimes a jurisdiction agreement specifies the courts in a country other than the country whose law is chosen for the matrix contract. The choice of courts is a reliable indicator of the parties' intention to submit to the procedural rules of the chosen forum but is not a good indicator of their intention to choose the law governing the validity of their jurisdiction agreement. As noted above, the parties do not usually address their minds to the law applicable to arbitration and jurisdiction agreements when they conclude the matrix contract. As an implied choice may only be founded on an actual intention, it may be concluded that the parties to an arbitration (or jurisdiction) agreement are unlikely to make, by means of voluntary *dépeçage*, an implied choice of law for the agreement.

It is true that when the parties make a choice of law for the matrix contract, they are just as unlikely to have an actual intention to extend the coverage of the law to an arbitration (or jurisdiction) agreement contained therein. For that reason, one author observes that the application of the law governing the matrix contract to the arbitration agreement would be no less arbitrary than the application of the law of the seat.[67] However, on the proposition that an arbitration (or jurisdiction) agreement should be treated as forming part of the matrix contract, it is a matter of course that a choice of law made by the parties for the matrix contract constitutes the choice of law for the arbitration (or jurisdiction) agreement.

Where the applicable choice of law rules contain rules for the protection of presumptively weaker parties, the approach of treating an arbitration (or jurisdiction) agreement as forming part of the matrix contract would be helpful for such parties. Suppose that a consumer wishes to challenge the validity of an arbitration (or jurisdiction) agreement contained in a contract he has concluded with a professional trader. If the applicable choice of law rules allow the consumer to rely on the mandatory rules of the law of the country where he has his habitual residence,[68] he may do so not only to challenge the validity of the matrix contract but also to challenge the validity of the arbitration (or jurisdiction) agreement[69] because, under this

---

[66] Briggs, *Private International Law in English Courts* (n 14) [14.41].
[67] Jonathan Hill, 'The law governing an arbitration clause' (University of Bristol Law School Blog) <https://legalresearch.blogs.bris.ac.uk/2017/03/the-law-governing-an-arbitration-clause> accessed 23 August 2020. For a similar view, see *Fouchard Gaillard Goldman* (n 15) [425].
[68] eg Art 6(2) of the Rome I Regulation.
[69] A consumer may invoke such rules as Art 3(1) and Annex 1(q) of the Council Directive 93/13/EEC of 5 April 1993 on Unfair Terms in Consumer Contracts [1993] OJ L95/29. This is extra ammunition in the armoury of a consumer, who may in addition be able to rely on the law of the forum if there are any rules denying effect to an arbitration agreement, such as s 91(1) of the English Arbitration Act 1996 (which is applicable 'whatever the law applicable to the arbitration agreement' (s 89(3))).

approach, the arbitration (or jurisdiction) agreement would be subject to the same law that governs the matrix contract.[70]

(b) Rival approach

Where the parties have made, expressly or impliedly, a choice of law for the matrix contract, if we follow the rival approach, that is, the approach of treating an arbitration (or jurisdiction) agreement as a distinct contract severed from the matrix contract, the choice of law for the matrix contract does not, in and of itself, constitute a choice of law for the arbitration (or jurisdiction) agreement. This is so even where, as is often the case, the choice of law clause uses all-embracing language purporting to cover all terms in the matrix contract, unless there is a specific indication that the arbitration (or jurisdiction) agreement is also covered.[71]

Treated as a distinct contract, an arbitration (or jurisdiction) agreement is subject to the law chosen by the parties, if any. In practice, though, hardly ever do they make an actual choice of law specifically for these agreements. This is because, as noted earlier, very rarely do the parties address their minds to the law applicable to these agreements when they conclude the matrix contract.

In the absence of choice of law by the parties, the governing law will have to be determined by objective connecting factors. The connecting factors adopted by the general choice of law rules for contracts may be either too vague or ill-suited to be used to designate the governing law of an arbitration (or jurisdiction) agreement. It would, therefore, be useful for the applicable choice of law rules to set out specific connecting factors for such agreements. This, however, leaves a difficult question of what the appropriate connecting factors are. It might be thought that an arbitration agreement should be subject to the law of the country of the arbitral seat or that a jurisdiction agreement should be subject to the law of the country of the chosen court. But these connecting factors are not entirely persuasive since at issue here is the validity of the agreement rather than the procedure of arbitration (or litigation).[72]

Where the applicable choice of law rules contain rules for the protection of presumptively weaker parties, the approach of treating an arbitration (or jurisdiction) agreement as a distinct contract would not be helpful for such parties. Suppose that a consumer wishes to challenge the validity of an arbitration (or jurisdiction) agreement contained in a contract he has concluded with a professional trader. If

---

[70] As the Rome I Regulation excludes arbitration and jurisdiction agreements from its scope of application (Art 1(2)(e)), Art 6(2) is only applicable to the matrix contract. The exclusion from the scope does not, however, preclude the possibility for the courts of Member States to deem these agreements to be subject to the same law that applies to the matrix contract (see the discussion of this point in Section I).

[71] As in the case of *Kabab-JI SAL v Kout Food* [2020] EWCA Civ 6, [2020] 1 Lloyd's Rep 269. Flaux LJ held, 'Governing law clauses do not necessarily cover the arbitration agreement. This one does because of the correct construction of the terms' [62].

[72] Briggs, *Private International Law in English Courts* (n 14) [14.40].

the choice of law rules allow the consumer to rely on the mandatory rules of the law of the country where he has his habitual residence,[73] he may do so to challenge the validity of the matrix contract but may not do so to challenge the validity of the arbitration (or jurisdiction) agreement because the governing law of the arbitration (or jurisdiction) agreement would, under this approach, have to be determined separately. Moreover, arbitration and jurisdiction agreements, treated as a distinct contract, may not qualify as a consumer contract since their procedural purposes do not easily square with the substantive considerations on which the definition of a consumer contract depends.[74]

3. Where there is no choice of law for the matrix contract

Having examined the scenario where the parties have made a choice of law for the matrix contract, let us now turn to the scenario where the parties have made no choice. In that scenario, the governing law of the matrix contract is determined by objective connecting factors.

If we follow the rival approach, that is, the approach of treating an arbitration (or jurisdiction) agreement as a distinct contract severed from the matrix contract, the law governing the matrix contract does not constitute the governing law of the arbitration (or jurisdiction) agreement. One consequence is that where the applicable choice of law rules contain rules for the protection of presumptively weaker parties,[75] the law specified by such rules may not be relied upon by such parties to challenge the validity of the arbitration (or jurisdiction) agreement. Under this approach, in order to find out what is the governing law of an arbitration (or jurisdiction) agreement, a separate analysis is necessary. As noted earlier, rarely in practice do the parties make an actual choice, expressed or implied, of law specifically for an arbitration (or jurisdiction) agreement. It makes it necessary to rely in virtually all cases on the objective connecting factors. As also noted earlier, the objective connecting factors adopted by the general choice of law rules for contracts may be either too vague or ill-suited to be used to designate the governing law of an arbitration (or jurisdiction) agreement. It would, therefore, be useful for the applicable choice of law rules to set out specific connecting factors for such agreements. This, however, leaves a difficult question of what the appropriate connecting factors are.

---

[73] eg Art 6(2) of the Rome I Regulation.
[74] The definition of a consumer contract under the Rome I Regulation, for example, depends on whether it is concluded by a natural person for a purpose outside his trade or profession with another party acting in the exercise of his trade or profession (Art 6(1)).
[75] eg Art 6(1) of the Rome I Regulation.

If, on the other hand, we follow the preferred approach, that is, the approach of treating an arbitration (or jurisdiction) agreement as forming part of the matrix contract, the law governing the latter, ascertained by objective connecting factors including those under any protective rules for the presumptively weaker parties, would in and of itself constitute the governing law of the arbitration (or jurisdiction) agreement. This conclusion is subject to the possibility of voluntary and involuntary *dépeçage*. In practice, it is unlikely for the parties to resort to voluntary *dépeçage* by means of either an express or implied choice. This is because, as noted earlier, they rarely address their minds to the law governing an arbitration (or jurisdiction) agreement when they conclude the matrix contract. As noted earlier in a different context, the court should only be allowed to resort to involuntary *dépeçage* where the applicable choice of law rules contain a clear and specific provision for an arbitration (or jurisdiction) agreement.

4. Observation

The above illustration has revealed some drawbacks of the approach of treating arbitration and jurisdiction agreements as a distinct contract severed from the matrix contract. That approach makes it necessary to tackle the difficult question of what the objective connecting factors should be for determining the governing law of these agreements. That approach is also not helpful for presumptively weaker parties as it does not allow them to rely on the law specified by the protective choice of law rules in challenging the arbitration and jurisdiction agreements. The preferred approach of rejecting severance excels in simplicity while, combined with the possibility of voluntary *dépeçage*, allowing for necessary flexibility. It is also conducive to appropriate results, including the protection of presumptively weaker parties. These advantages offer further support to the preferred approach along with its theoretical underpinnings examined in an earlier Section (Section D).

H. Analysis of English Cases on Arbitration Agreements

In this Section, we will examine some English cases on the law applicable to arbitration agreements to see which approach—the preferred approach or the rival approach—is favoured. The English authorities contain a number of irreconcilable decisions and statements.

Although the Supreme Court's decision is expected shortly, the most recent ruling at the time of writing is the Court of Appeal's decision in *Enka*.[76] Writing

---

[76] *Enka* (CA) (n 47). The Supreme Court delivered its ruling in the case on 9 October 2020 (see the postscript in Section K below).

ANALYSIS OF ENGLISH CASES ON ARBITRATION AGREEMENTS 163

for the court, Popplewell LJ held that the governing law of the matrix contract was generally not applicable to the arbitration agreement contained therein. His Lordship relied on the principle of severability to insulate the arbitration agreement for choice of law purposes.[77] His decision accordingly lends support to the rival approach. Based on the observation that the law applicable to an arbitration agreement is more closely connected with the curial law than with the law governing the matrix contract,[78] his Lordship asked rhetorically, where the parties have chosen 'the curial law of the arbitration agreement', why the governing law of the matrix contract should have anything to say about 'the closely related aspect of the very same arbitration agreement'.[79] But the expression 'the curial law of the arbitration agreement' strikes one as odd. The curial law of arbitration means the law applicable to arbitral proceedings, which may hardly be described as a closely related aspect of an arbitration agreement. His Lordship considered that there was an overlap between the curial law and the law applicable to arbitration agreements in terms of their scope. In his reasoning, 'the scope of the curial law is not limited to the exercise of purely procedural powers' but 'involves the curial court determining aspects of the substantive rights of the parties under their arbitration agreement by reference to the curial law'.[80] Though it is certainly true that the curial law affects the right to pursue arbitration in many ways, this reasoning merely confirms that the curial law is applicable not only to the tribunal's conduct but also to the national court's supervision, support, and control of arbitral proceedings. It does not seem to entail that there is an overlap of the scope of the curial law with that of the law applicable to arbitration agreements. It should also be noted that his Lordship's reasoning appears to presuppose that an implied choice of law may be made on a fictional basis. This is indicated by his statement that 'there is a strong presumption that the parties have impliedly chosen the curial law' as the law applicable to arbitration agreements and that this presumption could only be displaced 'where there are powerful countervailing factors'.[81] Such a presumption would be untenable if we take the position that an implied choice of law may only be ascertained by eliciting an actual intention rather than by imputing a fictional intention. As we have seen in Section G.1, confounding an implied choice with a fictional choice is difficult to defend in principle.

Prior to *Enka*, the leading English case was *Sulamérica CIA Nacional De Seguros SA v Enesa Engenharia SA*.[82] In this case, Moore-Bick LJ acknowledged that the concept of severability did not insulate an arbitration agreement from the matrix contract for all purposes. Yet, for the purpose of ascertaining the governing law of

---

[77] Ibid [92] and [94].
[78] Ibid [99].
[79] Ibid [94].
[80] Ibid [96].
[81] Ibid [105]. See also [100].
[82] [2012] EWCA Civ 638, [2013] 1 WLR 102 [26]–[32].

an arbitration agreement, his Lordship effectively treated the agreement as being severed from the matrix contract. This is indicated by his apparent acceptance of the appellants' concession that the express choice of law for the matrix contract did not amount to an express choice of law for the arbitration agreement.[83] His Lordship proceeded, after finding that the parties had made no choice of law for the arbitration agreement, to consider the law with which the agreement had the closest and most real connection.[84] Had the arbitration agreement been treated as forming part of the matrix contract, it would not have been necessary to do so; it should rather have been sufficient to say that the arbitration agreement was subject to the law chosen for the matrix contract. It was in a narrower context of ascertaining an implied choice of law for the arbitration agreement that his Lordship refused to insulate the arbitration agreement from the matrix contract. He took 'the assumption that, in the absence of any indication to the contrary, the parties intended the whole of their relationship to be governed by the same system of law'.[85] Taken as a whole, the choice of law approach followed by this decision may be described as a half-hearted rejection of the principle of severability (or a lukewarm embracement of it, if viewed from the opposite end). The result is a lack of clarity: whether the said assumption 'the parties intended the whole of their relationship to be governed by the same system of law' may be maintained is not clear where the parties made no choice of law for the matrix contract or where they made a choice only impliedly.

In *C v D*,[86] a case which predated *Sulamérica*, Longmore LJ took an unwavering stance in favour of treating an arbitration agreement as severed from the matrix contract. His Lordship held in *obiter* that '[i]t is necessary to distinguish between the proper law of the underlying insurance contract ... and the arbitration agreement which is ... a separable and separate agreement'[87] and that 'an agreement to arbitrate will normally have a closer and more real connection with the place where the parties have chosen to arbitrate than with the place of the law of the underlying contract'.[88] These remarks clearly support the rival approach. His Lordship's dicta was later explained by the Master of the Rolls in *Sulamérica* as resulting from 'the growing awareness of the importance of the principle that an arbitration agreement is separable from, in some ways almost juridically independent of, the underlying contract of which it physically is part'.[89]

In earlier cases, it is possible to find remarks in support of treating an arbitration agreement as forming part of the matrix contract. Thus, in *Sumitomo Heavy*

---

[83] Ibid [27].
[84] Ibid [32].
[85] Ibid [11], [26]–[27].
[86] [2007] EWCA Civ 1282, [2008] 1 Lloyd's Rep 239.
[87] Ibid [22].
[88] Ibid [26].
[89] Ibid [55].

Industries Ltd v Oil & Natural Gas Commission,[90] Potter J stated in *obiter* that 'since the arbitration agreement is part of the substance of the underlying contract', the proper law of the latter would 'usually be decisive' as to the proper law of the former 'in the absence of an express contrary choice'. This statement echoes the preferred approach.

As surveyed, the English case law shows a growing tendency in favour of the rival approach. But the signal is by no means uniform. It is hoped that in the shortly expected decision in *Enka*, the Supreme Court will see the sense of taking the preferred approach

I. Compatibility with Existing Instruments

This section will examine the compatibility of the preferred approach, as summed up in Section F, with existing instruments. This exercise is important since theories incompatible with established instruments risk being consigned to irrelevance. To this end, the following analysis will first examine the Rome I Regulation, a choice of law instrument for contracts generally. It will then turn to major international instruments on arbitration and jurisdiction agreements, respectively.

1. Rome I Regulation

Under the Rome I Regulation, arbitration and jurisdiction agreements are excluded from its scope of application (Art 1(2)(e)). At first sight, it might be thought that the preferred approach, that is, the approach of treating these agreements as forming part of the matrix contract, is inconsistent with the Regulation.

The Regulation follows its predecessor, the Rome Convention, which similarly excluded arbitration and jurisdiction agreements from its scope of application (Art 1(2)(d)). The background to the exclusion is explained in the Giuliano and Lagarde Report for the Convention.[91] With respect to jurisdiction agreements, the Report refers to two opposing views: the view that 'the matter lies within the sphere of procedure' and the view that jurisdiction agreements should be governed by the same law as the matrix contract. With respect to arbitration agreements, the Report again juxtaposes the view that 'severability is accepted in principle ... and the arbitration clause is independent' with the view that 'an arbitration agreement does not differ from other agreements as

---

[90] [1994] 1 Lloyd's Rep 45, 57.
[91] Giuliano and Lagarde Report (n 43) 11–12.

regards the contractual aspects'. The Report then mentions the adoption of the proposal that 'this matter should be studied separately'. The exclusion of arbitration and jurisdiction agreements should, accordingly, not be taken as indicating an approval of the proposition that they should be treated as a distinct contract severed from the matrix contract. Rather, it should be taken as leaving the matter to each Contracting State due to the failure to reach a consensus. Accordingly, it is open for the courts of each Member State to apply to arbitration and jurisdiction agreements the same law that governs the matrix contract as ascertained by the rules of the Rome I Regulation,[92] including protective rules for presumptively weaker parties such as those contained in Art 6. Put differently, the Regulation determines the governing law of the matrix contract which it is open for the courts of each State to deem also applicable to arbitration and jurisdiction agreements.[93] The possibility of treating these agreements as forming part of the matrix contract in this way is not precluded by their exclusion from the scope of application of the Regulation. It may, therefore, be concluded that the preferred approach of treating arbitration and jurisdiction agreements as forming part of the matrix contract is compatible with the Rome I Regulation.

2. Instruments on arbitration agreements

The New York Convention[94] provides that the recognition and enforcement of a foreign arbitral award may be refused if an arbitration agreement is not valid 'under the law to which the parties have subjected it or, failing any indication thereon, under the law of the country where the award was made' (Art V(1)(a)). The UNCITRAL Model Law provides for virtually the same choice of law rules for two contexts, namely the context of annulment as well as the context of the recognition and enforcement of awards (Arts 34(2)(a)(i)[95] and 36(1)(a)(i)).

These choice of law rules should, it is suggested, be applied both by national courts and by arbitral tribunals and irrespective of the context in which the issue arises, be it before the commencement of an arbitration, during the course

---

[92] For the same view in relation to arbitration agreements, see Adrian Briggs, *The Conflict of Laws* (4th edn, OUP 2019) 199; and in relation to jurisdiction agreements, see Francisco Garcimartin, 'Prorogation of Jurisdiction' in Andrew Dickinson and Eva Lein (eds), *The Brussels I Regulation Recast* (OUP 2015) [9.68] (hereafter Garcimartin, 'Prorogation of Jurisdiction')

[93] It should be noted that this is not what the English courts are actually doing. The recent cases proceed on the basis that the common law choice of law rules apply to determine the law applicable to arbitration agreements.

[94] United Nations Convention on the Recognition and Enforcement of Foreign Arbitral Awards (New York, 10 June 1958) (hereafter New York Convention).

[95] It refers, failing any indication on the law to which the parties have subjected the arbitration agreement, to 'the law of this State', which in the context of annulment points to the law of the country where the award was made (See Art 1(2)).

of an arbitration, or after the conclusion of an arbitration.[96] Otherwise, the same arbitration agreement may be found valid under one law in one context and invalid under another law in another context. This could not only make the time and money spent in arbitral proceedings wasteful but possibly also deprive the parties of the opportunity to resolve the dispute.

The following analysis will show that the preferred choice of law approach of treating an arbitration as forming part of the matrix contract is compatible with the Convention and the Model Law. We will look at the two expressions from the above-quoted choice of law rules in turn: 'the law to which the parties have subjected it' and 'the law of the country where the award was made'. Incidentally, it will be recalled that the principle of severability enshrined elsewhere in the Model Law (Art 16(1)) operates, as seen in an earlier section (Section C), in the sphere of substantive law.

(a) 'The law to which the parties have subjected' the arbitration agreement
The expression 'the law to which the parties have subjected it' may be interpreted in two ways.

On one reading, this expression only refers to the law chosen specifically for the arbitration agreement.[97] The law chosen for the matrix contract would not, on this reading, constitute a choice of law for the arbitration agreement. This reading is consistent with the approach of treating an arbitration agreement as a distinct contract severed from the matrix contract.

On another reading, this expression refers to either the law chosen for the matrix contract[98] *or* the law specifically chosen for the arbitration agreement. This reading is consistent with the preferred approach of treating an arbitration agreement as forming part of the matrix contract while accepting the possibility of voluntary *dépeçage*. It is suggested that this reading should be supported since it is possible to interpret the follow-up phrase 'failing any indication thereon', by reading it with an emphasis on 'any', as referring to the cases where there is absolutely no indication of a choice of law, not even in the guise of a choice of law for the matrix contract.

---

[96] For the same view, see eg Albert Jan van den Berg, *The New York Arbitration Convention of 1958: Towards a Uniform Judicial Interpretation* (Kluwer Law and Taxation 1981) 126 (hereafter van den Berg, *The New York Arbitration Convention*); and Ardavan Arzandeh and Jonathan Hill, 'Ascertaining the Proper Law of an Arbitration Clause Under English Law' (2009) 5 Journal of Private International Law 425, 426 (hereafter Arzandeh and Hill, 'Ascertaining the Proper law').

[97] See eg Hans-Viggo von Hülsen, *Die Gültigkeit von Internationalen Schiedsvereinbarungen* (J Schweitzer Verlag 1973) 100; van den Berg, *The New York Arbitration Convention* (n 96) 293 (It is, however, admitted that the wording of the Convention is somewhat ambiguous); and Arzandeh and Hill, 'Ascertaining the Proper law' (n 96) 441; Peter Schlosser, 'Rechtswahlvereinbarung für den Hauptvertrag auch gültig für die Schiedsvereinbarung?' [2020] 3 IPRax 222, 224.

[98] See apparently, Mayer 'The Limits of Severability' (n 16) 267.

(b) 'The law of the country where the award was made'
The expression 'the law of the country where the award was made' refers to the law of the country of the arbitral seat.

If we follow the approach of treating an arbitration agreement as a distinct contract severed from the matrix contract, this expression would be seen as simply specifying, by an objective connecting factor, the law applicable to an arbitration agreement.

On the other hand, if we follow the preferred approach, that is, the approach of treating an arbitration agreement as forming part of the matrix contract while accepting, where the parties have made no choice of law for the matrix contract, the limited possibility of involuntary *dépeçage* for an arbitration agreement, this expression would be seen as permitting the court to resort to involuntary *dépeçage*. It has been suggested earlier that the court should only be permitted to refer an arbitration agreement to a law different from that which governs the matrix contract where the applicable choice of law rules permit involuntary *dépeçage* for an arbitration agreement in clear and specific terms. The choice of law rules of the New York Convention and the UNCITRAL Model Law may be considered to be doing just that by means of this expression.

(c) Protective choice of law rules
It has been seen earlier that the preferred choice of law approach would allow presumptively weaker parties, such as consumers, to rely on the law ascertained by the protective choice of law rules for the matrix contract in challenging the validity of an arbitration agreement. Is it possible to derive this result under the New York Convention and the UNCITRAL Model Law?

The choice of law rules of the Convention and the Model Law should be seen as representing the *lex specialis* for arbitration agreements which overrides the *lex generalis*, the general choice of law rules for contracts such as those contained in the Rome I Regulation and the common law choice of law rules. Outside the scope of the *lex specialis*, the *lex generalis* is applicable. Since the Convention and the Model Law contain no special choice of law rules designed to protect presumptively weaker parties to a contract, the general choice of law rules for contracts are applicable to that extent. Suppose that a consumer has concluded a contract with a professional trader in which an arbitration agreement is contained. If the applicable general choice of law rules for contracts allow the consumer to rely on the mandatory rules of the law of the country where he has his habitual residence (as under Art 6(2) of the Rome I Regulation), he may do so not only to challenge the validity of the matrix contract but also to challenge the validity of the arbitration agreement because, under the preferred approach, the arbitration agreement would be subject to the same law that applies to the matrix contract. It should, therefore, be possible to derive, under the Convention and the Model Law, the result mentioned in the preceding paragraph.

3. Instruments on jurisdiction agreements

The Hague Choice of Court Convention grants jurisdiction to the courts of a Contracting State designated in a jurisdiction agreement (Art 5(1)), requires the courts of other Contracting States to suspend or dismiss proceedings (Art 6(a)), and provides that a judgment given by a court of a Contracting State designated in a jurisdiction agreement is recognised and enforced in other Contracting States (Art 8(1)). But it makes an exception where the jurisdiction agreement is null and void under the law of the State of the chosen court (Art 5(1), 6(a) and 9(a)), though this exception does not apply in the context of the recognition and enforcement of a judgment where the chosen court has determined that the agreement is valid (Art 9(a)).

At first sight, the reference to the law of the State of the chosen court might be considered to be incompatible with the preferred approach of treating a jurisdiction agreement as forming part of the matrix contract. But a closer examination reveals that it is not. The Explanatory Report, by Professors Hartley and Dogauchi, explains that the reference to the law of the State of the chosen court is meant to include its choice of law rules.[99] The Convention thus ensures that the same choice of law rules are applied to determine the law applicable to a given jurisdiction agreement irrespective of the Contracting State in which the issue arises. The aim is to ensure the same result among different fora. The Convention does not, however, seek to unify choice of law rules. It rather leaves each Contracting State to devise its own rules. Consequently, it is open for the courts of each State to take the approach of treating a jurisdiction agreement as forming part of the matrix contract for choice of law purposes. The preferred approach is, therefore, compatible with the Convention. Incidentally, it will be recalled that the principle of severability enshrined elsewhere in the Convention (Art 3(d)) operates, as seen in an earlier section (Section C), in the sphere of substantive law.

The same may be said of the Recast Brussels I Regulation. The Regulation refers the validity of a jurisdiction agreement to the law of the Member State designated by the agreement (Art 25(1)). It explains in the Recital that the reference to the said law is meant to include the choice of law rules (Recital (20)). This recital was introduced to align with the position of the Hague Choice of Court Convention.[100] It may, therefore, be concluded that the preferred approach is compatible with the Regulation. It will be recalled, incidentally, that the principle of severability enshrined elsewhere in the Regulation (Art 25(5)) operates in the sphere of substantive law.

---

[99] Hartley and Dogauchi, 'Explanatory Report' (n 31) [125] and [149].
[100] Garcimartin, 'Prorogation of Jurisdiction' (n 92) [9.62].

J. Concluding Remarks

The discussion in this essay bears a heavy theoretical overtone but has a practical significance. Take a typical scenario where the parties to a contract make a choice of law for the contract but make no specific choice of law for an arbitration (or jurisdiction) agreement contained in it. Such scenarios raise the question whether the arbitration (or jurisdiction) agreement is subject to the same law that governs the matrix contract. As views are genuinely divided and the text of existing instruments could accommodate both views, a principled approach to resolving this question is called for.

A key to providing an answer by a principled approach is to consider whether the principle of severability should be extended to the sphere of choice of law analysis. It is also important to reflect on the implications of *dépeçage*, a choice of law methodology for splitting up terms within a contract. This essay has suggested a preferred approach comprising these two major elements of consideration. It is hoped that it will stimulate further debate in this field.

K. Postscript

After the final manuscript of this essay was submitted, the UK Supreme Court delivered its judgment in *Enka*.[101] The Court dismissed the appeal by a majority (3–2) but renounced the Court of Appeal's approach of determining the law applicable to arbitration agreements.[102]

There is significant common ground between the majority and the dissenting judges in their reasoning on the latter issue. Most fundamentally, both refused to invoke the principle of severability to treat the arbitration agreement as a distinct contract severed from the matrix contract. Thus, the majority, led by Lord Hamblen and Lord Leggatt (with whom Lord Kerr agreed), held that 'the separability principle does not require that an arbitration agreement should be treated as a separate agreement for the purpose of determining its governing law'.[103] Similarly, the dissenting judges, led by Lord Burrows (with whom Lord Sales agreed), held that the purpose for which the principle of severability had been devised did 'not extend to working out the conflict of laws rules applicable to an arbitration agreement' and that 'in deciding on the proper law of the arbitration agreement, the arbitration agreement should be regarded as part of the main contract'.[104] These remarks

---
[101] *Enka Insaat Ve Sanayi AS v OOO Insurance Company Chubb* [2020] UKSC 38 (hereafter *Enka (SC)*). The Court of Appeal's decision is discussed at Section H above.
[102] Ibid [59]–[94].
[103] Ibid [41]; also [61].
[104] Ibid [233].

strongly support the preferred approach suggested by this essay.[105] A common ground also exists between the majority and the dissent in their basic acceptance of the possibility of *dépeçage*,[106] a position which again accords with the preferred approach.[107] Accordingly, both the majority and the dissent accept that the parties may, if they so wish, refer an arbitration agreement to a law different from the governing law of the matrix contract.[108]

The majority and the dissentients differed, however, in their conclusions: the majority held that the arbitration agreement in this case was governed by the law of the seat whereas the dissent held that it was governed by the governing law of the matrix contract. This disagreement stemmed primarily from their differing findings on whether the parties had made any choice of law for the matrix contract: the majority answered it in the negative but the dissentients' construction of the contract led them to the opposite finding.[109] Their disagreement in conclusion is also attributable to differing perspectives on *dépeçage*: while the dissentients stressed the exceptional nature of it,[110] the majority put a more positive gloss on it in relation to arbitration agreements, noting that the difficulty which could entail from applying different laws to different parts of a contract would be alleviated by the principle of severability: in their view '[a]n arbitration clause may ... more readily than other clauses be governed by a different law'.[111]

Had the majority found, as did the dissenting judges, that the parties had made a choice of law for the matrix contract, it is clear that they would have come to the same conclusion as the dissent, that the governing law of the matrix contract would serve as the law applicable to the arbitration agreement.[112] According to the dissentients, 'it is natural, rational and realistic' to regard the choice of law for the matrix contract as 'encompassing, or carrying across to, the arbitration agreement'.[113] Likewise, the majority held in *obiter* that a choice of law made by the parties for the matrix contract would constitute the choice of law for the arbitration agreement both as a matter of principle[114] and as a matter of interpretation of Article V(1)(a) of the New York Convention.[115] The majority considered that the choice of a different country as the seat of the arbitration would not be sufficient to displace this

---

[105] As an aside, a jurisdiction agreement was held in *obiter* to be generally governed by the same law as that governs the matrix contract by both the majority (ibid [53(v)]) and the dissentients (ibid [254]), a view which also accords with the preferred approach.
[106] For the majority's view, see ibid [38]. For the dissent's view, see ibid [193 (iii)].
[107] See Section E.1.
[108] For the majority's view, see esp *Enka (SC)* (n 101) [38]–[42], [170(iv)–(vi)]. For the dissentients' views, see ibid [193(iii)], [231], [257(ii)–(iv)]. See further text to nn 110–111.
[109] Ibid [155] (majority) and [205] (dissent). These findings are not a point of concern of this essay.
[110] Ibid [193] and [231].
[111] Ibid [40]–[41].
[112] Ibid [46], [53]–[54], [129], [170(iv)–(v)].
[113] Ibid [228].
[114] Ibid [53]–[54].
[115] Ibid [129].

conclusion.[116] The views of both the dissenting judges and the majority are consistent with the suggestion of this essay that where the parties have made a choice of law for the matrix contract, the court should not be allowed to resort to involuntary *dépeçage* to refer an arbitration agreement to a different law.[117]

Had the dissenting judges found, as did the majority, that the parties had made no choice of law for the matrix contract, they would still have differed with the majority in their conclusions: the majority concluded that the arbitration agreement was governed by the law of the seat whereas the dissent would have concluded that it was governed by the governing law of the matrix contract. Their disagreement in conclusion may be explained by their differing perspectives on *dépeçage*. The majority considered the law of the seat to be the law with which the arbitration agreement was most closely connected.[118] Given their rejection of the submission that an arbitration agreement should be treated as a separate contract, this reasoning, read in context, appears to rest on involuntary *dépeçage*. The dissenting judges, on the other hand, held in *obiter* that the governing law of the matrix contract, even if it had not been chosen by the parties, would also govern the arbitration agreement.[119] They would not allow the court to resort to involuntary *dépeçage*. The views of both the majority and the dissent—though disagreeing with each other in conclusion—are compatible with the suggestion of this essay[120] that the courts should be allowed to resort to involuntary *dépeçage* where the parties have made no choice of law for the matrix contract only if the applicable choice of law rules clearly provide what specific terms are referred, separately from the remainder of the matrix contract, to what laws. The majority apparently saw such choice of law rules in Article V(1)(a) of the New York Convention while the dissenting judges did not.[121] Thus, the majority prayed in aid that provision as a compelling reason for referring an arbitration agreement to the law of the seat where the parties had made no choice of law for the matrix contract.[122] The dissent, on the other hand, did not read the same provision as prescribing a mandatory choice of law rule separately referring an arbitration agreement to the law of the seat.[123]

From the foregoing analysis, it would be safe to conclude that the preferred approach suggested by this essay has found substantial favour with both sides of the Supreme Court in *Enka*.[124] The clarity of the Court's analysis would have been

---

[116] Ibid [46], [170(v)].
[117] Section E.2.
[118] *Enka* (SC) (n 101) esp [120]–[122] and [170(viii)].
[119] Ibid [256] and [260] (Lord Burrows); also ibid, [288], [292] (Lord Sales).
[120] Section E.2. and Section I.2.(b).
[121] Compare *Enka* (SC) (n 101) [125]–[141] (Lords Hamblen and Leggatt) with ibid [250]–[253] (Lord Burrows) and [289]–[291] (Lord Sales).
[122] Ibid [125].
[123] Ibid [251]–[253] and [260].
[124] The Court also gave consideration to other issues falling outside the scope of this essay, including the common law's so called 'validation principle' (ibid [95]–[109]) (Lords Hamblen and Leggatt), [198], [251], [257(iv)] (Lord Burrows), [266], [276]–[279], [284]–[285], [291] (Lord Sales)).

aided if, as attempted in this essay, a clearer presentation had been made of the two-tier scheme of analysis consisting, first, of the consideration whether an arbitration agreement should, by virtue of the principle of severability, be treated as a distinct contract severed from the matrix contract for choice of law purposes and, second, of the consideration whether an arbitration agreement should be split within the matrix contract by means of *dépeçage*. The clarity of the Court's analysis would also have been aided if, adopting the approach of this essay, a conscious distinction had been drawn between voluntary and involuntary *dépeçage* with the use of these expressions.

7
The Conflict of Laws and Unjust Enrichment

Andrew Burrows

A. Introduction

The relationship between the conflict of laws and the law of unjust enrichment (or, more widely, the law of restitution) continues to be of great academic interest as well as having practical importance. We need to distinguish two separate enquiries. First, in what circumstances do the English courts have jurisdiction to determine a claim in the law of unjust enrichment with a foreign element? Secondly, what law governs a claim in the law of unjust enrichment with a foreign element (often referred to as the 'applicable law' issue)? This essay will consider both jurisdiction and applicable law.

When Adrian Briggs and I were studying the conflict of laws in the same Oxford BCL seminars in 1979–1980, these questions were entirely a matter for English domestic law. In relation to applicable law, which the BCL course was then focussed on, the matter was entirely a matter for the common law without any relevant statutory input. Indeed, for some thirty years thereafter—until the coming into effect (on 11 January 2009) of the Rome II Regulation on the law applicable to non-contractual obligations[1]—the common law on the applicable law for unjust enrichment was a very hot topic. It caught the imagination of scholars because of the excitement of testing out, and applying, the newly articulated common law rules on unjust enrichment/restitution in the practical context of determining the common law rules on applicable law. The editors of the publication now known as *Dicey, Morris & Collins, The Conflict of Laws* had their say, with the relevant chapter being edited by Professor Briggs in the 13th and 14th editions.[2] In 2002, in his Clarendon series book *The Conflict of Laws*, Professor Briggs included a succinct overview of the applicable law covering unjust enrichment and restitution,

---

[1] Regulation (EC) No 864/2007 of the European Parliament and of the Council of 11 July 2007 on the law applicable to non-contractual obligations (Rome II) ([2007] OJ L199/40) (hereafter Rome II Regulation).

[2] Lawrence Collins and others (eds), *Dicey & Morris: The Conflict of Laws* (13th edn, Sweet & Maxwell 2000); Lawrence Collins and others (eds), *Dicey & Morris: The Conflict of Laws* (14th edn, Sweet & Maxwell 2006) (hereafter Dicey & Morris).

alongside equitable obligations, in a chapter headed 'Other Obligations'.[3] Several other commentators wrote articles or essays on applicable law and unjust enrichment/restitution.[4] Doctoral theses were written on this area.[5] And there was a sprinkling of court cases which will be mentioned below.

Alongside his characteristically sharp written comments, conversations with Adrian over the years (not least when we worked together on *The Myanmar Law of Contract*[6]) suggest that, while not a restitution-sceptic, he has viewed the fervent passion with which the law of unjust enrichment has been debated in academic circles during our academic careers as both amusing and bemusing. For him, it is clear that conceptual elegance and purity should, if necessary, bow to the need for a practically workable law that can flexibly respond to commercial needs. The language and concepts of unjust enrichment may be marginally better and clearer than quasi-contract but there is no need to get too worked up about it all.

Of course, the defining present issue for the conflict of laws in the United Kingdom is Brexit. Since the Referendum in 2016, UK private international law scholars have had to cope with massive uncertainty as to the future content of their subject. For, as Professor Briggs has explained, EU law had become central to English private international law:[7]

> Until recently it had been settled wisdom that private international law, as understood in England, was moving away from being a common law subject with European insertions and becoming a European subject with common law marginalia.

After the General Election of December 2019, the position in relation to the conflict of laws, including the subject matter of this essay, has become slightly clearer albeit that, at the time of writing, there is still significant uncertainty as to what, if anything, will replace the present EU legislation as far as the UK is concerned. To use Professor Briggs' analogy,[8] there is now sign of an omelette emerging (whether

---

[3] Adrian Briggs, *The Conflict of Laws* (1st edn, OUP 2002) 194–9 (hereafter Briggs, *The Conflict of Laws* (1st edn)). The book is now in its 4th edition (2019).

[4] eg Peter Hay, 'Unjust Enrichment in the Conflict of Laws' (1978) 26 AJ Comp L 3; T W Bennett, 'Applicable Law Rules in Claims of Unjust Enrichment' [1990] 39 ICLQ 136; Joanna Bird, 'Applicable Law' in Francis Rose (ed), *Restitution and the Conflict of Laws* (Mansfield Press 1995) 64–141 (hereafter Rose, *Restitution*); Peter Brereton, 'Restitution and Contract' in Rose, *Restitution* (n 4) 142–79; Robert Stevens, 'The Applicable Law Rules of Restitutionary Obligations' in Rose, *Restitution* (n 4) 180–220.

[5] eg George Panagopoulos, *Restitution in Private International Law* (Hart Publishing 2000) (hereafter Panagopoulos, *Restitution in Private International Law*). His approach was extensively criticised in a review essay by Stephen Lee, 'Applicable Law for Claims in Unjust Enrichment' (2002) 26 MULR 192.

[6] Adrian Briggs and Andrew Burrows, 'The Law of Contract in Myanmar' (2017) <https://www.law.ox.ac.uk/sites/files/oxlaw/briggsburrowsbook_-_thelawofcontractinmyanmar.pdf> accessed 16 September 2020, published by OUP on behalf of the Oxford Law Faculty (2017).

[7] Adrian Briggs, *The Conflict of Laws* (4th edn, OUP 2019) v.

[8] Ibid vi.

the taste is good or bad) although one may for ever feel that the main exercise has been in smashing the eggs.

As at 1 January 2021, the position on jurisdiction and applicable law for civil claims, including in unjust enrichment, can be summarised, with some simplification, as follows:

(i) Under the European Union (Withdrawal) Act 2018 and the European Union (Withdrawal Agreement) Act 2020, the implementation completion day ('IP completion day') is 31 December 2020.
(ii) As regards jurisdiction, for proceedings commenced after the IP completion day, the EU legislation on jurisdiction for civil claims including in unjust enrichment, in particular the Brussels I Regulation[9] and the Recast Brussels I Regulation,[10] is revoked by reason of the Civil Jurisdiction and Judgments (Amendment) (EU Exit) Regulations 2019, Part 5.[11] In addition, by Parts 2 and 4 of the 2019 Regulations, the Brussels Convention[12] and Lugano Convention[13] are deleted from the Civil Jurisdiction and Judgments Act 1982. However, the UK government has made clear that it intends to sign up again to the Lugano Convention;[14] and, on 8 April 2020, it submitted its application to do so to the EU and EFTA countries (the latter being Norway, Switzerland and Iceland).[15] The Lugano Convention is very similar to the Brussels I Regulation and, as far as unjust enrichment is concerned, it would appear that there are no significant differences. I shall assume for the purposes of this essay that the UK will again accede to the Lugano Convention.[16] Where the Lugano Convention rules on jurisdiction do not apply (because the defendant is not domiciled in the

---

[9] Regulation (EC) 44/2001 of 22 December 2000 on jurisdiction and the recognition and enforcement of judgments in civil and commercial matters [2001] OJ L12/1 (hereafter Brussels I Regulation).

[10] Regulation (EU) No 1215/2012 of the European Parliament and of the Council of 12 December 2012 on jurisdiction and the recognition and enforcement of judgments in civil and commercial matters [2012] OJ L351/1 (hereafter Recast Brussels I Regulation).

[11] SI 2019/479 (as amended) (hereafter 2019 Regulations) with 'exit day' (as defined in the European Union (Withdrawal) Act 2018 s 20) being replaced by 'IP completion day' by reason of the European Union (Withdrawal Agreement) Act 2020, s 41(4) and Sch 5, para 1.

[12] 1968 Brussels Convention of 27 September 1968 on jurisdiction and the enforcement of judgments in civil and commercial matters [1972] OJ L299/32 (hereafter Brussels Convention).

[13] Convention on jurisdiction and the recognition and enforcement of judgments in civil and commercial matters [2007] (OJ L339/3) (hereafter Lugano Convention).

[14] Ministry of Justice, 'Support for the UK's intent to accede to the Lugano Convention 2007' (28 January 2020) <https://www.gov.uk/government/news/support-for-the-uks-intent-to-accede-to-the-lugano-convention-2007> accessed 16 September 2020. The relevant version of the Lugano Convention is that of 2007.

[15] Separate permission must also be sought from Denmark.

[16] Even if this does not happen, by the Civil Jurisdiction and Judgments Act 1982, s 16 and Sch 4 similar issues presumably live on in respect of jurisdiction disputes within the different parts of the UK (and note that the important case of *Kleinwort Benson Ltd v Glasgow CC* [1999] 1 AC 153 (hereafter *Kleinwort Benson*), discussed in Section B.1.(b), dealt with a jurisdictional dispute as between Scotland and England).

UK, EU, Norway, Switzerland or Iceland) the law on jurisdiction for civil claims, including in unjust enrichment, is governed (subject to the Hague Convention on Choice of Court Agreements[17]) by the domestic Civil Procedure Rules (which are a form of delegated legislation).

(iii) As regards applicable law for non-contractual obligations, from IP completion day, the Rome II Regulation[18] is 'retained EU law'[19] within the law of the United Kingdom.[20] The same applies to the Rome I Regulation on the law applicable to contractual obligations[21] which, in Arts 12(1)(c), (d) and (e), has provisions covering respectively 'the consequences of breach', 'the various ways of extinguishing obligations' and 'the consequences of nullity'.

This essay is essentially concerned with examining the law after IP completion day. It will therefore focus on the Lugano Convention and the Civil Procedure Rules as regards jurisdiction; and on the Rome II Regulation and, to some extent, the Rome I Regulation as regards applicable law.

B. Jurisdiction

The special problems raised by unjust enrichment lie principally in determining which provision of the Lugano Convention applies; or, if the Civil Procedure Rules apply, in determining which sub-paragraphs of CPR Practice Direction 6B para 3.1 are applicable to unjust enrichment.

1. The Lugano Convention

(a) The exceptions in Arts 5(1) and 5(3)
One must be careful not to view the Lugano Convention through an exclusively domestic lens. An interpretation that ensures as uniform an interpretation as possible

---

[17] Hague Convention on choice of court agreements (2005) (hereafter Hague Choice of Court Convention). After IP completion day, this has the force of law in the UK by reason of the Private International Law (Implementation of Agreements) Act 2020, s 1(2) and Schedule 3F. The Hague Choice of Court Convention does not provide jurisdiction rules other than where there is a choice of court agreement; and it only applies where the court chosen is within a contracting state. The Hague Choice of Court Convention's material scope is subject to a number of limitations.
[18] Rome II Regulation (n 1).
[19] 'Retained EU law' is defined in the European Union (Withdrawal) Act 2018, s 6(7).
[20] Law Applicable to Contractual and Non-Contractual Obligations (Amendment etc) (EU Exit) Regulations (SI 2019/834); 'exit day' has been replaced by 'IP completion day' by reason of the European Union (Withdrawal Agreement) Act 2020, s 41(4) and Sch 5, para 1.
[21] Regulation (EC) No 593/2008 of the European Parliament and of the Council of 17 June 2008 on the law applicable to contractual obligations (Rome I) ([2008] OJ L177/6) (hereafter Rome I Regulation).

(across the EU and EFTA states) is required.[22] But of course it does not follow that the relevant meaning should be unprincipled; and, in this context, it is important that, in so far as the words allow it, and in so far as there is no conflicting relevant case law (eg, of the Court of Justice of the EU (CJEU)), it may be that the Lugano Convention can be interpreted in a way that respects the principled distinction between contract and unjust enrichment. After all, that is a distinction which is now recognised across civil and common law, even if there may be some differences in the precise demarcation lines between the two subjects.

As laid down in Art 2, the basic approach of the Lugano Convention (as analogously the Brussels I Regulation Art 2 and the Recast Brussels I Regulation Art 4) is that, subject to wide-ranging exceptions, a person domiciled in the UK, EU, Norway, Switzerland or Iceland, must be sued in that State. While there are exceptions for, for example, breach of trust,[23] salvage,[24] and rights *in rem* in immovable property,[25] the main exceptions into which unjust enrichment must be fitted, if at all, are contained in Art 5, sub-paragraphs (1) and (3) (Recast Brussels I Regulation, Arts 7(1) and (2)).

Art 5(1) and (3) reads as follows:

A person domiciled in a Contracting State may, in another Contracting State, be sued:

1. In matters relating to a contract, in the courts for the place of performance of the obligation in question; ...
3. In matters relating to tort, delict or quasi-delict, in the courts for the place where the harmful event occurred.

If one construes 'in matters relating to [contract or tort]' as meaning 'where the cause of action is based on [contract or tort]' these provisions cover restitution for wrongs (ie where the cause of action is a wrong such as a breach of contract or tort) but they do not apply to restitution of an unjust enrichment (ie where the cause of action is unjust enrichment).[26] That is, Art 5(1) applies to restitution *for* breach of contract: and Art 5(3) applies to restitution *for* torts. But, on this interpretation, they do not apply to the cause of action of unjust enrichment so that, for claims

---

[22] eg the Preamble of the Lugano Convention includes the recital: 'desiring to ensure as uniform an interpretation as possible of this instrument'.
[23] Lugano Convention (n 13) Art 5(6).
[24] Ibid Art 5(7).
[25] Ibid Art 22(1). This provision confers exclusive jurisdiction on the courts of the State where the property is situated. In Case C-294/92 *Webb v Webb* [1994] ECR I-1717, the CJEU held that a father's claim against his son to enforce a trust (created in England) over property in France did not fall within Brussels I (n 9) Art 24(1) (which was the equivalent of Art 22(1) Lugano Convention (n 13)) because the action was not based on a right *in rem*. Adrian Briggs, 'Trusts of Land and the Brussels Convention' (1994) 110 LQR 526, 530, described the decision as 'bizarre'.
[26] For the distinction between restitution for unjust enrichment and restitution for wrongs, see Andrew Burrows, *The Law of Restitution* (3rd edn, OUP 2011) 9–12.

based on the cause of action of unjust enrichment, there will be no special jurisdiction in another State and the claimant will have to fall back on the general rule of suing where the defendant is domiciled. That Art 5(1) does not extend to unjust enrichment is supported by the fact that 'the place of performance of the obligation in question' seems inapt given that the obligation to make restitution is imposed by law and is neither the performance of an implied contract or of a term implied into a contract. In other words, it would appear that the obligation referred to in Art 5(1) is the performance of the contract and not the performance of the obligation to make restitution.

Having said that, it is difficult to draw a sharp distinction between contract and unjust enrichment where rescission of a contract is the relevant remedy; the wiping away of the contract and the return of benefits rendered, or their value, can be viewed as one process. To have different courts deciding on the wiping away of the contract as opposed to the consequential reversal of benefits would be impracticable and wasteful. For that reason, the preferable view is probably that rescission of a contract including the consequential reversal of benefits for, for example, misrepresentation, duress or undue influence, should fall within Art 5(1). And the 'place of performance of the obligation' in question may be taken to refer to the place of performance of the contractual obligation that is being wiped away.

For similar reasons, one might argue for a still wider interpretation of Art 5(1) so that restitution (most obviously for failure of consideration) after the discharge of a contract for breach also falls within Art 5(1).

More controversially, one might argue, taking an even wider interpretation, that restitution consequent on a contract being void also falls within Art 5(1). Although this may seem an especially artificial interpretation, which fails to recognise the principled distinction between contract and unjust enrichment and runs into what appears to be the serious difficulty of attaching importance to the place of performance of a contractual obligation that never legally existed, it does have the merit of ensuring that there is no forum fragmentation (involving needless inconvenience and cost) between a court deciding whether a contract is void and a court deciding on the restitutionary consequences of the contract being void. In other words, once one has decided that the decision as to whether a contract is void is a matter relating to a contract (even though a purported contract) it may be thought pragmatically preferable to go on to apply the same approach—and hence to reach the same answer on jurisdiction—to a claim for restitution consequent on the contract being void.

Certainly such a wide interpretation of Art 5(1) (of the Brussels I Regulation) was favoured by the CJEU in *Profit Investment Sim SpA v Ossi*.[27] In that case, the

---

[27] Case C-366/13 [2016] 1 WLR 3832 (hereafter *Profit Investment*). See also Case C-417/15 *Schmidt v Schmidt* [2017] ILPr 6 (hereafter *Schmidt*) (a claim for the restitution of title to land, transferred under a contract that was invalid for the incapacity of the transferor, was held to fall within Art 7(1) Recast Brussels I Regulation (n 10) which is the equivalent to Art 5(1) Lugano Convention (n 13)).

claimant, an Italian company, had bought bonds issued by a German bank through a UK intermediary. Subsequently the German bank cancelled the bonds and the claimant sought, inter alia, a declaration that the agreements with the intermediary under which it had acquired the bonds were a nullity and restitution of the purchase price. Stressing that an autonomous EU law meaning should be given to Art 5(1) of the Brussels I Regulation, the CJEU held that the claims for a declaration and restitution were 'matters relating to a contract' within Art 5(1). The CJEU said the following:

> [53] [I]t must be recalled at the outset that the concept of 'matters relating to a contract' ... cannot be taken to refer to the classification under the relevant national law of the legal relationship in question before the national court. That concept must, on the contrary, be interpreted independently, regard being had to the general scheme and objectives of [the Brussels I Regulation], in order to ensure that it is applied uniformly in all the member states.
>
> ...
>
> [55] [A]s regards the link between the action for a declaration of nullity and the recovery of sums paid but not due, it suffices to note, as Advocate General Bot pointed out in ... his opinion, that, if there had not been a contractual relationship freely assumed between the parties, the obligation would not have been performed and there would be no right to restitution. That causal link between the right to restitution and the contractual relationship is sufficient to bring the action for restitution within the scope of matters relating to a contract.

That left the question of identifying the place of performance of the obligation in question. The CJEU took this to be the place of performance of the contract;[28] and Advocate General Bot had said that that was where the bonds were to be delivered to the purchaser (rather than, eg, where payment was to be made).[29] That may be thought an odd conclusion when one is talking about a non-existent contract and where the claim that one is concerned with is for the restitution of money paid under it. However, it is the sort of pragmatic, albeit somewhat artificial, conclusion that one is forced to reach if one takes such a wide interpretation of Art 5(1). The place of performance under the non-existent contract has no principled connection to the restitutionary obligation to repay. Despite the policy merits of avoiding forum fragmentation, one can therefore raise objections of principle to this approach of the CJEU.

There was no reference in that decision of the CJEU to the two leading English cases on this question. The first, in particular, took a significantly narrower—and, one might argue, more principled—interpretation of Art 5(1) and (3).

---

[28] *Profit Investment* (n 27) [54]–[57].
[29] Ibid, Opinion of Adv Gen Bot [85]–[86].

(b) The two leading English cases

Kleinwort Benson Ltd v Glasgow City Council[30] was one of the 'interest rate swap' cases. The claimant sought restitution of the payments it had made to the Scottish defendant under interest rate swap contracts that were agreed to be void as being outside the powers of the defendant local authority. The claimant brought proceedings in England arguing that the equivalent to Art 5(1) of the Brussels and Lugano Conventions (under Schedule 4 to the Civil Jurisdiction and Judgments Act 1982 applicable to jurisdiction within the UK) applied. The defendant wished to defend the claim in Scotland where it was domiciled and sought a declaration that the English courts had no jurisdiction. A majority of the House of Lords (Lords Nicholls and Mustill dissenting) held that Art 5(1) did not apply here. The claim for restitution of unjust enrichment was independent of contract. Any purported contract was void. The place of performance of the obligation in question was referring to the place of contractual performance whereas one was concerned with restitution not contractual performance. The general rule in Art 2 therefore applied and the claimant's action in unjust enrichment against the defendant had to be brought in Scotland.

In Lord Goff's words:[31]

> I turn to consider the question in the present case. That question is whether the claim of Kleinwort to restitution of the sums paid by it to Glasgow under a contract accepted to be void ab initio falls within article 5(1). I find it very difficult to see how such a claim can fall within article 5(1). It can only do so if it can properly be said to be based upon a particular contractual obligation, the place of performance of which is within the jurisdiction of the court. Where however, as here, the claim is for the recovery of money paid under a supposed contract which in law never existed, it seems impossible to say that the claim for the recovery of the money is based upon a particular contractual obligation.

While not deciding the point, Lord Goff left open the possibility that, in contrast, restitution following the discharge of a contract for breach might fall within Art 5(1).[32]

Lord Nicholls in the leading dissenting speech interpreted Art 5(1) in line with the policy of avoiding inconvenience and waste. He considered it unacceptable to have different courts dealing with the validity of a contract and its restitutionary

---

[30] *Kleinwort Benson* (n 16). See Andrew Dickinson, 'Restitution and the Conflict of Laws in the House of Lords' [1998] RLR 104; Robert Stevens, 'Conflict of Laws' in Birks and Rose (eds), *Lessons of the Swaps Litigation* (Mansfield Press 2000) 329–41. cf Adrian Briggs, *Civil Jurisdiction and Judgments* (6th edn, Informa Law 2015) [2.172] (hereafter Briggs, *Civil Jurisdiction and Judgments*).
[31] *Kleinwort Benson* (n 16) 167.
[32] Ibid 170–1.

consequences. In his view, Art 5(1) should therefore be interpreted as covering the claims for restitution.

It is noteworthy that the House of Lords in *Kleinwort Benson* rejected the view that a claim in unjust enrichment had to fall within either Art 5(1) or (3). The European Court of Justice in *Kalfelis v Bankhaus Schröder, Munchmeyer, Hengst & Co*[33] had earlier held that Art 5(3) included 'all actions which seek to establish the liability of a defendant and which are not related to a "contract" within the meaning of Art 5(1)'.[34] At first blush, this could be taken to mean that all personal restitutionary claims not falling within Art 5(1) fall within Art 5(3). However, in *Kleinwort Benson Ltd v Glasgow City Council* their Lordships were unanimous in the view that Art 5(3) does not apply to a claim based on unjust enrichment because such a claim does not involve a harmful event or a wrong. In other words, *Kalfelis* should be interpreted as meaning that Art 5(3) is concerned with liability for torts and other wrongs[35] (other than breach of contract), including restitution for wrongs, but not restitution of an unjust enrichment. That restitution of an unjust enrichment falls outside Art 5(3) was subsequently supported by the opinion of Advocate General Wahl in *Gazdasági Versenyhivatal v Siemens Aktiengesellschaft Österreich*.[36] The case concerned a claim for restitution where a regulatory authority had repaid a competition fine to the claimant. It subsequently transpired that the fine should have been paid. The authority brought a claim for restitution of the repaid fine (including interest). On the principal issue in the case, Advocate General Wahl took the view that the claim for restitution did not fall within 'civil and commercial matters' in Art 1 of the Brussels I Regulation. But he went on to explain that, in any event, an action for restitution of an unjust enrichment does not rest on a harmful event, damage or loss and therefore falls outside Art 5(3):[37]

> Unlike an action seeking to establish the defendant's non-contractual liability, which aims to undo damage or loss suffered by the applicant and for which the defendant is alleged to be liable owing to his conduct or omission or other reasons attributable to him, an action for restitution based on unjust enrichment aims to restore to the applicant a benefit which the defendant has acquired illegitimately at the former's expense (or the payment of its monetary equivalent).... [R]estitution on the ground of unjust enrichment therefore inherently focuses on the gain acquired by the defendant rather than the loss suffered by the applicant. Unjust enrichment is the cause of action, and restitution the remedy. Hence, I do

---

[33] Case 189/87 [1988] ECR 5565.
[34] Ibid [17].
[35] This should include equitable wrongs analogous to torts such as breach of fiduciary duty, breach of confidence and dishonestly assisting or procuring a breach of fiduciary duty. That 'dishonest assistance' falls within Art 5(3) was established by *Casio Computer Co Ltd v Sayo (No 3)* [2001] EWCA Civ 661; [2001] ILPr 43.
[36] Case C-102/15 [2016] 5 CMLR 14, Opinion of AG Wahl (hereafter *Gazdasági*).
[37] Ibid [61].

not subscribe to a vision according to which the mere non-receipt of a contested claim amounts to a 'harmful event' giving rise to a loss.

The decision of the CJEU upheld the opinion of Advocate General Wahl on the principal ground without discussing Art 5(3).

None of their Lordships in the majority in *Kleinwort Benson* clarified what the position would be in relation to rescission of a contract; that is, where the contract was voidable rather than void. This arose for decision in *Agnew v Lansförsäkringsbolagens AB*.[38] The claimants, who were London reinsurers, sought a declaration that they were entitled to set aside a reinsurance contract with the defendant Swedish insurers for the latter's misrepresentation or non-disclosure during the negotiation of the reinsurance contract in London. All of their Lordships agreed that a claim to rescind or set aside a contract was a 'matter relating to contract' within the first part of Art 5(1) of the Lugano Convention. The majority (Lords Woolf, Nicholls and Cooke) went on to decide that the place of performance of the obligation in question referred to the obligation to disclose the correct information or (per Lords Cooke and Nicholls but not Lord Woolf) not to make a misrepresentation. Those were obligations owed during the pre-contractual negotiations which had taken place in London. The English courts therefore had jurisdiction under Art 5(1).

Lords Hope and Millett dissenting did not think that the obligation referred to in Art 5(1) could be a pre-contractual obligation. As neither party had contended that the relevant obligation was that which the claimant sought to be relieved of under the voidable contract, Art 5(1) did not here apply and, applying the general rule under Art 2, the claimants would have to commence proceedings in Sweden as the defendant's domicile.

The minority's reasoning is persuasive in rejecting the majority's opinion that the relevant obligation was the obligation to disclose correct information. Moreover, where pre-contractual negotiations are carried on in different jurisdictions and over a period of time, it may be difficult to pinpoint the place where such an obligation should have been performed. Nor can it be rational to determine the ambit of Art 5(1) by drawing the distinction suggested by Lord Woolf between the negative obligation not to misrepresent facts, which he thought had no place of performance, and the positive obligation to disclose information, which he thought had a place of performance.[39] In any event, even if such a place of performance is identified (eg as being the only jurisdiction where contractual negotiations took place) it is far from clear that it is sufficiently significant to trigger jurisdiction.

---

[38] [2001] 1 AC 223.
[39] cf the negative 'exclusivity' contractual obligation in Case C-256/00 *Besix SA v Wasserreinigungsbau Alfred Kretzschmar GmbH & Co* [2003] 1 WLR 1113 which, because it required 'performance' everywhere, was held by the CJEU to fall outside Art 5(1).

The better view, therefore, is that Art 5(1) does apply to a claim to rescind a contract (in that respect the majority should be supported) but that, in respect of such a claim, the relevant obligation, and hence place of performance, is the contractual obligation from which the claimant seeks to be relieved.[40] In other words, Art 5(1) applies where the claimant seeks to enforce performance of a contract, including by claiming damages, or where the claimant seeks to deny (whether by a claim for rescission or a declaration of non-liability) that it is liable to perform a contract (subject to both parties agreeing that there was never a contract in which case *Kleinwort Benson v Glasgow CC* has laid down that there is no matter relating to a contract). In either case, it seems acceptable to link jurisdiction to the place where the contractual performance should have been carried out.

(c) Is *Kleinwort Benson v Glasgow CC* still good law?

At least at first sight, the narrow interpretation of Art 5(1) taken by the House of Lords in *Kleinwort Benson Ltd v Glasgow CC* has been superseded by the decision of the CJEU in *Profit Investment Sim SpA v Ossi*. Even if the argument that has been put forward above is accepted—that, in principle, one needs to distinguish between void and voidable contracts and that the reasoning of the majority of the House of Lords in *Kleinwort Benson* is correct in principle—it seems clear that that reasoning is inconsistent with the subsequent decision of the CJEU in *Profit v Ossi*. And, in any event, the latter decision has pragmatic policy on its side and was indeed the approach taken by the minority in *Kleinwort Benson*. As Uglesa Grusic has written, 'the House of Lords' decision in *Kleinwort Benson* concerning what is now Art 7(1) is untenable in light of recent authorities and should be regarded as wrongly decided'.[41]

However, without explicitly referring to *Profit v Ossi*, the argument that *Kleinwort Benson* is no longer good law was rejected at first instance and by the Court of Appeal in *Aspen Underwriting Ltd v Credit Europe Bank NV*.[42]

In that case, the claimants insured a vessel. The insurance policy contained an exclusive jurisdiction clause giving exclusive jurisdiction to the courts of England and Wales. The defendant bank, which had a mortgage over the vessel, was named

---

[40] This is therefore consistent with the decision of the Court of Appeal in *Boss Group Ltd v Boss France SA* [1997] 1 WLR 351 where the claim for a declaration that no contract was concluded was held to fall within Art 5(1) Brussels Convention (n 12). See also *Youell v La Reunion Arienne* [2009] EWCA Civ 175, [2009] 2 All ER (Comm) 1071.

[41] 'Unjust Enrichment and the Brussels I Regulation' (2019) 68 ICLQ 837, 859. The recent authorities particularly relied on by the author are *Profit Investment* (n 27) and *Schmidt* (n 27).

[42] [2018] EWCA Civ 2590, [2019] 1 Lloyd's Rep 221. For the judgment of Teare J at first instance, see [2017] EWHC 1904 (Comm), [2018] 1 All ER (Comm) 228 (he also gave a very short supplementary judgment at [2017] EWHC 3107 (Comm)). On the successful appeal in this case, the unjust enrichment issue was not dealt with by the Supreme Court: [2020] UKSC 11, [2020] 2 WLR 919.

as the loss payee and took an assignment of the policy. When the vessel sank, the claimant insurers settled the claim with the owners and managers of the vessel with the agreed sum being paid to the defendant bank. There was again a clause in the settlement agreement giving exclusive jurisdiction to the courts of England and Wales. It then transpired that the vessel had been deliberately sunk by the owners and the claimant insurers brought proceedings in England seeking, principally, damages for misrepresentation from the owners/managers and restitution of the sum paid out to the defendant bank.

The defendant bank argued that the English courts had no jurisdiction and that, under the Recast Brussels Regulation I, the claims could only be brought in the Netherlands, which is where the defendant was domiciled, because these were matters relating to insurance under Art 14 or because, even if that was wrong, the default position under Art 4 of the Recast Brussels I Regulation applied so that the claims should be brought in the courts of the defendant's domicile. It argued that, as a non-party to the insurance and settlements contracts, it was not bound by the exclusive jurisdiction clauses in those contracts.

The leading judgment in the Court of Appeal was given by Gross LJ. Agreeing with the decision and most of the reasoning of Teare J, at first instance, the Court of Appeal held as follows:

(i) The exclusive jurisdiction clauses did not bind the defendant bank because it was not a party to the insurance or settlement contracts; and it was not asserting claims to enforce those contracts and so did not fall within the 'conditional benefit' concept (ie that one cannot take a benefit without adhering to the condition attaching to that benefit).[43]

(ii) While these were matters relating to insurance within Art 14, that Art applied only to protect weaker parties and the defendant bank was not such a party.

(iii) The claim for damages for misrepresentation was a matter relating to 'tort, delict or quasi-delict' within Art 7(2) (rather than a matter relating to contract within Art 7(1)) and there was a good arguable case that the harmful event occurred within the jurisdiction of the English courts (as that was where the settlement agreement was signed and the loss suffered).

(iv) Applying *Kleinwort Benson Ltd v Glasgow CC*, the claim for restitution (which was based on mistake) did not fall within Art 7 so that that claim fell within Art 4 and therefore had to be brought within the jurisdiction of the defendant's domicile.

---

[43] The 'conditional benefit' concept was applied in the context of an arbitration clause by the Court of Appeal in *Schiffahrtsgesellschaft Detlev von Appen GmbH v Voest Alpine Intertrading GmbH (The Jay Bola)* [1997] 2 Lloyd's Rep 279.

Therefore, the conclusion of the Court of Appeal was that, unfortunate as forum fragmentation was, the English courts had jurisdiction in relation to the claim for damages for misrepresentation but no jurisdiction as regards the claim for restitution (which fell within the jurisdiction of the courts in the Netherlands).

It is significant that the Court of Appeal was faced with the argument that, as regards restitution, *Kleinwort Benson* had been overtaken by developments in EU law. It was not made clear precisely which developments in EU law were in mind although, given that *Kalfelis* preceded *Kleinwort Benson* and had been fully considered in it, one would have thought that the case of *Profit Investment Sim SpA v Ossi*, which was referred to by the Court of Appeal but not on this point, would have been particularly in mind. Gross LJ said that he was 'not at all persuaded'[44] that developments in EU law had overtaken *Kleinwort Benson*. But that, even if that was correct, the Court of Appeal was still bound, as a matter of precedent, by *Kleinwort Benson* as House of Lords authority.

With respect, the latter proposition is open to question. If the Court of Appeal had been clearly presented with the *Profit* case, as being a decision of the CJEU that was inconsistent with the decision of the House of Lords in *Kleinwort Benson*, it would surely have been bound to apply the decision of the CJEU.[45]

A further difficulty with this decision as far as unjust enrichment is concerned is the characterisation of the claim as being one for a mistake that was not a matter relating to contract under Art 7(1). Had the settlement contract been void so that the claimants were seeking restitution of money paid to the defendant bank mistakenly believing that they were bound to do so under a valid contract, *Kleinwort Benson* would have been directly in point. But it would appear that the settlement contract was voidable for misrepresentation not void for mistake and, unless and until that contract had been avoided for misrepresentation, the claimants were contractually bound to pay the money to the defendant bank albeit that the defendant bank was not a party to that contract. One might therefore strongly argue that, because the mistake claim was dependent on rescission of the settlement contract, the claim for mistake was a matter relating to that contract so that, even applying the English case law, Art 7(1) should have been applied because the important English case was *Agnew v Lansförsäkringsbolagens AB* not *Kleinwort Benson v Glasgow CC*.

Unfortunately, these interesting issues relating to unjust enrichment did not need to be discussed, and were not, in the judgment of the Supreme Court in this case. The Supreme Court agreed with the decision of the Court of Appeal that the exclusive jurisdiction clauses did not apply in relation to the defendant bank. But the Court of Appeal was overruled on the Art 14 issue. According to the Supreme Court, the claims were matters relating to insurance under Art 14 and, because the defendant bank was a beneficiary under the insurance policy, the 'weaker party'

---

[44] [2018] EWCA Civ 2590, [2019] 1 Lloyd's Rep 221 [152].
[45] See, eg, *ParkingEye Ltd v Beavis* [2015] UKSC 67, [2016] AC 1172 [105].

test—which was relevant only when considering the extension of those entitled to rely on Art 14—did not apply. As Art 14 applied, and as that is an exclusive provision where it applies, there was no scope for Art 7 and the question whether claims for restitution of an unjust enrichment fell within Art 7 fell away. It followed that, applying Art 14, all the claims against the defendant bank fell outside the jurisdiction of the English courts and within the jurisdiction of the courts in the Netherlands (as the domicile of the defendant bank). A principled decision was therefore reached which, at the same time, avoided the policy objections to forum fragmentation.

We therefore await clarification as to whether *Kleinwort Benson* remains good law. Certainly the Court of Appeal in *Aspen Underwriting Ltd v Credit Europe Bank NV* should not be regarded as having satisfactorily resolved that question.

2. The Civil Procedure Rules

Where the defendant is not domiciled in the UK, EU, Norway, Switzerland or Iceland, the rules as to jurisdiction laid down in the Lugano Convention do not apply and instead the Convention delegates the question of jurisdiction to the national rules of the relevant court.[46] In this situation, therefore, the position in England and Wales after IP completion day is that jurisdiction in relation to unjust enrichment is a matter for the Civil Procedure Rules 1998, as amended (CPR) (subject to there being a relevant choice of court agreement governed by the Hague Convention on Choice of Court Agreements). Under the CPR, there is jurisdiction where a claim form is served on a defendant within the jurisdiction or where a claim form is served out of the jurisdiction with the permission of the court given under CPR r 6.36 and Practice Direction 6B, para 3.1. By that paragraph, various 'jurisdiction gateways' are laid down under which service out may be permitted.

As regards claims in unjust enrichment, those jurisdiction gateways, until this century, were plainly unsatisfactory in that they did not expressly cover unjust enrichment (or restitution). Perhaps not surprisingly, given the historical emphasis on quasi-contract, the approach taken in the main cases on the question—*Bowling v Cox*,[47] *Rousou's Trustee v Rousou*[48] and *Re Jogia*[49]—was to force unjust enrichment claims into the contract jurisdiction gateway of what was then the Rules of the Supreme Court, Order 11.

---

[46] Lugano Convention (n 13) Art 4. As at 1 January 2021, the UK has not yet acceded again to the Lugano Convention although it has applied to do so; and it has been assumed for the purposes of this essay that the UK will again accede to that Convention (see text to n 16).
[47] [1926] AC 751.
[48] [1955] 3 All ER 486; See also *Re Intended Action, Rousou's Trustee v Rousou* [1955] 2 All ER 169 (hereafter *Rousou*).
[49] [1988] 1 WLR 484 (hereafter *Jogia*). See also *Finnish Marine Insurance Co Ltd v Protective National Insurance Co* [1989] 2 Lloyd's Rep 99, 102–3; *The Olib* [1991] 2 Lloyd's Rep 108, 118–19.

All three cases dealt with a specialised statutory example of unjust enrichment, namely a trustee in bankruptcy's right to recover money paid away by a bankrupt to the defendants.[50] In all of them it was reasoned that the trustee in bankruptcy's action for money had and received, albeit 'quasi-contractual', fell within the contract head of Order 11 so that one needed to determine whether the quasi-contractual obligation was 'made' (ie, arose) in England or whether the proper law of the quasi-contractual obligation was English. The former of these was somewhat inapt for unjust enrichment[51] and the whole approach was redolent of the now discarded implied contract theory of unjust enrichment.

Fortunately, the Supreme Court's Rules Committee recognised the inadequacy of the existing rules for unjust enrichment and restitution and, in 2000, CPR r 6.20(15) (now CPR r 6.36, coupled with Practice Direction 6B, para 3.1(16)), was implemented, which specifically deals with a claim for restitution. As subsequently amended (by adding paras (b) and (c)), it reads as follows:

The claimant may serve a claim form out of the jurisdiction with the permission of the court under rule 6.36 where...

(16) A claim is made for restitution where –

(a) the defendant's alleged liability arises out of acts committed within the jurisdiction; or
(b) the enrichment is obtained within the jurisdiction; or
(c) the claim is governed by the law of England and Wales.

As Professor Briggs has written:

[i]t is to be expected that paragraph (16) will now provide the natural home for restitutionary claims or those based on the law against unjust enrichment, and that earlier authorities which had allowed a quasi-contractual claim to be brought, for want of anything better, within the contract head, will not now need to be followed.[52]

Take a mistake case, where A in London sends a mistaken payment to B in New York, B's liability in unjust enrichment arises out of acts committed within England in the sense that the payment has been made from England.[53] So this falls

---

[50] The statutory provisions were previously laid down in the Bankruptcy Act 1914 and the Law of Property Act 1925, s 172. The modern equivalents are contained in the Insolvency Act 1986.

[51] In *Jogia* (n 49) Sir Nicolas Browne-Wilkinson V-C took the view that the obligation arose where the enrichment was received and that this was generally the same as the proper law of the quasi-contract.

[52] Briggs, *Civil Jurisdiction and Judgments* (n 30) [4.81].

[53] That not *all* the acts triggering liability have to take place within England is supported by, eg, *Polly Peck International Ltd v Nadir (No 3)* [1994] 1 BCLC 661 (CA). This dealt with 'knowing assistance' and 'knowing receipt' under what is now CPR 6B PD para 3.1(15).

within para 3.1(16)(a). If it is C in New York who sends a mistaken payment to D in London, this is covered by para 3.1(16)(b) because the enrichment is obtained in England. Therefore, in a mistaken payment case, the English courts may give permission for service out of the jurisdiction whether the payment was made from England or received in England.

It is noteworthy that para 3.1(16) does not use the words 'unjust enrichment' and focuses instead on a claim for restitution. Plainly restitution for unjust enrichment falls squarely within it. But what about restitution for wrongs, in relation to which it is now commonly accepted that the cause of action is the wrong not the wrongful (or unjust) enrichment?

Certainly one can argue that restitution for wrongs is naturally dealt with in other paragraphs covering the particular wrong. In other words, one might say that restitution for wrongs naturally falls within para 3.1(7) (for breach of contract), para 3.1(9) (for torts) and para 3.1(15) (for equitable wrongs where the defendant is alleged to be a 'constructive trustee'). These paragraphs essentially allow service out where the wrongful act was committed within England and Wales[54] or, in the case of tort, the damage was sustained within England and Wales.

The best approach is to accept that, in the context of restitution for wrongs, more than one of the jurisdiction gateways may apply. Paragraph 3.1(16) applies to any claim for restitution but, where restitution for a wrong is being claimed, there is another possible gateway. There is no good reason to take a narrow interpretation of para 3.1(16).[55] This is not least because, irrespective of there being a jurisdiction gateway, the courts may still refuse jurisdiction under the *forum non conveniens* doctrine.[56]

For similar reasons one can readily accept that, for restitution in the context of voidable or terminated contracts, there may be an overlap between paras 3.1(16) and 3.1(6), which applies to claims in respect of a contract.[57] Paragraph 3.1(6)

---

[54] CPR 6B PD para 3.1(15) reads: 'A claim if made against the defendant as constructive trustee, or as trustee of a resulting trust, where the claim arises out of acts committed or events occurring within the jurisdiction or relates to assets within the jurisdiction.'

[55] This is supported by *Nabb Brothers Ltd v Lloyds International (Guernsey) Ltd* [2005] EWHC 405 (Ch), [2005] ILPr 37 (hereafter *Nabb*): see n 56. cf Matthew Hoyle, 'Failures for Consideration: Re-Analysing Jurisdiction in Unjust Enrichment Claims' (2020) 83 MLR 1008, esp at 1018.

[56] In *Nabb* (n 55) this discretion was exercised in setting aside service out of the jurisdiction because England, as opposed to Guernsey, was not the appropriate forum. Had that not been so, it was held that, what were then, CPR r 6.20(14) and (15) would have applied as regards a claim for 'knowing receipt' because it was sufficient for those paragraphs that the transfer of funds had taken place in breach of trust from accounts held in London. See also *AstraZeneca UK Ltd v Albemarle Int Corp* [2010] EWHC 1028 (Comm), [2010] 2 Lloyd's Rep 61 in which a stay against proceedings in England was granted in an economic duress case that was held to fall within CPR 6B PD para 3.1(16).

[57] See, eg, taking a wide view of what is now CPR 6B PD 3.1(6) dealing with claims 'in respect of a contract', *Albon v Naza Motor trading Sdn Bhd* [2007] EWHC 9 (Ch), [2007] 2 All ER 719. See also CPR 6B PD 3.1(11) under which English courts may grant permission for service outside the jurisdiction if 'the whole subject matter of a claim relates to property located within the jurisdiction'. For a general discussion of the width of CPR 6B PD para 3.1(6), see *Alliance Bank JSC v Aquanta Corp* [2012] EWCA Civ 1588, [2013] 1 Lloyd's Rep 175 [56]–[73].

allows service out if, for example, the contract is governed by English law or was made within the jurisdiction or, very importantly, has a clause conferring jurisdiction on the English courts.[58]

As there are no objections to service out being granted under more than one jurisdiction gateway (ie the gateways are not mutually exclusive), the domestic law on jurisdiction in respect of the conflicts of law on unjust enrichment (or restitution) is relatively flexible. It follows that, if (contrary to the basis on which this essay has been written) the Lugano Convention were to fall away, reliance on the CPR would not be a disaster (albeit that one would lose the advantages of a unified approach across the EU and EFTA States). As it is, the likely position is that, after IP completion day, these CPR rules will continue to play only a residual role (ie they will apply only where the Lugano Convention does not).

3. Conclusion on jurisdiction

We have seen that, in relation to jurisdiction for claims in unjust enrichment, the courts are often required to decide difficult questions of legislative interpretation which reflect a tension between a principled approach, which recognises the independence of unjust enrichment from other causes of action (especially contract), and a pragmatic concern to avoid forum fragmentation. This may also be viewed as a tension between, on the one hand, the domestic approach to unjust enrichment and, on the other hand, the autonomous EU (and EFTA) approach to unjust enrichment that prevails in applying the Lugano Convention. We now turn to the applicable law for claims in unjust enrichment, where we shall see an analogous tension.

C. Applicable Law

As explained above,[59] after 'IP completion day' the Rome II Regulation on the applicable law for non-contractual obligations, with minor adjustments, becomes 'retained EU law' within the law of the United Kingdom. The same applies to the Rome I Regulation on the law applicable to contractual obligations,[60] which, in Arts 12(1)(c) and (e), has provisions covering respectively 'the consequences of breach' and 'the consequences of nullity' and which, therefore, may be applicable to what English law would treat as restitution within the law of unjust enrichment

---

[58] But where there is such a clause conferring jurisdiction on the English courts, the Hague Choice of Court Convention will, subject to its own restrictions, apply in any event: see n 17.
[59] See Section A.
[60] Regulation (EC) No 593/2008 on the law applicable to contractual obligations (Rome I) ([2008] OJ L177/6) (hereafter Rome I Regulation).

where a contract has been terminated for breach or is void or has been rescinded (eg, misrepresentation, duress or undue influence).

1. Art 10 of the Rome II Regulation

The most important provision for the law of unjust enrichment is Art 10 of the Rome II Regulation. This is headed 'Unjust Enrichment' and has four paragraphs as follows:

1. If a non-contractual obligation arising out of unjust enrichment, including payment of amounts wrongly received, concerns a relationship existing between the parties, such as one arising out of a contract or a tort/delict, that is closely connected with that unjust enrichment, it shall be governed by the law that governs that relationship.
2. Where the law applicable cannot be determined on the basis of paragraph 1 and the parties have their habitual residence in the same country when the event giving rise to unjust enrichment occurs, the law of that country shall apply.
3. Where the law applicable cannot be determined on the basis of paragraphs 1 or 2, it shall be the law of the country in which the unjust enrichment took place.
4. Where it is clear from all the circumstances of the case that the non-contractual obligation arising out of unjust enrichment is manifestly more closely connected with a country other than that indicated in paragraphs 1, 2 and 3, the law of that other country shall apply.

It can be seen, therefore, that the governing law for unjust enrichment is the law governing the underlying relationship; or, if that is inapplicable, the law of habitual residence of the parties if that residence is the same for both parties; or, if that is inapplicable, the law of the place where the unjust enrichment took place. However, where it is clear that the obligation arising out of the unjust enrichment is manifestly more closely connected with a different country than that indicated by the above three tests the law of that country applies. Rushworth and Scott neatly summarise this by saying that Art 10 'supplies three connecting factors and a flexible exception'.[61]

By Art 14 the law selected by those rules may be derogated from by agreement: that is, within certain limits, 'the parties may agree to submit non-contractual obligations to the law of their choice'. An express choice of law clause will therefore apply provided it covers the restitution claim.

---

[61] Adam Rushworth and Andrew Scott, 'Rome II: Applicable law for non-contractual obligations' [2009] LMCLQ 274, 285 (hereafter Rushworth and Scott, 'Rome II').

2. Art 12 of the Rome I Regulation

Although the Rome I Regulation is concerned with contractual obligations, it may be that Arts 12(1)(c) and (e) are applicable to what English law would classify as claims within the law of unjust enrichment. This is because, under Arts 12(1)(c) and (e), the law applicable to the contract applies to 'the consequences of breach' and to 'the consequences of nullity'. It may be, therefore, that restitution of benefits conferred under a contract that has been terminated or is void or has been rescinded falls within those provisions even though, in English law, restitution in those circumstances would be treated as part of the law of unjust enrichment.

By Arts 3 and 4 of the Rome I Regulation, the law applicable to the contract is the law chosen by the parties or, if there has been no such choice, the law which is specified in Art 4 for different types of contract or, if not specified, the law where the party required to effect the characteristic performance has his habitual residence or, as a default position, the law of the country with which the contract is most closely connected. There is no opt-out allowed from Art 12(1)(e) of the Rome I Regulation.[62]

Although one is very likely to come to the same result whether one applies, on the one hand, Art 12(1)(c) or (e) of Rome I Regulation or, on the other hand, Art 10 of Rome II Regulation, that is not inevitable because the rules laid down are different.

One cannot have overlapping applicable law rules leading to potentially different answers to the question of which is the applicable law. In other words, the legislative applicable law rules are mutually exclusive.[63] There is therefore an issue as to whether the Rome I Regulation or the Rome II Regulation should apply to restitution on the discharge of a contract for breach or where a contract is void or has been rescinded. The answer would appear to be that the provisions of the Rome I Regulation apply. This is because the words 'consequences of breach' and 'consequences of nullity' plainly extend to cover the restitutionary consequences of a contract being terminated for breach or being void; and it would be very odd then to treat differently restitution where a contract has been terminated for frustration or restitution consequent on rescission for, for example, misrepresentation, duress or undue influence. Although, at least in relation to void contracts, this is contrary to principle (and, as we have seen, the principled approach is reflected, in the different context of jurisdiction, in the decision of the House of Lords in *Kleinwort Benson v Glasgow CC*) the domestic approach must here give way to the clear words laid

---

[62] By the Contracts (Applicable Law) Act 1990, s 2(2) England and Wales had opted out of Art 10(1)(e) of the 1980 Rome Convention on the law applicable to contractual obligations (1980) (consolidated version [1998] OJ C27/34) (the predecessor of Art 12(1)(e) of the Rome I Regulation (n 60)) precisely to respect the distinction in English law between the law of contract and the law of unjust enrichment. But this possibility of an opt out was not extended to the Rome I Regulation.

[63] See also Recital (7) of the Rome II Regulation (n 1).

down in the relevant EU legislation. In any event, one can argue that, as a matter of policy, where restitution is consequent on a void, avoided or discharged contract, it is convenient, in avoiding having a different law for determining the validity of the contract and its consequences, to have the single applicable law for contract applying across the board.

3. Application of Art 10 of the Rome II Regulation

One of the commonest examples of unjust enrichment is where a payment is made mistakenly believing that it is owing under a valid contract between the parties. Although the words in Art 10(1)—'including payment of amounts wrongly received'—may not be the most appropriate,[64] it is tolerably clear that the governing law for restitution of the mistaken payment in this situation is the law of the underlying contract between the parties.[65]

While it is probably true to say that most examples of unjust enrichment occur in situations where there is a pre-existing relationship between the parties, whether a contractual or a purported contractual relationship, there are many situations where that is not so: for example, a mistaken payment of tax to the Revenue[66] or a mistaken payment to a charity or the compulsory discharge of another's liability. In those latter situations, Art 10(1) would not be applicable and, assuming Art 10(2) does not apply, one will fall back under Art 10(3), to the 'law of the country in which the unjust enrichment took place'.[67] That fall-back position appears to be very similar to the fall-back common law rule, formerly put forward by *Dicey, Morris & Collins: The Conflict of Laws*,[68] but criticised by many as

[64] The term 'wrongly' is unfortunate but the best interpretation is not that receipt must be in breach of a duty but rather that the receipt must be not due, ie, where the payment was not intended which does not suggest 'wrongdoing' in the legal sense. This appears to be supported by the texts in French ('*paiement indu*') and German ('*Zahlungen auf eine nicht bestehende Schuld*').

[65] For the same view, see Andrew Dickinson, *The Rome II Regulation* (OUP 2008) [3.109], [10.16].

[66] Assuming that this is a civil or commercial matter and not a revenue, customs or administrative matter or one concerning the liability of the State in the exercise of State authority: see Art 1 of the Rome II Regulation (n 1). See also the similar question, in the context of jurisdiction, discussed in *Gazdasági* (n 36).

[67] Rushworth and Scott, 'Rome II' (n 61) 287 for the argument that on the best view of Art 10(3) of the Rome II Regulation (n 1) it must be the location of the enrichment and not the location of the entire cause of action that is in mind.

[68] Dicey & Morris (n 2) rule 230(2)(c) (not repeated as a rule in subsequent editions because of the replacement of the common law by the Rome II Regulation but it is referred to in the present edition: Lord Collins of Mapesbury and others (eds), *Dicey, Morris & Collins: The Conflict of Laws* (15th edn, Sweet & Maxwell 2018) [36-008]) (hereafter Dicey, Morris & Collins). Their former approach derived judicial support from a number of cases. In *Jogia* (n 49) an action for money had and received was brought by a trustee in bankruptcy to recover money paid out by the bankrupt's agent to the defendant on or after the date of the receiving order. The central conflict of laws question was the jurisdictional one of whether leave to serve out should be granted. However, in determining this, Sir Nicolas Browne-Wilkinson V-C regarded the applicable law rule for 'quasi-contract' as relevant; and, at 495, he considered Dicey & Morris' residual rule—the place of enrichment—as 'sound in principle'. Applying it, the relevant law was French law because the enrichment was received in France. And he thought the

problematic,[69] of the law of the country where the enrichment occurs. Fortunately, and in contrast to Dicey, Morris & Collins' common law rule, any arbitrariness in applying that rule is removed by Art 10(4) which requires the court to apply the law of a country which is manifestly more connected to the obligation to make restitution than the country dictated by Arts 10(1), (2) and (3).[70]

It should be noted that there is nothing in the Rome Regulation II overtly dealing with proprietary rights created as a response to unjust enrichment, perhaps because in civilian jurisdictions unjust enrichment is never viewed as creating proprietary rights as such. In principle, it is strongly arguable that all rights (personal or proprietary) created by the same cause of action of unjust enrichment should be subject to the same applicable law. However, the language of Rome Regulation II, including, for example, Art 10, is purely framed in terms of non-contractual *obligations* arising out of unjust enrichment. It would appear, therefore, that, as with a vindicatio claim ('that property was and is mine') none of the legislative rules apply and one must fall back to the common law as to the applicable law for proprietary rights. This includes, for land, the law of the country where the land is (the *lex situs*).[71]

---

two decisions in *Rousou* (n 48) (a similar bankruptcy case) had been wrong because the receipt of the moneys had occurred in Cyprus not in England. In *El Ajou v Dollar Land Holdings plc* [1993] 3 All ER 717 (revd on other grounds [1994] 2 All ER 685 (CA)) which concerned a claim for 'knowing receipt', Millett J said, at 736, that the law governing receipt-based restitutionary claims is 'the law of the country where the defendant received the money' and he cited with approval Dicey & Morris' rule 230(2)(c). In *Kuwait Oil Tanker Co v Al Bader* [2000] 2 All ER (Comm) 271 (hereafter *Kuwait Oil*), Nourse LJ giving the judgment of the Court of Appeal in relation to a claim, inter alia, for restitution for breach of fiduciary duty by directors to their companies, said, at 338, '[T]he rule of English private international law is that the obligation to restore the benefit of an enrichment such as was obtained by the defendants in this case is governed by the law of the country where the enrichment occurred.' As 'authority' for that rule, he cited Dicey & Morris' rule 230(2)(c). For a comprehensive look at the relevant common law cases, and scrutiny of the Dicey & Morris rule, see *Barros Mattos v MacDaniels Ltd* [2005] EWHC 1323 (Ch) (Lawrence Collins J).

[69] Panagopoulos, *Restitution in Private International Law* (n 5) 166 summarised the arguments against the place of enrichment as follows: 'It is arbitrary; it gives a deceptively simple *locus*, yet it is often difficult to determine; it may not necessarily be connected with either of the parties, or events; and, finally, but most importantly, it can be manipulated by *mala fides* parties, who might ensure that they are "enriched" in jurisdictions with rules that will suit their aims.' See also Briggs, *The Conflict of Laws* (1st edn) (n 3) 198 (the point is not addressed in subsequent editions because of the replacement of the common law by the Rome II Regulation).

[70] Even at common law the arbitrariness of the 'place of enrichment' fall-back position was avoided by Christopher Clarke J in *OJSC Oil Co Yugraneft v Abramovich* [2008] EWHC 2613 (Comm) [239]–[245] by treating the underlying rule at common law as being the country which has the closest and most real connection to the unjust enrichment and the place of enrichment was merely one factor in applying that rule (on the facts the governing law for unjust enrichment was Russian). This was applied in *Dexia Crediop SpA v Comune di Prato* [2016] EWHC 2824 (Comm) (revd on a different point: [2017] EWCA Civ 428). Both those cases concerned facts which pre-dated the Rome II Regulation.

[71] In relation to the governing law for constructive trusts at common law, see, eg, *Trustor AB v Smallbone (No 3)* [2000] EWCA Civ 150; *Governor and Company of the Bank of Ireland v Pexxnet Ltd* [2010] EWHC 1872 (Comm).

However, in *Banque Cantonale de Geneve v Polevent Ltd*[72] it was simply assumed, without discussion, that Art 10 does apply to a claim for a restitutionary constructive trust to reverse an unjust enrichment. It was alleged that the claimant, a bank in Geneva, had been induced by the deceit of the defendant to transfer money to the defendant's account in London. The claimant brought proceedings against the first defendant based on two causes of action: damages for the tort of deceit and restitution of an unjust enrichment constituted by the mistaken payment. It was not in dispute that the tort claim fell within Art 4 of the Rome II Regulation so that the governing law for the tort of deceit was Swiss because Geneva was the place where the damage had occurred. But there was a dispute as to whether the governing law for the unjust enrichment claim was English law or Swiss law. This mattered because a third defendant, also a victim of the fraud, had obtained a freezing order over the first defendant's bank account in London. The claimant was seeking a restitutionary constructive trust (to reverse the mistaken payment) which would not be caught by the freezing order. English law recognises such a trust but Swiss law does not. The dispute was therefore in reality between two innocent victims of the first defendant's fraud. The claimant argued that the governing law was English law on the grounds that Art 10(3) applied and not Art 10(1). On a preliminary issue, Teare J decided that Art 10(3) applied.

While deceit explained why the transfer had been made, it was not a necessary ingredient of a claim for restitution; that, therefore, the claim was not a non-contractual obligation arising out of a tort for the purposes of Art 4 of Rome II Regulation. As regards 'relationship' for the purposes of Art 10(1) of the Rome II Regulation, this meant a relationship which had existed before the facts which had given rise to the claim had occurred, not the relationship of wrongdoer and victim created by the commission of a tort. Since there had been no relationship between the claimant and defendant before the events which had led to money being mistakenly paid into the latter's account in England, Art 10(3) applied. The result was that the law governing the restitution claim was the law of the country where the unjust enrichment had occurred, namely England. Art 10(3) was not displaced by Art 10(4) because one could not say that the unjust enrichment was manifestly more closely connected with Geneva than London; although the instructions to make the payment were made in Geneva and the claimant was a bank in Geneva, the defendant was enriched in London.

Had a personal claim to restitution been in issue, it would appear that all the above reasoning would have been correct. However, it was simply assumed that the proprietary restitution sought fell within Art 10 and there was no discussion of the difficult point raised above as to whether Art 10 is confined to personal restitution.

---

[72] [2015] EWHC 1968 (Comm), [2016] QB 394. For other examples of the application of Art 10 Rome II (n 1) see, eg, *OJSC TNK-BP Holding v Beppler and Jacobson Ltd* [2012] EWHC 3286 (Ch) [103].

4. Other claims for restitution outside Art 10 of the Rome II Regulation

It is important to recognise that there are specific articles, under the Rome II Regulation, dealing with *negotiorum gestio* (necessitous intervention) (Art 11) and non-contractual subrogation (Art 19) both of which are usually now regarded, in English law (but it would seem not in civilian jurisdictions), as falling within the law of unjust enrichment. Given that Arts 11 and 19 are explicitly geared to *negotiorum gestio* and non-contractual subrogation—and, in addition to the argument that the Regulation is here applying an autonomous EU meaning, standard interpretation would dictate that the general must give way to the particular—it is clear that those are the provisions to be applied where unjust enrichment rests on necessitous intervention or non-contractual subrogation.

What is the correct approach to the applicable law for restitution for wrongs? Although a matter of considerable debate, it is now commonly accepted in this jurisdiction, that restitution for wrongs is not part of the law of unjust enrichment because the cause of action in relation to restitution for wrongs is the wrong not unjust enrichment.[73] If one were to apply the English approach, it would logically follow that, instead of falling within Art 10 of Rome Regulation II, restitution for breach of contract would fall within Art 12(1)(c) of Rome Regulation I, restitution for a tort would fall within Art 4 of Rome Regulation II and restitution for an equitable wrong would fall within whatever law governs the equitable wrong.[74]

5. Conclusion on applicable law

The questions regarding the applicable law in respect of unjust enrichment have been largely answered by Art 10 of the Rome II Regulation and Art 12 of the Rome I Regulation which, after IP completion day, become 'retained EU law'. In some respects, especially restitution of an unjust enrichment consequent on a void

---

[73] n 26.
[74] See the discussion in Dicey, Morris & Collins (n 68) [34-083]ff. Some equitable obligations (fiduciary duties, duties of confidence in consensual relationships) are viewed as contractual within Rome I (n 21); others are viewed as non-contractual within Rome II (n 1) (although some tricky questions arise as to whether, for example, a knowing receipt claim is properly characterised as tort/delict (Art 4) or unjust enrichment (Art 10)). A third class (eg trusts created voluntarily) fall outside the Rome regime entirely (see Rome II Regulation (n 1), Art 1(2)(e)). For the common law on the applicable law for equitable wrongs, see *Grupo Torras SA v Al-Sabah (No 5)* [2001] Lloyd's Rep Bank 36, CA (appeared to apply a version of the 'double actionability' common law tort rule to a claim for compensation for the equitable wrong of dishonest assistance); *Arab Monetary Fund v Hashim* [1996] 1 Lloyd's Rep 589, CA (applied the law of the place where the dishonesty took place to govern a claim for restitution of a bribe acquired in breach of fiduciary duty); *Kuwait Oil* (n 68) (thought that the law of the place of enrichment was the applicable law for a claim for restitution for breach of fiduciary duty). See also *Thahir v Pertamina* [1994] 3 SLR 257 (law of place of enrichment applied to restitution of a bribe acquired in breach of fiduciary duty).

contract, the EU legislation cuts across English law's principled distinction between unjust enrichment and contract. However, it can be justified as opting for the pragmatic policy of avoiding the inconvenience of having one applicable law for determining the validity of the contract and a different applicable law for determining the consequences of that invalidity.

D. Concluding Remarks

This essay has attempted to identify, and offer some solutions to, the problems raised by jurisdiction and applicable law in relation to the law of unjust enrichment (and restitution). Both areas have revealed some tension between the English principled approach to unjust enrichment (unjust enrichment is a distinct cause of action from contract) and the approach dictated by the Lugano Convention and the Rome I and II Regulations which, as regards the interplay between contract and unjust enrichment, have tended to favour the policy of avoiding having different courts or laws dealing with issues arising out of contracts. Grappling with these very difficult questions merely serves to heighten my respect for those academic lawyers who have devoted themselves to the study of private international law. Pre-eminent among them, for his analytical rigour and perceptive concern for practical reality, has been my long-time friend and colleague, Adrian Briggs.

8
Choice of Law in the Shifting Sands of Securities Trading

Maisie Ooi

A. Introduction

This essay considers the choice of law issues relating to securities, an area of endless fascination for the writer, and for which she both credits and blames Adrian Briggs for two decades of exhilaration and agony. Her earlier works focused on the traditional and intermediated systems, in relation to which she advanced the theory that the solution for the proprietary issues arising out of cross border trading of these securities must lie in conflicts law and in the selection of the *lex creationis*, the law under which the thing, here a bundle of rights and obligations, was created, as the choice of law rule. She posited (but tentatively) that the *lex creationis* should be capable of application to new forms of securities and trading.[1]

Further research into the evolving Stock Connect and distributed ledger technology (DLT) platforms has not revealed any compelling reasons why a different conflicts treatment is required for new forms of securities holding. It will of course be an important outcome if the same rule is capable of application to the proprietary aspects of all types of securities and trading platforms particularly as existing choice of law for securities is mired by fragmentation and lack of coherence.[2] The bespoke rules created for intermediated securities have added to the complication,[3]

---

[1] The reader interested in following the development of the writer's theses in relation to securities may refer to Maisie Ooi, *Shares and Other Securities in the Conflict of Laws* (OUP 2003) (hereafter Ooi, *Shares and Other Securities*); Maisie Ooi, 'Intermediated Securities: The Choice of a Choice of Law Rule' in Louise Gullifer and Jennifer Payne (eds), *Intermediated Securities: Legal Problems and Practical Issues* (Hart Publishing 2010) ch 9 (hereafter Ooi, 'Intermediated Securities: The Choice of a Choice of Law Rule' and Gullifer and Payne, *Intermediated Securities* respectively); Maisie Ooi, 'Intermediation and its Effect on Investor Rights' (2015) 131 Law Quarterly Review 536 (hereafter Ooi, 'Intermediation and its Effect on Investor Rights'); Maisie Ooi, 'The Ramifications of Fragmentation in the Choice of Law for Shares' (2016) 12 Journal of Private International Law 411 (hereafter Ooi, 'Fragmentation in the Choice of Law for Shares'); Maisie Ooi, 'Rethinking the Characterisation of Issues Relating to Securities' (2019) 15 Journal of Private International Law 575 (hereafter Ooi, 'Characterisation of Issues Relating to Securities'); and Maisie Ooi, 'Re-enfranchising the Investor of Intermediated Securities' (2020) 16 Journal of Private International Law 69 (hereafter Ooi, 'Re-enfranchising the Investor of Intermediated Securities').

[2] As to which see Ooi, 'Fragmentation in the Choice of Law for Shares' (n 1).

[3] Discussed in Ooi, 'Intermediated Securities: The Choice of a Choice of Law Rule' (n 1).

and, as this essay will demonstrate, are not capable of application or logical extension to cryptosecurities. In a market where newly introduced securities and systems co-exist and commingle this creates choice of law issues that these rules do not address.

In *Private International Law in English Courts*, Professor Briggs flagged the need to treat securities, particularly complex securities, differently as a matter of conflicts law from the simple debt.[4] This essay will support that approach in relation to cryptosecurities where attempts to devise choice of law rules to fit existing characterisation categories of property and contract have not yielded a viable solution. This is because these categories are not equipped to deal with the new dimensions that cryptosecurities bring to choice of law. The writer's thesis is that a new characterisation category for securities is required that will encompass all forms of securities—traditional, intermediated and crypto—which will have its own choice of law rules manifesting the *lex creationis*.[5] In the case of cryptosecurities constituted within a cryptosecurities system, the applicable law will be the law of that system.

B. Existing Choice of Law Relating to Securities

It is helpful to start with a brief summary of the existing choice of law rules relating to securities in common law systems, with the principal focus on English law. Separate (property) rules apply to securities held in a traditional direct holding system[6] from those held in an intermediated (indirect) holding system.[7] Following the Court of Appeal's decision in *Macmillan Inc v Bishopsgate Investment Trust (No 3)*[8] issues of title to directly held securities are referred to the *lex situs* of the securities, being the *lex registri* (the law of the location of the register) in the case of registered securities and the *lex situs cartae* (the law of the location of the certificates) for bearer securities. The aspect of conflicts law that has received the most scrutiny has been issues of property in intermediated securities,[9] but the current conflicts

---

[4] Adrian Briggs, *Private International Law in English Courts* (OUP 2014) (hereafter Briggs, *Private International Law in English Courts*) [3.51] and [3.54], although cautioning against 'willy-nilly creation of new categories for general application'.
[5] See Ooi, 'Characterisation of Issues Relating to Securities' (n 1).
[6] Where the issuer is in a direct relationship with the legal holder of the securities.
[7] Where traditional securities are legally immobilised in the depository of the system who holds them as legal owner, and investors and financiers acquire intermediated securities on the system.
[8] [1996] 1 WLR 387 (hereafter *Macmillan*).
[9] See generally Roy Goode 'The Nature and Transfer of Rights in Dematerialised and Immobilised Securities' [1996] 11 Butterworths Journal of International Banking and Financial Law 172; Richard Fentiman 'Cross-Border Securities Collateral: Redefining Recharacterisation Risk' [1998] Butterworths Journal of International Banking and Financial Law (special supplement) 38; Ooi, 'Intermediated Securities: The Choice of a Choice of Law Rule' (n 1); Robert Stevens and Ben McFarlane, 'Interests in Securities: Practical Problems and Conceptual Solutions' in Gullifer and Payne, *Intermediated Securities* (n 1) ch 2 (hereafter Stevens and McFarlane, 'Interests in Securities').

approach which distinguishes between registered and bearer securities presents difficulties even to dispositions of traditionally held securities.[10]

There is as yet no consensus as to what the choice of law rule for property in intermediated securities should be despite the conviction of proponents of the 'Place of the Relevant Intermediary Approach' (PRIMA) that it is or should be the law of the immediate intermediary. The UK has implemented the EU legislated forms of PRIMA within the Settlement Finality Directive[11] and the Financial Collateral Directive[12] and retained them after Brexit.[13] There are differences in the scope and application of the two legislated forms of PRIMA but essentially PRIMA selects the law of the location of the account that the transferee has with its intermediary. This is an extension of the *lex registri* to intermediated securities.[14] The global solution offered for intermediated securities, in the Hague Securities Convention on the Law Applicable to Certain Rights in Respect of Securities Held with an Intermediary (hereafter Hague Securities Convention), has not found wide acceptance with just three ratifications to date after its finalisation in 2002.[15] The principal rule is the law chosen by the account holder and its intermediary. Concerns with this reliance upon party autonomy have led the EU to hold back on ratifying the Convention.

The 'no look through' approach which underpins both PRIMA and the Hague Securities Convention rule[16] was devised as an antidote to the malaise of the 'look through' approach, thought to be the consequence of *Macmillan*. The concern was that *Macmillan* would have required a financier taking collateral over a portfolio of securities to check and comply with the *lex registri* and *lex situs cartae* of nationally diverse securities. PRIMA and the Hague Securities Convention rule

---

[10] As to which see Ooi, 'Fragmentation in the Choice of Law for Shares' (n 1).
[11] Directive 98/26/EC of the European Parliament and of the Council of 19 May 1998 on settlement finality in payment and securities settlement systems [1998] OJ L166/45, as amended by Directive 2009/44/EC, [2009] OJ L146/37, Art 9 (hereafter Settlement Finality Directive). This is implemented in the UK by Financial Markets and Insolvency (Settlement Finality) Regulations (SI 1999/2979) (hereafter Settlement Finality Regulations).
[12] Directive 2002/47/EC of the European Parliament and of the Council of 6 June 2002 on financial collateral arrangements [2002] OJ L168/43, as amended by Directive 2009/44/EC, [2009] OJ L146/37), Art 9 (hereafter Financial Collateral Directive). This is implemented in the UK by Financial Collateral Arrangements (No 2) Regulations (SI 2003/3226) (hereafter Financial Collateral Regulations).
[13] The amendments under paras 4–10 of The Financial Markets and Insolvency (Amendment and Transitional Provision) (EU Exit) Regulations SI 2019/341 (hereafter EU Exit Regulations) do not remove the implementing regulations for the two directives nor the PRIMA rule which they legislate.
[14] Postulating that intermediated securities are located at the account with the intermediary because that is where a record is kept of them alone.
[15] The Hague Securities Convention came into effect on 1 April 2017 with the third ratification by the United States. Earlier ratifications were by Mauritius and Switzerland.
[16] For the reasons why the Hague Securities Convention legislates against the 'look through approach' see generally the Explanatory Report on the 2006 Hague Securities Convention. See also Francisco Garcimartin and Florence Guillaume 'Conflict of Laws Rules' in Thomas Keijser (ed), *Transnational Securities Law* (OUP 2014) (hereafter Garcimartin and Guillaume, 'Conflict of Laws Rules') where the authors state (at [10.43]): '[T]he applicable law cannot be found by treating the direct intermediary as transparent and referring to another higher-level intermediary, or by referring directly to the issuing company. The so-called "look-through approach" is not applicable.'

converge potentially diverse locations of securities into a single location or a single law, selected by reference to the financier's account with its intermediary. Whilst the benefit of this to the financier is undeniable, the consequence of making the financier's account the connecting factor is to effectively allow the financier to select the law by which its collateral will be judged. This must, the writer contends, undermine their suitability as the choice of law approach for issues of property in intermediated securities.

The issue of investor rights, perceived as distinct from issues of property and title, is excluded from the Hague Securities Convention, and not addressed by the EU's legislated forms of PRIMA. Whilst neither were relevant to *Secure Capital SA v Credit Suisse AG*,[17] the 'no look through' approach used to formulate them clearly underpinned the judgment of the Court of Appeal that the investor could not look through the intermediaries to the issuer for its rights. This was notwithstanding that by Luxembourg law, the law under which the intermediated (Clearstream) system in question was constituted and regulated, Secure Capital could sue the issuer. The consequence of applying 'no look through' to investor entitlement is to disenfranchise the investor of intermediated securities.[18]

The resolution of issues brought to bear by intermediation of securities has been put on the back burner in recent years by the pursuit of a choice of law rule for a new system of holding based on DLT.[19] This has yielded several options which this essay will scrutinise. As the DLT system is unlikely to completely replace the intermediated system in the foreseeable future, or disintermediate securities holding,[20] the need to find a solution to the intermediation problem remains.

---

[17] [2017] EWCA Civ 1486, [2017] EWCA Civ 1486 (CA) affirming [2015] EWHC 388 (Comm), [2015] 1 Lloyd's Rep 556 (Hamblen J) (hereafter *Secure Capital*).

[18] As to which see Ooi, 'Intermediation and its Effect on Investor Rights' (n 1) and Ooi 'Reenfranchising the Investor of Intermediated Securities' (n 1).

[19] The technical aspects of the DLT system are explained in Section E.

[20] This may not be desirable or viable, see Christopher Twemlow, 'Why are Securities Held in Intermediated Form?' in Louise Gullifer and Jennifer Payne (eds), *Intermediation and Beyond* (Hart Publishing 2019) ch 4, 104–7 (hereafter Twemlow, 'Why are Securities Held in Intermediated Form?' and Gullifer and Payne, *Intermediation and Beyond* respectively); ' ... it is possible to predict that a blockchained distributed ledger environment will not necessarily lead to less intermediation': Eva Micheler, 'Intermediated Securities from the Perspective of Investors: Problems, Quick Fixes and Long Term Solutions, in Gullifer and Payne, *Intermediation and Beyond* (above) ch 12, 252 (hereafter Micheler, 'Intermediated Securities from the Perspective of Investors').

C. Appraising the Elephant

And so these men of Indostan, disputed loud and long, each in his own opinion, exceeding stiff and strong, Though each was partly in the right, and all were in the wrong![21]

The parable of the blind men and the elephant may tell us something about the way issues relating to intermediated securities have been appraised and treated in the last two decades. The difficulty with the intermediated, and more recently the distributed ledger technology (DLT) system,[22] is that they are a cocktail of separate areas of law, each of which has its experts but for others may be perplexing.

This may perhaps explain the absolute truth of the 'no look through principle' claimed in the name of conflicts law, that the investor has rights only against its own intermediary, and not the issuer.[23] This is indubitably correct from a purely English law perspective,[24] and it may sometimes be appropriate to look to a domestic law conceptualisation of an issue, but one may and should ask why it underpins choice of law for intermediated securities, the purpose of which is to select the

---

[21] 'The Blind Man and the Elephant' from *The Poems of John Godfrey Saxe* (1816–87) <https://allpoetry.com/The-Blind-Man-And-The-Elephant> accessed 18 January 2021. In the parable some blind men who have never come across an elephant before conceptualise what the elephant is like by touching it, each a different part of the elephant's body. Each then appraises the elephant based on the part that he has touched and experienced.

[22] A distributed ledger is a digital record of who-owns-what that can be securely shared to and updated by multiple organisations so that every entity is sure that what it sees is what its counterparties see in near real time. But unlike traditional database technology, there is not necessarily a central administrator of the ledger, nor is there the need for a central data store: see <https://www2.asx.com.au/markets/clearing-and-settlement-services/chess-replacement/about-chess-replacement > accessed 18 January 2021. Section E elaborates upon the characteristics of the DLT system.

[23] English courts have said that this is inevitable as the intermediated system operates on the 'no look through principle' where the investor's right and recourse is only against its own intermediary, not the issuer of the securities. They have also reasoned that the investor at the end of a custodial chain has only the ultimate economic interests, or a right in a right (presumably the daisy chain of rights will lengthen with the number of intermediaries), but not in the securities. Finally, they have taken the view that addressing this unfortunate malaise is a matter for Parliament, not the courts. See *Eckerle v Wickeder Westfalenstahl GmbH* [2013] EWHC 68 (Ch) (hereafter *Eckerle*) where Norris J held that section 98 of the Companies Act 2006 was not available to the claimant investors who held English shares through intermediaries as they were not holders of the shares but only holders of 'the ultimate economic interests in the underlying securities.'; also Stevens and McFarlane, 'Interests in Securities' (n 9); *SL Claimants v Tesco Plc* [2019] EWHC 2858 (Ch) [19] (Hildyard J).

[24] For an English law analysis, see Sarah Green and Ferdisha Snagg, 'Intermediated Securities and the Distributed Ledger Technology' in Gullifer and Payne, *Intermediation and Beyond* (n 20) ch 16, 344 (hereafter Green and Snagg, 'Intermediated Securities'); Stevens and McFarlane, 'Interests in Securities' (n 9); Ben McFarlane, 'Intermediated Securities: Taking Stock' (2016) 31 Journal of International Banking and Financial Law 359. The position can be different under other laws: see Victoria Dixon 'The Legal Nature of Intermediated Securities: An Insurmountable Obstacle to Legal Certainty?' in Gullifer and Payne, *Intermediation and Beyond* (n 20) ch 3, s III.A (hereafter Dixon, 'Legal Nature of Intermediated Securities') and Philipp Paech, 'Conflict of Laws and Relational Rights' in Gullifer and Payne, *Intermediation and Beyond* (n 20) ch 14, ss I and II.A.

most appropriate law for determining the very question that the 'no look through principle' has answered in some legal systems.[25] Aside from questioning the principle as a matter of conflicts law, those involved in the creation of intermediated systems may well (if asked) question why 'no look through' is said to be the very basis of trading of a particular intermediated system in disregard of statements in the system's manual[26] that investors are entitled as against the issuers participating in the system.[27]

Experts in technology have also appraised the elephant that is intermediation and offered their own solution. The DLT system, they claim, can reduce if not also remove the need for intermediaries, and consequently the problem that is intermediation. The investor will then be reconnected to the issuer, as the corporate universe always intended.

This essay considers both the intermediated and crypto elephants.[28] It examines whether cryptosecurities and the DLT system can and will provide the solution to the intermediation woes, or instead create another metaphorical beast that is likely to baffle even more. It explores the collective wisdom of those who have assessed these animals in their particular area(s) of expertise, with the objective of gaining a better sense of the whole and facilitating more robust decisions on the treatment of the problem of choice of law relating to securities in all its present and future manifestations.

D. The Evolution of Securities and Trading Platforms

The companies legislation of most countries are enacted on the assumption that the investor is the owner of the shares, transfers of which are by delivery of certificates or registration depending on whether they are in bearer or registered form. Debt securities are contractually constituted but traditionally

---

[25] It is difficult to see how the analysis, made from an English law perspective, can as a matter of conflicts law apply outside of England, although it is reflected in the Hague Securities Convention and in EU legislation that have adopted PRIMA. England has not ratified the Hague Securities Convention but has retained the PRIMA rule following Brexit (see n 13). Because of the dichotomy that has been adopted between issues of property and entitlement neither legislations of the no look through apply to issues of entitlement.

[26] Setting out the terms and conditions of participation on the particular intermediated system for, *inter alia*, issuers, investors and intermediaries.

[27] 'No look through' has found its way into the UK Law Commission, *Intermediated Securities: who owns your shares? A Scoping Paper* (11 November 2020) <https://s3-eu-west-2.amazonaws.com/lawcom-prod-storage-11jsxou24uy7q/uploads/2020/11/Law-Commission-Intermediated-Securities-Scoping-Paper-1.pdf /> accessed 18 January 2021 where it is defined in the glossary as '[t]he principle that an ultimate investor may only make a contractual or trusts law claim against their immediate intermediary and not against the issuing company or intermediaries higher in the chain' and discussed in chapter 5.

[28] Space does not allow further investigation of the stock connect elephant save in relation to depository receipts that underpin the London-Shanghai Stock Connect.

also transferred the same way.[29] Execution of the prescribed transfers invest the acquiror with legal title in the securities, putting the investor in a direct relationship with the issuer.

Securities and trading platforms have since morphed to meet demands for cross-border trading activities. An intermediated system enables a more efficient settlement system and is today a requirement for listing on many stock exchanges. The system enables securities of multiple nationalities to seemingly transfer from one party to another without the requirement for paper, leading to the perception and (mis)representations of transactions on the system as electronic transfers of dematerialised securities. The securities transferred by the debiting and crediting of accounts held with intermediaries are in fact not the underlying securities legally immobilised in the depository of the system, but derivative interests in those securities. The conflation of the intermediated securities with their underlying securities has had regrettable consequences to the shape of choice of law for securities, as the essay will demonstrate.

Stock Connect systems are a specialised application of an intermediated system, recently introduced. There are currently three such systems, all intended to facilitate cross-border trading but between specific markets, namely Hong Kong and Shanghai, Hong Kong and Shenzhen, and London and Shanghai. The most recent of these, the London-Shanghai Stock Connect uses the device of depository receipts to allow listed companies in the UK and Mainland China access to each other's capital markets.[30] Choice of law analysis of these systems has been curiously lacking, the attention of analysts riveted towards the more intriguing cryptosecurities system.

The world is now being primed for cryptosecurities using DLT.[31] This is expected to improve efficiencies and speed and reduce cost. Those who have appraised this new elephant have found in it features that have the potential of resolving the problems created by intermediation, whilst others have cautioned that it will add complications to choice of law for securities.[32] This technologically created elephant is particularly difficult to appraise, as its technical aspects are still being worked upon for its wider use in securities trading but significant strides have been made in identifying and understanding the complexities involved to facilitate the choice of law analysis that this essay makes.[33]

---

[29] The contract constituting the debt securities will specify the way the securities will be transferred.
[30] Otherwise prohibited by Chinese restrictions against direct holding of Chinese securities by foreigners and conversely foreign securities by Chinese investors.
[31] Charles W Mooney Jr, 'Beyond Intermediation: A New (Fintech) Model For Securities Holding Infrastructures' (2020) 22(2) U of Pennsylvania Journal of Business Law 386 (hereafter Mooney, 'Beyond Intermediation') analysing this holding structure with reference to a relatively recent US stock traded as a cryptosecurity.
[32] See eg Green and Snagg, 'Intermediated Securities' (n 24) 353.
[33] Adopting and applying to cryptosecurities the caveat made by Andrew Dickinson in relation to cryptocurrencies that the sheer variety of [cryptocurrencies] systems does not permit a single, homogenous analysis: see Andrew Dickinson, 'Cryptocurrencies and the Conflict of Laws', in David Fox and

The metamorphosis of securities and trading platforms will not end with cryptosecurities and DLT platforms. Current trends indicate that the mechanics of trading platforms will become increasingly complex, paradoxically, to support simpler and more efficient trading. National laws have not kept pace with the changes to the way securities are held and traded, at least in a uniform way that will not discriminate and produce diametrically opposing outcomes in cross-border cases according to the holding structure.[34] The Shareholder Rights Directive II[35] and the UNIDROIT Convention on Substantive Rules for Intermediated Securities (hereafter Geneva Securities Convention)[36] both take a functional approach to facilitating the exercise of voting rights by the investor. Unless national corporate laws recognise the right of investors qua shareholder, no rights are created for the investor against the issuer.[37] Conflicts solutions devised for issues of title to intermediated securities have left issues of investor entitlement to the *lex incorporationis* (the law of the place of incorporation) of the issuer of the immobilised shares[38] and *lex contractus* (the governing law of the contract) of immobilised debt securities[39] with the consequence that the investor of intermediated securities who is not in a direct relationship with the issuer is disenfranchised.[40]

Sarah Green (eds), *Cryptocurrencies in Public and Private Law* (OUP 2019) [5.16] (hereafter Dickinson, 'Cryptocurrencies').

[34] Section 145 of the UK Companies Act 2006 which was intended to address the problem of disenfranchisement does work well in a purely domestic situation, but not where it arises in a cross border situation in relation to intermediated securities, see *Eckerle* (n 23).

[35] Directive (EU) 2017/828/EU amending Directive 2007/36/EC as regards the encouragement of long-term shareholder engagement (OJ L132/1) (hereafter Shareholder Rights Directive II).

[36] 9 October 2009. The Geneva Securities Convention has only been ratified by Bangladesh since its adoption in and is not yet in force.

[37] Thomas Keijser and Charles W Mooney Jr, 'Intermediated Securities Holding Systems Revisited: A View Through the Prism of Transparency' in Gullifer and Payne, *Intermediation and Beyond* (n 20) ch 15, 332, acknowledging that changes in the applicable law would be required to permit an ultimate account holder's right to claim even if a transparent information technology system allows the identification of the ultimate account holder.

[38] Whilst the Hague Securities Convention itself does not say so the Explanatory Report suggests this, see Goode, Kanda and Kreuzer, <https://www.hcch.net/en/publications-and-studies/details4/?pid=2955> accessed 18 January 2021. See also Garcimartin and Guillaume 'Conflict of Laws Rules' (n 16) [10.21]: 'The HSC does not apply to the rights and obligations of an issuer of securities, whether in relation to the holder of the securities or to any other person (Art 2(3)(c)). These rights depend on the legal status of the issuing company and are governed by the law applicable to the latter in accordance with the private international law rules of each State. The law applicable to the issuing company determines, for example, entitlement to income payments (eg dividends or interest); the type of voting rights attaching to securities; and the requirements with regard to granting free shares.'; Dixon, 'Legal Nature of Intermediated Securities' (n 24) 57.

[39] *Secure Capital* (n 17).

[40] The issue of investor rights, perceived as distinct from issues of property and title, is excluded from the Hague Securities Convention, and not addressed by EU legislation of PRIMA. Although the writer questions the divide drawn between issues of title and entitlement for securities, she does not advocate the extension of the Hague Securities Convention rule and PRIMA to issues of investor rights as to do so would be to subject issuers to a plethora of laws determined by reference to their investors' intermediaries.

E. Taxonomy of a DLT System

DLT which introduced Bitcoin into the financial markets is currently being considered for wider application for securities. It is said to have the potential of disintermediation, and consequently the ability to provide a targeted and comprehensive resolution to the problem of intermediation.[41] The exact mechanics of DLT platforms are complex and there are differences in the way writers have represented the application of the ledgers, nodes and tokens.[42] This is because there is some measure of speculation given that the system is still being evolved for applications beyond cryptocurrencies. Within these constraints, and the remit of this essay, the writer will nevertheless attempt a basic taxonomy of a DLT system, sufficient to provide some context to the analysis in the following sections.[43]

DLT systems involve distributed ledgers, records of electronic transactions which are maintained by a shared or 'distributed' network of participants (nodes) to provide a distributed validation system to store assets and validate transactions. Ledgers may evidence title transfers (record ledgers) or effect title transfers (title ledgers). Information and transactions on the ledgers are encrypted by master and user keys for security. Each user generates and takes responsibility for its own pair of encryption keys (akin to passwords). Information may be organised in chains of blocks containing transaction data (hence 'blockchains'), but it remains to be seen whether this organising tool will be used for securities. Tokens[44] which are the

---

[41] Evangelos Benos, Rodney Garratt and Pedro Gurrola-Perez, 'The Economics of Distributed Ledger Technology for Securities Settlement' (Bank of England, Staff Working Paper No 670, August 2017) 10, <https://papers.ssrn.com/sol3/papers.cfm?abstract_id=3023272> accessed 18 January 2021; Emilios Avgouleas and Aggelos Kiayias, 'The Promise of Blockchain Technology for Global Securities and Derivatives Markets: The New Financial Ecosystem and the 'Holy Grail' of Systemic Risk Containment' (2019) 20 European Business Organization Law Review 81, 105.

Charles Mooney advocates disintermediation via the DLT platform as the way to deal with impairments of investors' legal entitlements resulting from intermediated holding systems but suggests that this might well be adequately addressed by adopting DLT facilitated transparent intermediated holding systems even without the implementation of direct holding: see Mooney 'Beyond Intermediation' (n 31) 411–12, 414, 417; also Micheler 'Intermediated Securities from the Perspective of Investors' (n 20) 251–2.

[42] eg Green and Snagg, 'Intermediated Securities' (n 24) 341, describing a radical use of the DLT to transfer title directly on the distributed ledger so that the ledger would be 'the authoritative golden source or root of title of securities existing wholly within the DLT system' and noting that this will likely require a change of national securities laws to confer the requisite authority on the ledger. See also Financial Markets Law Committee (FMLC), *Distributed Ledger Technology and Governing Law: Issues of Legal Uncertainty* (Report, March 2018) <http://fmlc.org/wp-content/uploads/2018/05/dlt_paper.pdf> accessed 18 January 2021 (hereafter FMLC, *Distributed Ledger Technology and Governing Law*). These differences in treatment may have different choice of law considerations as this essay will seek to demonstrate.

[43] The following summary is principally drawn from the European Securities Markets Authority (ESMA) report, *The Distributed Ledger Technology Applied to Securities Markets* (Report, 7 February 2017) 4 <https://www.esma.europa.eu/sites/default/files/library/dlt_report_-_esma50-1121423017-285.pdf> accessed 18 January 2021 and FMLC, *Distributed Ledger Technology and Governing Law* (n 42) [3.2]–[3.4].

[44] Tokenisation of securities to offer them as cryptosecurities is how blockchain is applied to securities, so that they can be traded between parties with access to the same distributed ledger.

assets traded on the DLT system may represent or be pegged against 'real world' assets such as land, coffee beans or securities, or they could represent or be virtual assets created within a DLT system such as Bitcoin and other cryptocurrencies with a value derived entirely from that system and not any underlying assets.[45]

DLT systems may be centralised with an operating authority or decentralised with no central point of control and validation. Evidence from industry players suggest that activities related to tokens for securities would most likely be made in authorised centralised systems overseen by a central body or operator, the equivalent to the central security depositories of intermediated systems.[46]

F. Issues of Entitlement—the Technological Solution

The key potential advantage of cryptosecurities, in legal terms, is that an investor can be given a direct right in a specific, discrete and unique digital object and consequently retain direct control of any incidental benefits pertaining to it such as voting rights.[47] Few will argue against the logic that removing all intermediaries will re-enfranchise the investor and address the uncertainties as to issues of title created by intermediation and which remain despite PRIMA and the Hague Securities Convention rule. Total disintermediation is conceptually possible, but market analyses suggest it to be realistically unlikely given heavy investment in intermediated systems.[48] Abandonment of those systems, and concomitantly the convenience that they bring to portfolio transactions, is also likely to be in the way. The intermediated system enables transactions in portfolios of diverse securities to leapfrog the specific transfer requirements of the securities.[49] This is not a feature that technology alone can replicate.[50]

---

[45] FMLC, *Distributed Ledger Technology and Governing Law* (n 42) [3.3].

[46] European Commission, 'On an EU framework for markets in crypto-assets' (Consultation Document, 5 December 2019) 30, <https://ec.europa.eu/info/sites/info/files/business_economy_euro/banking_and_finance/documents/2019-crypto-assets-consultation-document_en.pdf> accessed 18 January 2021.

[47] Green and Snagg, 'Intermediated Securities' (n 24) 344; Eva Micheler, 'Custody Chains and Asset Values: Why Crypto-Securities Are Worth Considering' (2015) 74 CLJ 505, 508.

[48] This Utopia is however unlikely to materialise in the foreseeable future, industry players and their advisers pointing to the practical reality of a strong financial interest amongst market participants to maintain the system that they have invested heavily in. Investors who are not familiar with the operational aspects of the DLT platform may prefer to go through an intermediary. See Richard Salter, 'Enforcing Debt Securities' in Gullifer and Payne, *Intermediation and Beyond* (n 20) ch 7, 148 (hereafter Salter, 'Debt Securities'); Twemlow, 'Why are Securities Held in Intermediated Form?' (n 20) s III.A and Louise Gullifer and Jennifer Payne, 'Conclusion' in Gullifer and Payne, *Intermediation and Beyond* (n 20) ch 17, s I.C. (hereafter Gullifer and Payne, 'Conclusion').

[49] This is because intermediation by the immobilisation of securities in the depository creates a new form of securities (the intermediated securities) that are not subject to the individual transfer requirements of the securities in the portfolio.

[50] cf Gullifer and Payne, 'Conclusion' (n 48) s I.A.i where the editors suggest that the efficiencies of the intermediated system (electronic transfer and settlement) could be achievable with technology. The writer respectfully disagrees. Without a change to national laws, electronic transfers are only possible

What is more likely as a consequence of DLT is a significant reduction in the number of intermediaries in a chain of holding. From the standpoint of existing choice of law, reducing the number of intermediaries that interpose between the issuer and the investor can reduce the number of potentially applicable laws in a link by link analysis.[51] This ought to better the odds for the punter but is not a solution to the choice of law problem. Where the 'no look through' principle underlies the choice of connecting factor the investor is disenfranchised whether there is one intermediary or ten.[52] It has, nevertheless, been suggested that a DLT facilitated transparent intermediated holding systems will effectively extirpate the impairment of investor entitlement even without complete disintermediation.[53] Whilst DLT may help with the identification of investors and transmission of information (a look through the intermediaries), this will still be of limited utility without excising the aberration that is the 'no look through principle'. This is also the limitation of the functional approach of the Shareholder Rights Directive II.[54]

G. Issues of Entitlement—the Conflict of Laws Solution

Legal resolution to the problem of disenfranchisement of the investor of intermediated securities has mostly (if not entirely) been sought in substantive and not conflicts law. Existing solutions devised to treat the problem of disenfranchisement are mostly premised on 'no look through' restricting the investor's recourse to its immediate intermediary. The writer has demonstrated the limitations of treating disenfranchisement in this way in an earlier publication and will not repeat her reasons here.[55] Instead this section furthers her thesis that resolution of the problem of disenfranchisement, whether arising solely within an intermediated system or in the context of the DLT or Stock Connect platforms, must lie in the

because the securities transferred in an intermediated system are not the immobilised securities but intermediated securities that are not subject to the transfer requirements of the underlying securities.

[51] There have been contentions that PRIMA requires the choice of law analysis to be made at every tier of intermediation, see Ooi, Shares and Other Securities (n 1) [13.13]–[13.19]; for alternative approaches, see [13.20]–13.28], and for the writer's solution to the problem, [13.29]–[13.37].

[52] The result of *Secure Capital* (n 17) applying the *lex contractus* of the underlying securities is that the investor who is not privy to that contract has no rights against the issuer. This would be the case regardless of the number of intermediaries interposed between the investor and the issuer. See Section G below. The *lex contractus* may allow for third-party rights if the Contracts (Rights of Third Parties) Act 1999 is not excluded. This and other solutions are suggested in Ooi, 'Intermediation and its Effect on Investor Rights' (n 1).

[53] Mooney, 'Beyond Intermediation' (n 31) 414; Federico Panisi, Ross P Buckley and Douglas Arner, 'Blockchain and Public Companies: A Revolution in Share Ownership Transparency, Proxy Voting and Corporate Governance?' (2019) 2(2) Stanford Journal of Blockchain Law and Policy 189, 211–13.

[54] Text to n 35. Unless national corporate laws recognise the right of investors qua shareholder no rights are created for the investor against the issuer.

[55] Ooi, 'Re-enfranchising the Investor of Intermediated Securities' (n 1).

domain of the conflict of laws, and specifically in a choice of law rule applying the law of the system.

The law by which an intermediated system operates commonly provides the investor with rights against the issuer, some by deeming the investor the legal holder,[56] others by legislating for the conferment of rights on the investor.[57] These laws are national laws, but they may apply in a cross border context in one of two ways. First, the law may be invoked as a mandatory forum law exception to choice of law,[58] and secondly, it may be the law applicable under the choice of law rule covering issues of entitlement arising from acquisitions (including the taking of collateral) of securities traded in the system. The first is of more limited application as the forum has to be that whose law governs the system on which the securities are intermediated, the second would be an application of the law of the system. The second, the application of the law of the system, an application of the *lex creationis* in the context of securities holding systems, is not out of step with established choice of law rules for issues of entitlement arising out of traditional securities. The *lex incorporationis* for traditionally held shares and *lex contractus* for traditionally held debt securities are respectively the *lex creationis* of those securities.

Intermediated securities are often and incorrectly conflated with their underlying securities in representations of them as dematerialised securities.[59] Securities legally immobilised in the depository, the operator of the intermediated system, are likely to be certificated and are not extinguished but may be withdrawn from the system if permitted by the system's rules. The intermediated securities issued by reference to them are the creation of the law of the system, conceived and released into the system by the depository of the system *sans* certificates from inception. They are not the dematerialised souls of their underlying securities travelled (electronically) down intermediated chains having shed their corporeal remains (certificates) in the vaults of the central depository of the system. It thus makes little sense, as Professor Briggs has said, to look to the law applicable to the underlying securities for the choice of law rule:[60]

> Where shares are held in international deposit and clearing systems, and are therefore to be regarded as 'immobilized' (if there is a certificate but which is locked in a vault operated by or on behalf of the entity which operates the system) or as 'dematerialized' (where there is no share certificate at all), it would be possible, but it probably makes little sense, to say that the shares are situated in any particular place...

---

[56] As in the case of CREST and Singapore's CDP system.
[57] As in the case of the 2001 Luxembourg law, the law under which Clearstream operates.
[58] As Aedit Abdullah J had done in *Goldilocks Investment Co Ltd v Noble Group Ltd* [2018] SGHC 108.
[59] See for eg FMLC, *Distributed Ledger Technology and Governing Law* (n 42) [2.2].
[60] Briggs, *Private International Law in English Courts* (n 4) [9.24].

The conflation of intermediated securities with the underlying immobilised securities is seen in *Secure Capital* where the English Court of Appeal irreconcilably applied the 'no look through' approach to deny the investor rights against the issuer by 'looking through' the intermediated Notes (which the investor claimant held) to the underlying bearer Notes (a form of debt securities) to decide that the investor had no rights against the issuer since the Note certificates were with the Clearstream depository.[61]

Richard Salter QC has questioned whether the Court of Appeal's application of the 'no look through' principle in *Secure Capital* provided a choice of law rule that identifies the most appropriate law as it 'results in advantages to issuers ... whilst investors get the downside'.[62] This is of course a reference to Mance LJ's exhortation in *Raiffeisen Zentralbank Osterreich AG v Five Star Trading LLC*[63] that the overall aim of choice of law should be to identify the most appropriate law. The difficulty here is that both the 'no look through' approach and the *lex creationis*/law of the system may be said to select the most appropriate law, depending on whose interest English courts seek to advance.

Secure Capital has implications for Stock Connect platforms, which are also intermediated, and for DLT platforms, which are likely to use intermediation. If the UK should decide to use DLT within CREST as is being implemented for the Australian CHESS,[64] issues of investor rights may arise in the context of intermediation through the DLT platform. Whilst it may seem absurd that an English court would ignore the enfranchising provision for CREST (the UK's intermediated system),[65] the possibility cannot be dismissed that after *Secure Capital* it may be bound to decide that the enfranchising provision is not a mandatory law of the forum.

H. Issues of Title—Canvassed Solutions for Cryptosecurities

There are wide divergences in the conflicts solutions canvassed for the property aspects of transactions on the DLT system,[66] but predominantly these are, or purport to be, applications of the *lex situs* (the law of the location of the thing) rule.

---

[61] *Secure Capital* (n 17).
[62] Salter, 'Debt Securities' (n 48) 137, 138, 139.
[63] [2002] EWCA Civ 68, [26]–[29] ([2001] QB 825, 840–1).
[64] The plan is to replace the current system in the Clearing House Electronic Subregister System (CHESS) with a DLT based platform. The implementation has however been delayed to April 2023 see ASX media announcement 'ASX Announces New Scope and Go-Live Date for CHESS Replacement' of 28 October 2020 <https://www2.asx.com.au/about/media-centre> accessed 11 January 2021.
[65] Uncertificated Securities Regulations 2001 (SI 2001/3755), reg 24.
[66] The FMLC has considered an impressive range of potential solutions in FMLC, *Distributed Ledger Technology and Governing Law* (n 42) [6.2]–[6.28], and advanced their own proposal ([7.1]–[7.8]).

Not all of these are specific to cryptosecurities, as the DLT system can provide a trading platform for any property for which there is a market including tokenised coffee beans. Amongst those that are not specific to cryptosecurities are 'PROPA' (the place of the relevant operating authority/administrator approach), 'PREMA' (the place of primary residence of the encryption master keyholder approach), the location of the original coder of the DLT programme and the location of the private encryption key of the transferor. Solutions specific to securities such as the law of the assignment, the law of the location of the private user key (transferee) and the elective *situs* approach are respectively said to be applications of the *lex registri*, the *lex situs cartae* and PRIMA.

The writer questions the wisdom of devising generic conflicts solutions for DLT systems that do not consider the features that distinguish cryptosecurities from other tokenised assets. Securities including cryptosecurities represent bundles of entitlements against the issuer and derive their value from those entitlements.[67] Assets such as cryptocurrencies[68] by contrast are not entitlements against an issuer[69] but are generated by the cryptocurrency system and derive their value in a completely different way.[70] Cryptosecurities may be pegged against traditionally held or intermediated securities, whilst cryptocurrencies, at least those currently in issue, are not pegged against real world currencies. The way in which each are likely to be traded or used on and off platform[71] may also differ. The considerations underpinning the choice of the most appropriate property rule for cryptosecurities and cryptocurrencies may well be different as a consequence.

The sections that follow evaluate the extent to which the contending proposals are equipped to be the choice of law rule for the proprietary aspects of cryptosecurities. Those that share a common connecting factor are grouped together for analysis. The FMLC, in its 2018 report, considers all of the competing proposals save for the law of the system as a manifestation of the *lex creationis*.[72] The views stated in the sections that follow are the writer's own view save where they are specifically said to be those of the FMLC or another.

---

[67] Market conditions and manipulation may affect their value but these are not factors relevant to the conflicts considerations here.

[68] Cryptocurrencies are used to illustrate the point since they are the most common form of tokenised assets.

[69] Cryptosecurities differ markedly from Bitcoins and other virtual currencies which do not represent a claim against an issuer, see Philipp Paech, 'Securities, Intermediation and the Blockchain: An Inevitable Choice between Liquidity and Legal Certainty' (2016) 21 Unif L Rev 612, 635 (hereafter Paech, 'Securities').

[70] For an excellent consideration of the conflict of laws for cryptocurrencies, see Dickinson, 'Cryptocurrencies' (n 33).

[71] It has been suggested in relation to cryptocurrencies, that on platform property issues be treated by the cryptocurrency consensus law (the law of the system) whilst off platform property issues would be more appropriately referred to the law of the place of residence or business of the participant with which that participation is most closely connected, Dickinson, 'Cryptocurrencies' (n 33) [5.93] (on platform), [5.109] (off platform) and [5.110].

[72] FMLC, *Distributed Ledger Technology and Governing Law* (n 42).

1. Location of a named entity

'PROPA' (the place of the relevant operating authority/administrator), 'PREMA' (the primary residence of the encryption master keyholder) and the location of the original coder of the DLT programme each select a connecting factor by reference to the location of a particular entity. The advantage of these approaches is that they select a single law, but there are both practical and legal obstacles in the way of their application. The FMLC reports stakeholder representations of the cost and expense to market participants of ascertaining the location of these entities,[73] and questions why the original coder should impact the ongoing life of the distributed ledger where s/he is not also the system administrator.[74]

If a choice is to be made amongst them the location of the operating authority (PROPA) best fulfils the criteria of ascertainability and conflicts relevance, and this is perhaps the FMLC's reason for selecting it as a fallback rule should the elective *situs*, the FMLC's preferred rule, not gain wide acceptance because of objections to party autonomy underpinning the selection of the law.[75] It is particularly difficult to see the conflicts relevance of the originator of the computer code for the DLT system.

2. The locations of the private encryption key

The two approaches that apply the location of the private encryption key diverge in their points of contact, the transferee in one and the transferor in the other. The essay will demonstrate the very different outcomes that this brings to the rules. Both rules seek to address the problem of portfolio financing in a disintermediated environment where PRIMA does not apply.

(a) The location of the private encryption key of the transferee—application of the *lex situs cartae*

In a departure from conventional thinking, this rule equates cryptosecurities with traditional bearer securities on the basis that a cryptosecurity held directly from an issuer and recorded on the DLT system is treated as something that exists as

---

[73] In addition to the difficulties of establishing the location of the master key-holder for PREMA there is the also the problem of identifying a single master key, see ibid [6.18].
[74] Ibid [6.28].
[75] The elective *situs* and the party autonomy objections that may be in the way of its implementation are evaluated in Section H.4. PROPA is one of the FMLC's alternative choices 'where a truly elective *situs* or governing law (in the sense of a free choice) cannot readily or sensibly be implemented': ibid [7.5]. It has however cautioned that it may not be entirely clear who the operating authority is as the functions may be shared amongst two or more entities. The solution could also present problems if the operating authority moves jurisdiction: here the FMLC gives the example of a move necessitated by Brexit, [6.17] and [6.19].

a concrete thing in the world independent of relationships between persons. The argument is made that the cryptosecurity is not a claim but a tangible thing (being the encryption key) as although it may have been created by a transaction between individuals its existence once generated is not anchored to those individuals. Entitlement to the cryptosecurity is said to arise from possession (specifically of the private key) and is exhausted by the loss of the private key which transfers to the new holder of the private key.[76]

The rule, which is an application of the *lex situs cartae*, is immediately attractive in that it avoids the artificial analogies drawn between the register/intermediary account and the diffused DLT ledger that lacks geographical location and is not always a ledger of title. The proposal is backed by strong arguments for a different approach to cryptosecurities founded upon the concept of possession and control. The argument is made that in the same way that X does not have the bearer share if X does not have its certificate, X does not have the cryptosecurity if X does not have the encryption code to access the cryptosecurity.[77]

There are however several obstacles to its application as the connecting factor for cryptosecurities. First, it is impossible to draw a complete analogy with bearer securities as the private key is not the cryptosecurity.[78] It may be the key which together with another unlocks the virtual vault in which the cryptosecurity is kept but is in itself nothing more than that. The real world equivalent of the private user encryption key is the customer's key that must be used in combination with the bank's to open a safe deposit box. Professor Andrew Dickinson's explanation of the function of the private key in relation to cryptocurrencies may help illustrate the point made here:[79]

> The private key is simply a piece of information, and need not be held on a single device or any device at all. If a person held the key in their memory, or if a thumbprint is used to verify transactions: would the cryptocurrency be identified and located with that person? A copy of the blockchain is a record of transactions within the cryptocurrency system, and it plays an important role in maintaining the integrity of the system but in itself, is without value—it is its conformity with the consensus rules and identity with other copies held in other locations that matters.

The writer also questions the basis of the rule that '[a] cryptosecurity held directly from an issuer and recorded ... on DLT system, is something that exists as a concrete thing in the world' independent of relationships between persons'.[80] Even

---

[76] Green and Snagg, 'Intermediated Securities' (n 24) 345–7.
[77] Ibid 357.
[78] See text to n 82.
[79] Dickinson, 'Cryptocurrencies' (n 33) [5.97].
[80] Green and Snagg, 'Intermediated Securities' (n 24) 347.

ISSUES OF TITLE—CANVASSED SOLUTIONS FOR CRYPTOSECURITIES 215

cryptocurrencies generated by the cryptocurrency systems, which are not claims against an issuer, are nevertheless not completely divorced from the relationship of participants in their constitution as property. It is conceptually and legally not possible for cryptosecurities to have an existence independent of relationships between persons as they are bundles of entitlements and obligations defined by their terms of issue. There is, it is suggested, an analogy here with bearer securities. Whilst paper certificates are undeniably a thing, they are worthless as securities without their connection to the rights conferred by the issuer under their terms of issue. Likewise the key would be worthless without its connection to the rights attached to the cryptosecurities. In *Re Baku Consolidated Oilfields Ltd* [81] the ornamental certificates had collectors' value, but were worthless as securities in the issuer's liquidation. In the same way that bearer certificates are not the securities,[82] the encryption key is not the cryptosecurities.

Lastly, as Professor Dickinson has pointed out, the private key is a code and not any particular tangible device (which may be a physical token or mobile) which generates it or stores it. It may be attributed with the location of its holder, and this is what proponents of the rule have suggested, but this will only be known to the holder. An important feature of the *lex situs* rule is that it is ascertainable by third parties. The location of the user's key selects a law that is only capable of ascertainment at any particular time by the user of the key. The rule does make for time and cost efficiencies for portfolio financing,[83] as its proponents have highlighted, but this will be at the cost of an objectively ascertainable law to competing claimants. A similar benefit to financiers and corresponding impediment to competing claimants is seen in PRIMA and the Hague Securities Convention rule, where the relevant point of contact is also in the control of the transferee.[84] It is unsatisfactory for the choice of law approach to allow the applicable law to be ascertained easily and in advance by the financier alone. The applicable law must also be capable of ascertainment, and preferably with the same degree of certainty and predictability, by third parties as well.

(b) The location of the private encryption key of the transferor-application of the law of the assignor

The location of the private encryption key of the transferor aligns with the primary connecting factor in Art 4(1) of the European Commission, 'Proposal for a

---

[81] [1993] BCC 653.
[82] The fact that it is possible to have uncertificated securities lends weight to this argument. Traditionally held securities that are dematerialised and put on the DLT system do not cease to be entitlements against the issuer.
[83] As it substitutes one law for a multitude of laws that the financier may otherwise have to comply with for portfolio collateralisation.
[84] Which effectively allow the person whose interest is sought to be impugned to choose the law by which his entitlement will be determined by simply crediting the interest with an intermediary in the jurisdiction of that law.

Regulation of the European Parliament and of the Council on the law applicable to the third-party effects of assignments of claims'[85] and also the rule in the United Nations Convention on the Assignment of Receivables in International Trade,[86] both of which apply the law of the location of the assignor. The principal advantage of the law of the assignor, and the reason for its selection in the various instruments and this proposed rule for cryptosecurities, is the convenience that it brings to portfolio financing and assignments. It substitutes for the multiple laws that the financier/assignee would otherwise have to check and comply with, the single law of the location of the assignor or the assignor's private key in this case.[87]

It should be noted that the convenience to financiers/assignees is more circumscribed here in comparison to a rule which selects the private key of the financier/assignee. First, it is not as readily ascertainable to the financier/assignee[88] but this should not be an insurmountable problem as the assignor is likely to disclose the location to facilitate the transaction. Secondly, this rule applies a single law only where the cryptosecurities in question are all from one assignor. Lastly, the financier/assignee does not get to choose the law by which its entitlement to the cryptosecurities will be determined, which it can do if the law is selected by reference to its own location or that of its private key.

From the perspective of conflicts law, the selection by reference to the assignor or its private key[89] makes for a better choice of law rule for determining title as it does not put the financier/transferee at an advantage over competing claimants seeking to impugn the interest of the financier/transferee. In theory at least, the financier and others interested in acquiring the cryptosecurities should be investigating the source of the interest which is the transferor. It is however unclear that the DLT system's technologically driven checking system requires or enables disclosure of the location of the transferor or its key. Consequently in the context of the DLT system ascertainablity is not necessarily enhanced by the selection of the law by reference to the transferor rather than the transferee. Both will be particularly challenging in permissionless platforms where the identities of the parties and their locations are not easily ascertainable.

---

[85] COM (2018) 96 final, 2018/044 (COD), <https://eur-lex.europa.eu/legal-content/EN/TXT/?uri=COM%3A2018%3A96%3AFIN> accessed 11 January 2021 (hereafter Proposal for Regulation on third-party effects of assignment). The FMLC attributes the proposed solution to the EU's selection of the law of the assignment, FMLC, *Distributed Ledger Technology and Governing Law* (n 42) [6.22]. Note however that the FMLC paper preceded the Proposal and referenced the Consultation Document for the Proposal where the law of the assignment was the first of three choice of law rules that consultees were asked to consider (ibid [6.13]).
[86] Adopted 12 December 2001 but not as yet in force.
[87] These could be different save at the particular point of time when the assignor applies the private key for a transaction.
[88] The assumption is made that the financier/assignee (even an absent-minded one) knows where its own private key is since the transaction cannot be completed without it.
[89] The location of the private key as connecting factor does give rise to special concerns, see the discussion in relation to its use where the point of contact is the transferee, above Section H.2(a).

3. The law applicable to the assignment—purported application of the *lex registri*

This purports to be an application of the *lex registri* for traditionally held securities in the context of a DLT system. The law applicable to the transaction (contractual or otherwise) under which the assignment is made is given relevance, and said by its proponents to be the appropriate law, because the DLT ledger is a record of these transactions.[90] The other justification for its application is that it allows the parties to the transaction to choose the law which will govern its proprietary effects.[91]

The analogy drawn to the register of title of a ledger of transactions is obviously less than perfect, but the justification for the rule is the very reason why it is unsuited to be the choice of law rule for the proprietary effects of a transaction on the DLT system.[92] The law applicable to the assignment transaction is not ascertainable by competing claimants to the cryptosecurities[93] and to the issuer. One of the important criteria for the selection of an appropriate choice of law rule for cryptosecurities must be the protection of the issuer, the obligor. It would be unfair to the issuer that the law and terms pursuant to which the cryptosecurities were issued can be altered, potentially as many times as the cryptosecurities are assigned, by an act of assignment to which it is not party.

Significantly the law applicable to the assignment, the first rule in Art 14 of the Rome I Regulation, was one of the three options considered for, and the only one excluded from, the Commission's Proposal for Regulation on third-party effects of assignment.[94] The UK will not be opting into the proposed regulation[95] but this was not with a view to keeping the option of applying the law of the assignment to

---

[90] FMLC, *Distributed Ledger Technology and Governing Law* (n 42) [6.12].

[91] Ibid [6.14].

[92] The FMLC flagged the practical difficulties and inefficiencies that the rule will introduce to a system founded on technology intended to improve the speed and efficiency, and the fragmentation to the DLT system of subjecting it to multiple different laws: ibid [6.15].

[93] As acknowledged by Gerard Spindler, 'Fintech, Digitalization, and the Law Applicable to Proprietary Effects of Transactions in Securities (Tokens): a European Perspective' (2019) 24 Unif L Rev 724, 734 ('... even though such a freedom of choice of law is charming, as parties could adopt the best suited regime bilaterally, it does not provide a solution for third-party effects, such as competing entitlements').

There is also the question whether exclusion of questions governed by the law of companies contained in Art 1(2)(f) of the Rome I Regulation (Regulation (EC) No 593/2008 on the law applicable to contractual obligations [2008] OJ L177/6, hereafter Rome I Regulation) will exclude the application of Art 14 where the transaction on the DLT is of crypto-shares.

For debt securities, there are conflicting opinions as to whether Art 14 does apply to third-party effects of assignments. The view taken by the European Commission in drafting the new Proposal was that Art 14 of the Rome I Regulation does not apply (Proposal for Regulation on third-party effects of assignment (n 85)), a view endorsed by the European Court of Justice in *BGL BNP Paribas SA v TeamBank AG Nürnberg* (C-548/18) ECLI:EU:C:2019:848.

[94] n 85.

[95] This is because '[i]ts provisions would have significant unintended consequences for financial services market practices in the UK', see the statement from the Economic Secretary to the Treasury (HCWS836), 9 July 2018.

proprietary questions. Dicey, Morris & Collins[96] does not suggest the suitability of its Rule 135(1)(a)[97] for issues of property and for good reason.

4. The law of the system as a manifestation of the *lex situs*

Both the elective *situs* approach (the FMLC's preferred solution[98]) and the location of the token apply the law of the system, the solution advanced in this essay for cryptosecurities, but as manifestations of the *lex situs* rather than of the *lex creationis*. In the second approach the *situs* of the token or digital asset that possesses intrinsic value is deemed to be the law of the system.[99] The elective *situs* takes a more tenuous route to the law of the system. It is said to be an application of PRIMA through the adoption of the Hague Securities Convention approach to signpost a location or a *situs*. As the ledger in a DLT system is 'distributed' and not account specific, as PRIMA requires, the Hague Securities Convention approach applied to the DLT system has the applicable law selected by the network participants for the DLT system.[100]

Both the elective *situs* and *situs* of the tokens contemplate the selection of the law by the participants of the system collectively. In anticipation of objections to party autonomy[101] underpinning the selection of the law, the FMLC has suggested limiting options for participants' choice of the *situs*.[102] Notably the Hague Securities Convention also restricts unfettered choice (by the parties to the account agreement) but this has not persuaded the EU to adopt the Hague Securities Convention rule. It is difficult to see how the argument against party autonomy raised in relation to the Hague Securities Convention can be raised in the same way here where all participants have agreed to the law that would apply to their transactions on the cryptosecurities system. Whilst not all participants in the system at the time of a particular transaction would have participated in the selection by the originators

---

[96] Lord Collins of Mapesbury and others (eds), *Dicey, Morris & Collins: The Conflicts of Laws* (15th edn, Sweet & Maxwell, 2012) (hereafter Dicey, Morris & Collins).

[97] Rule 135(1)(a) is based on Art 14 of the Rome I Regulation (n 93). The common law rule concerning the law applicable to the proprietary effects of assignments of choses in action is much more difficult to pinpoint, see Andrew Dickinson, 'Assigning Priorities in the Conflict of Laws' [2020] LMCLQ 198.

[98] In combination with regulatory constraints on the election of the law where necessary: FMLC, *Distributed Ledger Technology and Governing Law* (n 42) [8.1].

[99] International Swaps and Derivatives Association (ISDA) and others, 'Private International Law Aspects of Smart Derivatives Contracts Utilizing Distributed Ledger Technology' (January 2020) 28–29, <https://www.isda.org/a/4RJTE/Private-International-Law-Aspects-of-Smart-Derivatives-Contracts-Utilizing-DLT.pdf> accessed 18 January 2021 (hereafter ISDA, DLT).

[100] FMLC, *Distributed Ledger Technology and Governing Law* (n 42) [6.5].

[101] For proprietary issues, party autonomy is generally not accepted as a choice of law principle, see Koji Takahashi, 'Implications of the Blockchain Technology for the UNCITRAL Works', 17–18, <http://www.uncitral.org/pdf/english/congress/Papers_for_Programme/30-TAKAHASHI-Implications_of_the_Blockchain_Technology_and_UNCITRAL_works.pdf> accessed 18 January 2021.

[102] FMLC, *Distributed Ledger Technology and Governing Law* (n 42) [6.9].

or initial participants, later participants may be said to have implicitly (if not expressly) agreed to the choice by dealing with cryptosecurities within the system. The equivalent of the contractually selected law of the cryptosecurities system would be the consensus rules of law applicable to relationships between participants of a cryptocurrency system which are said to answer questions relating to the proprietary effect of transactions in cryptocurrencies within the system.[103]

Participants in the cryptosecurities system, be they the issuer of the cryptosecurities or the financier who takes them as collateral or the investor, cannot complain about the application of that law since it is the law to which they had submitted. This is no different from expecting the rules of the stock exchange or Stock Connect or indeed the intermediated system to be relevant to transactions on that system. Clearly the law that has the closest and most real connection with transactions through the stock exchange and intermediated system would be the laws regulating the exchange or system in question. In the language of Dicey, Morris & Collins' Rule 135(2), the law of the system is that with which the cryptosecurities have their most significant connection. The option is always there for a participant to choose a different cryptosecurities system or a different holding and trading platform that applies a law more acceptable to it.[104]

The FMLC has said that the elective *situs* meets the requirements of being 'objective and easily ascertainable by the parties themselves and provides the clearest route for establishing the governing law within the context of this new technology'.[105] More importantly, the writer would add, it meets the criteria of ascertainability by competing third parties and the issuers, themselves likely to be participants of that system. Further advantages exist where the law of the system manifests the *lex creationis,* as will be demonstrated in the section that follows.

The formulation of the law of the system as the elective *situs* or the *situs* of the tokens has, however, no obvious advantage to the development of choice of law for securities beyond an incoherent expansion of the reach of the *lex situs* to cryptosecurities. This adds to the fragmentation of existing choice of law for securities, now a collection of disparate rules[106] given the appearance of coherence by the *situs* label attached to them. The approach of devising bespoke rules for new securities and ways of holding and trading makes for difficult application and less than coherent conflicts analysis. It will necessitate a multi-pronged approach to the choice of law treatment of cryptosecurities of different origins with the elective *situs* (or *situs*

---

[103] Dickinson, 'Cryptocurrencies' (n 33) [5.93], [5.100], [5.109].
[104] The Court of Appeal's grievance in *Secure Capital* (n 17) [58] that application of Luxembourg law would make relevant a foreign law is astonishing given that the issuer had selected to have the Notes held on a system constituted and regulated by that law.
[105] FMLC, *Distributed Ledger Technology and Governing Law* (n 42) [7.3].
[106] These include the *lex registri* and *lex situs cartae* for traditional securities, and the various legislated forms of PRIMA. For the difficulties in navigating amongst existing fragmented choice of law for shares, see Ooi, 'Fragmentation in the Choice of Law for Shares' (n 1).

of the token) applying to those issued within the cryptosecurities system, and the *lex registri* or *lex situs cartae* or PRIMA applying to those issued outside the system.

5. The law of the system manifesting the *lex creationis*

The law of the system as a manifestation of the *lex creationis* has several important advantages that its *lex situs* brethren and other options do not have. The law of the (cryptosecurities) system manifesting the *lex creationis* presents a rule that is not just pragmatic (a single ascertainable law) but also theoretically coherent.

Securities, whether traditional, intermediated or cryptosecurities, are created pursuant to a law. For traditionally held securities, the governing law of debt securities is contractually stipulated, for shares it is the *lex incorporationis*. Intermediated securities, which are derivatives of traditional securities, are created by the law of the intermediated system in which their underlying traditional securities are immobilised. The specific nature of cryptosecurities is not yet confirmed, but it is expected that there will be cryptosecurities systems that allow for cryptosecurities to be created and issued within the system which may or may not be pegged against traditional or intermediated securities (just as many cryptocurrencies are not pegged against traditional currencies). It also seems likely that cryptosecurities systems will accommodate dematerialised traditional securities tokenised on the system to enable the registry of securities to be maintained on a distributed ledger.[107] The *lex creationis* of the cryptosecurities would depend on whether the cryptosecurities in question are created and issued within a crytosecurities system or are tokens of dematerialised traditional securities issued outside the system.

The *lex creationis* of cryptosecurities constituted within a cryptosecurities system would be the law of that system by which they were created and defined, whether or not they are also pegged against securities (traditional or intermediated) issued outside the cryptosecurities system. Where the cryptosecurities are record tokens of dematerialised traditional securities, the *lex creationis* would be that of the dematerialised securities.[108] To illustrate the latter point, issues of property relating to transactions in Widget cryptosecurities which are dematerialised

---

[107] 'Under the most straightforward implementation of the collateralized DLT transaction, the real world collateral assets (such as cash or securities) are not replaced with on-ledger tokens or digital assets that possess intrinsic value. Rather, the tokens merely record the various forms of collateral provided and exchanged ... A more complex implementation of the collateralized DLT transaction could involve the replacement of the real-world collateral assets with a form of token or digital asset that possesses intrinsic value (such as a cryptocurrency)' ISDA, DLT (n 99) 28–9.

[108] A concern has been expressed that this would complicate portfolio holdings of off platform securities, since a single portfolio would then have many different governing laws applying to different securities therein, see Paech, 'Securities' (n 69) 636. Sometimes it is necessary for the solution to commercial problems arising from transnational transactions to be found in the realm of commercial law and devices if the integrity of the choice of law processes is to be sustained. Intermediation would address this problem since the law of the intermediated system (a single law) would apply then.

Widget (Ruritanian) shares put on a cryptosecurities system would be referred to Ruritanian law, their *lex creationis*. Here the Widget cryptosecurities are the Widget (Ruritanian) shares, the only change is that the registry of securities is maintained on a distributed ledger (a change that will require changes to Ruritanian corporate law).[109]

The *lex creationis*/law of the system approach is capable of rational application whatever the legal constituent of the cryptosecurities, and however they may evolve. Other approaches, on the other hand, are of more limited application. A majority of these approaches are said (by their proponents) to apply only to cryptosecurities issued within the cryptosecurities system, leaving issues relating to other cryptosecurities to the *lex situs* of the underlying securities, which 'could be the *lex incorporationis* (including the law of some place other than the *lex incorporationis* if the latter allows the securities to be dealt with there) or, where the securities are held in a centralized deposit system, the law of the country where the register, account or centralized deposit system is situated'.[110]

Objections to party autonomy[111] do not arise, as the reason for the law of the system manifesting the *lex creationis* is not to give effect to parties' choice but because it is the law which is the source of the cryptosecurities and to which the cryptosecurities owe their existence and legal characteristics. It need not be consensually selected even: cryptosecurities systems that are a creation of legislation may have the law of that legislation as the law of the system.[112] Objections to party choice may, conversely, be legitimately levelled in respect of the transferee's private key, the Hague Securities Convention rule, and indeed also PRIMA, as they select the law by reference to the key/account of the financier/transferee, the choice of which is within that financier/transferee's control.

The *lex creationis*/law of the system accommodates more than cryptosecurities, providing certainty and predictability to participants in the securities and financial markets where different securities co-exist and intermingle. Issues relating to traditionally held securities, whether debt or shares, registered or bearer, will be referred to the *lex creationis* of those securities.[113] Issues relating to intermediated securities will be referred to the law of the intermediated system, the *lex creationis* of the intermediated securities. The separate treatment of bearer and registered

---

[109] eg Delaware Corporations Law (8 Del C 1953) §224.
[110] ISDA, DLT (n 99) 28. The FMLC takes a similar approach, 'Finally, the FMLC also proposes that where the asset has an existence which is wholly independent of the system—such that the system serves purely as a means of recording the transaction and neither title nor the asset is constituted thereby—the proprietary effects of the transaction should be determined according to the conflicts of rules which would ordinarily apply outside the system.': FMLC, *Distributed Ledger Technology and Governing Law* (n 42) [7.8].
[111] See Section H.4; also text to n 83.
[112] There may be good reasons to restrict choices (where the system is not created by legislation) to align them with the regulatory controls, but these are measures to place the cryptosecurities within the jurisdiction of a regulator, and are not relevant to the conflicts analyses here.
[113] As bearer securities are not their certificates, see text to nn 81–82 above.

securities, and traditional and intermediated securities, under existing choice of law makes for uncertainties that compromise the integrity of securities transactions. The Court of Appeal in *Macmillan* had classified the Berlitz shares, the subject matter of the dispute, as registered in disregard of their classification as bearer by the laws of New York, the *lex incorporationis* of Berlitz Inc. The Berlitz shares had at different points of the disputed collateral transactions been placed on the DTC, an intermediated system, so that it was not obvious whether the issue of title was decided in relation to the directly held Berlitz shares or the intermediated Berlitz shares.[114] The convergence of separate connecting factors in the *lex creationis* will simplify and make for more coherent choice of law for securities.

Issues relating to the GDRs (general depository receipts) issued on the London-Shanghai Stock Connect will be referred to the *lex contractus* of the depository receipts and not the *lex incorporationis* of the Chinese shares to which they are pegged.[115] Should derivative GDRs be constituted within a cryptosecurities system in the future, the *lex creationis* of the derivative GDRs will be the law of the cryptosecurities system which created them. The *lex creationis*/law of the system approach which applies the *lex creationis* of the particular securities (instead of the underlying securities against which they are pegged as was done in *Secure Capital*) will produce outcomes that align with market expectations and ensure the integrity of the London-Shanghai Stock Connect and the intermediated and cryptosecurities systems.

The *lex creationis*/law of the system approach avoids the difficulties that arise from applying to securities the traditional characterisation categories and connecting factors for issues of property, contract and corporations by creating a category and rule specifically suited to securities.[116] This allows for issues of title and entitlement (against the issuer) to be treated together, as they should be for securities where the distinction is blurred.[117] Lawyers for the claimant in *Secure Capital* had sought to establish a right that lay between contract and property. This attempt to depart from established categories was rejected by the Court of Appeal and Hamblen J at first instance as 'inconsistent and to a significant extent legally incoherent',[118] the courts preferring to fit it within the contract category

---

[114] For a detailed analysis of the implications of these to the choice of law for securities, see Ooi, 'Characterisation of Issues Relating to Securities' (n 1) 584–5.

[115] The shares of Huatai Securities Co Ltd and China Pacific Insurance (Group) Co Ltd, both incorporated under the laws of the People's Republic of China, are currently the two stocks on the London-Shanghai Stock Connect. The GDRs for each issue are governed by English law, see the Huatai Securities Co Ltd GDR Prospectus (11 June 2019) <https://sec.report/nsm/Huatai-Securities-Co-L-T-D/data-migration/225239203> accessed 18 January 2021, and the China Pacific Insurance GDR Prospectus (12 June 2020) <www.cpic.com.cn/gdr/gdrggen/index_3.shtml> accessed 18 January 2021.

[116] As suggested by Professor Briggs in *Private International Law in English Courts* (n 4).

[117] Options other than the elective *situs* for cryptosecurities, if extended to issues of entitlement, will conversely alter the obligations of issuers unfairly by a law that they did not select to govern their obligations.

[118] *Secure Capital* (n 17) [28] (CA); also [36] (Hamblen J).

and apply its choice of law rule.[119] Insistence on applying to securities categories and rules that were not created with them in mind is the reason why investors are disenfranchised.

A dichotomised choice of law process makes for uncertainty that is inimical to the securities and financial markets. Issues of title are currently referred to an unwieldy collection of rules said to manifest the *lex situs* with no certainty to the investor/financier of which the court will apply where systems overlap, as they often do in today's securities transactions. Issues of investor rights are said to be the prerogative of the *lex incorporationis* of the issuer or treated as contractual in the case of debt securities (as in *Secure Capital*) even where the shares or debt securities are intermediated. The *lex creationis* avoids indiscriminate applications of the 'no look through' approach. It is one thing to say that 'no look through' underpins PRIMA and the Hague Securities Convention rule, or is the consequence of the English trust principle, and quite another to assume it where these do not apply and the links and contracts in the intermediated chain are not (all) governed by English law. The *lex creationis*/law of the system approach would have referred Secure Capital's claim arising from intermediated Notes to Luxembourg law, the law by which Clearstream and the intermediated Notes were constituted. By Luxembourg law investors of intermediated securities on Clearstream had rights against the issuers of traditional securities immobilised on the system.

The *lex creationis*/law of the system offers a unified coherent choice of law treatment for all securities and holding systems in their present and future expressions. This is critical as conflicts issues arise in increasingly complex ways in relation to securities, and traditionally held, intermediated and cryptosecurities come together in a cryptosecurities system which may itself change over time. The *lex creationis*/law of the system approach avoids the need to devise bespoke rules for every new form of securities and system, and the time and expense that the pursuit of such rules require.

I. Conclusion

The approach that has hitherto been employed for the choice of law treatment of securities has been to devise bespoke choice of law rules for different types of securities and platforms, sometimes explicitly and sometimes under the guise of applying existing rules and principles of the conflict of laws such as the *lex situs*. PRIMA and the Hague Securities Convention rule for intermediated securities have added to *Macmillan*'s legacy of fragmented choice of law rules for traditionally held securities.[120] This has resulted in different regimes of choice of law for

---

[119] No reasons were given in either judgment as to why the claim admitted of no other possible characterisation save contract.
[120] Discussed in Ooi, 'Fragmentation in the Choice of Law for Shares' (n 1).

securities which have no correlation with each other and do not work well save with respect to the particular securities and trading platforms (and arguably not even then) and from which no fundamental general principles can be drawn to any variations to securities and platforms.

The bespoke rules that have been canvassed for cryptosecurities,[121] if adopted, will further fragmentate and complicate choice of law for securities. These bespoke proposed rules bear no rational semblance to the rules from which they are said to derive and are of uncertain application where systems overlap. Where a cryptosecurities system remains intermediated, it is unclear whether the law of the cryptosecurities system or PRIMA applies. The lack of a uniform policy generates uncertainties for market players whenever different forms of securities commingle. Transactions on cryptosecurities systems may be of securities created within the system, or they could be of dematerialised traditionally held securities issued outside the system, or they could be of intermediated securities. Where specialised rules apply, it would be difficult for the investor or financier to predict with any certainty the applicable law that will be applied to determine its title to the securities. This is inimical to today's transactions in securities.

Brexit presents an opportunity for developing a principled conflicts approach to the many questions that present themselves in securities transactions.[122] It allows the UK to decide whether it should indeed keep the PRIMA rule in the Settlement Finality and Financial Collateral Regulations. The way forward for England to retain its competitive edge in attracting concentrations of cross border securities transactions is to ensure that it has cogent and clear choice of law rules that do not buckle under the pressures of new securities, and this can be achieved by adopting the *lex creationis*/law of the system approach.

---

[121] Sections H.1–4.

[122] The EU rules are particularly difficult to navigate due to the overlapping but not entirely consistent or reconcilable choice of law rules in the Financial Collateral Directive, the Settlement Finality Directive and the Winding-up Directive. The Proposal for Regulation on third-party effects of assignment (n 85) (which it appears highly unlikely that UK will follow) introduces two further rules whose sphere of application are not entirely distinct and which may potentially apply to intermediated and cryptosecurities. The provisions of the proposed Regulation do not explicitly exclude matters within the Directives and it is doubtful that there can be clear separation even if they do.

The European Commission, in its 'Communication from the Commission to the European Parliament, The Council, The European Economic and Social Committee and the Committee of the Regions on the applicable law to the proprietary effects of transactions in securities' COM (2018) 89 final <https://eur-lex.europa.eu/legal-content/en/TXT/?uri=CELEX%3A52018DC0089> accessed 11 January 2021, expresses the intention that these questions be kept separate from the proposed Regulation. The proposed Regulation is confined to claims but that does not in itself exclude cryptosecurities, as Recital (16) states that claims covered by the proposed Regulation include claims arising from securities and derivatives as 'financial instruments'.

9
Remedies and the Conflict of Laws

Adam Rushworth

A. Overview

Just before Christmas 2005, I met with Professor Briggs to discuss writing a doctorate on the conflict of laws. At that point, I had no specific topic in mind and said so. I was (literally) thrown a copy of Professor Boskovic's doctorate '*La réparation du préjudice en droit international privé*'.[1] Professor Boskovic argued that there should be a specific choice of law rule (neither the *lex causae* nor the *lex fori*) to determine the remedial consequences of the violated right. Professor Briggs had been the external examiner for the doctorate a few years before and it had inspired at least part of an article entitled '*Conflict of Laws and Commercial Remedies*' presented by him at the Sixth Oxford Law Colloquium.[2] At that time, the knee-jerk reaction of the English lawyer was that remedies were a matter for the *lex fori*. Professor Briggs summarised his thesis as follows:

> The line which separates right from final remedy is one which could usefully be eliminated, with the result that the lex causae would prevail generally [subject to an extreme case where an English court could not be expected to make an order of a kind wholly foreign to domestic English law[3]]; and where equitable claims and doctrines are concerned, some serious thinking-through of choice of law and its importance is now overdue. The granting of interim remedies should be governed by English law (if the trial will take place in England), but applications should take a very clear lead from the law of the court in which the trial will be taking place, if this is not England, but an order is still to be made. The coherence which this may tend to produce will be preferable to the rather archaic, or disjointed, current state of the law on commercial remedies.

That work itself inspired a doctorate, now completed some eleven years ago. The purpose of this paper is to sketch out the theory underpinning the approach to

---

[1] Olivera Boskovic, *La réparation du préjudice en droit international privé* (LGDJ 2003).
[2] Adrian Briggs, 'Conflict of Laws and Commercial Remedies' in A Burrows and E Peel (eds), *Commercial Remedies* (OUP 2003).
[3] Ibid, 275 where this caveat is explained.

remedies and the conflict of laws, to look at the present law under the Rome I[4] and Rome II[5] Regulations[6] and then to compare that to Professor Briggs' thesis of nearly twenty years ago. As will be seen, in large part, that thesis has been vindicated, albeit with some minor tinkering.

B. What is a *'Remedy'*?

It will be of some assistance to start by identifying what is being meant, at least in this paper, by *'remedy'*. The word is ambiguous and used by judges for different concepts. There is also extended academic commentary on its meaning with some arguing that certain uses of it, including the one primarily used in this paper, are incorrect or unhelpful.[7]

This paper proceeds on the basis that the word is ambiguous but does not seek to identify (or impose) any meaning which could be said to be correct as a matter of theory. Rather, the paper seeks only to be clear about what is being referred to when the word is used. It primarily focusses on remedies in the sense of court orders. Paradigm examples from contract law are the orders to pay a sum of damages to the claimant or to perform a contract (specific performance). The category is wide and would include, for example, an order for specific disclosure.[8] As part of this, it also discusses a sub-category of court orders referred to as 'interim remedies'. This terminology itself adds a further layer of ambiguity. It is used here to mean provisional remedies, in the sense of orders which, when ordered, expire on a given date (usually trial, unless renewed as a final order). Paradigm examples include an interim injunction prohibiting until trial a party from breaching a putative contractual term or a freezing injunction.

Finally, the paper also addresses, to some extent, the content of obligations to compensate a claimant for breach of a primary obligation, sometimes referred to as secondary obligations, which raises conceptually different issues.

---

[4] Regulation (EC) 593/2008 of 17 June 2008 on the law applicable to contractual obligations (Rome I) [2008] OJ L177/6 (hereafter Rome I Regulation).
[5] Regulation (EC) 864/2007 of 11 July 2007 on the law applicable to non-contractual obligations (Rome II) [2007] OJ L199/40 (hereafter Rome II Regulation).
[6] Which remain applicable post-Brexit with minor amendments: see the Law Applicable to Contractual Obligations and Non-Contractual Obligations (Amendment etc) (EU Exit) Regulations 2019.
[7] eg, P Birks, 'Rights, Wrongs and Remedies' (2000) 20 OJLS 1.
[8] eg, *Hewlett Packard Enterprise Company v Manchester Technology Data (Holdings) Ltd* [2019] EWHC 2089 (Ch), [22] referring to such an order as a *'remedy'*.

C. Theory

It is impossible to address remedies and the conflict of laws without also addressing the principle that the *lex fori* governs matters of procedure. This is because remedies sit on the fault line between substance and procedure.

The editors of Dicey, Morris & Collins explain that the 'principle that procedure is governed by the *lex fori* is of general application and universally admitted'.[9] Whilst universally admitted, the reason behind the principle is not universally agreed.

It was recently considered by the Court of Appeal, which gave the following explanation:[10]

> The distinction between substance and procedure is a fundamental one. The principle underlying it is said to be that a litigant resorting to a domestic court cannot expect to occupy a different procedural position from that of a domestic litigant. Thus, that litigant cannot expect to take advantage of some procedural rule of his own country to enjoy greater advantage than other litigants here. Equally he should not be deprived of some procedural advantage enjoyed by domestic litigants merely because such an advantage is not available to him at home. Thus, at common law, every remedy was regarded as procedure: see for example *Don v Lippmann* (1837) 2 Sh & MacL 682 at 724-5.

However, with respect, this does not actually provide any explanation. Litigants (both foreign and domestic) can sometimes expect to occupy a different substantive position from that of litigants in a purely domestic setting, otherwise there would be no choice of law rules at all. Two German companies (and, indeed, two English companies) can choose German law to govern their contract and the English court will then (subject to some caveats) apply German law to determine their rights. So why can they not expect the same with respect to the procedural position? The above explanation does not answer this.

The explanation provided by Dicey, Morris & Collins is as follows:[11]

> The primary object of this Rule is to obviate the inconvenience of conducting the trial of a case containing foreign elements in a manner with which the court is unfamiliar. In principle, therefore, if it is possible to apply a foreign rule, or to refrain from applying an English rule, without causing any such inconvenience,

---

[9] Lord Collins of Mapesbury and others (eds), *Dicey, Morris & Collins: The Conflict of Laws* (15th edn, Sweet and Maxwell 2012) [7-002] (hereafter Dicey, Morris & Collins or, in abbreviated form, Dicey).
[10] *Actavis UK Ltd v Eli Lilly & Co* [2015] EWCA Civ 555; [2016] 4 All ER 666, [132] (per Floyd LJ). The decision went on appeal to the Supreme Court but the issues with which this paper is concerned were not considered.
[11] Dicey, Morris & Collins (n 9) [7-004].

those rules should not necessarily, for the purpose of this Rule, be classified as procedural.

Critically, this explanation blends two different methods used to apply the *lex fori* in the context of procedure and, by doing so, conceals two different principles which are in operation.

The first method involves the characterisation of putative rights or obligations. Certain types of rights or obligations are characterised as procedural and so the *lex fori* is applied to determine the existence and extent of those rights or obligations. Suppose that a claimant claims in the English courts for breach of a contract governed by French law. It is unlikely anyone would dispute that the obligations on a defendant to serve a defence by a particular date or to disclose known adverse documents are to be characterised as procedural. This can be determined with limited, or no, inquiry into the precise content of the potentially relevant foreign law.

The second method involves the exclusion of otherwise applicable foreign law. This occurs at a subsequent stage of the conflict of laws inquiry to characterisation. After a right has been characterised as substantive and a foreign law is to be applied, in general it is best to apply all the foreign law rules which determine the existence, scope and extent of that right. However, there are circumstances in which a rule of the foreign law is disapplied because of its specific character. An example is where a rule of the otherwise applicable foreign law is disapplied by the court for public policy reasons. This method depends on the precise content of the relevant applicable law. There seems little doubt that there is also a rule of exclusion where it is procedurally too inconvenient to apply otherwise applicable foreign law. Its most obvious expression is in Arts 12(1)(c) of the Rome I Regulation and 15(d) of the Rome II Regulation, which both contain an express rule of exclusion based on the *'limits of the powers conferred on the court by its procedural law'*.

Having identified the two different methods used to apply the *lex fori* on procedural grounds, the next question is whether they share the same primary object.

There can be no doubt that the primary object of the rule of exclusion is the procedural inconvenience of applying the specific foreign law that would otherwise be applicable and, to this extent, Dicey must be correct. However, where it is respectfully suggested that Dicey errs, is in suggesting that the primary object of the characterisation of putative rights and obligations as procedural (ie the first method used to apply the *lex fori* on grounds of procedure) is also inconvenience. For this to be correct, there would have to be types or categories of right which can, in the abstract, be determined to be too inconvenient for the Court to apply foreign law in respect of them. However, there are two central difficulties with this. First, it is by no means obvious how, if at all, one can deem, for example, all foreign law obligations concerning the disclosure of documents in advance of a trial as being too inconvenient to apply whilst, at the same time, accepting that far more complex foreign law obligations in relation to trusts or fiduciary duties are not too inconvenient to apply. Secondly, if the purpose of the rule is to exclude rules of foreign laws which are too inconvenient to apply, then this could be achieved simply by a rule of exclusion. A characterisation-based approach is too blunt a tool to use and unnecessary given the existence of the rule of exclusion.

If the primary object of the characterisation of putative rights and obligations as procedural is not inconvenience, then what is it? The most cogent explanation is that those rights and obligations arise by virtue of a party being within a trial process and, in those circumstances, the *lex fori*, being the law of that trial process, is the most appropriate law to apply to those rights. Those procedural rights and obligations form a coherent system laid down by the *lex fori* to ensure a fair trial. If a defendant is sued in England for alleged damages due under a French law contract, his obligations to serve a defence by a particular date, or to provide certain disclosure in advance of the trial, do not, unlike his alleged obligation to pay damages, arise by virtue of the contract. They arise by virtue of the defendant being involved in English proceedings and are not dependent on whether the alleged contractual right actually exists. As these rights and obligations are created by English law to address being involved in English proceedings then it should follow that the appropriate law to govern those rights and obligations is English law.

The counter-argument is that applying anything other than the *lex causae* to all aspects of a dispute may encourage forum shopping and reduce certainty because different results to the dispute could be achieved in different jurisdictions due to procedural differences. However, the problem with this counter-argument is that, if accepted, it proves too much. In order to prevent forum shopping and to ensure certainty then, on the face of it, the whole of the procedural law of the *lex causae* must be applied. Moreover, if the determining Court did not apply the whole of the procedural law of the *lex causae* then it would mean that no one coherent system of procedural rights and remedies is applied to ensure a fair trial. It is unsurprising that this counter-argument has been rejected, in the context of the Rome II Regulation, by the Court of Appeal.[12]

Accordingly, it is suggested that there are two different principles in operation. The first rule is that rights or obligations arising by virtue of a party being involved in legal proceedings are characterised as procedural and so the rules of the *lex fori* should be applied to determine the existence and extent of those rights. It also follows from this that the court orders vindicating those rights are to be governed by the *lex fori*. The principle behind this rule is that the *lex fori* is the most appropriate law to govern those rights and remedies. The court is not interested in whether the specific foreign law right is too inconvenient to apply. The second principle is a rule of exclusion. Once the *lex causae* of a substantive right has been identified

---

[12] *Wall v Mutuelle de Poitiers Assurances* [2014] EWCA Civ 138; [2014] 1 WLR 4263 at [15] (Longmore LJ, with whom Jackson and Christopher Clarke LJJ agreed).

then, to the extent possible, all rules concerning the existence and extent of that right should be applied, including the relevant court order vindicating that right. However, in the rare case where the application of the *lex causae* is procedurally too inconvenient, it can be disapplied.

The following two sections look at the application of those principles in practice by looking at some issues which arise under the Rome I and Rome II Regulations.

D. Rights Arising by Virtue of Being Involved in Legal Proceedings

This section addresses the first principle and, in particular, the distinction between orders vindicating rights and obligations which arise by virtue of being in litigation and orders vindicating substantive rights. In particular, it discusses some of the difficult cases which have arisen in the case law including interim remedies and negative declaratory relief. The guiding question should always be: is the relevant party entitled to the order sought because it is involved in English litigation, or because it has a right which arose outside of the litigation process?

Before addressing the various instances where this has arisen, it would be helpful to set out the relevant legislative terms. Both the Rome I and Rome II Regulation contain, in Art 1(3) of each, a provision excluding from their scope 'evidence and procedure'. As will be seen, rights which arise by virtue of being in litigation fall within this provision and so it is for the domestic law of the determining court to determine the law applicable to them. This should always be the *lex fori*.

The Rome I and Rome II Regulations also contain specific provisions setting out a non-exclusive list of matters to which the law governing the relevant obligation applies.

Of particular relevance to this paper, Art 12(1)(c) of the Rome I Regulation provides that the law applicable to a contract shall govern 'within the limits of the powers conferred on the court by its procedural law, the consequences of a total or partial breach of obligations, including the assessment of damages insofar as it is governed by rules of law'.

Further, Arts 15(c) and (d) of the Rome II Regulation provide that the law applicable to non-contractual obligations shall govern:

(c) the existence, the nature and the assessment of damage or the remedy claimed;

(d) within the limits of the powers conferred on the court by its procedural law, the measures which a court may take to prevent or terminate injury or damage or to ensure the provision of compensation;

There can be no doubt from these provisions that the final remedy which vindicates the claimant's substantive right should be governed by the *lex causae* and so the central aspect of Professor Briggs' thesis is correct under the Regulations. However, difficult questions still arise over the limits of this principle.

1. Evidence

In English civil courts, parties have qualified rights to call evidence to establish their factual case. The rights are qualified[13] because they often depend on the court giving a party permission to do so, albeit the court's decision on whether to give permission follows well-established rules or guidelines. One example is expert evidence. Under Part 35 of the Civil Procedure Rules (CPR), a party can seek permission from the court to call expert evidence to support its case. In determining the application, the court will follow the well-established guidance concerning whether permission should be granted.[14]

Rights to call evidence arise by virtue of being a party to litigation in order to ensure a fair trial. They apply irrespective of whether one's right is contractual, tortious or some other substantive right. Accordingly, they are to be characterised as procedural and the *lex fori* should be applied to determine their scope and the Court orders to which a party is entitled.

This can be seen from the Court of Appeal decision in *Wall v Mutuelle de Poitiers Assurances*.[15] Mr Wall took a holiday to France and was severely injured in a road traffic accident by the negligent driving of the defendant's insured. It was common ground that, by virtue of the Rome II Regulation, French law applied to the non-contractual obligation which arose and the only issue between the parties concerned the quantum of damages. The claimant asked for permission, under Part 35 of the CPR, to call evidence from a number of experts. The defendant argued that French law applied to the expert evidence which could be called, under which the Court would appoint two medico-legal experts to assist the judge. The Master ordered a preliminary issue to be tried on whether the type of expert evidence to be ordered fell to be determined by English law on the basis it was procedural and so fell within Art 1(3) of the Rome II Regulation, or by French law on the basis that it fell within Art 15 of the Rome II Regulation.

The Court of Appeal upheld the decision of Tugendhat J that this was a matter of evidence or procedure falling within Art 1(3) of the Rome II Regulation. The Court explained that, whilst rules as to the kind of loss which is recoverable were to be imported from the *lex causae*, mere methods of proving recoverable loss were not to be. The reasoning of the Court of Appeal was that the English courts are

---

[13] H Malek (ed), *Phipson on Evidence* (19th edn, Sweet and Maxwell 2018) [11–15] refers to these as 'restrictions on the right to call evidence'.
[14] eg *British Airways Plc v Spencer* [2015] EWHC 2477 (Ch); [2015] Pens LR 519 [21]–[25].
[15] [2014] EWCA Civ 138; [2014] 1 WLR 4263.

ill-equipped to receive expert evidence given in the French manner because the other procedures used by the English courts (such as disclosure and the giving of oral evidence) could not easily sit aside the approach taken by French law to the giving of expert evidence.[16] This is the same reasoning as explained in Section C above. A domestic law of procedure has a unified integrity where individual foreign law rules of procedure cannot coherently replace those of the *lex fori*. Whilst one could loosely refer to this as procedural inconvenience, it is not inconvenience in the sense of the practical difficulties of applying a specific foreign law (which the rule of exclusion covers) but rather the detrimental effect of applying that specific foreign law on the coherence of the procedural law to be applied.

It also follows from this that applications for evidential orders, such as for specific disclosure, will be governed by the *lex fori*. In short, the (qualified) rights to such orders arise by virtue of being in litigation rather than due to the existence of a specific substantive right.

2. Damages and interest

As explained in Section B above, there is a distinction between a court order and a secondary obligation to pay a sum of money for breach of an obligation (which is then vindicated by a court order). When one refers to '*damages*' it is possible to be referring to either: a court order to pay a sum of money determined to be due as compensation; or the secondary obligation to compensate a person for the breach of a primary obligation. The actual court order to pay a sum of money due as compensation raises little complexity. However, the determination of the content of the secondary obligation to compensate a person for breach of a primary obligation does raise some problems, particularly as it can be difficult to identify which rules of the foreign law concern the extent of the secondary obligation and which concern the right to call and establish facts before the relevant tribunal, which has already been discussed above.

As is well known, under the common law, which was then apparently ossified by the Private International Law (Miscellaneous Provisions) Act 1995,[17] all questions of the quantification of damages were procedural and a matter for the *lex fori*. That position was difficult to justify and has now largely been replaced by the European Regulations.[18]

Under the European Regulations, the position is now clear. Any rules of the *lex causae* concerning the assessment of damages should be applied: see Art 12(1)(c)

---

[16] See, in particular, the decision of Jackson LJ: [2014] EWCA Civ 138; [2014] 1 WLR 4263 [43]–[44].

[17] *Harding v Wealands* [2006] UKHL 32; [2007] 2 AC 1.

[18] The most notable area of commercial private law where the courts still apply the old common law rules is in respect of claims for breach of fiduciary duties against directors: see *AS Latvijas Krajbanka v Antonov* [2016] EWHC 1679 (Comm) [7]–[8].

of the Rome I Regulation and Art 15(c) of the Rome II Regulation set out above. These rules include '*soft law*' such as foreign law equivalents to the Judicial College Guidelines which set out guidelines for the English courts for the assessment of damages in personal injury cases.[19] Further, if a foreign law contains discount rates for specific claims, then these are to be applied.[20] The rate of interest on recoverable damages should also be a matter for the *lex causae*.[21]

There had been some debate over whether Recital (33) of the Rome II Regulation varied this in the context of road traffic accidents. That provides:

> According to the current national rules on compensation awarded to victims of road traffic accidents, when quantifying damages for personal injury in cases in which the accident takes place in a State other than that of the habitual residence of the victim, the court seised should take into account all the relevant actual circumstances of the specific victim, including in particular the actual losses and cost of after-care and medical attention.

This provision was the product of a compromise between the European Commission and European Parliament.[22] It was considered in some detail by Nelson J in *Stylianou v Toyoshima*, who concluded (correctly in the view of this author), that its effect was simply that the court should look at the actual costs, for example, of aftercare in the victim's place of residence, and take those into account when assessing damages, but *only* insofar as the applicable law permits it to do.[23] That is, it is a 'reminder'[24] or a 'wish'[25] on the part of the drafters that, subject to the rules of the applicable law, the courts should take the actual losses into account and that a victim, resident abroad, may be in a different economic position from a locally resident victim.

Recital (33) was also considered in *Wall v Mutuelle de Poitiers Assurances*, the facts of which have been explained in the previous sub-section above. As part of the determination of the preliminary issue, the parties had submitted expert

---

[19] *Wall v Mutuelle de Poitiers Assurances* [2014] EWCA Civ 138; [2014] 1 WLR 4263 [24].

[20] *Stylianou v Toyoshima* [2013] EWHC 2188 (QB) [91]–[96].

[21] *AS Latvijas Brakbanka v Antonov* [2016] EWHC 1679 (Comm) [10]. cf *Troke v Amgen Seguros Generales Compania de Seguros Y Reaseguros Sau* [2020] EWHC 2976 (QB), [2020] 4 WLR 159 in which Griffiths J held that the power to award interest under s 69 of the County Courts Act 1984 and s 35A of the Senior Courts Act 1981 was procedural and so fell within Art 1(3) of the Rome II Regulation. With respect, it is suggested that *Troke* is wrong because it fails to distinguish between the position prior to Rome II and the position after Rome II, and also misunderstands paragraphs [10] and [13] of the judgment in *Antonov*.

[22] A detailed explanation of the *travaux preparatoires* on this can be found in Adam Rushworth, 'Remedies and the Rome II Regulation' in John Ahern and William Binchy (eds), *The Rome II Regulation on the Law Applicable to Non-Contractual Obligations* (Martinus Nijhoff Publishers 2009) 207–8 (hereafter Rushworth, 'Remedies and the Rome II Regulation').

[23] *Stylianou v Toyoshima* [2013] EWHC 2188 (QB) [78].

[24] Dicey, Morris & Collins (n 9) [34-057].

[25] Rushworth, 'Remedies and the Rome II Regulation' (n 22) 209.

reports on French law, which the Court of Appeal considered when determining what expert evidence should be permitted to be adduced for trial. The claimant's expert report explained that the general principle was that all losses resulting directly and unequivocally from the injuries sustained in the accident must be compensated for in full. It also explained that the French courts used an itemised list of potential pecuniary and non-pecuniary losses (the 'Dintilhac Headings') when assessing the losses for which compensation was payable, and sought to give evidence of the figures *'normally adopted'* by the Paris Cour d'Appel in respect of at least the non-pecuniary items on the list. It is unclear from the law report whether this evidence included figures for pecuniary loss as well. The Court of Appeal gave permission for the parties to adduce evidence of the figures normally adopted by the French courts for non-pecuniary loss, but not for pecuniary loss, relying for this distinction on Recital (33).[26] A full explanation for this is not given. It seems the likely explanation is that the Court considered, on the face of the evidence before it, that under French law the determination of the amount of pecuniary loss was purely a factual inquiry and so the figures adopted in other cases by the French courts would be of no assistance to the English court, which just had to proceed to perform its own factual inquiry. If that is the explanation of the Court of Appeal's decision, then it is unobjectionable and entirely consistent with the decision of Nelson J in *Stylianou*.

Accordingly, Recital (33) does not change the underlying choice of law rules themselves: any rules of the *lex causae* concerning the assessment of damages should still be applied. However, a distinction must be drawn between, on the one hand, rules concerning the assessment of damages and, on the other hand, rules concerning the methods of proving recoverable loss. The latter remain a matter for the *lex fori*.[27] This is a straightforward application of the first principle explained in Section C above. Rules concerning the assessment of damages concern the extent of the relevant substantive right. Accordingly, the *lex causae* should apply to determine those rights. However, rules concerning the proof of facts at trial concern the parties' qualified rights to call evidence to establish their factual case and these arise by virtue of being in litigation. They are governed by the *lex fori*, as explained in the previous sub-section. The devil is in the detail and, no doubt, harder cases will arise. However, the principled distinction between the two categories remains.

3. Interim relief

The categorisation of interim relief is, on the face of it, more difficult. One must also be particularly alive to the fact that the same answer may not apply to all forms

---

[26] *Wall v Mutuelle de Poitiers Assurances* [2014] EWCA Civ 138; [2014] 1 WLR 4263 [29].
[27] Ibid, [16].

of interim relief. An interim injunction which replicates, albeit temporarily, the final injunction sought to vindicate the relevant substantive right has much greater claim to be governed by the *lex causae* than, for example, an injunction whose purpose is to allow a party to obtain evidence for trial (eg a search order), the treatment of which is difficult to distinguish for choice of law purposes from a simple order for specific disclosure.

(a) English authority

No English case has considered this issue in detail but some recent decisions have touched on it. None provides a conclusive answer.

In *OJSC TNK-BP Holding v Lazurenko*, the defendant had agreed an employment contract with the claimant which was governed by Russian law. It was alleged by the claimant that the defendant had threatened to misuse confidential information in breach of that employment contract and the claimant sought injunctive relief, both as a final remedy and by way of interim relief. The claimant obtained an *ex parte* interim injunction restraining the disclosure of the relevant information. Morritt C had to address an application from the claimant to continue the interim injunction, and an application from the defendant for a declaration that the Court had no jurisdiction. He discharged the injunction and struck out the claim. The relevant part of the reasoning for present purposes was as follows:[28]

> ... both experts make it clear that under Russian law no *quia timet* injunction, interim or final, to restrain a threatened disclosure of confidential information is available. Rome I Article 10.1 *(sic)* and Rome II Article 15 may have changed the common law position under which the availability of remedies was a matter for the *lex fori*. They appear to make the availability of remedies a matter for the *lex causae*. In this case that is Russian law. It would follow that TNK-BP has not demonstrated any cause of action or serious question to be tried in respect of its claim for an interim *quia timet* injunction. However, there is no authority to that effect, the issue was not fully argued before me and doubts have been expressed in Dicey and Morris [14th edn, para 32-203] and 19 Halsbury's Laws [5th edn para 646 note 9]. Nevertheless, the doubt as to the availability of an injunction as a remedy shows that TNK-BP is unable to demonstrate a sufficient likelihood of success to satisfy the requirements of s.12(3) Human Rights Act 1998. For these reasons I will discharge the orders made by Roth and Vos JJ and dismiss the application of TNK-BP for their continuance.

The current supplement to Dicey, Morris & Collins suggests that this is some authority for the proposition that, under both the Rome I and Rome II Regulations,

---

[28] [2012] EWHC 2781 (Ch), [20].

interim remedies are governed by the applicable law.[29] However, there are reasons to pause before coming to that conclusion and it is probably wrong. The key sentence is that TNK-BP had not demonstrated any cause of action or serious question to be tried in respect of its claim for an *'interim quia timet injunction'*. The requirement to demonstrate a putative cause of action in respect of which there is a serious issue to be tried is a requirement under English law for most interim injunctions. The requirement concerns the cause of action (and relief) sought at trial, not the interim relief. Put simply, if an applicant seeks an interim injunction, he does not have to establish that there is a serious issue to be tried as to whether he is entitled to the interim injunction. Rather, he must satisfy the Court that the requirements for an interim injunction are made out and, as part of that, he has to establish that there is a serious issue to be tried on the cause of action for which he is seeking relief at trial (or a higher standard for certain types of interim relief). Accordingly, the most likely interpretation of the sentence is that the judge's (*obiter*) reasoning was that, if the claimant could not establish, under the agreed applicable law, that it was entitled to the final (and only) remedy sought in its Particulars of Claim, then the claimant had not satisfied the English law requirements of obtaining interim relief. This also appears to be how the decision was understood by Arnold J in *Actavis UK Ltd v Eli Lilly & Co*.[30] Further, it is the only coherent interpretation of the paragraph when one looks at the references in the following sentence. Dicey, Morris & Collins, in the paragraph (32-203) referred to by the judge, states that 'with some hesitation' orders for a final injunction or specific performance are to be governed by the *lex contractus*. However, it states (in no uncertain terms) that 'There can be no doubt that the availability of interlocutory relief remains essentially a matter of procedure governed by the *lex fori*'. Similarly, the footnote of Halsbury's Laws does not refer to interim remedies.

If the above is correct, then the judge was not actually making any specific comment about the applicable law to interim relief, even *obiter*, and it is no authority of any sort for the governing law of interim remedies.

Since *OJSC TNK-BP Holding*, there have been two further decisions of the High Court, neither of which refers to *OJSC TNK-BP*, nor do they provide any detailed discussion of the law, and they are, in fact, inconsistent with each other.

In *Republic of Angola v Perfectbit Limited*,[31] Bryan J had to hear a number of applications at a return date in respect of proprietary injunctions, worldwide freezing orders and disclosure orders which had been made against a number of defendants. One of the defendants argued that there had been a failure of full and frank disclosure by the claimants on the *ex parte* application because they had failed to

---

[29] L Collins (ed), *Fifth Cumulative Supplement to Dicey, Morris & Collins: The Conflict of Laws* (15th edn, Sweet and Maxwell 2018) [32-155] and [34-056] (Note 343) (hereafter Dicey Supplement).
[30] [2014] EWHC 1511 (Pat); [2015] Bus LR 154 [228].
[31] [2018] EWHC 965 (Comm).

draw the Court's attention to the possibility that Angolan law applied both to the substance of the cause of action and to the availability of interim relief. The judge appeared to accept, without any discussion or argument, the claimants' position that the applicable law governs the availability of interim relief, and in that case the availability of a freezing injunction.[32]

Subsequently, in *Folkes v Generali*,[33] Nicol J had to determine an application for an interim payment in respect of a tort arising from a road traffic accident which it was common ground was governed by French law. The judge's reasoning on the issue was as follows:[34]

> Since the process for making an order for an interim payment is part of the 'procedure' which Article 1(3) and Article 15(d) leave to be determined by the law of the forum, I agree with Mr Doherty that it is to English law that I must look. For this reason, I did not find helpful the references which Ms Crowther QC, for the defendant, made, on this topic, to the report of the Defendant's expert on French law, Madame Witvoet. Thus the standard of proof which French law would set for interim payments, (to be made only for matters which are not challenged by a grounded defence or where the Judge can identify 'what goes without saying' or is beyond reasonable challenge) is strictly speaking immaterial. That said, perhaps unsurprisingly, English and French procedural law in this regard are very similar.

The result of all of this is that there is no obvious answer to be drawn from the case law. Dicey also does not give a strong steer.

In the chapter of the main work on Rome I, Dicey says that: 'There can be no doubt that the availability of interlocutory relief remains essentially a matter of procedure governed by the lex fori.'[35] In the most recent supplement,[36] it states that that sentence should be deleted and suggests that interim relief 'may be' governed by the applicable law, relying on *OJSC TNK-BP Holding*. However, as explained above, it is likely that is not authority for the proposition.

With respect to the position under the Rome II Regulation, the editors of Dicey, Morris & Collins refer to the explanatory memorandum on the original proposal which became Rome II. That memorandum stated in respect of what is now Art 15(d) of the Rome II Regulation that the wording 'refers to ... ways of preventing or halting the damage, such as an interlocutory injunction ...'.[37] In the supplement, it again refers to *OJSC TNK-BP Holding v Lazurenko*.

---

[32] Ibid, [203] and [210].
[33] [2019] EWHC 801 (QB).
[34] Ibid, [16].
[35] Dicey, Morris & Collins (n 9) [32-155].
[36] Dicey Supplement (n 29) [32-155].
[37] Dicey, Morris & Collins (n 9) [35-059].

Professor Dickinson tentatively concludes that, under the Rome II Regulation, interim measures are governed by the *lex causae*, emphasising the importance that the grant or refusal of measures of this kind may have in practice in promoting settlement before trial.[38]

Due to the paucity of authority, it is necessary to analyse the position under the Regulations from first principles.

(b) Textual and contextual interpretation

Starting with the textual interpretation, although the Rome II Regulation may be read as leaning closer to the proposition that interim remedies are governed by the *lex causae*, neither Regulation is clear.

It is difficult to see how interim remedies naturally fall within the words of Art 12(1)(c) of the Rome I Regulation: interim remedies are not the consequences of a total or partial breach of obligations. First, they are granted before a Court has determined that there has been a total or partial breach of any obligation. Secondly, even if a breach has been determined, save for some possible exceptions (such as interim remedies seeking provisionally to vindicate the substantive right, eg an award of an interim payment), they are not easily analysed as a consequence of a breach. However, the items listed in Art 12(1)(c) as being governed by the *lex causae* are non-exhaustive and so the fact that they are not expressly listed does not rule them out as being governed by the *lex causae*.

Art 15(d) of the Rome II Regulation is also unclear and raises a number of ambiguities.

First, as to the measures that a Court may take to 'prevent or terminate injury or damage', one would naturally expect that 'injury or damage' is intended to refer to 'injury or damage' due to the breach of a non-contractual obligation, rather than 'injury or damage' at large. However, an interim injunction may or may not prevent or terminate injury or damage due to the breach of a non-contractual obligation. At the time the injunction is awarded, it is unknown whether any such breach has occurred. Accordingly, for interim injunctions to fall within Art 15(d), one must read 'prevent or terminate injury or damage' to mean injury or damage due to the putative breach of a non-contractual obligation. That is not immediately obvious from the words.

Secondly, as to the measures that a court may take to ensure the provision of compensation, plainly an order for the payment of damages is the paradigm measure. However, how far outside of this category do these words extend? A post-judgment order that a defendant's assets can be seised to satisfy a judgment debt is, on one view, a measure to ensure the provision of compensation. Yet no one would argue that the *lex causae* should govern such orders, matters of enforcement being

---

[38] Andrew Dickinson, *The Rome II Regulation* (OUP 2008) [14.35].

a matter for the *lex fori*. A more difficult example is an English freezing injunction. The purpose of such an injunction is to ensure the defendant has sufficient assets available to satisfy the ultimate Court order. On one view, such an injunction (pre-emptively) 'ensure[s] the provision of compensation'.

Thirdly, when Art 15(d) refers to the measures that a Court 'may take' does this mean that the governing law is relevant only to determining the measures which are in principle available, or does it mean that the determining Court must apply the same measure that a court sitting in the jurisdiction of the *lex causae* would have applied were it to have been seised with the dispute? To take an example, if either an injunction or damages are available under the *lex causae*, and a court in the jurisdiction of the *lex causae* would normally award injunctive relief, is the determining court bound to follow this, or is the limit of the reference to the *lex causae* to determine only the measures available (here, injunctive relief and damages), and then the determining court can choose which to apply on the principles existing under the *lex fori*?

As regards contextual interpretation, neither Regulation applies to evidence and procedure: Art 1(3) of each of the Regulations.[39] Accordingly, if interim measures properly fall within the scope of Art 1(3), they must fall outside the scope of Art 15(d). However, this then begs the question of whether they fall within Art 1(3).

Separately, the substantive scope and provisions of the Regulations should be interpreted consistently with one another: Recital (7) of each of the Regulations.[40] Accordingly, as there is no coherent basis for having a different solution under each Regulation, the solution under both must be the same.

(c) Purposive interpretation

Given the lack of assistance from textual and contextual interpretation, it is likely that the answer is to be found in a purposive interpretation of the provisions.

One of the key underlying principles of the Regulations, and the choice of law process itself, is that substantive rights should be treated the same whichever Court has jurisdiction over the dispute. Further, as explained in Section C above, the law of procedure is a coherent body of rules which inter-relate. The application of these principles suggest that there may not be one simple answer for all interim remedies.

If one starts with what is probably the easier category, some interim remedies do not, even provisionally, seek directly to vindicate a party's putative substantive right. Two examples can be given. The first example is a freezing injunction in support of English substantive proceedings. Such an order seeks to preserve

---

[39] Art 1(3) of each Regulation (Rome I (n 4) and Rome II (n 5)) states: 'This Regulation shall not apply to evidence and procedure...'.
[40] Recital (7) of the Rome II Regulation (n 5) states that: 'The substantive scope and the provisions of this Regulation should be consistent with ... the instruments dealing with the law applicable to contractual obligations.' Recital (7) of the Rome I Regulation (n 4) states that: 'The substantive scope and the provisions of this Regulation should be consistent with ... [the Rome II Regulation].'

the defendant's assets pending judgment so that, if the claimant is ultimately successful, there are assets against which to execute any judgment. It does not matter whether the claimant's claim is in contract, tort or for some other non-contractual obligation. The right arises out of the fact that the claimant is, or is imminently about to be, in court proceedings and the court provides an order to ensure the effectiveness of the potential future judgment. The second example is a search order. Such an order seeks to preserve evidence for use at the ultimate trial. Again, it does not matter whether the claimant's substantive right is contractual, tortious or some other non-contractual right. The right arises out of the fact the claimant is in, or is imminently about to be in, litigation, and the courts wish to ensure that the trial process is fair.

Such interim remedies do not seek provisionally to vindicate the applicant's substantive right. Rather, they seek to ensure a fair trial and that the outcome of the trial process is effective. Accordingly, they should not be governed by the *lex causae*. This is also consistent with even the more expansive wording of Art 15(d) of the Rome II Regulation. Provisional remedies which seek to vindicate procedural rights are not naturally to be considered measures which may be taken to prevent or terminate injury or damage, or to ensure the provision of compensation.

However, even once one has decided that the *lex causae* should not apply to such remedies, there is a further question of which *lex fori* should be applied. The answer is simple if an English court is granting the interim remedy in support of English substantive proceedings: English law will apply. However, what happens if the English court is acting in support of foreign substantive proceedings? Should the English court apply the *lex fori* of the substantive proceedings? This is a matter outside the scope of the Rome I and Rome II Regulation and so is outside the scope of this paper. However, it is tentatively suggested that the law of the court being asked to determine the application should still be applied, albeit with reference to what the court with substantive jurisdiction over the dispute would do.[41] Such measures are usually confined to the territory of that court,[42] and the granting of this type of measure requires particular care on the part of the court in question and a detailed knowledge of the actual circumstances in which the measures sought are to take effect.[43]

---

[41] See s 25(2) of the Civil Jurisdiction and Judgments Act 1982, which provides that the court may refuse to grant relief 'if, in the opinion of the court, the fact that the court has no jurisdiction apart from this section in relation to the subject-matter of the proceedings in question makes it inexpedient for the court to grant it'. What the Court with substantive jurisdiction over the dispute would do is one of the considerations which should fall within the test of inexpediency.

[42] eg Recital (33) of Regulation (EU) No 1215/2012 of 12 December 2012 on jurisdiction and the recognition and enforcement of judgments in civil and commercial matters [2012] OJ L351/1 (hereafter Recast Brussels I Regulation).

[43] C-391/95 *Van Uden Maritime BV v Kommanditgesellschaft in Firma Deco Line* [1998] ECR I-7091 [38].

The more difficult issue under the Regulations is the law applicable to interim remedies which do provisionally seek to vindicate substantive rights. An example of such an interim remedy is an interim injunction ordering a party to refrain from interfering with an alleged intellectual property right. There are arguments both ways and it is finely balanced. On one view, such remedies arise by virtue of the trial process because they seek only to preserve the parties' position whilst the litigation process reaches its conclusion. Further, at least under English law, it is not necessary that the applicant demonstrates the existence of the substantive right in order to obtain such a remedy: an applicant need usually[44] only show a real prospect of success which is a threshold requirement for being able to proceed with a claim in any event. The contrary argument is that such interim relief is merely the provisional vindication of the substantive right and so is closely connected to that right.

Ultimately, and given how finely balanced this is, in light of the *travaux préparatoires* of the Rome II Regulation which explain that the wording of Art 15(d) was intended to include interim injunctions, one would expect a court to conclude that, under the Regulations, such remedies are governed by the *lex causae*.

However, the application of the *lex causae* to at least a category of interim relief can cause practical difficulties to arise. Two in particular come to mind. First, if an applicant is seeking urgent interim relief, there may be insufficient time to obtain evidence of the relevant foreign law. Secondly, the *lex causae* may be in dispute at the time the applicant seeks interim relief.

It is suggested that these practical difficulties can be resolved through the (careful) application of Art 1(3) of the Rome II Regulation. In particular, case management powers are matters of procedure, and so matters for the *lex fori*. Accordingly, so long as the application of those powers does not undermine the purpose of the Regulations, the Court has some room to take appropriate steps in the context of practical difficulties.[45] For example, if a party seeks urgent interim relief and there is no time to obtain evidence of the *lex causae*, the Court could grant the interim relief under the *lex fori* until a hearing at a later date at which the issue of the interim relief available under the *lex causae* can be addressed. So long as the initial interim relief is not determinative of the dispute, it hard to see how such an approach could undermine the purpose of the Regulations. Perhaps the more difficult issue is whether, in the event of an applicant seeking an interim injunction provisionally vindicating a substantive right and there being a dispute as to the *lex causae*, the Court must make a full and final determination as to the *lex causae*, as it would at trial. Under English law, this normally requires disclosure of documents relevant to any relevant factual dispute concerning the applicable law and could

---

[44] Putting aside applications which will be determinative of the dispute.
[45] See by analogy the approach of the Courts to stays on case management grounds under the Brussels I Regulation (see eg *Curtis v Lockheed* [2008] EWHC 260 (Comm); [2008] 1 CLC 219) and the Maintenance Regulation (*Villiers v Villiers* [2020] UKSC 30; [2020] 3 WLR 171 [34] (Lord Sales), [73] (Lady Black)).

even involve expert evidence. It is suggested that the court is not required to do so. The rules applicable to the proof of the applicable foreign law and its content must fall within the scope of Art 1(3) of the Regulation. Accordingly, following the present procedures, the English court should normally be able to make a provisional determination as to the *lex causae* on an application for interim relief on the basis of the witness evidence provided, without such determination having to be the final such determination. However, there may be instances where such an approach would undermine the purpose of the Regulations. For example, if the effect of the grant or refusal of the injunction is to determine the dispute finally, then the appropriate approach for the court is likely, if at all possible, to engage in a full and final determination of the applicable law at the stage of the application being made.

(d) Conclusion on interim relief

In summary, the answer, at least on the present law, is that the Court should first ask whether the relief applied for seeks to vindicate rights arising from being in English litigation or whether it seeks provisionally to vindicate the substantive rights of the applicant. If the former, the *lex fori* should be applied. If the latter, the *lex causae* will apply to determine whether the applicant is entitled to the remedy. However, as explained above, there is some room for the application of the *lex fori* on a case management basis so long as this does not undermine the purpose of the Regulations.

4. Declaratory relief

Another area of some difficulty is declaratory relief, which was considered by the Court of Appeal in *Actavis UK Limited v Eli Lilly & Company*.[46] Actavis claimed for declarations of non-infringement of a European patent and the corresponding national designations in France, Italy and Spain. One issue which arose is whether it was sufficient for Actavis to establish that it had satisfied the UK statutory requirements to obtain declarations of non-infringement or whether Actavis had to establish that it could satisfy the relevant provisions in French, Italian and Spanish law.

The specific foreign law rules in issue concerned the following requirements: to seek an acknowledgement of non-infringement from the patentee; to give particulars of the proposed allegedly non-infringing act; to show some form of interest or degree of preparation in respect of the allegedly non-infringing act; and to show some form of useful purpose in the resolution of the dispute. The Court of Appeal held, *obiter*, that these types of rules concerned whether the court should hear a

---

[46] [2015] EWCA Civ 555; [2016] 4 All ER 666.

dispute about the substance and were not directly concerned with the substance itself.[47]

The Court of Appeal's analysis is correct. The rules concerned whether there was a right to engage the court process, rather than defining or limiting the substantive rights themselves, and so the *lex fori* applied. If (contrary to the present position in English law which only provides for potential costs consequences) a party could not issue a claim until the pre-action protocol had been satisfied, that would not be a rule concerning the extent of any substantive rights. The fact that certain patent actions essentially have a very specific pre-action protocol does not change that analysis.

However, it is unclear from the Court of Appeal's judgment whether the availability (or not) of declaratory relief is always to be considered a matter of procedure. Floyd LJ (giving the only judgment of the Court) stated that Art 15 of the Rome II Regulation was not a 'safe guide' to whether matters which are not within its scope are procedural or substantive,[48] but also decided *obiter* that the availability of a negative declaration fell outside of the categories listed in Art 15 of the Rome II Regulation.[49]

It is suggested that this will depend on the specific rule in question. If the relevant rule defines or limits the substantive right, then the *lex causae* will apply. For example, if a foreign law refuses to give declaratory relief for breach of non-contractual obligations absent proven loss because that law considers no breach of non-contractual obligation arises until loss has occurred, then that foreign law should be applied. However, if the relevant rule defines or limits a party's ability to engage the court process, then the *lex fori* should be applied. *Actavis* is a useful example of the latter type of rule.

E. Inconvenience: The Rule of Exclusion

As explained in Section C above, in addition to a rule which characterises certain rights as procedural or substantive, there is also a rule of exclusion whereby the otherwise applicable foreign law will be disapplied due to inconvenience. The rule of exclusion is contained within Art 12(1)(c) of the Rome I Regulation and Art 15(d) of the Rome II Regulation.

In terms of how these rules are to be applied in practice, it seems unlikely that an English court would actually make an order precisely in the terms of, for example, a French order. An element of adaptation into the domestic system's legal order inevitably must occur. Practically, the English court has to find the English order (or set

---

[47] Ibid, [135].
[48] Ibid, [131].
[49] Ibid, [141]–[145].

of orders) which most closely replicates the order or orders that would have been made under the *lex causae*. This idea of adaptation is not novel to choice of law. The same applies in the context of the enforcement of European judgments under the Recast Brussels I Regulation. Art 54 thereof provides:

> If a judgment contains a measure or an order which is not known in the law of the Member State addressed, that measure or order shall, to the extent possible, be adapted to a measure or an order known in the law of that Member State which has equivalent effects attached to it and which pursues similar aims and interests.
>
> Such adaptation shall not result in effects going beyond those provided for in the law of the Member State of origin.

The aim of the Court in the context of choice of law is the same. The only limit to the determining Court is its procedural powers. In order to fulfil the purpose of the provisions, this must be narrowly construed and it is expected that it will only arise in a rare case. For example, although adequacy of damages is sometimes referred to as a 'threshold requirement' for an order for specific performance,[50] an English court could and should not refuse to order specific performance which would be granted under the *lex causae* because the court does not consider damages to be inadequate. Such a rule is not a procedural limitation on the scope of the court's power but is a reason for the English court to refrain from exercising its powers in a particular case.[51]

The classic example of the type of case in which the rule of exclusion could be applied is *Phrantzes v Argenti*.[52] In that case, the claimant sued the defendant, her father, for a declaration that she was entitled, under Greek law, to a dowry, an account of the defendant's property and an inquiry as to the amount of dowry properly payable by the defendant and such further inquiry, judgment or order as might be required to give effect to the declaration. Lord Parker CJ dismissed the claim. The right claimed was not a right to the payment of a sum of money, but an order condemning the father to draw up a dowry contract in accordance with the directions of the court, and to enter into that contract with the son-in-law who was not a party to the proceedings. The judge explained that the English court did not have the relief appropriate to the enforcement of the foreign right. There was no right in English law to obtain an order condemning someone to enter into a contract with a person not party to the proceedings.

The same should apply under the Regulations in respect of contractual and non-contractual obligations falling within their scope. If A and B conclude a contract

---

[50] eg John McGhee and S Elliot (eds), *Snell's Equity* (34th edn, Sweet and Maxwell 2020) [17-007].

[51] This can be seen from, eg, paragraph 30 of the speech of Lord Neuberger PJSC in *Cavendish Square Holding v Makdessi* [2015] UKSC 67, [2016] AC 1172, where it is stated that 'specific performance should *ordinarily* be refused where damages would be adequate remedy' (emphasis added).

[52] [1960] 2 QB 19.

requiring B to negotiate and conclude a contract with C, the English court has no procedural mechanism to order the specific enforcement of this obligation even if is available under the *lex causae*. Whilst, theoretically, the English court could order a mandatory injunction under section 37 of the Senior Courts Act 1981, the court could not enforce such an injunction and, therefore, it is suggested it lies outside of its procedural powers for the purposes of the Regulations.

It is very difficult to find other examples which have arisen in English law. *Phrantzes v Argenti* has been relied on in some subsequent cases for a slightly different distinction, which is whether English law has a method of assessment of damages which harmonises with the head of loss identified under the *lex causae*. This arises under the pre-Regulation, common law position because the line between the *lex causae* and the *lex fori* is drawn differently and so should not be relevant under the Regulations.

In *Cox v Ergo Versicherung AG*,[53] the claimant widow sued the defendant insurer for bereavement and loss of dependency after her husband died in a car accident in Germany caused by the insured person. The accident occurred prior to 11 January 2009 and so the Private International Law (Miscellaneous Provisions) Act 1995 applied, rather than the Rome II Regulation. Liability was not in dispute but a preliminary issue was ordered as to the law applicable to damages.

There were two relevant differences between German and English law. First, under German law damages awarded to a widow under the BGB will take account of any legal right to maintenance by virtue of a subsequent remarriage or a subsequent non-marital relationship following the birth of a child, whereas section 3(3) of the Fatal Accidents Act 1976 expressly excludes remarriage or the prospect of remarriage as a relevant consideration. Secondly, unlike under the Fatal Accidents Act, section 844 of the BGB confers no right to a solatium for bereavement. Under section 823 of the BGB, the widow may in principle be entitled to compensation for her own pain and suffering but this required proof of additional matters.

The Court of Appeal characterised the German rules as substantive and the English rules as procedural. They were, as explained by Lord Sumption, 'much exercised'[54] by the difficulties of applying the damages rules of the Fatal Accidents Act to a cause of action under the BGB given the considerable differences between them, and ultimately applied the German damages rules by analogy. Lord Sumption, referring to *Phrantzes v Argenti*, explained that there were cases in which English law has no suitable remedy for breach of a foreign law duty but this was not one of them. English law did provide a remedy which harmonised with the German law right, 'namely damages',[55] and that, as the Fatal Accidents Act did not apply on its own terms, the general principles for the assessment of damages from

---

[53] [2014] UKSC 22; [2014] AC 1379.
[54] Ibid, [18].
[55] Ibid, [21].

the common law were to be applied. Here, Lord Sumption is not concerned only with the availability of a court order for damages, but whether English law contains rules for the assessment of damages which harmonise with the substantive right. As Lord Sumption explained,[56] this is no longer relevant under the Rome II Regulation because Art 15(c) applies the applicable law to the 'existence, the nature and the assessment of damage or the remedy claimed'.[57]

Similarly, in another case under the pre-Regulation law, in *Iraqi Civilians v Ministry of Defence*,[58] Leggatt J explained, in addressing a foreign law claim for aggravated damages, that English law provided a suitable remedy which harmonises with the liability because it had the remedy of damages, the assessment of which would be carried out in the same way as the Court would assess aggravated damages in a case where liability had been established under English law. Again, under the pre-Regulation case law, the focus is not on whether the English court has an available order, but on whether English law has a method of assessment which harmonises with the substantive right.

Accordingly, under the approach of the Regulations, it is expected that the rule of exclusion will only be applied in an exceptionally rare case.

F. Conclusion

As explained in the introduction, almost two decades ago Professor Briggs set out his thesis that, subject to an extreme case where an English court could not be expected to make an order of a kind wholly foreign to domestic English law, the *lex causae* should apply to determine both the right and final remedy sought, and the *lex fori* would determine only interim remedies. That thesis has largely remained intact but, following the above analysis, two caveats are suggested.

First, Professor Briggs was concerned in his thesis only with substantive rights. However, there is an anterior issue as to which rights are substantive and which are procedural. In particular, one must be careful to identify whether the remedy (in the sense of court order) sought vindicates a right arising by virtue of being in English litigation, or whether it vindicates some other right. The *lex fori* should govern both the right and final remedy in respect of the former. The *lex causae* should govern the right and final remedy in respect of the latter.

Secondly, at least under the Rome I and Rome II Regulations, it is likely that the position on interim remedies is more nuanced. In particular, a distinction must be drawn between interim remedies which vindicate rights arising from being in English litigation, such as a freezing injunction or a search order, and interim

---

[56] Ibid, [23].
[57] n 5.
[58] [2014] EWHC 3686 (QB); [2015] 2 All ER 714.

remedies which provisionally vindicate the substantive rights of the applicant. The former will be governed by the *lex fori* but it seems likely that, subject to there being some room for the application of the *lex fori* on a case management basis, the *lex causae* will govern the latter.

The only thing left to be said in conclusion is that it is entirely characteristic of the scholarship of Professor Briggs that he managed to foresee a rational future path for the law and, after two decades of legislation and case law, so little needs adding to that original work.

PART III
RECOGNITION AND ENFORCEMENT OF FOREIGN JUDGMENTS

10
Foreign Judgments and Contracts: The Anti-enforcement Injunction

Tiong Min Yeo

A. Introduction: From Anti-suit to Anti-enforcement Injunctions

The protection of contractual rights stands out as one of the most important themes in the common law approach to private international law across the frameworks of jurisdiction, jurisdiction agreements, choice of law agreements, and the recognition and enforcement of foreign judgments.[1] One objective of having choice of court (or arbitration) clauses in contracts is to prevent judgments from materialising from non-chosen jurisdictions. Thus, choice of court (or arbitration) clauses have at least an indirect effect on the issue of the recognition and enforcement of foreign judgments. Indeed, a foreign judgment obtained in breach of an agreement will not be recognised or enforced in the United Kingdom if the Civil Jurisdiction and Judgments Act 1982, s 32 applies.[2] Agreements directly relating to foreign judgments have not yet made substantial appearances in international commercial litigation, but may well present the next battlefront even as the principles relating to the enforcement of jurisdiction agreements settle. This essay reviews common law developments[3] in England and Singapore (where

---

[1] It stands out as a recurring theme in the prolific writings of Adrian Briggs on private international law including his seminal work: Adrian Briggs, *Agreements on Jurisdiction and Choice of Law* (OUP 2008); and numerous articles and notes on the enforcement of jurisdiction agreements. On the link between agreements and judgments, see eg Adrian Briggs, 'Recognition of Foreign Judgments: A Matter of Obligation' (2013) 129 LQR 87; Adrian Briggs 'Distinctive Aspects of the Conflict of Laws in Common Law Systems: Autonomy and Agreement in the Conflict of Laws' (2005) 308 The Doshisha Hogaku (The Doshisha Law Review) 21; Adrian Briggs 'Crossing the River by Feeling the Stones: Rethinking the Law on Foreign Judgments' (2008) 8 Sing YB Int L 1. It is a theme of Adrian Briggs' work that is explored further in Edwin Peel's essay in this collection (ch 12).

[2] On the issues arising from this provision, see Adrian Briggs, *Civil Jurisdiction and Judgments* (6th edn, Informa 2015) [7.67] (hereafter Briggs, *Civil Jurisdiction and Judgments*).

[3] This essay focuses on the common law and does not address the interface between the common law and the European jurisdiction regime. On the latter, see Case C-159/02 *Turner v Grovit* [2004] ECR I-3565 (hereafter *Turner v Grovit*); Case C-185/07 *Allianz SpA v West Tankers Inc* [2009] ECR I-663; Case C-536/13 *Re Gazprom OAO* [2015] 1 WLR 4937 (ECJ). It also does not address issues arising from post-Brexit disengagement from the European jurisdiction regime.

English common law is generally closely tracked[4]) in relation to anti-enforcement injunctions.[5]

The availability of the anti-suit injunction as a tool of the common law[6] court to regulate cross-border litigation is well-established. An anti-suit injunction may be granted by the court against a respondent within its jurisdiction, when the forum has a legitimate or sufficient interest to be protected.[7] Commonly, the respondent sought to be restrained from starting or continuing foreign legal proceedings has breached a legal duty or has acted in a 'vexatious or oppressive' manner in the conduct of the foreign proceedings.[8] In particular, if the respondent is acting in breach of contract (the usual and clearest example is the breach of an exclusive choice of forum court agreement), that legitimate interest is established by the need to protect the contractual rights of the applicant. The remedy is ultimately discretionary, but the applicant's contractual right not to be sued in the foreign jurisdiction will normally be protected by an injunction unless strong reasons can be demonstrated otherwise.[9] International comity is normally an important consideration in the court's exercise of discretion, but it has been repeated often that international comity recedes considerably when the court is concerned with ordering the respondent to honour its contractual obligation.[10] The most important practical consideration is that an applicant who has waited too long in making its application, resulting in the foreign proceedings being very far advanced, is unlikely to get a remedy from the English court.[11]

Case authorities on the anti-suit injunction are plentiful, and the principles are relatively settled in both England and in Singapore.[12] Matters take a more

---

[4] Application of English Law Act (Cap 7A, Rev Ed 1994).

[5] An injunction may be sought to prevent recognition rather than enforcement. 'Anti-enforcement injunction' is used here to encompass both types of injunctions in the interest of brevity as the same principles apply.

[6] 'Common law' is used in this essay to include principles of equity.

[7] *Turner v Grovit* [2001] UKHL 65, [2002] 1 WLR 107 [27] (hereafter *Turner*); *Airbus Industrie GIE v Patel* [1999] 1 AC 119 (HL) 138–9 (hereafter *Airbus Industrie*). The further reference in *Turner* to the additional need for existing proceedings pending in the forum is not supported by *Airbus Industrie* or the practice of the English courts. It is widely thought that this gloss was an unsuccessful attempt to persuade the European Court of Justice to accept the anti-suit injunction (*Turner v Grovit* (n 3), noted in Adrian Briggs, 'Anti-suit Injunctions and Utopian Ideals' (2004) 120 LQR 529), and it is 'not to be taken literally': Briggs, *Civil Jurisdiction and Judgments* (n 2) [5.42].

[8] The categories are not closed: *Castanho v Brown & Root (UK) Ltd* [1981] AC 557 (HL) 573; *Bank of Tokyo Ltd v Karoon* [1987] AC 45 (CA) 58–9. See Andrew Dickinson's essay in this collection (ch 4).

[9] *Donohue v Armco Inc* [2001] UKHL 64, [2002] 1 All ER 749 [24], [53] (hereafter *Donohue*); *AES Ust-Kamenogorsk Hydropower Plant LLP v Ust-Kamenogorsk Hydropower Plant JSC* [2013] UKSC 35, [2013] 1 WLR 1889 [25]–[27].

[10] The observation of Millett LJ to this effect in *The Angelic Grace* [1995] 1 Lloyd's Rep 87 (CA) 96 (hereafter *The Angelic Grace*) is frequently cited. The high-water mark was reached in *Deutsche Bank AG v Highland Crusader Offshore Partners LP* [2009] EWCA Civ 725, [2010] 1 WLR 1023 [50]: 'An injunction to enforce an exclusive jurisdiction clause governed by English law is not regarded as a breach of comity, because it merely requires a party to honour his contract.' See further Edwin Peel's essay in this collection (ch 12), Section B.2(b), but compare Andrew Dickinson's essay in this collection (ch 4), Section C.3.

[11] *The Angelic Grace* (n 10) 96.

[12] Although still open to question: see Andrew Dickinson's essay in this collection (ch 4). It took a while longer to settle in Singapore, as authorities initially did not distinguish clearly between anti-suit injunctions on *forum conveniens* grounds and an anti-suit injunctions to protect a contractual right.

complicated turn, however, when one party seeks to recognise or enforce a foreign judgment against the other in a foreign country, and it is alleged that the recognition or enforcement is or at least involves a breach of the parties' contractual agreement. In recent years, two decisions in the Court of Appeal of England and Wales and one in the Court of Appeal of Singapore have addressed this issue. There appears to be no substantive difference in the approaches between the two jurisdictions. In both, the difference between an anti-suit injunction and the anti-enforcement injunction is that there are additional considerations to be taken into account in the latter because of the contexts in which the injunction arises. It should follow that contractual obligations continue to be strongly enforced by injunctions, though comity could play a larger role in the case of anti-enforcement injunctions.

It will be argued that the anti-suit injunction differs from the anti-enforcement injunction not in principle, but in how international comity is engaged by the differences in the underlying factual matrices. Furthermore, it is as much against comity to interfere with foreign jurisdiction as it is to interfere with foreign judgments, and the biggest practical difference between the anti-suit injunction and the anti-enforcement injunction is how the factor of delay plays out within the different underlying factual matrices. It will also be argued that there is a difference of principle as well as context between a situation where the foreign judgment had been obtained by a breach of contract, and the situation where the enforcement of the foreign judgment would be a breach of contract.

B. The Law on Anti-enforcement Injunctions

There are very few cases on the anti-enforcement injunction,[13] and even fewer where an application has succeeded. The recent synthesis of the law on

---

This distinction is now clearly drawn in the case discussed below: *Sun Travels & Tours Pvt Ltd v Hilton International Manage (Maldives) Pvt Ltd* [2019] 1 SLR 732 (CA) [67]–[68] (hereafter *Sun Travels*).

[13] Examples of cases not involving breach of contract in obtaining or enforcing the foreign judgment are: *ED & F Man (Sugar) Ltd v Yani Haryanto (No 2)* [1991] 2 Lloyd's Rep 429 (CA) (hereafter *ED & F Man*); *Mamidoil-Jetoil Greek Petroleum Co SA v Okta Crude Oil Refinery AD* [2003] 1 Lloyd's Rep 1 (QB); *The Eastern Trader* [1996] 2 Lloyd's Rep 585 (QB) (hereafter *The Eastern Trader*) (no finding of breach of the arbitration clause). In *Masri v Consolidated Contractors International Co SAL (No 3)* [2008] EWCA Civ 625, [2009] QB 503 [94] (not an anti-enforcement injunction case) (hereafter *Masri*) Lawrence Collins LJ opined that it will be in rare and exceptional circumstances that an anti-enforcement injunction would be granted. In *Interdigital Technology Corp v Xiaomi Corp* IA 8772/2020 in CS (Comm) 295/2020 (Delhi High Court, 9 October 2020), the plaintiff was granted an (interim) anti-enforcement injunction to prevent the defendant from relying on an anti-suit injunction—which the defendant had obtained against the plaintiff from the Chinese court in related proceedings—to stop the Indian proceedings. The anti-enforcement injunction appeared to be confined to the enforcement of the Chinese injunction in India ([50]). It appears that foreign injunctions may be enforceable under Indian law: Narinda Singh, 'Country Report: India', in Adeline Chong (ed), *Recognition and Enforcement of Foreign Judgments in Asia* (Singapore: Asian Business Law Institute, 2017) 70, [39].

anti-enforcement injunctions by the Court of Appeal *SAS Institute Inc v World Programming Ltd*[14] is significant. It is the first time that an anti-enforcement injunction was granted in a situation not involving a breach of contractual obligation in obtaining or enforcing the foreign judgment. S lost its claim against W for copyright infringement and breach of contract in the English court. It was held that the licensing terms in questions were null and void according to English legislation giving effect to the Software Directive of the European Union.[15] Before the English proceedings were concluded, S sued W in North Carolina on various claims including breach of contract. Judgment was given against W. S then sought to enforce the judgment in respect of the claims other than breach of contract, recognising that the judgment on the breach of contract claim would clearly not be enforceable in England because of cause of action estoppel from the prior English judgment. The enforcement claim of S, even when so limited, failed as a result of, *inter alia*, issue estoppel, abuse of process, and contravention of English public policy. Subsequently, S took steps to enforce the North Carolina judgment in California. Enforcement procedures under California law included assignment orders (requiring the judgment debtor to assign specified assets to the judgment creditor) and turnover orders (directing the judgment debtor to transfer specified assets to an officer of the court), all taking effect *in personam*. W obtained *ex parte* an anti-enforcement injunction restraining W from seeking such orders in any court in the United States, but it was discontinued at the *inter partes* hearing. On appeal, the injunction was granted, but strictly confined to the restraint of such overseas enforcement that purported to affect assets located within the jurisdiction of the English court.[16]

Males LJ (Flaux and Popplewell LJJ agreeing) considered the anti-enforcement injunction to have developed incrementally from the same underlying principles as the anti-suit injunction. There was no additional jurisdictional requirement that the case should be an exceptional one. This was in response to the argument by counsel seeking to uphold the reasoning of the trial judge that the anti-enforcement injunction should only be available in exceptional cases involving fraud and other cases of similar gravity. Accordingly, anti-enforcement injunctions are only granted very infrequently because the conditions for granting such injunctions are rarely satisfied and not because of an additional threshold requirement of exceptionality. Further, such a requirement would impose a 'vague and somewhat elastic criterion'.[17] Thus, the power to grant an anti-enforcement injunction should be exercised when required by the ends of justice. The categories are not closed,

---

[14] [2020] EWCA Civ 599 (hereafter *SAS Institute*), noted by Andrew Dickinson, 'The Interference Paradox' (2020) 136 LQR 569.

[15] Council Directive 91/250/EEC of 14 May 1991 on the legal protection of computer programs [1991] OJ L122/42, Art 5(3).

[16] Essentially, debts situated in England in the private international law sense.

[17] *SAS Institute* (n 14) [93].

though great caution should be exercised in the granting of such injunctions as a matter of comity.[18]

Comity requires that the court should have a sufficient interest in the matter in question before it grants an anti-suit injunction.[19] Sufficient interest may be shown by the need to protect the jurisdiction or process of the English court, or to prevent the litigant's evasion of important public policies of the forum.[20] This was satisfied on the facts. The foreign judgment could not be enforced in England because of *res judicata* and abuse of process as it was inconsistent with prior English judgment between the same parties on substantive liability issues, and enforcement would not only undermine the English judgment but also lead to contravention of English public policy.[21] On this approach, it follows that the court has a sufficient interest to act to enforce contractual rights in an appropriate case.

Comity requires the forum to respect the work of foreign courts.[22] The significance of this aspect of comity will depend on the circumstances. Where the injunction is not sought on grounds which involve a breach of contract, the comity that leans against interference with foreign court processes will always require careful consideration. Comity, however, has to work both ways. Thus, it will be a less weighty consideration if the foreign judgment in question involves a breach of customary international law.[23] The court considered that it would be against comity for a foreign court to enforce its judgments against assets situated in England which are subject to the jurisdiction of the English court.[24] Hence, the foreign enforcement orders were exorbitant to the extent that they purported to affect property within the jurisdiction of the English court without the safeguard of being conditional upon effect given to them under English law, thus infringing the sovereignty of the United Kingdom.[25]

Comity requires that the applicant for an anti-enforcement injunction should act without undue delay. Delay is a multifaceted factor in the context of an anti-suit or anti-enforcement injunction. As the injunction is an equitable remedy, delay is evidence of dilatoriness of the applicant which can defeat an application for an injunction if there is requisite knowledge of the relevant circumstances and prejudice or detriment.[26] The detriment could be that of the respondent, or of third parties, including particularly foreign courts of law.[27] Males LJ said:[28]

---

[18] Ibid [90]–[91].
[19] Ibid [108], following *Airbus Industrie* (n 7) 138.
[20] *SAS Institute* (n 14) [108]–[110].
[21] Ibid [88].
[22] Ibid [101]–[103]. See further James Edelman and Madeleine Salinger's essay in this collection (ch 13).
[23] *SAS Institute* (n 14) [111]–[112]. See also *Airbus Industrie* (n 7) 140.
[24] *SAS Institute* (n 14) [112].
[25] Ibid [72]–[89].
[26] *Sun Travels* (n 12) [106]–[108].
[27] *Ecobank Transnational Inc v Tanoh* [2015] EWCA Civ 1309, [2016] 1 WLR 2231 [122]–[123] (hereafter *Ecobank*).
[28] *SAS Institute* (n 14) [104].

In general, the greater the delay in seeking relief, the further the foreign proceedings would have advanced, and the more justifiable will be the foreign court's objection to an order by the English court which is liable to frustrate what has gone before and waste the resources which have been expended on the foreign proceedings.

On the facts, the injunction granted was not regarded as leading to wastage because it was limited only to enforcement against specified English assets, and the foreign judgment remained enforceable against assets elsewhere.[29]

C. Interference with Foreign Legal Systems

In addition, two related considerations have generally been regarded as highly relevant in inhibiting the exercise of the power to grant anti-enforcement injunctions. First, it would be against international comity because it should be up to each legal system to decide whether to recognise or enforce judgments from other countries.[30] Second, in the case of restraint operating in the originating state of the foreign judgment, the anti-enforcement injunction is regarded as an even more serious infringement of international comity in indirectly interfering with the recognition and enforcement of the country's own judgments.[31] On the facts of *SAS Institute*, however, they were not regarded as weighty factors insofar as the injunction sought only to prevent enforcement against assets considered to be within the jurisdiction of the English court,[32] contrary to a prior English judgment and English public policy.

These are indeed serious encroachments, albeit indirect. But it is also a serious encroachment for an anti-suit injunction to prevent a party from litigating in a foreign court instead of letting the foreign court decide for itself whether it would take jurisdiction to hear the case and to apply the relevant rules of private international law and the resulting substantive law to determine the parties' rights and liabilities. As a matter of principle, it is not clear why it is obviously more serious to interfere with recognition or enforcement of judgments by foreign courts than to interfere with the recognition and enforcement of laws by foreign courts,[33] apart

---

[29] Ibid [106].
[30] Ibid [105]; *Ecobank* (n 27) [136]; *ED & F Man* (n 13) 437; *Sun Travels* (n 12) [92]; *Akai Pty Ltd v People's Insurance Co Ltd* [1998] 1 Lloyd's Rep 90 (QB) 108 (hereafter *Akai*).
[31] *SAS Institute* (n 14) [97]–[98]; *ED & F Man* (n 13) 437–8; *Ecobank* (n 27) [136]; *Sun Travels* (n 12) [92], [98]; *Masri* (n 13) [93].
[32] cf *SAS Institute* (n 14) [99].
[33] Neither is the opposite view—that interfering (indirectly) with a foreign court's jurisdiction is 'inherently more invasive' than interfering (indirectly) with the enforcement of its judgments (*ICC Case No 17176, Final Award* [2016] 41 YB Comm Arb 86–126)—sustainable in principle.

from the common law courts being more familiar with, and used to, the latter.[34] Moreover, the fact that the foreign court has given judgment affirming its own jurisdiction is not regarded as a bar to the court of the forum granting an anti-suit injunction,[35] even though the injunction will clearly interfere with the effect of the foreign court's judgment within its own territory, albeit on a jurisdiction point.

The difference between the anti-suit injunction and the anti-enforcement injunction is not one of kind but of degree. There is a spectrum.[36] As Rix J noted in *The Eastern Trader*:[37] 'to injunct a party from reliance on its foreign judgment is a far greater interference in the judicial process than occurred in *The Angelic Grace*, where the foreign proceedings were still in their infancy'.

The point on the spectrum at which the application for an injunction is made will have implications for the very important consideration of wastage of resources of the litigants as well as courts and witnesses. The earlier it is sought, the less is the damage done to international comity. The anti-enforcement injunction is usually sought after the foreign judgment has been given, which is why applications tend to occur at the wrong end of the spectrum. Indeed, an attempt to seek one early is likely to fail on the basis that the application is premature. In *Akai Pty Ltd v People's Insurance Co Ltd*,[38] an application for an anti-enforcement injunction to restrain the enforcement of a future judgment from a foreign court taking jurisdiction in proceedings started in breach of an exclusive English jurisdiction agreement was rejected by the English court, as there was no judgment yet and no suggestion that the anti-suit injunction which the court had granted would not be obeyed.

It is far from being suggested that indirect interference with foreign processes does not raise important considerations of comity; it is only suggested that it is of equal importance or unimportance whether the court is dealing with an anti-suit or anti-enforcement injunction.[39] Thus, to the extent that comity in the sense of interference with foreign laws is a reduced factor in anti-suit injunctions when the court is concerned with enforcing contractual obligations, it should operate in the same way whether what is sought is an anti-suit or anti-enforcement injunction. On the other hand, delay causing wastage remains a significant factor in

---

[34] At least at the giving, though perhaps not the receiving, end: Adrian Briggs, 'The Principle of Comity in Private International Law' (2012) 354 *Recueil des Cours* 65, 125–6.
[35] *Ecobank* (n 27) [133]; *Lakshmi v Jhaveri* [2019] 2 SLR 372 (CA) [102]–[105].
[36] Helpfully illustrated in *Ecobank* (n 27) [133].
[37] *The Eastern Trader* (n 13) 603.
[38] *Akai* (n 30) 108.
[39] This essay does not address the important related question whether anti-suit (and anti-enforcement) injunctions should give way to damages: *Starlight Shipping Company v Allianz Marine & Aviation Versicherungs AG* [2014] EWCA Civ 1010, [2014] 2 Lloyd's Rep 544 (hereafter *Starlight Shipping*) and perhaps even declarations of the existence and breach of choice of court agreements (*Starlight Shipping Co v Allianz Marine & Aviation Versicherungs AG* [2014] EWHC 3068 (Comm) and Piraeus Court of Appeal Nr 89/31.01.2020) as a matter of international comity. See further Edwin Peel's essay (ch 12).

international comity even when the injunction is sought to enforce an obligation, at least to the extent that the wastage is caused by the applicant's lack of vigilance.

D. The Importance of Primary Obligations

There is, however, an important difference between enforcing an agreement by putting the parties in the position as if the agreement had been performed, and enforcing an agreement by compelling performance. While it remains an open question what role choice of law has in injunctions to protect contractual rights, courts have generally proceeded on the application of the *lex fori*.[40] Most relevant cases coming before the English courts have involved English jurisdiction or arbitration agreements governed by English law.[41] In principle, the question whether there is a contractual obligation and if so whether it has been breached is a substantive contract law question governed by the applicable law of the contract,[42] but whether the injunction will be ultimately granted raises a question of procedure governed by the *lex fori*. On the basis of English common law, injunctive relief is more readily available when it is sought to protect a negative covenant than when it is sought to undo the consequences of a breach of contract. In the context of domestic contract law in *Doherty v Allman*, Lord Cairns explained that no question of balance of convenience is involved when it is a simple matter of getting the contracting party to perform the negative bargain.[43] In *Hampstead & Suburban Properties Ltd v Diomedous*,[44] Megarry J applied this principle even to interim injunctions, stating that where there is a plain and uncontested breach of a clear negative covenant, then in the absence of special circumstances the contracting party should be restrained from its breach. The common law's robust attitude towards enforcing negative contractual obligations can explain the ready availability of the anti-suit injunction to protect a contracting party's right not to be sued in a

---

[40] Adrian Briggs, 'The Unrestrained Reach of an Anti-suit Injunction: A Pause for Thought' [1997] LMCLQ 90 (hereafter Briggs, 'The Unrestrained Reach of an Anti-suit Injunction'); Richard Garnett, *Substance and Procedure in Private International Law* (OUP 2012) [4.57]; Cameron Sim, 'Choice of law and Anti-suit Injunctions: Relocating Comity' (2013) 62 ICLQ 703; Thomas Raphael, *The Anti-Suit Injunction* (OUP 2008) [7.06]–[7.07]; Tiong Min Yeo, *Choice of Law for Equitable Doctrines* (OUP 2004) [4.49]–[4.78].

[41] The English court (*Akai* (n 30) 108) approved of the practice in Singapore (*People's Insurance Co Ltd v Akai Pty Ltd* [1998] 1 SLR 206 (HC)) of not intervening with an anti-suit injunction when the substantive dispute in question is subject to the exclusive jurisdiction of a foreign court.

[42] See especially Briggs, 'The Unrestrained Reach of an Anti-suit Injunction' (n 40). This raises a common law choice of law question since Regulation (EC) No 593/2008 of the European Parliament and of the Council of 17 June 2008 on the law applicable to contractual obligations (Rome I) [2008] OJ L177/6 (hereafter Rome I Regulation) does not apply to choice of court agreements: Art 1(2)(e). See further *Enka Insaat Ve Sanayi AS v OOO Insurance Company Chubb* [2020] UKSC 38, [2020] 1 WLR 4117.

[43] (1878) 3 App Cas 709 (HL) 719–20; see also *Jaggard v Sawyer* [1995] 1 WLR 269 (CA).

[44] [1969] 1 Ch 248 (Ch D). This principle is also part of Singapore law: *RGA Holdings International Inc v Loh* [2017] 2 SLR 997 (CA).

foreign jurisdiction,[45] whether of a permanent or interlocutory nature. The traditional justification that damages would naturally be manifestly inadequate[46] may not survive modern developments on damages for breaches of choice of court agreements.[47] On the other hand, contractual enforcement may be defeated by strong reasons[48] because of the procedural context of anti-suit injunctions and the additional dimension of international comity that applies.

If there is a primary obligation in a contract not to enforce or rely on a foreign judgment,[49] then equity acts *in personam* not just in the operational sense that it is the only way equity can operate, but in the substantive sense that it is enforcing a contractual obligation between the parties.[50] The justification for the reduced role of international comity when the court is enforcing a primary obligation is that the court is only ordering the party in breach to refrain from doing what he promised not to do. This is how an anti-suit injunction traditionally works, and the similarity between the anti-suit injunction to enforce a promise not to sue in a particular court(s) and a promise not to enforce a foreign judgment has been judicially noted.[51] The analogy with the Chancery court enforcing personal equities to justify taking jurisdiction over disputes involving foreign immovable property[52] is the strongest when the court is concerned with enforcing a primary obligation.[53]

It is a different situation if the enforcement of the foreign judgment is not itself a breach of a primary obligation, but a consequence of a prior breach of a primary obligation in the commencement of foreign proceedings. An injunction that is granted not to enforce a primary right but to reduce the losses suffered by the innocent party to a breach of contract (or any wrong, for that matter) cannot be explained in the same way. The secondary obligation to pay compensatory damages does not correlate to a right to performance. It is a policy decision how to balance the protection of rights with an acceptable level of interference with foreign legal

---

[45] *Clearlake Shipping Pte Ltd v Xiang Da Marine Pte Ltd* [2019] EWHC 2284 (Comm) at [18].
[46] *Continental Bank NA v Aeakos Compania Naviera SA* [1994] 1 WLR 588 (CA) 598; *The Angelic Grace* (n 10) 96; *Schiffahrtsgesellschaft Detlev Von Appen GmbH v Voest Alpine (The Jay Bola)* [1997] 2 Lloyd's Rep 279 (CA) 190; *OT Africa Line Ltd v Magic Sportswear Corpn* [2005] EWCA Civ 710, [2006] 1 ALL ER (Comm) 32 [33].
[47] *Donohue* (n 9) [48]; *Starlight Shipping* (n 39). See further Edwin Peel's essay in this collection (ch 12).
[48] Text to n 9. Thus, the reference to the lack of judicial discretion in the award of such remedy in *Doherty v Allman* (n 43) has been described as an oversimplification at least in the context of anti-suit injunctions: *Skype Technologies SA v Kasesalu* [2009] EWHC 2783 (Ch) at [29]–[31] and *Hamilton-Smith v CMS Cameron McKenna LLP* [2016] EWHC 1115 (Ch) at [71].
[49] Text to n 54.
[50] *Penn v Baltimore* (1750) 1 Ves Sen 444, 27 ER 1132 (hereafter *Penn*) is the classic case where the Chancery court justified taking jurisdiction over the defendant to order the performance of a contractual promise to go to arbitration on a dispute relating to title to immovable property overseas.
[51] Text to n 79. See, however, Andrew Dickinson's essay in this collection (ch 4)—esp Section C.3.
[52] *Penn* (n 50).
[53] See also Edwin Peel, 'The Legacy of *Penn v Lord Baltimore*', in Timothy Endicott, Joshua Getzler, and Edwin Peel (eds), *Properties of Law: Essays in Honour of Jim Harris* (OUP 2006) 218, 237 (fn 111); Adrian Briggs, 'Trusts of Land and the Brussels Convention' (1994) 110 LQR 526, 527.

processes. It is suggested that it is prudent to confine the reduced role of comity to cases where primary contractual rights are being enforced. On the other hand, it is harder to see a justification to differentiate between a primary obligation not to sue and a primary obligation not to rely on a judgment.

Where the foreign judgment has been obtained by a breach of contract (whether jurisdiction or arbitration clause), it is a separate question whether taking steps to recognise or enforce that judgment would amount to a breach of a contractual right. This involves a question of construction (in the broad sense encompassing both interpretation and implication of terms) of the jurisdiction or arbitration clause in question, but it will probably be an exceptional case that the clause incontrovertibly includes disputes as to judgments obtained in proceedings that contravened the clause. In many cases, the law applicable to the jurisdiction agreement will be relevant to extract the contractual intention either by way of interpretation of express terms or implication of terms.[54] Even if the clause is broad enough to include such disputes, it is also likely that the breach will be regarded as a continuing one that started from the commencement of the proceedings in breach of the clause resulting in the foreign judgment in question, and thus an application to enforce even this primary right will, even on reduced comity considerations, easily be defeated by delay in the application in the absence of exceptional circumstances.

If the reliance on the foreign judgment is not itself a breach of contract, then the basis of the injunction is not to enforce a primary obligation, but it is in the nature of an injunction to repair or undo the consequences of breach of contract. The purpose of such an injunction is not to prevent a breach of contract (which has already occurred) but to prevent or reduce the loss to the innocent party.[55] As a matter of domestic law, the threshold for the grant of such injunctions is higher than for an injunction to enforce a primary negative contractual obligation.[56] Economic waste even when not the result of the applicant's lack of vigilance can be an important consideration.[57] From the private international law perspective, the protection of a contractual right can still justifiably provide the sufficient interest for the forum to act, so that it will not be necessary to show vexatious and oppressive conduct independently, though it is thought that the latter will in any event be easily satisfied based on the prior breach in commencing and continuing the foreign proceedings. Wastage of resources is a highly relevant factor both as a matter of domestic law of injunctions and international comity considerations whether they are caused by

---

[54] In domestic English law, the relationship between interpretation and implication of contractual terms is a controversial one: *Marks and Spencer plc v BNP Paribas Securities Services Trust Co (Jersey) Ltd* [2015] UKSC 72, [2015] 3 WLR 1843; L Hoffman, 'Language and Lawyers' (2018) 134 LQR 553. For the position in Singapore law, see *Sembcorp Marine Ltd v PPL Holdings Pte Ltd* [2013] 4 SLR 193 (CA).

[55] It has the incidental effect of preventing the party in breach from benefiting from the breach of contract, though it is doubtful that this is the goal of the remedy in English contract law, at least in the absence of highly exceptional circumstances: *Attorney General v Blake* [2001] 1 AC 268 (HL).

[56] *Charrington v Simons & Co* [1970] 1 WLR 725 (Ch) 730.

[57] *Wrotham Park Estate Co Ltd v Parkside Homes Ltd* [1974] 1 WLR 798 (CA).

unwarranted delay in making the application, and should bear greater weight than when the forum is enforcing a primary contractual right. In the latter case, wastage should bear less weight if not caused by unwarranted delay of the applicant.

E. *Ellerman Lines*: Breach of Contract and Fraud

Given the constraints of international comity discussed in Sections B and C, it is not surprising that there are few cases on the anti-enforcement injunction in contrast to the rich body of case law on anti-suit injunctions. In recent years, however, there have been two Court of Appeal cases from England and Wales and one Court of Appeal decision from Singapore addressing the anti-enforcement injunction in contexts involving a breach of contract. All three cases relied heavily on one older case, involving both breach of contract and fraud.

Ellerman Lines Ltd v Read[58] was the first case where an application for an anti-enforcement injunction succeeded, and remains a leading case today. The defendant had contractually agreed to salvage the claimant's ship, and not to arrest the salvaged ship unless there was an attempt to remove it before security for the defendant's claim was provided. The defendant arrested the vessel in Turkey in spite of the provision of security, claiming to the Turkish court that he had not authorised his lawyers to agree to the amount of security offered. The claimant sued for damages for breach of contract in England and also sought an injunction to restrain the defendant from enforcing a Turkish judgment which had awarded a sum of money to the defendant for the salvage services. The High Court found that the defendant had committed a 'deliberate and shameless' breach of contract in arresting the vessel and had lied to the Turkish court about not having authorised his solicitors to agree to the security amount. The judge allowed the injunction to restrain against enforcement in England and refused the injunction claim for enforcement outside England on the basis that it had no power to do so, but nevertheless granted an interim injunction to the same effect pending appeal.

The Court of Appeal varied the decision, allowing the injunction to operate both in and out of England. Scrutton LJ, delivering the main judgment (Atkin LJ and Eve J concurring), granted the injunction without any territorial limitation on the basis that the defendant had commenced proceedings in the foreign jurisdiction in breach of contract, and had obtained the foreign judgment by fraud.[59] While it has not been questioned that the injunction could have stood on the basis of fraud alone, it is not clear whether the injunction could have stood on the basis of the breach of contract alone.

---

[58] [1928] 2 KB 144 (CA) (hereafter *Ellerman*).
[59] Ibid 152–3, 154, 156, 158.

The judgment of Atkin LJ is the clearest in suggesting that a breach of obligation on its own can justify an anti-enforcement injunction: [60]

> If the English Court finds that a person subject to its jurisdiction has committed a breach of covenant, or has acted in breach of some fiduciary duty or has in any way violated the principles of equity and conscience, and that it would be inequitable on his part to seek to enforce a judgment obtained in breach of such obligations, it will restrain him, not by issuing an edict to the foreign Court, but by saying that he is in conscience bound not to enforce that judgment. It was everyday procedure at one time for the Court of Chancery to restrain a person from proceeding upon a judgment obtained in a common law Court where it was necessary to do so.

Two further points are noteworthy. First, initially upon the merger of the administration of the common law and chancery jurisdictions, there would have been no need for an injunction to prevent the objectionable judgment from being recognised or enforced in the forum, because the equity upon which the Chancery court restrained parties by the common injunction against proceedings in the common law court could operate by way of defence after the merger of administration of the courts of common law and equity.[61] Indeed such an injunction was prohibited.[62] However, as a result of subsequent legislation, it is not entirely clear whether such an injunction is permissible under present English law.[63] In the modern context, the statutory defence will in any event apply to prevent recognition or enforcement in the United Kingdom.[64] Second, like the anti-suit injunction, the anti-enforcement injunction operates *in personam*, but likewise there will obviously be indirect interference with foreign jurisdictions, thus calling for caution as a matter of international comity. The '*in personam*' description only refers to the *modus operandi* of equity in preventing the enjoined party from asserting legal rights. It does

---

[60] Ibid 155.
[61] Judicature Act 1873, s 24(5). The equivalent provision in Singapore law is the Civil Law Act (Cap 43, Rev Ed 1999), s 3(e). A declaration would be a more appropriate remedy: *ED & F Man* (n 13) 437.
[62] Judicature Act 1873, s 24(5).
[63] The prohibition of the injunction in the Judicature Act 1873 (n 61) was continued by the Supreme Court of Judicature (Consolidation) Act 1925, s 41, but the latter provision was in turn repealed by the Senior Courts Act 1981 (originally named the Supreme Court Act 1981). Two High Court decisions have considered that the former restriction against granting injunctions in relation to pending proceedings before the High Court and Court of Appeal had been removed: *South West Trains Ltd v Wightman* [1997] EWHC 1160 (Ch), [1998] Pens LR 113, [96]–[97] (Neuberger J) and *Omega Engineering Inc v Omega SA* [2010] EWHC 1211 (Ch), [2010] FSR 26, [86]–[93] (Arnold J). The jurisdiction to treat the equity as a defence or a reason to stay proceedings remains: Senior Courts Act 1981, s 19(2)(b) and s 49(3). I am grateful to Andrew Dickinson for pointing me to these statutory provisions and authorities.
[64] Text to n 2. In Singapore law, an equivalent provision exists under the Reciprocal Enforcement of Foreign Judgments Act (Cap 265, Rev Ed 2001) (hereafter REFJA), which currently only applies to judgments from Hong Kong SAR. The position for other foreign judgments remains unclear, but if it had been possible to obtain an injunction from the chancery side to restrain the recognition or enforcement of the foreign judgment in the forum, then it should be a defence at common law today (n 61).

not necessarily mean that the injunction in question is one to enforce a personal obligation.

Although it can be said that the injunction in *Ellerman* was granted to enforce an agreement,[65] with the benefit of hindsight it would appear to be difficult to justify the decision on the basis of breach of contract alone. Whether the enforcement of the foreign judgment is considered a continuing breach of the agreement not to arrest the ship or is simply the consequence of the breach of the agreement (which could call for different considerations of comity), the delay in the application would in any event probably not have been excusable without the additional consideration of the fraudulent conduct of the defendant in the foreign proceedings. The prevention of the injustice of allowing a party to rely on a fraudulently obtained judgment weighs heavily in favour of the injunction. It tips the balance in favour of the innocent party who may have been careless in failing to discover the fraud or to act promptly.[66] International comity considerations are still relevant, but the objection based on interference with foreign legal systems would be outweighed by the personal order against the enjoined party from taking advantage of the fraudulently obtained judgment.[67] That the judgment has been obtained by fraud also means that the economic wastage argument is not applicable since the judgment should not be recognised or enforced in any jurisdiction. The economic wastage arises not from the grant of the injunction but from the fraud.

F. Three Modern Cases Involving Breach of Contract

Bank St Petersburg OJSC v Arkhangelsky[68] bears a superficial similarity to *Ellerman*.[69] The claimant had obtained judgments against the defendants in Russia and sought to enforce them in France and Bulgaria. After a number of cross-suits in other jurisdictions, the parties entered into a settlement agreement that all their substantive disputes would be resolved exclusively in the English court. Pursuant to this agreement, both sides commenced actions in England. The defendants then sought an interim anti-enforcement injunction, pending the outcome of the English proceedings, to stop the claimant from enforcing the Russian judgments in France and Bulgaria, alleging, *inter alia*, that the Russian judgments had been obtained by fraud. The injunction was denied by the High Court, but

---

[65] *SAS Institute* (n 14) [94].
[66] In the analogous (domestic) context of setting aside a domestic judgment, the party who had obtained the judgment by fraud cannot complain that the other party had been careless in not discovering and preventing the fraud: *Takhar v Gracefield Developments Ltd* [2019] UKSC 13, [2020] AC 450. A similar point was made in *Ellerman* (n 58) 153–4 in the context of assessing contractual damages.
[67] See further text to n 75.
[68] [2014] EWCA Civ 593, [2014] 1 WLR 4360 (hereafter *Bank St Petersburg*).
[69] *Ellerman* (n 58).

allowed by the Court of Appeal. There were two strands of reasoning in the judgment of Longmore LJ (with whom Kitchin and McCombe LJJ concurred). First, if the claimant were to lose in the substantive proceedings in England, it would have been contractually bound not to enforce the Russian judgments anywhere in the world, and this would prima facie justify an interim injunction.[70] Second, since a permanent anti-enforcement injunction would have been granted on the basis of *Ellerman* if the English court had found in the substantive trial that the Russian judgments had been obtained by fraud of the claimant, an interim injunction could properly be granted to maintain the status quo.[71]

Bank St Petersburg is similar to *Ellerman* in having two possible bases for an anti-enforcement injunction: breach of contract and fraud in obtaining the foreign judgment. The procedural difference between the interlocutory and final injunction respectively in the two cases is practically important as balance of convenience plays a significant role in the former case. This essay is, however, concerned with the impact of the contractual agreement on the availability of the anti-enforcement injunction in principle, that is, the permanent injunction. Like *Ellerman*, *Bank St Petersburg* does not unequivocally answer the question whether the contractual ground was a sufficient basis for the anti-enforcement injunction.

Longmore LJ thought that the facts of *Ellerman* were stronger because the English court in that case had already made a finding that the foreign judgment had been obtained by fraud, but he was able to justify an *interim* injunction as a holding position pending investigation by the court.[72] However, the facts of *Bank St Petersburg* are actually stronger than *Ellerman* on the contractual reasoning: while in *Bank St Petersburg* the hypothetical permanent injunction which justified the actual interim injunction aims to enforce a primary obligation in the contract not to enforce the Russian judgments anywhere,[73] the injunction in *Ellerman* was not to enforce the primary obligation not to sue in Turkey (it was too late for that), but to undo the consequences of that breach.[74] Longmore LJ did not appear too concerned about the indirect intrusions of the English injunction on the laws of France and Bulgaria on the recognition and enforcement of judgments. The injunction was not considered to cause unwarranted interference with the process of the French or Belgian courts, because it only operated *in personam* on the claimant.[75] Since all injunctions operate *in personam*, the reason must be found elsewhere. It is easily found in the enforcement of the negative primary contractual obligation not to rely on the foreign judgment.

---

[70] *Bank St Petersburg* (n 68) [29].
[71] Ibid [38].
[72] Ibid [38].
[73] Ibid [31].
[74] See Section D.
[75] *Bank St Petersburg* (n 68) [35]. See, however, the discussion of this point in Andrew Dickinson's essay in this collection (ch 4), Section C.3.

Ecobank Transnational Inc v Tanoh[76] was decided by the Court of Appeal shortly after *Bank St Petersburg*. The defendant was employed by the claimant under a contract which contained a London arbitration clause. After the defendant's employment was terminated, he sued the claimant in the Togolese Republic and the Ivory Coast. The claimant had defended on the merits of the dispute in the two proceedings as required by the laws of the two countries in order to maintain its objection to their respective jurisdictions on the basis of the arbitration clause, but lost on both jurisdiction and merits in both cases. The claimant had served notice of arbitration on the defendant about six or seven months after the commencement of the foreign proceedings. Nearly a year after the Togolese proceedings were commenced, the claimant sought and obtained an *ex parte* interim injunction from the English court to restrain the defendant from taking action to recognise or enforce the Togolese and Ivorian judgments anywhere in the world, pending the outcome of the arbitration proceedings. Subsequently, the High Court had found the claims in Togo, but not the claims in the Ivory Coast, were within the scope of the arbitration clause, but in any event discharged the interim injunction on the basis of the delay of the claimant in applying for the relief. The decision was affirmed on appeal.

Christopher Clarke LJ (with whom Etherton C and Patten LJ agreed), held that both sets of proceedings fell within the scope of the arbitration clause, but affirmed the High Court's exercise of discretion that the application failed on the basis of delay of the claimant in making the application to the English court. He reviewed the authorities, and dismissed the argument of the claimant that delay was not an obstacle where the object of the injunction was to protect the contractual rights of the claimant. His Lordship's extensive discussion of the comity factors, in particular of the wastage of resources caused by delay, was largely tracked in the later decision of *SAS Institute*.[77] He also stressed the importance of avoiding interference with the processes of foreign courts in recognising and enforcing foreign and local judgments:[78] the fact that the injunction would only operate *in personam* did not appear to cure that problem, in contrast with the situation in *Bank St Petersburg*. In distinguishing *Bank St Petersburg*, three points in particular were noted. First, the parties in *Bank St Petersburg* had agreed, after the foreign judgments had been obtained, not to enforce the judgments pending the outcome of the English proceedings. Secondly, there was no question of delay in the application for the injunction. Thirdly, the anti-enforcement injunction in that case served a similar function as an anti-suit injunction.[79] The first and third points emphasised that the injunction in *Bank St Petersburg* was to enforce a primary contractual obligation,

---

[76] *Ecobank* (n 27).
[77] *SAS Institute* (n 14). See Section B.
[78] *Ecobank* (n 27) [136].
[79] Ibid [117].

and delay was not an issue because the primary obligation arose after the foreign judgments had been obtained.

Ecobank was substantially followed in Singapore in *Sun Travels and Tours Pvt Ltd v Hilton International (Maldives) Pvt Ltd*.[80] An arbitral tribunal seated in Singapore had made two awards in favour of the claimant. The claimant sought to enforce the awards in the Maldives but there had been some confusion about which court had jurisdiction over the enforcement process. In the midst of the confusion, the defendant commenced legal proceedings against the claimant in the Maldives, basically relitigating the issues decided by the tribunal in Singapore. The claimant defended on the merits as it was the only way to maintain its objection to the jurisdiction of the court. By the time the claimant had found the right judicial route to enforce the arbitral awards (the enforcement proceedings), the Maldivian court had given judgment in the defendant's favour in the substantive proceedings, resulting in the Maldivian court in the enforcement proceedings refusing enforcement of the awards because of *res judicata* effect of the prior judgment of its own jurisdiction in the substantive proceedings. The claimant appealed in both proceedings in the Maldives, and in the meantime sought remedies from the Singapore court. The High Court granted an anti-enforcement injunction to restrain the defendant from relying on the Maldivian judgment from the substantive proceedings in the Maldivian enforcement proceedings.[81] In the Court of Appeal, the main question[82] was the correctness of the grant of this anti-enforcement injunction.

Delivering the judgment of the Court of Appeal, Chong JA refused to grant the anti-enforcement injunction. After reviewing the case law discussed above,[83] he held that an anti-enforcement injunction will only be granted if, over and above the requirements for an anti-suit injunction, there were exceptional circumstances to justify making an order of this kind.[84] He accepted that the Maldivian proceedings started by the defendant was a breach of the arbitration agreement[85] and was also vexatious and oppressive in the circumstances.[86] However, following closely the analysis of comity in *Ecobank*, he refused the injunction in view of the delay of the claimant in making the application to the Singapore court, allowing the Maldivian

---

[80] *Sun Travels* (n 12).

[81] *Hilton International Manage (Maldives) Pvt Ltd v Sun Travels & Tours Pvt Ltd* [2018] SGHC 56.

[82] The claimant had also obtained a declaration that the proceedings in the Maldives were in breach of the arbitration agreement between the parties, with the rider that the defendant was free to raise defences to the enforcement of the awards under Maldivian law. This was readily affirmed by the court.

[83] With the exception of *SAS Institute* (n 14) which had not been decided at that time.

[84] *Sun Travels* (n 12) [67], [97]–[99], [116].

[85] The relevant breach was an implied obligation not to take steps to undermine the award (other than to defend in enforcement proceedings) in any other jurisdictions than the seat of the arbitration. It was regarded as 'contrived' to characterise the defendant's Maldivian proceedings (on liability) as a breach of the arbitration clause after the arbitration process had concluded: *Hilton International Manage (Maldives) Pvt Ltd v Sun Travels & Tours Pvt Ltd* (n 81) [54]–[55], [58], applying *C v D* [2007] EWCA Civ 128, [2008] 1 Lloyd's Rep 239 [17].

[86] *Sun Travels* (n 12) [116], [125].

proceedings to proceed to judgment and even to appeal. The fact that it had entered the merits because it needed to do so to continue protesting jurisdiction cut no ice with the court; it should have sought the injunction from the Singapore court early on, even if it was content to carry on with the Maldivian proceedings simultaneously.[87] The court did not directly address the question whether the claimant had submitted to the jurisdiction of the Maldivian court in objecting to the jurisdiction on the basis on the arbitration agreement[88] or entering the merits in order to maintain its jurisdictional objection,[89] as the delay was already fatal to its claim.

Chong JA opined that while the categories of exceptional circumstances required over and above the requirements for an anti-suit injunction are not closed, they include fraud,[90] or when the applicant is not guilty of unconscionable delay, for example where it did not know of the foreign proceedings until the delivery of the judgment.[91] The characterisation of the lack of unconscionable delay as amounting to exceptional circumstances to justify granting an injunction appears odd at first blush because unconscionable delay is a general *defence* to the remedy of injunction, and its absence should be characteristic of all successful injunction applications. This demonstrates that, consistent with the English law approach in *SAS Institute*,[92] the exceptional circumstances in the Singapore approach is in substance not an independent jurisdictional requirement. Instead, as an application for an anti-enforcement injunction in the context of a foreign judgment obtained in breach of a jurisdiction or arbitration clause would ordinarily be made too late, exceptional circumstances are required to overcome that practical hurdle.

However, Chong JA was also reluctant to endorse the justification of the anti-enforcement injunction in *Bank St Petersburg* based on the parties' agreement made after the foreign judgments had been obtained, preferring to justify it on the basis that there had been no unconscionable delay in the claimant's application for the injunction,[93] in spite of the observation in *Ecobank* that this alone provided strong grounds to justify the injunction in that case.[94] He observed that 'it is not easy to understand why party autonomy should gain primacy merely because it manifested after a judgment'.[95] With respect, the primacy has nothing to

---

[87] Ibid [118].
[88] This could have raised somewhat troublesome issues because the common law rule in *Henry v Geoprosco International Ltd* [1976] QB 726 (CA) that objecting to the exercise of jurisdiction of a foreign court amounts to submission to its jurisdiction, has not been statutorily overruled in Singapore except in the very limited context of the REFJA (n 64), which did not apply to the case.
[89] Submission was regarded as a strong factor against granting an injunction in *SAS Institute* (n 14) [114], adopting the view of Professor Briggs in Briggs, *Civil Jurisdiction and Judgments* (n 2) [5.36].
[90] *Sun Travels* (n 12) [100], following *Ellerman* (n 58).
[91] *Sun Travels* (n 12) [105].
[92] *SAS Institute* (n 14).
[93] *Sun Travels* (n 12) [104].
[94] *Ecobank* (n 27) [117]. See also Steven Gee, *Commercial Injunctions* (6th edn, Sweet & Maxwell 2016) [14-055]; Richard Fentiman, *International Commercial Litigation* (2nd edn, OUP 2015) [16.04]; David Joseph, *Jurisdiction and Arbitration Agreements and Their Enforcement* (Sweet & Maxwell 2015) [12.98].
[95] *Sun Travels* (n 12) [104].

do with timing. It arose because of the undertaking of a primary obligation not to enforce the foreign judgment, which is readily enforced in equity as a negative covenant and which has traditionally been regarded as an enforcement of a personal right which justifies the indirect interference with foreign legal processes. In both *Ecobank* and *Sun Travels*, the case for the injunction was based on the breach of an obligation not to sue which resulted in the judgment, and not the breach of an obligation not to rely on the judgment.[96] This explains why the interference with foreign laws on the recognition and enforcement of judgments was an important factor in *Ecobank*[97] and *Sun Travels*[98] but not in *Bank of Petersburg*.[99]

Instead, Chong JA explained *Bank St Petersburg* on the basis of absence of delay on the part of the applicant and an application of the exception in *Ellerman*[100] (which he interpreted as resting solely on the ground of fraud[101]). It is not entirely clear whether these were considered as alternative or cumulative reasons. Logically they need not be cumulative, since they are listed as alternative grounds for justifying an anti-enforcement injunction.[102] If they are alternative, then since absence of delay only removes a barrier to getting an injunction and does not explain the basis of the injunction, the basis is either contract enforcement or fraud. But since fraud is the alternative ground, the absence of delay logically references the contractual enforcement ground anyway. One hopes for future clarification from the Singapore Court of Appeal.

G. Agreements to Discharge Judgment Debts

An agreement not to rely on a foreign judgment is not the same as an agreement to discharge or release a judgment obligation. If the discharge or release of a judgment debt is valid under the law (including private international law) of the originating country of the foreign judgment, then there is no enforceable judgment at source. The discharge will be valid by its law only if the contract is valid under its choice of law rules. This resembles an 'incidental question' analysis in the application of the contract choice of law rules of the originating country. In fact, it is not a choice of law question but a question of determining whether the foreign judgment has legal effect under the law of the originating country.[103] If the judgment debt is discharged under the law of the originating country, even if there is no promise not to

---

[96] See Section D.
[97] *Ecobank* (n 27) [136].
[98] *Sun Travels* (n 12) [92]–[93].
[99] *Bank St Petersburg* (n 68) [35].
[100] *Sun Travels* (n 12) [104].
[101] Ibid [100].
[102] Ibid [100]–[101], [105].
[103] It therefore avoids the question whether the Rome I Regulation (n 42) can be bypassed if the contract choice of law question arises as a true incidental question.

enforce the judgment anywhere in the world, it will not be difficult to make out a case of vexatious and oppressive conduct if the judgment creditor insists on trying to enforce it against the judgment debtor in a foreign country.[104] If the discharge is valid under the law applicable to the contract as determined in the forum where the judgment is sought to be enforced, there is a defence to the enforcement of the judgment debt in the forum.[105] Under the common law, the judgment debt in the forum is a distinctive legal creation of the law of the forum to enable the enforcement of foreign judgment. It does not necessarily follow that the judgment debt will be regarded as discharged in the originating country, or in other countries.

Whether a promise not to rely on the judgment anywhere in the world can be implied from a contract of release or discharge is a question of interpretation or of the implication of a term according to the law applicable to the contract.[106] This may depend to some extent on whether the parties had negotiated with reference to the effect of the judgment in one country only, or with respect to the effect of the judgment across borders.[107]

H. Conclusion

The breach of a choice of court or arbitration agreement presents one typical scenario where an anti-enforcement injunction may be sought. The case law has demonstrated that it will be difficult to obtain, primarily because of delay in the application giving rise not only to the question of the conduct of the party seeking the injunction but also to important implications for comity, particularly in terms of wasted resources for the respondent and foreign courts. In the absence of such inhibiting factors, the question is the weight to be given to the separate consideration of interference with the foreign court's legal processes. The general proposition, at least in the context of anti-suit injunctions, is that this factor recedes in significance when the court is enforcing contractual rights. The position for anti-enforcement injunctions appears to be less clear.

---

[104] Except perhaps if there is evidence that the foreign country would allow the enforcement notwithstanding its having no effect in the originating country, but this might invoke the public policy considerations of perversity: *Carl Zeiss Stiftung v Rayner & Keeler* [1967] 1 AC 853 (HL), 922; *Air Foyle Ltd v Center Capital Ltd* [2003] 2 Lloyd's Rep 753 (QB), 761.

[105] In *Kuhadas v Gomez* [2014] FCCA 1130, a contract assumed by the Federal Circuit Court of Australia to be governed by the law of the forum (at [41]) was held to discharge a judgment debt arising from a Singapore judgment. The court was only concerned with the effect of the Singapore judgment in the forum. The decision was affirmed on appeal in *Gomez v Kuhadas (No 2)* [2015] FCA 561, the Federal Court ruling that it made no difference even if the contract was governed by Singapore law (at [58]) (on the same premise of the application of Australian choice of law rules for contracts).

[106] Text to n 54.

[107] In a different context, because the parties in *Bank St Petersburg* (n 68) were negotiating with reference to the cross-border effect of the Russian judgments, it was not difficult for the English court to reach the conclusion that the jurisdiction agreement encompassed a promise not to enforce the Russian judgments should the defendant lose in the substantive proceedings in the English court.

This essay has suggested that the emerging case law is consistent with differentiating between enforcing a primary negative obligation and enforcing contractual rights in the broader sense of making orders to put the innocent party in the position as if the breach had not occurred. The former calls for stronger protection and is traditionally the basis for the court justifying the indirect interference with foreign jurisdictions: the court is only ordering the party injuncted to refrain from doing what he has promised or undertaken not to do. It is a different thing to make an order to remedy the consequences of breach of contract (or any other wrong) which includes refraining from taking steps to assert legal rights available in foreign jurisdictions.

It has also suggested that a contractual promise not to rely on a judgment should be protected to the same extent as a contractual promise not to sue. For example, it is not uncommon for settlement agreements to contain clauses not to sue anywhere on matters covered by the settlement, and these are readily enforceable by anti-suit injunctions.[108] It will also not be uncommon for settlement agreements to contain promises not to enforce judgments or awards already obtained.[109] These promises should be protected to the same extent. There will be other situations in which a contractual promise or other undertaking deserves the same level of judicial protection. Atkin LJ in *Ellerman* gave the examples of a person assigning his rights in a foreign judgment to another for value and agreeing not to enforce the judgment abroad except for the benefit and with the consent of the assignee, and an agent who has obtained a foreign judgment on behalf of his principal and who then seeks to enforce it for his own benefit contrary to the instructions of his principal.[110] These are primary obligations in contract and fiduciary law[111] respectively. The weight of other comity factors will vary from case to case. For example, the waste of resources is not cured in the settlement agreement example, but is arguably excusable in the interest of finality of dispute resolution. In the examples of Atkin LJ, there is arguably no real problem of wastage of resources as the only question is who is the right party to enforce the foreign judgment.

An additional dimension in Singapore (but not English) law is the Singapore Convention on Mediation,[112] taking legal effect in Singapore from September 2020.[113] Singapore will be obliged to enforce[114] an international mediated

---

[108] eg *Ashlock v SetClear Pte Ltd* [2012] 2 SLR 625 (CA).

[109] *Ecobank* (n 27) is one example.

[110] *Ellerman* (n 58) 154–5.

[111] While inadequacy of damages is not a serious consideration for injunction to enforce a negative contractual obligation (see text to nn 43–46), it is irrelevant to an injunction to restrain a breach of fiduciary duty.

[112] United Nations Convention on International Settlement Agreements Resulting from Mediation, GA Res 73/198, UN GAOR, 73rd session, 62nd plenary meeting, Agenda item 80, UN Doc A/RES/73/198 (20 December 2018) (adopted 20 December 2018, entered into force 12 September 2020) (hereafter Singapore Convention on Mediation).

[113] Singapore Convention on Mediation Act 2020, Act No 4 of 2020 (hereafter Singapore Convention Act).

[114] Singapore Convention on Mediation (n 112), Art 3(1).

settlement agreement falling within the scope of the statute. Such an agreement will be recorded as an order of court and enforced in the same manner as a judgment or order granted by the High Court.[115] If the settlement agreement contains a promise not to enforce a judgment (whether Singapore or foreign) anywhere, it will have the effect of a worldwide anti-enforcement injunction granted by the Singapore court, unless one of the defences apply. The relevant defences for this purpose are where enforcement of the agreement would be contrary to the public policy of Singapore, or where the subject matter of the dispute purported to be settled is not capable of settlement by mediation under Singapore law.[116] It is difficult to see how holding the parties to their bargain can be against Singapore public policy, or how judgments cannot be the subject of a mediated settlement.

---

[115] Singapore Convention Act (n 113), s 5(2)(a).
[116] Ibid s 7(3).

11
'A Peculiarly Pointless Line of Division': Recognition of Proceedings and Non-proceedings Divorces under the Family Law Act 1986

Máire Ní Shúilleabháin

A. Introduction

The overseas divorce recognition scheme laid down in Part II of the Family Law Act 1986 hinges on a distinction between divorces obtained by 'judicial or other proceedings'[1] (hereafter 'proceedings divorces') and divorces obtained 'otherwise than by means of proceedings'[2] (hereafter 'non-proceedings divorces').[3] The Act extends generous recognition to divorces falling within the first category, and much more limited recognition to those within the second. Extra-judicial divorces straddle the two categories.

This essay will explore the rationality and impact of this distinction, and its tortuous development through the case-law of the English courts.[4] The essay will interrogate the policy interests cited in justification of these statutory filters, and evaluate their contemporary relevance. It will be argued that the disparate treatment of proceedings and non-proceedings divorces has led to a skewed scheme of divorce recognition which is incapable of realising its own stated policy objectives.

This 'peculiarly pointless line of division', as Professor Briggs terms it,[5] has, in turn, corrupted the rationality of related statutory schemes: the allocation of financial relief under Part III of the Matrimonial and Family Proceeding Act 1984, and the recognition of civil partnership dissolutions under the Civil Partnership Act 2004. These secondary repercussions will be analysed—and it will be argued

---

[1] Family Law Act 1986, s 46(1) (with 'proceedings' defined in s 54(1)) (hereafter FLA 1986).
[2] Ibid s 46(2).
[3] Ibid Pt II entered into force on 4 April 1988.
[4] While FLA 1986 (n 1) Pt II applies throughout the UK, this essay will focus on its implications for English law.
[5] Adrian Briggs, *Private International Law in English Courts* (OUP 2014) [12.102] (hereafter Briggs, *Private International Law in English Courts*).

Máire Ní Shúilleabháin, *'A Peculiarly Pointless Line of Division': Recognition of Proceedings and Non-proceedings Divorces under the Family Law Act 1986* In: *A Conflict of Laws Companion*. Edited by: Andrew Dickinson and Edwin Peel, Oxford University Press. © Máire Ní Shúilleabháin 2021. DOI: 10.1093/oso/9780198868958.003.0011

that this segregation of proceedings and non-proceedings divorces has exerted a profoundly negative influence, not only on the development of UK divorce recognition policy, but also on these related fields of statutory regulation.

This essay argues for a more thoughtful realignment of divorce recognition norms, and for the discontinuation of this irrational dichotomy, in particular at a time when the geographical scope of Part II of the 1986 Act has been enlarged as a result of the UK's departure from the EU.

Finally, the essay will also explore another related, and equally problematic, line of division affecting recognition of extra-judicial divorces under the 1986 Act, and criticised by Professor Briggs as 'beyond rational explanation':[6] the line drawn between 'mono-territorial'[7] and transnational divorces, precluding recognition of the latter.

B. An Historical Exegesis: The Origins of the Distinction between Proceedings and Non-proceedings Divorces

The 1970 Hague Convention on the Recognition of Divorces and Legal Separations (hereafter the 1970 Convention) provided for the recognition in one Contracting State of divorces 'obtained in another Contracting State' following 'judicial or other proceedings officially recognised in' that Contracting State.[8] Most of the countries participating in the negotiation of the 1970 Convention were European and common law states with a tradition of judicial divorce, but as the Chair, Professor Graveson, noted, it was possible to consider religious (non-judicial) divorces, 'Through the fortunate presence of the delegations of the United Arab Republic and Israel'.[9]

The 1970 Convention did not offer any definition of 'judicial or other proceedings', and the *Actes et Documents*[10] suggest that there was considerable disagreement on the scope of coverage of 'other proceedings'. While some delegates expressed concern at the inclusion of administrative and religious divorces,[11] others (particularly the United Kingdom) argued for a broad definition of proceedings, contesting the need for any 'officiality of the divorce procedure'[12] and submitting that 'a change of marital status ought to be recognized whatever may be the

---

[6] Ibid [12.104].
[7] Adrian Briggs, *The Conflict of Laws* (4th edn, OUP 2019) 323 (hereafter Briggs, *The Conflict of Laws*).
[8] Hague Convention on the Recognition of Divorces and Legal Separations (1970), Art 1 (hereafter 1970 Convention).
[9] Ronald Harry Graveson, 'The Tenth Session of the Hague Conference of Private International Law' (1965) 14 ICLQ 528, 552.
[10] Hague Conference on Private International Law, *Actes et Documents de la Onzième Session, Tome II, Divorce* (7–26 October 1968).
[11] Ibid 32, 100.
[12] Ibid 32.

method of divorce which the State provides or permits'.[13] The Explanatory Report of Professors Bellet and Goldman[14] is also inconclusive on this question, with some passages supporting a broad construction ('The nature and form of a divorce are of no importance: it may be judicial, administrative, religious or legislative')[15] and others suggestive of a more restrictive conception of 'proceedings' ('a State can refuse to recognize a dissolution of marriage even where it is legally effective in the State of origin, if it does not result from "proceedings"').[16] Thus, it seems 'judicial or other proceedings' was left deliberately vague and the negotiators accepted a fudge on this issue.[17] Nonetheless, it is important to note that pursuant to Art 17, the 1970 Convention would not 'prevent the application in a Contracting State of rules of law more favourable to the recognition of foreign divorces'. So, it was clear from the outset that there was no barrier to an interpretation of 'judicial or other proceedings' which was *more expansive* than that envisaged by the Convention (assuming a Convention meaning could be discerned).

The UK ratified the 1970 Convention and adopted the Recognition of Divorces and Legal Separations Act 1971 to give effect to its Convention obligations (making statutory provision for recognition of overseas divorces obtained in 'judicial or other proceedings',[18] alongside the retention of some traditional common law recognition principles).[19] Wildly differing interpretations of 'judicial or other proceedings' emerged in the case-law on the 1971 Act, with some judges preferring an inclusive, non-exhaustive definition (whereby any divorce effective under a foreign legal order could qualify)[20] and others articulating a sharp distinction between proceedings and non-proceedings divorces.[21]

In time, the 1971 Act was replaced by Part II of the Family Law Act 1986,[22] with Parliament choosing to perpetuate this distinction between proceedings and

---

[13] Ibid 83.
[14] Pierre Bellet and Berthold Goldman, *Explanatory Report on the 1970 Hague Convention on the Recognition of Divorces and Legal Separations* (English translation) (1971).
[15] Ibid 4.
[16] Ibid 7.
[17] See Susan Nott, '"Judicial or Other Proceedings": the Story to Date' (1985) 34 ICLQ 838, 838, 847 (hereafter Nott, 'Judicial or Other Proceedings'); A E Anton, 'The Recognition of Divorces and Legal Separations' (1969) 18 ICLQ 620, 627; Peter North, *The Private International Law of Matrimonial Causes in the British Isles and the Republic of Ireland* (North-Holland 1977) 226–7.
[18] Recognition of Divorces and Legal Separations Act 1971, ss 2–5 (hereafter RDLSA 1971).
[19] RDLSA 1971 (n 18), s 6.
[20] See eg Lord Scarman in *Quazi v Quazi* [1980] AC 744, 824 (HL) (hereafter *Quazi* (HL)); Bush J in *Zaal v Zaal* [1983] 4 FLR 284, 288 (HC); Taylor J in *R v Secretary of State for the Home Dept, ex p Fatima* [1985] QB 190, 195 (HC) (hereafter *Fatima* (HC)).
[21] See eg Wood J in *Sharif v Sharif* (1980) 10 Fam Law 216 (HC); Oliver LJ in *Chaudhary v Chaudhary* [1985] Fam 19 (CA) (hereafter *Chaudhary*).
[22] FLA 1986 (n 1) was originally intended 'to tidy up a number of difficulties of the earlier legislation' and to bring annulments (excluded from the scope of the 1970 Convention (n 8)) into the statutory scheme: see David Pearl, 'Family Law Act 1986, Part II' [1987] CLJ 35, 37 (hereafter Pearl, 'Family Law Act 1986'); Law Commission (and Scottish Law Commission), *Private International Law: Recognition of Foreign Nullity Decrees and Related Matters* (Law Com No 137 (Scot Law Com No 88), 1984) 5 (hereafter Law Com No 137).

non-proceedings divorces and to enshrine it in legislation (against the advices of the Law Commission in their 1984 Report[23]).

C. Two Distinct Schemes of Recognition under Section 46(1) and 46(2) of the 1986 Act

The Family Law Act 1986 provides for recognition of overseas 'proceedings' divorces (divorces obtained by means of 'judicial or other proceedings') where either spouse was habitually resident or domiciled[24] in, or a national of, the country where the divorce was obtained at the date of commencement of the proceedings (s 46(1)(b)). Thus, section 46(1) allows for recognition of almost all proceedings divorces,[25] although recognition may be refused where there is a public policy objection, an earlier irreconcilable judgment, or where there was a lack of notice or opportunity to take part in the divorce proceedings (s 51). It is also necessary to show that the divorce 'is effective under the law of the country in which it was obtained' (s 46(1)(a)).

The 1986 Act, at section 46(2), provides a much narrower window of recognition for non-proceedings divorces (divorces obtained 'otherwise than by means of ... judicial or other proceedings').[26] Such a divorce is recognised only if it is effective 'under the law of the country in which it was obtained' and if, at the date on which it was obtained, either both spouses were domiciled in that country, or one was domiciled there and the other was domiciled in a country which recognises the divorce (s 46(2)(a) and (b)).[27] It is also a pre-condition of recognition of non-proceedings divorces that neither party to the marriage was habitually resident in the UK throughout the period of one year immediately preceding the date on which the divorce was obtained (s 46(2)(c)). Section 51 sets out various grounds upon which non-proceedings divorces which are eligible for recognition under section 46(2) may be denied recognition after all: where there is a public policy objection, or an earlier irreconcilable judgment, or where there

---

[23] Law Com No 137 (n 22) 52.
[24] In FLA 1986 (n 1) s 46(1) (and in s 46(2)), 'domicile' refers to both the traditional common law conception and to any local conception within the family law system of the jurisdiction of origin of the divorce (s 46(5)).
[25] FLA 1986 (n 1) (and RDLSA 1971 (n 18)) went further than was required by the 1970 Convention (n 8), in discarding some of the additional requirements for divorce recognition (intended by the Convention as safeguards against forum shopping), and in extending the scheme to all foreign divorces (not just those from Contracting States). As indicated above, this more generous recognition of foreign divorces was permitted by Art 17 of the 1970 Convention (n 8).
[26] FLA 1986 (n 1) s 54 defines 'proceedings'.
[27] FLA 1986 (n 1) s 45(1) indicates that overseas divorces should be recognised 'if, and only if' they are entitled to recognition under s 46 (or another enactment), and the implication is that there is no further role for the common law recognition doctrine (previously retained under RDLSA 1971 (n 18) s 6): Law Com No 137 (n 22) 49, 93.

is no official document to certify effectiveness in the country of obtainment (or, where there was not a shared domicile in the country of obtainment to certify recognition in the country of domicile of a spouse domiciled outside of the country of obtainment).

The Law Commission had recommended a single scheme which would have allowed for the recognition of *all* overseas divorces (judicial, administrative, and informal) on the terms ultimately adopted for proceedings divorces under section 46(1).[28] Recognising the need to respect the UK's ratification of the 1970 Convention,[29] the Law Commission proposed a statutory formula facilitating recognition of foreign divorces obtained by means of 'judicial or other proceedings' but with a broad inclusive definition of 'judicial or other proceedings'.[30] This would have allowed for the extension of the same (s 46(1)) recognition criteria to divorces obtained in countries where 'there need be no proceedings before a court or indeed any other body at all' and even to 'bare *talaqs*' (repudiations taking effect simply through private pronouncement).[31] This latitude chimed with the Law Commission's 'general underlying policy ... of recognising the validity of divorces ... and of any later marriage entered into by the parties',[32] and it was envisaged that the public policy defence could be invoked to preclude recognition, where appropriate.[33]

In the event, however, Parliament declined to follow this recommendation, and as indicated above, the 1986 Act made separate provision for recognition of non-proceedings divorces on a much more restrictive basis. It is argued in this essay that this was a serious error, and that the Law Commission recommendations ought to have been heeded.

The Lord Chancellor gave the following reasons for declining to accept that non-proceedings divorces should be recognised on the same basis as other divorces:

> There are public policy elements here. Such divorces are informal, arbitrary and usually unilateral. More importantly, there is often no available proof that what is alleged to have taken place has taken place at all. In addition, these divorces are almost exclusively obtained by men and therefore discriminate against women. Finally, particularly where the wife is resident abroad, such divorces provide little or no financial protection for the wife and family.[34]

---

[28] Law Com No 137 (n 22) 94, 122.
[29] Ibid 5.
[30] Ibid 122: the Law Commission proposed that 'judicial or other proceedings' be defined as including 'acts which constitute the means by which a divorce ... may be obtained in that country and are done in compliance with the procedure required by the law of that country'.
[31] Ibid 50, 52.
[32] Ibid 6.
[33] Ibid 52.
[34] HL Deb 22 April 1986, vol 473, col 1082.

The Lord Chancellor also justified the 'more restricted recognition of such decrees' and the adoption of section 46(2) on the basis that it would 'give greater protection to wives resident in the United Kingdom whose husbands have obtained an informal divorce abroad' and that '[i]t would be wrong to deny a wife living here recourse to the protection of our own courts'.[35]

D. Rationality of the Disparate Treatment of Proceedings and Non-proceedings Divorces: A 'Peculiarly Pointless' Line of Division?

As has been seen in Section C., the restricted recognition of non-proceedings divorces (under section 46(2)) was motivated by concerns relating to gender-discrimination and protection of financially-dependent wives, and also by objections to informality, arbitrariness, unilateralism, and a lack of proof in foreign dissolutions. The soundness of these justifications will be interrogated in this section and it will be argued that, in fact, they cannot support the 'line of division' drawn in section 46.

1. Gender discrimination and financial provision

Parliament had every reason to be concerned about gender discrimination in the recognition of overseas divorces. Many foreign legal systems gave men preferential access to divorce, and in some systems based on Islamic traditions (or 'Sharia'), men could divorce their wives simply by oral repudiation (the 'bare *talaq*'), while women were confined to divorce by agreement or judicial divorce based on fault.[36] Divorce by repudiation or *talaq* was widely acknowledged to be the most common form of divorce in countries applying Islamic law, although increasingly, in the second half of the twentieth century, men pronouncing *talaq* were bound by obligations of notification or registration in most jurisdictions permitting this form of divorce.[37]

While it was entirely legitimate that Parliament would attempt to curtail recognition of gender-discriminatory divorce forms, it is submitted that the restricted

---

[35] Ibid.
[36] Najma Moosa, 'An Overview of Divorce and Dispute Resolution in Islamic Law' [2004] International Family Law 225, 227 (hereafter Moosa, 'Divorce in Islamic Law'); Judith Tucker, *Women, Family and Gender in Islamic Law* (CUP 2008) 86–100 (hereafter Tucker, *Women, Family and Gender*); Dawoud Sudqi El Alami and Doreen Hinchcliffe, *Islamic Marriage and Divorce Laws of the Arab World* (Kluwer 1996) 22–32 (hereafter El Alami and Hinchcliffe, *Islamic Marriage*).
[37] Moosa, 'Divorce in Islamic Law' (n 36) 225; El Alami and Hinchcliffe, *Islamic Marriage* (n 36) 22, 24; Tucker, *Women, Family and Gender* (n 36) 116–17; *H v S (Recognition of Overseas Divorce)* [2012] 2 FLR 157 [18]–[19] (HC) (hereafter *H v S*).

recognition of non-proceedings divorces was not the rational means to achieve this goal. The 1986 Act appeared to be underpinned by a Parliamentary assumption that formality in the divorce process protects women, and that informality is detrimental to their interests, when this is not necessarily true.[38] This misconceived assumption has distorted the logic of section 46, leading to over-inclusivity under both section 46(1) and section 46(2).[39]

Indeed it was anticipated by the Lord Chancellor that the section 46(2) non-proceedings category (viewed with suspicion and afforded limited recognition) would include not only traditional 'bare' *talaqs*, but also informal divorces concluded with the agreement of the wife, and in some cases at her instigation.[40] So it was accepted from the outset that section 46(2) would capture consensual divorce forms which are relatively unobjectionable from a gender equality perspective.[41] This should have prompted a re-evaluation of the approach being taken, but apparently it did not.

If section 46(2) was over-inclusive from the perspective of avoiding gender-discrimination, so too was section 46(1). This privileged category of 'proceedings divorces', afforded relatively untrammelled recognition under the 1986 Act, would include many unproblematic divorce forms—but also some kinds which are highly objectionable from a gender equality perspective, for instance, unilateral *talaqs* notified to state or religious authorities but not necessarily to the wife herself.[42]

The reality is that increased formalisation of the divorce process does not of itself ensure increased protection of women. If men have superior access to divorce in an overseas legal system, requirements of notification and registration may do little to redress that fundamental gender-imbalance.[43]

In dividing overseas divorces into proceedings and non-proceedings categories, and viewing the former with favour and the latter with disfavour, section 46 was,

---

[38] See James Young, 'The Recognition of Extra-Judicial Divorces in the United Kingdom' (1987) 7 Legal Studies 78, 82: 'the criterion of whether the divorce was obtained by proceedings fails to identify the offending class of divorces' (hereafter Young, 'Recognition of Extra-Judicial Divorces').

[39] See James Fawcett, Máire Ní Shúilleabháin, and Sangeeta Shah, *Human Rights and Private International Law* (OUP 2016) 690–4 for an assessment of the human rights implications of FLA 1986 (n 1) s 46 (hereafter Fawcett and others, *Human Rights and Private International Law*).

[40] HL Deb 22 April 1986, vol 473, col 1082.

[41] Young, 'Recognition of Extra-Judicial Divorces' (n 38) 82.

[42] See *H v H (Talaq Divorce)* [2007] EWHC 2945 (Fam), [2008] 2 FLR 857 [38] (hereafter *H v H (Talaq Divorce)*) indicating that the failure to notify the wife is not fatal to the validity of the *talaq* divorce under the 1961 Ordinance procedure in Pakistan. It was always envisaged that these divorces would be characterised as 'proceedings' divorces under FLA 1986 (see HL Deb 22 April 1986, vol 473, col 1082 referring to the case-law under RDLSA 1971 (n 18), and see *Quazi* (HL) (n 20) and the 1961 Ordinance discussed in Section E. below). See also *El Fadl v El Fadl* [2000] 1 FLR 175, 184 (HC) (hereafter *El Fadl*) where it is noted that Lebanese law did not require that the wife be given notice of a 'proceedings' *talaq* recognised under s 46(1).

[43] See Pearl, 'Family Law Act 1986' (n 22) 38 arguing that the radically different treatment under FLA 1986 (n 1) of (informal) Indian and Kashmiri *talaqs* by comparison with (more formal) Pakistani and Bangladeshi *talaqs* is 'certainly not justified by the limited reforms introduced into Pakistan and Bangladesh law'.

from a gender-equality perspective, off-target from the outset. This legislative approach over-estimated the value of formality and took no account of a woman's own assent to a divorce. Women were faced with recognition of objectionable 'proceedings' divorces and non-recognition of non-proceedings divorces instigated by themselves, or accepted by them. In the latter case, a woman who had remarried in reliance on a non-proceedings divorce, could find her second marriage invalidated on account of its non-recognition, [44] and her interests thwarted—notionally for the purpose of achieving gender equality.

Aside from the gender implications which were intrinsic to the structure of the 1986 Act itself (and discussed above), the section 46 categorizations have also had *external* consequences—under Part III of the Matrimonial and Family Proceedings Act 1984—which are equally problematic from the perspective of affected women. Part III of the 1984 Act had been adopted with a view to ensuring that dependent wives who had been divorced abroad (by *talaq* or otherwise) could still apply to the English courts for ancillary financial relief (and that this facility was not extinguished by their inability to petition for a domestic divorce).[45] Part III of the 1984 Act was particularly aimed at women who would otherwise 'face destitution' in circumstances where the foreign divorce law made no provision for financial support (a situation which was most likely to arise in the context of extra-judicial divorce).[46] However, the wording of Part III of the 1984 Act confined this relief to those who had been divorced overseas by way of 'judicial or other proceedings'.[47] At the time, it was almost certainly envisaged that this would be an inclusive formula (as per the Law Commission's recommendations, as discussed above)[48] but following the separate treatment of proceedings and non-proceedings divorces in the 1986 Act, the orthodox view is that Part III can only be invoked following the recognition of a proceedings divorce under section 46(1), and where a non-proceedings divorce is entitled to recognition under section 46(2), there can be no relief under Part III

---

[44] There is some uncertainty as to whether the recognition of the second marriage would depend on the divorce-recognition policies of FLA 1986 (n 1) in all circumstances or whether the status of the non-proceedings divorce under the law of her domicile at the time of the second marriage might have a role. Pearl, 'Family Law Act 1986' (n 22) 38 argues that FLA 1986 (n 1) would be generally determinative—but, in any event, it seems clear that s 46(2) could invalidate the second marriage if the woman remarries in England, or has become domiciled in England by the time of the remarriage. See Paul Torremans (ed), *Cheshire, North & Fawcett Private International Law* (15th edn, OUP 2017) 920, 926 (hereafter *Cheshire, North & Fawcett*).

[45] Law Commission, *Family Law: Financial Relief After Foreign Divorce* (Law Com No 117, 1982) 1–2, 21.

[46] Ibid 1–2. See also Lucy Carroll, 'Muslim Women and "Islamic Divorce" in England' in Ann Laquer Estin (ed), *The Multi-Cultural Family* (Ashgate 2008) 192.

[47] Section 12(1)(a) Matrimonial and Family Proceedings Act 1984 (hereafter MFPA 1984).

[48] Sebastian Poulter, 'Divorce—Recognition of Foreign Divorces—The New Law' (1987) Law Society Gazette 84 (253) (hereafter Poulter, 'Divorce-Recognition of Foreign Divorces'). At the time of adoption of MFPA 1984 (n 47), the case-law tended to favour an expansive definition of 'judicial or other proceedings': see n 20 above. The Court of Appeal decision in *Chaudhary* (n 21) advocating a sharp distinction between proceedings and non-proceedings divorces was handed down a few weeks after the adoption of MFPA 1984.

of the 1984 Act.[49] Thus, the line of division drawn in the 1986 Act appears to have subverted the aims of the 1984 Act to the detriment of women who were intended to be protected by that Act—and the Lord Chancellor's stated ambition (in terms of safeguarding the financial welfare of women) has been turned on its head (albeit unintentionally). Poulter argued that this 'flaw in the 1984 Act ... should have been put right as soon as it was discovered' but more than thirty years later, this gap in protection remains.[50]

2. Informality, arbitrariness, and unilateralism

As has already been mentioned, the 'proceedings' category includes many unilateral divorces—while the non-proceedings category includes many consensual ones. It therefore follows that the restricted recognition of non-proceedings divorces is not logically connected to the curtailment of unilateralism and the promotion of bilateralism in divorce—although this was one of the stated aims of the section 46 bifurcation.

At a more fundamental level, one must also question the legitimacy of the Lord Chancellor's objection to informal, arbitrary, and unilateral overseas divorces given that, at the time of the adoption of the Family Law Act 1986, English divorce law had already become a 'paper-based ... procedure' and 'primarily an administrative process'.[51] Whilst notionally divorce was by court order, in reality there was 'not a judicial inquiry into the truth'[52] and England had (since the introduction of the 'special procedure' in the 1970s[53]), 'something tantamount to immediate unilateral divorce on demand'.[54]

In 2017, English law began to move towards the digitisation of divorce,[55] with applicants invited to apply online.[56] The entitlement to unilateral divorce, without having to give reasons, and with minimum formality, has now been copper-fastened by the Divorce, Dissolution and Separation Act 2020. Thus, if concerns regarding unilateralism, informality, and arbitrariness in foreign divorce were ever

---

[49] See eg *H v S* (n 37) [8], [16]; *MET v HAT* [2013] EWHC 4247 (Fam); [2014] 2 FLR 692 [10]–[11] (hereafter *MET v HAT*) although it was suggested in *El Fadl* (n 42) 191 that 'judicial or other proceedings' might be given a different interpretation within the context of MFPA 1984 (n 47).

[50] Poulter, 'Divorce-Recognition of Foreign Divorces' (n 48). It seems, however, that this point is often overlooked in applications for relief under MFPA 1984 (n 47) Pt III: see eg *MAH v ZS* [2012] EWHC 3271 (Fam); *Z v A (Financial Remedies: Overseas Divorce)* [2012] EWHC 467 (Fam); [2012] 2 FLR 667.

[51] Liz Trinder and others, *Finding Fault? Divorce Law and Practice in England and Wales* (Nuffield Foundation 2017) 13, 72.

[52] Ibid 13.
[53] Ibid 28, 55.
[54] Ibid 10, 33.
[55] Ibid 31.
[56] See <https://www.gov.uk/apply-for-divorce> (accessed 24 July 2020).

really warranted, any such justification has been substantially eroded by subsequent developments in English divorce law and in the domestic consensus of how divorce should be administered.

3. Lack of proof

The Lord Chancellor advocated a restricted recognition of non-proceedings divorces on the basis that 'there is often no available proof that what is alleged to have taken place has taken place at all'.[57] He also noted the inclusion of a discretion 'to refuse to recognise one of these informal divorces where there is no official certificate that it is effective under the relevant law'[58] (a defence which is now enshrined in s 51(3)(b)(i) of the 1986 Act). The necessity for this discretion was questioned by Lord Meston who noted that the defence refers not to documentary evidence of divorce as such, but to certification of the effectiveness of the divorce under the legal system of origin.[59] He surmised 'that the real reason for a requirement of the official documentation is to make the job of officials, and in particular immigration officials, easier'.[60] He noted that 'There was no need for documentation before' and that 'Expert evidence in appropriate cases usually sufficed' and expressed concern that 'this requirement may well cause hardship to those who come from countries where there is simply no mechanism for producing such documentation ... Even in sophisticated legal systems such a document may not be easy to obtain.'[61] These criticisms were echoed in the literature: Professor Briggs describes this defence as 'baffling'[62] and McClean and Ruiz Abou-Nigm observe that 'it is not clear what policy is served by requiring a particular form of proof'.[63]

It is also interesting to note that while the 1986 Act can make divorce-recognition contingent on the availability of official certification of validity, the English common law rules impose no such requirement in the domain of foreign marriage recognition. Informal customary marriages—which are not documented in any way—are entitled to be recognised on the same terms as officially certified

---

[57] HL Deb 22 April 1986, vol 473, col 1082.
[58] Ibid, col 1083.
[59] Ibid, col 1094. FLA 1986 (n 1), s 51(3)(b)(i) and s 51(4) allow for non-recognition where there is no 'document certifying that a divorce ... is effective': this suggests that the certificate must affirm that the parties in question are validly divorced under the law in question (and that a more general confirmation of the effectiveness of a particular type of divorce would not suffice). Section 51(3)(b)(ii) also allows for non-recognition—in cases where one party was domiciled outside of the country of obtainment—on the basis of lack of certification of the effectiveness of the non-proceedings divorce in this other country.
[60] HL Deb 22 April 1986, vol 473, col 1094.
[61] Ibid.
[62] Briggs, *The Conflict of Laws* (n 7) 325.
[63] David McClean and Veronica Ruiz Abou-Nigm, *Morris: The Conflict of Laws* (9th edn, Sweet & Maxwell 2016) [12.036]. See also *Cheshire, North & Fawcett* (n 44) 1033; Pearl, 'Family Law Act 1986' (n 22) 36: Young, 'Recognition of Extra-Judicial Divorces' (n 38) 89.

marriages.[64] If Lord Meston is correct in suggesting that this section 51(3)(b)(i) defence is likely to be of particular relevance in the immigration context, it seems odd that there is considerable flexibility respecting proof of foreign marriage (which will be routinely invoked as a basis for entry) but less so for divorce (which must arise for consideration only in a small minority of cases where there is reliance on a second marriage).

4. Conclusion

It is entirely reasonable that UK law should seek to restrict recognition of gender-discriminatory divorces, in particular where there were strong party connections to the UK at the time of the divorce. However, the Act's prioritisation of formality did not advance this agenda—and in fact, in its interactions with the Matrimonial and Family Proceedings Act 1984, section 46 has been retrogressive. Concerns with unilateralism and arbitrariness were misplaced when they had already been abandoned within the domestic legal order. The focus on proof of foreign divorce is also perplexing when there is no equivalent requirement with respect to foreign marriage.

E. Practical Difficulty in Distinguishing Proceedings and Non-proceedings Divorces

The courts have experienced great difficulty[65] in devising a consistent, coherent legal test for distinguishing proceedings and non-proceedings divorces,[66] and the jurisprudence has often been unconvincing and contradictory.[67] Furthermore, even if the law were clear on how the line should be drawn, the classification of individual divorces requires (as Professor Briggs terms it) 'some intricate analysis of religious and foreign law'.[68] Thus, the difficulty in defining 'proceedings' is compounded by the complexities entailed in mapping this conception onto the relevant foreign law. This can lead to expensive, protracted proceedings involving multiple experts on foreign law.[69]

---

[64] *McCabe v McCabe* [1994] 1 FLR 410 (CA) (hereafter *McCabe*); *Alfonso-Brown v Milwood* [2006] EWHC 642 (Fam); [2006] 2 FLR 265 (hereafter *Alfonso-Brown*).
[65] See *H v S* (n 37) [23]; *El Fadl* (n 42) 186; *Quazi v Quazi* [1980] AC 744, 784–5, 788–9 (CA) (hereafter *Quazi* (CA)).
[66] FLA 1986 (n 1) provides no guidance beyond defining 'proceedings' as meaning 'judicial or other proceedings' (s 54). Arguing for a definition of 'the constituents of proceedings', see Alan Reed, 'Extra-Judicial Divorces Since *Berkovits*' [1996] Fam Law 100, 101.
[67] See EM Clare Canton, 'The Court of Appeal and Non-Judicial Divorces' (1985) 48 MLR 212, 220 (hereafter Canton, 'Non-Judicial Divorces'); Nott, 'Judicial or Other Proceedings' (n 17) 847.
[68] Briggs, *The Conflict of Laws* (n 7) 323.
[69] *Quazi* (CA) (n 65) 784; *Quazi* (HL) (n 20) 804, 819; *NP v KRP (Recognition of Foreign Divorce)* [2013] EWHC 694 (Fam), [2014] 2 FLR 1 [2] (hereafter *NP v KRP*); *H v H (The Queen's Proctor*

1. Defining 'proceedings': first interpretative steps in *Quazi* and *Chaudhary*

The only appellate authorities on the meaning of 'judicial or other proceedings' are *Quazi v Quazi*[70] and *Chaudhary v Chaudhary*,[71] both cases decided under the 1971 Act.[72] While these two cases provided some useful guidance—which is still routinely cited in the case-law on the 1986 Act—the value of these precedents is somewhat diminished by the lack of uniformity in the various judgments in each of the two cases[73] (with individual judgments conceptualising 'proceedings' in different ways). *Chaudhary* is also criticised for its 'questionable'[74] and 'dubious'[75] reasoning insofar as it seems to contradict aspects of the House of Lords judgments in *Quazi*. Nonetheless, it is possible to extract a consensus on certain questions from these two cases, and to identify a number of other common points of emphasis.

The House of Lords in *Quazi* confirmed (unanimously) that divorce in accordance with the formalised *talaq* procedure of Pakistan (and Bangladesh[76])—under the 1961 Muslim Family Laws Ordinance—should be considered a 'proceedings' divorce, and this has been accepted ever since.[77] Thus, there are 'proceedings' (and the divorce is eligible for s 46(1) recognition) where the husband is required to give notice to the Chairman of the Union Council of his pronouncement of divorce by *talaq*, and where the divorce can only become effective after the giving of such notice, and after the expiration of ninety days during which a reconciliation hearing may be convened.[78] In accepting a 'proceedings' characterisation for this process, the House of Lords were also unanimous in rejecting the Court of Appeal suggestion[79] that a state (or state-sanctioned) authority must have a right of veto over the divorce (in the sense that the external authority can deny a party's (or the parties') wish to be divorced).

Intervening) (Validity of Japanese Divorce) [2006] EWHC 2989 (Fam), [2007] 1 FLR 1318 [11] (hereafter *H v H (Japanese Divorce)*).

[70] *Quazi* (HL) (n 20).
[71] *Chaudhary* (n 21).
[72] These were confirmed as the only available appellate authorities on point in 2011 in *H v S* (n 37) [28]. To the author's knowledge, there has been no appellate authority on point since.
[73] See *H v S* (n 37) [26], [28].
[74] Canton, 'Non-Judicial Divorces' (n 67) 218.
[75] Lord Collins of Mapesbury and others (eds), *Dicey, Morris & Collins: The Conflict of Laws* (15th edn, Sweet & Maxwell 2012) [18.106] (hereafter Dicey, Morris & Collins).
[76] Poulter, 'Divorce-Recognition of Foreign Divorces' (n 48): the 1961 Ordinance is also in force in Bangladesh.
[77] See eg Dicey, Morris & Collins (n 75) [18.107]; *H v H (Talaq Divorce)* (n 42).
[78] *Quazi* (HL) (n 20) 806. The 1961 Ordinance also provides for notice to the wife, but while failure to give notice to the Union Chairman is fatal to the validity of the divorce, failure to give notice to the wife is not: *H v H (Talaq Divorce)* (n 42) [38].
[79] *Quazi* (CA) (n 65) 789.

The Court of Appeal in *Chaudhary* were unanimously of the view that a bare *talaq* (the classic Islamic divorce by oral repudiation only—effective in Kashmir) was not a proceedings divorce. (The House of Lords in *Quazi* had expressed mixed views—*obiter*—on the same question).[80] A majority of the Court of Appeal in *Chaudhary* thought that 'proceedings' required the involvement of 'some agency, whether lay or religious, of or recognised by the state'.[81] Oliver LJ (echoing Lords Diplock and Salmon in *Quazi*[82]) also emphasised that the effectiveness of the divorce must be contingent on the completion of the formalized process, and that adherence to an elaborate ritual (involving witnesses, pronouncement in a temple, execution in writing) would not alter a non-proceedings characterisation if the divorce was effective on the simple pronouncement of *talaq* and the additional proceedings were 'mere surplusage' and not required by law for the dissolution to take effect.[83] One must focus on the 'essential elements' of an effective divorce under the law of the country of origin.[84]

Beyond these points of agreement, the appellate judges offered a number of conflicting views as to what constituted a 'proceedings' divorce and what the core identifiers were. Lords Diplock and Salmon in *Quazi* highlighted, for example, the presence of criminal sanctions under Pakistani law: a man who failed to comply with the procedure laid down in the 1961 Ordinance was liable to be fined or imprisoned and this pointed towards a 'proceedings' classification.[85] Lord Fraser, by contrast, emphasised the 'regular definite form' of the Ordinance procedure.[86] Oliver LJ in *Chaudhary* opined that the external state (or state-sanctioned) authority must have a role which is 'more than simply probative' in order for the divorce to attract a 'proceedings' characterisation.[87]

2. Defining 'proceedings': interpretative disarray under the 1986 Act?

As indicated above in Section E.1., there has been no appellate consideration of the demarcation between proceedings and non-proceedings divorces since the coming into force of the 1986 Act. The English High Court has considered the matter on

---

[80] See *Quazi* (HL) (n 20) 817 (Lord Fraser, leaving the question open), 824 (Lord Scarman, implying that bare *talaqs* were proceedings divorces).
[81] *Chaudhary* (n 21) 41 (Oliver LJ). This idea was echoed by Balcombe J (at 46) who thought that 'proceedings' required 'some form of state machinery to be involved in the divorce process: not necessarily machinery established by the state, since existing religious machinery recognised by the state is sufficient'.
[82] *Quazi* (HL) (n 20) 809 (Lord Diplock), 812 (Lord Salmon).
[83] *Chaudhary* (n 21) 41–2.
[84] *Chaudhary* (n 21) 42.
[85] *Quazi* (HL) (n 20) 809 (Lord Diplock), 812 (Lord Salmon).
[86] Ibid 814.
[87] *Chaudhary* (n 21) 41.

a number of occasions since 1988;[88] however, these High Court judgments have offered a variety of different views as to where the 'line of division' should be drawn, some relatively faithful to the guidance in *Quazi* and *Chaudhary*,[89] others much less so.[90]

In *H v H*[91] it was determined (contrary to the view of the Lord Chancellor at the time of adopting the 1986 Act,[92] and contrary to the submissions of the Queen's Proctor[93]) that a Japanese *kyogi rikon* was a proceedings divorce. This is a form of divorce which flows from the private agreement of the parties, but crucially the fact of party agreement is required to be registered with a state authority—so, as the judge termed it, the policy was one of 'no registration, no divorce',[94] and the principles laid down in *Quazi* and *Chaudhary* were thought to have been complied with. The judge was troubled by Oliver LJ's suggestion that the state authority must have a role that is more than 'simply probative' and was initially inclined towards a non-proceedings characterisation on this basis:[95] however, he was subsequently convinced that the registration was fundamental to the effectiveness of the divorce, and not simply a record of what the parties had agreed.[96]

Two recent cases suggest a willingness to pull free from the shackles of *Quazi* and *Chaudhary* and a tendency to afford a 'proceedings' classification whenever a customary form involves a certain level of public ritual, or where supplementary formalities are mandated by law—even if the divorce itself is constituted without any direct involvement of a state (or state sanctioned) authority.

In *H v S* a Saudi *talaq* was accepted as a 'proceedings' divorce on the basis that registration at the Sharia court was 'overwhelmingly convenient' and standard practice[97]—and because lack of registration attracted criminal sanction.[98] Little emphasis was given to the fact that the change in status could precede these steps, taking effect simply by virtue of the pronouncement of *talaq*.[99] Indeed the judge

---

[88] As indicated above (see n 3), FLA 1986 (n 1) Pt II entered into force on 4 April 1988.
[89] See eg *Wicken v Wicken* [1999] Fam 224, 236–7 (HC) where a 'divorce by letter', a valid method of dissolving a marriage of Muslims under Gambian law, was considered a non-proceedings divorce (the divorce was effected by simple delivery of the letter to the wife in Gambia; and while registration at the Sharia Court was formally obligatory, non-registration did not affect the validity of the divorce); also *El Fadl* (n 42): in this case a Lebanese *talaq* which became effective in law only after registration at the Sharia court, and pronouncement before two witnesses, was considered a proceedings divorce. See also *H v H (Talaq Divorce)* (n 42) confirming recognition of a Pakistani *talaq* under the 1961 Ordinance as a proceedings divorce and *MET v HAT* (n 49) [8]–[9] confirming that a 'bare *talaq*' was a non-proceedings divorce.
[90] *H v S* (n 37); *NP v KRP* (n 69).
[91] *H v H (Japanese Divorce)* (n 69).
[92] HL Deb 22 April 1986, vol 473, col 1082.
[93] *H v H (Japanese Divorce)* (n 69) [14].
[94] Ibid [96].
[95] Ibid [94]–[95].
[96] Ibid [98].
[97] *H v S* (n 37) [32], [41].
[98] Ibid [41], [61].
[99] Ibid [32], [36]–[41].

opined that 'the purpose and policy of s 46(1)' was to provide 'a mechanism to afford recognition to a Sharia divorce which is more than, and has developed from mere oral delivery, so that there can be no issue that it has been pronounced'.[100] This dictum comes close to suggesting that *any* formalised *talaq* should be recognised as a proceedings divorce, at least if the formalisation provides proof of the divorce—and goes well beyond *Quazi* and *Chaudhary* insofar as they envisaged mandatory involvement of a state (or state-sanctioned) authority as a pre-requisite to any change in status.[101]

NP v KRP was also very generous in its interpretation of 'proceedings', and while *Quazi* and *Chaudhary* were cited and purportedly followed, in reality the constraints of those authorities were disregarded.[102] In this case (*NP v KRP*), it was accepted that a *panchayat* (Hindu customary) divorce was a proceedings divorce in the face of evidence that there was no 'fixed' or 'definite procedural requirement' for such a customary divorce[103] (and certainly no 'regular definite form' as envisaged by Lord Fraser in *Quazi*). The divorce would usually be effected in writing with some involvement by community members, as was reflected in the deed of divorce at hand[104]—and Parker J thought this was sufficient to satisfy the 'proceedings' criterion.[105]

Parker J also attached significance to the fact of registration of the deed even though registration was voluntary and did not 'create the divorce':[106] 'The registrar's ... participation in the process also entitles me to treat the registration in this case as more than a mere administrative record. In a jurisdiction where the only essential elements are (i) divorce and (ii) community involvement, and there are no prescribed procedures, I am entitled to and do treat this as an important part of the process.'[107] This approach sits very uncomfortably alongside *Chaudhary*, which would suggest that any such voluntary registration (post-dating the change in status) was 'mere surplusage'.

---

[100] Ibid [63].
[101] The focus on proof of status is curious. While this aligns with the Lord Chancellor's emphasis of proof of divorce in devising a separate non-proceedings category, it is at odds with *Chaudhary* (n 21) and *Quazi* (HL) (n 20) insofar as these authorities did not seem to see facilitation of proof as a key indicator of a proceedings divorce. On the contrary, as has been seen, Oliver LJ in *Chaudhary* (n 21) (at 41) emphasised that the role of the external authority must go beyond the purely probative in order for a divorce to qualify as a proceedings divorce—and in *Quazi* (HL) (n 20), the House of Lords accepted that the 1961 Ordinance procedure, which qualified as a proceedings divorce, would not necessarily produce any reliable proof of status. (Rather it was acknowledged (at 817) that the husband was free to revoke the *talaq* without notifying the Chairman of the Union Council, and that the Chairman's certificate could be 'entirely misleading').
[102] *NP v KRP* (n 69).
[103] Ibid [106].
[104] Ibid [106].
[105] It is interesting to note that the Lord Chancellor—at the time of adopting FLA 1986 (n 1)—envisaged that *panchayat* divorces would be non-proceedings divorces: HL Deb 22 April 1986, vol 473, col 1082.
[106] *NP v KRP* (n 69) [106].
[107] Ibid [122].

In *NP v KRP* there is no clear identification of the relevant external state (or state-sanctioned) authority (considered a vital element of a 'proceedings' divorce in *Chaudhary*). As indicated by Parker J, there was some sense that the Registrar might fulfil this role—but elsewhere in the judgment it was suggested that the 'community elders' played this part.[108] Finally, it was also suggested that the Indian state sanction of these customary divorces constituted 'state participation in the process'[109] but this appears to confuse, or conflate, the 'proceedings' criterion in the opening words of section 46(1) with the requirement of effectiveness under the law of origin (under s 46(1)(a)).

3. Defining 'proceedings': future prospects

There is considerable uncertainty as to the appropriate classification of extra-judicial divorces having regard to the English case-law under the 1971 and 1986 Acts. While there is judicial guidance on the characterisation of *certain* extra-judicial divorces,[110] others have yet to be considered[111]—and even in those cases which have enjoyed judicial consideration, the lack of recent appellate authority (and the inconsistency of the judicial guidance) creates a degree of doubt.

This cloud of uncertainty is a matter of grave concern because the question of recognition of extra-judicial divorces is not a peripheral matter, relevant to the very few on the fringes, but rather is very much a mainstream legal problem. The reality is that extra-judicial divorces are the standard form of divorce in many very populous countries with which the UK has strong ties.[112]

Divorces granted in EU Member States now fall for consideration under the Family Law Act 1986 following the UK's departure from the EU.[113] This change has

---

[108] See Ibid [122] referring to 'public affirmation of the parties' divorce by members of the community'.

[109] Ibid [121].

[110] eg Pakistani and Lebanese *talaqs* (*Quazi* (HL) (n 20) and *El Fadl* (n 42)); Jewish *gets* (confirmed *obiter* to be 'proceedings divorces' in *Berkovits v Grinberg* [1995] Fam 142, 145–6 (HC)) (hereafter *Berkovits*); Russian administrative divorces (confirmed *obiter* to be 'proceedings divorces' in *Solovyev v Solovyeva* [2014] EWFC 1546, [2015] 1 FLR 734 [18], [30]) (hereafter *Solovyev*). See further n 89 above.

[111] eg consent divorces under African customary law: see Poulter, 'Divorce-Recognition of Foreign Divorces' (n 48).

[112] In *NP v KRP* (n 69) [106] it is estimated that 80% of Hindu divorces are *panchayat* divorces. In *H v H (Japanese Divorce)* (n 69) [6] it is noted that the *kyogi rikon* is the most frequently used method of divorce in Japan (and Morley estimates that more than 90% of Japanese divorces are in this form: see Jeremy Morley, 'Non-Recognition of Japanese Consent Divorces in the UK' [2005] International Family Law 159). The (formalised) *talaq* is thought to be the most common method of dissolution in many Muslim majority countries: see n 37 above.

[113] The Jurisdiction and Judgments (Family) (Amendment etc) (EU Exit) Regulations 2019, SI 2019/519, reg 15(7). Having ceased to be an EU Member State, the UK no longer participates in the Brussels II *bis* scheme for mutual recognition of divorces within the EU: Council Regulation (EC) No 2201/2003 of 27 November 2003 concerning jurisdiction and the recognition and enforcement of judgments in matrimonial matters and the matters of parental responsibility, repealing Regulation (EC) No 1347/2000 [2003] OJ L338/1.

the potential to open a whole new set of challenges for the English courts insofar as European states are increasingly moving away from judicial divorce and accepting administrative forms and notarised instruments for non-contentious cases.[114] Of course, these dissolutions are most unlikely to fall within the mischief at which section 46(2) was aimed—insofar as they are secular divorces, available to men and women on equal terms, and the subject of state records.[115] However, if this European trend towards 'dejuridification' of divorce continues,[116] English judges may encounter difficulty in characterising these consent divorces as 'proceedings divorces'—if, for example, there is evidence that registration has a purely probative character.

It may be that, in time, there is appellate confirmation of the liberalising tendency that has been seen in more recent cases like *H v S*[117] and *NP v KRP*,[118] bringing most extra-judicial divorces into the 'proceedings' fold, and leaving the non-proceedings category as the exclusive preserve of the 'bare *talaq*' and other divorces which are entirely lacking in public ritual. This would result in a more targeted application of section 46(2) (one which is better aligned to the objectives articulated by the Lord Chancellor in 1986). Also, in view of the increased regulation of divorce in countries applying *Sharia* law, and a discernible shift away from divorce by bare *talaq*,[119] one might reasonably anticipate that the problematic section 46(2) 'non-proceedings' category might eventually wither away into insignificance, ultimately becoming a dead letter. On this hypothesis, English law might organically move towards the position advocated by the Law Commission in 1984, making law reform less pressing.

It is, however, contended in this essay that law reform is necessary, even if the above suppositions are well-founded. While the obtainment of divorce by bare *talaq* may now be increasingly rare (eg following its constitutional condemnation

---

[114] On the new extra-judicial divorce in France, see Bastien Baret and others, 'A Chronicle of French Family Law' in Margaret Brinig (ed), *The International Survey of Family Law 2017 Edition* (LexisNexis 2017) 99: 'The judge's decision is replaced by a contract called a convention, which takes the form of a private agreement countersigned by two lawyers ... Once signed, a notary registers the convention and that confers to it a certain date and enforceability. This recording frees the effects: divorce and all its consequences.'
On the requirements for administrative divorce in Spain, Portugal, and Estonia, see <https://e-justice.europa.eu/content_divorce-45-en.do> (accessed 24 July 2020).
[115] See Ibid.
[116] Masha Antokolskaia, 'Divorce Law in a European Perspective' in Jens Scherpe (ed), *European Family Law, Volume III: Family Law in a European Perspective* (Edward Elgar 2016) 72.
[117] *H v S* (n 37).
[118] *NP v KRP* (n 69).
[119] The reforms in Pakistan and Bangladesh under the 1961 Ordinance have been discussed above (see text to n 76ff). On reforms in other countries, see eg Abdullahi An-Na'im, *Islamic Family Law in a Changing World* (Zed 2002) 47 (Tanzania), 100 (Iran), 159 (Tunisia). On the 2004 reforms in Morocco, see Veronique Chaveau, 'The New Moroccan Legislation in Family Matters: The New Moudawana' [2005] International Family Law 230, 231.

290 RECOGNITION OF PROCEEDINGS AND NON-PROCEEDINGS DIVORCES

in India in 2017[120]), there will, for many years to come, be questions of recognition of bare *talaqs* pronounced in the recent past and affecting the status of those who remain alive and may have remarried in reliance on the *talaq*. Also, even if most extra-judicial consent divorces can henceforth be characterised as 'proceedings' divorces, the Islamic *khula* usually lacks any element of publicity[121] and seems destined to remain in the non-proceedings category—even though, as a divorce initiated by the wife, and concluded with the consent of the husband, it largely falls outside of the mischief targeted by the non-proceedings category, as outlined by the Lord Chancellor in 1986.

Furthermore, as things stand at present, there is no such appellate guidance on the horizon (and no guarantee that an appellate court would favour the more liberal interpretation adopted in *H v S* and *NP v KRP*). Accordingly, for now at least, UK family judges are left to struggle with an indeterminate line of division between proceedings and non-proceedings divorces, and with a very onerous obligation of interpretation of foreign law, in a context of increasingly limited legal aid budgets.[122] If *Chaudhary* remains good law, the hapless judge faces the task of determining the essential elements of the overseas divorce process, and the extent to which the change in status is contingent on engagement with an external authority. This may involve grappling with what may be uncodified, customary laws (where there are conflicting views as to what is essential).[123] This is an unenviable task indeed and one may reasonably question the value of these interpretative wrangles.

F. Replication in the Civil Partnership Act 2004

The Civil Partnership Act 2004 was intended to replicate the laws governing marriage and to extend them into the domain of civil partnership.[124] Therefore, it was perhaps no surprise to find that the 2004 Act allowed (in s 235(1)) for recognition of overseas civil partnership dissolutions 'by means of proceedings' on terms echoing section 46(1) Family Law Act 1986; and that it made separate provision (in s 235(2)) for recognition of overseas civil partnership dissolutions 'otherwise than by means of proceedings' in a provision duplicating section 46(2).

---

[120] The Indian Supreme Court on 22 August 2017 struck down the law allowing for traditional divorce by *talaq* for Indian Muslims as a violation of art 14 of the Constitution of India (guarantee of equality before the law): see *Bano v Union of India* [2017] INSC 677.
[121] *Quazi v Quazi* [1980] AC 744, 766 (HC); *Quazi* (HL) (n 20) 824; Tucker, *Women, Family and Gender* (n 36) 99.
[122] See *Tufail v Riaz* [2013] EWHC 1829 (Fam) [4]–[8].
[123] On the susceptibility of customary laws to different interpretations, see *McCabe* (n 64) and *Alfonso-Brown* (n 64) (two cases on marriage formation).
[124] HC Deb 9 November 2004, vol 426, col 776.

This line of division makes even less sense than its counterpart in the Family Law Act 1986.[125] Civil partnership tends to exist only in secular family law systems and was borne of a commitment to non-discrimination[126] which tends, of itself, to exclude the kind of gender discrimination which prompted the adoption of section 46(2) Family Law Act 1986. This has led the editors of Dicey, Morris & Collins to observe that section 235(2) took 'The replication of provisions appropriate to marriage ... to extreme lengths'.[127] In the authors' view: 'The notion of "non-proceedings" dissolutions ... in the case of civil partnerships seems fanciful ... These provisions do the legislator no credit.'[128]

The views expressed in Dicey, Morris & Collins might suggest that section 235(2) was always destined to be a dead letter, and open to criticism on that basis, but not likely to give rise to any practical difficulties. Perhaps this will prove to be the case, if, for example, there is an appellate judgment giving a wide interpretation to the concept of 'proceedings' under section 46 Family Law Act 1986 and, by extension, section 235 Civil Partnership Act 2004. However, it is important to note that there is a long-established tendency towards greater informality in civil partnership dissolution by comparison with dissolution of marriage.[129] This informality might, potentially, provoke difficulty in classifying civil partnership dissolutions under section 235, with judges becoming entangled in deliberations as to the precise meaning of 'proceedings' in this context. This risk is heightened by the burgeoning spread of civil partnership as an institution,[130] and, in particular, by the UK's departure from the EU, insofar as this has brought European civil partnership dissolutions back under the remit of section 235.[131] Section 235 has therefore

---

[125] It was accepted at the time of adopting the Civil Partnership Act 2004 that the policy of replicating marriage laws should not be pursued where 'there was an objective justification for a difference in the approaches taken to civil marriage and civil partnership': HC Deb 9 November 2004, vol 426, col 776. One might suggest that there was such justification where the question was one of replication of FLA 1986 (n 1) s 46(2) but Parliament appeared not to share this view.

[126] Jens Scherpe and Andy Hayward 'The Future of Registered Partnerships: An Introduction' in Jens Scherpe and Andy Hayward (eds), *The Future of Registered Partnerships: Family Recognition Beyond Marriage* (Intersentia 2017) 2–4 (hereafter Scherpe and Hayward, *Future of Registered Partnerships*).

[127] Dicey, Morris & Collins (n 75) [18.136].

[128] Ibid [18.136].

[129] eg Ian Sumner, 'Registered Partnerships in the Netherlands' 148; Laurence Francoz Terminal, 'Registered Partnerships in France' 167–8; Dafni Lima, 'Registered Partnerships in Greece and Cyprus' 323; Josep Ferrer-Riba, 'Registered Partnerships in Spain' 365; Geoffrey Willems, 'Registered Partnerships in Belgium' 391, all in Scherpe and Hayward, *Future of Registered Partnerships* (n 126); also Ian Curry-Sumner, *All's Well that Ends Registered? The Substantive and Private International Law Aspects of Non-Marital Registered Relationships in Europe* (Intersentia 2005) 110–2; 150–2.

[130] See the ILGA-Europe table at <https://rainbow-europe.org/#0/8682/0> (accessed 30 December 2020). The expansion of registered partnership has been encouraged by the judgment of the European Court of Human Rights in *Oliari v Italy* (2017) 65 EHRR 26 where it was held that there was a violation of art 8 ECHR in denying same-sex couples an opportunity for formalisation of their relationship.

[131] See the Civil Partnership and Marriage (Same Sex Couples) (Jurisdiction and Judgments) (Amendment etc) (EU Exit) Regulations 2019, SI 2019/495, reg 5(6). Civil partnership dissolutions obtained in EU Member States were previously subject to separate bespoke rules matching the rules applicable to divorces under the Brussels II *bis* Regulation (see n 113 above) pursuant to the Civil Partnership (Jurisdiction and Recognition of Judgments) Regulations 2005, SI 2005/3334.

an ever-increasing scope of application and sub-section (2) throws an entirely unnecessary shadow of uncertainty over the recognition of extra-judicial civil partnership dissolutions.

G. Another Pointless Line of Division? Transnational Divorces

Adrian Briggs is also critical of another related line of division which is embedded into the fabric of the Family Law Act 1986, rather less explicitly than that drawn between proceedings and non-proceedings divorces, but no less problematic for that.

As observed by Professor Briggs, the legislative wording of the Family Law Act 1986 appears to assume that divorces are always obtained in a single country, when reality does not conform to that template.[132] Extra-judicial divorces, in particular, have frequently involved steps being taken in different countries, reflecting the universal nature of religious laws, and their transcendence of national borders.[133] As a result, many Jews and Muslims, wherever they live, have divorced under religious laws with civil effect in countries to which they retain strong connections (and where acts of perfection may be completed).[134] Any insistence on 'mono-territorial overseas divorces'[135] will thus lead to limping status for many UK residents who have divorced in this way.

Problems with recognition of transnational religious divorces emerged under the 1971 Act, and it was determined by the House of Lords in *Re Fatima* that a *talaq* pronounced by a Pakistani national in England, and notified under the 1961 Ordinance procedure in Pakistan, was not entitled to recognition in England.[136] This non-recognition of transnational divorces initiated in England was justified by reference to the language of the 1971 Act (which envisaged that overseas divorces would be obtained in a single country) and the policy interest (articulated in the Domicile and Matrimonial Proceedings Act 1973) in requiring 'persons within the jurisdiction' to divorce 'in a United Kingdom court'.[137] The Law Commission made no recommendation for the reform of this position,[138] and the 1986 Act used similar statutory language, confining recognition under section 46 to divorces 'obtained in a country outside the British Islands',[139] and continuing to insist on judicial divorce as the only mode of divorce within the UK.[140] Thus, it came as no

---

[132] Briggs, *The Conflict of Laws* (n 7) 321.
[133] Prakash Shah, 'Inconvenient Marriages, or What Happens When Ethnic Minorities Marry Transjurisdictionally' (2010) 6(2) Utrecht Law Review 17, 24.
[134] Bernard Berkovits, 'Transnational Divorces: The Fatima Decision' (1988) 104 LQR 60, 78, 84.
[135] Briggs, *The Conflict of Laws* (n 7) 323.
[136] *In re Fatima* [1986] 1 AC 527 (HL) (hereafter *Fatima* (HL)).
[137] Ibid 534.
[138] Law Com No 137 (n 22) 52.
[139] FLA 1986 (n 1) s 45(1).
[140] Ibid, s 44(1).

surprise when the High Court determined, in *Berkovits v Grinberg*, that a transnational Jewish *get* divorce written in England and delivered to the wife in Israel was not entitled to recognition under the 1986 Act.[141]

This policy of non-recognition of transnational divorces commenced in England is difficult to defend when—as the High Court freely acknowledged in *Fatima*— it can easily be side-stepped by a brief trip abroad.[142] Taylor J accepted that the decision seemed in that regard 'technical and even hollow',[143] and in *Berkovits* it was further acknowledged that the policy favoured the wealthy: 'a rich man could avoid its effects by flying to Pakistan to pronounce *talaq* whilst a poor man could not'.[144] Nonetheless, it was recognised that Parliament sought to reverse *Qureshi v Qureshi*[145] (which had allowed for divorce by pronouncement of *talaq* within the UK) and that this policy, by logical extension, prohibited recognition of UK-pronounced *talaqs* perfected abroad.[146] There are echoes here of the more recent debate concerning recognition of informal marriages by telephone—and similar arguments that persons physically present within the UK should not be entitled to marry (or divorce) in non-compliance with domestic law.[147]

Whatever the merits of demanding compliance with domestic law on domestic soil, it is (as Professor Briggs argues) impossible to justify non-recognition of transnational divorces where all steps are taken overseas in countries which recognise the divorce[148] (and where there is no anti-evasion consideration). Of course, this scenario has yet to come before the English courts, but the statutory construction adopted in *Berkovits* (and the insistence on obtainment in a single country) logically precludes recognition of transnational divorces even in these circumstances.[149] Furthermore, as Professor Briggs points out, this interpretation must logically extend to judicial divorces (which are governed by the same statutory criteria).[150] Thus, in principle, and as a matter of interpretative consistency, the English courts must deny recognition to judicial divorces where any essential step took place outside the granting jurisdiction.[151]

---

[141] *Berkovits* (n 110). See also *Sulaiman v Juffali* [2002] 1 FLR 479 [45] confirming (*obiter*) the non-recognition of transnational divorces under FLA 1986.
[142] *Fatima* (HC) (n 20) 199.
[143] Ibid 199.
[144] *Berkovits* (n 110) 159.
[145] *Qureshi v Qureshi* [1972] Fam 173 (HC).
[146] *Fatima* (HL) (n 136) 534.
[147] *City of Westminster v IC* [2008] EWCA Civ 198; [2008] 2 FLR 267 [39]–[42], [50]; *MRA v NRK* [2011] ScotSC CSOH 101; Fawcett and others, *Human Rights and Private International Law* (n 39) 619–22; Elizabeth Crawford and Janeen Carruthers, 'Dual Locality Events: Marriage by Telephone' [2011] SLT 227.
[148] Briggs, *The Conflict of Laws* (n 7) 322.
[149] David McClean, 'The Non-Recognition of Transnational Divorces' (1996) 112 LQR 230, 231 (hereafter McClean, 'Non-Recognition of Transnational Divorces').
[150] Briggs, *The Conflict of Laws* (n 7) 323.
[151] Ibid 323.

Like the line of division between proceedings divorces and non-proceedings divorces, the boundary between transnational and non-transnational divorces is not always easy to draw. Commentators have queried as to whether taking evidence abroad,[152] or service abroad,[153] might be sufficient to preclude recognition of a judicial divorce obtained overseas—or whether more elaborate external 'steps' might be necessary.[154] Administrative divorce obtained through a consular outpost might be considered a paradigm transnational divorce—but in *Solovyev v Solovyeva*, it was held that a divorce obtained at the Russian Consulate in London was not transnational, but rather was obtained in London (only).[155] The divorce in *Solovyev* was therefore denied recognition in England, not as a transnational divorce, but as a divorce obtained in the UK other than through the UK courts.[156] The English Family Court accepted that 'the divorce was obtained from the Russian Federation by an administrative process of the Russian bureaucracy' but held 'that is not the point'.[157] What was significant was that the events which had culminated in the legal dissolution of the parties' marriage 'all took place in London, albeit in the Russian Consulate, and not in Russia'.[158]

With this focus on the place of acting—and the de-emphasis of the identity of the sovereign authority dissolving the marriage—the digitisation of divorce may lead to an increase in the incidence of transnational divorce, and a corresponding increase in the incidence of limping marriages. The facilitation of online filing[159] (and a move away from physical filing) will inevitably lead to a dispersal of activity away from the administrative hub of the dissolving authority. Expatriate couples will be able to file for divorce at a remove (where they would previously have arranged for the physical filing of paperwork in their homeland). If an application for divorce is made via a computer in one overseas country and processed via a computer in another overseas country, the logic of *Fatima*, and *Berkovits*, and *Solovyev*, would suggest that the resultant divorce cannot be recognised under the Family Law Act 1986, although, as discussed in this Section, there is no rational justification for non-recognition.

---

[152] McClean, 'Non-Recognition of Transnational Divorces' (n 149) 231.
[153] Briggs, *Private International Law in English Courts* (n 5) [12.106].
[154] McClean, 'Non-Recognition of Transnational Divorces' (n 149) 231.
[155] *Solovyev* (n 110). In line with previous case-law, the court immediately dismissed any suggestion that a consular premises should be treated as foreign territory (at [20]).
[156] FLA 1986 (n 1) s 44(1).
[157] *Solovyev* (n 110) [33].
[158] Ibid. Curiously, the court appeared to focus on the locus of the final 'events' immediately preceding the Russian dissolution, and not on earlier steps—but in any event all steps had been taken in London. The record of the divorce was received at the central archive in Moscow a year after the divorce had been certified by the Russian Consulate in London—but this was considered irrelevant to the question at hand—because it had no bearing on the coming into effect of the divorce as a matter of Russian law.
[159] See Sahil Aggarwal, 'Online Divorce Petitions' [2019] Family Law 985, pointing out that in adopting online divorce in 2017, the UK was following in the footsteps of various US States and Australia.

While digitisation of divorce may, on this hypothesis, lead to an increase in the incidence of (limping) transnational divorces, it is, however, equally possible that digitisation will pose a challenge to the existing focus on the place of acting (and therefore to the entire policy of non-recognition of transnational divorces).

As has been observed in other contexts,[160] physical realities are obscured and side-lined in the context of any online transaction and the global ubiquity of the internet tends to diminish the significance of geographical localizing factors. There is a heightened sense of artificiality in any focus on the place of acting when the very same online act could be carried out in the very same way from any corner of the earth. These considerations (in the event of a marked shift towards digitisation[161]) might encourage a reassessment of the existing treatment of transnational divorces and a renewed focus on the locus of the sovereign authority granting the divorce, or the perfecting authority (in the case of religious divorces).

H. Conclusion

Part II of the Family Law Act 1986 is in urgent need of reform. The Act lays down a satisfactory scheme of recognition where judicial divorces are concerned, but is wholly unsatisfactory in its treatment of extra-judicial divorces.

The Law Commission advocated a legislative framework which would allow for recognition of all foreign divorces, judicial and extra-judicial, on the terms currently laid down in section 46(1) of the 1986 Act, with the public policy doctrine acting as a filter for wholly objectionable divorces.[162] This is the approach advocated in this essay—and it is suggested that women should have an explicit entitlement to invoke the public policy clause where the overseas divorce law gives men exclusive access to divorce on demand. Other European countries make recognition contingent on the wife's assent in these circumstances[163]—and the UK should not be afraid to make liberal use of the public policy clause where a woman objects to an overseas divorce in a gender-discriminatory form.[164]

---

[160] eg Paul Schiff Berman, 'The Globalization of Jurisdiction' (2002) 151 University of Pennsylvania Law Review 311; also Pedro de Miguel Asensio, 'Internet: Jurisdiction' in Jürgen Basedow and others (eds), *Encyclopedia of Private International Law* (Edward Elgar 2017).

[161] See William Healing, 'Divorce in the Time of Covid-19 – an English Perspective' [2020] International Family Law 118, arguing that the Covid-19 pandemic has radically accelerated the digitisation of family justice.

[162] Law Com No 137 (n 22).

[163] Cristina González Beilfuss, 'Islamic Family law in the European Union' in Johan Meeusen and others (eds), *International Family Law for the European Union* (Intersentia 2007) 433.

[164] Indeed it is arguable that the UK owes an obligation to allow a public policy objection pursuant to art 14 ECHR (non-discrimination in the exercise of Convention rights) taken with art 8 ECHR (right to respect for private life and family life): see Fawcett and others, *Human Rights and Private International Law* (n 39) [12.69]. Where the foreign divorce is obtained by way of a court proceeding giving preferential treatment to men, art 6 ECHR may be engaged: see *Pellegrini v Italy* (2001) 35 EHRR 44. Some existing English case-law suggests a reluctance to deny recognition on public policy grounds even in the face of gender-discrimination in an overseas divorce law: *El Fadl* (n 42); *Lachaux v Lachaux* [2019]

The repeal of section 46(2) (and its counterpart in the Civil Partnership Act 2004) will simplify the law on divorce recognition, providing much greater certainty of status for those who have divorced abroad, whilst also preserving court resources (and avoiding lengthy interpretative battles over the precise meaning of 'proceedings').

The 1970 Convention has a greater significance for the UK now that it has left the EU and has ceased to be party to the Brussels II *bis* Regulation on mutual recognition of divorces[165]—but, as has been seen in Section B., the reforms outlined can be achieved in full compliance with the 1970 Convention. While the term 'judicial or other proceedings' originates in that Convention, the separate treatment of non-proceedings divorces was a home-grown initiative, and Art 17 of the 1970 Convention allows for a broad definition of 'judicial or other proceedings' which encompasses all foreign divorces, judicial and extra-judicial. With a broad, inclusive definition of 'judicial or other proceedings', the unintended loophole in the operation of Part III of the Matrimonial and Family Proceedings Act 1984 will be remedied, and dependent spouses will no longer be deprived of financial relief simply on account of the informality of the overseas divorce.

The treatment of transnational divorces should also be reconsidered. While the 1970 Convention frames the obligation to facilitate recognition of divorces 'obtained in another ... State', the UK authorities are free to focus on the principal place of obtainment (or the place of perfection) and to attach no significance to the locus of earlier 'steps' taken in the obtainment of the divorce.[166]

Domestic divorce practices have shifted on their axes since the adoption of the 1986 Act, with decreased formality in Britain and other European states, and increased formality in countries applying Islamic principles. The reforms outlined will allow for a better alignment with the contemporary divorce landscape, whilst also ensuring that the UK complies with its obligations under the 1970 Hague Convention.

EWCA Civ 738, [2019] 4 WLR 86 [54], [118], [123], [179]. Art 10 of the 1970 Convention (n 8) allows for non-recognition on public policy grounds.

[165] See Jayne Holliday, 'The Urgent Need for the UK to Accept the Accessions of EU and Non-EU Contracting Parties to the 1970 Hague Convention on Recognition of Divorces and Legal Separation' Working Paper 2019/1, University of Stirling Working Paper Series, see <https://www.stir.ac.uk/about/faculties/arts-humanities/law-and-philosophy/law-research/law-working-papers/> (accessed 24 July 2020). See also David Hodson, 'Family Law in England and Wales after Fully Leaving the EU' [2020] International Family Law 103, 106, referring to a desire that the EU participate in the 1970 Convention (n 8). Insofar as more than half of the other Contracting States are EU Member States, the 1970 Hague Convention was of more limited significance whilst the UK was an EU Member State: pursuant to art 60(c) of the Brussels II *bis* Regulation (n 113), the Regulation took precedence over the 1970 Convention (n 8) as between Member States.

[166] If the reference in the 1970 Convention (n 8) to divorces 'obtained in another Contracting State' is to be understood narrowly (as excluding transnational divorces), then the UK is at liberty (pursuant to art 17) to allow for recognition of transnational divorces.

PART IV
CONFLICT OF LAWS WITHIN THE LEGAL SYSTEM

12
How Private is English Private International Law?

Edwin Peel

A. Introduction

This essay takes as its starting point some of the observations which were made by Adrian Briggs at a meeting of the Swiss Jurists Association in 2005. The fact that they were made to an audience of largely non-English lawyers did not prevent them from being made with characteristic bluntness. For example:

> ... there is a tendency to see rules of civil jurisdiction as just rules, as prescriptions which produce a particular outcome, lacking any more fundamental justification. It is in this blindness that we fail to see the truth. The truth, so far as English law is concerned, is that a very large amount of the law on jurisdiction, but also on choice of law, is dependent on the very private law notions of consent and obligation.[1]

Adrian Briggs went on to explain that it is 'necessary' to understand this because 'it explains much of what is truly fundamental to the common law approach' to private international law. It is also necessary at the outset of this essay to say what it intends to cover in light of this sort of comment, and others like it. They were made in 2005 in response to a triumvirate of decisions of the European Court of Justice[2] on the interpretation of the Brussels Convention (now Regulation), in which it could be said (and most definitely was said by our honorand) that the Court had failed, or refused, to approach questions of jurisdiction as if they were as much concerned with the vindication of the rights, or the enforcement of the obligations, of *the parties*, as with regulation of the jurisdiction of *the courts*. It would be a rather sterile debate to re-visit that particular

---

[1] Adrian Briggs, 'The Impact of Recent Judgments of the European Court on English Procedural Law and Practice' (2005) 124 (2005) II Zeitschrift fur Schweizerisches Recht 231, 235 (hereafter Briggs, 'Recent Judgments').
[2] Case C-116/02 *Erich Gasser GmbH v Misat srl* [2003] ECR I-14963 (hereafter *Gasser*); Case C-159/02 *Turner v Grovit* [2004] ECR I-3565 (hereafter *Turner v Grovit*); Case C-281/02 *Owusu v Jackson* [2005] ECR I-1383 (hereafter *Owusu*).

Edwin Peel, *How Private is English Private International Law?* In: *A Conflict of Laws Companion.* Edited by: Andrew Dickinson and Edwin Peel, Oxford University Press. © Edwin Peel 2021.
DOI: 10.1093/oso/9780198868958.003.0012

issue, in part because there is no prospect of the Court of Justice changing its mind in relation to the issues in question[3] and in part because, in an English court, what the Court of Justice has to say may no longer matter after Brexit (more, but mercifully not too much more, on that later). Nor does this essay engage more generally in an exercise in comparative law, but it is important nonetheless to begin with a preliminary point of comparative law.

As Adrian Briggs has himself acknowledged, it is perfectly possible to approach questions of jurisdiction and applicable law in terms of public law. Take jurisdiction as an example. If the parties agree (or consent) to the jurisdiction of a particular court, that may be the basis upon which the court in question decides that it has and/or will exercise jurisdiction (prorogation). If the parties agree (or consent) that only a particular court should be regarded as having jurisdiction over their dispute, that may be the basis upon which any other court decides that it does not have and/or will not exercise jurisdiction (derogation). In this sense, consent is not irrelevant, but it only informs the question of whether the court in question has or will exercise its jurisdiction; or, in the context of applicable law, the question of what law to apply. It is, however, possible to go further and ask whether what the parties have done, in the manifestation of their consent, is create an obligation on their part to produce or avoid a certain result and a corresponding right in the other party to a particular result or outcome. What has just been described may sound a lot like a contract, because that is what it is. While such a contractual analysis, or something like it, is not unheard of even in civil law systems where the public law conception of jurisdiction and applicable law is to the fore,[4] it is central to the regulation of jurisdiction and applicable law in English law. This essay addresses the question of just how far the privatisation of English private international law has gone and what are the appropriate limits of such privatisation. The particular topics to be addressed are jurisdiction and jurisdiction agreements and choice of law and choice of law agreements. Its principal focus is on contracts and remedies for breach of contract.

---

[3] Though the decision in *Gasser* (n 2) has been met by legislative amendment: see Art 31(2) of Regulation (EU) No 1215/2012 of 12 December 2012 on jurisdiction and the recognition and enforcement of judgments in civil and commercial matters [2012] OJ L351/1 (hereafter Recast Brussels I Regulation), discussed below: text to n 125.

[4] As stated, this is not a comparative study, but see eg Horatia Muir Watt, 'Injunctive Relief in the French Courts: A Case of Legal Borrowing' [2003] CLJ 573; cf *GreCon Dimter Inv v JR Normand Inc* [2005] 2 SCR 401 (Québec).

B. Jurisdiction and Jurisdiction Agreements

1. Jurisdiction

The most obvious way in which the question of jurisdiction may be conceived of in terms of private rights is when it is subjected to the redistributive will of the parties. The extent to which the parties are entitled to buy and sell their options as to particular jurisdictional outcomes in the same way that they sell their goods and services, and the remedies in support of such redistribution, is the main focus of this part. But even short of a contract, there is room to conceive of jurisdiction in terms of the private rights, or at least the private interests, of the parties. As Adrian Briggs pointed out in the paper with which this essay began, if the parties wish to confer jurisdiction which the English court would not otherwise have, they may do so by their submission; and it is the defendant's 'right' to invite the court not to exercise the jurisdiction it might already have based on presence, or satisfaction of one of the 'gateways' for service on a defendant who is not so present. For recognition of this in the Scottish courts (from whom the doctrine of *forum non conveniens* was imported by the English courts), see the observation of Lord Sumner that 'the court has to proceed until the defender objects, but, as against the pursuer's *right*, the defender has an equal *right* to plead forum non conveniens'.[5] That this is the defendant's right which he may, or may not, choose to invoke appears to have eluded the European Court of Justice in *Owusu*[6] in reaching the decision that there is no room for the courts of a Member State with jurisdiction under the Regulation[7] to consider whether a stay might be appropriate in favour of the courts of a non-Member State.[8]

That the question of whether to exercise jurisdiction should be answered in terms of the private rights, or interests, of the parties still seems to be the prevailing view of the English courts. The extent to which the focus in applying the doctrine of *forum (non) conveniens* should increasingly be on public interest factors, rather than those of private interest, is one of the principal aspects of Martin Davies's essay (ch 2), but no serious attempt appears as yet to have been made in the English courts to depart from the view expressed by Lord Hope that 'the principles on which the doctrine of forum non conveniens rest leave no room for considerations of public interest or public policy which cannot be related to the private interests of any of

---

[5] *Société du Gaz de Paris v Société Anonyme de Navigation "Les Armateurs Francais"* 1926 SC 13 (HL), 21 (emphasis added).
[6] *Owusu* (n 2).
[7] By which is meant one of the jurisdictional rules of the Recast Brussels I Regulation itself; not Art 6 under which the question of jurisdiction is delegated to national law.
[8] The principal mis-step can be found in [42]. English commentators certainly did not hold back: 'nonsensical': Briggs, 'Recent Judgments' (n 1) 245; 'Curiosity ... turns to disbelief on reading paragraph 42': Andrew Dickinson, 'Legal Certainty and the Brussels Convention' in Pascal de Vareilles-Sommiéres (ed), *Forum Shopping in the European Judicial Area* (Hart Publishing 2007) 130.

the parties or the ends of justice in the case which is before the court'.[9] Of course, under the doctrine of *forum non conveniens* the defendant's 'right' is only to invoke the exercise by the courts of an even-handed discretion based on the private interests of both parties. If a party wishes to obtain any more than this and 'enhance' the rights which an English court might enforce,[10] it will be necessary to have bargained for it in the form of a jurisdiction agreement; and it is to such agreements that we now turn.

2. Jurisdiction agreements

This part is primarily concerned with remedies, rather than rights, but it is necessary to deal briefly with the underlying right. The remedies to be considered below are awarded for breach of contract,[11] but for any breach to have occurred one party must have defaulted in the performance of its obligations. In the present context, we are therefore concerned only with *exclusive* jurisdiction agreements, that is, where the parties (or one of them[12]) have undertaken not to sue in any court other than those designated by the agreement. For the purpose of this essay and its focus on remedies, we shall assume that the jurisdiction agreement is exclusive. Whether it is, in practice, is simply a question of construction, but it is not seriously questioned, at least by the English courts, that the outcome of a jurisdictional dispute may be made the subject of a promissory obligation. As we shall see below, such a question is still to be asked in the context of a choice of law agreement.

One further preliminary point needs to be made. At least some of the remedies which might be available to the English courts have been curtailed where the breach by one party is to have commenced proceedings in the courts of an EU Member State. For example, the English courts have no power to order the remedy

---

[9] *Lubbe v Cape Plc* [2000] 1 WLR 1545, 1566. This notwithstanding the 'overriding objective' of dealing with cases 'justly and at proportionate cost' (Civil Procedure Rules 1998 (CPR) r 1.1(1)), which includes allotting to the case 'an appropriate share of the court's resources, while taking into account the need to allot resources to other cases' (CPR r 1.1(2)(e)). For a creative attempt to bridge the gap between the public interest and the private interest, see the speech of Lord Hoffmann in *Connelly v RTZ Corp* [1998] AC 854 which (disappointingly) did not appeal to the majority in that case: see Edwin Peel, 'Forum Non Conveniens Revisited' (2001) 117 LQR 187.

[10] See Adrian Briggs, 'The Hidden Depths of the Law of Jurisdiction' [2016] LMCLQ 236 and the distinction drawn therein, by reference to Hohfeldian terminology, between the 'claim right' not to be sued abroad in breach of contract which founds an anti-suit injunction and the 'right' to seek a stay as a 'liberty' to request the court to exercise a power to alter the procedural relationship of claimant and defendant.

[11] But not necessarily only for breach of contract. They may be awarded for other forms of wrong, or the infringement of other forms of right: see eg the award of an anti-suit injunction for so-called 'equitable wrongs', discussed in Andrew Dickinson's essay in this collection (ch 4).

[12] English law has not, as yet, shown the hostility seen in some legal systems to the use of one-sided or 'asymmetrical' exclusive jurisdiction agreements, ie exclusive for one party, but not for the other: see eg *Commerzbank AG v Liquimar Tankers Management Inc* [2017] EWHC 161 (Comm), [2017] 1 WLR 3497.

of an injunction to restrain the party in question from commencing or continuing with such proceedings.[13] But the United Kingdom is no longer an EU Member State and when the transition period (which treats it as if it still is a Member State) comes to an end, the provisions of the Brussels I Regulation and the rulings of the European Court of Justice will, or may,[14] no longer curtail. To deal with this in a manageable way, this part first assumes that there is no such curtailment, that is, it considers the practice of the English courts on the basis that, where relevant, any foreign proceedings are taking place in the courts of a non-Member State. It will then conclude with a brief summary of what has been curtailed and what might be the outcome of the United Kingdom's withdrawal from the EU.

On the assumption that an exclusive jurisdiction agreement has been breached, there are four 'remedies' which might follow. Two of them are instantly recognisable as remedies for breach of contract: an injunction to restrain the party in breach from persisting in it,[15] in the form of an 'anti-suit injunction', and damages for any loss proved to have resulted from the breach. But in the context of breach of a jurisdiction agreement, the English courts may be faced with two further questions: whether to allow English proceedings to continue or whether to order a stay; and whether to deny recognition to a foreign judgment where that stage has been reached in proceedings commenced in breach of contract. Each of those may be addressed in terms of a 'remedy', at least in the sense of an order of the court which is required to take into account the effect of the breach. The former is not considered in any detail, save for two observations. First, what is involved is a form of specific relief: to stay, or not to stay. Whether such relief is granted is at the discretion of the court. It is a discretion which allows the court to take into account other circumstances, in addition to any breach. The same is true where an application is made for an anti-suit injunction.[16] While the circumstances in which an English court decides whether or not to stay its own proceedings are not a 'mirror-image' of those in which an anti-suit injunction may be awarded,[17] there is a parallel to be drawn between the two 'remedies'. In each case, the order sought may be denied, but this is not a finding that there was no underlying breach, such that an alternative remedy may not be available, for example damages. Second, as a general rule, as one would expect, the parties' contract is enforced, and there is no obviously detectable chauvinism involved when the English courts decide not to enforce by granting, or refusing, a stay. Thus, where English proceedings have been commenced in breach of an agreement to the jurisdiction of a foreign court, a stay will not be ordered if there is 'strong cause'[18] to allow the proceedings to

---

[13] *Turner v Grovit* (n 2).
[14] See text to nn 124–6.
[15] Or going ahead with any threatened breach.
[16] *Donohue v Armco Inc* [2001] UKHL 64; [2002] 1 Lloyd's Rep 25 (hereafter *Donohue*).
[17] *SNI Aérospatiale v Lee* [1987] AC 871.
[18] More often than not, the 'strong cause' lies in the fact that enforcement of the agreement as between the parties to it will lead to the unwelcome fragmentation of multi-party litigation. There are

continue;[19] but if such cause can be shown as to why foreign proceedings are more appropriate, a stay will be ordered even if such proceedings would be in breach of an agreement to the jurisdiction of the English courts.[20]

As far as the three remaining 'remedies' are concerned, the traditional approach has been to consider them in the following order: anti-suit injunction; damages;[21] and non-recognition of foreign judgments (sometimes only in passing, when discussing the first two). In this essay that order is reversed, in part to give greater focus to section 32 of the Civil Jurisdiction and Judgments Act 1982 and what that may tell us about the priority given in English private international law to the parties' bargain; and in part because a clearer understanding of the scope of that provision is relevant to the scope of the remedy in damages.

(a) Non-recognition of foreign judgments

It is helpful to set out the relevant provisions of s 32 of the 1982 Act at the outset:[22]

(1) ... a judgment given by a court of an overseas country in any proceedings shall not be recognised or enforced in the United Kingdom if—
  (a) the bringing of those proceedings in that court was contrary to an agreement under which the dispute in question was to be settled otherwise than by proceedings in the courts of that country; and
  (b) those proceedings were not brought in that court by, or with the agreement of, the person against whom the judgment was given; and
  (c) that person did not counterclaim in the proceedings or otherwise submit to the jurisdiction of that court.
  ...

(3) In determining whether a judgment given by a court of an overseas country should be recognised or enforced in the United Kingdom, a court in the United Kingdom shall not be bound by any decision of the overseas court relating to any of the matters mentioned in subsection (1) or (2).

The provenance of this provision is curious, in that it does not really have one, at least as a matter of common law. According to Dicey, Morris & Collins, it

---

questions of privity at work in such cases (see Briggs, 'Recent Judgments' (n 1) 236), but more obviously these are cases where there is a 'strong public interest in preventing conflicting judgments from coming into existence': Adrian Briggs, *Civil Jurisdiction and Judgments* (6th edn, Informa 2015) [4.53].

[19] *The Eleftheria* [1970] P 94; *The El Amria* [1981] 2 Lloyd's Rep 119; *The Sennar (No 2)* [1985] 1 WLR.
[20] *Bouygues Offshore SA v Caspian Shipping Co (Nos 1, 3, 4 and 5)* [1998] 2 Lloyd's Rep 461.
[21] Injunction before damages, largely on the basis that the practical availability of the latter is a much more recent development than the former: see Section B.2(c) below.
[22] Section 32(1) does not apply to a judgment from an EU Member State court which is required to be recognised under the Recast Brussels I Regulation (n 3): s 32(4)(a).

adopted and extended a similar provision in the Foreign Judgments (Reciprocal Enforcement) Act 1933[23] 'on which there was no authority at common law'.[24] The latter is a telling observation given that it has been said that the grounds for setting aside the registration of a foreign judgment under the 1933 Act 'reflect those of the common law'.[25] If one simply refers to the relevant provision in the 1933 Act itself, which was repealed by the 1982 Act,[26] the principal 'extension' to which Dicey Morris & Collins refers is that there was no equivalent of section 32(3).

The effect of section 32(3) is best illustrated by a simple example: C and D are parties to a contract. D commences proceedings in a foreign court[27] and does so when C is present within the jurisdiction of the foreign court. The contract includes a term which, before the English courts, amounts to a valid and enforceable agreement to the exclusive jurisdiction of the English courts, the scope of which extends to the claim made by D against C. The foreign court enters judgment on the substantive merits against C and also rules that it did not refrain from exercising its jurisdiction[28] because of the jurisdiction agreement on the basis that the claim did not fall within the scope of the agreement. In such a case C would have a defence to the recognition of the foreign judgment in England under section 32(1)(a). Since the foreign court was otherwise jurisdictionally competent to adjudicate, based on C's presence,[29] ordinarily any ruling of the court which is final and

---

[23] s 4(3)(b). There is no explicit discussion of this ground for setting aside registration in the 'Greer Report' upon which the 1933 Act is based (Foreign Judgments (Reciprocal Enforcement) Committee, *Report* (Cmd 4213, 1932)), nor in the earlier Report of Lord Sumner (Committee appointed by the Lord Chancellor to consider the conduct of legal proceedings between parties in this country and parties abroad, and the enforcement of judgments and awards, *Report* (Cmd 251, 1919)) which led to the Administration of Justice Act 1920. The wording of what is now s 32(1)(a) seems to originate in a convention negotiated with Belgium: *Convention providing for the Reciprocal Enforcement of Judgments in Civil and Commercial Matters* (Cmd 4618, 1934). I am grateful to Andrew Dickinson for drawing my attention to these materials and furnishing me with copies. In the case of the 1933 Act, it only extends to a foreign country when a bilateral treaty has been made to provide for substantial reciprocity of treatment. The same principle of reciprocity underpins the Recast Brussels I Regulation (n 3), but it is notable that breach of a jurisdiction agreement is not one of the limited grounds on which recognition of a foreign judgment may be refused: Art 45.

[24] Lord Collins of Mapesbury and others (eds), *Dicey, Morris & Collins: The Conflict of Laws* (15th edn, Sweet & Maxwell 2012) [14-098] (hereafter Dicey, Morris & Collins). Though see *Ellerman Lines Ltd v Read* [1928] 2 KB 144 (hereafter *Ellerman*) where an injunction against enforcement of a foreign judgment was obtained on the basis of 'breach of contract and fraud'. And in Canada, see *Old State Brewing Co v Newlands Service Inc* (1998) 155 DLR (4th) 250 (BCCA).

[25] Adrian Briggs, *Private International Law in English Courts* (OUP 2014) [6.131] (hereafter Briggs, *Private International Law in English Courts*).

[26] Sch 14.

[27] ie the court of a non-Member State of the EU: see n 22 above.

[28] It is now widely accepted that it is not a question of whether such agreements oust the jurisdiction of the court, in which case they might be regarded as void on that basis. They are relevant to the question of how the court should exercise its jurisdiction (see most notably the analysis of Chief Justice Burger in *M/S Bremen v Zapata Off-Shore Company* 407 US 1, 12 (1972): 'No one seriously contends in this case that the forum selection clause *"ousted"* the District Court of jurisdiction over Zapata's action. The threshold question is whether that court should have *exercised* its jurisdiction to do more than give effect to the legitimate expectations of the parties, manifested in their freely negotiated agreement, by specifically enforcing the forum clause.' (emphasis added)).

[29] *Adams v Cape Industries Plc* [1990] Ch 433.

conclusive would be treated as *res judicata*, including the ruling that there had been no breach of the jurisdiction agreement.[30] But this is where section 32(3) applies. The English court is free to reach its own determination. It is a vivid illustration of the priority given to the parties' bargain in English private international law.

To make good on this observation we might turn to Adrian Briggs' masterly series of lectures at the Hague Academy of International Law on '*The Principle of Comity in Private International Law*'. As he observed: 'the most significant illustration of comity as a central component of private international law comes in the manner in which we give effect at home to the adjudications of foreign courts.'[31] The 'manner' in which effect is given to foreign judgments in English private international law is to 'recognise' (by conferring the status of *res judicata* on) judgments given against a person who was present within the territorial jurisdiction of the foreign court when the proceedings were begun. Adrian Briggs leaves one in no doubt as to the best explanation for this:

> The *recognition* of judgments against those who were present when the process was opened is the most fundamental of rules in English private international law; it is the most fundamentally justified by the principle of comity and territorial sovereignty. It embodies the oldest and most deeply seated sense that sovereign acts are territorial, and when a sovereign has so acted, his act is to be respected, and if our courts are asked to do it, his judgments are to be recognised.[32]

These are precisely the circumstances of the example above. In reaching its decision that there was no breach of the jurisdiction agreement, the foreign court acted in relation to one (C) who was present when the process was opened, that is, in accordance with the principle of territorial sovereignty. Why then should its decision that there was no breach of the jurisdiction agreement not be respected by the English courts? One answer to this question is simply that this is what section 32 says. In their essay in this collection, which reflects more generally on the principle of comity, James Edelman and Madeleine Salinger submit that comity is based on 'the implied consent of the forum state to give effect to acts of another sovereign within the forum state's territory'.[33] From this it follows that, since the principle of comity derives from consent, it 'would not prevent a court from enforcing a law passed by the forum state that prohibits the recognition of any foreign judgment'.[34] In the present circumstances the law passed by the forum state is section 32. This is not quite a full answer to the question put in that it does not address *why*,

---

[30] cf *The Sennar No 2* [1985] 1 WLR 490.
[31] Adrian Briggs, 'The Principle of Comity in Private International Law' (2012) 354 *Recueil des Cours de l'Académie de Droit International* 65 (hereafter Briggs, *Hague Lectures*).
[32] Ibid 150.
[33] Ch 13, Section B.1.
[34] Ibid.

consistently with the principle of comity as articulated, the parties' bargain should be prioritised over the sovereign act of the foreign court by section 32(3).

A fuller answer may be derived from the very concept of 'recognition' which is adopted by the English courts in giving effect to foreign judgments. At common law, foreign judgments, as such, are not enforced in the English courts. Only English judgments are enforced, but where a foreign judgment is recognised, the cause of action which results in an English judgment is breach of the obligation to comply with the foreign judgment. This is the so-called 'doctrine of obligation' and it is right to acknowledge that it has been questioned.[35] If, however, it is a question of which foreign judgments a party is obliged to observe, it may seem an obvious proposition to say that no party is obliged to observe a judgment which the other party was obliged not to have obtained in the first place. If one reverts to the essay by James Edelman and Madeleine Salinger, the proposition is made therein that a court will only be justified in refusing to recognise a foreign sovereign act where it is 'contrary to a fundamental principle of justice'.[36] Such principles are those which are 'so fundamental, or so basic, that any legal system would be unjust without them'.[37] In the present context, one might point to a version of the principle that no party should be entitled to benefit from her own breach of contract.[38] In English law there is some debate about whether such a principle is applied by way of an implied term or rests on a 'positive rule of the law of contract that conduct of either promisor or promisee which can be said to amount to himself "of his motion" bringing about the impossibility of performance is in itself a breach'.[39] The most recent view of the courts is that it rests on a term implied 'in fact', that is, where necessary to give effect to the intention of the parties,[40] but the suggestion that what is in play is a 'positive rule of law' hints at the sort of 'fundamental principle' which is required. In more colloquial form, one cannot pull oneself up by one's own bootstraps and this quite nicely explains section 32(3) in particular. In the example above, D cannot rely on the judgment of the foreign court that there was no breach

---

[35] *Hilton v Guyot* 159 US 113, 201 (1895); *Rubin v Eurofinance SA* [2012] UKSC 46, [2013] 1 AC 236 [9] ('purely theoretical and historical'); Andrew Dickinson, '*Schibsby v Westenholz* and the Recognition and Enforcement of Foreign Judgments in England' (2018) 134 LQR 426; cf Adrian Briggs, 'Recognition of Foreign Judgments: A Matter of Obligation' (2013) 129 LQR 87.

[36] Ch 13, Section C.1.

[37] Ch 13, Section C.3. An analogy is suggested with *ius gentium* and one of the examples referred to, from Hermogenian, is the 'proliferation of commerce': Alan Watson (tr), *The Digest of Justinian* (University of Pennsylvania Press 1985) vol 1, 1–2. Certainly one does not need to look too far, not least in the published works of Adrian Briggs, for the view that the robust and predictable enforcement of jurisdiction agreements (and choice of law agreements) is crucial to 'the proliferation of commerce'. This is, in many ways, the *raison d'etre* of his book: Adrian Briggs, *Agreements on Jurisdiction and Choice of Law* (OUP 2008) (hereafter Briggs, *Agreements*).

[38] The fundamentality of the principle is reflected in the observation that 'the justification may be one of the specific defences, but might as easily be public policy': Briggs, *Private International Law in English Courts* (n 25) [6.189] (citing *Kendall v Kendall* [1977] Fam 208).

[39] *Southern Foundries (1926) Ltd v Shirlaw* [1940] AC 701, 717 (Lord Atkin).

[40] *Duval v 11-13 Randolph Crescent Ltd* [2020] UKSC 18, [2020] 2 WLR 1167 (hereafter *Duval*).

of the jurisdiction agreement, such that C cannot invoke section 32(1)(a), in circumstances where C can establish before the English court that no such question should have been put to the foreign court in the first place.[41]

Before turning to injunctions and damages, two further points should be made in relation to section 32 of the 1982 Act. For the first, we may return to Adrian Briggs' *Hague Lectures*, in which there is no specific reference to section 32 in the chapter on 'Comity in the Enforcement of Judgments',[42] perhaps on the basis that detailed consideration of a statutory provision of English law was inappropriate for an audience of international lawyers. There is however a section entitled: 'Asking for judicial adjudication in breach of an agreement not to ask for it'.[43] That giving effect to such an agreement by withholding recognition of a foreign judgment obtained in breach of the agreement is not inconsistent with the principle of comity is rationalised on the basis of what is referred to as the 'relativity of legal relationships'. It is the same rationalisation which explains the award of an anti-suit injunction,[44] as we shall see below. No attempt is made to improve on the following analysis:[45]

> ... although it could not rule on another court's jurisdiction according to its law, an English court was entitled to say to the parties that they had violated an agreement which they had assumed to each other, or another obligation which they owed to each other,[46] and that *this* was what should be given effect by the English court, acting *in personam* and directing a person subject to the English court's personal jurisdiction to comply with his obligations.

It is the *in personam* nature of the relief available from the English courts which is said to both justify and explain the limits of the privatisation of private international law. This is not a new idea.[47] In the context of section 32, it means there

---

[41] There is an element of circularity involved here, as to which see text following n 97.

[42] It is said 'simply in passing' that the same reasoning which is applied to breach of an agreement to ask for adjudication, as discussed in the text following, might be used to 'justify relief for breach of an agreement on choice of court or even choice of law': Briggs, *Hague Lectures* (n 31), 155. That may be taken as a reference to s 32. Whether it extends to an agreement on choice of law is considered below.

[43] Given the specific reference to '*judicial* adjudication', this may refer to arbitration agreements (which certainly fall within s 32 of the 1982 Act), though the discussion which follows makes no reference to arbitration.

[44] An obvious contrast between the two forms of relief is that there is nothing discretionary about the relief available under s 32. If the conditions set out in s 32(1) are met, the judgment debtor is entitled to the withholding of recognition. The converse suggestion that, if the conditions have *not* been met because the judgment debtor submitted to the foreign court, the English court may, but is not bound to, recognise the foreign judgment (see *AES Ust-Kamenogorsk Hydropower Plant LLP v AES Ust-Kamenogorsk Hydropower Plant JSC* [2011] EWCA Civ 647, [2011] 1 Lloyd's Rep 233 [149] (Rix LJ) (hereafter *AES*)) cannot be supported.

[45] Briggs, *Hague Lectures* (n 31) 155.

[46] Our main concern is with obligations assumed by agreement, particularly in the context of s 32, but this is clearly a reference to the award of an anti-suit injunction based on an equitable wrong; as to which, see Andrew Dickinson's essay in this collection (ch 4).

[47] See, most famously, *Penn v Baltimore* (1750) 1 Ves Sen 444.

is no question of the English courts interfering with the jurisdiction of the foreign court, or impugning the foreign judgment as such. It may be recognised and enforced in any other jurisdiction. It is simply that within the jurisdiction of the English courts the judgment creditor is precluded from invoking it against the judgment debtor.

The second point with which to finish before leaving section 32 is to lay down a marker for an issue which is particularly relevant to the availability of damages. As set out in section 32(1)(c) above, a judgment debtor may not rely on section 32 as a defence to recognition if she has submitted to the jurisdiction of the foreign court. If she has done so, she has waived the right to resolution of the dispute only in the court(s) designated by the jurisdiction agreement. What remains contentious is what it means to have 'submitted' for this purpose. This is considered in Section B.2(c) below.

(b) Anti-suit injunctions

The remedy of an anti-suit injunction can be dealt with relatively briefly in this essay for two reasons. First, it is a remedy which is assessed in detail in Andrew Dickinson's essay in this collection (ch 4). Second, our principal focus is on remedies for breach of contract and here the law, as it is, is relatively settled. Where an injunction is sought on the basis that foreign proceedings have been commenced in breach of a jurisdiction agreement (or an arbitration agreement), it will be granted unless 'strong reasons' can be shown why it should be refused.[48] In terms of a purely contractual analysis, this is entirely orthodox. The obligation which has been breached is in the nature of an express negative stipulation, that is, *not* to sue in the court in which proceedings have been commenced, and 'in such cases, an injunction is normally granted as a matter of course';[49] the court is not normally concerned with 'the balance of convenience or inconvenience'.[50] In any event, while damages may now be more widely available (see Section B.2(c) below), it remains the case, if only on the basis that the assessment of loss is difficult, that they will often not represent an adequate, or the most adequate, remedy.[51]

Of course, a purely contractual analysis will not suffice. As acknowledged by Adrian Briggs, and picked up by Andrew Dickinson in his essay, to order an anti-suit injunction 'looks very much like an act of interference with proceedings before [the] foreign court, and the appearance does not mislead'.[52] The 'strong reasons' which might result in the refusal to order an injunction can, broadly speaking, be

---

[48] *Donohue* (n 16) [24] (jurisdiction agreements); *Aggelki Charis Compania Maritima SA v Pagnan SpA (The Angelic Grace)* [1995] 1 Lloyd's Rep 87 (arbitration agreements).

[49] Edwin Peel (ed), *Treitel: The Law of Contract* (15th edn, Sweet & Maxwell 2020) [21-059] (hereafter *Treitel*).

[50] *Doherty v Allman* (1878) 3 App Ca 709, 720.

[51] cf *Continental Bank NA v Aeakos Compania Naviera SA* [1994] 1 WLR 588, 598 ('relatively ineffective remedy', but said before the developments referred to below).

[52] Briggs, *Private International Law in English Courts* (n 25) [5.89].

divided into those which turn on the conduct of the party seeking the injunction and those which go to the due administration of justice. A recurring example of the latter is that to restrain a party from commencing or continuing foreign proceedings may lead to the unwelcome fragmentation of multi-party litigation involving non-parties to the jurisdiction agreement.[53] In other cases, the two categories may overlap as in the case of a party who seeks an injunction when the foreign proceedings are well advanced.[54] But these possibilities do not address a more fundamental issue which is why enforcement of the parties' agreement should be a matter for the English courts, rather than the foreign court before which proceedings have been commenced. To stress that any relief only applies *in personam*[55] may be met by pointing to judicial recognition that 'an English court has no superiority over a foreign court in deciding what justice *between the parties* requires …'.[56] To say that the parties agreed to, or chose, the English courts, but not the foreign court, begs the question since, in the view of the foreign court, there may have been no valid agreement, or the claim may fall outside its scope; and we are reminded in Andrew Dickinson's essay that comity requires the English court to accept that 'different judges operating under different legal systems with different legal policies may legitimately arrive at different answers, without occasioning a breach of customary international law or manifest injustice'.[57]

Against this, one cannot underestimate the compelling simplicity of the submission that an English court should sanction the wrongs committed by those within its personal jurisdiction. This should, of course, be tempered by a degree of circumspection in determining whether any wrong has been committed. This is particularly so in cases where no breach of contract is alleged and an injunction is sought, instead, on the basis that a party is guilty of an 'equitable wrong', based on what has variously been described as 'vexatious and oppressive' or 'unconscionable' conduct.[58] But when it comes to breach of contract, one is left with the same point which was made in relation to section 32.[59] If the parties *appear* to have agreed to

[53] *Donohue* (n 16).
[54] *Ecobank Transnational Inc v Tanoh* [2015] EWCA Civ 1309, [2016] 1 WLR 2231 [132]–[137].
[55] Relief in the form of an anti-suit injunction is perhaps less *in personam* than relief under s 32 of the 1982 Act. The effect of the latter is that any foreign judgment will not be recognised *in England*, but it does not impugn the foreign judgment itself which may be enforced elsewhere, whereas the effect of an anti-suit injunction may be to restrain the party in question from obtaining a judgment in the first place; cf *Ellerman* (n 24) where an injunction was sought and obtained preventing the judgment creditor from taking steps to enforce a Turkish judgment obtained in circumstances amounting to 'breach of contract and fraud' against the judgment debtor's vessels, ie it does not seem to have been confined to property within the jurisdiction. Of course, the sanctions for not observing the order are confined to those within the personal jurisdiction of the English courts. See also *SAS Institute Inc v World Programming Ltd* [2020] EWCA Civ 599.
[56] *Barclays Bank plc v Homan* [1992] BCC 757, 762 (Hoffmann J, emphasis added).
[57] *Deutsche Bank AG v Highland Crusader Offshore Partners LLP* [2009] EWCA Civ 725; [2010] 1 WLR 1023 [50] (Toulson LJ).
[58] See further Andrew Dickinson's essay in this collection (ch 4).
[59] In this context a degree of circumspection might require that the English court decline to grant an injunction in the exercise of its discretion in cases where there is 'enough room for overseas disagreement': Briggs, *Agreements* (n 37) [6.55–6.57].

the exclusive jurisdiction of the English courts (or, perhaps more accurately, have agreed not to take proceedings in the foreign court in question) and it is the view of the English courts that *they have so agreed*, the party seeking relief has established the right which it is the duty of the court to enforce, without interference on the basis of consequences which follow only as a result of a breach of the underlying right itself. In the case of an anti-suit injunction, such relief remains discretionary, but we finish this part by considering the remedy to which a party is entitled as of right.

(c) Damages

Adrian Briggs has been one of the foremost advocates of the remedy of damages for breach of contract in the context of jurisdiction agreements[60] (or arbitration agreements). As recently as 2014, he conceded that 'actual decisions to this effect are few'[61] and, elsewhere, that 'there may be a point at which the private international law context overshadows the contradictory logic of ordinary contractual principle'.[62] But while decisions have not arrived in a torrent, those which have appear to bear out the prediction that it is not 'easy to see where such a damages claim may be deflected or derailed'.[63] The first definitive step was, perhaps not surprisingly, taken in a case which could not have been more straightforward, even in private international law terms. In *Union Discount Co v Zoller*[64] the claimant successfully applied to the New York courts for an order striking out the proceedings there as being in breach of an agreement to the exclusive jurisdiction of the English courts, but recovered none of the costs of so doing. Not only did the Court of Appeal allow an appeal against a decision striking out a claim for damages to recover such costs in the English court as loss flowing from the defendant's breach of contract, it went further in expressing its opinion that such a claim was perfectly good.[65] The House

---

[60] 'In the context of jurisdiction agreements', rather than 'for breach of an exclusive jurisdiction agreement' in acknowledgement of his view that in some circumstances one might breach a 'non-exclusive' jurisdiction agreement: see eg his analysis of *Sabah Shipyard (Pakistan) Ltd v Islamic Republic of Pakistan* [2002] EWCA Civ 1643, [2003] 2 Lloyd's Rep 571 in Briggs, *Agreements* (n 37) [4.52]; cf *Catlin Syndicate Ltd v Adams Land & Cattle Co* 2065 (Comm), [2006] 2 CLC 425.

[61] Briggs, *Private International Law in English Courts* (n 25) [4.428].

[62] Briggs, *Agreements* (n 37) [8.03].

[63] Ibid. The focus in this essay is on the analysis of Adrian Briggs. For the analyses of others, see eg Edwin Peel, 'Exclusive Jurisdiction Agreements: Purity & Pragmatism in the Conflict of Laws' [1998] LMCLQ 182; Daniel Tan and Nik Yeo, 'Breaking Promises to Litigate in a Particular Forum: Are Damages an Appropriate Remedy?' [2003] LMCLQ 435; Louise Merrett, 'The enforcement of jurisdiction agreements within the Brussels regime' [2006] ICLQ 315; Koji Takahashi, 'Damages for Breach of a Choice-of-Court Agreement' (2008) 10 Yearbook of Private International Law 57; and Koji Takahashi, 'Damages for Breach of a Choice-of-Court Agreement: Remaining Issues' (2009) 11 Yearbook of Private International Law 73. For a tortious analysis, see Chee Ho Tham, 'Damages for breach of English Jurisdiction Clauses: More Than Meets the Eye' [2004] LMCLQ 46.

[64] [2001] EWCA Civ 1755, [2002] 1 WLR 1517 (hereafter *Zoller*).

[65] The potential obstacle was the decision in *Quartz Hill Consolidated Gold Mining Co v Eyre* (1883) 11 QBD 674 (CA) which prevents a further action to recover as damages the sums not covered by a costs order in an earlier decision of the English courts. The Court of Appeal in *Zoller* (n 64) did not consider that the policy reasons behind that decision (such as abuse of process, or comity) applied to a claim for

of Lords in *Donohue v Armco Inc*[66] may subsequently have accepted as correct counsel's concession that an award of damages might go beyond recovery of the wasted costs which represented the loss in *Zoller*, but just how far is demonstrated by the more recent decision of the Supreme Court in *The Alexandros T*[67] and of the Court of Appeal, in the same litigation, in *Starlight Shipping Co v Allianz Marine & Aviation Versicherungs AG*.[68]

The owners of a damaged vessel (the defendants) settled a claim against their insurers (the claimants) and did so without any recovery in damages for the loss they said flowed from the failure of the claimants to pay under the policy.[69] The defendants received 100% of the claim, but no interest and costs. The settlement agreement was stated to be 'in full and final settlement' of the defendants' claims and was subject to English law and the exclusive jurisdiction of the English courts (as were the underlying insurance policies). Three years later, proceedings were commenced in Greece by the defendants against the claimants. In the Greek proceedings, the defendants made 'materially identical' allegations to those made in England prior to the settlement, which were said to amount to breaches of the Greek Civil and Criminal Code. The claims were for US$150m for loss of opportunity and €1m for moral damage. The claimants sought relief in the English courts in the form of declarations that the Greek proceedings were in breach of the release in the settlement agreement and damages for such breach, damages for breach of the jurisdiction agreement, and a claim under an indemnity clause. Our principal concern is with the claim for damages for breach of the jurisdiction agreement.

An initial obstacle to the claim for damages is that the Greek courts were first seised, resulting in the possible application of what was then Art 27 of the original Brussels I Regulation.[70] Under that provision any court second seised in proceedings involving the same parties and the same cause of action must decline jurisdiction (once established) in favour of the court first seised. We shall return, briefly, to the 'EU dimension' in Section D. For now we need only note that this obstacle was overcome by the Supreme Court on the basis that the claims for relief before the English courts were held not to amount to the same cause of action as the claims

---

breach of an exclusive jurisdiction agreement, at least in circumstances where no order for costs was available from the foreign court at all.

[66] *Donohue* (n 16).
[67] [2013] UKSC 70, [2014] 1 Lloyd's Rep 223 (hereafter *The Alexandros T*).
[68] [2014] EWCA Civ 1010, [2014] 2 Lloyd's Rep 544 (hereafter *Starlight*). See the comments on both cases by James Ruddell, 'Monetary Remedies for Wrongful Foreign Proceedings' [2015] LMCLQ 9 and Andrew Dickinson, 'Once Bitten—Mutual Distrust in European Private International Law' (2015) 131 LQR 542.
[69] Not available as a matter of English law because failure to pay is regarded as a breach by the insurer and one cannot claim damages for the failure to pay damages: *The Fanti* [1991] 2 AC 1. This is contentious: Law Commission, *Insurance Contract Law: Post Contract Duties and Other Issues: Joint Consultation Paper* (Law Com CP No 201, 2011) para 2.87.
[70] Regulation (EU) 44/2001 [2001] OJ L12/1.

before the Greek courts.[71] The Supreme Court was not itself concerned with the claim for damages for breach of the jurisdiction agreement; only with whether it could get past Art 27. Two further obstacles potentially stood in the way.

First, the potential effect of any submission before the Greek courts that the jurisdiction clause did not preclude the Greek proceedings. If such a submission was advanced and the Greek court were to rule that there was no preclusion,[72] would the automatic recognition of such a ruling under the Regulation prevent the claim for breach in the English courts? No such claim was advanced,[73] but the questions which arise from the interaction of the rules for the recognition of foreign judgments and the claim for damages are not straightforward. They are dealt with below.

Second, could the English courts go so far as to award damages for breach of the jurisdiction agreement, the practical effect of which would be to reverse any judgment on the merits in favour of the defendants in the Greek courts? The 'logic of ordinary contractual principle' provides a clear and obvious answer which appears to have been accepted by both Lord Clarke and Lord Neuberger with alacrity. According to the latter:[74]

> I accept that, if they were successful, the English indemnity and damages claims could be fairly said to neutralise, at any rate in commercial terms, any benefit to [the defendants] of a judgment in the Greek claims. However, crucially in my view, success for [the claimants] in the English indemnity and damages claims would not be logically inconsistent in any way with success for [the defendants] in the Greek claims. It is not inconsistent (although it is commercially pointless) to say that a defendant is liable to pay a claimant a sum by way of damages, while the claimant is bound to indemnify the defendant in respect of the whole of that sum (or is bound to pay an equivalent sum to the defendant). Indeed, the indemnity is not merely logically consistent with the liability: it is positively meaningless

---

[71] Lord Clarke (*The Alexandros T* (n 67) [38]) referred to an 'established line of cases in England to the effect that claims based on an alleged breach of an exclusive jurisdiction clause or an arbitration clause are different causes of action from claims for substantive relief based on a breach of the underlying contract': see eg *Continental Bank NA v Aeakos Compania Naviera SA* [1994] 1 WLR 588, 595–6; *Alfred C Toepfer International GmbH v Molino Boschi Sarl* [1996] 1 Lloyd's Rep 510, 513; *Toepfer International GmbH v Société Cargill France* [1997] 2 Lloyd's Rep 98, 106; *WMS Gaming Inc v Benedetti Plus Giocolegale Ltd* [2011] EWHC 2620 (Comm) [32].

[72] Its mere advancement would, of course, mean that the same cause of action was before the two courts so that the English court at the time (see now Recast Brussels I Regulation (n 3), Art 31(2) and n 125), would have been required to decline jurisdiction.

[73] Lord Clarke (*The Alexandros T* (n 67) [37]) did not hide his suspicion that the reason for this was because it would be met with the response that a dispute as to the meaning and effect of the settlement agreements was subject to the English jurisdiction clause, such that the court in Greece would decline jurisdiction (under Art 23 of the original Brussels I Regulation (n 70); now Art 25 of the Recast Brussels I Regulation (n 3)). It is understood that this is the view which the Greek courts subsequently came to.

[74] *The Alexandros T* (n 67) [132]. The view expressed mirrors the earlier view of Burton J in *CMA CGM SA v Hyundai Mipo Dockyard Co Ltd* [2008] EWHC 2791 (Comm), [2009] 1 Lloyd's Rep 213 [40].

without the liability for damages, and the liability for damages, though rendered nugatory by the indemnity, is not logically inconsistent with the indemnity.

This seems clearly to have registered with the Court of Appeal which had little hesitation, in a very brief judgment, in ordering summary judgment for damages to be assessed when this claim was made before them after a stay had been lifted by the ruling of the Supreme Court. Furthermore, Longmore LJ saw no need for any reference to the European Court of Justice:[75]

> The Greek court is free to consider the Greek claims; it will, of course, have to decide whether to recognise ... any judgment awarding damages for breach of the Settlement Agreements and the jurisdiction clauses in both the settlement agreements and the insurance policies. But that is not an interference with the jurisdiction of the Greek court but rather an acknowledgment of the Greek court's jurisdiction. In these circumstances there is no infringement of EU law, nor is there any need for a reference to the Court of Justice of the European Union ...

In principle, both decisions endorse the widest possible scope for an award of damages for breach of a jurisdiction agreement (or an arbitration agreement), whether the offending proceedings are commenced in a Member State court, or a non-Member State court; including the prospect of, in effect, reversing a decision of the foreign court on the merits.

The practical difficulties which may be involved in any assessment of the relevant 'loss' for the purpose of such a claim cannot be underestimated. The same simple formula may be applied as in any claim for damages for breach of contract, being a comparison between the factual (or breach) position and the counterfactual (or non-breach) position, but what exactly does the latter consist of? If a claimant succeeds in establishing that a claim should have been heard in the English courts rather than in the foreign courts, does it have to go on to contest the merits to prove that it would have obtained a more advantageous outcome in the English courts?[76] That may not be necessary. There is an obvious parallel here with purely 'domestic' claims which may be made against one's lawyer for the negligent prosecution of a

---

[75] *Starlight* (n 68) [16]. The suspicion looms large that the English courts, having already 'lost' two weapons in the armoury of English civil procedure in previous references (the anti-suit injunction (*Turner v Grovit* (n 2) and see also: *Allianz SpA v West Tankers Inc* Case C-185/07 [2009] ECR I-663 (no injunction to enforce an arbitration agreement)) and the power to stay (*Owusu* (n 2))), were not keen to risk losing the last weapon available for the enforcement of a jurisdiction or arbitration agreement.

[76] In the Court of Appeal Longmore LJ noted that the 'claims in England' had already 'failed' when Tomlinson J refused permission to the defendants to amend their original English claim to include the losses said to flow from the insurers failure to pay (see n 69), but also commented that, since the owners breach was to bring the claims in Greece, '[w]hether they succeed in Greece or would have failed in England is irrelevant': *Starlight* (n 68) [16]. No explanation is provided as to why the counterfactual of suing in England (or at least not in Greece) should be regarded as 'irrelevant'.

case, where the case itself will not be heard again, but damages may be awarded for 'loss of chance'.[77] But one still has to evaluate the chance.

There are several potential practical solutions to this very practical problem of valuation which might briefly be considered before finishing with a more fundamental point of principle. First, might the courts be persuaded to resort to one of the solutions they have adopted, or accepted, in other situations to deal with the uncertainty of establishing, or valuing, loss?[78] One such solution is the award of 'negotiating damages', that is, the sum which represents the 'fee' which the parties would hypothetically have agreed to release the defendant from the obligation not to sue in the foreign court in question, assuming them to have acted as a reasonable 'seller' and a reasonable 'buyer'.[79] Such awards are not confined to the breach of negative stipulations,[80] but they are particularly well-suited to such a breach, where loss is often hard to quantify. After the decision of the Supreme Court in the *One Step* case,[81] it seems very unlikely that a jurisdiction agreement (or arbitration agreement) will be found to represent the sort of 'asset' which now seems necessary to attract an award of negotiating damages, but they might be awarded in lieu of the injunction to which the claimant is otherwise entitled;[82] and there is also the suggestion of Lord Sumption that, in 'non-asset' cases where damages may only be awarded for conventional financial loss, 'negotiating damages' may simply represent the best technique for assessing the relevant loss. The problem with such an award, even if available, is that it does little more than move the underlying uncertainty to a different stage. Even a willing and reasonable buyer (the defendant) will only be prepared to pay what she would otherwise have been required to 'pay' by way of damages which brings us back to where we started. In effect, negotiating damages represent a hypothetical settlement and, for the purpose of that settlement, the parties (and therefore the courts) need some sense of what the seller (the claimant) stands to lose by the breach of the jurisdiction agreement.

One way to avoid this uncertainty, of course, is for the parties to agree the 'fee' in advance, by way of a fixed sum.[83] After the decision of the Supreme Court in

---

[77] See eg *Kitchen v Royal Air Force Association* [1958] 1 WLR 563.
[78] More generally, the 'solution' is to engage in 'the exercise of sound imagination and the practice of the broad axe': *Watson, Laidlaw & Co Ltd v Pott, Cassels & Williamson* [1914] SC 18 (HL) 29–30 (Lord Shaw).
[79] *Pell Frischmann Engineering Ltd v Bow Valley Iran Ltd* [2009] UKPC 45, [2010] BLR 73 [49] (Lord Walker).
[80] See eg *Guido van der Garde BV v Force India Formula One Ltd* [2010] EWHC 2373 (QB). For the suggestion that they should be so confined, see *Turf Club Emporium Pte Ltd v Yeo Boong Hua* [2018] SGCA 44.
[81] *Morris-Garner v One Step (Support) Ltd* [2018] UKSC 20, [2019] AC 649.
[82] This 'category' for the award of negotiating damages is not without its own difficulty: Edwin Peel, 'Negotiating Damages after *One Step*' (2019) 35 JCL 216; Andrew Burrows, 'One Step Forward?' (2018) 134 LQR 515.
[83] Another possibility is to agree an indemnity; such a provision may not be vulnerable to the rule against penalties (*Jervis v Harris* [1996] Ch 195), but does it assist with the problem of uncertainty if the sum against which the indemnity is provided still has to be established?

Cavendish Square Holding BV v El Makdessi,[84] the prospect of such a provision amounting to an unenforceable penalty must have receded a little further. It might be upheld on any of three grounds: (i) that as an attempt to address the loss flowing from breach, it is not 'out of all proportion' given the very uncertainty of estimating loss at the time of the contract;[85] (ii) that it makes no attempt to address loss, as such, but should be upheld as a provision which purports to go 'beyond compensation' in order to protect a 'legitimate interest in performance' in a way which is not extravagant or unconscionable;[86] or (iii) that it is not subject to the rule against penalties at all, that is, there is no breach in suing in a non-designated court if the party in question pays the price for exercising such an option. Writing in 2008 in his book on *Agreements on Jurisdiction and Choice of Law*, Adrian Briggs speculated about whether such provisions might become more common-place. This essay is not the occasion for the empirical research to establish whether this has happened, but one senses that it has not. If that is correct and one speculates why, the answer may be that drafters are concerned that this may prove to be counter-productive. Notwithstanding developments in the law of damages for breach of a jurisdiction agreement, it seems clear that an ant-suit injunction remains the more effective remedy (at least for proceedings in courts outside the EU). Is there a risk that, if damages have been agreed, they may be regarded as 'adequate' and therefore become the more common remedy?[87]

If it seems clear that there is a willingness in the English courts to take the award of damages for breach of a jurisdiction agreement to its logical conclusion, including reversing the consequences of a foreign judgment on the merits, and that there are practical solutions available to the practical problem of how to assess such damages, it is necessary to return to the fundamental point of principle which was raised above in the context of *The Alexandros T*. What is the effect if the foreign court has already ruled that there was no breach of the jurisdiction agreement by the party which commenced proceedings before it? Does such a ruling mean that the question of breach is *res judicata* and no claim for damages is available? The *status* of such a ruling is our principal concern, but it is necessary to point out that it must be a ruling, in terms, that there was *no breach*. For example, if the foreign court concludes that there was no valid or enforceable agreement, or that the claim made before it fell outside the scope of the jurisdiction agreement, there

---

[84] [2015] UKSC 67, [2016] AC 1172.
[85] *Dunlop Pneumatic Tyre Co Ltd v New Garage & Motor Co Ltd* [1915] AC 79, 87–8 (Lord Dunedin).
[86] *Cavendish Square Holding BV v El Makdessi* [2015] UKSC 67, [2016] AC 1172 [28] (Lord Sumption and Lord Neuberger).
[87] The risk may be unfounded. In *Bath & North East Somerset DC v Mowlem Plc* the Court held that, despite the inclusion of a liquidated damages clause in a building contract, the claimant was entitled to rely on the probable higher level of the actual loss that it would suffer to justify the award of an injunction allowing another builder access to the site. Mance LJ distinguished between a 'claim to recover damages' where the parties' agreement is conclusive and 'a claim for an injunction which is designed to avoid ... any cause for a claim to such damages' where it is not: [2004] EWCA Civ 115, [2004] BLR 153 [15].

is a ruling that no breach was committed. If, however, the foreign court proceeds on the basis that the agreement was valid, binding, and applicable but it was necessary to 'override' it for some reason (as, occasionally, we have seen the English courts will sometimes do, eg because of the multi-party nature of the litigation), there is no ruling that no breach was committed.

As far as the status of any foreign ruling is concerned, we might begin by reverting to the example set out above where D commences proceedings in a foreign court and obtains a ruling that this does not constitute the breach of an agreement with C only to sue in England (or some other court).[88] We saw that the effect of section 32(3) of the Civil Jurisdiction and Judgments Act 1982 is that the English courts are not bound by the ruling of the foreign court, notwithstanding that its rulings would otherwise be entitled to recognition because of C's presence at the time proceedings began. However, if the foreign court is an EU Member State court and the proceedings fall within the scope of the Recast Brussels I Regulation, section 32 does not apply[89] and it would seem to follow that the automatic recognition afforded to the court's ruling would undermine any claim for damages.[90] We also saw that the protection of section 32 can be lost by one who has submitted. To test what this might mean, in practice (and in principle), we need to consider two variations to the earlier example.

In the first variation, C is not only present at the time when proceedings are begun in the foreign court, she also appears in the proceedings and does so to try and persuade the foreign court that it should not hear the claim on the merits because of the jurisdiction agreement. There is obvious good sense to this, since the anti-suit injunction which might be available is only effective against a party who is amenable to the sanction of the English courts and any claim for damages is, as we have seen, not free from difficulty. It is also consistent with the principle of comity to at least first *ask* the foreign court to recognise and give effect to the parties' agreement and this no doubt, in part, explains why this step alone will not be regarded as submission under section 33 of the 1982 Act. If C does no more than appear for the 'purpose' of contesting jurisdiction, she has not submitted, and she will not be bound by the answer from the foreign court to the question which was asked of it.[91]

In the second variation, C appears to contest the jurisdiction of the foreign court, but having failed to persuade it to decline, or not exercise, jurisdiction because of a ruling which amounts to the conclusion that there is no breach of the jurisdiction agreement, C goes on to contest the merits. One can also see the good

---

[88] See text following n 27.
[89] s 32(4)(a). Nor does it apply to judgments which are required to be recognised and enforced under the Lugano Convention, or the Hague Convention on Choice of Court Agreements.
[90] Even this might be debated: see Briggs, *Agreements* (n 37) [8.63–8.76].
[91] Some doubt about this conclusion is created by the reasoning of Stuart-Smith and Evans LJJ in *Desert Loan Corp v Hill* [1996] 2 All ER 847. The short and compelling reasoning of Roch LJ as to the scope of s 33 is much to be preferred.

sense in this. While C may have the protection of section 32 for any assets located in England should she withdraw without contesting the merits, that will not assist with assets in other jurisdictions which may be vulnerable if she allows the foreign proceedings to conclude in a judgment in default. It is in this scenario that the conflict between 'the private international law context' and 'the contradictory logic of ordinary contractual principle' is at its most acute. The principle of comity appears to be wearing a bit thin if a party can ask a foreign court if there has been a breach of contract, get the answer that there has not been, and still ask the English courts to ignore that answer if she also gets a decision from the foreign court on the merits, after contesting them, to which she objects. What then is the position, and what should it be?

In *The Atlantic Emperor*[92] the view of the Court of Appeal was that such conduct goes beyond that which is permitted under section 33 and does amount to submission; furthermore, such submission is applied retrospectively to the commencement of proceedings. On this basis, a ruling of the foreign court at any time during the proceedings on whether there has been a breach of the jurisdiction agreement should be recognised, and no claim for damages should be available. The argument to the contrary by Adrian Briggs is one which is firmly based on the distinction to be drawn between 'personal rights, created by the agreement about jurisdiction, and the jurisdiction of a foreign court as a matter of public law'.[93] In short, it is that no step is taken by C which amounts to a waiver of his rights against D *under the jurisdiction agreement*, including those taken after any jurisdictional challenge has failed, because they are necessary only as a result of the breach of contract committed by D.[94] It is not entirely clear whether this leads to the conclusion that the judgment on the merits is not entitled to recognition, or only the judgment that there is no breach of the jurisdiction agreement.[95] It seems that it is the latter and this is, it is submitted, the better view. Recognition of the judgment on the merits is no bar to damages. Indeed, it provides the basis for it, if that judgment leaves C in a worse position than if the jurisdiction agreement had been observed.[96] The

---

[92] *Marc Rich & Co AG v Societa Italiana Impianti pA (The Atlantic Emperor) (No 2)* [1992] 1 Lloyd's Rep 624.

[93] Briggs, *Agreements* (n 37) [8.38].

[94] This may be seen as a further example in which C 'had no real option but to act as [she] did' (*AES* (n 44) [200] (Burnton LJ), but in that case C's conduct was aimed at sustaining a jurisdictional challenge; in the example considered in the text C's jurisdictional challenge has been exhausted: cf Dicey, Morris & Collins (n 24) [14-073] fn 280 ('it will not be open to a defendant to give himself a lifeline by complaining about the jurisdiction in circumstances where there is no basis for making a challenge to it').

[95] There is a degree of ambiguity in the way the point is put (or perhaps in the way I choose to read it): Briggs, *Agreements* (n 37) [8.38].

[96] cf the view of Burton J, in the context of breach of an arbitration agreement where a judgment of the French courts was entitled to recognition under the original Brussels I Regulation: 'This is not a question of not recognising a judgment, but concluding that, as the parties were obliged to go to arbitration, it is only the outcome of arbitration which is of any relevance': *CMA CGM SA v Hyundai Mipo Dockyard Co Ltd* [2008] EWHC 2791 (Comm) [40].

judgment of the foreign court that there is no breach of the jurisdiction agreement is not entitled to recognition on the basis that, in relation *to it*, there was no submission: 'For the claimant to defend the proceedings after the foreign court has ruled that there is no sustainable jurisdictional objection does not tell the outside world that he has given up the right not to be sued in the foreign court.'[97]

Can this conclusion be supported? As a matter of authority, it would be necessary to qualify the decision in *The Atlantic Emperor* by denying the retrospective effect of any submission, or by accepting the idea of a submission only on the substantive merits, both of which arguments were put to the Court of Appeal and rejected. As a matter of principle, it is difficult. C maintains that she had a right not to be sued in the foreign court and, as a result, should at the very least not be bound by any decision of that court about that right; but if the decision of the foreign court is recognised, the very premise of this argument falls away. The appearance of a degree of circularity is all too obvious and one is left with a question of priority which can only be answered almost as a matter of assertion. The assertion is that the private right should trump private international law. The principle of comity is met, to some extent, by encouraging C to ask the foreign court itself whether there has been a breach of the jurisdiction agreement, but does not extend to binding C to the answer provided. We have already seen that C is not bound where she makes no appearance at all,[98] or where she asks the question only for the purpose of challenging jurisdiction,[99] so it may, at least, appear consistent to assert that C is no more bound when she then chooses to contest the merits. The argument that D seeks to gain from what, *in the eyes of the English courts*, is a wrong is just as applicable here, as in those other situations.

C. Choice of Law and Choice of Law Agreements

The role of party autonomy in determining the law applicable to a contract and claims thereunder is not open to doubt, even if there have been periods of resistance.[100] The clue is in the name: *choice* of law. But what, if anything, are the parties *promising* if they *choose* an applicable law. We have seen that a 'choice of court' agreement is readily accepted as an obligation-generating provision; the debate has centred around the extent to which such an obligation can be enforced, given the private international law context. The debate when it comes to choice of law is whether there is any promissory obligation in play at all. Writing in 2008, Adrian Briggs conceded that common law authority in support of a claim for breach of

---

[97] Briggs, *Agreements* (n 37) [8.38].
[98] See text following n 30.
[99] See text to n 91.
[100] For a short summary of the history, see Dicey, Morris & Collins (n 24) [32-004]ff.

choice of law is 'almost non-existent',[101] though it was possible to point to cases which, on a generous interpretation, provide some indirect support.[102] And that remains true today. One is left to approach the question as a matter of principle.

The customary practice in my working relationship with Adrian Briggs over the last thirty years is that we are more often in agreement than disagreement; but if we disagree initially, I am usually persuaded to his point of view. This is, in part, a testament to his skill as an advocate and, in part, a legacy of my time as one his students. However, I have long resisted the prospects of a successful claim for breach of choice of law. It is important to stress that this is a disagreement about prospects; it is not a disagreement about the very concept of such a claim. Adrian Briggs' view is that it should be available if the parties have promised that they will not take steps that would lead to the application of a law other than the chosen law (in particular, that they will not sue in a court where this will be the outcome); and whether they have so promised is just a matter of construction. I agree. For example, consider a provision which states: 'This contract and any disputes arising under or in connection with it shall be governed by English law and the parties agree not to commence proceedings in any court where the outcome of so doing is that English law will not be applied.' If one of the parties then commences proceedings in a court where English law will not be applied, they are guilty of the breach of such a provision. The relief available may include an anti-suit injunction, or damages, or even, at a push,[103] the non-recognition of any judgment in the English courts, if obtained from a foreign court. But if the wording before 'and' is common-place, the wording after it is unheard of, or at least has not been heard of by me.

The real question for debate therefore would appear to be whether the requisite promise can be established simply on the basis of the more common-place wording. While this is undoubtedly a question of construction, that is, it is a contract question, it is once again one which has to be answered in a private international law context. In that context, establishing the necessary promise seems unlikely, for several reasons.

First, what is required, in effect, is a form of jurisdiction agreement: instead of a promise not to sue in any court other than that expressly agreed, which is the promise made, or implied, in a jurisdiction agreement itself, one identifies a promise not to sue in any court which will not result in the application of the chosen law. If there is also an express jurisdiction agreement, or at least an express exclusive jurisdiction agreement, that must presumably have overriding effect, that

---

[101] Briggs, *Agreements* (n 37) [11.46].
[102] See, in particular: *Ellerman* (n 24); *Cadre SA v Astra Asigurari SA* [2005] EWHC 2626 (Comm), [2006] 1 Lloyd's Rep 560.
[103] This seems a 'push' because there is not only the question of the construction of the parties' agreement, but also the interpretation of s 32 Civil Jurisdiction and Judgments Act 1982. Does the example provision amount to an agreement 'under which the dispute in question was to be settled otherwise than by proceedings in the courts of that country', as required by s 32(1)(a)?

is, the parties can only have agreed, or promised, that the law chosen will be applied to the extent that it is applicable by the chosen court. That still leaves contracts in which the parties have chosen only to agree the applicable law (or have only agreed to the non-exclusive jurisdiction of the English courts[104]).

Second, in such a case it seems unlikely, at least as a matter of English law, that a choice of law agreement would be regarded as a jurisdiction agreement of the type required as a matter of *interpretation*, given a certain emphasis in recent cases on the primacy of the language used, or 'textual analysis', particularly in cases where some reliance can be placed on the quality of the drafting.[105] The submission that a particular interpretation of a contract term should not be rejected simply on the basis that if that is what the parties meant they could easily have said it may have been denigrated in some quarters,[106] but it has a certain resonance in this context.[107]

Third, if not a question of interpretation, there are formidable obstacles in the way of an implied term of the type required,[108] not least of which are the vagaries of the applicable law process in any court. This is not the place for a general and in-depth analysis of choice of law rules; suffice it to say, notwithstanding a degree of uniformity brought about by instruments such as the Rome I Regulation,[109] a significant degree of unpredictability attends the determination of the law applicable to a contract and claims arising thereunder. For example, one court may characterise the claim as contractual, while another prefers a different characterisation, or the law chosen may be overridden by one court on the basis of public policy, or mandatory rules, but not by another; or overridden in favour of a different set of mandatory rules. This may be met by emphasising that the unpredictability of an outcome, indeed the very possibility of an outcome, is not necessarily a bar to an implied promise that it shall be achieved. Thus, as far as the unpredictable is concerned, it has been said by a court that there is nothing to stop a party warranting

---

[104] In such a case, the jurisdiction agreement may still have a more limited overriding effect, ie there is no breach if proceedings commenced in the non-exclusive court results in the application of a law other than that chosen, or is the better construction that the non-exclusive jurisdiction can only be invoked if it is consistent with the application of the chosen law? The very uncertainty of the outcome in such a case does not bode well for the interpretation, or implication, which Adrian Briggs seeks to draw from the choice of law.

[105] *Wood v Capita Insurance Services Ltd* [2017] UKSC 24, [2017] AC 1173 [10] (Lord Hodge).

[106] See eg *Spire Healthcare Ltd v Royal & Sun Alliance Insurance plc* [2018] EWCA Civ 317, [2018] 1 CLC 327 [21].

[107] cf *Black Diamond Offshore Ltd v Fomento de Construcciones y Contratas SA* [2016] EWCA Civ 1141, [2017] 1 BCLC 196.

[108] It might be regarded as a variation of the type of implied term considered above: text to nn 39–40. We have seen that this is viewed as a term implied 'in fact' (*Duval* (n 40)), meaning that it would need to be shown that it is 'necessary for business efficacy', or 'so obvious that it goes without saying'. This is an 'ambitious undertaking' at the best of times (*Philips Electronique Grand Public SA v BSkyB Ltd* [1995] EMLR 472, 480 (Lord Bingham MR)) and looks no less ambitious here.

[109] Regulation (EC) 593/2008 of 17 June 2008 on the law applicable to contractual obligations (Rome I) [2008] OJ L177/6 (hereafter Rome I).

that 'it would snow next Christmas',[110] but the point that was being emphasised is that this would 'represent a bet' and it seems unlikely that such a bet can be implied, if not provided expressly. As far as the impossible is concerned, one can point[111] to a case such as *McRae v Commonwealth Disposals Commission*[112] where the non-existence of an oil tanker for salvage resulted in the liability of the Commission for breach of an implied warranty that it did exist. But such a conclusion was only reached on the basis that the Commission had ample opportunity to investigate what was a question of past fact (or non-fact as it happens); any analogy with the outcome of future proceedings does not seem entirely apt. This may be met, in turn, by narrowing down the nature of the term to be implied to one not deliberately to take steps with the intention of ensuring that the chosen law is not applied,[113] but claims which depend on establishing a 'deliberate' breach have not been well received in English law;[114] and the inherent uncertainty of establishing just what is the scope or nature of the obligation owed, and whether it has been breached, does not sit well with the requirement that before a term can be implied it 'must not be too vague, and it must be possible to formulate its content with "adequate precision"'.[115]

So, I remain unconvinced about the prospects, if not the underlying principle. Also writing in 2008, Adrian Briggs observed that, when it came to a claim for breach of choice of law, it was surprising that it was an argument that no one had tried, given the imagination (desperation?) of commercial litigators and the sums of money which may be at stake.[116] And still no one seems to have tried, at least not in the English courts,[117] which may in itself be telling.

D. Brexit

The temptation simply to ignore the potential consequences of the UK's withdrawal from the EU on the issues addressed in this essay is enormous. As it is, this is still an exercise in saying as little as possible. This is not without justification, if only because one is confined to discussion of the *potential* consequences. They are most likely to be felt in the context of jurisdiction agreements.[118] What is known is that

---

[110] *Avrora Fine Arts Investment Ltd v Christie, Manson & Woods Ltd* [2012] EWHC 2198 (Ch), [2012] PNLR 35 [133] (Newey J).
[111] As does Adrian Briggs: Briggs, *Agreements* (n 37) [11.81].
[112] (1951) 84 CLR 377.
[113] For this suggestion, see Briggs, *Agreements* (n 37) [11.53].
[114] See eg *Kudos Catering (UK) Ltd v Manchester Central Convention Complex Ltd* [2013] EWCA Civ 38, [2013] 2 Lloyd's Rep 270 [28] (Tomlinson LJ).
[115] See *Treitel* (n 49) [6-064] and the cases cited in support.
[116] Briggs, *Agreements* (n 37) [11.49].
[117] cf *Ace Insurance Ltd v Moose Enterprise Pty Ltd* [2009] NSWSC 724.
[118] As we have seen, the prospects of private law relief for a 'breach of choice of law' remain a matter of speculation and the EU instrument which might have any bearing on this (the Rome I Regulation)

the Recast Brussels I Regulation no longer applies to proceedings commenced after the transition period to implement the UK's exit comes to an end on 31 December 2020.[119] At present, the Regulation, and the decisions of the European Court of Justice thereunder, have outlawed the anti-suit injunction and section 32 of the 1982 Act does not apply to the judgment of an EU Member State court which is entitled to recognition under the Regulation.[120] If nothing replaces it, then damages will continue to be available as they are at present, even if that is only because the European Court of Justice has not had the opportunity to say what it thinks of that development. An anti-suit injunction will, presumably, also be available, in which case the need to resort to a claim for damages will be less acute; and the non-recognition of a judgment from an EU Member State under section 32 of the 1982 Act will also be possible. More intriguing is the prospect that the UK becomes a party to the Lugano Convention[121] alongside the EU, Norway, Iceland, and Switzerland.[122] Section 32 of the 1982 Act does not apply to a judgment required to be recognised under the Lugano Convention,[123] and although the courts of a contracting state are only required to 'pay due account' to the case law of the European Court of Justice on the Recast Brussels I Regulation,[124] it seems unlikely that the English courts would see the opportunity to revive the anti-suit injunction as the solution to breach of a jurisdiction agreement. The temptation to do so may stem from the fact that the amendment made to the Recast Brussels I Regulation under which a court seised second pursuant to an exclusive jurisdiction may continue to hear the case[125] has not been made to the Lugano Convention.[126] That amendment is no doubt the reason why a claim for damages does not appear to have been much resorted to (at least in terms of reported decisions), notwithstanding the expansive approach of the English courts in *The Alexandros T* litigation. It may be anticipated that more will be seen of it if the United Kingdom does accede to the Lugano Convention.

---

will, at least initially, be retained as part of English law: Law Applicable to Contractual Obligations and Non-Contractual Obligations (Amendment etc) (EU Exit) Regulations 2019, SI 2019/834.

[119] The hope of sense prevailing and some form of extension being agreed upon between the two sides turned out to be forlorn.
[120] s 32(4)(a).
[121] Convention of 30 October 2007 on jurisdiction and the recognition and enforcement of judgments in civil and commercial matters [2007] OJ L339/3 (hereafter Lugano Convention).
[122] The UK has deposited a request for accession in its own right, though it is understood that the European Commission is not too keen.
[123] s 32(4)(a).
[124] Lugano Convention (n 121) Protocol 2, Art 1.
[125] Recast Brussels I Regulation (n 3), Art 31(2), in effect reversing the decision in *Gasser* (n 2).
[126] Nor is it available through a creative interpretation of the Lugano Convention in accordance with the principle of harmonisation: *Mastermelt Ltd v Siegfried Evionnaz SA* [2020] EWHC 927 (QB).

E. Conclusion

If the question addressed in this paper is how private is English private international law, the answer is: very. It is perhaps more accurate to say that it is not so much that the *law* is private since, ultimately, even in England, jurisdiction, applicable law, and the recognition of enforcement of foreign judgments are aspects of public law. Rather, the English courts seem very much at ease with the idea that the outcomes of these questions of public law may be made the subject of the enforceable rights and duties of the litigating parties. If anything, Adrian Briggs considers that it might be possible for the courts to go further even than they have already done. I, and others, may not (yet) have been persuaded to go quite as far, but it seems appropriate to allow him the final characteristically blunt word (albeit couched in terms specifically about jurisdiction): 'Contracts are made to be performed and the fact that they may be contracts about jurisdiction is nothing to the point.'[127]

---

[127] Briggs, *Agreements* (n 37) [6.05].

13
Comity in Private International Law and Fundamental Principles of Justice

James Edelman and Madeleine Salinger

A. Introduction

In 2011, Adrian Briggs delivered a ground-breaking series of lectures concerning the common law principle of comity in private international law.[1] The published version of these lectures represent the most careful consideration of this principle in the history of private international law. This essay focuses upon the same topic. As is usual with consideration of any of Professor Briggs' work on private international law, this essay owes a great debt to his work. We do not purport to, and cannot in the space of this essay, descend to the detail of his comprehensive examination of the principle of comity in his published lectures. Instead, as Australians for whom legal notions of comity are embedded in s 118 of our Constitution, we develop his approach by considering the underlying rationale for the principle of comity and explaining the meaning and operation of a widely accepted limit to the principle.

As Professor Briggs has observed, the foundation for the principle of comity in private international law is the respect for the territorial sovereignty of other states.[2] In an international legal system based upon competing sovereignties, it is generally implied that each state consents to respect each other. But there are limits to this implied consent. The perspective we offer in this essay concerns the limit where comity runs contrary to fundamental principles of justice. We consider why this limit exists and how to identify such fundamental principles. The difficulty of identification of such fundamental principles is then illustrated by reference to the principle of privacy, a principle which, almost uniquely in Australia, has not been instantiated directly into a legal rule.

The essay is divided into three parts. The first part considers the meaning of comity and the role that it should play in a court's decision-making process in

---

[1] Adrian Briggs, 'The Principle of Comity in Private International Law' (2012) 354 *Recueil des Cours* 65 (hereafter Briggs, *Hague Lectures*).
[2] Adrian Briggs, *Private International Law in English Courts* (OUP 2014) [3.139] (hereafter Briggs, *Private International Law in English Courts*).

private international law cases. As Briggs has powerfully argued, although comity is difficult to define because it has been used in different senses over time it has a core meaning concerned with mediating respect for the territorial sovereignty of all states with a stake in a private international law matter.[3] Understood in this way, comity is the basal principle underlying many rules of private international law. However, it is not a principle that is capable of direct application in any particular case. Rather, it is one consideration to be taken into account in the application of open-textured rules and in deriving and developing concrete rules.

The second part of this essay considers one limit to the principle of comity which in turn limits the development and application of rules based upon that principle. Given that the principle of comity is based upon one sovereign impliedly consenting to respect the territorial sovereignty of another, comity only operates to the extent that consent can reasonably be implied. No reasonable implication of consent could be implied for a state to give effect within its territory to actions of another sovereign taken within that sovereign's territory if those acts are contrary to fundamental principles of justice. This is often referred to, somewhat misleadingly, as a 'public policy' exception to certain rules of private international law. There are relatively few cases in which courts have applied this exception, and as a result there is a lack of clarity about how courts ascertain when a foreign act is contrary to a fundamental principle of justice. Fundamental principles are usually directly reflected in legal rights and freedoms in all just systems of law. But different states protect these rights and freedoms to different degrees when resolving their conflict with other principles. It is always possible to countenance a degree of departure from fundamental rights and freedoms in a foreign legal system without concluding that the foreign system has failed to respect an underlying fundamental principle of justice. The ultimate limit to the concept of comity therefore depends upon an exercise of judgment about the extent to which a derogation from a fundamental right or freedom means that the foreign legal system does not respect a fundamental principle of justice. Such a conclusion will be rare.

The third and final part of the essay considers how new fundamental principles of justice might be identified. From the perspective of Australia, where the law recognises no direct right to privacy, the principle of privacy forms the ideal case study to assess whether new fundamental principles of justice might arise and, if so, how they might be recognised.

---

[3] See Briggs, *Hague Lectures* (n 1) 80; Briggs, *Private International Law in English Courts* (n 2) [3.139].

B. The Meaning and Role of Comity

The principle of comity is a concept of 'very elastic content'.[4] It has variously been described as a principle 'formulated by reference to the principles of sovereignty and territoriality',[5] a principle of 'deference and respect due by other states to the actions of a state legitimately taken within its territory',[6] a principle of 'respect for ... legitimate authority',[7] a 'a species of accommodation' which 'involves neighbourliness, mutual respect, and the friendly waiver of technicalities',[8] and a principle that is conditioned upon the reciprocal treatment by states of one another's judgments.[9] As Professor Briggs has observed, the varying definitions have led some writers to express the view that the principle of comity is unusable or useless as a component of legal reasoning.[10] Nevertheless, as he also observes, it has an important purpose.[11] That purpose is common to all principles that underlie legal rules. They provide reasons for rules and elucidate how the rule might be developed. At its core, comity is a principle concerned with respect for the territorial sovereignty of all nations. As Millett LJ said in *Crédit Suisse Fides Trust v Cuoghi*,[12] 'It is becoming widely accepted that comity between the courts of different countries requires mutual respect for the territorial integrity of each other's jurisdiction'. This principle informs the existence and development of many rules of private international law.

1. Respect for territorial sovereignty based upon implied consent

As a general principle of such elastic content, comity is not susceptible of precise definition in the same way as most legal rules that are capable of direct application.

---

[4] Lord Collins of Mapesbury and others (eds), *Dicey, Morris and Collins: The Conflict of Laws* (15th edn, Sweet & Maxwell 2015) [1-008] (hereafter Dicey, Morris & Collins).
[5] Briggs, *Private International Law in English Courts* (n 2) [3.139].
[6] *Morguard Investments Ltd v De Savoye* [1990] 3 SCR 1077, 1095. See also *Nevsun Resources Ltd v Araya* 2020 SCC 5 [45], [50] (hereafter *Nevsun*); Donald Earl Childress III, 'Comity as Conflict: Resituating International Comity as Conflict of Laws' (2010) 44 University of California Davis L Rev 11, 31 (hereafter Childress, 'Comity as Conflict').
[7] Timothy Endicott, 'Comity among Authorities' (2015) 68 Current Legal Problems 1, 10.
[8] James Crawford, *Brownlie's Principles of Public International Law* (OUP 2019) 21 (hereafter *Brownlie's Principles of Public International Law in English Courts*).
[9] *Hilton v Guyot* 159 US 113, 228 (1895) (hereafter *Hilton*).
[10] Briggs, *Private International Law in English Courts* (n 2) [3.138], referring to Albert Venn Dicey, *A Digest of the Law of England with Reference to the Conflict of Laws* (Stevens and Sons, Sweet and Maxwell 1896) 10; also Briggs, *Hague Lectures* (n 1) 80–1, discussing James Fawcett, Janeen Carruthers, and Peter North, *Cheshire, North & Fawcett, Private International Law* (14th edn, OUP 2008) 5.
[11] Briggs, *Private International Law in English Courts* (n 2) [3.138].
[12] [1998] QB 818.

It would be futile to attempt a precise definition that could be directly applied.[13] However, in order to understand the boundaries of the principle and the way that it influences the development of legal rules it is necessary to understand its theoretical foundations. These were cogently outlined in the seminal works of Ulrich Huber and Joseph Story from which the common law conception of comity developed. The theoretical foundation of comity is that it mediates respect for the territorial sovereignty of both the forum state and all other states with an interest in a private international law matter based upon the implied consent of the forum state to give effect to acts of another sovereign within the forum state's territory. This understanding of comity has been adopted by courts throughout the common law world and continues to inform their use of comity in the development of legal rules.

In *De Conflictu Legum Diversarum in Diversis Imperiis*,[14] Ulrich Huber outlined three basic axioms of private international law. Huber's first two axioms were concerned with the sovereignty that each state has within its own borders:[15]

1. 'The laws of each state have force within the limits of that government and bind all subjects to it, but not beyond.'
2. 'All persons within the limits of a government, whether they live there permanently or temporarily, are deemed to be subjects thereof.'

However, Huber's focus on territorial sovereignty gave rise to a problem:[16] if a state has absolute sovereignty within its own territory (and, it follows, in relation to the laws to be applied in its courts), how can that court apply a law of another sovereign state? This was resolved by a third axiom, or the principle of comity, which permits respect for rights acquired within the territorial sovereignty of another state:[17]

3. 'Sovereigns will so act by way of comity that rights acquired within the limits of a government retain their force everywhere so far as they do not cause prejudice to the power or rights of such government or of its subjects.'

Huber's axioms were adopted as 'general maxims' by Joseph Story.[18] Story then explained the ultimate foundation of the principle of comity as lying in implied

---

[13] Childress, 'Comity as Conflict' (n 6) 13; Thomas Schultz and Niccolò Ridi, 'Comity in US Courts' (2018) 10 Northeastern University L Rev 280, 285–6 (hereafter Schultz and Ridi, 'Comity in US Courts'); also Briggs, *Hague Lectures* (n 1) 181.

[14] Ernest G Lorenzen, 'Huber's *De Conflictu Legum*' in Ernest G Lorenzen (ed), *Selected Articles on the Conflict of Laws* (Yale University Press 1947) 162 (hereafter Lorenzen, 'Huber's *De Conflictu Legum*').

[15] Ibid 164.

[16] Childress, 'Comity as Conflict' (n 6) 21.

[17] Lorenzen, 'Huber's *De Conflictu Legum*' (n 14) 164.

[18] J Story, *Commentaries on the Conflict of Laws* (Hillard, Gray, and Company 1834) (hereafter Story, *Commentaries*). See Childress, 'Comity as Conflict' (n 6), 23–5.

consent. Referring to the third axiom or maxim, he argued that the recognition or local enforcement of a foreign sovereign act within the territory of another state required the consent of the latter state:[19]

> [W]hatever force and obligation the laws of one country have in another, depends solely upon the laws, and municipal regulations of the latter, that is to say, upon its own proper jurisprudence and polity, and upon its own express or tacit consent.

It followed, according to Story, that comity 'is derived altogether from the voluntary consent of [the state where the law is sought to be recognised]; and is inadmissible, when it is contrary to its known policy, or prejudicial to its interests'.[20] Story emphasised that it was for the 'nation', rather than the 'courts', to consent to giving the laws of another nation force within its borders, but considered that courts could assess whether the 'nation' had consented by 'presum[ing] the tacit adoption of [foreign laws] by their own government, unless they are repugnant to its policy, or prejudicial to its interests'.[21]

By treating comity as a principle that is founded upon implied consent of the sovereign and capable of influencing the development of legal rules, Story's approach explains why comity does not require the recognition or local enforcement of a foreign sovereign act in every circumstance. Since the principle of comity derives from consent it would not prevent a court from enforcing a law passed by the forum state that prohibits the recognition of any foreign judgment.[22] Nor would a court recognise or enforce a foreign sovereign act where to do so would undermine the operation of the laws of the forum state.[23] And, in perhaps the most significant limit upon the operation of comity, it could not require a state to 'enforce doctrines, which, in a moral, or political view, are incompatible with its own safety or happiness, or conscientious regard to justice and duty'.[24] The way in which this limitation has been adopted by the courts is discussed in part two of this essay.

In the two centuries since the publication of his *Commentaries*, three key criticisms of Story's theory have emerged. None undermines it, although they require the theory to be adapted. The first criticism is that the first maxim is contradicted by the power of states to legislate extraterritorially in certain circumstances.[25] This is undoubtedly true but there is usually a general presumption that a state's jurisdiction is territorial. Story's territorial theory of jurisdiction can be refined so

---

[19] Story, *Commentaries* (n 18) § 23.
[20] Ibid § 38.
[21] Ibid § 38.
[22] Briggs, *Hague Lectures* (n 1) 145.
[23] Compare the majority and the minority in *XX v Whittington Hospital NHS Trust* [2020] UKSC 14, [2020] 2 WLR 972.
[24] Story, *Commentaries* (n 18) § 25.
[25] See eg Ernest G Lorenzen, 'Story's Commentaries on the Conflict of Laws—One Hundred Years After' (1934) 48 Harvard L Rev 15, 37 (hereafter Lorenzen, 'Story's Commentaries').

that it is now perhaps better expressed as requiring a 'genuine connection between the subject matter of jurisdiction and the territorial base or reasonable interests of the state in question'.[26] The decision of the Supreme Court of the United States in *Hartford Fire Insurance Co v California*,[27] discussed below, illustrates that a state may legitimately legislate extraterritorially in relation to matters that have a substantial effect within the state's territory. However, even with this refinement of the territorial principle, the principle of comity will still be required in most cases to explain how a sovereign act in one state can have force in another.

The second criticism takes aim at Story's view that states consent (albeit often implicitly) to afford comity to one another. It has been suggested that this view is based upon a misunderstanding of Huber, who, properly understood, argued that comity is an imposed legal obligation.[28] Putting aside the question of whether Story did in fact diverge from Huber in this respect,[29] Story's conception of comity as a matter of consent is entirely consistent with the view in Anglo-American law that rules of private international law are not imposed on states by some superior authority, but are rather 'voluntarily accepted by each sovereign state'.[30]

The third criticism is that it is unclear what Story's third maxim requires of courts in determining whether the 'nation' had impliedly consented to giving effect to the laws of another state within its borders. Story's suggestion that there was no implied consent where affording comity was not in the forum state's 'interests' is said to create difficulty for courts to assess.[31] This is also undoubtedly true. But it merely illustrates the nature of Story's maxims as principles from which concrete rules are derived or open-textured rules are applied. They are not rules that are to be applied directly to the facts of a case. As Schultz and Ridi argue, 'it is unthinkable to resolve cases involving comity considerations with the simple application of Story's maxims'.[32] Or, as Schultz and Holloway put it, comity is 'a springboard from which [courts] proceeded to develop a highly organized and sophisticated set of choice of law rules'.[33] This aligns with the role of comity for which Briggs powerfully argued in his Hague lectures.

---

[26] *Brownlie's Principles of Public International Law in English Courts* (n 8) 440–1.
[27] 509 US 764 (1993) (hereafter *Hartford*).
[28] Alan Watson, *Joseph Story and the Comity of Errors: A Case Study in Conflict of Laws* (University of Georgia Press 1992) 22 (hereafter Watson, *Comity of Errors*); also Lorenzen 'Story's Commentaries' (n 25), 35–6.
[29] Watson, *Comity of Errors* (n 28) 22; Schultz and Ridi, 'Comity in US Courts' (n 13) 298; also Hessel E Yntema, 'The Comity Doctrine' (1966) 65 Michigan L Rev 9, 29–30. cf Lorenzen, 'Huber's *De Conflictu Legum*' (n 14) 138–9.
[30] Lorenzen, 'Story's Commentaries' (n 25) 36. This principle has long been established: see eg *Holman v Johnson* (1775) 1 Cowp 341, 343; 98 ER 1120, 1121; *Dalrymple v Dalrymple* (1811) 2 Hagg Con 54, 58–9; 161 ER 665, 667.
[31] Childress, 'Comity as Conflict' (n 6) 29–30.
[32] Schultz and Ridi, 'Comity in US Courts' (n 13) 300.
[33] Thomas Schultz and David Holloway, '*Retour sur la comity, deuxième partie: La comity dans l'histoire du droit international privé*' (2012) 139 Journal du Droit International 571, 593–4, quoted in Schultz and Ridi. 'Comity in US Courts' (n 13) 355.

Story's theory has been referenced by courts throughout the common law world,[34] including in the decision of the Supreme Court of the United States *Hilton v Guyot*[35] which has remained a central authority for more than a century, both in the United States and abroad.[36] In that case, a French court had given judgment against Hilton and others, who removed their assets to the United States during the course of the litigation. The issue before the Supreme Court of the United States was whether to enforce the French judgment. The Court's starting point was in essence a restatement of Story's first and third maxim: it held that '[n]o law has any effect, of its own force, beyond the limits of the sovereignty from which its authority is derived', and it followed that 'the extent to which the law of one nation ... shall be allowed to operate within the dominion of another nation, depends upon what our greatest jurists have been content to call "the comity of nations" '.[37] In what remains the most cited statement on the principle of comity in the United States,[38] the Court held that comity 'is neither a matter of absolute obligation, on the one hand, nor of mere courtesy and good will, upon the other' and that it entailed 'the recognition which one nation allows within its territory to the legislative, executive, or judicial acts of another nation, having due regard both to international duty and convenience, and to the rights of its own citizens or other persons who are under the protection of its laws'.[39]

From this general statement, the Court distilled a number of more specific rules relating to the enforcement of foreign judgments: for example, a judgment *in rem* adjudicating the title to a ship or other movable property is treated as valid everywhere, as is a judgment affecting the status of persons, such as a decree confirming or dissolving a marriage unless this is contrary to the policy of the forum state.[40] Childress suggests that the Supreme Court in *Hilton* set the principle of comity adrift from its historical moorings by stating a number of rules which required the application of foreign law in certain circumstances without consideration of what was in the forum state's sovereign interests.[41] This may be so, but in our view the manner in which the Supreme Court used Story's theory of comity largely aligns with what we say remains its most appropriate use today. Comity is not a principle of direct application: it is insufficiently hard-edged for a Court to determine

---

[34] See eg United States: *Bank of Augusta v Earle* 38 (13 Peters) US 519, 569, 589 (1839); *Walworth v Harris* 129 US 355, 364 (1889); *Hartford* (n 27) 817. United Kingdom: *Castrique v Imrie* (1870) Law Rep 4 HL 414, 428–29; *British South Africa Co v Cia de Moçambique* [1893] AC 602. Canada: *Spar Aerospace Ltd v American Mobile Satellite* [2002] 4 SCR 205, 217–18 (hereafter *Spar Aerospace*). Australia: *Potter v Broken Hill Proprietary Co Ltd* (1906) 3 CLR 479, 501–2.
[35] *Hilton* (n 9).
[36] The Supreme Court of Canada has adopted the definition of comity outlined in *Hilton*: see *Spar Aerospace* (n 34) 219.
[37] *Hilton* (n 9) 163.
[38] Joel R Paul, 'Comity in International Law' (1991) 32 Harvard Law Journal 1, 9.
[39] *Hilton* (n 9) 163–4.
[40] *Hilton* (n 9) 167.
[41] Childress, 'Comity as Conflict' (n 6), 33–4.

a case on the basis of what 'comity' requires by some global assessment of whether affording comity is in the sovereign's interests in a given case. Rather, it is a general principle that explains the theoretical basis for one sovereign giving effect to the laws of another, from which concrete rules are distilled.

The *Hilton* decision did however depart from the concept of comity we advocate here in one respect: the Court ultimately refused to enforce the French judgment on the basis that France would not have enforced an equivalent judgment of the United States, and thus conditioned comity upon reciprocity.[42] As Briggs argues, comity has nothing to do with reciprocity.[43] This has now been recognised in the United States.[44]

Although it has been suggested that, as a result of the criticisms discussed above, comity is no longer the ground of conflict of laws theory,[45] the powerful force of Story's theory maintained its gravitational pull upon the Supreme Court in *Hartford Fire Insurance Co v California*,[46] a century after its decision in *Hilton*. In that case, the principle's operation in relation to statutory interpretation was effectively based by both the majority and by the minority upon the implied consent of the United States to treat with respect the territorial sovereignty of another state.

In *Hartford Fire Insurance*, the State of California brought proceedings against reinsurers who were based in London under a law of the United States, the Sherman Act 1890, alleging that the reinsurers had engaged in various conspiracies to impact the American insurance market. The relevant conduct had occurred in London and was not prohibited under English law. On its face the Sherman Act was not limited to conduct that occurred in the United States. This raised questions as to whether comity required that the Sherman Act not apply to activities undertaken in London, and whether, even if it did so apply, the Court should refrain from exercising its jurisdiction for reasons of comity. The Court divided and, as Briggs notes, both camps appeared to understand that comity was on their side.[47]

The majority, comprised of Rehnquist CJ, White, Blackmun, Stevens, and Souter JJ, considered that the Act applied to the foreign acts in issue due to their 'substantial' effect on the markets of the United States.[48] The majority did not appear to view considerations of comity as any impediment to the Act having extraterritorial effect. Further, the majority considered that it was not necessary to determine whether it would be appropriate for the court to 'refrain from the exercise of jurisdiction on grounds of international comity' because, given that the conduct

---

[42] *Hilton* (n 9) 228.
[43] Briggs, *Hague Lectures* (n 1) 89–91.
[44] See *Direction der Disconto-Gesellschaft v US Steel Corp* 300 F 741, 747 (1925); *Johnston v Compagnie Générale Transatlantique* 152 NE 121, 123 (NY 1926).
[45] Childress, 'Comity as Conflict' (n 6) 30; Eugene F Scoles and others, *Conflict of Laws* (4th edn, Thomson West 2004) 20.
[46] *Hartford* (n 27).
[47] Briggs, *Hague Lectures* (n 1) 102.
[48] *Hartford* (n 27), 796.

was not prohibited in England, there was no true conflict between the laws of England and the United States.[49] It has been suggested that in so holding the majority 'dealt comity a near death blow'.[50] However, as Briggs notes, on one view the majority's holding is consistent with comity: as noted above, the refinement of the territorial principle suggests that it is legitimate for states to regulate matters that have a substantial impact within their territory, and on this basis it could be argued that 'international comity tolerated the application of US law'.[51]

The minority, comprised of O'Connor, Scalia, Kennedy, and Thomas JJ, held that the question was not whether the court should 'refrain' from exercising its jurisdiction but was instead how the legislature intended the Act to apply, which included considerations of comity.[52] Citing Story, the minority held that 'comity is exercised by legislatures when they enact laws, and courts assume it has been exercised when they come to interpreting the scope of laws their legislatures have enacted'.[53] Since the foreign acts were committed by British subjects in Britain, and Britain had 'established a comprehensive regulatory scheme governing the London reinsurance markets', it was 'unimaginable that an assertion of legislative jurisdiction by the United States would be considered reasonable' and 'inappropriate to assume, in the absence of statutory indication to the contrary, that Congress has made such an assertion'.[54] The minority's decision was therefore also influenced by considerations of respect for England's territorial sovereignty to regulate conduct within its borders without foreign influence. Similarly, the Supreme Court of Canada has suggested that courts may use comity as 'an interpretive tool' that requires laws to be interpreted 'in a manner respectful of the spirit of international co-operation and the comity of nations'.[55]

The nature of comity as a principle of respect for territorial sovereignty based upon implied consent is also evident in the United Kingdom. In *Kuwait Airways Corporation v Iraqi Airways Co (Nos 4 and 5)*,[56] the Court of Appeal considered whether it should recognise an Iraqi decree that purported to divest Kuwait Airways of its aircraft present within Iraqi territory as one part of Iraq's purported annexation of Kuwait. In a decision that was upheld by the House of Lords, the Court of Appeal held that there is a rule of English law, 'founded primarily on a view as to the comity of nations', that 'a foreign sovereign is to be accorded that absolute authority which is vested in him to act within his own territory as a sovereign

---

[49] Ibid 799.
[50] Spencer Weber Waller, 'The Twilight of Comity' (2000) 38 Columbia Journal of Transnational Law 563, 564; also Schultz and Ridi, 'Comity in US Courts' (n 13) 312–13.
[51] Briggs, *Hague Lectures* (n 1) 102.
[52] *Hartford* (n 27) 813, 817.
[53] Ibid 817, citing Story, *Commentaries* (n 18) § 38.
[54] Ibid 819.
[55] *R v Hape* [2007] SCR 292 [47]–[52].
[56] *Kuwait Airways Corp v Iraqi Airways Co* [2002] UKHL 19, [2002] 2 AC 883 [318] (hereafter *Kuwait Airways*); see also *Belhaj v Straw* [2017] UKSC 3, [2017] AC 964 [225] (hereafter *Belhaj*).

acts'. The implied consent reflected in this rule was however limited. As the Court of Appeal noted, each sovereign affords comity to the other by saying: 'We will respect your territorial sovereignty. But there can be no offence if we do not recognise your extraterritorial or exorbitant acts'. We return to what exactly constitutes an exorbitant act in part two of this essay. We conclude then, with Adrian Briggs, that:[57]

> [T]he principle or doctrine of comity may be formulated by reference to the principles of sovereignty and territoriality: as a principle which asserts or admits and avers, according to context, that the exercise of jurisdiction and legislative power, by state and court, is properly territorial and that exercises of sovereign power within the sovereign's own territory are bound and entitled to be respected by other states and other courts.

2. A principle that influences the development of legal rules

Some authors consider that the implied consent of sovereigns to respect the territorial jurisdiction of other States is a matter of concern to executive government and legislatures but not to courts because 'comity is a matter for sovereigns, not for judges required to decide a case according to the rights of the parties'.[58] As Perram J said in *Habib v Commonwealth*,[59] considering the Commonwealth of Australia's argument that international comity was relevant to whether to *exercise* jurisdiction to consider allegations of the Australian government's complicity in alleged acts of torture: 'No doubt comity between the nations is a fine and proper thing but it provides no basis whatsoever for this Court declining to exercise the jurisdiction conferred on it by Parliament'.

Story agreed that is for the nation rather than the courts to afford comity, but argued that it is nevertheless appropriate for a court's reasoning to be informed by considerations of whether the nation had implicitly consented to affording comity in certain situations.[60] This was to be 'ascertained in the same way, and guided by the same reasoning, by which all other principles of the municipal law are ascertained and guided'.[61] Since comity can be taken into account in the application of open-textured rules such as the process of statutory interpretation undertaken by the minority in *Hartford Fire Insurance*, so too it should be able to be taken into

---

[57] Briggs, *Private International Law in English Courts* (n 2) [3.139], [6.137]–[6.138]. See also Briggs, *Hague Lectures* (n 1) 181; Adrian Briggs, 'Recognition of Foreign Judgments: a Matter of Obligation' (2013) 129 Law Quarterly Review 87, 91.
[58] Paul Torremans and others (eds), *Cheshire, North & Fawcett, Private International Law* (15th edn, OUP 2017) 4.
[59] (2010) 183 FCR 62 [37].
[60] Story, *Commentaries* (n 18) § 38.
[61] Ibid § 38.

account in the assessment of other open-textured rules such as whether jurisdiction should be exercised. In *Mannington Mills Inc v Congoleum Corporation*,[62] a decision cited by the majority in *Hartford Fire Insurance*,[63] the United States Court of Appeals (Third Circuit) indicated that it was appropriate for courts to take considerations of comity into account when determining whether to exercise jurisdiction. Further, as a general principle it should be capable of influencing the development of legal rules in private international law.[64] Schultz and Mitchenson argue that comity 'will be relevant in any circumstances where the application of law or the exercise of judicial power (be it domestic or foreign) has the potential to have an effect outside the jurisdictional boundaries of the State'.[65] They analyse in detail the various areas of private international law in which the principle of comity plays an important role including: statutory and treaty interpretation; adjudication on the laws and acts of foreign states; recognition of foreign judgments; judicial co-operation; request for pre-trial discovery orders; and assistance in bankruptcy and insolvency proceedings. For present purposes, it suffices to consider in the second part of this essay the influence that comity has had on the development of the rules of private international law in two areas that are particularly relevant to the discussion of the limits of the principle comity.

The first area concerns the true principle underlying the common law recognition of foreign judgments and enforcement of them by local orders. There is a line of English authority, described by Briggs as based upon the adoption of a 'thoughtless non-definition of what comity really is',[66] in which courts have rejected comity as a basis for the common law recognition of foreign judgments.[67] For instance, while recognising that comity was the original rationale for common law recognition of foreign judgments it has been said that, in 1845, Baron Parke placed recognition of foreign judgments on the different footing that the foreign judgment gave rise to a legal obligation.[68] But this does not explain *why* the foreign legal obligation is recognised by the local court. As Lord Collins said, the principle of comity can be said to be 'the basis for the enforcement and recognition of foreign judgments'.[69] When comity is understood as a principle of respect for territorial sovereignty based upon implied consent, there is an undeniable link between the principle of comity and the rules governing common law recognition of foreign judgments. As

---

[62] 595 F2d 1287, 1296 (3rd Cir 1979).
[63] *Hartford* (n 27) 797 fn 24.
[64] See Briggs, *Hague Lectures* (n 1); Briggs, *Private International Law in English Courts* (n 2) [3.139]. See also D P [Daniel Patrick] O'Connell, *International Law* (2nd edn, Steven & Sons 1970) vol 1, 20.
[65] Thomas Schultz and Jason Mitchenson, 'Rediscovering the Principle of Comity in English Private International Law' (2018) 28 European Review of Private Law 311, 315.
[66] Briggs, *Hague Lectures* (n 1) 148.
[67] See eg *Adams v Cape Industries plc* [1990] Ch 433, and discussion in Dicey, Morris and Collins (n 4) [14.007]–[14.009].
[68] *Rubin v Eurofinance SA* [2010] EWCA Civ 895, [2011] Ch 133 [34]-[35], citing *Williams v Jones* (1845) 13 M & W 628, 633. See also *Rubin v Eurofinance SA* [2012] UKSC 46, [2013] 1 AC 236 [9].
[69] *Agbaje v Agbaje* [2010] UKSC 13, [2010] 1 AC 628, 671 [54].

outlined above, the Supreme Court's decision in *Hilton* gives examples of various rules, distilled from the principle of comity, relating to the common law recognition of various kinds of judgments. The same can be said of English rules on common law recognition of foreign judgments. As to recognition of foreign judgments, a judgment given in a foreign court has no application on its own within England.[70] Only English judgments can directly apply within England, so in order to be given force the judgment must be converted to a local judgment.[71] As to recognition of foreign judgments at common law, an English court will generally recognise a foreign judgment given against a person who was within the foreign territory at the time that proceedings were commenced.[72] As Briggs argues, these rules are 'fundamentally justified by the principle of comity and territorial sovereignty' because they embody 'the oldest and most deeply seated sense that sovereign acts are territorial, and when a sovereign has so acted, his judgments are to be recognized'.[73]

The second area in which the application of the principle of comity is particularly relevant to illustrate its limits is the rule that courts will not enquire into the validity of foreign sovereign acts (whether legislative or executive) done in relation to property that is within the foreign sovereign's territory.[74] As the High Court of Australia acknowledged in *Attorney-General (UK) v Heinemann Publishers Australia Pty Ltd*,[75] this rule rests partly on international comity. In England this rule has been referred to as a part of the act of state doctrine.[76] An example of the application of this rule is that courts are generally required to accept as valid confiscations of property by foreign governments within the territory of a foreign state. Hence, in *Aksionairnoye Obschestvo A M Luther v James Sagor & Co*,[77] the House of Lords refused to inquire into the validity of a Russian decree issued during the Russian Revolution that purported to vest property in all mechanical sawmills above a certain capital value and all woodworking establishments in the Republic because the United Kingdom had recognised the Soviet Government as the de facto Government of Russia before the date of the decree. The House of Lords also applied this rule in refusing to assess the validity of the seizure on behalf of the Sultan of Muscat of British goods on board a British ship that was located within the territorial waters of Muscat.[78]

---

[70] Dicey, Morris & Collins (n 4) [14.002].
[71] Briggs, *Hague Lectures* (n 1) 149.
[72] Dicey, Morris & Collins (n 4) [14R.054].
[73] Briggs, *Hague Lectures* (n 1) 150.
[74] See eg *Oetjen v Central Leather Company* 246 US 297, 304 (1917) (hereafter *Oetjen*); *Aksionairnoye Obschestvo A M Luther v James Sagor & Co* [1921] 3 KB 532 (hereafter *Luther*).
[75] (1988) 165 CLR 30, 41 (hereafter *Heinemann*). See also *Belhaj* (n 56) [225] (Lord Sumption).
[76] See *Belhaj* (n 56) [35] (Lord Mance), [228]–[229] (Lord Sumption), although Lord Neuberger queried whether this particular rule actually falls within the doctrine at [120].
[77] *Heinemann* (n 75). See also *Princess Paley Olga v Weisz* [1929] 1 KB 718.
[78] *Carr v Fracis Times & Co* [1902] AC 176.

This rule is however limited by the same factors that limit the principle of comity upon which the rule of non-enquiry into foreign sovereign acts derives. Courts have refused to apply this rule where to do so would be contrary to fundamental principles of justice, as the discussion of *Oppenheimer v Cattermole*[79] in Section C.2 below illustrates. But, as a further illustration of its foundations in the principle of comity, the rule is limited to the exercise of sovereignty within territory. For instance, in *Laane and Balster v Estonian State Cargo & Passenger SS Line*,[80] the Supreme Court of Canada refused to give extraterritorial effect to a 1940 decree of the Estonian Soviet Socialist Republic that purported to nationalise all Estonian ships (including those in foreign ports) in respect of a ship that was docked in a Canadian port.

C. Fundamental Principles of Justice as a Limit on Comity

1. The limit as a matter of principle

The principle of comity, or respect for sovereign acts taken within the territory of another state, is not absolute. Although this respect is so well established as to be nearly ubiquitous, it is still only a principle that arises by implication rather than a mandatory rule. As a principle that is implied based upon assumed consent of the sovereign it cannot operate where it would be unreasonable for that consent to be implied. It is plainly reasonable for many differences in legal result to be tolerated by a local legal system on the ground that although the local system does things differently it can respect the different approach taken by others. Hence, a court will not be justified in refusing to recognise a foreign sovereign act merely because that act is contrary to either a principle of the domestic law of the forum state or of international law. It will only be so justified where the foreign act is contrary to a fundamental principle of justice. Cardozo J made this point in respect of domestic law in *Loucks v Standard Oil Co of New York*:[81]

> We are not so provincial as to say that every solution of a problem is wrong because we deal with it otherwise at home ... The courts are not free to refuse to enforce a foreign right at the pleasure of the judges, to suit the individual notion of expedience or fairness. They do not close their doors, unless help would

---

[79] [1976] AC 249 (hereafter *Oppenheimer*).
[80] [1949] SCR 530. Cf *Lorentzen v Lydden & Co* [1942] 2 KB 202, a decision not followed by the Court of Appeal in *Peer International Corporation v Termidor Music Publishers Ltd* [2003] EWCA Civ 1156, [2004] Ch 212.
[81] 120 NE 198, 201–2 (NY 1918). See also *Kuwait Airways* (n 56) [114].

violate some fundamental principle of justice, some prevalent conception of good morals, some deep-rooted tradition of the common weal.

2. Recognition of this limit by courts

Courts have variously suggested that they would be justified in refusing to recognise foreign laws that are 'so barbarous or monstrous',[82] 'so contrary to moral principle'[83] or 'so repugnant to British ideas of international personal morality'[84] that they should not be recognised, or where the recognition of the law would 'outrage [a court's] sense of justice or decency'[85] or 'would lead to a result wholly alien to fundamental requirements of justice as administered by an English court'.[86] Although examples where the courts have actually done so are relatively rare, there are three cases in which the House of Lords and Supreme Court of the United Kingdom have given detailed consideration to the issue in the course of developing what is widely described as a 'public policy' exception to rules of private international law based on comity. The examples are valuable although the label, 'public policy', is unfortunate given that the court's task in considering whether the exemption is applicable (and the judicial task generally[87]) is to make decisions based upon principle, rather than policy. As Lord Radcliffe said:[88]

> [p]ublic policy suggests something inherently fluid, adjusted to the expediency of the day, the proper subject of the minister or the member of the legislature. The considerations which we accept as likely to weigh with them are just not those which we expect to see governing the decisions of a court of law. On the contrary, we expect to find the law indifferent to them, speaking for a system of values at any rate less mutable than this.

However, despite the unfortunate label of the public policy exception, the courts' focus is as a matter of substance upon questions of principle.

The first case is *Oppenheimer v Cattermole*.[89] The issue was whether the appellant, a naturalised British subject, was also a German national for the purpose of claiming an income tax exemption. This required the Court to consider whether to recognise a 1941 German decree that purported to deprive all German Jewish

---

[82] *Cammell v Sewell* (1860) 5 H & N 728, 743; 157 ER 1371, 1377.
[83] *Luther* (n 74) 559.
[84] *Empresa Exportadora de Azucar v Industria Azucarera Nacional SA ('The Playa Larga')* [1983] 2 Lloyd's Rep 171, 190.
[85] *In the Estate of Fuld, decd (No 3)* [1968] P 675, 698.
[86] *Kuwait Airways* (n 56) [16].
[87] Ronald Dworkin, *A Matter of Principle* (Harvard University Press 1985) 69.
[88] Lord Radcliffe, *The Law & Its Compass*, (Northwestern University Press 1960) 43–4.
[89] *Oppenheimer* (n 79).

people who were living overseas of both their citizenship and any property within Germany. The Court ultimately dismissed the appeal on the basis that the appellant had ceased to be a German citizen by operation of a later, non-discriminatory, law. However, Lord Cross, with whom Lords Hailsham, Hodson, and Pearson agreed, observed that the 1941 decree 'constitute[d] so grave an infringement of human rights that the courts of this country ought to refuse to recognise it as a law at all'.[90] Lord Salmon did not state the principle so broadly, but rather considered that the Court would be justified in refusing to give effect to the Nazi decree because England was at war with Germany at the time the decree was made and it would not be contrary to 'international comity ... for our courts to decide that the 1941 decree was so great an offence against human rights that they would have nothing to do with it'.[91]

The second case is *Kuwait Airways Corporation v Iraqi Airways Co (Nos 4 and 5)*.[92] When Iraq invaded and occupied Kuwait in August 1990 it directed the defendant to fly ten of the claimant's aircraft from Kuwait to Iraq. The Iraqi government then passed Resolution of the Revolutionary Command Council No 369 ('RCC 369'), which purported to dissolve the claimant and transfer its assets to the defendant. One issue was whether to recognise RCC 369 as part of the *lex situs*. The House of Lords unanimously held that RCC 369 should not be recognised in the United Kingdom. Each of their Lordships considered that the decree was contrary to public policy on the basis that (a) the seizure and assimilation of the planes 'were flagrant violations of rules of international law of fundamental importance';[93] and (b) all member states of the United Nations had been called upon to refrain from actions that may be taken as an indirect recognition of the annexation of Kuwait.[94] For Lord Nicholls, there was also an analogy with *Oppenheimer*, whereby an English court would not enforce or recognise 'a law depriving those whose property has been plundered of the ownership of their property in favour of the aggressor's own citizens'.[95]

The third case is *Belhaj v Straw*,[96] where the Supreme Court heard together two cases, both concerning individuals who had been subject to severe mistreatment, including unlawful abduction and torture, by foreign States. It was alleged that officers of the United Kingdom had been complicit in these acts. One issue was whether the defendants could rely on the non-justiciability limb of the doctrine of foreign act of state to bar the claims. The defendants relied upon the doctrine,

---

[90] Ibid 278.
[91] Ibid 282–3.
[92] *Kuwait Airways* (n 56).
[93] Ibid [20] (Lord Nicholls), [114] (Lord Steyn), [125] (Lord Hoffmann), [148] (Lord Hope), [192] (Lord Scott).
[94] Ibid [20] (Lord Nicholls), 1102–3 (Lord Steyn), [125] (Lord Hoffmann), [146] (Lord Hope), [192] (Lord Scott).
[95] Ibid [29].
[96] *Belhaj* (n 56).

asserting that the adjudication of the claims would necessarily involve English courts adjudicating on the lawfulness of acts of foreign sovereigns taken within the territory of those sovereigns. A majority of the court (Lord Sumption dissenting on this point)[97] held that the foreign act of state doctrine did not apply because the claims were only brought against United Kingdom officials, so it was not strictly necessary for the court to consider the public policy exception. However, Lord Mance, Lord Neuberger, and Lord Sumption (with whom Lord Hughes agreed) each concluded that the public policy exception would have applied to this case. Whilst this case related to the non-justiciability limb of the foreign act of state doctrine, rather than the question of whether a foreign law applies, the Court's discussion of the public policy exception is equally informative as to how that exception might apply to a claim for the application of a foreign law.

3. The Source of fundamental principles of justice

In *Belhaj*, Lord Mance, Lord Neuberger and Lord Sumption each accepted that whether the public policy exception applied was a matter of domestic law.[98] This is plainly correct because, as we outlined in part one of this essay, a corollary of each state's territorial jurisdiction is that it can determine when to give acts of other sovereigns effect within its own territory. Rules such as the act of state doctrine, and any exceptions to those rules, are a matter of domestic law. But this does not answer the question of how courts ascertain what are 'fundamental principles of justice'.

The Court in *Belhaj* took varied approaches to this question. Lord Mance looked to 'individual rights recognised as fundamental by English statute and common law', rather than considering whether the conduct in issue was contrary to *ius cogens* norms.[99] His Lordship noted that freedom from arbitrary detention was enshrined in Magna Carta, and that freedom from torture was another long-standing fundamental right in English law.[100] In contrast, Lords Neuberger and Sumption considered international law to be relevant or decisive in determining whether the conduct was contrary to principles that were sufficiently fundamental.[101] Lord Sumption considered that, generally speaking, if a norm is *ius cogens* then it will be a fundamental principle of justice.[102] For this proposition his Lordship adopted the words of Le Bel J in *Kazemi Estate v Islamic Republic of Iran*,[103] where, in the context of determining whether an international obligation was a fundamental principle of

---

[97] Ibid [233], [238].
[98] Ibid [98] (Lord Mance), [154]–[155] (Lord Neuberger), [257] (Lord Sumption).
[99] Ibid [107].
[100] Ibid [98]–[99].
[101] Cf Lord Mance: ibid [107].
[102] Ibid [257].
[103] [2014] 3 SCR 176, 248 [150]–[151].

justice for the purposes of section 7 of the Canadian Charter of Rights and Freedoms, His Honour observed that 'not all commitments in international agreements amount to principles of fundamental justice' but that 'jus cogens norms can generally be equated with principles of fundamental justice'. On this basis, Lord Sumption concluded that the allegations of torture enlivened the public policy exception,[104] but that the allegations of ill-treatment falling short of torture did not.[105]

Lord Mance acknowledged that the differences in approach between his Lordship and Lord Sumption did not make any difference to the outcome of the case and was unlikely to make a difference in any case.[106] This instinct is revealing. It illustrates the point that fundamental principles of justice do not truly derive from either domestic or international law. Fundamental principles of justice are principles that are so fundamental, or so basic, that any legal system would be unjust without them. An example illustrates this point. English common law generally insists upon consideration before an agreement will be binding. Continental law generally does not. In a sense, the legal principle of consideration might be said to be fundamental to the English law of contract. But it is not a principle that is fundamental to the justice of the legal system. By contrast, a legal principle that is truly fundamental to the English legal system is one without which English lawyers would consider any legal system to be fundamentally unjust. The existence of such basic principles ought not, therefore, be identified solely by reference to the legal system of the forum. Such principles ought to be derived from reason and evident in many legal systems, and particularly in international law. Today they might be described as 'natural law'.

4. The Roman roots of fundamental or natural principles of justice

In Book One of his Institutes, Justinian, borrowing almost verbatim from Gaius,[107] wrote:[108]

> All peoples with laws and customs apply law which is partly theirs alone and partly shared by all mankind. The law which each people makes for itself is special to its own state. It is called 'state law', the law peculiar to that state. But the law which natural reason makes for all mankind is applied the same everywhere. It is called 'the law of all peoples' because it is common to every nation.

---

[104] *Belhaj* (n 56) [268].
[105] Ibid [280].
[106] Ibid [107].
[107] W M Gordon and O F Robinson (trs), *The Institutes of Gaius* (Duckworth 1988) 19 (hereafter Gordon and Robinson, *Institutes of Gaius*).
[108] Peter Birks and Grant McLeod (trs), *The Institutes of Justinian* (Duckworth 1987) 37, para 1.2.

These fundamental principles later came to be described as natural law. But to the Romans they were the law of 'peoples' or *ius gentium*. The law of peoples was not then given the label 'natural law' because it did not come naturally or instinctively. It required the hard work of reason. Since the rules of basic reason required an advanced mind, they were not natural to all animals. Hence, the rules derived by reason, fundamental to all peoples, were described as *ius gentium* or the laws of peoples. Natural law, as the Romans called it, was more like the law of base instinct. In a more detailed compilation in Justinian's Digest, on 'Justice and Law', there is a passage from the first Book of Ulpian's Institutes defining the two branches of public and private law. 'Private law', it was written, 'is tripartite, being derived from principles of *jus naturale, jus gentium,* or *jus civile*'.[109] *Ius naturale* for the Romans is the law common to all animals.[110]

Ulpian's exposition of *ius gentium* is followed by a number of examples: from Pomponius, 'religious duties toward God, or the duty to be obedient to one's parents and fatherland'; from Florentinus, 'the right to repel violent injuries', the protection of bodily security, and the 'grave wrong for one human being to encompass the life of another'; from Ulpian again, 'manumissions' (the granting of freedom to slaves); and from Hermogenian, the proliferation of commerce, 'including contracts of buying and selling and letting and hiring'.[111] For completeness, Ulpian continued: 'whenever to the common law we add anything or take anything away from it, we make a law special to ourselves, that is, *jus civile,* civil law.'

As Justinian and Gaius recognised, the law of a nation or a people is 'partly its own and partly common to all mankind'.[112] When we speak of the common law in this sense, we speak literally of fundamental principles derived from reason that are *common* to the law of all peoples. Some of the ancient examples highlighted earlier—self-defence, the prohibition on murder, and the law of contracts—still hold true today. There is, of course, divergence in the manner in which those principles manifest themselves in rules in the law that becomes the *ius civile*, the State law. But the same fundamental principles underlie these rules across all jurisdictions.

Fundamental principles should not be identified merely by an examination of important matters of contemporary forum public policy. Rather their existence should be able to be derived by reason from the society in which we live and the rules which govern it. The notion of fundamental principles of law conceived by reason is both outward and inward facing. From an outward face, John Rawls described a doctrine of 'public reason' as that which a citizen may reasonably expect

---

[109] Alan Watson (tr), *The Digest of Justinian* (University of Pennysylvania Press 1985) vol 1, 1 (hereafter Watson, *Digest*).
[110] Ibid 1.
[111] Ibid 1–2.
[112] Gordon and Robinson, *Institutes of Gaius* (n 107) 19. See Watson, *Digest* (n 109), 1.

other citizens to endorse.[113] As to the inward facing aspect, John Locke defined reason as:[114]

> [T]he discovery of the certainty or probability of such propositions or truths, which the mind arrives at by deduction made from such ideas, which it has got by the use of its natural faculties; viz by the use of sensation or reflection.

Whilst these principles are not determined by reference to contemporary public policy, what is considered to be a fundamental principle of justice can change over time because the source of these principles, reason, is imperfect. However, if, by the application of reason, it is deduced that one ought to have certain rights, it must follow that although the boundaries of those rights might vary, the underlying basic rights ought to be recognised universally regardless of the existence of national borders.

5. Fundamental principles of justice in international law

From roots in Roman law the earliest descriptions of the 'law of nations' in international law also distinguished the law of all nations derived by reason, or *ius gentium*, from the 'law of nature'. For instance, Grotius[115] and Blackstone[116] spoke not merely of compacts within communities or the benefits of all people but also of the compacts *between* communities and between cities that are deducible by reason. As international law developed, the 'law of nations' was not confined to those principles within a State by which natural reason would dictate that people were entitled to expect others and the State to behave. It came also to include those principles by which States were entitled to expect other States to behave. As Judge Crawford expressed the expansion, the influential forebears of international law—in addition to Grotius there were Vitoria, Gentili, Pufendorf, Wolff, Vattel, and others—led to the inclusion of the 'specialized body of legal thinking about the relations between rulers, reflective of custom and practice in such matters as treaty-making, the status of ambassadors, the use of the oceans, and the modalities of warfare.'[117]

International arbitral tribunals also recognised and applied the general principles of the law of nations between nations. In the *Antoine Fabiani Case* between France and Venezuela, the arbitrator defined these principles as 'the rules *common* to most legislations or taught by doctrines [sic]'[118] (emphasis added). Such

---

[113] John Rawls, 'The Idea of Public Reason Revisited' (1997) 64 University of Chicago L Rev 765, 773.
[114] John Locke, *An Essay Concerning the Human Understanding* (Clarendon Press 1894) vol 2, bk IV, ch VXIII, 416.
[115] William Evans (tr), *De Jure Belli ac Pacis* (Thomas Baffet 1682) viii.
[116] Blackstone, *Commentaries on the Laws of England* (1769) bk IV, 66–7.
[117] *Brownlie's Principles of Public International Law in English Courts* (n 8) 3–4.
[118] *Antoine Fabiani Case* (1905) 10 RIAA 83, 117.

principles were also recognised in preamble to the Convention (IV) respecting the Laws and Customs of War on Land in 1907 at the Hague.[119] It was against this background that Art 38(1)(c) of the Statute of the Permanent Court of International Justice declared the 'law of nations' as a basic source of international law. Art 38 of the Statute of the Permanent Court of International Justice was the foundation for Art 38 of the Statute of the International Court of Justice, the only addition to which was words in the chapeau which were calculated to emphasise the Court's function to apply the enumerated sources as *international* law.[120] Art 38(1) of the ICJ Statute provides for four categories of source: (a) international conventions; (b) international custom, as evidence of a general practice accepted as law; (c) the general principles of law recognized by civilized nations; and (d) subject to the provisions of Art 59, judicial decisions and the teachings of the most highly qualified publicists of the various nations, as subsidiary means for the determination of rules of law.

Art 38(1)(c) uses the adjective 'civilized' apparently to describe the nations that accept these common principles. Today this is an unfortunate adjective. As Judge Crawford said in the latest edition of *Brownlie's Principles of Public International Law*, 'it is easy to see how that term could possess an unfortunate, even colonialist, connotation'.[121] And as Judge Ammoun, in a separate opinion in the *North Sea Continental Shelf* cases, said, this distinction was 'unknown to the founding fathers of international law'.[122] Rather than focusing upon the adjective 'civilized' in Art 38(1)(c), the importance of the subsection should be recognised as lying in the reference to the general nature of the principles of law. The reference to civilised nations is really a loose expression of that which Hersch Lauterpacht called the 'ultimate assumption of international law', namely that general principles exist within an 'interdependent community' of States.[123] Lauterpacht described this assumption as combining two essential elements: 'the law conceived as reason and the law conceived as will imposing itself upon the subjects'.[124] General principles of law are thus identified by reason and applied, by rules developed from those common principles, in all legal systems.

---

[119] See Permanent Court of International Justice: Advisory Committee of Jurists, *Procès-verbaux of the Proceedings of the Committee June 16th–July 24th 1920 with Annexes* (Van Langenhuysen Brothers 1920) 323–4.

[120] Al-Farsy, 'Report of the Rapporteur (Nasrat al-Farsy, Iraq) of Committee IV/1' in *Documents of the United Nations Conference on International Organization San Francisco, 1945* (UN Information Organizations 1945) vol 13, 381, 392; Hugh Thirlway, 'The Sources of International Law' in Malcolm D Evans (ed), *International Law* (3rd edn, OUP 2010) 95, 98–9 (hereafter Thirlway, 'Sources of International Law').

[121] *Brownlie's Principles of Public International Law in English Courts* (n 8) 31 fn 89.

[122] *North Sea Continental Shelf* [1969] ICJ Rep 3, 132–3 (Sep Op Ammoun).

[123] Lauterpacht (ed), *International Law: being the Collected Papers of Hersch Lauterpacht* (1970) vol 1, 58.

[124] Ibid 58.

During the 1960s legal scholars began to recognise that some of the certain general principles of law were peremptory or *ius cogens* norms.[125] Although there remains dispute about the source of *ius cogens* norms as superior norms of international law,[126] and although there is no general agreement as to which rules have this character,[127] such norms are identified in Art 53 of the Vienna Convention on the Law of Treaties as any 'norm accepted and recognized by the international community of States as a whole as a norm from which no derogation is permitted and which can be modified only by a subsequent norm of general international law having the same character'. Despite the difficulties in characterising a norm as *ius cogens*, the fact that such principles are accepted by the international community and are non-derogable, highlights that they are principles without which a legal system is unjust. Although Lord Sumption suggested in *Belhaj*[128] that there could be instances where *ius cogens* norms did not fall within the 'public policy' exception based on fundamental principles of justice, the better approach is that they are a necessary part of a just legal system and can be equated with fundamental principles of justice, as Le Bel J recognised in *Kazemi*.[129]

The rules to which these *ius cogens* norms have given rise represent a tiny fraction of those rules of customary international law, derived from general state practice and *opinio iuris*. The less fundamental rules of customary international law, based on general principles, are sometimes described as having been 'automatically incorporated' into domestic law unless inconsistent with other extant rules such as legislation or judicial decisions.[130] But in 'view of the importance of the rights involved' the obligations to which *ius cogens* norms have given rise are those in which 'all States can be held to have a legal interest in their protection; they are obligations *erga omnes*' which derive 'from the principles and rules concerning the basic rights of the human person, including protection from slavery and racial discrimination'.[131] They are not principles from which any just legal system can permit departure in formulating its legal rules other than to the extent that the contours of the rules may be affected by other fundamental legal principles. Indeed, when Story recognised that 'comity cannot prevail in cases, where it violates the law of our own country, the law of nature or the law of God'[132] he relied upon Barnewall and Cresswell's King's Bench Report of *Forbes v Cochrane*,[133] where Best J had

---

[125] *Brownlie's Principles of Public International Law in English Courts* (n 8) 581.
[126] See Thirlway, 'Sources of International Law' (n 120) 173–86.
[127] Robert Jennings and Arthur Watts (eds), *Oppenheim's International Law* (9th edn, Longman 2008) vol 1, para 2.
[128] *Belhaj* (n 56) [257].
[129] *Kazemi Estate v Islamic Republic of Iran* [2014] 3 SCR 176.
[130] *Chung Chi Cheung v The King* [1939] AC 160, 168; *Trendtex Trading Corp v Central Bank of Nigeria* [1977] 1 QB 529; *Nevsun* (n 6) [86]–[87], [211].
[131] *Case Concerning Barcelona Traction, Light and Power Company (Belgium v Spain)* [1970] ICJ 1 [33]–[34].
[132] Story, *Commentaries* (n 18) § 244.
[133] (1824) 2 B & C 448, 472–3; 107 ER 450, 459–60.

concluded that the slavery laws of East Florida were 'against the law of nature and the law of God' and therefore could not be recognised in an English court.

6. Fundamental principles of justice are illustrated by both international and domestic law

Within a domestic legal system, fundamental principles of justice might be concerned with regulating conduct within a nation: between people themselves and between people and the State. They are now also concerned with regulating principles of international conduct. In many cases, at an even higher level of generality, the same norms might govern both. For instance, the international principles that are the part of the law of nations which give rise to the prohibition of slavery or genocide,[134] self-determination,[135] and *uti possidetis iuris*[136] might also be seen as akin to interpersonal norms concerned with bodily liberty and integrity, freedom of expression, and private ownership of land—adapted to the scale and discourse of international relations.

In an interdependent international system, marked by comity, it would be unusual for fundamental principles of justice to differ across domestic legal systems and from international law. Such fundamental principles, deduced by reason, are usually therefore a source of both domestic law and international law. This is why the diverging paths taken by Lord Mance and Lord Sumption in *Belhaj* ultimately led to the same conclusion. The question will not usually be whether the relevant principle is a principle *of* domestic law or *of* international law. Rather, the question is whether the principle is a fundamental principle of justice which generally underlies domestic and international law.

7. The identification of fundamental legal principles and the balancing of them

The legal principles which are fundamental to systems of law can usually be identified by reference to rights or freedoms to which a legal system gives direct effect. As to the rights that arise from fundamental principle, more than a century ago in *Allen v Flood*[137] Cave J, following Blackstone, said

---

[134] *Reservations to the Convention on the Prevention and Punishment of the Crime of Genocide* [1951] ICJ Rep 15, 23.
[135] *Western Sahara* [1975] ICJ Rep 12 [59].
[136] *Frontier Dispute (Burkina Faso/Republic of Mali)* [1986] ICJ Rep 554 [20].
[137] [1898] AC 1, 29.

The personal rights with which we are most familiar are: 1. Rights of reputation; 2. Rights of bodily safety and freedom; 3. Rights of property; or, in other words, rights relative to the mind, body, and estate; and, if the general word 'estate' is substituted for 'property', these three rights will be found to embrace all the personal rights that are known to the law; but in that case it must be admitted that the third class is very general, and embraces a good many subdivisions, which, however, like causes in natural science, are not to be unnecessarily multiplied.

To these basic rights can be added those that are based on the fundamental principle that binding undertakings should be respected and the principle that there will be circumstances where justice requires that a person be entitled to restitution of another's unjust enrichment at a person's expense. In *Fibrosa Spolka Akcyjna v Fairbairn Lawson Combe Barbour Ltd*[138] Lord Wright described the latter as a principle for which 'any civilized system of law is bound to provide remedies'. Basic freedoms to be added to this list are general liberties against the world at large although they are often expressed as freedoms from interference by the State. Freedoms that are generally recognised as fundamental include freedom of expression, freedom of association, and freedom of religion.

Although these fundamental rights and freedoms can be seen in many legal systems and in international law, as direct instantiation of fundamental principles of justice, comity will not always be limited by a foreign legal system's derogation from a fundamental right or freedom. One reason for this is that fundamental rights or freedoms are not absolute. For instance, one person's right to reputation qualifies another's right to freedom of expression. A person's right to exclude others from property is qualified by another's right to bodily safety. Another reason is that the extent to which the rights and freedoms are qualified by each other will be heavily dependent upon other characteristics of a society and its existing legal system. The extent to which fundamental legal principles are protected by the rights recognised by a legal system will vary across legal systems and also within a legal system over time.

In *Kuwait Airways*, Lord Nicholls held that 'The acceptability of a provision of foreign law must be judged by contemporary standards'.[139] In *Belhaj v Straw*, Lord Sumption acknowledged that 'the standards which public policy applies in cases with an international dimension have changed a great deal in the past half-century',[140] noting that United States courts abstained from adjudicating the lawfulness of the arbitrary detention and expropriation of property by foreign states in *Hatch v Baez*,[141] *Underhill v Hernandez*,[142] and *Oetjen v Central Leather Co*[143] on

---

[138] [1943] AC 32, 61.
[139] *Kuwait Airways* (n 56) [28], citing Lord Wilberforce in *Blathwayt v Baron Cawley* [1976] AC 397, 426.
[140] *Belhaj* (n 56) [251]–[252].
[141] 7 Hun 596 (1876).
[142] 168 US 250 (1897).
[143] *Oetjen* (n 74).

the basis that it was more appropriate that those matters be resolved by diplomats. Such an outcome in 1917 was necessitated by 'the highest considerations of international comity and expediency'.[144] One hundred years later, the Supreme Court of the United Kingdom came to a very different conclusion in *Belhaj* and *Kuwait Airways* as to how it should weigh the same fundamental principles in issue in the American cases—the rights to liberty and property—against rules that were based upon considerations of comity.

A forum legal system can sometimes tolerate a different balance being struck between fundamental rights and freedoms without necessarily reaching the conclusion that the underlying principle is not respected by the foreign legal system. The question of whether the balance is one that denies sufficient respect to a fundamental principle of justice may depend upon the importance of the embedded principle in the forum. This is illustrated by *Bachchan v India Abroad Publications Inc*.[145] In that case the Supreme Court of New York refused to enforce an English judgment against the defendant for defamation on the basis that English laws of defamation lacked an equivalent to the First Amendment and 'The protection to free speech and the press embodied in that amendment would be seriously jeopardized by the entry of foreign libel judgments granted pursuant to standards deemed appropriate in England but considered antithetical to the protections afforded the press by the US Constitution'.[146]

D. New Fundamental Principles of Justice and the Example of Privacy

Many of the fundamental principles of justice outlined above have been recognised for centuries. But what about new fundamental principles of justice? There are two ways in which new fundamental principles of justice might be recognised. The first way is if the principle had always existed but took many years or centuries to be recognised. For instance, in a Roman society that thought deeply about which principles counted as fundamental due to natural reason, slavery was a shocking inconsistency. But that does not mean slavery only later became contrary to basic principle when society progressed. Rather, slavery was always contrary to natural reason. Even in Roman law, Ulpian had recognised this and, Justinian's Institutes had recorded that slavery was contrary to natural right.[147] A future society might think the same way about the right to life for animals other than humans. A second way is where a fundamental principle of justice develops due to changes in society

---

[144] Ibid 303–4.
[145] 585 NYS 2d 661 (1992).
[146] *Bachchan v India Abroad Publications Inc* 585 NYS 2d 661, 665 (NY 1992).
[147] Inst 1.III.2.

creating a basic need that did not exist before. The line between the two is not always clear. This part focuses upon the possible recognition of a new fundamental principle of justice that might arguably fall within either category. The example is the principle of privacy which has only been afforded direct recognition relatively recently and in some domestic legal systems has not yet been treated as fundamental nor been given direct effect.

In the United States in 1890, Samuel Warren and Louis Brandeis published an article in the Harvard Law Review that was later described as having 'the unique distinction of having initiated and theoretically outlined a new field of jurisprudence'.[148] In it, they advocated a 'right "to be let alone" '.[149] They said that this right was necessitated by the invasion of 'the sacred precincts of private and domestic life' by 'Instantaneous photographs', 'newspaper enterprise', and 'numerous mechanical devices'.[150] However, their argument was not really that the principle of privacy only came into existence with mass media. Instead, their argument was that mass media meant that the existing protections afforded by common law and equitable doctrines were no longer adequate to protect individual privacy.[151] Privacy had become too fundamental to be protected only indirectly.

The ground-breaking article of Warren and Brandeis had little immediate effect in the courts. In 1902, the Court of Appeals of New York rejected a more generalised right of privacy.[152] That case concerned the unauthorised use of a minor's image in a flour advertisement disseminated with 25,000 copies. A demurrer was allowed on the basis that she had no right to privacy. The decision was met with public outcry and a legislative prohibition upon the use of the name, portrait, or picture of another for commercial purposes without written consent.[153] Three years later, a Supreme Court of Georgia decision concerning essentially the same question recognised a distinct right of privacy 'derived from natural law'.[154] By 1931, the Restatement of Torts was able to say that '[a] person who unreasonably and seriously interferes with another's interest in not having his affairs known to others or his likeness exhibited to the public is liable to the other'.[155] By the time of Dean Prosser's famous article in 1960 there were 'over three hundred cases in the books'.[156]

---

[148] Wilbur Larremore, 'The Law of Privacy' (1912) 12 Columbia L Rev 693, 693.
[149] Samuel D Warren and Louis D Brandeis, 'The Right to Privacy' (1890) 4 Harvard L Rev 193, 195 (hereafter Warren and Brandeis, 'Right to Privacy') quoting Thomas M Cooley, *A Treatise on the Law of Torts or the Wrongs which arise Independent of Contract* (2nd edn, Callaghan & Company 1888) 29.
[150] Warren and Brandeis, 'Right to Privacy' (n 149) 195.
[151] Ibid 211.
[152] *Roberson v Rochester Folding Box Co* 64 NE 442, 443, 447 (NY 1902).
[153] W Page Keeton and others (eds), *Prosser and Keeton on The Law of Torts* (5th edn, West Publishing Co 1984) § 117, 850–1 (hereafter *Prosser and Keeton*).
[154] *Pavesich v New England Life Insurance Co* (50 SE 68, 70 (Ga 1905). See *Prosser and Keeton* (n 152) § 117, 851.
[155] Restatement (First) of Torts (1939) § 867. See also *Melvin v Reid* (1931) 297 P 91, 92.
[156] William L Prosser, 'Privacy' (1960) 48 California L Rev 383, 388.

As in the United States, the development of a right to privacy in Germany began with distinguished academics in the late nineteenth century, particularly Josef Kohler in 1893 and Otto von Gierke in 1895.[157] However, at the turn of the century their advocacy for a right of general protection against interferences with personal interests was rejected by the drafting committee of *Bürgerliches Gesetzbuch* (BGB) on the basis that it would unacceptably 'place non-material values on the same level as property interests'.[158] Consistently with this approach, s 823(1) of the BGB was said to be concerned only with proprietary rights.[159] That subsection provides that compensation is payable for unlawful injury to 'the life, body, health, freedom, property or another right of another person'. However, following Arts 1 and 2 of the *Grundgesetz für die Bundesrepublik Deutschland* (Basic Law) of 1949 which provided that '[h]uman dignity shall be inviolable' and that '[e]very person shall have the right to free development of his personality insofar as he does not violate the rights of others', the German courts held that s 823(1) contained a general protection against 'invasions of the right of personality'.[160] The privacy of an individual is regarded as an aspect of this all-encompassing protection of the individual 'in the exercise of his faculties in every conceivable direction'.[161] As the Constitutional Court said in another right of personality case in 1973 concerning Princess Soraya:[162]

> Occasionally, the law can be found outside the positive legal rules erected by the state; this is law which emanates from the entire constitutional order and which has as its purpose the 'correction' of written law. It is for the judge to 'discover' this law and through his opinions give it concrete effect.

The German right of personality is broader in scope than the American right to privacy.[163] They both instantiate the general principle of privacy but Germany does so with a much broader right. An example of its breadth is the Constitutional Court's 1973 *Lebach* decision.[164] The petitioner was an accessory to an armed

---

[157] Basil S Markesinis and Hannes Unberath, *The German Law of Torts: A Comparative Treatise* (4th edn, Hart Publishing 2002) 74 (hereafter Markesinis and Unberath, *German Law of Torts*).
[158] Ibid 74.
[159] H C [Harold Cooke] Gutteridge, 'The Comparative Law of the Right to Privacy' (1931) 47 Law Quarterly Review 203, 206 (hereafter Gutteridge, 'Comparative Law'). Cf the particular provision of the Kunsturhebergesetz, s 22.
[160] '*Verletzungen des Persönlichkeitsrechts*': Konrad Zweigert and Hein Kötz, *Introduction to Comparative Law* (Tony Weir tr, 3rd edn, OUP 1998) 687 (hereafter Zweigert and Kötz, *Introduction to Comparative Law*).
[161] Gutteridge, 'Comparative Law' (n 159) 203–4.
[162] BVerfGE 34, 269 (1973). See Markesinis and Unberath, *German Law of Torts* (n 157) 31; Donald P Kommers and Russell A Miller, *The Constitutional Jurisprudence of the Federal Republic of Germany* (3rd edn, Duke University Press 2012) 165–9.
[163] Harry D Krause, 'The Right to Privacy in Germany—Pointers for American Legislation?' [1965] Duke Law Journal 481, 484.
[164] BVerfGE 35, 202 (1973). See Zweigert and Kötz, *Introduction to Comparative Law* (n 160) 707; Markesinis and Unberath, *German Law of Torts* (n 157) 423–9.

robbery of a military arsenal, in which four soldiers were killed. Shortly before his release from six years' imprisonment, a television station commissioned a documentary about the robbery, incorporating the petitioner's name and likeness. The petitioner successfully obtained an interim injunction from Constitutional Court restraining broadcast of those details due to the documentary's likely impact on his ability to reintegrate into society.

During this period of development, international law also began to recognise a fundamental principle of privacy. In 1948 the General Assembly of the United Nations adopted the Universal Declaration of Human Rights which reflected 'general principles of law or elementary considerations of humanity'.[165] Art 12 includes protection against 'arbitrary interference' with privacy, family, home, or correspondence.[166] There was little discussion about the inclusion of this principle. It was said to be 'an obvious choice in a bill of rights that was supposed to reassert some venerable rights as well as come up with some new ones appropriate for a modern society'.[167] Although the Universal Declaration is not binding, a right to privacy was recognised in almost identical terms[168] in Art 17 of the International Covenant on Civil and Political Rights which was adopted by the General Assembly in 1966 and came into force in 1976, after its thirty-fifth ratification.[169] Today there are 173 State Parties.[170] The Universal Declaration was also the 'most significant normative influence' on the European Convention on Human Rights[171] which was adopted in 1950 and came into force in 1953. Article 8(1) of that Convention, entitled 'Right to respect for private and family life', provides, subject to qualification in Art 8(2), that as against public authorities:[172] 'Everyone has the right to respect for his private and family life, his home and his correspondence.'[173] The Supreme Court of the United Kingdom has recognised one of the 'fundamental values' protected by Art 8 to be 'the inviolability of ... the personal and psychological space within which each individual develops his or her own sense of self and relationships with other

---

[165] *Brownlie's Principles of Public International Law in English Courts* (n 8), 612.

[166] Universal Declaration of Human Rights (adopted 10 December 1948) UNGA Res 217 A(III) (UDHR) Art 12.

[167] Megan Richardson, *The Right to Privacy: Origins and Influence of a Nineteenth-Century Idea* (CUP 2017) 113. See also Oliver Diggelmann and Maria Nicole Cleis, 'How the Right to Privacy Became a Human Right' (2014) 14 Human Rights L Rev 441, 443 (hereafter Diggelmann and Cleis, 'Human Right').

[168] James Michael, *Privacy and Human Rights* (UNESCO 1994) 19; Diggelmann and Cleis, 'Human Right' (n 167) 449.

[169] See International Covenant on Civil and Political Rights (adopted 16 December 1966, entered into force 23 March 1976) 999 UNTS 171 (ICCPR) Art 49.

[170] United Nations, 'Multilateral Treaties Deposited with the Secretary-General' ch IV, 4 <https://treaties.un.org/doc/Publication/MTDSG/Volume%20I/Chapter%20IV/IV-4.en.pdf> accessed 14 September 2020.

[171] William A Schabas, *The European Convention on Human Rights: A Commentary* (OUP 2015) 1.

[172] *P and S v Poland* App no 57375/08 (ECtHR, 30 October 2012) [94]. See also *Nunez v Norway* (2014) 58 EHRR 17, 534 [68].

[173] Convention for the Protection of Human Rights and Fundamental Freedoms (European Convention on Human Rights, as amended) (ECHR) Art 8.

people'.[174] Finally, Art 7 of the Charter of Fundamental Rights of the European Union, which took legal effect with the entry into force of the Treaty of Lisbon in 2009, has broadly the same meaning and scope as Art 8 of the ECHR.[175]

In contrast with the direct application of the principles of privacy over this period in the United States, Germany, and international law, Anglo-Australian jurisprudence traditionally gave effect to principles of privacy, if at all, only indirectly by various rights that directly protected other interests. For instance, one way in which a privacy principle might be said to have been indirectly protected was through the protection given to property rights. In *Prince Albert v Strange*, the Prince Consort tried to prevent the exhibition of unauthorised copies of etchings made of the Royal Family. The Lord Chancellor, echoing earlier statements by Lord Eldon, said:[176]

> Upon the principle, therefore, of protecting property, it is that the common law, in cases not aided or prejudiced by statute, shelters the privacy and seclusion of thoughts and sentiments committed to writing, and desired by the author to remain not generally known.

Other ways in which the privacy principle might be said to have been given some indirect effect is through the protection given by legal doctrines including implied contract terms,[177] defamation,[178] trespass,[179] nuisance,[180] copyright,[181] and breach of confidence.[182] This incidental protection of privacy in the course of protecting other interests left gaps in any protection of privacy. For instance, in *Corelli v Wall*,[183] the Court refused an injunction to restrain publication and sale of postcards depicting the plaintiff in imaginary scenes in her life. The postcards were not defamatory and there was no authority to establish a right to restrain

---

[174] *Sutherland v Her Majesty's Advocate (Scotland)* [2020] UKSC 32, [2020] 3 WLR 327 [27], quoting *R (Countryside Alliance) v Attorney-General* [2007] UKHL 52, [2008] 1 AC 719 [116].

[175] 'Explanations Relating to the Charter of Fundamental Rights' (2007) OJ C303/17, 20. See also Convention on the Rights of the Child (adopted 20 November 1989, entered into force 2 September 1990) 1577 UNTS 3, Art 16; American Declaration of the Rights and Duties of Man, OAS Res XXX adopted by the Ninth International Conference of American States (1948) reprinted in *Basic Documents Pertaining to Human Rights in the Inter-American System* OEA/Ser L V/II.82 Doc 6 Rev 1 at 17 (1992) Art V; American Convention on Human Rights 'Pact of San José, Costa Rica' (adopted 22 November 1969, entered into force 18 July 1978) 1144 UNTS 1979 Art 11.

[176] (1849) 2 De G & Sm 652, 695; 64 ER 293, 312 (hereafter *Prince Albert*). See also *Southey v Sherwood* (1817) 2 Mer 435, 438; 35 ER 1006, 1007.

[177] *Pollard v Photographic Co* (1888) 40 Ch D 345 (hereafter *Pollard*).

[178] *Monson v Tussauds Ltd* [1894] 1 QB 671, 687 (CA); *Pryce & Son Ltd v Pioneer Press Ltd* (1925) 42 TLR 29.

[179] *Morris v Beardmore* [1981] AC 446, 464 (HL).

[180] cf *Bernstein v Skyviews & General Ltd* [1978] QB 479, 489.

[181] See eg *Williams v Settle* [1960] 1 WLR 1072 (CA).

[182] *Prince Albert* (n 176); *Pollard* (n 177); *Argyll v Argyll* [1967] Ch 302; *Stephens v Avery* [1988] Ch 449.

[183] (1906) 22 TLR 532 (Ch).

publication of an unauthorised photograph.[184] In 1930, Greer LJ said in *Tolley v J S Fry & Sons Ltd*:[185]

> I have no hesitation in saying that in my judgment the defendants in publishing the advertisement in question, without first obtaining Mr Tolley's consent, acted in a manner inconsistent with the decencies of life, and in doing so they were guilty of an act for which there ought to be a legal remedy. But unless a man's photograph, caricature, or name be published in such a context that the publication can be said to be defamatory within the law of libel, it cannot be the subject-matter of complaint by action of law.

That decision was overturned on appeal to the House of Lords, but only on the basis that the imputation was defamatory.[186] In between the Court of Appeal's decision and the decision on appeal to the House of Lords, Winfield urged the recognition of an independent tort of privacy.[187] Although his plea was not accepted, the law of confidence developed in England to provide something close to direct protection of a central aspect of privacy by a tort of misuse of private information. This development arose after the House of Lords held that an obligation of confidence could arise from the knowing receipt of confidential information[188] and then subsequently, in a development influenced by the presence of European law, held that misuse of private information fell within the scope of this wrong.[189] In the latter case, which has been seen as the recognition of distinct causes of action protecting privacy on one hand and confidential information on the other,[190] Lord Nicholls said:[191]

> Now the law imposes a 'duty of confidence' whenever a person receives information he knows or ought to know is fairly and reasonably to be regarded as confidential. Even this formulation is awkward. The continuing use of the phrase 'duty of confidence' and the description of the information as 'confidential' is not altogether comfortable. Information about an individual's private life would not, in ordinary usage, be called 'confidential'. The more natural description today is that such information is private. The essence of the tort is better encapsulated now as misuse of private information.

---

[184] See also *Sports and General Press Agency Ltd v "Our Dogs" Publishing Co Ltd* [1917] 2 KB 125 (CA).
[185] [1930] 1 KB 467, 478 (CA).
[186] *Tolley v J S Fry and Sons Ltd* [1931] AC 333 (HL).
[187] Percy H Winfield, 'Privacy' (1931) 47 Law Quarterly Review 23.
[188] *Attorney General v Guardian Newspapers Ltd (No 2)* [1990] 1 AC 109, 281 (HL).
[189] *Campbell v MGN Ltd* [2004] UKHL 22, [2004] 2 AC 457 (hereafter *Campbell*). In addition to the influence of the European Convention on Human Rights see also C-131/12 *Google Spain SL v Agencia Espanola de Proteccion de Datos* ECLI:EU:C:2014:317 where the CJEU applied the right to privacy to search engine providers, and held that there is a temporal aspect to the right (ie a 'right to be forgotten').
[190] *Douglas v Hello! Ltd (No 3)* [2007] UKHL 21, [2008] 1 AC 1 [255].
[191] *Campbell* (n 189) [14].

In contrast with English law, Australian law has not yet developed any tort of misuse of private information or any other direct instantiation of a principle of privacy. The course of Australian law has been heavily influenced by a decision in 1937 when the High Court refused, in the *Victoria Park Racing* case, an injunction restraining the broadcast of a race meeting from a makeshift tower on land adjoining the race course.[192] Before his retirement from the High Court, Callinan J extrajudicially called for that decision to be revisited[193] and judicially described the decision as having 'the appearance of an anachronism, even by the standards of 1937'.[194] Two other justices have referred to the description of invasion of privacy as 'one of the "developing torts"',[195] and have observed that the *Victoria Park Racing* case involved a commercial company, not a private person, and that the claim against it was not based upon any breach of privacy but was concerned with breach of copyright, nuisance, and the rule in *Rylands v Fletcher*.[196]

It is not necessary to consider in this essay how Australian law might develop. It suffices to say that there are at least four paths. First, it may be that Australian law will continue to follow the path of *Victoria Park Racing* on the basis that privacy is not a principle worthy of protection, with the argument that legal wrongdoing is not established by causing misery to others if that misery does not amount to established psychological harm that constrains independent action.[197] Secondly, it may be that Australian law could recognise privacy as a principle worthy of protection but not as one that gives rise to any direct right, thus preserving the status quo which only protects the principle in a patchwork way. Thirdly, it may be that Australian law will further develop other wrongs including the equitable wrong of breach of confidence to include the misuse of private information so as to directly instantiate a principle of privacy. There are suggestions of this in a decision in Victoria allowing recovery in an action arising from the publication of a videotape of sexual activities between the defendant and his ex-partner.[198] Fourthly, and finally, it may even be that direct protection of privacy is recognised in a new and independent tort. Whatever the view that is taken, the key point is that in many areas the development of such basic legal rules will need to proceed by considering

---

[192] *Victoria Park Racing and Recreation Grounds Co Ltd v Taylor* (1937) 58 CLR 479. Whilst English law has given effect to the principle of privacy by the rules outlined above, like Australia it does not recognise that a person has a cause of action in nuisance arising from overlooking: *Fearn v Board of Trustees* [2020] EWCA Civ 104, [2020] 2 WLR 1081, 1100 [69].

[193] I D F (Ian David Francis) Callinan, 'Privacy, Confidence, Celebrity and Spectacle' (2007) 7 Oxford University Commonwealth Law Journal 1, 2.

[194] *Australian Broadcasting Corporation v Lenah Game Meats Pty Ltd* (2001) 208 CLR 199 [318] (hereafter *Lenah Game Meats*).

[195] Ibid [106], quoting *Church of Scientology v Woodward* (1982) 154 CLR 25, 68.

[196] *Lenah Game Meats* (n 194) [107]–[111].

[197] Robert Stevens, 'Damages for Wrongdoing in the Absence of Loss' in Jason N E Varuhas and Nicole A Moreham (eds) *Remedies for Breach of Privacy* (Hart Publishing 2018) 97, 107–8. See *Day v Brownrigg* (1878) 10 Ch D 294.

[198] *Giller v Procopets (No 2)* (2008) 24 VR 1.

whether there exists, as many foreign jurisdictions and international law have recognised, an underlying principle of privacy.

The manner in which the law develops in countries such as Australia which have no direct privacy protection might be important for the limits of the principle of comity and the application of rules based upon those limits. The important point for the purposes of this essay is that if the increasing recognition of the fundamental nature of a principle of privacy by national and international courts and in basic human rights instruments were to lead now to its recognition as a fundamental principle of justice then a failure sufficiently to respect this fundamental principle could lead to denial of the application of the principle of comity.

A loose analogy might be drawn with the jurisprudence of the European Court of Human Rights which has held member States to be in violation of Art 8 of the Convention for the Protection of Human Rights and Fundamental Freedoms for insufficiently affording protection to an individual's right to privacy. For instance, in *von Hannover v Germany*,[199] the European Court of Human Rights considered the decision of the German Constitutional Court which had held that the publication of photographs of Princess Caroline in public places was constitutionally valid. The European Court of Human Rights concluded that despite the margin of appreciation afforded to the German State, the Princess' privacy rights under Art 8 had been infringed and her privacy should be protected outside 'the sphere of any political or public debate'.[200]

An analogy with these Convention cases might be drawn if the principle of privacy comes to be recognised as a fundamental principle of justice. Then, to return to the two examples of the application of the fundamental principle of justice exception to principle of comity considered in this essay, the exception might be a basis for invoking a rule that denies common law recognition or local enforcement to a foreign judgment or foreign sovereign act which, despite a similar margin of appreciation as afforded in Convention cases, fails to afford sufficient respect to that fundamental principle of privacy.

E. Conclusion

Comity is not a hard-edged rule. It is a general principle that is based upon the implied consent manifested by one state to respect another's territorial sovereignty. Understood in this way, comity is a source for the development of many of our concrete rules of private international law. However, one instance where comity ends

---

[199] ECHR 2004-VI 41. See Donald P Kommers and Russell A Miller, *The Constitutional Jurisprudence of the Federal Republic of Germany* (n 162) 491–2.

[200] *von Hannover v Germany* ECHR 2004-VI 41, 70. See also, *Bărbulescu v Romania* App no 61496/08 (ECtHR, 5 September 2017) [108], [113]. *López Ribalda v Spain* App nos 1874/13 and 8567/13 (ECtHR, 17 October 2019) [110]–[113].

is where it is inconsistent with respect for fundamental principles of justice. The certainty of legal rules developed by reference to the principle of comity must give way where it would conflict with the 'public policy' of the legal system, particularly the foundational principles that make that system just. As Professor Briggs notes, 'Public policy and legal certainty will never be the easiest of bedfellows, but no judge worth his or her salt will accept that an uncivilised answer is called for, and there is small sense in decrying the fact'.[201] Hence, whilst it ordinarily does so, comity does not require that courts always accept without inquiry the validity of sovereign acts in another territory.

The identification of those fundamental principles of justice that underlie a legal system is not always a simple task. These fundamental principles are not solely principles of domestic or international law. They are principles reflected by the legal system which can only be discerned from natural reason based upon the society in which we live. They can often be seen in the widespread direct effect that they are given by enforceable legal rights and freedoms in many jurisdictions. However, two caveats must be made. First, the absence within a foreign legal system of rights and freedoms that directly apply a particular fundamental legal principle in a particular case is not always sufficient to deny the operation of legal rules based on comity to that foreign legal system if it still has some rules that uphold the fundamental principle. A domestic legal system can sometimes tolerate a different balance being struck between rights and freedoms by a foreign legal system without concluding that the foreign legal system has contravened a fundamental principle of justice. Secondly, in exceptional cases, fundamental principles might exist or develop even if there is not universal recognition of those principles or universal application of them through directly enforceable rights and freedoms. Those new principles will then form instances where insufficient protection is sufficient for a court to deny the application of the general principle of comity in areas such as common law recognition and local enforcement of foreign judgments or recognition of the acts of a foreign sovereign. A principle of privacy might become one such example.

---

[201] Adrian Briggs, 'Public Policy in the Conflict of Laws: A Sword and a Shield?' (2002) 6 Singapore Journal of International & Comparative Law 953, 978.

APPENDIX

List of Publications

Publications are sole authored unless otherwise stated. This list excludes book reviews.

1. Conflict of Laws—General

The Conflict of Laws (4th edn, Clarendon Press 2019) (1st edn, 2002; 2nd edn, 2008; 3rd edn, 2013)
Private International Law in Myanmar (2016; published in electronic form on the website of the Oxford Law Faculty)
Civil Jurisdiction and Judgments (6th edn, Informa Law 2015) (1st edn, Lloyd's of London Press 1993, with Peter Rees under the title *Norton Rose on Civil Jurisdiction and Judgments*; 2nd edn, 1997 with Rees; 3rd edn, 2002, with Rees; 4th edn, 2005, with Rees; 5th edn, 2009)
Private International Law in English Courts (OUP 2014)
Dicey, Morris & Collins: The Conflict of Laws (15th edn, Sweet & Maxwell 2012, with responsibility for chapters 2, 3, 4, 9, 12, 14, 24, 26 and 28 under the general editorship of Lord Collins of Mapesbury) (14th edn, 2006, with responsibility as above; 13th edn, 2000, with responsibility for chapters 9, 12 (jointly with Lawrence Collins), 14, 24, 26 to 28 and 34)
'Private International Law and the Privy Council' in Charles Mitchell and Stephen Watterson (eds), *The World of Maritime and Commercial Law: Essays in Honour of Francis Rose* (Hart Publishing 2020)
'The Principle of Comity in Private International Law' (2012) 354 *Receuil des Cours: Collected Courses of the Hague Academy of International Law* 65
'The Development of Principle by a Final Court of Appeal in Matters of Private International (Common) Law' in James Lee (ed), *From House of Lords to Supreme Court* (Hart Publishing 2011)
'The Rejection of Abuse in International Civil Procedure' in Rita de la Feria and Stefan Vogenauer (eds), *Prohibition of Abuse of Law* (Hart Publishing 2011)
'Decisions of British Courts: Private International Law' (annually 1996–2009), British Yearbook of International Law
'Private International Law' in Andrew Burrows (ed), *English Private Law* (3rd edn, OUP 2013) (1st edn, 2000; 2nd edn, 2007)
'Learning to Learn from Others in Europe in Commercial Litigation' in Birgitt Bachmann (ed), *Grenzueberschreitungen Beitraege zum Internationalen Verfahrensrecht und zur Schiedsgerichtsbarkeit: Festschrift fuer Peter Schlosser zum 70. Geburtstag* (Mohr Siebeck 2005) (with Barbara Dohmann QC)

2. Common Law Rules of Jurisdiction/Service Out of the Jurisdiction/*Forum Non Conveniens*

'Holiday Torts and Damage within the Jurisdiction' [2018] LMCLQ 196
'Service out in a Shrinking World' [2013] LMCLQ 415
'*Forum Non Satis*: *Spiliada* and an Inconvenient Truth' [2011] LMCLQ 329
'The Cost of Suppressing Insurrection' (2007) 123 LQR 182
'Public-Private Law Protective Schemes and the Conflict of Laws' [2004] LMCLQ 313
'The Duke of Brunswick and Defamation by Internet' (2003) 119 LQR 210
'The Legal Significance of the Place of a Tort' (2002) 2 OU Commonwealth Law Journal 133
'The Revenue Rule in the Conflict of Laws: Time for a Makeover' [2001] Singapore Journal of Legal Studies 280
'Service Out of the Jurisdiction Gets Easier: Defendant, Beware!' [1994] LMCLQ 1
'*Forum Non Conveniens* in Australia' (1989) 105 LQR 200
'Wider Still and Wider: The Bounds of Australian Exorbitant Jurisdiction' [1989] LMCLQ 216
'*Forum Non Conveniens*: The Last Word?' [1987] LMCLQ 1
'Forum Non Conveniens: An Update' [1985] LMCLQ 360
'The Staying of Actions on the Ground of *Forum Non Conveniens*' [1984] LMCLQ 227
'*Forum Non Conveniens*—Now We Are Ten?' (1983) 3 Legal Studies 74

3. EU (Brussels I) Rules of Jurisdiction

'Carriage of Goods by Road and the Brussels Diversion' [2016] LMCLQ 197
'Arbitration and the Brussels Regulation Again' [2015] LMCLQ 284
'The Brussels I Bis Regulation Appears on the Horizon' [2011] LMCLQ 157
'*Timeo Danaos* on the Rock of Gibraltar' (2010) 126 LQR 20
'Fear and Loathing in Syracuse and Luxembourg' [2009] LMCLQ 161
'Who is Bound by the Brussels Regulation?' [2007] LMCLQ 433
'Jurisdiction over Defences and Connected Claims' [2006] LMCLQ 447
'*Forum Non Conveniens* and Ideal Europeans' [2005] LMCLQ 378
'The Impact of Recent Judgments of the European Court on English Procedural Law and Practice' 124 (2005) II *Zeitschrift fur Schweizerisches Recht* 231
'Anti-suit Injunctions and Utopian Ideals' (2004) 120 LQR 529
'Two Undesirable Side-effects of the Brussels Convention?' (1997) 113 LQR 364
'The Uncertainty of Special Jurisdiction' [1996] LMCLQ 27
'The Brussels Convention Tames the Arrest Convention' [1995] LMCLQ 161
'How Soon is an English Court Seised (Revisited)?' [1994] LMCLQ 470
'Trusts of Land and the Brussels Convention' (1994) 110 LQR 526
'Anti-European Teeth for Choice of Court Clauses' [1994] LMCLQ 158
'Jurisdiction over Restitutionary Claims' [1992] LMCLQ 283
'Get Your Writs Out?' [1992] LMCLQ 150
'The Brussels Convention Reaches the House of Lords' (1992) 108 LQR 186
'Foreign Judgments, Fraud and the Brussels Convention' (1991) 107 LQR 531
'The Brussels Convention' (annually 1988–1997), Yearbook of European Law

4. The Common Law's Relationship with the Brussels I Regime, including Brexit-related Matters

'Brexit and Private International Law: An English Perspective' (2019) *Rivista di diritto internazionale privato e processuale* 261
'Service Out: *Communis Error Frangit Ius*' [2019] LMCLQ 195
'Seccession from the European Union and Private International Law: The Cloud with the Silver Lining', COMBAR lecture, 25 January 2017
'No Need to Panic over Impact of Brexit on English Law' Lloyd's List Insurance Day, 17 November 2016, 9
'The Hidden Depths of the Law of Jurisdiction' [2016] LMCLQ 236
'The Death of *Harrods*: *Forum Non Conveniens* and the European Court' (2005) 121 LQR 535
'Some Points of Friction between English and Brussels Convention Jurisdiction', ch 19 in Mads Andenas and Francis Jacobs (eds), *European Community Law in the English Courts* (OUP 1998)
'*Forum Non Conveniens* and the Brussels Convention Again' (1991) 107 LQR 180
'*Spiliada* and the Brussels Convention' [1991] LMCLQ 10

5. Recognition and Enforcement of Foreign Judgments

'Recognition and Enforcement of Judgments (Common Law)' in Jürgen Basedow, Giesela Rühl, Franco Ferrari and Pedro de Miguel Asensio (eds), *Encyclopaedia of Private International Law* (Edward Elgar 2017)
'Recognition of Foreign Judgments: A Matter of Obligation' (2013) 129 LQR 87
'Foreign Judgments: The Common Law Flexes its Muscles' (2011) 17 Trusts & Trustees 328
'Enforcing and Reinforcing an English Judgment' [2008] LMCLQ 421
'Recognition and Enforcement of Russian Judgments in England' (2006) 2006-3 Vyestnik: Journal of International Legal Institute of the Ministry of Justice of the Russian Federation 77 (with Tatian Neoupokoeva (trs))
'Foreign Judgments and Human Rights' (2005) 121 LQR 185
'Crossing the River by Feeling the Stones: Rethinking the Law on Foreign Judgments' (2004) 8 Singapore Yearbook of International Law 1
'Bring All Your Claims in One Court, or Lose Them ...' [1993] LMCLQ 451
'Foreign Judgments: More Surprises' (1992) 108 LQR 549
'Foreign Judgments, Fraud and the Brussels Convention' (1991) 107 LQR 531
'Which Foreign Judgments Should We Recognise Today?' (1987) 36 ICLQ 240

6. Anti-suit Injunctions

'Direct Actions and Arbitration: All at Sea' [2016] LMCLQ 327
'Enforcing and Reinforcing an English Judgment' [2008] LMCLQ 421
'Anti-suit Injunctions in a Complex World', ch 12 in Francis Rose (ed), *Lex Mercatoria: Essays on International Commercial Law in Honour of Francis Reynolds* (Informa Law 2000)
'The Further Consequences of a Choice of Law' (2007) 123 LQR 18

'Anti-suit Injunctions and Utopian Ideals' (2004) 120 LQR 529
'Self-restraint in the High Court of Australia' (1998) 114 LQR 27
'The unrestrained reach of an anti-suit injunction' [1997] LMCLQ 90
'Anti-European teeth for choice of court clauses' [1994] LMCLQ 158
'Restraint of foreign proceedings' [1987] LMCLQ 391
'No interference with foreign courts?' (1982) 31 ICLQ 189

7. Agreements on Choice of Court and Arbitration Agreements

Agreements on Jurisdiction and Choice of Law (OUP 2008)
'What do You Mean, "Non-exclusive"?' [2019] LMCLQ 329
'Choice of Forum and Submission to Jurisdiction' in Jürgen Basedow, Giesela Rühl, Franco Ferrari and Pedro de Miguel Asensio (eds), *Encyclopaedia of Private International Law* (Edward Elgar 2017)
'One-sided Jurisdiction Clauses: French Folly and Russian Menace' [2013] LMCLQ 137
'The Subtle Variety of Jurisdiction Agreements' [2012] LMCLQ 364
'What Should be Done about Jurisdiction Agreements?' (2011) 12 Yearbook of Private International Law 311
'Construction of an Arbitration Agreement: Deconstruction of an Arbitration Clause' [2008] LMCLQ 1
'Jurisdiction Clauses and Judicial Attitudes' (1993) 109 LQR 382
'The Validity of Floating Choice of Law and Jurisdiction Clauses' [1986] LMCLQ 50

8. Agreements on Choice of Law

Agreements on Jurisdiction and Choice of Law (above)
'Floating Choice of Law' in Jürgen Basedow, Giesela Rühl, Franco Ferrari and Pedro de Miguel Asensio (eds), *Encyclopaedia of Private International Law* (Edward Elgar 2017)
'Contractual Agreements on Choice of Law' in Andrew Burrows and Edwin Peel (eds), *Contract Terms* (OUP 2007)
'On Drafting Agreements on Choice of Law' [2003] LMCLQ 389

9. Choice of Law in Contract (see also Agreements on Choice of Law, Above)

Adrian Briggs, 'Restitution and Not-so-local Authority Swaps' (2010) 126 LQR 500 (with James Edelman)
'When in Rome, Choose as the Romans Choose' (2009) 125 LQR 191
'Choice of Choice of Law' [2003] LMCLQ 12
'The Formation of International Contracts' [1990] LMCLQ 192

10. Choice of Law in Tort

'When in Rome, Choose as the Romans Choose' (2009) 125 LQR 191
'The Meaning and Proof of Foreign Law' [2006] LMCLQ 1
'Choice of Law in Tort and Delict: The Private International Law (Miscellaneous Provisions) Act 1995' [1995] LMCLQ 519
'*The Halley*: Holed, but Still Afloat? (1995) 111 LQR 18
'Tort in the Conflict of Laws' (1989) 105 LQR 359
'What Did *Boys v Chaplin* Decide?' (1983) 12 Anglo-Am LR 237

11. Choice of Law—General/Other

'Misappropriated and Misapplied Assets and the Conflict of Laws' in Simone Degeling and James Edelman (eds), *Unjust Enrichment in Commercial Law* (Lawbook Co 2008)
'A Map or a Maze: Jurisdiction and Choice of Law in the Court of Appeal' (2007) 9 Singapore Year Book of International Law 123
'The Meaning and Proof of Foreign Law' [2006] LMCLQ 1
'A Note on the Application of the Statute Law of Singapore within its Private International Law' [2005] Singapore Journal of Legal Studies 189
'Distinctive Aspects of the Conflict of Laws in Common Law Systems: Autonomy and Agreement in the Conflict of Laws' (2005) 308 *Doshisha Hogaku* (The Doshisha Law Review) 21
'Public-Private Law Protective Schemes and the Conflict of Laws' [2004] LMCLQ 313
'Owing, Owning, and the Garnishing of Foreign Debts' [2003] LMCLQ 418
'The Real Scope of European Rules for Choice of Law' (2003) 119 LQR 352
'Choice of Choice of Law' [2003] LMCLQ 12
'Conflict of Laws and Commercial Remedies' in Andrew Burrows and Edwin Peel (eds), *Commercial Remedies: Current Issues and Problems* (OUP 2003)
'Public Policy in the Conflict of Laws: a Sword and a Shield?' (2002) 6 Singapore Journal of International and Comparative Law 953
'In Praise and Defence of Renvoi' (1998) 47 ICLQ 877
'From Complexity to Anti-Climax: Restitution and Choice of Law' [1996] Restitution LR 88
'Restitution Meets the Conflict of Laws' [1995] Restitution LR 94
'The International Dimension to Claims for Contribution' [1995] LMCLQ 437
'Garnishment of an English Debt: Foreign Complications' [1988] LMCLQ 429

12. Cross-border Insolvency

'Judicial Assistance Still in Need of Judicial Assistance' [2015] LMCLQ 179
'In For a Penny, in For a Pound' [2013] LMCLQ 26
'Recognition: Foreign Judgments or Insolvency Proceedings?' [2010] LMCLQ 523

13. Family Law

'Polygamous marriages and English domiciliaries' (1983) 32 ICLQ 737

14. Other Subject Matter

The Law of Contract in Myanmar (OUP 2017) (with Andrew Burrows)
'Co-ownership and an Equitable Non-Sequitur' (2012) 128 LQR 183
'Provocation Re-reassessed' (1996) 112 LQR 403
'Judges, Juries and the Meaning of Words' (1985) 5 Legal Studies 314
'In Defence of Manslaughter' [1983] Crim LR 764

Index

abuse of process
  Australia 19
admiralty
  forum non conveniens 31
agreements
  arbitrate, to 17
anchor defendants
  see also co-defendants, jurisdiction over
  Brussels I Regulation (recast) 111–112
  co-defendants, jurisdiction over
    Brussels I Regulation (recast) 111–112
    domestic rule 114
    liquidation 119
    proper forum 123
  natural forum 9
anti-enforcement injunctions 251–271
  anti-suit injunction compared 253
  assessment of 269–271
  breach of contract 252, 263–268
  comity 252, 255
  conclusions 269–271
  contracts 251–271
  copyright infringement 254
  delay 255
  development 254–255
  discretionary remedy 252
  foreign judgments 251–271
  fraud 261–263
  generally 251–256
  interference with foreign legal systems 256–258
  nature of remedy 252
  primary obligations 258–261
  principles 252–253
  respecting foreign courts 255
  sufficient interest 255
  vexatious or oppressive proceedings 252
anti-suit injunctions 77–110
  anti-enforcement injunctions 253
  Australia 94, 95
  background 88–92
  breach of contract 95
  character 78
  choice of law 107–108, 109
  combining justice and convenience 87

combining statutory conditions 87
comity 83–86, 87
conditions 81–87
contempt of court 78
contractual rights 84–85
convenience 83–86
due administration of justice 83
duty of restrained party 78
effect 80
emergence of the injunction 88–92
ends of justice 96
equitable principles 109–110
exceptions to power to grant 92–96
exclusive jurisdiction agreements 303, 304, 309–311
foreign choice of court agreements 85
forum conveniens 87, 92
framework uncertainty 92–96
growth 10
interference with foreign proceedings 80
in personam character 80
just and convenient 81–86
justice 78, 81–83, 96
last resort, as 104
legal basis 81–87, 109
limits on power to grant 82
meaning 77
natural forum 10
nature of injunction 80
origins 79
overview 77–79
protecting jurisdiction of English courts 95, 102–104
public interest 84, 85
public policies 102–104
reasons for grant 78
remedy for wrongdoing 101–102
role 77, 78
rule uncertainty 96–107
sanctions 78, 80
SNI Aerospatiale 105–107
special circumstances 83
statutory conditions 81–87
sufficient interest 81, 86–87, 109
terminology 79–81

364 INDEX

anti-suit injunctions (*cont.*)
  unconscionable conduct 93, 94, 96–97, 109
  undertakings 106–107
  United States 79
  use 79
  vexatious and oppressive conduct 78, 93, 95, 99–101, 109
applicable law
  see also **choice of law; governing law**
  cryptosecurities 217–218
  unjust enrichment
    claims outside Art 10 Rome II Regulation 197
      conclusions 197–198
    IP completion day 191
    negotiorum gestio 197
    non-contractual subrogation 197
    overview 175–176
    Rome I Regulation 193–194
    Rome II Regulation 191, 192, 194–197
arbitration and jurisdiction agreements
  see also **exclusive jurisdiction agreements**
  expectation of the parties 145–146
  free-standing agreement, as 145–146
  matrix contract, as 145
  midnight clauses 145
  negotiation 145
  severability
    applicable law 147–148
    autonomy 142
    Brussels I Regulation (recast) 141, 169
    contract, as 152–153
    dual character of agreements 150–152
    English cases 162–165
    existing instruments, compatibility of preferred approach with 165–169
    exists, where choice of law for the matrix contract 158–161
    expectations of parties 145–146
    generally 140
    governing law 147–148
    Hague Choice of Court Convention 169
    illustrations of approaches 156–162
    instruments on arbitration agreements 166–168
    invalid matrix contract 142
    law of the country where award was made 168
    law to which the parties have subjected the arbitration agreement 167
    matrix contract 140, 145, 148
    meaning of severability in context of 141
    midnight clauses 145
    no choice of law for the matrix contract 161
    observations 162
    preferred analysis 156, 170–171, 170–173
    protective choice of law rules 168
    purpose of severability 148–150
    substantive terms 146–147
    UNICTRAL Model Law 141, 148
    use of severability 142
Australia
  abuse of process 19
  anti-suit injunctions 94, 95
  clearly inappropriate forum 19–20, 25, 30, 32, 35–36, 49
  forum non conveniens 32
    clearly inappropriate forum 35–36, 49
    convenience of the parties 39–40
    discretion to refuse leave 37–38
    leave 36
    nature of the decision 47, 48, 49–50
    permission of court 35
    service of process 35
    statutory rules 35–36
    witness evidence 39–40
  fundamental principles of justice 326
  hard cases 25–26
  natural forum 10, 11, 18–21
  oppression 19
  parallel proceedings 20
  personal injury cases 18, 19
  policy considerations 21
  privacy 354–355
  professional negligence 19, 20
  renvoi 11
  Spiliada 8–9, 11, 18–19, 21
  vexatious or oppressive use of jurisdiction 19
  witness evidence 39–40
aviation industry
  COVID-19 pandemic 4

Bahamas 37
Bermuda 37
Bitcoin 207
blockchains
  distributed ledger technology 207
breach of confidence 352
breach of contract
  anti-enforcement injunctions 252, 263–268
  anti-suit injunctions 95
  exclusive jurisdiction agreements 302
  foreign judgments 261–268
  fraud 261–263
breach of trust
  unjust enrichment 179
Brexit 74, 176–178, 191, 224, 300, 303, 322–323

Brunei
Spiliada 8
Brussels Convention 125, 299
Brussels I Regulation 57, 74, 177
Brussels I Regulation (recast) 57, 74, 77, 177
  anchor defendants 111–112
  co-defendants, jurisdiction over
    anchor defendants 111
    connection between the claims 125–128
    development 125–128
    merits 132–136
    motives 132–136
    origins 125–128
    rationale 125
    scope of rule 128–132
    sole object test 132–136
  severability 141, 169
bundles
forum non conveniens 38

Canada
  approach of courts 21–22
    general rule 21–22
  Beals 22–23
  changes in law 22
  comity 22, 57
  common law 22–23
  development of common law 22
  discretion
    certainty 59, 60–64
    common law and civil law approaches 56–57
    constitutional principles 60
    consumer law 66–69
    damage sustained in the forum 60–62, 74
    generally 53–54
    holiday torts 64–66, 69–71, 72–73
    indeterminacy 56
    jurisdiction 54, 56
    legal standards 56
    necessary and proper party 63, 64, 73, 113
    real and substantial connection 60, 61, 62–63
    residual jurisdiction 63
    role of discretion 53–75
    standards for direct and indirect jurisdiction 60–64
    statutory rules 62–64
    understanding international jurisdiction 73–75
  equality of treatment to local and foreign judgments 22–23
  gateways 60, 63, 64, 66, 74
  jurisdiction
    discretion 54, 56
    residual jurisdiction 63
    standards for direct and indirect jurisdiction 60–64
    understanding international jurisdiction 73–75
  law reform, recognition of need for 22
  natural forum 8, 21–23
  necessary and proper party 63, 64, 73, 113
  parallel proceedings 73–74
  product liability 66–67
  real and substantial connection test 22, 23
  Spiliada 8, 21–23
case management
  developments 4
  natural forum 13–15
Cayman Islands
Spiliada 8
centre of main interests
  natural forum 12
charterparties 94
choice of court agreement *see* arbitration and jurisdiction agreements
choice of law
  see also applicable law; choice of law agreements; governing law; severability
  anti-suit injunctions 107–108, 109
  breach 319–320
  equity 11
  meaning 319
  party autonomy 319
  securities
    Clearstream 202
    cryptosecurities 200, 205, 211–222, 224
    directly held securities 200
    distributed ledger technology 199, 202, 203, 204
    entitlement 209–211
    existing law 200–202
    Hague Securities Convention 201–202, 223
    intermediated securities 199, 200–201, 203
    lex creationis 199, 200
    lex registri 200
    lex situs cartae 200
    'no look through' approach 201, 202, 203, 204, 209
    overview 199–200
    Place of the Relevant Intermediary Approach (PRIMA) 201–202, 223, 224
    Stock Connect 199, 205
  severability 143–153
    applicable law 147–148
    Brussels I Regulation (Recast) 169

choice of law (cont.)
    contract, meaning of 152–153
    dual character of arbitration and jurisdiction agreements 150–152
    existing instruments, compatibility of preferred approach with 165–169
    exists, where choice of law for the matrix contract 158–161
    expectation of the parties 145–146
    governing law 147–148
    Hague Choice of Court Convention 169
    instruments on arbitration agreements 166–168
    law of the country where award was made 168
    law to which the parties have subjected the arbitration agreement 167
    midnight clauses 145
    no choice of law for the matrix contract 161
    observations 162
    practical significance 170
    preferred analysis 156, 170–173
    protective choice of law rules 168
    purpose 148–150
    substantive terms 146–147
  unjust enrichment
    generally 175
choice of law agreements
  see also choice of law
  applicable law, determination of 321
  boiler plate clauses 44
  breach of agreement 319–320
  characterisation of claims 321–322
  English law 44–45
  exclusive jurisdiction agreements 320
  implied terms 321, 322
  interpretation 321
  jurisdiction agreements 320
  promissory obligation, whether 319–322
  unpredictability of outcome 321
civil partnerships
  foreign judgments 290–292
Civil Procedure Rules 33, 34, 35, 36, 57, 114, 115, 122, 123, 178, 188–191
clearly inappropriate forum
  Australia 19–20, 25, 30, 32, 35–36, 49
  cogent evidence 26–27
  meaning 36
  natural forum 19–20, 25, 26–27
  nature of test 36
Clearstream 202
closest and most real connection
  natural forum 28

cloud storage 39
co-defendants, jurisdiction over 111-136
  anchor defendants
    Brussels I Regulation (recast) 111
    domestic rule 114
    liquidation 119
    proper forum 123
  Brussels I Regulation (recast) 111
    anchor defendants 111
    connection between the claims 125–128
    criticism 111–112
    development 125–128
    merits 132–136
    motives 132–136
    origins 125–128
    rationale 125
    scope of rule 128–132
    sole object test 132–136
  conditions 111
  domestic rule
    anchor defendant 114
    Civil Procedure Rules 114, 115, 122, 123
    development 112–115
    generally 112
    improper purposes 118
    Manx version 113, 120
    merits 116–122
    motives 116–122
    origins 112–115
    proper forum 122–125
    proper parties 116
    'properly brought' 113–114, 117, 118, 119
    purpose of rule 112–113
    real issue for court to try 117
    real issue which it is reasonable to try 121
    requirements 113
    RSC Order XI 113–114
    scope 116
    sole purpose of bringing in foreign defendant 119–121
    Spiliada 114–115
  EU law 111
  liquidation, defendant in 119
  merits
    Brussels I Regulation (recast) 132–136
    domestic rule 116–122
  motives
    Brussels I Regulation (recast) 132–136
    domestic rule 116–122
  overview 111–112
  proper forum 122–125
  Spiliada
    domestic rule 114–115

INDEX

comity 325–356
  anti-enforcement injunctions 252, 255
  anti-suit injunctions 83–86, 87
  Canada 22, 57
  development of common law conception 328
  development of legal rules 334–337
  foreign sovereign acts 336–337
  foundations 325
  fundamental principles of justice 325, 337–348, 356
  Huber, Ulrich 328
  justice
    development of legal rules 334–337
    fundamental principles 325, 337–355
    meaning of comity 327–337
    territorial sovereignty 327–334
  meaning 83–84, 326, 327–337
  natural forum 24–30
  nature of principle 355–356
  public interest 84
  role 85, 327–337
  scope 328
  Story, Joseph 328–331
  territorial sovereignty 326, 327–334
connecting factors
  natural forum 15
  stay of proceedings 15
consent 300
  territorial sovereignty 326, 327–334
consumer law
  Canada 66–69
  product liability 66–67
  social media 67
  travel industry 67–68
contracts
  see also **breach of contract; severability**
  dépeçage distinguished 154
  foreign judgments
    anti-enforcement injunction 251–271
    breach of contract 263–268
    Ellerman Lines 261–263
    primary obligations 258–261
  proper law 44
  unjust enrichment 179–181
copyright 352
COVID-19 pandemic
  aviation industry 4
  effect 4
  technology 39, 40
  video evidence 39
  witness evidence 39, 40
cryptosecurities
  advantages 208
  applicable law 217–218
  choice of law 200

lex creationis 220–223
lex registri 217–218
lex situs 218–220, 223
location of the private encryption key 213–216
named entity, location of 213
place of the relevant operating authority/administrator (PROPA) 212, 213
primary residence of the encryption master keyholder (PREMA) 212, 213
securities trading
  applicable law 217–218
  choice of law 200, 205, 211–222
  distributed ledger technology 205
  lex creationis 220–223
  lex registri 217–218
  lex situs 218–220, 223
  location of the private encryption key 213–216
  named entity, location of 213
  place of the relevant operating authority/administrator (PROPA) 212, 213
  primary residence of the encryption master keyholder (PREMA) 212, 213
value 212

damages 232–234
  exclusive jurisdiction agreements 303, 304, 311–319
declaratory relief
  remedies 242–243
defamation 352
dépeçage
  choice of law and 153
  contract, distinguished from 154
  involuntary dépeçage 154–155
  meaning 141
  objective dépeçage 154
  Rome Convention 154, 155
  Rome I Regulation 154
  voluntary dépeçage 154–155
digitization 39
discretion 53–75
  advantages of suing at home 71–73
  Canada
    certainty 59, 60–64
    constitutional principles 60
    consumer law 66–69
    damage sustained in the forum 60–62, 74
    generally 53–54
    holiday torts 64–66, 69–71, 72–73
    indeterminacy 56
    jurisdiction 54, 56
    legal standards 56
    necessary and proper party 63, 64, 73, 113
    real and substantial connection 60, 61, 62–63

discretion (cont.)
  residual jurisdiction 63
  role of discretion 53-75
  standards for direct and indirect
      jurisdiction 60-64
  statutory rules 62-64
  understanding international
      jurisdiction 73-75
  England and Wales
    Brownlie case 58-59, 69
    Brussels I Regulation 57
    certainty 58-59
    Civil Procedure Rules 57
    common law and civil law
        approaches 56-57
    generally 53-54
    indeterminacy 56
    jurisdiction 54-56
    Practice Direction 6B 55, 58-59
    role of discretion 53-75
    service 57
  gateways
    certainty 58, 60
    damage sustained in the forum 60, 72
    equal treatment 74
    exceptional nature 54
    generally 54, 55
    proper forum 54
    purpose 55
    relevant connections 55
    tort 60-61, 73
    unobjectionable 74
  natural forum 16, 27
  public interest 72
  Spiliada 16
dispute resolution
  changes 4
  funding 4
  technology 4
distributed ledger technology
  assets 208
  blockchains 207
  centralised systems 208
  chain of holding 209
  choice of law 199
  cryptosecurities 205
  encryption 207
  ledgers 207
  mechanics of platforms 207-208
  nodes 207
  securities trading
    difficulties with system 203
    use 204
  tokens 207-208

divorce, recognition of 273-296
  Family Law Act 1986
    arbitrariness 281-283
    defining proceedings 283-290
    financial provision 278-281
    gender discrimination 278-281
    generally 273-274
    historical background 274-276
    law reform 295-296
    proceedings and non-proceedings
        divorces 276-290
    schemes of recognition 273-283
    transnational divorces 292-295
  financial provision 278-283
  foreign judgments
    civil partnerships 290-292
    definition of proceedings 284-290
    financial provision 278-283
    gender discrimination 278-283
    generally 273-274
    historical background 274-276
    law reform 295-296
    overview 295-296
    proceedings and non-proceedings
        divorces 276-290
    recognition of judgments 273-296
    schemes of recognition 276-283
    transnational divorces 292-295
  proceedings and non-proceedings
      divorces
    arbitrariness 281-283
    defining proceedings 283-290
    financial provision 278-281
    gender discrimination 278-281
    informality 281-283
    practical difficulties 283-290
    proof 282-283
    rationale of differing treatment 278-283
    schemes of recognition 276-283
    unilateralism 281-283
  recognition of foreign judgments 273-296
    civil partnerships 290-292
    definition of proceedings 284-290
    financial provision 278-283
    gender discrimination 278-283
    generally 273-274
    historical background 274-276
    law reform 295-296
    overview 295-296
    proceedings and non-proceedings
        divorces 276-290
    schemes of recognition 276-283
    transnational divorces 292-295
double actionability rule 11

e-bundles 38
electronic communications
  forum non conveniens 38
England and Wales
  Civil Procedure Rules 33, 34, 35, 36, 57, 114,
    115, 122, 123, 178, 188–191
  discretion
    Brownlie case 58–59, 69
    Brussels I Regulation 57
    certainty 58–59
    Civil Procedure Rules 57
    common law and civil law
      approaches 56–57
    generally 53–54
    indeterminancy 56
    jurisdiction 54–56
    Practice Direction 6B 55, 58–59
    role of discretion 53–75
    service 57
  forum non conveniens
    change of rules 34
    Civil Procedure Rules 33, 34, 35, 36
    frontloaded decisions 34
    legitimate expectation 36
    nature of the decision 48
    origins of doctrine 31
    private interest factors 34
    proper place in which to bring a
      claim 34, 35
    public interest factors 34–35
    service out of the jurisdiction 34
    source of power 33
    Spiliada 34, 35
  jurisdiction
    discretion 54–56
  parallel proceedings 73–74
  privacy 353
equity
  anti-suit injunctions 109–110
  choice of law 11
  natural forum 11
European Convention on Human Rights
  effect 5
  privacy 355
European Court of Human Rights
  privacy 355
European Union
  Brexit 74, 176–178
evidence
  see also witness evidence
  clearly inappropriate forum 26–27
  COVID-19 pandemic, during 39, 40
  electronic evidence 40–41
  natural forum, of 17
  remedies 231–232
  technology 40–41
  video evidence 39
exclusive jurisdiction agreements
  anti-suit injunctions 303, 304, 309–311
  breach of contract 302
  Brexit 322–323
  choice of law agreements 320
  damages 303, 304, 311–319
  EU Member State, breach in 302–303
  generally 324
  meaning 302
  non-recognition of foreign judgments 303,
    304–309
  remedies 302–304
  stay of proceedings 303

family law 41
Family Law Act 1986
  divorce
    arbitrariness 281–283
    defining proceedings 283–290
    financial provision 278–281
    gender discrimination 278–281
    generally 273–274
    historical background 274–276
    law reform 295–296
    proceedings and non-proceedings
      divorces 276–290
    schemes of recognition 273–283
    transnational divorces 292–295
financial provision 27
foreign choice of court agreements
  anti-suit injunctions 85
foreign judgments
  agreement to discharge judgment
    debts 268–269
  anti-enforcement injunction 251–271
  breach of contract 261–268
  civil partnerships 290–292
  contracts
    anti-enforcement injunction 251–271
    breach of contract 263–268
    Ellerman Lines 261–263
    primary obligations 258–261
  divorce
    civil partnerships 290–292
    definition of proceedings 284–290
    financial provision 278–283
    gender discrimination 278–283
    generally 273–274
    historical background 274–276
    law reform 295–296
    overview 295–296

foreign judgments (*cont.,*)
    proceedings and non-proceedings
        divorces 276–290
    recognition of judgments 273–296
    schemes of recognition 276–283
    transnational divorces 292–295
  fraud 261–263
  non-recognition 303, 304–309
  obtained in breach of agreement 251
  status 23
foreign main proceeding 12
forum of necessity 29–30
forum non conveniens 3-30, 31-51
see also **natural forum;** *Spiliada*
  adequacy of alternative forum 45–46
  admiralty 31
  anti-suit injunctions 87, 92
  application of tests 31–51
  assessment of approaches 50–51
  Australia
    background 32
    clearly inappropriate forum 35–36, 49
    convenience of the parties 39–40
    discretion to refuse leave 37–38
    leave 36
    nature of the decision 47, 48, 49–50
    permission of court 35
    service of process 35
    statutory rules 35–36
    witness evidence 39–40
  Bahamas 37
  Bermuda 37
  bundles 38
  change of rules
    England and Wales 34
    United States 33
  comparative interest analysis 43–44
  conduct of litigation 32
  convenience of the parties 38–41
    Australia 39–40
    bundles 38
    cloud storage 39
    commercial matters 38
    cost of witness attendance 38
    digitization 39
    e-bundles 38
    ease of access to sources of proof 38–39
    electronic communications 38
    proof 38
    Spiliada 38
    technology 38
    translations 39
    United States 38, 39, 41
    witness attendance 38, 39–40
  discretion to refuse leave 37–38
  e-bundles 38
  electronic communications 38
  electronic evidence 40–41
  England and Wales
    change of rules 34
    Civil Procedure Rules 33, 34, 35, 36
    frontloaded decisions 34
    legitimate expectation 36
    nature of the decision 48
    origins of doctrine 31
    private interest factors 34
    proper place in which to bring a
      claim 34, 35
    public interest factors 34–35
    service out of the jurisdiction 34
    source of power 33
    Spiliada 34, 35
  evidence
    electronic evidence 40–41
    witnesses 39–40
  governing law 42–45
  interpretative difficulties 33–38
  lex causae 42, 43
  Malaysia 46
  nature of the decision 47–50
    Australia 47, 48, 49–50
    'balancing' 48–49
    correctness standard 47, 48
    deferential standard 47–48
    discretion 47, 48
    England and Wales 48
    United States 47
    'weighing all the factors' 48, 49
  nature of rights 302
  'not unless' rules 36–37
  private interest factors 32
    England and Wales 34
    meaning 34
    United States 34
  proper law of a contract 44
  public interest factors 32–33, 41–47, 301
    adequacy of alternative forum 45–46
    administrative burden 45
    burden on local juries 45
    comparative interest analysis 43–44
    docket congestion 45
    England and Wales 34–35
    evidence, nature of 41–42
    foreign law 42
    governing law 42–45
    lex causae 42, 43
    localized disputes 43
    Malaysia 46

meaning 34
political value judgements 46
United States 32–33, 34, 42–43, 45
source of court's power 33
Spiliada 31, 34, 35
convenience of the parties 38
technology 32, 38–41
translations 39
United States 31–32
  best evidence rule 38–39
  change of rules 33
  comparative interest analysis 43–44
  convenience of the parties 38–39, 41
  discretion 47
  dismissal of proceedings 33
  docket congestion 45
  due process 33
  ease of access to sources of proof 38–39
  frontloaded decisions 34
  long arm statute 33
  nature of the decision 47
  private interest factors 32–33, 34
  public interest factors 32–33, 34, 42–43, 45
  service of process 33
  source of court's power 33
  witness attendance 39
  witness attendance 38, 39–40
forum shopping 12
  meaning 12
France 27
fraud
  anti-enforcement injunctions 261–263
  breach of contract 261–263
freezing injunctions 80, 82, 92
fundamental principles of justice 337–355
  Australia 326
  balancing principles 346–348
  comity 325, 337–348, 356
  domestic law, regulation of 346
  identification 346–348, 356
  international conduct, regulation of 346
  international law 343–346
  law of nations 343–344
  natural principles of justice 341
  new principles 348–355
  privacy 348–355, 356
  public policy exception 326, 338–340
  Roman roots 341–343
  source 340–341
funding
  litigation 4
  natural forum 24

gateways
  Canada 60, 63, 64, 66, 74
  discretion
    certainty 58, 60
    damage sustained in the forum 60, 72
    equal treatment 74
    exceptional nature 54
    exorbitant 74, 75
    generally 54, 55
    proper forum 54
    purpose 55
    relevant connections 55
    tort 60–61, 73
    unobjectionable 74
  jurisdiction 54, 55, 58, 60–61, 73–75, 301
Germany
  privacy 350–351
Gibraltar
  Spiliada 8
Giuliano and Lagarde Report 154
governing law
  choice of law agreements 44–45
  English law 44–45
  forum non conveniens 42–45

Hague Choice of Court Convention 141, 148, 149, 169, 178
Hague Judgments Convention 74
Hague Securities Convention 201–202, 223
Hong Kong 27–28
  Spiliada 8, 27
human rights
  privacy 351–352

India
  Spiliada 8
injunctions
  see anti-enforcement injunctions; anti-suit injunctions
  background 88–92
  Chancery, role of 88–89
  freezing injunctions 80, 82, 92
  United States 89
insolvency
  foreign main proceeding 12
insurance 69
interest
  remedies 232–234
interest rate swaps 182–184
interim relief
  remedies 234–242
intermediated securities
  disintermediation 208, 209
  securities trading 199, 200–201

intermediated securities (*cont.*)
  difficulties with system 203
  entitlement 208–211
  EU law 201
  Place of the Relevant Intermediary
    Approach (PRIMA) 201–202, 223, 224
  purpose 205
  Stock Connect 205
  Stock Connect 205
  technology 204, 208–209
international commercial arbitration
  growth 17–18
  natural forum 17–18, 29
international commercial courts
  developments 4
Isle of Man 29

Jenard Report 125, 126
judgment debts
  agreement to discharge 268–269
jurisdiction
  see also co-defendants, jurisdiction over
  anti-suit injunctions 95, 102–104
  Canada
    discretion 54, 56
    residual jurisdiction 63
    standards for direct and indirect
      jurisdiction 60–64
  Civil Procedure Rules 178, 188–191
  consent 300
  England and Wales
    Civil Procedure Rules 178, 188–191
    discretion 54–56
  gateways 54, 55, 58, 60–61, 73–75, 301
  private rights 301–302
  public law concept 299–300
  unjust enrichment
    *Agnew v Lansförsäkringsbolagens
      AB* 184–185
    breach of trust 179
    Civil Procedure Rules 178, 188–191
    contractual matters 179–181
    exceptions in Arts 5(1) and 5(3) 178–181
    generally 175
    Kleinwort Benson 182–184, 185–188
    Lugano Convention 178–181
    rights *in rem* 179
    salvage 179
    tort/delict 179–180
jurisdiction agreements *see* arbitration and
    jurisdiction agreements; exclusive
    jurisdiction agreements
justice
  anti-suit injunctions 78, 81–83, 96
  comity
    fundamental principles 325, 337–355

  fundamental principles 335, 337–355
    balancing 346–348
    domestic law, regulation of 346
    identification 346–348
    international conduct, regulation of 346
    international law 343–346
    law of nations 343–344
    natural principles of justice 341–343
    privacy 348–355
    public policy exception 326, 338–340
    Roman roots 341–343
    source 340–341
  natural forum 15, 16, 24, 26–27, 28
  quality 17
  substantial justice 15, 16, 24

kompetenz-kompetenz 148
  severability distinguished 143
Kuwait 27

legal professional privilege 119
lex causae
  forum non conveniens 42, 43
  remedies 229–230
lex creationis 199, 200, 220–223
lex fori
  remedies 225, 227–228, 229
lex registri 200, 217–218
lex situs 218–220, 223
lex situs cartae 200
Lugano Convention 125, 127, 131
  unjust enrichment 178–181, 191

Malaysia 46
  forum non conveniens 46
  Spiliada 8
matrix contract
  arbitration and jurisdiction agreements 140
  severability
    invalidity 142
mediation
  Singapore 270–271
midnight clauses 145

Namibia 24
natural forum
  see also forum non conveniens; Spiliada
  anchor defendants 9
  anti-suit injunctions 10
  assassination risks 28, 29
  assessment of outcomes 16–17
  Australia 10, 11, 18–21
  availability of foreign forum 16, 17
  Canada 8, 21–23
  case management 13–15
  centre of main interest 12

clearly inappropriate forum 19–20, 25, 26–27, 32
closest and most real connection 28
comity 24–30
commercial cases 15
common law techniques 10–11
connecting factors 15
consequences of unsuccessful applications 17
discretion 16, 27
disposal of decisions 14
equity 11
evidence 17
foreign law issues 17
forum-dependant outcomes 10
funding 24
hard cases 24–30
identification 15–17
international commercial arbitration 17–18, 29
justice 15, 16, 24, 26–27, 28
length of hearings on appropriate forum 13–14
natural justice 29
parallel proceedings 10
parochialism 27
pleadings 16
purpose of doctrine 10, 12
quality of justice 17
reputation 11
risk of injustice 28–29
service out of the jurisdiction 15
Singapore 8, 15, 23, 28, 30
strategic advantages 15
substantial justice 15, 16, 24
test 6
'unattainable perfection' 9–18
UNCITRAL Model Law 12
undertakings 16
uniformity 9
natural justice 29, 84
necessary and proper party 63, 64, 73, 113
negotiorum gestio 197
New Zealand
Spiliada 8, 11
non-contractual subrogation 197
non-recognition of foreign judgments
exclusive jurisdiction agreements 303, 304
nuisance 48, 352

oppression
Australia 19
optical character recognition 38
overseas civil restraint orders 80, 109

parallel proceedings
Australia 20
Canada 73–74

England and Wales 73–74
natural forum 10
personal injury
Australia 18, 19
place of the relevant intermediary approach (PRIMA) 201–202, 223, 224
place of the relevant operating authority/administrator (PROPA) 212, 213
primary residence of the encryption master keyholder (PREMA) 212, 213, 223
private law, relationship with 300–324
privacy
Australia 354–355
confidentiality 353
England and Wales 353
European Court of Human Rights 355
fundamental principles of justice 348–355, 356
Germany 350–351
human rights 351–352
legal doctrines giving effect to 352
United States 349
private nuisance 48
product liability
Canada 66–67
professional negligence
Australia 19, 20
proper law
contract 44
public interest factors
discretion 72
forum non conveniens 32–33, 41–47, 301
adequacy of alternative forum 45–46
administrative burden 45
burden on local juries 45
comparative interest analysis 43–44
England and Wales 34–35
evidence, nature of 41–42
lex causae 42, 43
localized disputes 43
meaning 34
political value judgements 46
United States 32–33, 34, 42–43
public policy
fundamental principles of justice 326, 338–340

real and substantial connection test
Canada 22, 23
Singapore 23
recognition of foreign judgments
divorce
civil partnerships 290–292
definition of proceedings 284–290
financial provision 278–283
gender discrimination 278–283
law reform 295–296
transnational divorces 292–295

374　INDEX

reinsurance　131–132
remedies　226-247
　characterisation of rights/obligations　228, 229
　damages　232–234
　declaratory relief　242–243
　exclusion of applicable foreign law　228–229
　exclusionary rule　243–246
　exclusive jurisdiction agreements　302–304
　inconvenience　243–246
　interest　232–234
　interim relief　234–242
　involvement in legal proceedings
　　damages　232–234
　　declaratory relief　242–243
　　evidence　231–232
　　generally　230–231
　　interest　232–234
　　interim relief　234–242
　lex causae　229–230
　lex fori　225, 227–228, 229
　meaning　226
　Rome I Regulation　228, 246
　Rome II Regulation　228, 246
　scope　226
　terminology　226
　theory　227–230
renvoi
　Australia　11
reputation
　natural forum　11
restraining orders　80
rights *in rem*
　unjust enrichment　179
Rome Convention　154, 155
Rome I Regulation　108, 154, 178, 193–194, 228, 246, 321
Rome II Regulation　72, 108, 178, 191, 192, 194–198, 228, 246
rule of law　79
Russia　28

salvage
　unjust enrichment　179
sanctions
　anti-suit injunctions　78, 80
securities　199-224
　choice of law
　　Clearstream　202
　　cryptosecurities　200, 205, 211–222, 224
　　directly held securities　200
　　distributed ledger technology　199, 202, 203
　　entitlement　209–211
　　existing law　200–202
　　Hague Securities Convention　201–202, 223

　　intermediated securities　199, 200–201, 203
　　lex creationis　199, 200
　　lex registri　200
　　lex situs cartae　200, 223
　　'no look through' approach　201, 202, 203, 204, 209
　　overview　199–200
　　Place of the Relevant Intermediary Approach (PRIMA)　201–202, 224
　　Stock Connect　199
　cryptosecurities
　　advantages　208
　　applicable law　217–218
　　choice of law　200, 205, 211–222
　　distributed ledger technology　205
　　lex creationis　220–223
　　lex registri　217–218
　　lex situs　218–220, 223
　　location of the private encryption key　213–216
　　named entity, location of　213
　　place of the relevant operating authority/administrator (PROPA)　212, 213
　　primary residence of the encryption master keyholder (PREMA)　212, 213
　distributed ledger technology
　　choice of law　199, 202
　　difficulties with system　203
　　mechanics of platforms　207–208
　　use　204
　evolution of securities　204–206
　immobilised debt securities　206
　immobilised shares　206
　intermediated securities　199, 200–201
　　difficulties with system　203
　　EU law　201
　　Place of the Relevant Intermediary Approach (PRIMA)　201–202, 223, 224
　　purpose　205
　　Stock Connect　205
　　technology　208–209
　platforms　204–206
　Stock Connect
　　choice of law　199
　　meaning　205
　　technology　208–209
　trading platforms　204–206
separability *see* **severability**
service out of the jurisdiction
　England and Wales　34
　natural forum　15
severability　139-173
　see also **dépeçage**
　arbitration and jurisdiction agreements

applicable law 147–148
autonomy 142
Brussels I Regulation (recast) 141, 169
contract, as 152–153
dual character 150–152
dual character of agreements 150–152
English cases 162–165
Enka 162–163
existing instruments, compatibility of preferred approach with 165–169
exists, where choice of law for the matrix contract 158–161
expectations of parties 145–146
generally 140
governing law 147–148
Hague Choice of Court Convention 169
illustrations of approaches 156–162
instruments on arbitration agreements 166–168
invalid matrix contract 142
law of the country where award was made 168
law to which the parties have subjected the arbitration agreement 167
matrix contract 140, 145, 148
meaning of severability in context of 141
midnight clauses 145
no choice of law for the matrix contract 161
observations 162
preferred analysis 156, 170–173
protective choice of law rules 168
purpose of severability 148–150
substantive terms 146–147
UNCITRAL Model Law 141, 148
use of severability 142
Brussels I Regulation (recast) 141, 169
choice of law 143–153
applicable law 147–148
Brussels I Regulation (Recast) 169
contract, meaning of 152–153
dual character of arbitration and jurisdiction agreements 150–152
existing instruments, compatibility of preferred approach with 165–169
exists, where choice of law for the matrix contract 158–161
expectation of the parties 145–146
governing law 147–148
Hague Choice of Court Convention 169
illustrations of approaches 156–162
law of the country where award was made 168
law to which the parties have subjected the arbitration agreement 167

no choice of law for the matrix contract 161
observations 162
practical significance 170
preferred analysis 156, 170–173
protective choice of law rules 168
purpose 148–150
substantive terms 146–147
Hague Choice of Court Convention 141, 169
kompetenz-kompetenz distinguished 143
matrix contract 140
invalidity 142
substantive law 141–143
UNCITRAL Model Law 141, 143
use 142
ships 40–41
Singapore 251, 270–271
forum 4, 10
mediation 270–271
natural forum 8, 15, 23, 28, 30
real and substantial connection test 23
Spiliada 8
stay of proceedings 15
slavery 348
SNI Aerospatiale
anti-suit injunctions 105–107
social media 67
South Africa 24–25
Spiliada
see also *forum non conveniens;* **natural forum**
Australia 8–9, 11, 18–19, 21
background 5–6
Brunei 8
Canada 8, 21–23
Cayman Islands 8
co-defendants, jurisdiction over domestic rule 114–115
connecting factors 12
discretion 16
foreign law issues 17
forum non conveniens 31, 34, 35
Gibraltar 8
Hong Kong 8, 27
India 8
internationalist spirit 3–4
judicial involvement 12–13
jurists 7–8
Malaysia 8
natural forum 3, 5–9
New Zealand 8, 11
prequels 6–7
quality of justice 17
reflections on decision 30
Singapore 8
substantial justice 15, 16

376 INDEX

stay of proceedings
  connecting factors 15
  length of hearings on appropriate
    forum 13–14
  Singapore 15
Stock Connect
  choice of law 199
  meaning 205
subrogation 94
sufficient interest
  anti-suit injunctions 81, 86–87, 109

technology
  cloud storage 39
  COVID-19 pandemic 39, 40
  digitization 39
  dispute resolution 4
  electronic evidence 40–41
  forum non conveniens 32, 38–41
  intermediated securities 204, 208–209
  optical character recognition 38
  securities trading 208–209
  social media 67
  witness attendance 39–40
territorial sovereignty
  comity 326, 327–334
  implied consent 327–334
tort/delict
  gateways 60–61, 73
  holiday torts 64–66, 69–71, 72–73
  unjust enrichment 179
translations 39
travel industry 67–68
trespass 352

UNCITRAL Model Law
  foreign main proceeding 12
  severability 141, 143
unconscionable conduct
  anti-suit injunctions 93, 94, 96–97, 109
  background 96–98
  meaning 96–97
undertakings 106–107
  natural forum 16
United States 29
  anti-suit injunctions 79
  forum non conveniens 31–32
    best evidence rule 38–39
    change of rules 33
    convenience of the parties 38–39, 41
    discretion 47
    dismissal of proceedings 33
    due process 33
    ease of access to sources of proof 38–39
    long arm statute 33
    nature of the decision 47
    private interest factors 32–33, 34
    public interest factors 32–33, 34,
      42–43, 45
    service of process 33
    source of court's power 33
    witness attendance 39
  injunctions 89
unjust enrichment 175-198
  academic treatment 175–176, 198
  *Agnew v Lansförsäkringsbolagens
    AB* 184–185
  applicable law
    claims outside Art 10 Rome II
      Regulation 197
      conclusions 197–198
    IP completion day 191
    negotiorum gestio 197
    non-contractual subrogation 197
    overview 175–176
    Rome I Regulation 193–194
    Rome II Regulation 191, 192, 194–197
  breach of trust 179
  Brexit 176–177
  choice of law
    generally 175
    importance 175
  jurisdiction
    *Agnew v Lansförsäkringsbolagens
      AB* 184–185
    breach of trust 179
    Civil Procedure Rules 178, 188–191
    contractual matters 179–181
    exceptions in Arts 5(1) and 5(3) 178–181
    generally 175
    Kleinwort Benson 182–184, 185–188
    Lugano Convention 178–181, 191
    rights *in rem* 179
    salvage 179
    tort/delict 179
  Kleinwort Benson 182–184, 185–188
  Lugano Convention 178–181, 191
  non-contractual subrogation 197
  rights *in rem* 179
  salvage 179

vexatious and oppressive conduct
  anti-enforcement injunctions 252
  anti-suit injunctions 78, 93, 95, 99–101, 109
  Australia 19
  historical development 99

meaning 99–100
modern approach 99
oppressive 100
ulterior motives 100, 101
vexatious 100
video evidence 39

witness evidence
  Australia 39–40
  COVID-19 pandemic 39, 40
  forum non conveniens 38, 39–40
  video evidence 39
Woolf Report 37